Archbishop John Stratford, Political Revolutionary and Champion of the Liberties of the English Church, ca. 1275/80-1348

by

Roy Martin Haines

John Stratford, born ca. 1275 in the Warwickshire town of that name, is arguably the most important Englishman in the ecclesiastical and political life of the fourteenth century. Prominent in the political revolution which overthrew Edward II, he was to act as diplomatic envoy, "opposition leader," and finally – once Edward III was freed from the leading strings of Queen Isabella and her lover Mortimer – as chancellor of England. In the ecclesiastical sphere, thanks to papal cooperation, he acquired the wealthiest English bishopric, Winchester, from which he progressed in 1333 to the archbishopric of Canterbury, a position he combined for some years with the chancellorship. He was also instrumental in founding an ecclesiastical dynasty, for his brother Robert became bishop of Chichester (also royal chancellor), and his nephew Ralph bishop of London.

The middle phrase of Stratford's career, which spans the initial stage of the Hundred Year's War, includes a remarkable if bizarre two years on the continent as diplomatic agent and spy, and also a period of directing royal government at home. It closes with the crisis of 1341, a titanic struggle between archbishop and king. The outcome was a partial victory for Stratford and his rehabilitation as Edward III's principal councillor. Despite such preoccupation with state affairs, Stratford produced the most extensive provincial constitutions of the later middle ages, devised detailed ordinances for the Court of Canterbury, in which he had earlier served, founded the college of St. Thomas the Martyr in his native town, preached some memorable sermons, and had a notable impact as fearless defender of the liberties of the *Ecclesia Anglicana*.

The present study is much more than a biography of Stratford. With the aid of a wide range of manuscript and printed sources, backed by a comprehensive array of secondary studies, the author charts the course of a complex and controversial character through the volatile and faction-ridden later years of Edward II and the first two decades or so of the reign of his son. Stratford's death in 1348 can be fairly said to mark the end of an era in English history.

STUDIES AND TEXTS 76

ARCHBISHOP JOHN STRATFORD

Political Revolutionary and
Champion of the Liberties of
the English Church
ca. 1275/80 - 1348

BY

ROY MARTIN HAINES
Canada Council Killam Senior Research Scholar
1978-1980

PONTIFICAL INSTITUTE OF MEDIAEVAL STUDIES

ACKNOWLEDGMENT

This book has been published with the help of a grant
from the Canadian Federation for the Humanities,
using funds provided by the Social Sciences and
Humanities Research Council of Canada.

CANADIAN CATALOGUING IN PUBLICATION DATA

Haines, Roy Martin
  Archbishop John Stratford

(Studies and texts, ISSN 0082-5328 ; 76)
Includes index.
Bibliography: p.
ISBN 0-88844-076-6.

1. Stratford, John, d. 1348.   2. Catholic Church - England - Bishops -
Biography.   3. England - Church history - Medieval period, 1066-1485.
I. Pontifical Institute of Mediaeval Studies.   II. Title.   III. Series: Studies
and texts (Pontifical Institute of Mediaeval Studies) ; 76.

BR754.S87H34 1986   282'.42'0924   C85-098448-3

© 1986 by

Pontifical Institute of Mediaeval Studies
59 Queen's Park Crescent East
Toronto, Ontario, Canada M5S 2C4

PRINTED BY UNIVERSA, WETTEREN, BELGIUM

Distributed outside North America by
E. J. Brill, Leiden, The Netherlands
(Brill ISBN 90 04 07917 3)

DULCE BELLUM INEXPERTIS

In memory of my father
Evan George Martin Haines
who died in 1929 after an illness attributable
to service with the Welsh Guards
in the First Great War

26 November 1915 – 15 April 1919

Byr eu hoedyl, hir eu hoet ar eu carant
* * *
Brief were their lives, long the grieving
for them among their kinsmen

(*The Gododdin* ca. 600 AD)

Contents

Preface

Somewhat more than three and a half years ago, in the March of 1977, I was engaged in writing the preface to *The Church and Politics in Fourteenth-Century England*, which was in effect a biography of Adam Orleton, one of the most maligned of English bishops. Orleton's career brought me into contact with his contemporary and rival, John Stratford, and it is interesting to note that both came from the west midlands of England, indeed from contiguous dioceses. Clearly Stratford was an even more important figure than Orleton, for he became both archbishop and chancellor, recalling to mind Thomas Becket, whom he revered and whom at a moment of crisis he strove to emulate. I think it can be said that the resolution to attempt another biography, so soon after the first, was rashly conceived in the summer of 1977 at Oxford in the congenial atmosphere of the buttery at Worcester College and in the course of conversation with Mr. James Campbell. The resolution took on a more practical aspect when in 1978 I was awarded a Killam Senior Scholarship. It was the generosity of the Killam trust, which I gratefully acknowledge, that provided me with the time and opportunity to accomplish what would otherwise have been a protracted task.

The present biography is intended to be a companion study to *Church and Politics*. Obviously they overlap here and there, for the respective subjects are almost exact contemporaries, but I have tried hard to avoid duplication. Although *Archbishop Stratford* is a book complete in itself, *Church and Politics* will be found to be complementary, and I have deliberately followed a similar structure in each. But whereas Orleton's career in the world beyond his diocese of Winchester was over by the mid-1330s, Stratford continued to be influential in public affairs almost until the time of his death in August 1348.

Some have claimed that I made too much of a hero out of Orleton. I would not wish to deny that he had his heroic moments and was a stubborn resister of oppression, but I did not envisage more than that. If such qualities and actions constitute a hero, then he has been rightly portrayed. Stratford's case is not dissimilar. He too had his moments of heroism, he too was a brave man who did not back down when he felt principles to be at stake. But neither, some would urge, were cast in the

heroic mould of earlier times. Perhaps that is rather beside the point. Both
men upheld the law and condemned actions that contravened it, regardless of the eminence of those responsible for such contravention. By men
of that stamp are liberties preserved. It seems to be less than just to argue
that they sought only their own interests. Clearly they did not.
Conformity to authority, perverse though it might be, is almost invariably
an easier road than resistance. Both chose resistance, when such a course
was forced upon them. Both suffered as a consequence, but Stratford less
so than Orleton, because vindictiveness was not an element in Edward
III's character; it was in that of his father.

Unless I am much mistaken, assessment of Stratford as a royal
administrator is likely to remain largely beyond the capacity of present-
day historians to determine. It is too difficult to disentangle the precise
influence of an individual. That Stratford was far from incompetent is
clear, but that he failed to live up to Edward III's expectations as a war-
financier is equally so. But in this it could be that the blame is attributable
more to the king for demanding too much, than to Stratford for
accomplishing too little. As for Stratford's regimen as archbishop and
Canterbury diocesan, we are severely handicapped by the loss of his
register.

Despite attempts to belittle Stratford, and to be cynical about his
donning of Becket's mantle, he was a man who achieved much. He
largely dominated English political life at two particularly crucial
moments: in 1326-1327, when Edward II's future (some would suggest
even that of the royal line itself) lay in the balance, and again in 1340-
1341, when Edward III had to learn a hard lesson at the hands of his
minister. He did so, and his reign though long was, until near the end,
unmarred by the political strife, personal incompetence, and military
failures of that of his father. Stratford deserves some credit for this
outcome. It would seem too, that in his insistence on the necessity of
bringing matters before parliament he deserves to be allotted a place in the
centuries-long development of that institution.

As a churchman it must be admitted that by our standards he is less
satisfactory, though typical of his day. He sought to serve two masters, the
king and the papacy; friction was inevitable in view of the heavy clerical
taxation following from the king's determination to wage war with
France. Another outcome of this conflict was the need for purposes of
defence to draw a line between the indigenous and alien elements in the
English church. The Roman or Western church was an all-embracing
institution which did not readily take account of distinctions of a national
or nationalistic kind. It can be said, however, that Stratford made a

surprisingly effective attempt to serve both the interests of the church
and the political ambitions of his secular master. Naturally there were
moments when the gap was too difficult to bridge and conflict ensued.
Stratford's provincial constitutions are monuments to his concern for right
order in the church, so too are his regulations for the Court of Canterbury.
It was fitting that a lawyer with practical experience of both diocesan
administration and the process of the ecclesiastical courts should legislate
in this fashion.

Stratford's biography reveals that he gave a high priority to the
preservation of the liberties of the English church as expressed in canon
law and in the charters of England's monarchs. That he was not a spiritual
man in any deep or consistent sense is self evident. Those who can live up
to our ideals in all facets of their lives are few indeed.

Roy Martin Haines
Halifax, Nova Scotia

The feast of St. Denys, 9 October 1980.
The six-hundred-and-forty-sixth
anniversary of John Stratford's
enthronement as archbishop of Canterbury.

Acknowledgments

It is with sadness that I record my debt to the late Professor Walter Ullmann for allowing my *Church and Politics* to appear in *Cambridge Studies in Medieval Life and Thought*, under his general editorship, and then adding to his kindness by supporting my project for a biography of Archbishop Stratford. Two other scholars to whom I have a special obligation for acting as referees in my submission to the Canada Council are Mr. James Campbell, Fellow of Worcester College, Oxford, and Professor Christopher Crowder of Queen's University, Kingston. Professor Leonard Boyle of the Pontifical Institute of Mediaeval Studies was most helpful in smoothing the path of admission to the Vatican Archives. It is superfluous to add that I carried as my *vade mecum* his own indispensable guide to those records of the central administration of the medieval church. To Fr. Charles Burns of the Vatican Archives I am indebted for his help and interest during my researches in Rome, and to the nuns of the Casa di Santa Brigida for their hospitality, which made my stay in that city much more pleasurable than it might otherwise have been. Dr. Roger Highfield, librarian of Merton College, Oxford, was kind enough to respond more than once to my queries about Stratford's university education, and I am indebted to other college and university librarians for allowing me to read the manuscripts in their charge or to have them copied. The extent of these obligations may be gauged from the Bibliography of Manuscript Sources.

Among the many archivists and custodians of documents whom I have encountered while in pursuit of John Stratford I should like to thank particularly Mr. Davey of the Hampshire Record Office, Mr. Nicholas Bennett of the Lincolnshire Archives Office, Miss Melanie Barber, deputy librarian and archivist of Lambeth Palace Library, who brought to my notice Stratford *acta* in the Dover cartulary, Canon Paul Britton, Winchester Cathedral librarian, Mr. N. H. MacMichael FSA and the staff of the Westminster Abbey Muniment room, the staff of Shakespeare's Birthplace Trust Records Department at Stratford, Miss Anne Oakley, archivist of Canterbury Cathedral Library, Miss Penelope Morgan, who allowed me to read the sermons attributed to Stratford in the unique atmosphere of the chained library at Hereford, the staff of the West Sussex

Record Office at Chichester and of the Joint Record Office at Lichfield, and once again, Miss Margaret Henderson of the Hereford and Worcester Record Office at St. Helen's Worcester. Dr. Kathleen Major, learning of my quest at Lincoln, kindly sent details of the house which Stratford occupied in Minster Yard whilst archdeacon, now 4 and 5 Pottergate. The chapter accounts (LAO Bj/2/5, fol. 23^r) show that £2 12s 4³/₄d was expended on its repair during Stratford's tenancy (1320-1321).

Like so many other researchers I owe an immense debt to the British Library and the Public Record Office, and I welcome the opportunity to express my gratitude for being able to work in the Institute of Historical Research, London University, and in the library of the Society of Antiquaries, where much of my reading of secondary material was accomplished. Mr. John Hopkins FSA, the Antiquaries' librarian, was quick to respond to my enquiries and to provide copies of material. In Halifax the former librarian of King's College was most helpful in permitting me to borrow the relevant volumes of the Record Commission's edition of *Foedera*.

My debt to other scholars is evidenced by the footnotes. Professor Robert Wright I should like to thank for a timely gift of his book, *The Church and the English Crown*, which has saved me from many a pitfall, and also Professor Charles Donahue of Harvard University for offprints of his articles which have relevance to Stratford. Professor C. R. Cheney kindly read the section on Stratford's constitutions with beneficial results. In the final stages many obscurities and errors were removed as a result of the diligence and acuity of one of the readers for the press.

* * *

Unpublished Crown Copyright material is reproduced by permission of the Controller of H. M. Stationery Office. For permission to print transcripts of documents, or portions of documents, and particularly those in Appendix 1, I thank the bishop of Worcester and the Hereford and Worcester County Archivist, the Lincolnshire Archivist, the Hampshire County Archivist and Diocesan Record Officer, the British Library Board, and the Directorate of the Vatican Archives.

Abbreviations

In the footnotes the authors of articles and books are given together with abbreviated titles. Fuller details can be found in the Bibliography, where abbreviations for printed chronicles are likewise extended, but not those for episcopal registers (for which see Smith, *Guide to Bishops' Registers*).

al.	aliter (otherwise)
APS	*Acts of the Parliament of Scotland*, ed. T. Thomson and C. Innes (Edinburgh 1814-1875)
BIHR	*Bulletin of the Institute of Historical Research*
Biog. Cantab.	A. B. Emden, *A Biographical Register of the University of Cambridge to 1500* (Cambridge 1963)
Biog. Oxon.	idem, *A Biographical Register of the University of Oxford to 1500*, 3 vols. (Oxford 1957-1959)
BJRL	*Bulletin of the John Rylands Library*
BL	British Library
BRT	Shakespeare's Birthplace Trust Records Department, Stratford-on-Avon
ca.	circa
Cal. Inqu. Misc.	*Calendar of Inquisitions Miscellaneous 1307-1349* (PRO C.145)
Cal. PMR	*Calendar of Plea and Memoranda Rolls ... of the City of London 1323-1364*, ed. A. H. Thomas (Cambridge 1926)
Cant. Admin.	I. J. Churchill, *Canterbury Administration*, 2 vols. (London 1933)
CCC	Corpus Christi College, Cambridge
CChR	*Calendar of Charter Rolls*
CChW	*Calendar of Chancery Warrants 1244-1326* (PRO C.81)
CCL	Canterbury Cathedral Library
CCR	*Calendar of Close Rolls*
CFR	*Calendar of Fine Rolls*
CMRE	*Calendar of Memoranda Rolls (Exchequer) 1326-1327*
CPL	*Calendar of Papal Letters*
CPP	*Calendar of Papal Letters, Papal Petitions*
CPR	*Calendar of Patent Rolls*
CUL	Cambridge University Library
CYS	Canterbury and York Society
Decretum	*Decretum Gratiani*
DHGE	*Dictionnaire d'histoire et de géographie ecclésiastiques*

DNB	*Dictionary of National Biography*
DRO	Devon Record Office, Exeter
Ds.	Dominus (Sir)
EcHR	*Economic History Review*
ECL	Exeter Cathedral Library
EETS	Early English Text Society
EHR	*English Historical Review*
excusaciones	of Archbishop Stratford in 1341: see *Vitae Arch. Cant.*, pp. 27-36. Lambeth MS 99, fols. 136^r-146^v
Extra	*Decretales Gregorii P. IX*
Extrav. Commun.	*Extravagantes communes*
fl.	floruit
Foedera	*Foedera, Conventiones, etc.*, ed. T. Rymer, 3rd. ed., 10 vols. (The Hague 1739-1745)
Foedera (R.C.)	*Foedera, Conventiones, etc.*, ed. T. Rymer, new ed., ed. A. Clarke, F. Holbrooke, J. Caley, 4 vols. in 7 (London: Record Commission 1816-1869)
fol., fols.	folio(s)
GEC	G. E. Cokayne, *The Complete Peerage*, 12 vols. (London 1910-1959)
HBC	*Handbook of British Chronology*, ed. F. M. Powicke and E. B. Fryde, 2nd ed. (London 1961)
HCL	Hereford Cathedral Library
HCM	Hereford Cathedral Muniments
HD	*Handbook of Dates*, ed. C. R. Cheney (London 1948)
HMCR	*Historical Manuscripts Commission's Report*
HMSO	Her Majesty's Stationery Office
HRO	*Hereford Register Orleton*
JEH	*Journal of Ecclesiastical History*
l., ll.	line(s)
LAO	Lincolnshire Archives Office, Lincoln
Le Neve	*John le Neve, Fasti Ecclesiae Anglicanae 1300-1541*, 12 vols. Institute of Historical Research (London 1962-1967)
Lit. Cant.	*Literae Cantuarienses*, ed. J. B. Sheppard, 3 vols. RS 85. (London 1887-1889)
Lydford	*John Lydford's Book*, ed. D. M. Owen, HMSO and Devon and Cornwall Record Soc. new ser. 20 (1975) (DRO MS 723)
M.	Magister (Master). For other university degrees I have followed Emden's abbreviations in *Biog. Oxon.* and *Biog. Cantab.*
m., mm.	membrane(s)
n., nn.	note(s)
NNRO	Norfolk and Norwich Record Office, Norwich
no., nos.	number(s)

ob.	obiit (died)
OHS	Oxford Historical Society
Parl. Writs	*Parliamentary Writs* (see Bibliography)
PHE	*Political History of England*, 12 vols.
pl.	plate(s)
PRO	Public Record Office
PSA	*Proceedings of the Society of Antiquaries*
RA	*Registra Avenionensia* (Vatican Archives)
RDP	*Reports ... Touching the Dignity of a Peer* (see Bibliography)
responsiones	of Bishop Orleton in 1334: see Twysden, *Historiae Anglicanae Scriptores Decem* (London 1652) cols. 2763-2768. Lambeth MS 1213, pp. 300-306; also *Winch. Chart.* nos. 233-234
RS	Rolls Series
RSV	(*Worcester*) *Registrum Sede Vacante* (printed) (see Bibliography)
RV	*Registra Vaticana* (Vatican Archives)
SA	Society of Antiquaries
s.a.	sub anno
SCH	*Studies in Church History*
SCKB	*Select Cases in the Court of King's Bench under Edward II*, ed. G. O. Sayles, vol. 4. Selden Soc. 74 (London 1957) — *under Edward III*, vol. 5. Selden Soc. 76 (London 1958); vol. 6. Selden Soc. 82 (London 1965)
SCKC	*Select Cases before the King's Council 1243-1482*, ed. J. S. Leadam and J. F. Baldwin. Selden Soc. 35 (Cambridge Mass. 1918)
Sext	*Liber sextus decretalium Bonifacii P. VIII*
s.v.	sub voce
TCC	Trinity College, Cambridge
TRHS	*Transactions of the Royal Historical Society*
VCH	*Victoria History of the Counties of England* (Individual volumes are readily identifiable from the abbreviated titles and are not included in the Bibliography.)
Vitae Arch. Cant.	"Birchington." See Bibliography, Manuscript Sources (Lambeth Palace Library), and Printed Sources.
WAM	Westminster Abbey Muniments
WHS	Worcestershire Historical Society
Winch. Chart.	*Chartulary of Winchester Cathedral*, ed. A. W. Goodman (Winchester 1927)
WinPR	Winchester Pipe Rolls (Hampshire Record Office). See MS Bibliography
WinRO	{ Winchester Registers Orleton and Stratford
WinRS	{ See MS Bibliography

WoCL	Worcester Cathedral Library
Worc. Admin.	R. M. Haines, *The Administration of the Diocese of Worcester in the First Half of the Fourteenth Century* (London 1965)
WRO	*A Calendar of the Register of Adam de Orleton, Bishop of Worcester 1327-1333*, ed. R. M. Haines, HMSO and WHS (London 1979)
WSRO	West Sussex Record Office, Chichester
YB	*Year Books, 11-12 Edward III*, ed. A. J. Horwood, RS 31. (London 1883)
	Year Books, 12-20 Edward III, ed. L. O. Pike, 14 vols., RS 31. (London 1885-1911)
	(see Graves, *Bibliography of English History*, pp. 545-547, for details of year books Edward I-III)

All the calendars of national documents and the Rolls Series (Chronicles and Memorials of Great Britain and Ireland during the Middle Ages) are listed in *Government Publications, British National Archives*, sectional list no. 24, HMSO 1983.

1

The Making of a Career

Stratford-on-Avon in the late-thirteenth century was a small compact town with a regular pattern of streets, approached from the southeast, the direction of Oxford and London, by a wooden bridge across the River Avon, towards the reconstruction of which the subject of this biography was to make a substantial contribution in his will. The town and surrounding area constituted a manor of the bishops of Worcester.[1] John de Stratford, the future archbishop of Canterbury and chancellor of England, was born there into a propertied burgher family. His father's name, like that of his younger brother, was Robert, his mother's Isabel; information which he himself provides in the regulations for his chantry, first drawn up in the autumn of 1331, by which time both parents had died.[2] Thus far we are on safe ground.

John's father is commonly assumed[3] to have been that Robert de Stratford who, as a member of the fraternity of the Holy Cross, early in 1270[4] secured Bishop Godfrey Giffard's confirmation of a plan to build a

---

[1] According to the author of *VCH Warwicks.* 3, p. 222, "The layout of the older part of the town has changed little since the 15th century. It consists of three streets running parallel and three at right angles to the river, and seems to be an example on a small scale of medieval town planning." For extents of "Old Stratford" manor (which lay to the southwest) dated 1252 and 1299 see *Red Book of Worcester*, pp. 243ff., 471ff.; also *Extenta Manerii de Veteri Stratford* (1252). The 1252 extent lists all the burgage tenements. The bridge is first mentioned in 1235 and was of timber until the building of Clopton Bridge in Henry vii's time. See *VCH Warwicks.* 3, p. 224.

[2] Worcester Reg. Montacute 1, fol. 56^{v}ii (al. p. 124). Dated 8 October 1331, while Stratford was bishop of Winchester.

[3] For instance, in the modern commemorative stained-glass window depicting John Stratford on the north side of the sanctuary of the Guild Chapel at Stratford (Robert de Stratford's foundation). The adjacent window depicts John's brother Robert.

[4] The date is invariably given as 1269. In fact Giffard's confirmation is dated 10 January 1270. Worcester Reg. Polton, fol. 85^r (al. p. 173). The author of *VCH Warwicks.* 2, p. 113, writes of Robert de Stratford and "15 of the confraternity of the Holy Cross," giving his reference as "Reg. Polton, fol. 149 [sic]." I can only suppose that the "15"

hospital with an oratory or chapel, complete with bells.[5] As in all such medieval foundations there was an element of chantry; divine service was to be celebrated on behalf of the forbears of the brethren and sisters of the fraternity. The immediate purpose, however, was the care of the poor, both members of the fraternity and others. Unusual was the additional provision for such needy priests as might be promoted with insufficient title by the Worcester bishops. This clearly reflects the interests of the local diocesan, Giffard, who is alleged to have been excessively liberal in the ordination of clerks; so much so that his successor, William Gainsburgh, was forced to seek Pope Clement v's dispensation from the canonical obligation to support them.[6]

But there are problems in identifying the cofounder and first master of the hospital with John Stratford's father. In the first place he is termed *Magister* Robert de Stratford, as though a graduate; secondly, the members of the new institution were bound to observe the Rule of St. Augustine, which would certainly have been inconsistent with marital union and the procreation of children.[7] John's birth can be assigned to the later 1270s or at a stretch to the early 1280s, his life span being roughly congruent with that of Adam Murimuth, the chronicler, who was born

derives from Dugdale's use of the word "sistren," which from the printing of long "s" appears very much like "fifteen." There is no such number in the Reg. Polton entry. See Dugdale, *Warwickshire* 2, pp. 695-697.

[5] The original document has been lost. We owe our text to Bishop Polton's confirmation (27 September 1430) following a dispute about parochial rights between the warden of Stratford collegiate church, Richard Praty, and the guild. See Worcester Reg. Polton, fols. 149[v], 85[r] (al. pp. 302, 173) – the folios are bound incorrectly. The documents are translated in the preface to Harvey Bloom, *The Gild Register*. On 12 March 1270 Bishop Giffard licensed the fraternity of the Holy Cross to elect a collector and distributor of alms. Another mandate of the same date directed the Stratford bailiffs to aid and protect the new hospital. Regs. Giffard, fol. 26[r]; Polton, fol. 85[r]. The Polton entry of the former seemingly was not copied from Giffard's register.

[6] *Worc. Admin.*, p. 168 n. 6. At the time of ordination clerks were often made to take an oath to the effect that they would not claim support from the bishop on the basis of *Cum secundum apostolum* (*Extra* 3, 5, 16), which obliged him to make provision for those whom he had ordained. There was a poor priests' hospital at Canterbury (part of the buildings can still be seen) and in some other places. See Clay, *Mediaeval Hospitals*, pp. 23-25.

[7] Giffard appointed "Magister Robert de Stratford" as "dicti hospitalis magistrum ... et custodem." Had he been a graduate (the term *magister* is also used in other contexts) this would not have precluded him from fathering children, but John does not accord his parent any such title. Giffard decreed: "Conversantes in hospitali regulam teneant beati Augustini." Those admitted were to promise obedience to the master and to take a vow of chastity and poverty (continencie et proprietatis non habende). Worcester Reg. Polton, fol. 85[r]. It is true that Giffard is not as explicit as one would wish and the master of a hospital could on occasion be a layman. See Clay, *Mediaeval Hospitals*, pp. 149, 174-175.

1274-1275 and who died in 1347.[8] In other words John was born within a decade or so after Master Robert's assumption of the governance of the new hospital. Despite the survival of a sprinkling of late-thirteenth-century deeds and other documents concerned with the guild of the Holy Cross and the transfer of land and property in Stratford, there is no firm evidence connecting the two Roberts.[9]

The Rochester chronicler William Dene[10] rightly considered John Stratford (hence also his brother Robert) to be uncle to the bishop of London, Ralph (de) Stratford, who bore the family name Hatton. The relationship is confirmed by Archbishop Stratford in his will and later, in 1354, by Robert, then bishop of Chichester, who in a document granting forty days' indulgence to those who prayed for his nephew's soul, describes him as "Ralph Hatton de Stratford." [11] There being no indication of a third brother, the suggestion has been made that a sister of John and Robert was Ralph Hatton's mother. John Stratford's will mentions a sister Alice, but whether she was married or not is left to our conjecture. She may not have been, for one of the complaints made (in 1342) against Abbot Hereward of Cirencester by the townsmen was that he had granted an annual pension of £40 to the archbishop's sister, presumably Alice. Of course, by that time she could have been a widow. Another possibility is that she was the Alice, wife of Philip de Barton, who during her lifetime was entitled to hold the manor of Caldecote, Cambridgeshire, which belonged to John Stratford and on his death was inherited by Robert, subject to Alice's interest.[12] Another "nephew" of the Stratford brothers

---

[8] For Murimuth see Emden, *Biog. Oxon.*, s.v. It is difficult to be more precise about Stratford, but it looks as though Murimuth was a few years his senior – four or five at most.

[9] The residual archives of the guild are housed with the Stratford borough records in Shakespeare's Birthplace Trust Records Department (BRT). See Wellstood, "Stratford: Calendar of Medieval Records" (typescript). Items were transcribed and/or translated by W. J. Hardy in a handwritten calendar ("Hardy's Calendar"). For later guild records see Harvey Bloom, *The Gild Records*. Fisher, *Antient Paintings*, has reproductions of many guild documents, notably the indulgences. The Gough edition (1838) has a descriptive letterpress.

[10] I have accepted the attribution to Dene, which appears to carry conviction, although the *Historia Roffensis* has yet to be analyzed with a critical eye on the question of authorship. See below, "Stratford and the Chroniclers."

[11] BL Cotton MS Faustina B.v, fol. 88ʳ (*Anglia Sacra* 1, p. 374); BRT 1/3/16; Fisher, *Antient Paintings*, pl. IX no. 7; and see below, "Beneficiaries of Stratford's Will."

[12] *Cirencester Cartulary* 1, p. 103 no. 124: "item le dite abbe ad graunte annuele pension de xl *l.* a la soere le erchevesque de Canterb' pour maintener lui et les maueisis enprises qe il usent en countre reson et encountre le droiture de roi et de sa corone"; BL Harleian Ch. 43 H 1.

was Thomas Laurence de la More, an Oxfordshire knight, the son of John Laurence de la More and husband to a lady of the same name as Stratford's mother – Isabel.[13]

With the Hatton family we return to firmer ground; its members were remarkably influential in early-fourteenth-century Stratford. Between 1309 and 1318, apart from the two-year interval 1314-1316, Henry de Hatton occupied the office of bailiff or mayor of the borough.[14] A contemporary but distinguishable man of the same name had been one of Bishop Giffard's clerks, who was rewarded for his services by a grant of land in nearby Shottery.[15] Bailiff Hatton made a substantial transfer of property in Stratford to a William de Hatton, son of Thomas de Hatton,[16] and in some of the deeds this William is designated "clerk." [17] Seemingly he was only in minor orders, since he was married to yet another Isabel, who survived him. It was Ralph Hatton of Stratford, then bishop of London, who in 1345 was to secure a reversion of the lands which the widow Isabel held for life from John de Peyto, senior,[18] an influential man in the neighbourhood who was evidently acting as trustee.[19]

---

[13] *CPR 1327-1330*, p. 184; ibid. *1330-1334*, pp. 88, 115; WinRS, fol. 183ᵛ. Details of his life are collected below, "Stratford and the Chroniclers." It is possible, however, that *nefeu* in More's case was used in an imprecise sense. Sometimes it can refer to a great nephew or even a mere kinsman.

[14] Wellstood, "Calendar," fols. 7ff.: list of bailiffs, and subbailiffs or catchpolls.

[15] Worcester Reg. Giffard, fol. 443ʳ; *Red Book of Worcester*, p. 253. Cf. BRT 1/2/79.

[16] BRT 1/2/119.

[17] E.g. BRT 1/2/132.

[18] For the Peyto family see Dugdale, *Warwickshire* 2, pp. 471-472ff. Because of his services to Bishop Bransford John de Peyto, junior, was rewarded with the farm of Stratford manor for £60 p.a. (*Worcester Reg. Bransford*, p. 16, no. 80). Though a lawyer, Peyto failed to secure royal confirmation and the unfortunate aftermath is related in *VCH Warwicks.* 3, pp. 258-259. In Worcester Reg. Maidstone, fol. 17ʳ, the bishop addresses Peyto (senior) as bailiff of Stratford (London, 27 November 1314).

[19] BRT 1/3/167-168. The surviving deeds suggest that Henry de Hatton (fl. ca. 1295 × 1318) and Thomas de Hatton (fl. ca. 1294 × 1328) were contemporaries, possibly brothers. Thomas is recorded as having two sons, William (fl. 1310, ob. by 1344) and Ralph (mentioned 1315), who could be the future bishop. The "Thurstan messuage" in Old Stratford was granted to William by Bishop Maidstone and the grant confirmed by Bishop Cobham and the Worcester chapter in 1319. *Red Book of Worcester*, p. 252; Liber Albus, fols. 97ᵛ-98ʳ; BRT 1/3/167. A John son of William de Hatton was granted letters dimissory to all minor and holy orders in January 1338 (Worcester Reg. Hemenhale, fol. 13ᵛ). William de Hatton accompanied John Stratford on his journeys abroad in the 1320s and in 1342 acted as one of the archbishop's attorneys. *CPR 1324-1327*, pp. 50, 94, 129; ibid., *1340-1343*, p. 374. Probably the man, given the status "donzel," who was appointed constable of Farnham in 1328. WinRS, fol. 183ᵛ (*bis*) and see below, "Stratford's *Familia* and Administration." In general, see Wellstood, "Calendar"; "Hardy's Calendar"; Dugdale Soc. 6 (Lay subsidy rolls), pp. 90-96, and cf. ibid., pp. 5-6 (Rolls of a tenth and fifteenth, 1332).

Connected with the Hattons were the Prests or Priests. In 1311 Robert "called Prest" granted two parts of a messuage with reversion of a third to the William son of Thomas de Hatton who has just been mentioned, and it was to this William that in 1314 and 1319 Helen or Ellen Elysse, daughter and heiress of John Prest, quitclaimed property in the town of Stratford.[20] Here we encounter the same combination of names prevalent among the Stratfords. It may be added that although John occurs in the Hatton family, the combination of John and Robert seemingly does not.[21]

Another local family which could claim kinship with the Stratfords was the Gerauds. Henry "de Stratford," a chancery clerk who during the political crisis of 1341 is described as the archbishop's – that is John Stratford's – cousin, bore the name Geraud. Henry was kinsman, possibly brother, of the John Geraud who became "custos" of the Stratford chantry.[22]

A bewildering number of John de Stratfords occurs in records of the time in question.[23] It is not always easy to distinguish them. For instance, a John de Stratford was ordained subdeacon in Worcester diocese at the Trinity ordination of 1284,[24] and he could have been the clerk who, at the petition of the then dean of St. Paul's, William de Montfort, was granted a bull of provision seven years later.[25] By the latter date he is entitled "magister" and the bull secured for him the rectory of Badminton, though not without opposition from a presentee of the regular patron.[26] On the strength of the title provided by his benefice Master John proceeded to the

---

[20] BRT 1/2/112, 132.

[21] E.g. a John Hatton occurs in 1229, *Red Book of Worcester*, p. 248; others in the 1330s, 1340s and 1360s: Wellstood, "Calendar," fols. 223-224 (cf. Dugdale Soc. 6, pp. 94-96), 262, 351-352.

[22] *French Chronicle*, pp. 84-85. For the Gerauds alias "de Stratfords" see below, "Stratford's *Familia* and Administration," and for chantry warden John Geraud, "The College of St. Thomas the Martyr, Stratford." For other Geroudes or Gerauds see Dugdale Soc. 6, pp. 94-95.

[23] Br. John de Stratford was a Worcester monk. See indexes s.v. to the Worcester *RSV* and *Liber Albus*. A secular clerk of this name was ordained subdeacon and deacon in May and June 1319. *Worcester Reg. Cobham*, fols. 47ʳ, 49ᵛ; pp. 52, 62. A John Nore "alias dictus Johannes de Stratford," son of Adam of Shottery, occurs in a list of deacons in Worcester Reg. Hemenhale, fol. 23ʳ. He alienated property in Stratford to the warden of Stratford's chantry (*CPR 1348-1350*, p. 281). A M. John de Stratford was in 1340 sent by the king to Norwich Priory as a corrodian (*CCR 1339-1341*, p. 482), and another M. John "alias Keu," a king's yeoman, was granted a pension of ten marks from St. Augustine's, Canterbury (*CPR 1340-1343*, p. 520). A John de Keu went abroad with Stratford in 1325 (ibid. *1324-1327*, p. 129). A John de Stratford was comptroller (controller) of the pipe in the early 1330s. PRO E.430/259, 267, 276.

[24] Worcester Reg. Giffard, fol. 210ᵛ, p. 238.

[25] Ibid., fols. 240ᵛ-241ʳ, p. 395: bull of 1 March 1291, Orvieto.

[26] Ibid., fols. 367ᵛ, 372ʳ; pp. 427, 433.

diaconate,[27] an order to which yet another John de Stratford was promoted in 1295.[28] It must have been Master John, in company with a colleague, who informed the Worcester cathedral chapter of the death of the diocesan bishop, Godfrey Giffard, with the request that his body be received for burial.[29] He occurs also as the proctor of M. Thomas de Wilton for the latter's institution to Lapworth rectory in 1303.[30]

Our John Stratford emerges from the obscurity of his early years at about the time we lose trace of his namesake.[31] He must surely be the "J. de S.," professor of civil law, who bore testimony to the character of a secular clerk who was seeking to become a monk. The document was copied into the *Liber Albus* of Worcester Cathedral Priory, and as the entries are regularly in chronological order, it has been usual to ascribe this one to 1308.[32] However, it so happens that a similar entry was made in another of the priors' letter-books, the *Liber Ecclesiae Wigorniensis*, now in the Public Record Office in London.[33] This time the entry is preceded by a letter addressed to Archbishop Reynolds, which points to a date at least five years after 1308. But as this volume is far from being in chronological order, the evidence is inconclusive.

Particulars of John Stratford's education are sparse. We know nothing of his schooling, though it is a reasonable guess that the schoolmaster thought to have been attached to the parish church of Holy Trinity in his home town instructed him in the rudiments of Latin grammar.[34] Subsequently he studied at Oxford.[35] In the seventeenth century Anthony

---

[27] Ibid., fol. 370^r, p. 431. Not entitled "magister" in this instance.

[28] Ibid., fol. 391^r, p. 459.

[29] *Liber Ecclesiae Wigorniensis*, p. 25 (PRO E.315/63/fol. 28^v).

[30] *Worcester Reg. Gainsburgh*, fol. 32^v, p. 122: 8 October 1303.

[31] Possibly the last occasion on which he is mentioned is in 1310, when a royal writ was issued on the plaint of "John, parson of Great Badminton." *Worcester Reg. Reynolds*, fol. 105^r, p. 170.

[32] *Liber Albus*, fol. 32^r, no. 422. It is in the form of a letter from the abbot of Winchcombe to Prior John de Wyke. The clerk concerned is a "Magister R. de D. clericus," who in view of the description cannot be equated with the monk of Worcester, Robert de Diclesdon, who is mentioned in 1317 (ibid., fol. 83^v). See next note.

[33] *Liber Ecclesiae Wigorniensis*, pp. 21-22 (PRO E.315/63/fol. 24^{r-v}). This time the editor incorrectly extends the "W" of the manuscript to "Westminster." The clerk is named as "Magister Ricardus de D. clericus."

[34] See Leach, *VCH Warwicks*. 2, p. 297, quoting Worcester Reg. Giffard, fol. 390^v. The Giffard entry is an ordination list of 28 May 1295 (eve of Trinity). Among the deacons appear M. William de Grenefeld, rector of Stratford, and much lower down "Ricardus rector scolarum de Stratford." The assumption that the latter functioned in connection with the parish church is however not unreasonable.

[35] *Biog. Oxon.* s.v. A letter from the Oxford chancellor to "John bishop of Winchester," mentioning suits in the Roman curia, is now considered to refer to John de

Wood, out of misguided loyalty to his own college, Merton, "tried to fit in a number of extra planets which had never been there." [36] One such luminary was John Stratford, whose name Wood claimed to have found in the bursarial accounts among those of the fellows. [37] Admittedly there are lacunas during the relevant years, but these seem to have been present already in Wood's time. A pointer in another direction is provided by Stratford's legacy of ten marks to Balliol Hall. [38] We do get an inkling of Stratford's Oxford reputation from a fellow lawyer. In his gloss on the phrase "quod habita possessione," which occurs in Cardinal Ottobon's regulation *Christianae religionis* about institution and the plurality of benefices, the noted canonist John de Athon (or Acton) quotes from Stratford's *repetitio* and dubs him "doctorem meum." [39] Athon though was of a later generation; the *repetitio* must have been delivered well before his student days. Indeed, it has been argued that the canonist's claim to pupillage may in fact mean only that Stratford, when bishop of Winchester, honoured Athon by presiding at his inception. [40] The *repetitio* itself survives in a somewhat ill-written copy on what had been one of the blank leaves prefacing a manuscript now in the British Library. [41]

Leaving aside the questionable instance in the *Liber Albus* at Worcester, it would seem that Stratford is first mentioned as a doctor of civil law in 1312. [42] The context is provided by another episode in the perennial struggle between the mendicant friars and the secular masters of Oxford

Sandale and not Stratford. BL. Royal MS 11 D.vi, fol. 24ᵛ; *Oxford Formularies* 1, pp. 84-85.

[36] Highfield, *Early Rolls of Merton College*, intro. p. 77.

[37] Brodrick, *Memorials of Merton College*, pp. 183 n. 1, 197.

[38] The lacunas are between 1292/3 and 1296/7, first bursar's accounts; 1290/1 and 1295/6, second bursar's accounts; and 1290/1 and 1294/5, third bursar's accounts. See the table in Highfield, *Early Rolls of Merton College*, p. 198. For the will, see CCL MS W.219 and below, "Beneficiaries of Stratford's Will."

[39] *Constitutiones Legatinae*, p. 129. "Solutio secundum venerabilem patrem dominum Johannem de Straford, doctorem meum, nuper Wintoniensem episcopum, jam vero Cantuariensem, in sua repet[it]ione dictae decretalis, *commissa* lib. 6." The question involved the interpretation of "possession" of a benefice, necessitating the surrender of all "prior benefices." Stratford's solution was: "Quoad commodum litis sufficit possessio quaecumque, licet non pacifica .... Sed quoad perpetuum praejudicium generandum, vel evitandum per possessionem, oportet, quod sit possessio, etiam pacifica." See Brownbill, "An Old English Canonist," pp. 164-167.

[40] *Biog. Oxon.*, s.v. Acton, John de. Athon was MA by 1327, DCnL by 1335. See also his "Prologus" to the *Constitutiones Legatinae*.

[41] BL. Royal MS 11 D.vi, the second leaf before the text. I owe this reference to *Biog. Oxon.*, s.v. Stratford, John de. The MS is a copy of the *Digestum Vetus*.

[42] In his credentials as proctor for Oxford University (June 1312). See *Collectanea* 2, pp. 207, 229-230, 236-237.

University. The secular masters were attempting to insist on regency in Arts as a preliminary to a theological degree; a measure strongly resisted by the Dominicans who considered themselves capable of providing such instruction in their own houses. Riccardo Petroni, cardinal deacon of St. Eustachius, heard the case on 27 January 1313, Stratford appearing as proctor for the university. The cardinal's decision is not extant, but the case was shortly afterwards referred to judges delegate in England.[43]

Legal expertise such as Stratford possessed was in considerable demand in the litigious world of the fourteenth century. What is more, there were local openings of which the young lawyer took full advantage. Some time before 1313 he became one of the legal advisers to the prior and chapter of Worcester. In September of that year his position was recognized by the grant of an annual pension of five marks (£3 6s 8d), with the right to claim hospitality at the convent's expense.[44] Stratford's enhanced status involved the taking of the customary oath of fidelity, with an acknowledgment of the obligation to give appropriate counsel and a promise not to reveal the chapter's affairs or to do anything to its detriment.[45] The roll of the cellarer and bursar from about this time shows Stratford heading the list of the priory's pensionary clerks, only one of whom, M. Andrew de Brugges, received a higher pension.[46] Among the *iuris periti* was M. John Bloyou, shortly to become Bishop Walter Maidstone's diocesan official at Worcester.[47] It was this bishop who in 1315 appointed Stratford one of his advocates in the Court of Canterbury. This responsible position also earned him a pension of five marks, payable for as long as he held office.

[43] See inter alia, *Collectanea* 2, pp. 206-251; *Oxford Formularies* 1, pp. 18 n. 1, 24-28; *Councils and Synods*, p. 1357 and n.; *CPL 1305-1342*, pp. 111-112; and the general account in Rashdall, *Universities* 3, pp. 70-75. Wright, *Church and Crown*, p. 323 no. 26 summarizes the whole case, concluded in 1321.

[44] *Liber Albus*, fol. 60ᵛ, no. 599: vigil of St. Matthew, i.e. 20 (not 2nd) September 1313. Cf. Wilson, *Worcester Liber Albus*, p. 129.

[45] *Liber Albus*, fol. 60ᵛ, no. 600: 21 September 1313. Wilson, *Worcester Liber Albus*, p. 130, takes the feast to be St. Matthias, hence 24 February 1313/1314. The form is the regular one. Compare, for instance, the declaration of M. William de Hyntes "of Ludlow" at fol. 63ᵛ of the *Liber Albus*.

[46] *Early Compotus Rolls*, p. 36 (WoCL ᴍꜱ C.482). This has been dated ca. 1313/1314. M. Andrew received £5 p.a. He was very senior; he is named official of Winchester diocese in 1316 and had died by January 1325. See *Biog. Oxon.* 3, App. s.v. Brigges; Wright, *Church and Crown*, index s.v. Bruges.

[47] Appointed in 1318 to serve Bishop Cobham in the same capacity: *Worc. Admin.*, p. 324. He became official of the Court of Canterbury in 1328: *Cant. Admin.* 2, p. 237. Another of the group, M. Thomas Teffunte or Teffonte, became a clerk of Bishop Maidstone and of Archbishop Reynolds and also dean of the Arches. See *Biog. Oxon.*, s.v. Teffonte; *Worc. Admin.*, index s.v.; *Cant. Admin.* 2, p. 239; *Councils and Synods*, p. 1295.

Once again Stratford found himself in the company of talented legists, among them M. Adam Murimuth, the chronicler, likewise a doctor of civil law.[48]

Thanks to the *Liber Albus* we are able to view some of Stratford's activities in the cathedral priory's service; activities which soon earned him promotion to a benefice in lieu of the pension he had so far enjoyed. Opportunity arose as a consequence of the vacancy of the Worcester see caused by Walter Reynolds' translation to Canterbury,[49] but the business was fraught with complications. Following the death of the rector of the episcopal church of Kempsey in Worcestershire, Bishop Reynolds granted the commend, or temporary enjoyment of the revenues, to Roger de Wingfield, but this was cancelled forthwith,[50] custody of the sequestration being granted instead.[51] Both mandates were dated 7 October 1313 from London, but the following day Reynolds changed his mind again and sealed letters of collation in their place.[52] What happened then is obscure. Already Reynolds' bulls of translation were on their way to England,[53] but it was not until some time after his successor had obtained possession of Worcester that Prior John de Wyke collated Kempsey to Stratford, claiming that the right to do so had devolved on him as a consequence of the recent vacancy.[54] Whether the new rector gained possession is doubtful. We do know that his position was contested and that an attack was made on his rectory. Following a petition to John de Sandale, the royal chancellor, a commission of oyer and terminer was set up to deal with the matter.[55] So far as Stratford is concerned the incident was closed by Bishop Maidstone's collation of Kempsey on 19 December 1316 to M. Richard of Chaddesley, who was already the incumbent of Chipping

[48] A future official of the Court of Canterbury. See *Cant. Admin.* 2, p. 238; Worcester Reg. Maidstone, fols. 29[r], 37[r]; and, in general, *Biog. Oxon.*, s.v. Murimouth. Other advocates were Teffunte and John Oseworth. For the latter: *Worc. Admin.*, pp. 284, 324.

[49] Prior John de Wyke assumed the *sede vacante* jurisdiction about 26 November 1313, relinquishing it ca. 25 February 1314. *Worc. Admin.*, p. 292. During that period Gloucester abbey renewed its resistance to the prior's exercise of visitation as official *sede vacante*. Murimuth and Brugges were accepted as arbitrators (18 July 1314), with Stratford as a third in case the other two failed to agree. See *Liber Pensionum Prioratus Wigorn.*, pp. 28-29; Haines, "*Sede vacante* Administration," pp. 168-171.

[50] Worcester Reg. Reynolds, fol. 95[r].

[51] Ibid., fol. 95[v], printed *Worc. Admin.*, p. 202 n. 4.

[52] Worcester Reg. Reynolds, fol. 94[v].

[53] Dated 1 October 1313. *Worc. Admin.*, p. 281.

[54] *Liber Albus*, fols. 67[v], 68[r]; nos. 661, 663. The form used was set down as a precedent.

[55] PRO S.C.1/37/109: London, 19 September 1316. Stratford was granted protection 24 September and the commission was issued 10 October. *CPR 1313-1317*, pp. 550, 593.

Norton church, which he expressed himself reluctant to surrender because of the possibility of litigation.[56]

We can do no more than speculate about movements behind the scenes. It is conceivable that Bishop Maidstone sought to compensate Stratford for the loss of Kempsey by making him dean of the collegiate church of Westbury-on-Trym, just outside Bristol.[57] On the other hand, the brevity of his tenure of the deanery could indicate that this was merely a temporary expedient.[58] Whatever the reason, Stratford was without a benefice and thus deprived of the measure of financial security it would have afforded. But not for long. By February 1317 he had tapped another source of patronage; he was presented to a canonry of the king's free chapel within Hastings Castle. Furthermore, it was probably in early May during the renewed vacancy in the see of Worcester – this time occasioned by Maidstone's death – that Stratford secured Holy Trinity rectory in his native town. Doubtless this was due to the good offices of Prior John de Wyke; one of his last, for the prior died before the year was out. There is no record of Stratford's institution, but on 12 May he obtained letters dimissory for the subdiaconate, such ordination being by canon law incumbent on holders of benefices.[59] A few months later, 4 August 1317, he received letters dimissory to all holy orders from M. James de Cobham, the vicar general of the incoming bishop, the scholarly Thomas de Cobham.[60]

It was common for highly qualified clerks to remain in minor orders until such time as they secured a benefice with cure of souls, but after ordination to the subdiaconate they could obtain licence to continue their

---

[56] Worcester Reg. Maidstone, fol. 49ᵛ. "Et dictus magister Ricardus tunc publice protestabatur se nolle ipsam ecclesiam admittere ut litigiosam, nec propriam ecclesiam de Chepingnorton dimittere, antequam sciret se posse ecclesiam Chepingnorton pacifice retinere [sic]."

[57] Ibid.: 14 December 1316. At fol. 48ᵛ there is an earlier institution of Stratford to the deanery (11 November 1316, Alvechurch). For a list of the deans of Westbury at this time see *Worc. Admin.*, pp. 28-29 n. 7.

[58] Nicholas de Gore became dean 31 January 1317. The deanery was then said to be vacant by the resignation of Gilbert de Kirkeby. It is worth noting that Chaddesley, the new rector of Kempsey, was Gore's proctor. Worcester Reg. Maidstone, fol. 50ʳ.

[59] Stratford was presented to the Hastings canonry 19 February. The mandate to install, following admission by John Langton, bishop of Chichester, is dated 22 May. *CPR 1313-1317*, pp. 619, 654. Emden, *Biog. Oxon.*, s.v. Stratford, John de, thought he became rector of North Piddle, but this arose from a misunderstanding of *RSV*, fol. 103ʳ (p. 188), which runs: "Memorandum quod iiii Idus [12th] Maii anno supradicto magister Johannes de Stratforde rector ecclesie eiusdem [i.e. Stratford, not the North Piddle of the previous entry] obtinuit litteras dimissorias de ordine subdiaconatus."

[60] Worcester Reg. Maidstone, fol. 52ʳ.

studies, thus shelving the necessity of advancing to the priesthood. As we have seen, by 1317 Stratford had committed himself fully to an ecclesiastical career, but bearing in mind his qualifications one is inclined to suggest that he had been somewhat slow in acquiring a benefice.

With the death of Stratford's patron, John de Wyke, the process of electing a successor as prior of Worcester began. This followed the lines of the composition drawn up in 1224 between bishop and chapter, and the complexity of the legal procedures required that they be thoroughly understood and meticulously followed.[61] Stratford was available to make sure that this was the case. As proctor of the subprior and convent he gave preliminary warning that all those who were disqualified from voting should take no part in the election. The *acta* or formal notarial exemplification of the process bore his name as one of the witnesses.[62] The electors' task was to nominate seven of their confrères, from whom the bishop was to select the new prior. In Cobham's absence his vicar general, James de Cobham, chose Wolstan de Bransford, who was installed in the cathedral choir on 30 November 1317, the feast of St. Andrew. Stratford's position was unaffected by this change of command. He must have known Wolstan long before the election and the new prior, himself a competent administrator, had every confidence in the abilities of the chapter's established legal adviser.[63]

Shortly afterwards the *Liber Albus* records a lengthy but enigmatic letter from Prior Wolstan to Stratford, whom he addresses as his "special friend." [64] First of all the writer hints at matters touching Stratford's own position, about which he intends to speak at their next meeting.[65] The letter continues with the claim that the diocesan official, M. John Bloyou, was angry with the prior and had it in mind to damage his interests and those of his church.[66] Stratford is asked to come to his aid by erecting a defensive wall for the house of the Lord – an expression not uncommon

[61] For the process see *Worc. Admin.*, pp. 220-221ff. It was usual to have at least one qualified secular clerk on hand to ensure adherence to canonical procedure.

[62] Liber Albus, fols. 83ᵛ, 84ʳ. The election document is summarized (with some inaccuracies) by Wilson, *Worcester Liber Albus*, pp. 162-166, no. 750.

[63] Haines, "Wolstan de Bransford," p. 98; *Worcester Reg. Bransford*, pp. vi-vii.

[64] Liber Albus, fol. 92ʳ. "Eximie discrecionis viro et amico si placeat speciali magistro J[ohanni] de S[tratford] W[olstanus] prior...."

[65] "Propter aliqua personam vestram tangencia de quibus vos plenius informabimus in futurum."

[66] "Nosque ac ecclesiam nostram intendit gravare, et modis quibus poterit molestare prout publice comminatur." The language is somewhat immoderate. It is likely that this refers to the officials' claim to procuration during sessions of the consistory court. See *Worc. Admin.*, p. 108.

at this time.[67] The prior then goes on to say that he has learned of the intention to remove the official of the Worcester archdeacon.[68] He urges Stratford to secure an appointee favourably disposed towards him, or better still, one of the priory's own clerks.[69] The writer concludes with a request that Stratford use his influence to secure for the prior the farm of the archdeaconry, which would be advantageous to the church of Worcester. Although undated, the letter can probably be assigned to the year 1318.[70] At that time the Worcester archdeaconry was occupied by the eminent nobleman Henry de la Tour, uncle of the Dauphin Guigue VIII, who became bishop of Metz the following year.[71] Normally the official of the archdeacon would have been deputed by his principal. Of course, the bishop could have stepped in because of default and assigned someone – Stratford for example – to deal with the matter. In this instance, however, the prior's statements would bear the interpretation that Stratford was acting as proctor of the absentee archdeacon and thus able both to appoint the official and to arrange for the farm of the archdeaconry.[72]

Other letters followed, which illustrate the close liaison between Stratford and Prior Wolstan. Meetings of the kind referred to in such correspondence help to explain why the letters themselves are less explicit than one would wish. Already the more sensitive aspects of particular negotiations had been examined, and decisions taken, in private. For example, this was so in the case of a certain "Dominus N.," to whom at the prior's request Stratford had given advice at Grimley[73] and elsewhere. This man had allegedly suffered at the hands of Bishop Orleton, the

---

[67] "Vobis ... specialiter supplicamus quatinus per vos murum pro domo domini in hiis que poteritis velitis opponere, loco et tempore oportunis, quo minus minas adversantium timeamus." Cf. Ezek. 13.5.

[68] For these officers see *Worc. Admin.*, pp. 39-43. Stratford is said to have appointed the official himself (officialis domini .. archidiaconi Wygorn. eidem officio per vos hactenus deputatus).

[69] "Rogamus quatinus talem eidem in eodem officio subrogare velitis qui statum nostrum et ecclesie nostre predicte in suis negociis favorabiliter et benigne velit et valeat promovere. Sane dilectum clericum nostrum speramus, si vobis placuerit, dictum officium occupare...."

[70] In a further letter (Liber Albus, fol. 92ʳ) Prior Wolstan asks for the farm of the archdeaconry to be given "Magistro W. de B.," should he be removed from his office (of official of the archdeacon?). Mention in the earlier letter of John de Bloyou argues a date subsequent to his appointment as diocesan official, i.e. *post* 31 January 1318. See *Worc. Admin.*, p. 324.

[71] *Worc. Admin.*, p. 33 n. 7.

[72] See above, nn. 68-69. For some temporary arrangements: *Worc. Admin.*, p. 40.

[73] Liber Albus, fol. 92ʳ. Grimley was one of the priory's manors.

Hereford diocesan; an incident which cannot be traced at present. There is no need to give the statement a sinister interpretation, despite Orleton's (largely undeserved) notoriety. Very probably it concerned some beneficial irregularity; Orleton had a reputation for rigorous implementation of canon law.[74] In the same letter the prior reiterated his request for the farm of the Worcester archdeaconry and concluded with profuse apologies for failing to accede to Stratford's petition on behalf of one of his kinsmen.[75] The eventual outcome of these various negotiations does not transpire.

Stratford was next involved in a particularly intricate negotiation, arising from the prospective visitation of the monastic houses of Evesham, Worcester and Gloucester by visitors deputed by the presidents of the provincial chapter of the Black or Benedictine monks. Prior Wolstan and his fellow prelates were reluctant to endure the inconvenience and expense of a visitation, so Stratford was asked for his opinion. He argued that there were adequate legal grounds for an appeal in that the presidents had determined on visitation without consulting the general chapter. On the other hand, he said, processes of that kind could well give rise to "popular tumult" and eventually they might be faced with much sterner visitors. It would be wiser to seek a temporary postponement on the basis that the notice of visitation had been too brief. This irenic counsel was adopted by the three religious houses and postponement was conceded; an outcome which speaks well for the common sense of all concerned.[76]

When Prior Wolstan was summoned to appear in person before Archbishop Reynolds to account for payment of the current tenth, he preferred – as was usual with him – to remain at home, pointing out that very little money had still to be collected. It was to Stratford that he entrusted the compilation of letters dealing with the affair.[77] The essentially practical and seemingly disinterested nature of Stratford's advice emerges from another delicate matter; delicate because it involved

---

[74] Notably with respect to plurality regulations. See Haines, *Church and Politics*, p. 47. The allegation runs: "Quod dominus .. Hereford. iuxta opinionem wlgi et clamorem populi dominum N. infestat minus racionabiliter et iniuste" (Liber Albus, fol. 92ʳ). Nicholas de Aka (later one of Stratford's clerks) was deprived of his benefice about this time. The case went to the Court of Canterbury.

[75] This person is described as "A." Could he have been Alexander de Stratford? See *Lit. Cant.* 2, p. 217, and below, "Stratford's *Familia* and Administration."

[76] *Liber Albus*, fol. 92ᵛ, no. 850. The whole of this correspondence is printed in Pantin, *Documents* 1, pp. 186-192.

[77] *Liber Albus*, fol. 94ʳ, no. 863: "Nos domi valeamus manere," and "Mittimus ... litteras ... dilecti magistri Johannis de Stratford eidem patri directas ob illud."

Archbishop Reynolds' kinsman and protégé, Ralph of Windsor. Thanks to his sponsor Ralph had secured the episcopal benefice of Tredington, but subsequently complained to the same quarter that the prior's officers were abstracting a portion of the tithes. These in fact came from the priory's demesne lands in nearby Shipston, within Tredington parish, and had for long been paid to the sacrist, though not without contention. Prior Wolstan attempted to mollify the archbishop, but made the point that as long ago as the time of Bishop Mauger (1200-1212) judges delegate of Pope Innocent III had secured an agreement apportioning tithes between rector and sacrist. It was easier, he concluded, to explain by word of mouth than by letter, so he was sending the details to Stratford so that he could contact the archbishop. Wolstan then wrote to Stratford, enclosing copies of the relevant documents and of his own letter to Reynolds, with the request that he examine the situation. There was no question, wrote the prior, of claiming anything to which his house was not entitled. From the priory's point of view the initial response was disappointing. Stratford gave his opinion that as the result of a new constitution a privilege of the kind claimed did not extend to those lands which had been handed over to others for cultivation. His advice was that the rector should be permitted to enjoy the tithes without hindrance, but if the affair went otherwise the prior should write to him so that it could be settled without altercation. He promised to find some satisfactory way out of the difficulty.[78] The legal adviser proved over-sanguine; as late as 1363 the dispute was to be an element in the composition between the then rector and the cathedral chapter.[79]

The practice of exchanging benefices was common among career clerks of the day. The real reasons for specific exchanges are often hidden from us, the series engineered by the Stratford family in the autumn and winter of 1319 being no exception. We can surmise, however, that John Stratford, whose centre of gravity had by that time moved from Worcester diocese, found the prospect of Lincoln archdeaconry attractive. It offered income without the onerous conditions of residence which were being enforced by more rigorous bishops in the case of parish churches. It was regular practice for archdeacons to rely on deputies, called officials, to carry out the everyday duties of their office. It must also have been by design that the family retained the incumbency of Holy Trinity in Stratford, for which later an ambitious plan was to be conceived. It was

---

[78] Ibid., fol. 99^{r-v}, nos. 893-894. The new constitution referred to was incorporated in Clement. 3, 8, 1 *Religiosi quicumque.*

[79] Printed Nash, *Worcs.* 2, pp. 434-436, from the *Liber Albus.*

on 30 May 1319 that Bishop Cobham of Worcester set the process in motion, at the request of the parties concerned, by authorizing the Lincoln diocesan, John Dalderby, to bring about the exchange of the archdeaconry held by the persistently non-resident William de Estaviaco [Estavayer], for John Stratford's rectory of Holy Trinity.[80] The proper procedure was well established; enquiry had to be made (in theory at any rate) and the respective patrons induced to give what amounted to a nominal assent. The date of Stratford's assumption of the archdeaconry has been taken to be 30 May,[81] but it is not until 13 September that Bishop Dalderby concluded the formalities by issuing his certificate, which recited the action taken by virtue of Cobham's mandate.[82] The order for Estaviaco's induction to Stratford was issued four days later.[83] The next exchange must already have been under way for it was effected by 27 October, when Estaviaco gave up Holy Trinity for the benefice of Overbury, which had been in Robert Stratford's possession for just under two years.[84] Three days afterwards John Stratford was among those present in the prior's chamber at Worcester for Estaviaco's resignation of Overbury.[85] The final stage was reached when M. John Geraud, himself as we have seen a Stratford man, exchanged Nettleham rectory in Lincoln diocese for Overbury, to which he had been presented by a cooperative Worcester chapter. This time is was Bishop Cobham who was authorized by his colleague to carry out the exchange. He did so on 31 December 1319.[86] As the benefices in this concatenation of exchanges were of disparate value, we are left to imagine the means by which financial equivalence was achieved.

[80] *Worcester Reg. Cobham*, fol. 40^r, pp. 40-41; Lincoln Reg. Dalderby 2 (Reg. 3), fol. 417^v, where Estaviaco is said to have been non-resident for more than twenty years. Archdeacon Stratford himself, though with a house in Minster Yard, was also to be a non-residentiary. See the lists in Edwards, *Secular Cathedrals*, App. 1, from LAO Bj/2/4-10.

[81] *Worcester Reg. Cobham*, fol. 40^r, pp. 40-41: Dalderby's certification of Cobham's mandate (Alvechurch, 30 May 1319). Much later, 29 February 1320, the king presented Stratford by reason of the vacancy following Dalderby's death (12 January). See *Le Neve* 1, p. 6.

[82] *Worcester Reg. Cobham*, fol. 40^r, pp. 40-41: Stow Park.

[83] Ibid., fols. 16^v, 40^r: Bredon, 17 September 1319.

[84] Ibid., fols. 17^r, 40^r-41^r. Robert Stratford was instituted to Overbury 4 October 1317 (Worcester Reg. Maidstone, fol. 53^r) and in April 1318 Bishop Dalderby licensed the bishop of Llandaff to ordain him to the subdiaconate and any lesser orders within Lincoln diocese (Reg. Dalderby 2 [Reg. 3], fol. 348^v).

[85] *Liber Albus*, fol. 96^v, no. 877: 30 October 1319.

[86] *Worcester Reg. Cobham*, fol. 18^r, pp. 22, 233; Lincoln Reg. Dalderby 2 (Reg. 3), fol. 430^r. Cf. *Liber Albus*, fol. 94^v, no. 869; *RSV*, fol. 124^r, p. 226.

By the early 1320s Stratford's portfolio of benefices, with its aggregation of canonries held in plurality by papal dispensation, had come to resemble that of the typical up-and-coming clerk with his way to make in a competitive world. The initial prebend of Stone in the chapel of Hastings Castle had soon to be relinquished for that of Wartling,[87] which in turn was exchanged for Tachbrook prebend in Lichfield Cathedral.[88] As canon of Lichfield Stratford, together with a fellow canon and two monks from Coventry Cathedral Priory, brought news of the death of Bishop Walter Langton (9 November 1321) to the king's officers at Ongar in Essex, where royal licence was issued for the election of a successor.[89] Meanwhile, at the end of 1317, Stratford had become a canon of Lincoln and prebendary of Caistor there.[90] To this canonry and the archdeaconry of Lincoln was added a canonry of York by virtue of papal provision.[91] Finally in June 1322, thanks to the king's presentation, came the prospect of a canonry of Salisbury with the attendant prebend of Charminster and Bere. This time Stratford's luck was out. The royal letters were countermanded and Bishop Martival was prohibited from doing anything about the canonry until the right of advowson, disputed between bishop and king, should be determined in the royal court. Once the king had made good his claim, Martival was instructed to admit Stratford. Three

[87] *CPR 1313-1317*, pp. 619, 654; ibid., *1317-1321*, pp. 133, 150. Stratford was presented to Wartling, Walter de Harpham to Stone, 15 April 1318. Mandate for their induction is dated 22 May 1318.

[88] Coventry and Lichfield Reg. Langton (B/A/1/1), fol. 79^r: 4 June [1320]; *CPR 1317-1321*, p. 451.

[89] *CPR 1317-1321*, p. 33. The complexity of the delegation arose from the fact that the diocese had both a monastic and a secular cathedral.

[90] Lincoln Reg. Dalderby 1 (Reg. 2), fol. 299^v; *Le Neve* 1, p. 48, where Stratford is wrongly styled "D.Cn. & C.L.": see correction ibid. 12, pp. 14, 22. The fact that Stratford presented Gilbert de Normanby to Caistor vicarage 4 February 1324 suggests that he was slow to relinquish the prebend (PRO S.C.1/38/204). At Lincoln the fruits of the vacancy were claimed by the dean and chapter as soon as they heard of Stratford's consecration, i.e. on 26 July 1323, until 1 July 1324, when he received the Winchester temporalities. LAO Bj/2/5, fol. 61^v. There was much delay in admitting M. Eduardo Sapiti to succeed Stratford in the Tachbrook prebend at Lichfield. Coventry and Lichfield Reg. Northburgh (B/A/1/2), fol. 21^v: mandate of 5 May 1328.

[91] *CPL 1305-1342*, p. 220: 27 April 1322; York Reg. Melton, fol. 78^v (cited Emden, *Biog. Oxon.*). Stratford does not figure in *Le Neve* as holder of a York prebend. This provision was made *motu proprio* [for which see Boyle, *Survey Vatican Archives*, p. 151], "non ad tuam vel alterius pro te nobis oblate peticionis instantiam sed de mera nostra liberalitate." Stratford is here (as elsewhere in the Vatican Registers) called "Johannes de Sterford"; execution was entrusted to the abbot of Evesham, the prior of Worcester and the archdeacon of Winchester. As executor of a bull for Benedict de Paston Stratford is styled "canon of York." Vatican Archives, *RA* 16, fol. 329^{r-v}; 17, fol. 107^r; *RV* 73, fols. 239^r, 366^v.

months later the presentation was revoked on the grounds that the canonry was not vacant but held by M. Giorgio dei Saluzzi, the king's kinsman, who was still alive and well![92]

The improvement in Stratford's beneficial, hence his financial position, was symptomatic of a widening of horizons. He had first come to the notice of the central government in 1317, when he was summoned to attend royal councils at Clarendon, Westminster and Nottingham.[93] To these we shall have to return.[94] For the moment suffice it to say that nothing is known of Stratford's contribution to the councils' proceedings, but they marked his political baptism of fire. The year 1317 was also marked by the controversial advancement of a fellow lawyer, Adam Orleton, to the see of Hereford, and it is in this connection that Stratford is first styled "king's clerk."[95]

We have seen that royal service soon brought tangible rewards, but other avenues of employment remained open. By late 1317 Stratford was diocesan official at Lincoln in the service of Bishop Dalderby (1300-1320), for whom he was to perform the office of executor, and whose canonization he was to advocate.[96] Lincoln diocese, being second in size to that of York, the most extensive of English dioceses, must have provided an arduous challenge to any official. No court records have survived, but there is much information about the more general aspect of Stratford's work in the diocese. He was one of those delegated in 1318 to visit the dean and chapter and city of Lincoln – its religious houses, clergy and people. In addition he was appointed a penitentiary with power to absolve in serious cases reserved for the bishop's attention, and to impose suspension and excommunication where appropriate.[97] When in the

---

[92] *Salisbury Reg. Martival* 1, pp. 261-264; 3, pp. 96, 192; *Le Neve* 3, p. 41. For Saluzzi see Wright, *Church and Crown*, pp. 324-325, nos. 29, 36.

[93] *CCR 1313-1318*, p. 455; *Parl. Writs* 2, ii, pp. 170-171, nos. 9, 10, and 1; *RDP* (App.) 3, pp. 263, 266-267.

[94] See below, "Councillor and Diplomatic Envoy."

[95] *CChW*, p. 468 (PRO C.81/99/4194); *Foedera* 2, i, p. 129.

[96] Stratford's commission is dated 9 December 1317. Two days later he was empowered to proceed *ex officio* against the bishop's secular subjects with authority to correct, punish and reform. Lincoln Reg. Dalderby 2 (Reg. 3), fol. 376[r]. For the canonical necessity to specify such powers see *Worc. Admin.*, pp. 110-111ff. For notices of Stratford as executor see *CPR 1321-1324*, p. 41; Lincoln Reg. Burghersh 3 (Reg. 5B), fols. 4[r]-5[r], 9[r], 69[v]. Stratford's part in the Dalderby canonization process when bishop of Winchester (he sent four letters to three cardinals and M. Andrea Sapiti respectively) is recorded in LAO Dj/20/2/B3 (which includes two letters of thanks sent to Stratford by the chapter at mm. 14[r-v] and 15[r]). Cf. Dj/20/2/B1-2.

[97] Lincoln Reg. Dalderby 2 (Reg. 3), fols. 384[r] (4 April 1318), 391[r] (24 June 1318). The latter commission refers specifically to the visitation process. See below, Appendix 1.

summer of 1318 Bishop Dalderby's blindness and advancing senility prevented the proper performance of his duties, it was Stratford and his fellow canon, M. Thomas de Langtoft, who were commissioned to negotiate with the chapter for the provision of a coadjutor.[98] Stratford was a witness to the customary oath of canonical obedience taken by the archdeacon of Lincoln's official at the time of his appointment[99] and as diocesan official was empowered (with the coadjutor's assent) to hear the case of M. John de Spanby, who was claiming the rectory of South Hykeham despite an irregularity in his birth for which he had not received dispensation.[100] He was likewise commissioned to hear the suit against the Hospitallers, who were alleged to have erected a chapel at Shabbington and to have celebrated there without authority.[101] A task which regularly engaged the official's attention was that of holding enquiry into the presentation of clerks to benefices.[102] On another occasion he was deputed to examine the rector of Fingest for his failure to proceed to the priesthood as required by canon law.[103] Stratford also represented the bishop at the level of provincial and parliamentary assembly; he was proctor for the convocations of February 1318 and of April in the following year,[104] as well as for the York parliament of May 1319.[105] Dalderby's death in January 1320 meant the end of Stratford's period of office at Lincoln, but he was shortly to be found in Archbishop Reynolds' service, more particularly as dean of the Court of Arches, a forum in which he had previously exercised his talents as advocate.[106]

[98] Ibid., fol. 393[r] (27 July 1318). On 30 July Bishop Dalderby received a letter from the dean and chapter nominating M. Jocelyn de Kirmington. But in January 1319, at the appointment of an *yconomus* or temporary custodian of Creslow church, M. Thomas de Bray is named coadjutor and precedes Stratford in the list of witnesses. Ibid., fol. 407[v].

[99] Ibid., fol. 411[r]: Buckden, 28 February 1319 (also M. William de Stanbridge's oath on 4 March, likewise witnessed by Stratford).

[100] Ibid.: 3 March 1319.

[101] Ibid.: 1 March 1319.

[102] E.g. ibid., fols. 417[v]-418[r] (Dillington, Weston); 422[v] (Peakirk).

[103] Ibid., fol. 426[v].

[104] Ibid., fols. 381[r], 415[r]. Both were summoned to St. Paul's.

[105] Ibid., fol. 416[v]. Appointed 28 April together with Simon de Chaumberleyn, knight, and M. Thomas de Langtoft, canon of Lincoln. See below, "Councillor and Diplomatic Envoy."

[106] In Churchill's list (*Cant. Admin.* 2, p. 239) Stratford follows M. R[ichard] de Stanou (1315-1317), whose death on 11 October 1318 is recorded by *Annales Paulini* (p. 284), and he is said to have resigned about April 1323. Archbishop Reynolds appointed a commissary to act in the deanery of Arches in view of Stratford's absence in the Roman curia in that year. Canterbury Reg. Reynolds, fol. 130[r]: Mortlake, 11 April 1323. Stratford is mentioned as dean in *CPR 1317-1321*, p. 577: 14 April 1321.

The chance survival of some isolated documents permits us to glimpse Stratford as defender of the rights of his archdeaconry. In October 1319 Archbishop Reynolds, fortified by a special privilege from the apostolic see, had determined to visit Lincoln diocese. In company with M. Gilbert de Middleton, the archbishop's official,[107] Stratford was deputed to examine the title of the dean and chapter to their appropriated churches, a regular feature of visitations but one which could give rise to conflict.[108] It must have been in the course of these or similar investigations that Stratford discovered various religious houses and colleges, on the pretext of appropriation, to have exercised jurisdiction during vacancies which by long-established custom belonged to the archdeacon. At Stratford's promotion the encroachment was brought to the archbishop's notice.[109] The overall outcome is unknown, although we do have Stratford's ratification (dated 21 July 1321) of the appropriation to Spalding Priory of the church of Spalding itself, as well as of the rectories of nearby Pinchbeck, Moulton and Weston.[110]

In the secular sphere Stratford was able to exert influence at a high level. He secured pardon for Walter de Paxford of Birmingham, who had been sentenced to abjure the realm on account of the death of his wife.[111] It was at his instance that M. Richard Bachiler from Warwickshire was pardoned for not appearing before the king on a charge of rape and breach of the peace. The accusation, made by Joan daughter of Robert de Eston, is possibly misleading.[112] At Stratford's intervention too, Sir John de Bishopton on payment of a fine of forty pounds was pardoned for his

[107] He was archdeacon of Northampton in Lincoln diocese.
[108] *Cant. Admin.* 1, pp. 311-314. See also LAO Dij/62/(i), nos. 12 and 13 (draft): *inspeximus* by the archbishop (6 January 1320) of Stratford's proceedings in the recent visitation; Lincoln Reg. Dalderby 2 (Reg. 3), fol. 423^{r-v} (papal privilege); Wright, *Church and Crown*, p. 73.
[109] PRO S.C.1/55/56: 16 December 1321. Much of this document (a mandate of Archbishop Reynolds for M. John de Harrington and M. Thomas de Langtoft to proceed against those having appropriated churches) is indecipherable. The final part runs: "... in usus proprios habentes ipsasque ecclesias et beneficia tacite iure archidiaconali quod ad archidiaconum loci eiusdem racione vacacionum ecclesiarum et beneficiorum huiusmodi in eodem archidiaconatu vacancium de consuetudine in dicto archidiaconatu optenta et antiquitus approbata spectare dinoscitur optinuisse appropriata, dictosque religiosos et collegia predicta ad promocionem magistri Johannis de Stratford nunc archidiaconi Lincoln. occasione premissa f... ad iudicium evocari [?] ad nonnullos actus iudiciales in hac parte procedendo."
[110] BL Add. MS 5844, p. 329, citing "a most noble register of the abbey of Spalding," fol. 286^r (now Add. MS 35296). There is quite a lot about this Benedictine house in Owen, *Church and Society*.
[111] *CPR 1317-1321*, p. 497: 9 August 1320.
[112] Ibid., *1321-1324*, p. 139: 26 June 1322.

adherence to the contrariant lords during the uprising of 1321-1322.[113] It will be observed that all these were from Stratford's point of view "local men."

Many clerks of ability comparable to or even exceeding Stratford's might at this point have reached their pinnacle of achievement, with the prospect of continued employment in royal service, the ecclesiastical courts, or diocesan and provincial administration, as opportunity offered. Stratford's expectations were to be radically transformed by his unexpected elevation to the great bishopric of Winchester. It is to his activities as diocesan bishop therefore that we must next turn our attention.

---

[113] Ibid., p. 181: 20 July 1322. This was certainly a considerable fine. Many of the fines recorded in PRO Just. 1/1388 are quite small. Sir John was witness to one of Bishop Orleton's grants for the benefit of Stratford's chantry. *CPR 1330-1334*, p. 213.

2

Bishop and Primate

WINCHESTER 1323-1333

The circumstances of John Stratford's appointment to the see of Winchester precipitated a minor political and diplomatic crisis, discussion of which is deferred until a later stage.[1] For the present we must confine our examination to the more restricted sphere of his activities as diocesan bishop. The principal source of information for this purpose is Stratford's episcopal register, complemented mainly by the Winchester cartulary.[2] The latter comprises a greater variety of material than its title suggests. It bears a close resemblance to a type of register sometimes described as the monastic letter-book.[3] In other words, it contains copies of letters and documents which concern current administrative business. Although Stratford's episcopal register, in contrast with that of his successor, Orleton, is not particularly remarkable for the period, it is carefully subdivided and sufficiently detailed to give as full a picture of diocesan business as one could reasonably expect.[4]

---

[1] See below, "Councillor and Diplomatic Envoy."

[2] Cited as *Winch. Chart.* This is edited in English by A. W. Goodman from the MS in the cathedral library. There is some Stratford material in a book compiled by the lawyer John Lydford, ob. 1407 (cited as *Lydford*).

[3] See Pantin, "English Monastic Letter-Books."

[4] The division is as follows: Introductory – mandates, commissions, licences, record of enthronement – fols. 1^r-8^v; General register prefaced by separate rubric recording Robert Stratford's appointment as vicar general, fols. 9^r-88^v; Register of institutions and collations of benefices, dispensations for study etc., fols. 89^r-139^v; Ordinations, fols. 140^r-159^r; Register of causes (quaternus causarum), fols. 160^r-168^r (followed by blank leaf); Foundation of St. Thomas, Southwark, and visitation injunctions, fols. 170^r-180^r (followed by blank leaf); Register of temporalities (together with Bishop Peter des Roches' foundation of a chantry at Marwell and Bishop Henry of Blois' foundation of Holy Cross hospital, fols. 185^v-186^r, 186^v), fols. 182^r-186^v (followed by three blank leaves); Register of royal writs (quaternus brevium), fols. 190^r-219^v. Fol. 133 is repeated in the numeration.

Stratford was informed of his provision to Winchester by a bull dated 20 June 1323. The customary bulls announcing his elevation, all bearing the same date, were addressed to the cathedral prior and chapter, the clergy, the vassals of the see, and to Archbishop Reynolds and the king.[5] Six days later, on the feast of St. John and St. Paul, Stratford was consecrated at Avignon by Bertrand de la Tour, cardinal bishop of Tusculum, and given leave to depart for his diocese.[6] In practice there was no question of his returning home until the furore aroused by his acceptance of the papal grace had subsided. In the meantime he had to contain himself in patience at Avignon, continuing the king's business pending the abrogation of his master's authority. Pope John XXII stood firm behind his appointee, excusing his failure to return to England by claiming that he was needed at the curia (apud nos instando) on account of business which could not have been completed earlier.[7] Towards the end of August and in September the pope circularized English notables – the king, the bishops, Hugh le Despenser, and the earls of Kent, Pembroke, Winchester, Arundel and Warenne – with missives in which he expatiated upon Stratford's merits and urged his acceptance as bishop.[8]

At Avignon Stratford, like all newly provided bishops, was faced with the problem of meeting the financial obligations to pope and cardinals arising from his promotion – to a see moreover which was heavily assessed by the papal camera. With papal permission he proceeded to raise a loan on the security of his bishopric of up to two thousand pounds, repayable in four years.[9] This was to prove insufficient. In January 1324 he secured a further bull, which enabled him to contract a debt of four thousand pounds, subject to suspension from his bishopric and to

[5] Vatican Archives, *RA* 19, fols. 108^v-109^v; *RV* 75, fols. 26^v-27^v; *CPL 1305-1342*, p. 230.

[6] Vatican Archives, *RA* 19, fols. 81^v-82^r; *RV* 75, fols. 46^r-47^v; *CPL 1305-1342*, p. 230. The cardinal's own promotion was recent; see Cristofori, *Storia dei Cardinali*, pp. 27, 72 (tt. St. Martinus in Montibus 1320-1323), 303.

[7] Vatican Archives, *RV* 112, fol. 184^r; *CPL 1305-1342*, p. 455 (13 September 1323). "Propter occupaciones tamen multiplices quibus anxiamur continue supra vires ipsum nequivimus cicius expedire."

[8] Vatican Archives, *RV* 111, fols. 238^r-241^v. "Considerantes eciam quod vir est litterarum sciencia preditus, in rebus agendis expertus, vite laudabilis et multis graciarum dotibus insignitus, et de regno Anglie oriundus, et quod per eius conversacionem placidam et honestam quam in Romana curia nobiscum et cum eisdem fratribus nostris habuerat" (fol. 238^r: pope to king and *mutatis mutandis* in a letter to Hugh le Despenser [the younger], fols. 238^r-239^r). Cf. *CPL 1305-1342*, pp. 452 (20 August 1323), 453 (3 September 1323).

[9] Vatican Archives, *RA* 19, fol. 391^r; *RV* 75, fols. 165^v-166^v; *CPL 1305-1342*, p. 231 (1 September 1323).

excommunication should he fail to make repayment.[10] At the same time he was making preliminary plans for his enthronement, though this was bound to be delayed. Stratford foresaw some difficulty being raised by the regular inductor in the province, the archdeacon of Canterbury.[11] Its nature is not stated, but the archdeacon-elect was M. John de Bruton, formerly chancellor of Archbishop Reynolds, who had been presented by the king on the grounds of the previous vacancy at Canterbury.[12] To circumvent the problem Stratford petitioned the pope for permission to be enthroned by someone other than his "ordinary." [13] At first there was reluctance to grant such a licence,[14] but eventually (18 July 1324) the new bishop was authorized to make his own choice.[15] The precise date of Stratford's return to England is unknown, but it must have been some time in November 1323, for towards the end of that month proceedings were being taken against him at Nottingham on the king's orders.[16] He set foot in his manor of Southwark on or about 23 February 1324 in time to make preparations for the Lenten ordination, which he conducted in the priory there on 10 March.[17]

Since the season of Lent was at hand, the bishop's most pressing task was to make arrangements for the spiritual needs of his subjects. He appointed M. Nicholas de Heytesbury, one of the monks of the cathedral priory and a doctor of theology, to hear the confessions of those coming to

[10] Vatican Archives, *RA* 21, fol. 145^v; *RV* 77, fol. 130^{r-v}: "Nolentes quod tu propter ipsarum expensarum defectum indigenciam paciaris"; *CPL 1305-1342*, p. 239 (18 January 1324). Subsequently (25 July 1325) a bull permitted Stratford's absolution from ecclesiastical sentences which he might have incurred for non-payment of such debts. *CPL 1305-1342*, p. 473.

[11] For his right see *Cant. Admin.* 1, pp. 276-278 and the leaves following the *Historia Roffensis* in BL Cotton MS Faustina B.v. There is an interesting instance of Bishop Grandisson of Exeter's cavilling at the archdeacon's perquisites at such times. Bishop Orleton (himself newly enthroned) urged his colleague to respect the invariable custom of the province. *Exeter Reg. Grandisson*, pp. 391-392.

[12] For him see *Cant. Admin.*, index s.v. Bruton, John de, canon of Wells, and for Reynolds' mandate for implementing the royal presentation, 2 August 1323, Canterbury Reg. Reynolds, fol. 130^v. Bruton was superseded by a papal provisor.

[13] The term ordinary here must be interpreted as referring to the person with jurisdiction in this specific matter, i.e. the archdeacon of Canterbury.

[14] Vatican Archives, *RV* 112, fol. 192^v: "Sane si circa installacionem committendum alii quam ordinario tuo quem asseris tibi esse suspectum precibus tuis annu[eri]mus proculdubio non interis cum id nullatenus honestati congruet." Cf. *CPL 1305-1342*, p. 460 (5 May 1324), and see Appendix 1 below.

[15] Vatican Archives, *RA* 21, fol. 81^r (where a marginal rubric is obscured by the binding); *RV* 112, fol. 88^r al. 93^r; ibid., 91^v al. 96^v (duplicate); ibid. 77, fol. 229^{r-v} (slight verbal differences); WinRS, fol. 8^v.

[16] See below, "Councillor and Diplomatic Envoy."

[17] WinRS, fol. 140^{r-v}.

the cathedral church of St. Swithun.[18] Other penitentiaries were appointed in the two archdeaconries, Winchester and Surrey, and in the deanery of the Isle of Wight. In addition friars were licensed in the customary manner both to hear confessions and to preach.[19]

The episcopal register gives an unusually comprehensive view of the administrative arrangements involved in Stratford's assumption of authority, both spiritual and temporal. An initial formality was to receive the obedience of his subjects. M. William Inge, the archdeacon of Surrey, took the prescribed oath at Southwark in the presence of Stratford's brother, Robert, and also of M. John de Malmesbury and M. William Mees, the notary public destined to continue long in Stratford's service and to acquire a measure of fame, or perhaps notoriety, as the person who recorded the articles in justification of Edward ii's deposition.[20] Inge's fellow archdeacon, of Winchester, Jacopo di Firenze, was a more or less permanent absentee. What arrangements were made with respect to his oath are not recorded, but it could have been taken by proxy.[21] Instructions for the citation of the clergy, regular and secular, as well as of other subjects of the bishop, were despatched on 12 March.[22] The official of the archdeacon of Surrey, M. John de Hoghton,[23] and the deans of Ewell and Southwark took the oath at Kingston-on-Thames, the deans of Guildford and Farnham in Holy Trinity church, Guildford, whilst the official of the Winchester archdeacon, M. Nicholas de Middleton, joined the deans of his archdeaconry for a ceremony in Winchester cathedral.[24] M. Richard of Chaddesley, who was to play a vital part in Stratford's administration, was appointed to receive all such oaths on his principal's behalf.[25]

[18] Ibid., fol. 1ʳ.

[19] Ibid., fol. 1ᵛ. The prior of Chertsey was penitentiary in Surrey, the rector of St. John *supra montem* (in montibus) in Winchester archdeaconry, Thomas vicar of [Alton] in the Isle of Wight (29 February 1324).

[20] Ibid.; *Responsiones*, col. 2765.

[21] However, he may have been in England about this time since he had safe conduct to accompany Stratford abroad in November 1324. *CPR 1324-1327*, p. 49.

[22] WinRS, fol. 1ᵛ.

[23] Not mentioned in *Biog. Oxon.* or *Biog. Cantab.* He was rector of Cobham, Surrey, e.g. WinRS, fol. 77ᵛ.

[24] WinRS, fol. 1ᵛ. There were three rural deaneries in Surrey archdeaconry: Southwark, Ewell and Guildford. Deans of the first two took the oath on 23 March (Et ad observandum statuta sinodalia episcopatus Wynton' et ad fideliter exequendum mandata episcopalia offic*ialium* et ministrorum suorum). The rural dean of Guildford joined the dean of the jurisdiction of Farnham (an episcopal church) to take it on 24 March. (Farnham church had come to be appropriated to the archdeaconry of Surrey, a cause of friction. See below, pp. 39-40.)

[25] Ibid.: commission dated from Southwark, 19 March 1324.

Another pressing obligation was to ensure the continuity of proceedings in the courts. In line with regular English practice there were
two distinct episcopal courts in the diocese: the consistory court presided
over by the official or his assessor, who was commonly the commissary
general, and the audience court, presided over by the bishop himself, if as
in Stratford's case he were a competent lawyer, by his chief legal officer
the chancellor, or in the latter's absence some ad hoc commissary. On 19
March M. Richard of Chaddesley was deputed to hear consistory court
cases, both those brought by virtue of the bishop's office and those
initiated by outside parties.[26] By another commission of the same date
Chaddesley was appointed commissary general of the official, with
powers which included the sequestration of vacant benefices, custody of
the goods of those who died intestate, the probate of wills of clerks and
knights and of such other wills as fell within the bishop's competence, as
well as enquiry into, correction and punishment of offences.[27] Similar
commissions, though omitting the authority to correct and punish the
bishop's subjects, were issued to sequestrators general in the two archdeaconries and in the Isle of Wight.[28] This was because the archdeacons
themselves had limited rights of a corresponding kind within the areas of
their jurisdiction. No copy of the appointment of either a chancellor or of
an official is to be found in the register at this time, or indeed later, but
Chaddesley is termed chancellor in February 1325 and M. Richard of
Gloucester official in the following year.[29] We may assume with
confidence that what we can call Stratford's spiritual and judicial
administration was complete before the end of 1324, by which time he
had issued his first appointment of a vicar general.[30]

As one might expect of a bishop heavily engaged in diplomatic and
political affairs, Stratford was frequently forced to abandon his diocese for
both long and short periods. At such times he adopted the current practice

---

[26] Ibid., fol. 2^v: "Ad audiendum causas, lites et controversias consistorii nostri
Wynton' quascumque ad parcium quarumcumque instanciam vel ex officio motas et
movendas in futurum fine debito terminandum."

[27] Ibid., fol. 2^r. Chaddesley is not actually named "commissary" in the body of the
commission, but the marginal rubric is "Commissio generalis." A "special commissary,"
M. John de Lecch, was appointed (Stockwell, 5 November 1324) with like powers of
enquiry, correction and punishment.

[28] Ibid., fol. 7^v. Richard de Rudeham, rector of Compton-by-Guildford, in Surrey
archdeaconry (Farnham, 10 October 1324); Thomas, vicar of Alton, in Winchester
archdeaconry (Farnham, 29 November 1324); Nicholas de la Flode in the Isle of Wight (as
for Rudeham).

[29] Ibid., fols. 93^r, 164^r.

[30] Ibid., fol. 9^r: Robert Stratford's appointment, 2 December 1324.

of appointing one or more vicars general empowered to act on his behalf in all spiritual and judicial matters. On no fewer than eleven occasions[31] Stratford was constrained to make such appointments. The bishop's registrar was meticulous in recording them, as also the precise dates of his master's comings and goings and the conduct of affairs by the various vicars general. It is probably true to say that in the fourteenth century a bishop deputed such officers only when he anticipated being out of the country, or at least a considerable distance from his diocese, and for a long period. Stratford did so not merely when abroad in France or elsewhere, but also when he was in close attendance on the king and the business of the chancery, which was for a time in Norfolk and for much longer in York.[32] The ready availability of university-trained lawyers with experience of diocesan administration meant that during such enforced absence routine functions could be performed precisely as though the diocesan himself were present. For sacramental duties the services of a suffragan were not difficult to obtain.

It could be credited to Stratford that despite worldly preoccupations he undertook twenty-four of the twenty-eight general ordinations listed in the register.[33] For the others he employed first Peter of Bologna, bishop of Corbavia, and then Benedict, bishop of Sardica.[34] There was a moderate amount of delegation of episcopal functions, more particularly with respect to the reconciliation of sacred places which had been desecrated and to the dedication of altars.[35] In addition licences were issued at intervals to the bishop of Exeter, authorizing him to ordain and correct clerks from his own diocese within the bounds of that of Winchester.[36]

The temporalities of the bishopric formed the essential counterpart of the spiritualities. Without them the bishop could not discharge his functions save by becoming an excessive financial burden to his flock, a fact which was fully appreciated by the king into whose hands such

[31] See below, Appendix 2.

[32] See, for instance, the rubrics in WinRS at fols. 56^r, 57^v, 122^v, 123^r, 123^v.

[33] See Appendix 2 for list of ordinations.

[34] Bishop Peter held two ordinations in 1325, one in 1327; Bishop Benedict one in 1333. See Appendix 2. Peter de Corbavia acted for Archbishop Reynolds: Wright, *Church and Crown*, p. 241 n. 141. For many details of him see Stubbs, *Chronicles of Edward I and II* 1, pp. xci-xcii. Record of his death (19 January 1332) at the Greyfriars in London is in *Annales Paulini*, p. 356.

[35] E.g. WinRS, fols. 21^v, 47^r, 58^r, 64^r, 65^r. In 1331 Bishop Peter was commissioned to dedicate the high altar in the choir of Bermondsey Priory, a Cluniac house. Ibid., fol. 64^r. Cf. the commission (1328) to the new bishop of St. David's (Gower). Ibid., fol. 39^r.

[36] E.g. Ibid., fols. 2^r, 37^r.

temporalities came at times of vacancy.[37] A special quaternion devoted to
the temporal aspect of the bishop's administration is to be found in his
register. This provides much detailed information about appointments;
information that dovetails with the extensive manorial accounts which
have survived for the whole of Stratford's episcopate.[38] As a consequence
of piecemeal endowment over the centuries the property of the bishopric
was scattered through some eight or more counties, although the bulk of it
was concentrated in Surrey and Hampshire, counties which basically
constituted the diocese.

The Winchester manors were for the most part well sited for the
diocesan's purposes. He, by nature of his office and indeed of the social
custom of the times, was peripatetic. Closest to the city of London, just
across the River Thames in fact, was the manor of Southwark, in the
shadow of the great priory church of St. Mary Overy.[39] Here was the
bishop's London residence, shielded by the river in times of conflict, but
sufficiently close to enable the diocesan to take his place in parliament or
convocation.[40] A short distance upstream lay Stockwell and Battersea,
places patronized by Stratford to a much lesser extent. West of London the
bishop regularly stayed at Esher, less frequently at nearby Walton[-on-
Thames?]. In Berkshire he found Wargrave to be the most convenient
base, though from time to time he stayed at Brightwell. Were he to be
setting out for the north, the Berkshire manors and that of Witney in
Oxfordshire provided handy staging posts. On the other hand, if he were
making his way south to his cathedral city, Farnham at the southwestern
extremity of Surrey was directly on the road. Here was a substantial castle
built on high ground dominating the town. Its twelfth-century shell keep
was still prominent, though other more comfortable and commodious
buildings had been added to the site, while Farnham chase provided a
convenient source of food for the episcopal table.[41] There was an

[37] Edward II, as is well known, adopted a policy of temporary confiscation or tardy
release with respect to temporalities. Stratford was one of several to experience such
punitive measures.
[38] WinRS, fols. 182r-186v. The manorial accounts or pipe rolls are for the half year
1323 and the years 1324 to 1332, being numbered 159336 to 159345. See below, n. 46
and "Stratford's Familia and Administration."
[39] The manor was important for its situation rather than for its monetary value, which
ca. 1290 was assessed (for purposes of papal taxation) at just over £25 p.a. Taxatio, p. 215.
[40] St. Paul's and the Tower (almost opposite) as well as Westminster (the royal palace)
and Lambeth (the archbishop's London residence) were readily accessible by barge. In
1326 the bishops considered it safer to meet at Southwark than St. Paul's. See below,
"From Conformist to Revolutionary."
[41] At Esher Stratford secured royal licence to divert a public way so that he could
enlarge the house. CPR 1330-1334, p. 99: 8 April 1331. Thomas de Bradeston was

extensive block of property in the northern part of Hampshire at
Burghclere, Kingsclere and Highclere. At the last the bishop had the use of
a substantial residence with its adjoining park.[42] A number of properties
encircled Winchester: of these Marwell was Stratford's favourite, though
he also stayed from time to time at Waltham. While in his cathedral city
he resided at his castle of Wolvesey adjacent to the close of St. Swithun's.
So far as is known, many of the remoter properties were not visited by
their lord. Some of these were substantial, notably the castle and town of
Taunton in Somerset. It was to be expected that individual bishops would
have their favourite houses and Stratford, as we have seen, was no
exception; but the cost of maintaining so many residences was high and
increasingly uneconomic. In consequence, adequate facilities for receiving
the bishop and his entourage were available only at certain places.[43]

Instructions for the restoration of the Winchester temporalities by the
royal custodians were not issued until 28 June 1324, some four months
after Stratford's arrival in the diocese, and the registrar records that it was
on 1st July that the new diocesan was formally admitted to them at
Westminster.[44] All the same, Stratford's itinerary shows that he made use
of certain residences at an earlier date.

We have seen that in the case of the spiritualities it was customary for
episcopal officers to administer oaths of obedience; for the temporalities
there were corresponding commissions for the taking of homage. The task
was entrusted to Robert Stratford, subsidiary commissions being added
for the remoter counties of Buckinghamshire and Oxfordshire on the one

---

ordered to repair the palings of the park at Farnham out of the issues of the neighbouring
manor of Itchell, of which he was tenant. *CCR 1330-1333*, p. 387: 20 January 1332. At
Farnham Stratford inherited what was basically a motte-and-bailey castle, the motte of
which had been flattened towards the end of the twelfth century and a stone wall built to
form a shell keep, to this day an impressive structure. Towards the base of the triangular
bailey, away from the keep, was a hall and other domestic buildings. See Robo, *Mediaeval
Farnham*. Many details are contained in H. R. Hubbard's typescript, "Farnham Castle" (SA
MS 845). Both Stratford and Orleton were engaged in building the "new chapel" and
adjacent chamber (ibid., pp. 69, 76).

[42] A commission to the official of the archdeacon of Winchester, dated 29 August
1331, ordered the proclamation of *de facto* excommunication and citation of those who
broke into the episcopal park at Highclere.

[43] Retrenchment with respect to manor houses is observable in a number of dioceses,
e.g. Hereford (*Charters and Records*, pp. 226-228); Coventry and Lichfield (Reg. Booth,
fol. 54^r) – mid-fifteenth century examples.

[44] *Foedera* 2, ii, p. 101; WinRS, fol. 182^r: "Qui primo die Julii admissus fuerat ad
temporalia sua apud Westmonasterium anno domini M°CCC^{mo}XXIIII^{to}." The matter is
more fully examined below. See "Councillor and Diplomatic Envoy," nn. 139, 143.

hand, and for Wiltshire and Somersetshire on the other.[45] Robert was also
empowered to hold the courts of the manors, to remove bailiffs and other
temporal officers, and to appoint others in their stead. He is not named
here as steward – the principal officer of the temporalities – but it is
evident from the Winchester pipe roll for the first half-year of Stratford's
episcopate that he was acting as such.[46] Another key appointment was that
of Thomas de Fulquardeby as treasurer of Wolvesey. This man was also
responsible for keeping the episcopal prison in the castle.[47] By a separate
commission of 9 August 1324 Thomas was authorized to purchase all the
goods and chattels from the royal custodians, Richard Ayrminne and
William de Pillaunde.[48] It would seem that he was made to pay dearly for
the stock, though it is difficult to be precise without studying comparable
accounts over a period.[49] In any case Stratford did not receive his full
quota. Since the episcopate of Peter des Roches (1205-1238) there had
been a fixed complement of stock on the manors, which was supposed to
pass undiminished from one bishop to the next. But on Bishop Sandale's
death in 1319 Edward II seized his stock on the pretext that money was
owed to him. On livery of the temporalities to Sandale's successor, Rigaud
d'Assier, there was a substantial deficit, and this was still the case when
Stratford succeeded in his turn. Nothing could be done while Edward
lived, but when his son succeeded Stratford petitioned in parliament for
restoration of the confiscated property and in 1331 Edward III, for the
benefit of his father's soul and of his own, promised restitution of £537
13s 2d, a sum based on the estimated value of the missing animals. This
was advanced to Stratford by the merchants of the Bardi on the king's
behalf.[50]

His spiritualities and temporalities safely ordered, Stratford's next duty
should have been to launch a primary visitation of the diocese. The

[45] WinRS, fol. 182ʳ. Thomas de Breilles (Brailes) was appointed for Buckinghamshire
and Oxfordshire, Adam de Draycote for Wiltshire and Somerset.
[46] Ibid.: "Commissio ad supervidendum maneria et ad recipiendum fidelitates."
WinPR 159336, m. 1ʳ. M. Robert received just over ten shillings for three days while
holding the court at Taunton. This pipe roll is dated the first year of the bishop's
consecration, both on the cover and the first membrane. This is inaccurate. The roll in fact
dates from the second year of consecration (first of investiture), which means that each
roll is dated one year in arrears. The last one should be 1333, the eleventh year of
Stratford's consecration. Cf. Beveridge, "Memoranda," pp. 99-112.
[47] WinRS, fol. 182ʳ: 8 July 1324. See also ibid., fol. 11ʳ, for a commission to release
prisoners.
[48] Ibid., fol. 182ʳ.
[49] *Foedera* 2, ii, p. 174; *CCR 1323-1327*, pp. 203, 355. The fact that Stratford was later
(February 1327) allowed to be quit of the unpaid balance of the £2,460 5s 10d levied for
stock perhaps speaks for itself. *CMRE*, no. 333.
[50] *CPR 1330-1334*, pp. 230-231, 255-256; *CCR 1330-1333*, pp. 439-440.

nation's business was to prevent him doing so. It is true that he was at Winchester towards the end of November 1324, when he took the opportunity of having himself enthroned by the man of his choice, M. William Inge, in accordance with the papal grace mentioned above,[51] but there was no time to attend to other matters. Almost immediately he returned to London to make profession at Mortlake to his ecclesiastical superior, Archbishop Reynolds.[52] It was necessary to do this before his departure for France on the king's business. En route to the coast he paused at Canterbury to repeat his profession before the high altar in the customary manner.[53] Although back in England by late-January 1325, Stratford scarcely had time to make his preparations before re-crossing the channel.[54] At last, at the end of April, he was able to spend some time in Winchester and its neighbourhood. Even then the respite was short-lived. Soon he was re-embarking at Dover, not to return to his manor of Southwark until 22 November 1325. From there, after attending to some pressing business, he made his way to Farnham in time to hold an ordination in the parish church on the Ember Saturday in December.[55] From Farnham he moved south to Waltham, where on 11 January 1326 – disregarding the season – he issued his mandate to the cathedral prior, warning him of his intention to visit the monastery "in head and members" on 3 February.[56]

The visitation was to prove no formality; indeed by his rigorous approach the new bishop was in danger of precipitating a long-term rupture with the cathedral chapter. On the day appointed Stratford arrived at St. Swithun's and preached the customary introductory sermon. After his mandate of citation had been read out a formal warning was published; under penalty of excommunication all were to reveal whatever required reformation. With him Stratford brought all the leading figures of his spiritual administration: a theologian, M. John Brabazoun, whose position in the hierarchy is unclear, the diocesan official, M. Richard of

[51] WinRS, fol. 8ᵛ; n. 15 above. He was enthroned on the feast of St. Katherine the Virgin (25 November). Present were M. Thomas de Astley, canon of Lichfield, M. Robert de Canterbury, canon of London, two barons, John de St. John and Ralph de Camoys, and M. William Mees.

[52] On 1 December 1324. Geographically Mortlake lay within the diocese.

[53] *Canterbury Professions*, p. 96 no. 272. "Coram magno altare professionem suam coram domino archiepiscopo prius factam publice et solempniter recitavit et innovavit."

[54] The bishop is said to have crossed on 11 January, to have returned to Southwark about the 20th, and to have left again on 14 February (Illo die arripuit iter suum versus Franciam). WinRS, fols. 92ᵛ, 93ʳ, 93ᵛ.

[55] Ibid., fols. 97ʳ, 142ᵛ-143ʳ.

[56] Ibid., fols. 13ᵛ, 171ᵛ.

Gloucester, the chancellor, M. Richard of Chaddesley, and the official's commissary, M. John de Lecch. These men and their associated clerks were deputed to assist the bishop in the examination of the personnel and affairs of the house.[57]

It was the beginning of Lent, in some respects an inconvenient time for visitation. On Ash Wednesday the bishop broke off the proceedings to preach in his cathedral, to which he had summoned his "parishioners" from the deanery of Winchester.[58] The examination continued until 7 February, when the monks assembled in their chapter house to be told that Monday the 10th was appointed for the publication of the *comperta* – findings derived from the *detecta* or depositions. The visitation took the form of a legal enquiry with assignment of days for further hearings, the presentation on the bishop's behalf of written articles alleging faults or omissions of duty, and the response by way of denial or confession on the part of the prior or individual monks. If articles were denied then purgation on oath would be enjoined. The whole affair dragged on for a considerable time, in fact until 15 March, though proceedings were by no means continuous. One of the more intractable problems concerned the apportioning of income from certain appropriated churches and other property. It was alleged that much of such revenue had been diverted from the community to the prior. After some stalling on the plea of further consultation with his council, the prior at last agreed to submit to the bishop's regulation in this respect. The eventual outcome was the issue on 1 July 1326 of what was termed the "election decree," a lengthy series of injunctions. There is nothing particularly remarkable about the content of these injunctions, but despite a degree of stereotyping, perhaps inevitable in such cases, they do throw light on the specific circumstances of the priory.[59]

[57] Ibid., fols. 171^v-172^r.

[58] Ibid., fol. 15^r: mandate to the dean of Winchester. "Angit nos cura potissima inter ceteras sollicitudines quibus assidue premimur ut nostris subditis exhibeamus nostram presenciam corporalem ipsos iuxta datam a Deo nobis prudenciam prout convenit instruendo verbis pariter et exemplis."

[59] Ibid., fols. 172^v-174^r. Briefly they concern the proper regulation of the churchyard and the erection of a cross there, the celebration of the divine office, the keeping of silence as enjoined by the Rule, the prevention of easy access to church and high altar (the surrounding iron gates of which were to be kept shut), the transaction of secular business in the "house of God," the condemnation of partitions in the dormitory and of eating outside refectory or misericord, the maintenance of distributions to the convent, the consigning of remains of food and drink to the almoner, the unacceptable practice of giving money to monks instead of clothes or other necessaries, the receiving by monks of manors at farm, the obedient undertaking of offices, the relationship with the nuns of St. Mary's, wandering outside the cloister, the necessity for discussion and common consent

A prompt reaction came from Prior Richard de Enford and his chapter. The bishop had made the tactical mistake of imposing definitive penalties, not merely for current *detecta* and *comperta* but also in the event of their repetition. This was interpreted as an intolerable intrusion on the internal administration of the house. It was claimed – without elucidation – that the regulations which Stratford sought to impose disregarded the Rule of St. Benedict and would brand all the monks as guilty of misconduct![60] The bishop relented to the extent of granting a suspension of the sentences until Michaelmas, then for a further month, and finally until Christmas.[61] Towards the end of February 1327 he reimposed them with only minor modifications.[62] Provoked by this, the prior and chapter prepared an appeal to the Court of Canterbury.[63] Had both sides proved adamant years of litigation in the papal curia might have been the outcome, but moderation prevailed. On 26 June the future prior, Alexander Heriard, came before the bishop as proctor of Prior Richard for the purpose of renouncing the appeal and reaching an amicable compromise. In his turn Stratford was magnanimous, agreeing to withdraw the vexatious penalties "of special grace." He declared that contrary to what had been alleged he had no wish to impose anything which conflicted with the compositions between his predecessors and those of the prior. However, he did not withdraw the injunctions themselves.[64]

Though Stratford had avoided a legal confrontation, he remained determined to reform the monks by other means – the replacement of the prior. At the papal curia he urged Prior Richard's incapacity to rule, and expressed the view that even were he to be removed the monks, who had been allowed to slip into laxity, would in all likelihood elect someone equally unsatisfactory. On this basis he secured a bull, dated 10 May 1328, which empowered him to choose a suitable successor for the apparently senile and incompetent Richard.[65] We can only guess what use he made of

---

in important business, the improper use of the prior's seal on its own, the presentation of annual accounts by obedientiaries, the granting of corrodies, the observance of chapters or constitutions, the sending of monks to the university, and the appropriate distribution of certain manors between convent and prior.

[60] *Winch. Chart.*, no. 250.

[61] WinRS, fols. 174[r], 177[v].

[62] Ibid., fols. 177[v]-178[r]. The modifications concern the custody of the keys of the church, the conducting of people through the cloister and communication with the nuns of St. Mary's.

[63] *Winch. Chart.*, no. 250. The public instrument incorporating the proceedings and the appeal was dated 11 March 1327.

[64] WinRS, fol. 178[r]; *Winch. Chart.*, no. 251.

[65] Vatican Archives, *RA* 30, fol. 609[v]; *RV* 87, fol. 155[v]: "Et licet idem Ricardus prior

it; probably it was kept in reserve as a threat. Prior Richard was prevailed upon to resign in Stratford's presence and the consequent election seemingly took a normal course. The bishop concluded the proceedings by confirming Alexander Heriard as the new prior on 13 July 1328.[66] It would seem that this was a choice eminently agreeable to Stratford.

The Winchester injunctions of 1326 provide the exemplar for those which Stratford issued to Hyde Abbey in the same year.[67] The New Minster, as it was at one time called to distinguish it from the cathedral priory, had been established at Hyde just to the north of the city, where the entrance gate can still be seen. Stratford visited the place on 21 February during a lull in the proceedings at St. Swithun's. This time there were no violent repercussions though there was much for the visitor to amend, and once again the head of the house was the chief stumbling block to good discipline. The *acta* or judicial process began three days after the opening formalities, that is on 24 February,[68] and preliminary enquiries continued until 1 March. For this purpose the bishop associated with himself the same persons as he had employed earlier at St. Swithun's, with the exception of the official, Richard of Gloucester, who must have been engaged elsewhere. Publication of the *comperta* followed on 3 March. The legal process then continued until 29 May when, as Stratford was not available, the dean of Winchester and the subprior of the cathedral monastery were commissioned to appoint further days for the hearing.[69] Meanwhile on 3 July at Wargrave the bishop published his injunctions. He deputed M. John de Lecch to continue the case and it was before this officer that the whole process was rehearsed on the 24th. Some months later, on 7 October, Stratford pronounced his verdict. The most serious charge against Abbot Walter de Hyde was that before his election he had promised – not without taint of simony – to release all the manors belonging to the portion of the prior and convent. Once elected he had proceeded to retain them in his own hand, thus adding perjury to his original offence. And he was said to have confessed as much to the

huiusmodi simplicitatem et impericiam suam cognoscens ad voluntatem tuam ut asseris prioratui suo eiusdem ecclesie in manibus tuis cedere sit paratus, times tamen quod admissa huiusmodi cessione dilecti filii capitulum eiusdem ecclesie ad quos eleccio prioris ipsius ecclesie dicitur pertinere, alium eligerent minus bonum." Stratford argued that without a suitable head correction was impossible.

[66] WinRS, fols. 107ʳ-108ʳ.

[67] Ibid., fol. 174ᵛ. These are much shorter than the ones for the cathedral priory (see n. 59 above), comprising fourteen items instead of twenty-one (omitting the instruction to publish).

[68] Ibid., fols. 162ʳ-163ʳ.

[69] Ibid., fol. 162ᵛ.

archbishop during his *sede vacante* visitation.[70] Despite these and other faults Stratford found it necessary to release Abbot Hyde from his examination, though reserving the right to pursue further articles of indictment at a later stage.[71]

Stratford also drew up injunctions for the Benedictine nunnery of St. Mary at Winchester,[72] and for the Augustinian priories of Breamore[73] and Twynham.[74] There is a strong family likeness about them. He had hoped to present injunctions to the Augustinian canons of St. Denys, but a summons to attend a parliament at York prevented him. He had time only for a hurried note of explanation coupled with an admonition against wandering outside the cloister without licence.[75] At the end of July in the same year, 1328, he wrote to the prior of St. Denys protesting that "suspect women" of whom he had complained to the former head of the house had not been removed but were interfering in its affairs.[76] Stratford was obviously incensed by a report from Twynham that certain canons, in defamation of himself and of their fellows, were claiming that during his visitation he had proceeded falsely and with malice, and he gave orders for the offenders' names to be sent to him.[77] There are other indications of irregularity at Twynham. Early in 1326 the bishop had issued a mandate for the absolution of one of the canons, Thomas de Montagu, who was said to have assaulted a clerk, John called "Wastour." Five years later the same canon was still causing trouble, but his friends complained that excessive penalties had been imposed on him. Stratford appears to have concurred with this view, but his intervention brought an aggravation rather than a relaxation of the punishments, so he was obliged to take a firm line with the prior.[78]

It will be apparent already that Stratford's episcopal register provides a wealth of information, random though much of it is, about the state of the religious houses in his diocese and his determination to take action against

---

[70] Ibid., fols. 162ᵛ-163ʳ. That Archbishop Reynolds conducted a *sede vacante* visitation is also suggested by the commission for M. Hugh Prany to collect the arrears of procuration "nobis per eundem assignata et donata" (Ibid., fol. 3ᵛ: 10 April 1324). Churchill, *Cant. Admin.* 1, p. 214, mentions the commission, but no activity by virtue of it.

[71] WinRS, fols. 22ʳ, 163ʳ.

[72] Ibid., fols. 176ʳ-177ʳ: Waltham, 2 September 1326.

[73] Ibid., fol. 178ᵛ: Farnham, 11 December 1327.

[74] Ibid., fols. 179ʳ-180ʳ: Waltham, 25 January 1328.

[75] Ibid., fol. 34ᵛ.

[76] Ibid., fol. 40ʳ.

[77] Ibid., fol. 39ᵛ.

[78] Ibid., fols. 13ᵛ, 63ʳ.

laxity. There are many other instances. Thus, following a visitation of Tandridge priory he found it necessary to appoint a coadjutor for the prior, John Hausard or Hansard, whose election he had confirmed only a few years before.[79] Hausard was probably an elderly man for Stratford's successor, Adam Orleton, persuaded him to resign on the grounds of bodily infirmity.[80] Very close to the bishop's heart were the affairs of the hospital at Southwark; it was not only dedicated to St. Thomas the Martyr, but also situated right on the doorstep, as it were, of his manor. Its condition demanded his personal attention as early as 1324, when he is said to have made a recent visitation of the house only to find that one of its brothers, Walter de Merelawe, was guilty of apostasy and other crimes. Stratford prescribed a penance and assigned commissaries to ensure that this was performed with appropriate humility.[81] The following year he appointed one of his clerks, John of Windsor, to administer the spiritualities and temporalities.[82] A further visit resulted in episcopal action in the October of 1327. One of the inmates, this time a woman, in disregard of her oath to abide by the religion and custom of the house had left it without cause and assumed the dress of a secular. The bishop's letters patent denounced her apostasy to the general public in the hope that she would return to her duty and not imperil her soul further.[83] Despite episcopal efforts the affairs of the house were so much in disarray that in August 1330 coadjutors were again imposed on the master, though the order was withdrawn some six or seven months later.[84]

There was a problem of a different kind at the magnificent hospital of St. Cross just south of Winchester. There M. Peter de Galiciano's claim to be master was disputed by Stratford, whose vicar general gave instructions for the house to be sequestered. It was alleged that the *soi-disant* master, a papal chaplain, was endeavouring to divert its resources to alien purposes.[85] But this was a straightforward matter compared to the intricacy of the problems which beset the small secular college of St. Elizabeth by Winchester. In September 1324 Stratford ordered an enquiry

---

[79] Ibid., fols. 3[r-v], 51[r].

[80] Haines, "Adam Orleton and Winchester," p. 24.

[81] WinRS, fols. 3[v]-4[r]: 25 April 1324. This visitation would seem to have been a special one prompted by adverse reports relayed to the diocesan.

[82] Ibid., fol. 12[v]: 29 December 1325. He was also licensed to admit two women inmates.

[83] Ibid., fol. 32[v].

[84] Ibid., fols. 50[v] (8 August 1330), 51[r] (revocation: 28 February 1331).

[85] Ibid., fol. 78[r]. Following his appeal, Galiciano was cited before the Court of Canterbury by the agency of Prior Heriard then (1333) vicar general. The official of Winchester was unable to find him. *Winch. Chart.*, nos. 156-159, 161.

to be held into the state of the college and correction made. His commissary discovered that the provost, John de Gorges, was absent abroad and without him the defects could not effectively be remedied. It appears that the provost had borrowed a large sum of money from foreign bankers. Failing to make repayment both he and other clerks of the house had been excommunicated. The bishop absolved them by virtue of a papal bull, but appointed one of his clerks to act as coadjutor to Gorges, whom he caused to be cited before him. When to dilapidation of the goods of the college Gorges added contumacy, Stratford proceeded to his deprivation. This took place at Southwark on 2 October 1326.[86]

As is frequently the case, remarkably little information can be gathered about episcopal visitation of the secular clergy. However, it is clear from a number of mandates to initiate the process, or to continue what had been left unfinished by the bishop, as well as from scattered allusions to subsequent action, that visitation was carried out, though only in small part by Stratford himself.[87] A diocesan bishop was supposed to undertake visitation every three years. That Stratford did so is possible, but if so it could only have been in a perfunctory manner; his other commitments were too pressing. There was some visitatorial activity in 1328,[88] presumably the aftermath of wider enquiries begun somewhat earlier. There is no record of any admonition to the cathedral chapter in 1329 – a canonical prerequisite – but evidence exists of visitation in both archdeaconries during that year.[89]

The cathedral priory received the diocesan as visitor for the last time on 8 July 1332.[90] Stratford arrived in the thick of an internal conflict. A few months previously one of the monks, Peter de Basyng, who must have commanded some degree of support,[91] had launched an appeal against

---

[86] WinRS, fols. 8ᵛ (commission to visit: 13 September 1324), 17ᵛ, 18ᵛ-19ʳ. Thomas de Breilles was appointed coadjutor 21 September 1326 (ibid., fol. 18ᵛ) and his oath as provost was subsequently relaxed for a time (ibid., fol. 20ʳ: 13 October 1326). The bishop appointed Richard atte Watere as *dean*, 8 September 1327 (ibid., fol. 105ᵛ).

[87] E.g. WinRS, fols. 39ᵛ, 46ʳ, 46ᵛ-47ᵛ, 50ʳ, 59ᵛ.

[88] E.g. in Southampton deanery; WinRS, fols. 33ʳ, 35ᵛ, 39ᵛ.

[89] WinRS, fols. 46ʳ, 46ᵛ-47ᵛ. M. John de Lecch, the official, was deputed to continue the business arising out of visitation in both archdeaconries, ibid., fol. 50ʳ. It seems probable that all three relevant entries on this folio should be dated 1329 (rather than the 1330 implied by the MS *ut supra*). See also PRO C.115/K2/6681, fol. 17ʳ⁻ᵛ.

[90] WinRS, fol. 69ᵛ.

[91] Two of the monks, Nicholas de Eneforde and Thomas Fromond attested Basyng's notarial instrument (*Winch. Chart.*, no. 176), but according to the prior's account in a letter to Andrea Sapiti (acting as his proctor in the curia), Stratford found no one who supported the appeal (ibid., no. 200).

Prior Alexander, alleging that he had contravened the constitutions of Bishops Giffard and Blois[92] and listing eight specific charges, some of which echo Stratford's injunctions.[93] But all was not what it appeared. Stratford is said to have uncovered a number of serious crimes perpetrated by Basyng, though one imagines he did no more than bring them to public notice of the chapter. Basyng had allegedly embezzled two hundred pounds' worth of silver belonging to his office, removed a pyx from the infirmary chapel, and finally absconded from the house.[94] Basyng's destination was the curia, where he sought ineffectually to promote his complaints against the prior. Underlying this matter seems to have been the policy of Prior Alexander, who had the bishop's confidence,[95] to reverse the drift towards financial insolvency in some of the monastery's offices – a drift his predecessor had done nothing to arrest.[96]

Two problems which closely affected the ordinary parishioner were given serious attention by Stratford: absenteeism from benefices with cure of souls, and the ordination of adequate vicarages. In the fourteenth century there was considerable lawful absenteeism among rectors, much of it for purposes of study in compliance with the Bonifacian constitution *Cum ex eo*.[97] There are many licences for study in Stratford's register,[98] and it is reasonable to suppose that petitions of this kind fell on a receptive ear, for Stratford was a university-trained man himself. Vicars though were bound by oath to continual residence and licences permitting their absence are exceptional. What the bishop attempted to remedy was unlicensed absence, since in such cases there was unlikely to be adequate provision for the needs of the parishioners, which was a prerequisite of licensed absence.[99] The regular machinery of archidiaconal and episcopal

[92] William Giffard or Gifford (1107-1129); Henry de Blois (1129-1171).

[93] *Winch. Chart.*, no. 176. These concern particularly the financial affairs of the house and the alleged appropriation of revenues by the prior.

[94] Ibid., nos. 197-198, 200.

[95] He appointed him vicar general, 7 February 1333 (with the chancellor, M. Richard of Chaddesley). WinRS, fols. 77^r, 133^r; *Winch. Chart.*, nos. 159-161, 174.

[96] The measures taken for this purpose are revealed in *Winch. Chart.*, no. 180.

[97] For its operation see Boyle, "The Constitution *Cum ex eo*"; Haines, "Some Observations on *Cum ex eo*."

[98] Notably in the introductory quaternion (WinRS, fols. 1ff.) and in the third, the register of institutions etc. (ibid., fols. 89^{r}ff.), but also in the general register (ibid., fols. 9ff.). See n. 4 above.

[99] Stratford did license Peter, vicar of Godalming, to be abroad for three months in fulfilment of a vow (WinRS, fol. 15^v), while the vicar of Portsmouth was permitted to take a short holiday away from the seaside twice in a year: "infirmitati tue qua propter aeris intemperiem iuxta mare plus solite pregravaris paterno compacientes affectu ut ad partes tuas de quibus oriundus existis causa recreacionis et sanitatis habende bis in anno iam instanti licite valeas accedere" (ibid., fols. 18^v, 38^r).

visitation, reinforced by the vigilance of the bishop's permanent officers, proved insufficient to eradicate the abuse. Towards the end of 1324 Stratford gave instructions to the commissary of his official – for Winchester archdeaconry – and to the archdeacon of Surrey – for his archdeaconry – to order all rectors and vicars to be resident within a month.[100] Possibly it was a failure to respond to this citation that brought M. Nicholas de Aka, rector of Brighstone in the Isle of Wight, before M. John de Lecch, the special commissary deputed to deal with the case. We are not told what happened at the hearing, but M. Nicholas continued to be absent from his rectory, though now under the bishop's licence and with the proviso that on its expiry he should return to his parochial duties.[101] Some three years or more later, 30 January 1328, further mandates were issued for the citation of non-residents, with the instruction that offenders' names should be sent to the bishop by the feast of the Holy Cross (3 May).[102] It was in November of the same year that another incumbent from the Isle of Wight, Richard de Bourn, rector of Shalfleet, was summoned for persistent absence and contempt of the bishop's admonitions. He was directed to show cause why he should not be removed from his benefice, whilst the fruits were sequestered by the rural dean. But certain persons defied the order and carried off some of the goods, thereby incurring excommunication. The rector claimed that on the pretext of a royal writ sued out by someone in London and transmitted by the diocesan, the vicar of Godshill, acting as the bishop's sequestrator, had extracted a much larger sum than was due – to Bourn's substantial damage.[103] Quite what happened after that is not clear, but Bourn does not figure among those who suffered sequestration in 1333 when the bishop's vicar general, Richard of Chaddesley, made another effort to stamp out the abuse of absenteeism. This time the schedule of absentees in the southern archdeaconry is recorded by the registrar, who names nine.[104] There is no corresponding list for Surrey, unless it be

[100] Ibid., fol. 10^r, Marwell, 23 November 1324: "Monicio generalis super residencia." The other mandate "sub forma predicta" for the Surrey archdeaconry was dated from Southwark, 25 November.

[101] Ibid., fol. 11^r. In fact M. Nicholas received two licences, each for two years, in 1326 and 1328 respectively. Ibid., fols. 16^r, 41^v. He was one of the bishop's clerks, being termed "dilectus clericus suus" in 1328 (ibid., fol. 115^r). See below, "Stratford's *Familia* and Administration."

[102] WinRS, fol. 35^r.

[103] Ibid., fols. 41^v-42^r.

[104] Ibid., fol. 80^v. The rectors of Shorwell (Isle of Wight), Upham, Pittleworth, Stratfield Saye, Elvetham, Newton (Valence), Linkenholt, Bradley and Swarraton. It is noteworthy that these are all rectors.

represented solely by one, the rector of Buckland, in which case there was a marked divergence between the state of affairs in the two archdeaconries.[105]

The problem of vicarages was even more intransigent because it involved the great monastic corporations. In the course of time religious houses had appropriated, that is converted to their own uses, large portions of the rectoral income of those churches of which they had obtained the advowsons. By law the diocesan was obliged to see that in each instance a fixed portion, which could not be encroached upon by the appropriator, was set aside for a "perpetual vicarage." It was during visitation[106] that Stratford discovered that the vicarages of Chertsey, Cuddington and Addington had not been properly ordained. The archdeacon of Surrey was therefore directed to make preliminary enquiry as to the value of the churches concerned and the division made between vicars and appropriators.[107] It was left for the bishop's vicar general, Wybert de Littleton, to take the matter further in 1331, though one imagines that he had discussed the problem with Stratford beforehand. Littleton's mandate to the archdeacon of Surrey lists no fewer than eighteen vicarages which demanded attention, the responsibility of seven individual monasteries.[108] That something positive was done is evidenced by the Chertsey cartulary, which records the ordination or augmentation at this time of vicarages at Chertsey, Egham, Chobham, Epsom and Horley.[109] It was in 1331 also, that Stratford drew up a vicarage ordination for Morden, a church united to Westminster the year before as part compensation for the destruction wrought in the abbey by a disastrous fire.[110] Stratford also took action with respect to Farnham

---

[105] Ibid., fol. 81[r]. That there was such a wide divergence seems unlikely, but the Isle of Wight and the coastal area of Hampshire suffered from piratical raids, which could well have had an effect on absenteeism. The return of the writ of 1325 against alien incumbents reveals that Ds. Stephen, rector of Buckland, was an alien (ibid., fols. 192[v]-193[r]).

[106] His mandate is undated, but the original probably bore the same date as the previous entry in the register, viz. 18 June 1330. This could refer to the visitation of 1329, for which see WinRS, fol. 50[r] and n. 89 above.

[107] Ibid., fol. 53[r].

[108] Ibid., fol. 56[r], and cf. fol. 53[r]. The abbeys of Chertsey, Waltham and Westminster, and the priories of Merton, Southwark, Bermondsey and Newark, were the houses concerned.

[109] *Chertsey Cart.*, pp. 46ff. These are all said to have been implemented in the ninth year of Stratford's episcopate, i.e. 1331-1332. For the Chertsey ordination (21 August 1331) see also WinRS, fol. 71[v].

[110] WinRS, fol. 71[v]: 21 August 1331; WAM, 1851. See also Haines, "Appropriation of Longdon Church."

church, which though in his gift was appropriated to the Surrey arch-deaconry.[111] Both vicar and archdeacon were summoned before the bishop's audience. During the process which followed the archdeacon was temporarily suspended from office by the bishop's commissary.[112] Such matters could be time-consuming, particularly if contested, as can be seen in the case of Kingston, appropriated to Merton priory, where the monks objected to the vicarage arrangements made by the official, M. Richard of Gloucester, and appealed to the audience court.[113] It was the commissary of the official who, following visitation, reported that insufficient revenue was available for supporting the burdens incumbent on the vicar.[114]

At this point one obvious question needs to be raised, and some endeavour made to answer it. How does Stratford's reputation stand as a ruler of the see of Winchester? The bishop himself was to suggest an answer much later, in 1341, by his sorrowing admission that he had allowed temporal affairs to absorb the greater part of his time.[115] The truth of this is emphasized by the scribe of his register in the meticulous distinction he makes between what was performed by the bishop and what by his vicars general. But there is much to be entered on the credit side. Stratford was a businesslike man who did a great deal in the time available. For example, as a trained lawyer he presided over many sessions of his audience court. We know this because his register has a rare quaternion of proceedings in that court.[116] As a monastic visitor Stratford was undoubtedly thorough; too thorough in the eyes of the monks of his cathedral, who considered him to be overstepping the bounds appropriate to his office. But conflicts of the kind were not unusual. This one was resolved amicably, thus paving the way for a

---

[111] WinRS, fol. 65[v].

[112] Who was M. Gilbert de Kyrkeby. See also WinRS, fol. 32[v]: commission for the official of Winchester to proceed with the case (Brightwell, 30 October 1327).

[113] WinRS, fols. 7[r], 164[r]-165[v]. "In negocio appellacionis directe a magistro Ricardo de Gloucestr." (ibid., fol. 164[r]). This was not an (unprecedented?) appeal from the consistory to the bishop's audience as might seem at first glance. The official in this case had acted as an ad hoc commissary.

[114] Ibid., fol. 7[r]. "Prout in visitacione commissarii officialis nostri in archidiaconatu Surr' iuxta consuetudinem legitime prescriptam." This appears to be a reference to a "general inquisition" held in the diocese in the years when there was no episcopal visitation. See Haines, "Orleton and Winchester," p. 21.

[115] See below, "The Crisis of 1341."

[116] WinRS, fols. 160[r]-168[r]. In one case (a dispute about the right to the benefice of Andover) it was noted apropos of a hearing scheduled for 26 June 1324: "Propter absenciam extra diocesim nostram Wynton. dictus dies periit sine fructu" (ibid., fol. 161[r-v]).

constructive relationship between Stratford and a subsequent prior, to their mutual benefit. When the bishop moved to Canterbury Alexander trusted that his church of Winchester had gained a friend in high places.[117]

The prior's confidence was not misplaced. It weighed with Stratford's contemporaries that he was a firm defender of the rights and property of his see and of its monastic chapter.[118] To this end he supported the cathedral prior's claim to exercise certain privileges or "pontificalia" – the right to use the ring, the mitre and the pastoral staff and to reconcile the churchyard at Winchester as need arose, though with due respect for the episcopal dignity.[119] Similarly he forwarded the union of Crondall and Wonston churches to the priory, although both were in episcopal collation, so that ostensibly the priory's gain would involve the bishop's loss. Stratford's purpose in attempting to unite Wonston to the priory was to ensure that a sum amounting to over half its value would be provided in perpetuity for the support of St. Mary Magdalene's hospital, previously subsidized from the treasury at Wolvesey.[120] Bulls appropriating both churches were duly obtained by Stratford's agency, though in the event the monks received neither, mainly because of their benefactor's promotion to Canterbury. Bishop Orleton was not disposed to forward his predecessor's schemes, so the rectories received new incumbents. Wonston was to remain unappropriated, whereas Crondall passed

[117] See, for example, *Winch. Chart.*, nos. 255, 264, 273-276. As the prior expressed it, the church of Winchester formerly spouse to Stratford, was now his daughter.

[118] These were closely connected, despite divisions which had grown up between bishop and chapter or prior and convent. Their inter-relationship is shown, for instance, in Stratford's petition to the pope for confirmation of the composition between his predecessor, Bishop Pontissara, and the then prior and chapter. See *Winch. Chart.*, no. 187. Of course, bishop and chapter did not always agree. A form of composition concerning tithes settled between the abbot and convent of Chertsey and the rector of Esher, and approved by Stratford as bishop, did not receive the Winchester chapter's assent, "Sic hec composicio non est realisata." *Lydford*, p. 55 (no. 91), dated from Esher, 19 May 1330. Cf. the composition of 18 June 1330 in *Chertsey Cart.*, p. 46, 18 June 1330. Stratford was equally meticulous. Wood-Legh, *Perpetual Chantries*, p. 59, comments on his refusal to approve the abbot of Titchfield's chantry ordination (usually a routine process): "Quia quedam in huiusmodi ordinacione contenta videntur nobis quodam modo preiudicialia et subsistere non posse de iure" (WinRS, fol. 71ᵛ). The objection seems to have been to the serving of the Crofton chantry by a regular canon.

[119] *Winch. Chart.*, nos. 190-191; PRO 31/9/17A, fols. 12ʳ, 35ᵛ-36ᵛ. The prior was not to use the staff within the city or diocese. For the faculty to reconcile the churchyard see Vatican Archives, *RA* 43, fol. 664ʳ; *RV* 104, fol. 430ʳ; *CPL 1305-1342*, p. 381 (9 March 1333); PRO 31/9/17A, fol. 12ᵛ.

[120] This meant that the hospital suffered when the see fell vacant. The processes are carefully documented in the priory's records. See *Winch. Chart.*, nos. 183-186, 192-194, 202, 255, 257, 276, 419-423, 437-438.

eventually to St. Cross.[121] So Stratford and the priory had expended large sums of money and much labour in vain.

Another area of concern was the exercise of royal rights over temporalities. Stratford's personal experience convinced him of the enormous wastage that occurred when, during vacancies, the property of the see fell into the hands of royal custodians. In an attempt to avoid this pitfall for the future he petitioned the king and council that custody should be granted to the cathedral priory at such times, subject to the payment of a proportion of the profits to the exchequer. The response was favourable, but royal custodians continued to be appointed.[122] Stratford fared better with respect to the revenues of the churches of East Meon and Hambledon. His argument was that these had at one time fallen to the priory during vacancies, but that the custom had been ignored by Edward II's officers, who insisted on treating them as part of the temporalities. Stratford's petition was granted under Mortimer and Isabella's regime and Pope John XXII confirmed the concession with penalties for those who infringed it.[123] Following Stratford's translation to Canterbury the undertaking was honoured by Edward III.[124]

The bishop also had a care for less powerful institutions. Due to his intervention the parishioners of St. Olave, whose church was so dangerously close to the River Thames that both its fabric and cemetery suffered at every turn of the tide, were granted a sixty days' indulgence by

[121] Wonston: Vatican Archives, *RA* 43, fols. 562ᵛ-563ʳ; *RV* 104, fol. 466ʳ⁻ᵛ; *CPL 1305-1342*, p. 381 (9 March 1333). Crondall: Vatican Archives, *RA* 45, fol. 332ᵛ; *RV* 106, fol. 248ʳ⁻ᵛ; *CPL 1305-1342*, p. 400 (1 April 1334). And see Haines, "Orleton and Winchester," pp. 12-13 n. 13; 17 n. 9; 18 n. 2. Even in Stratford's time the churches could not be kept free of royal presentees. Thomas de Staunton claimed Crondall, where he is said to have been guilty of dilapidations. He was proceeded against in the audience court and appealed to Canterbury. M. Robert de Ayleston was presented to Wonston. WinRS, fols. 20ᵛ, 35ᵛ, 64ʳ, 164ʳ (Crondall); 91ʳ, cf. 93ʳ (Wonston). For these clerks see *Hemingby's Register*, pp. 171-172, 232-233; *Biog. Oxon.*, s.v. Aylestone.

[122] Apparently in 1327, when Edward III was a minor under tutelage. PRO S.C.8/15/719. The petition is endorsed "Coram magno consilio" with the order to the treasurer and barons of the exchequer to search the rolls in order to find out the practice at past voidances. The chancellor then summoned the treasurer and others of the king's council to make a charter in accordance with the petition.

[123] *Winch. Chart.*, nos. 188, 199, 424-425, 427-430; *Rot. Parl. Inediti*, p. 173 (petitions of 1327); *CPR 1327-1330*, p. 65 (grant of 6 April 1327); ibid., *1330-1334*, p. 73 (reiteration of 6 February 1331); Vatican Archives, *RV* 106, fol. 77ʳ⁻ᵛ (refers to 1327 petition and 1331 grant); *CPL 1305-1342*, p. 397 (31 October 1333). See also Howell, *Regalian Right*, pp. 115-116.

[124] *Winch. Chart.*, no. 429: writ of 22 February 1334 to John de Scures and John de Hampton as custodians of the temporalities.

the pope in aid of their expenses in shoring up the bank. The bull was issued "Gratis pro Deo" – quit of the usual fees.[125]

Perhaps the crowning achievement of Stratford's efforts on behalf of Winchester was Edward III's confirmation in 1335 of its rights and liberties. Admittedly credit should be given to the bishop at the time, Adam Orleton, but it was Stratford, as archbishop, who witnessed the charter and secured the "further grace" that no Winchester diocesan should be impeded in the enjoyment of the liberties because of earlier default in their exercise.[126] When three years later the charter was confirmed, this was said to have been at Stratford's behest.[127]

At the best of times the task of a fourteenth-century diocesan was a difficult one. Stratford's episcopate spanned a politically volatile period of English history. Some idea of the violence of the times and of the clergy's involvement in crime seeps through from various entries in the episcopal register. These illustrate the working of the machinery for claiming clerks from the secular justices, for enjoining purgation for the offences of which they stood indicted, and for invoking the secular arm against those who remained obdurate, in the face of ecclesiastical censure.[128] Even the bishop's retinue and property were not sacrosanct. Late in December 1327 a commission of oyer and terminer was set up on Stratford's complaint that various persons had prevented the exercise of episcopal rights at the fair on St. Giles' hill above Winchester, which was held annually for sixteen days from the eve of St. Giles (i.e. 31 August).[129] One of those on the commission was Robert de Hungerford, a man frequently called upon to act in such a capacity. It was while staying in Robert's house in Hungerford, Berkshire, that a mob of men and women is said to have broken down doors and windows, carried off the bishop's goods, and assaulted his servants.[130] The places are far apart and different people

[125] Vatican Archives, *RA* 27, fol. 89ᵛ; *RV* 83, fol. 109ᵛ; *CPL 1305-1342*, p. 256 (23 March 1328).

[126] An *inspeximus* of the confirmatory charter of 4 July 1317 entered in Stratford's register. WinRS, fols. 184ʳ-185ᵛ.

[127] WinRO, 1, fols. 134ᵛ-135ʳ; *CChR 1327-1341*, pp. 340-341: York, 8 June 1335. The confirmation of liberties of 8 March 1338 was "ad requisicionem venerabilis patris Johannis archiepiscopi Cant.": WinRO 1, fols. 144ᵛ-145ʳ.

[128] E.g. WinRS, fols. 11ʳ, 12ʳ, 16ᵛ, 41ʳ. Copy of the writ *pro capcione* against Roger de Hertford, clerk, can be matched with the petition for his livery from secular power. WinRS, fol. 42ᵛ; PRO S.C.8/236/11778. On the legal procedure in general see Logan, *Excommunication*, where at p. 26 n. 8 the reference should be to "Archbishop Stafford" rather than to "Archbishop Stratford."

[129] *CPR 1327-1330*, pp. 292-293: Gloucester, 22 December 1327.

[130] Ibid., pp. 279-280: York, 28 February 1328. Thomas de Breilles was a member of the commission.

were implicated, so it may be that Stratford's involvement in both incidents is merely a coincidence.[131]

Against this unhelpful background Stratford did what lay in his power to encourage the devotion and charity of his subjects. In this he expectedly followed the trends of the time rather than attempting to set them. One important tendency concerned devotion to Our Lady. Stratford issued letters granting forty days' indulgence to those who recited the "Angelic Salutation" daily on bended knee,[132] and ordered their publication in every church, annually in general convocation, and on festivals of the Virgin.[133] Papal indulgences for the observance of Corpus Christi were announced in 1325, and early in 1329 Stratford granted one of his own for those who visited Westminster Abbey in order to venerate the relics or to recite the Lord's Prayer and Angelic Salutation at the tomb of King Henry III, whose piety had prompted the rebuilding of so much of the church's fabric.[134] Echoing Archbishop Mepham's constitution, Stratford reacted strongly against those who sought to interfere with the traditional practice, indeed duty, of making offerings at times fixed by local custom. Such misbehaviour he condemned as sacrilegious, those culpable being declared excommunicate.[135] The bishop's special devotion to St. Thomas of Canterbury is exemplified by his foundation in 1331 of a chantry in the parish church of his native Stratford, a foundation which will be examined at a later stage.[136] He also had opportunity to raise money for his alma mater, Oxford University; a subsidy having been authorized by

[131] In any case, it was a politically volatile time. Stratford was on his way to the York parliament. At York various matters were dealt with, including the unpopular Scottish treaty, the rehabilitation of Thomas of Lancaster, and Orleton's promotion to the see of Worcester.

[132] "Rogamus et hortamur in Christo quatinus singulis diebus habita trina pulsacione modica inchoacione pulsacionis ignitegii in ecclesiis et locis in quibus ipsum pulsari contigerit, necnon in aliis locis quibuscumque hora vespertina vel saltim circiter noctis tenebras, in qualibet pulsacione modico intervallo interveniente cum omni devocione possibili salutacionem beate Virginis Marie trinis viabus dicant genibus flexis ubilibet existentes, ita quod novies perdixerint ante finem pulsacionis complete. Si vero in loco tam distanti extiterint quod campanam audire non poterunt ut est dictum tunc hora ad huiusmodi pulsacionem assueta dictam salutacionem perdicant iuxta modum et formam superius annotatam."

[133] WinRS, fol. 5ʳ. Episcopal letters patent of 23 May; executory mandate to archdeacon of Surrey, Battersea, 29 May 1324.

[134] Ibid., fol. 11ᵛ: Farnham, 20 June 1325; WAM 6672, which enumerates Westminster's relics.

[135] WinRS, fol. 11ᵛ: Waltham, 5 January 1326. Cf. *Const. Prov.*, p. 42; *Concilia* 2, pp. 553-554.

[136] WinRS, fols. 66ᵛ-67ᵛ; and see below, "The College of St. Thomas the Martyr."

the Canterbury convocation, its collection was entrusted to the prior of Merton.[137]

In episcopal registers of this date one expects to find conventional mandates for the preservation of peace.[138] There could be something more particular about the mandate "Pro serenitate aeris," a plea for prayers on behalf of the tranquillity of the English church, of the king, and of the kingdom. It was issued 9 August 1330, not long before Mortimer's fall, and those who complied with its terms were offered a relaxation of forty days' penance.[139] At the other extreme, as it were, there was little apparent hesitation in invoking the ultimate ecclesiastical penalty of excommunication. At Alton on a particular occasion Stratford, supported by the prior of Winchester, the abbot of Hyde, and the clergy of the local deaneries, solemnly published a series of sentences. The intention was to combat the use of churches and churchyards for secular purposes, but the form may well have been that in regular use in the diocese.[140] It is interesting to note in this connection that when Bishop Grandisson of Exeter proposed to take action against widespread theft and vandalism in his manors, he applied to Stratford for a copy of the form of sentence he used.[141]

In short Stratford may be said to have made effective use of the ecclesiastical machinery of his day, whether punitive or persuasive, to have encouraged the devotion of his subjects in ways which were in vogue at the time, and to have administered the see in a manner calculated to ensure that the law was obeyed and abuses rooted out. For one who was in no position to put spiritual matters first his record is a commendable one, so far as the nature of our evidence permits judgment.

In any case, Stratford's involvement in spiritual and judicial activities was not confined to his diocese. Like many other bishops his services were invoked by a series of bulls in which he was named as one of several

---

[137] WinRS, fol. 42ᵛ. Orleton's mandate to Worcester diocese, the body of which is the same (*Oxoniensis universitas velud ager fertilis*) is printed in Haines, *Church and Politics*, pp. 212-213, from Coventry and Lichfield Reg. Northburgh 3, fol. 102ʳ. Cf. *Concilia* 2, p. 551. The prior of Merton appears to have acted as collector for the province.

[138] E.g. WinRS, fol. 10ᵛ: Merton, 22 March 1325 (issued by the vicar general); *Quoniam iuxta sanctorum patrum*. Wright, *Church and Crown*, App. 11 (pp. 348-360), gives a useful list of "Prayers for the crown" between 1305 and 1334. It is a pity that the incipits were not included. See also Jones, "English Church and Royal Propaganda."

[139] WinRS, fol. 45ᵛ.

[140] Ibid., fol. 51ᵛ. Mandates for the attendance of the Winchester prior, the abbot of Hyde and others are dated 13 August 1330. Cf. Ibid., fol. 45ᵛ: excommunication of those who infringed the rights of the church of Winchester.

[141] *Exeter Reg. Grandisson*, pp. 172-173 (1328).

executors.[142] Most of these were routine provisions to benefices, sometimes involving persons in whom the bishop had a particular interest,
such as M. Thomas de Astley,[143] or his own brother Robert.[144] Of much
wider significance was his investigation during 1327 of the dispute
between William Melton, archbishop of York, and his cathedral chapter.
On Melton's attempting to conduct a visitation of his cathedral church the
canons had refused to admit him, claiming exemption. Stratford and
Bishops Orleton of Worcester and Gravesend of London were delegated
by the apostolic see to ascertain the truth of the affair and either to grant
protection to the chapter, if it were able to sustain its contention, or to
compel obedience to the archbishop. Orleton excused himself, so the
conduct of the case was left to Stratford and Gravesend. Enquiry was
made with the help of religious houses in the dioceses of York and
Lincoln, but the cathedral chapter could produce no evidence of
exemption. Instead it launched an appeal to the curia from the two
delegates, which Stratford denounced as unlawful and contrary to the
intention of delegation.[145] No further details of the bishop's activity in the
affair are given in his register, but in 1328 other delegates successfully
arranged a composition between the contending parties.[146]

Another problem which Stratford was appointed to investigate, in
conjunction with Bishop Orleton, was the failure of M. Gilbert de Brueria,
proctor of Gailhard de la Mothe, to render the income from that cardinal's
benefices.[147] Stratford's expertise was also called upon in connection with
the seemingly interminable dispute about the treasurership of York be-

---

[142] It is noticeable that certain bishops are frequently named as executors, Stratford
and Orleton prominent among them, while other names seldom occur. An examination of
this phenomenon is overdue. Among bishops provided by the apostolic see there was
recognition of a debt of gratitude. In *CPL* the "foreign" executors are deliberately omitted.

[143] Vatican Archives, *RA* 30, fol. 109ᵛ; *RV* 86, fol. 125ᵛ. The co-executors were the
bishop of Hereford (Thomas Charlton) and the dean of Angoulême (M. Bertrand de
Genest, papal chaplain). Cf. *CPL 1305-1342*, p. 269 (14 July 1328), also p. 263 for an
earlier bull.

[144] Vatican Archives, *RA* 38, fols. 469ᵛ-470ᵛ; *RV* 97, fol. 38ʳ:"Episcopus Wintonien.
cuius germanus existis nobis super hoc humiliter supplicantes," rendered in *CPL 1305-
1342*, p. 325 (20 January 1331), as "at the request of his kinsman, John, bishop of
Winchester."

[145] WinRS, fols. 26ᵛ-27ᵛ. "Illegitimam et contra intencionem delegantis reputamus"
(ibid., fol. 27ᵛ). Vatican Archives, *RV* 83, fol. 200ᵛ; *CPL 1305-1342*, p. 257 (22 April
1327).

[146] See Edwards, *Secular Cathedrals*, pp. 129-130.

[147] Vatican Archives, *RA* 32, fol. 64ʳ; *RV* 89, fol. 61ʳ; *CPL 1305-1342*, p. 282 (13
October 1328); Vatican Archives, *RA* 29, fols. 226ᵛ, 257ʳ; *RV* 85, fol. 90ʳ⁻ᵛ; *CPL 1305-
1342*, p. 264 (12 December 1327).

tween Francesco Gaetani, a papal chaplain, and Walter de Bedewynde, the royal nominee. In the event the conflict resolved itself; by 1333 Francesco was intent on marriage, while his rival had died.[148] Non-controversial, but presumably close to Stratford's own inclinations, was the execution of a bull for the appropriation of West Wittenham church to Stapeldon Hall in Oxford, an intention of the bishop of that name, which his murder had frustrated.[149]

I have left until last the most intriguing of Stratford's assignments outside his diocese – arbitration in the case of the prior of Llanthony-by-Gloucester, which lay in Thomas Cobham's diocese of Worcester. Prior William de Pembury had been implicated in the rebellion of 1321-1322, whether rightly or wrongly it would be hard to determine.[150] Imprison-ment was used as a means to force him to resign his office, which he did early in 1324, at about the same time that Stratford and Orleton were under pressure in the courts. The custody of the priory was given to Adam de Helnak or Halfnaked – the curious name occurs also in the manor of Halnaker in Sussex – who was certainly inimical to Orleton and probably for political reasons.[151] Pembury did not give up easily. The subsequent election at Llanthony resulted in a conflict between two candidates, Walter de Langeneye and Robert de Gloucester, to both of whom Pembury objected. Bishop Cobham turned to Stratford and authorized him to arbitrate. He did so, and ruled that Pembury was the true prior and ought to be accepted as such. The judgment was delivered at Southwark on 8 July 1325, immediately before Stratford's departure for France.[152] Cobham ratified the document the same day, for he was in London, but apparently feared to implement it. It was not until 24 September 1326, the day of Queen Isabella's landing (though the bishop

---

[148] Vatican Archives, *RA* 38, fols. 136^v-137^r; *RV* 99, fols. 210^r-211^r; *CPL 1305-1342*, p. 344 (13 August 1331); Vatican Archives, *RV* 104, fol. 368^{r-v}; *CPL 1305-1342*, p. 379 (6 February 1333). For a summary of the case see Wright, *Church and Crown*, p. 320, no. 10.

[149] Vatican Archives, *RV* 105, fol. 377^v; *CPL 1305-1342*, p. 393 (8 August 1333). See Buck, *Walter Stapeldon*, pp. 103-105. There was opposition from the bishop of Salisbury, however.

[150] The case against him is made out in considerable detail in PRO Just. 1/1388/m. 8^r, marked *vacat* (like the process against Bishop Orleton) as being enrolled among the pleas *coram rege*. He is said to have helped the earl of Hereford in various ways; joining him at Tewkesbury and remaining in his company for ten days before the king's arrival at Gloucester, and also paying him ten marks a day for his journey from Gloucester to the north.

[151] See Haines, *Church and Politics*, index s.v. Halfnaked. Adam, however, was a Herefordshire knight.

[152] See below, "Councillor and Diplomatic Envoy."

could not have known of the fact) that Cobham informed Pembury of his acceptance of the arbitrator's findings and openly admitted that the prior's resignation had been extorted. A further letter of 15 December urged the subprior and canons to accept Pembury, in whose absence the house had suffered grievously from lack of discipline and the loss of spiritualities and temporalities.[153] It looks as though Stratford had been sufficiently confident to overlook the political repercussions of his decision. Cobham, on the other hand, shows up badly. Fully aware of the injustice to Pembury and of the illegal use of force, he yet refrained from acting until there was little fear of reprisal.

Weighed down though Stratford had been at Winchester, what with secular affairs and the concerns of the church both within and without his diocese, the burden was slight compared with that which he was to shoulder as metropolitan.

ARCHBISHOP OF CANTERBURY 1333-1348

Simon Mepham's turbulent archiepiscopate closed with his death in a state of excommunication at Mayfield about the hour of Vespers on 12 October 1333.[1] The former archbishop was buried in his cathedral church on the 26th and on the following day, in the presence of two notaries, the prior determined that Wednesday after the feast of All Saints – 3 November – should be set aside for the election of a successor. A legal instrument was drawn up to that effect. Meanwhile, two monks were deputed to secure the king's licence to proceed to an election. They found Edward III at Windsor, but returned empty-handed because the great seal was with the chancery clerks at York.[2] Fortunately the proceedings did not have to be postponed because the *congé d'élire* arrived from the north on the last day of October. On the election day prime was sung in the morning, followed by a mass of the Holy Spirit and then all the canonical hours to vespers. This done, the summons to chapter was made in the

---

[153] *Worcester Reg. Cobham*, fols. 95ʳ, 117ᵛ-119ᵛ; pp. 170, 208-212. The case is discussed by Pearce, *Thomas de Cobham*, pp. 195-197.

[1] CCL Reg. Q, fol. 187ʳ (al. 191); BL Cotton MS Faustina B.v, fol. 66ᵛ. The chronicle has: "as dawn was breaking."

[2] CCL Reg. Q, fol. 188ʳ⁻ᵛ (al. 192); cf. Reg. G, fol. xxxiiiᵛ. The letter to the king was dated 15 October. At the Society of Antiquaries (*PSA* 2nd ser. 4, 1867-1870, pp. 413-415) J. B. Sheppard exhibited an "original" of this letter. J. Y. Akerman argued that the deed was not executed – "a very early example of a dead letter." But it is quite clear both that petition was made and that Stratford was subsequently elected.

usual manner. The monks trooped into the chapter house and all the doors of the church were closed except the great doors of the nave. Following the reading of the martyrology and the performance of everything else appropriate to the office of the day, there was a brief sermon by one of the monks, the *Veni Creator* was sung, and Br. James de Oxene (Oxney) read out the royal licence tested *me ipso* at Windsor on 19 October. At that point Br. Simon de Petro, who had been deputed for the purpose the day before, warned all those who were disqualified from taking part in the election to withdraw. After a brief interval Oxney proceeded to recite the constitution *Quia propter* of the Fourth Lateran Council (1215), which laid down the permitted forms of election.[3] It was decided to adopt the way of compromise – election by a committee. The decision was announced by M. John de Wymbourne, a secular clerk. Three monks were selected, the subprior and two others, with the responsibility of choosing seven of their fellows on whom would devolve the task of election. The seven compromisers took an oath to act faithfully according to God and their consciences (*secundum Deum et puras conscientias*). One of them, Br. Richard de Icham (Ickham), was deputed to announce the outcome of their deliberations. Apparently these did not take long. Ickham re-entered the chapter house and announced the result – known technically as a postulation – to the applause of the prior and brethren. Rising from their seats the monks processed to the choir, intoning the *Te Deum laudamus* as they went. From the *pulpitum* or stone screen above the nave (in pulpito dicte ecclesie) Br. Hugh de Sancto Yvone declared the result in the vulgar tongue to clergy and people – John Stratford, the bishop of Winchester had been postulated.[4]

It was determined that Prior Oxenden should inform Stratford of the outcome as soon as possible. But is was not until the eve of St. Martin, 10 November, that a deputation from the cathedral priory found the bishop at Farnham, where they delivered a letter to him in his chapel. Stratford replied that on their return from informing the king of the postulation he would, God willing, give his final answer.[5] Matters moved swiftly. On 12

---

[3] *Extra* 1, 6, 42 (Lateran iv, cap. 24). The three forms were: scrutiny (by vote), compromise (delegation to a committee), and inspiration by the Holy Spirit.

[4] The term "postulation" was used when someone required a dispensation from a canonical defect or, as in this case, if there was translation by the pope from another see. *Extra* 1, 5, 6; *HBC*, p. 203. For the use of the *pulpitum* on such occasions see Vallance, *Greater English Church Screens*, pp. 24-26, 30 ff.

[5] CCL Reg. Q, fol. 191ʳ (al. 195). See also the notarial copy of the process, ibid., fols. 193ʳ-194ᵛ (al. 197-198), *Concilia* 2, pp. 564-566, and cf. Reg. G, fols. xxxviiʳ-xxxviiiᵛ. When the process of postulation (with the letter of 7 November) was delivered to

November both Oxenden and the proctors of Christ Church set out for the court, arriving at the royal palace of Clarendon two days later. The prior spoke to King Edward and other magnates in the chapel, while the proctors presented the formal processes. Precisely what was said is not revealed, but on 5 December a private letter was written by the prior to Pope John and on the following day the process of election was recorded in a notarial instrument. Robert Hathbrand (the future cathedral prior) and M. Andrea Sapiti were appointed to prosecute the affair in the curia and authorized to defray their expenses by raising a loan of up to five hundred marks. Just in case everything was not technically in order a further legal instrument empowered notaries to modify the chapter's submission.

Meanwhile, on 16 November, Stratford is reported to have given his considered response to the prior and chapter; he would neither consent to nor dissent from the postulation, but submitted himself entirely to the will of the pope.[6] The king's letters close recommending Stratford to Pope John are dated 18 November from Clarendon. As was customary, he sent various other letters requesting the pallium for his nominee and asking for the cardinals' support. The pope needed no such prompting. On 26 November 1333, before the arrival of the royal letters or indeed of the sealing of the prior and chapter's public instruments, he had issued a bull providing Stratford to Canterbury, as well as corresponding bulls for the chapter of Canterbury, the clergy of the city and diocese, the people of the diocese, the archbishop's vassals and his suffragans. But it was not until 11 February 1334 that these instruments were formally published at Canterbury by M. Nicholas de Tharenta (Tarrant), provost of the collegiate church of Wingham.[7]

Stratford he spoke a few words on the text of Jeremiah 1.6, "Puer ego sum; nescio loqui." Eventually his proctor, M. Richard de Chaddesley, replied, "Quod super hiis deliberare volebat."

[6] CCL Reg. Q, fol. 194ʳ (al. 198): "Huic postulacioni ut dicitur de me facte nec consencio, nec dissencio, sed in hoc beneplacito domini pape totaliter me submitto."

[7] The above account is derived from CCL Reg. Q, fols. 187ʳ-197ʳ (al. 191-201). Cf. Reg. G, fols. xxviʳ, xxxiiiᵛ, xxxviʳ-xxxviiiᵛ. The process is printed from Reg. Q (formerly P pt. 2) in *Concilia* 2, pp. 564-566, as is the "instrumentum ad conficiendum et reficiendum instrumenta in curia Romana postulacionem tangencia," ibid., pp. 566-567. See also ibid., pp. 567-569; Somner, *Antiquities*, App. to Supplement, pp. 16-17 no. v; *Foedera* 2, iii, pp. 102-103. CCL MS A.196, endorsed "Potestas instructorum," is a copy of the notarial instrument drawn up by Simon of Charing, dated 6 December 1333 and witnessed by M. Thomas of Canterbury and Alexander de Hanekyn or Hauekyn. In it the monks Richard de Willardesey and Hugh de Sancto Yvone are named as presentors of the postulation to the pope.

So much for the evidence of the records. What lies behind them? According to Murimuth, the Canterbury monks in postulating Stratford made a virtue of necessity, for they already knew that the king had written on his behalf to Pope John, who regarded him with considerable favour. Doubtless the chapter had more than an inkling of what was in the king's mind, but the *congé d'élire* is regular in form and did not nominate Stratford as Dean Hook asserted.[8] Certainly his promotion was politically acceptable; he was after all the royal chancellor. But the pope exercised his authority without direct reference to Westminster or Canterbury, and Stratford himself was determined to await first royal approval and then papal provision. To all outward appearances there was a rare unanimity between the three parties, though the manner of appointment was open to objection both by chapter and king. As for the complex and expensive process at Canterbury, it had proved little more than an empty form.

In the meantime Stratford continued to act as bishop of Winchester, holding an ordination at Farnham on 18 December and consecrating Richard de Bury as bishop of Durham shortly thereafter.[9] Arrangements for parliament and convocation were under way through the agency of Prior Oxenden, in his capacity as *sede vacante* guardian of the see of Canterbury.[10] But he seems to have been less than competent. Altercation took place between legal experts about irregularities in the form of the prior's mandates to the clergy, which allegedly gave rise to a degree of obscurity.[11] Stratford at this point set out for Woodstock, where his temporalities were restored on 4 February. Two days later, in an informal and friendly letter under his privy seal, he assured the prior that he would make his excuses for absence from parliament and look after the interests of Canterbury. Arrived at York, Stratford received back the great seal from the chancery clerks and subsequently took part in parliamentary proceedings.[12]

[8] *Murimuth*, p. 69: "Faciendo de necessitate virtutem." Hook, *Lives* 4, p. 22; Akerman, "Note on election of Archbishop Stratford" (n. 2 above).

[9] *Murimuth*, p. 71, and see "Itinerary" below.

[10] CCL Reg. Q, fol. 181^r-v (al. 185); *Concilia* 2, pp. 562-563, 570; *CCR 1333-1337*, p. 177.

[11] Words were used "modo obscuro," the town of Northampton was specified but not the actual place of assembly (ne clerus vagaret sub incerto), and there was no provision for certification by the bishop of London of the other suffragans. CCL Reg. Q, fols. 181^v-182^v (al. 185-186).

[12] *CPR 1330-1334*, p. 510: mandate for livery, Woodstock, 5 February 1334; *CCR 1333-1337*, p. 296: seal delivered 17 February; CCL Reg. Q, fol. 183^v (al. 187): "amice carissime."

The archbishop-elect's next step was to secure the pallium from the pope. This constituted the symbol of his authority as metropolitan and was held to be a prerequisite for the performance of certain functions.[13] The procedure in this instance is particularly well documented, owing to the choice of Bishop Hethe as an executor of the bull for the delivery of the pallium and the receiving of the archbishop's oath to the apostolic see. Details are to be found both in Hethe's episcopal register and in Dene's *Historia Roffensis* – Hethe being the central character in the chronicler's narrative. On mid-Lent Sunday (6 March 1334) Hethe received Stratford's mandate requiring him to bring the pallium to York. He then waited at his manors of Trottiscliffe and Halling for more than five weeks. Meanwhile, Stratford was sent on a mission to the continent, and from Rue in Ponthieu wrote again and with more than a trace of asperity. Hethe was to bring the pallium in all haste. At long last, on 18 April, the pallium reached Halling in the care of M. Andrea Sapiti, the king's proctor in the Roman curia. The reluctant Hethe was obliged to brave tempestuous seas and to cross the channel in accordance with the archbishop's imperious instructions. Stratford was still at Rue when Hethe arrived on 23 April. The ceremony of conferring the pallium and performing the oath took place in the local church. His duty discharged, Hethe certified the pope of the fact and hastened home. Stratford was detained by negotiations until the first week of June.[14]

Clearly there was to be a conflict of interest. Stratford was anxious to assume his new ecclesiastical duties, but the king's business allowed him scant time so to do. Having reported to Edward in the north he issued, on 12 August, a mandate for convocation, and eight days later a summons to his fellow bishops and other clergy to attend his enthronement. Parliament met on 20 September, convocation six days later at St. Paul's. On the 28th, at Westminster, Stratford divested himself of the burden-

---

[13] See *Cant. Admin.* 1, pp. 158-159; *Extra* 1, 8, 3 *Nisi specialis dilectio*. Stratford declared it was customary to receive papal graces at the time of receiving the pallium, but that he had not done so. PRO 31/9/17A, fol. 80ʳ: *Supplicationes* entrusted to M. Andrea Sapiti.

[14] *Rochester Reg. Hethe*, pp. 549-551; BL Cotton MS Faustina B.v, fols. 75ʳ, 76ʳ⁻ᵛ; Kirsch, "Andreas Sapiti," p. 593. On 13 June 1334 M. Richard de Langdon, Stratford's treasurer, received from the prior the privilege of Pope Innocent "Quod ipse archiepiscopus posset uti pallio suo extra provinciam suam, cuius privilegii copia est in quadam cedula huic quaterno annexa." CCL D.E.3, fol. 25ʳ. It will be noted that Stratford received the pallium by virtue of a special bull naming particular executors, Hethe and the bishop of London, Gravesend. According to *CPL 1305-1342*, p. 411, the pallium was being sent by Br. Robert Hathbrand. The usual procedure, whereby the Canterbury monks secured the pallium and handed it to the archbishop, is recorded in CCL Reg. Q, fol. 197ᵛ (al. 201). See also CCL MS A.40a.

some duties of chancellor; the great seal passed to a new holder of the office, Bishop Bury of Durham.[15]

Perhaps it was a freak of chance that the feast of St. Denys (9 October), the patron of France, was chosen for Stratford's enthronement in Christ Church, Canterbury, by Prior Richard Oxenden. Such an event was traditionally of national importance, regularly attended by the king and other notables. On this occasion Edward was otherwise engaged, defending the northern border against the Scots. However, his younger brother John of Eltham, earl of Cornwall, was present. By custom the earl of Gloucester acted as steward and butler for the festivities. Here too there was a change because Earl Gilbert de Clare had died at Bannockburn in 1314, leaving three co-heiresses. One of these was married to Hugh Audley,[16] and as her portion of the inheritance included tenure of the archbishop's castle of Tonbridge and other manors, from which the services were due, her husband assumed the responsibilities usually assigned to the earl. He determined to exercise his duties in person; a necessity if he were to receive the perquisites of office. For Audley's fee and liveries – both robes and other items which by composition[17] belonged to the steward and butler – Stratford is said to have given a hundred pounds, or more reliably, a hundred marks. In the event, Audley not only provided the number of scarlet robes prescribed,[18] but also five more with fur trimming. In addition to Cornwall two other earls participated in the ceremonies, Surrey (John de Warenne) and Arundel (Richard FitzAlan).[19] The clerical order was better represented by six

[15] Summonses to attend convocation are entered in WinRO 1, fols. 7r-8r; Worcester Reg. Montacute 2, fols. 2v-3v. See Appendix 3. For Stratford's replacement by Bury and his subsequent diplomatic mission: below, "In the Seat of Power," at nn. 135-136ff.

[16] Hugh Audley married Margaret de Clare, widow of Piers Gaveston, earl of Cornwall, and second daughter of Gilbert de Clare (ob. 1295).

[17] See Canterbury Reg. Reynolds, fol. 4r: "Littera de feodo domini comitis Glouc. in intronizacione" (7 February 1314). The earl was Gilbert de Clare II. Because of former disputes an indenture was drawn up, part of which was to remain in the earl's wardrobe, the other with John de Ringwood, the archbishop's clerk. The agreement itself is not recorded there. As steward the earl was to provide seven scarlet robes, thirty sextars of wine and fifty pounds of wax for candles; as butler another seven scarlet robes, twenty sextars of wine and a further fifty pounds of wax. See CCL Reg. G, fols. 23v-24r; also Dugdale, *Monasticon* 1, pp. 103-104 (from BL Cotton MS Galba E.iv, fols. 34v-35r); Somner, *Antiquities*, App. pp. 56-57, no. 45; and nn. 18, 20 below.

[18] See *Monasticon* 1, pp. 103-104, (BL Cotton MS Galba E.iv, fols. 34v-35r) for the thirteenth-century composition which seems to have been largely reiterated in the arrangement of Reynolds' time.

[19] Warenne died the year before Stratford. Richard FitzAlan was Warenne's nephew and assumed the title of earl of Surrey on the death of the dowager countess in 1361. *HBC*, p. 451.

suffragan bishops, those of Coventry and Lichfield (Northburgh), Salisbury (Wyville), Rochester (Hethe), London (Gravesend), St. David's (Gower), and Winchester (Orleton), as well as by the "local" abbots of St. Augustine's Canterbury, Faversham, Langdon and St. Radegund's, Dover. The enthronement was followed by the usual conviviality, but of this we hear nothing specific. It was in any case of short duration, since before the end of the month Stratford was again at Dover on his way to France.[20]

Stratford's new titles were archbishop of Canterbury, primate of all England and legate of the apostolic see,[21] which epitomize the various aspects of his authority. Within his own diocese of Canterbury he was much like any other bishop; within the province of Canterbury, which included the four Welsh sees, he exercised a general oversight with capacity to act if any of his suffragans proved negligent, and also claimed a prerogative jurisdiction over testaments of persons of status who left property in various dioceses.[22] When sees within the province fell vacant,

[20] CCL Reg. Q, fol. 197^r (al. 201); Lambeth Registrum Album, fols. 32^{r-v}, 33^v; BL Cotton MS Faustina B.v, fol. 75^v; *Murimuth*, p. 73; also "Itinerary" below. For Winchelsey's enthronement (1294), attended by the king, his son, his brother, and by seven bishops and six earls, see Somner, *Antiquities*, App. pp. 57-58 no. 47. The magnificence of a much later enthronement, that of Archbishop Warham in 1504, can be seen from the document in Dugdale, *Monasticon* 1, pp. 113-118, where it is also noted that Audley had received 100 marks from Stratford (as in Lambeth Registrum Album). Reg. Q states that it was £100. The composition referred to in the *Monasticon* is that between Archbishop Boniface and Richard de Clare. The Bodleian MS cited by Dugdale (*Monasticon* 1, p. 118) accords with CCL Reg. G, fols. 23^v-24^r, in which Stratford is termed "lately archbishop"; in both the sum paid to Audley is given as 100 marks, (Gilbert de Clare received 200). See also n. 17 above.

[21] "Johannes Dei gracia Cantuariensis archiepiscopus tocius Anglie primas et apostolice sedis legatus." In general see *Cant. Admin.* 1, pp. 153-160; also Kemp, "History and Action," p. 361. For earlier titles of bishops and archbishops see Cheney, *English Bishops' Chanceries*, pp. 61-66.

[22] See *Cant. Admin.* 1, esp. chap. 7; Denton, *Winchelsey*, pp. 46-47; *Canterbury Reg. Chichele* 2, intro. pp. 1ff. Churchill, *Cant. Admin.* 1, pp. 380-386, discusses the prerogative jurisdiction, which she considers was "stated with greater precision by Archbishop Reynolds." Lambeth Registrum Album has this rubric at fol. 32^v (duplicating that in CCL Reg. G, fol. 24^r): "Insinuaciones testamentorum diversorum qui bona tam in diocesi Cant. et in iurisdiccionibus domino Cant. archiepiscopo immediate subiectis quam in diversis diocesibus Cant. provincie habuerunt facte et approbate coram venerabili patre domino Johanne Dei gracia Cant. archiepiscopo ac eius vicario generali ipso in remotis agente." There follows Stratford's repudiation of probate by Bishop Hethe in the case of the lady Alice de Columbers. She had held goods in more than one diocese, hence probate belonged "ad nos de prerogativa ecclesie nostre Cant." The archbishop then approved the will (16 June 1334). Ibid. fols. 32^v-33^r. But elsewhere (*Bath and Wells Reg. Shrewsbury*, p. 367), and as late as 13 March 1340, Alice's son and executor is cited to appear with a copy of the will. Murimuth as vicar general granted probate of the testaments of M. John de Everdon, dean of St. Paul's, 3 February 1336 (*Biog. Oxon.* s.v. wrongly says that he

the archbishop was responsible for their administration, though in some his authority was circumscribed by composition.[23] Although the position of *legatus natus* gave him a special relationship with the Roman see it is not clear what additional powers this conferred in practice. Dr. Churchill thought that Simon Mepham was the first archbishop to adopt this designation as part of his official style; Stratford followed him and the practice was continued until the Reformation.[24]

Examination of Stratford's activities in the individual spheres is handicapped by the loss of his archiepiscopal register.[25] The lacuna can be filled in part by recovering his *acta* from other sources, principally the registers of his suffragans, the letter-books of the priors of Canterbury, cartularies, and other miscellaneous records.[26] A provisional list of *acta* is included among the appendices; provisional because additional items will assuredly come to light from time to time and the present writer does not claim to have made a systematic search. Inevitably the composition of the surviving sources imposes a limitation on the scope of Stratford's bio-graphy. Political aspects apart, we learn much of the archbishop's relations with his cathedral priory of Christ Church, something of his work as metropolitan, particularly in those sees for which the registers are extensive, but very little indeed about the administration of Canterbury diocese. Unless by some unlikely chance the missing register reappears, little can be done to remedy the imbalance. Bearing this in mind, we can

died 15 January 1337; *Le Neve* 5, p. 5, has "by 24 July 1335"), and of Pagan Bursar of London, 18 November 1334. In the latter case he repudiated the insinuation made by William Inge, archdeacon of Surrey. See ccl. Reg. G, fol. 24^{r-v}; Lambeth Registrum Album, fols. 32^v-33^r; Ducarel, "Fragmenta," fol. 72^{r-v}; also for the composition between Archbishop Reynolds and Bishop Dalderby of Lincoln, 8 January 1320, Lincoln Reg. Bek 2 (Reg. 7), fols. 215^v-216^r (part of process re will of Henry, earl of Lancaster, in 1346), ccl. Reg. G, fols. 12^v-17^r. Bishop Wyville resisted Stratford's claims and sought his chapter's support for appeals and provocations in the curia. The chapter urged a peaceable solution. *Hemingby's Register*, pp. 124-125 (215), undated.

[23] In Archbishop Boniface's time compositions were made for Lincoln, London and Salisbury between 1261 and 1263, that for Worcester following in 1268. The Norwich composition is of Mepham's time. See *Cant. Admin.* 1, chap. 1.

[24] *Cant. Admin.* 1, pp. 155-158. That Winchelsey may have claimed such authority is suggested by Denton, *Winchelsey*, p. 45 n. 41 (citing *Salisbury Reg. Gandavo*, pp. 262-262; *Reg. Boniface VIII* 2, p. 627); but his usual "style" did not reflect this.

[25] Both Stratford's register and that of his immediate predecessor Mepham are lost, leaving a gap between 1328 and 1348. Archbishop Wittlesey or Whittlesey consulted Stratford's register in 1370 (*Thorne*, col. 2108). Lambeth Registrum Album, a collection of miscellaneous material culled from various medieval registers and bearing the date 1570 on the label, seemingly does not mention Stratford's register, the details of testamentary jurisdiction (n. 22 above) apparently coming from elsewhere.

[26] For an earlier attempt at this see Ducarel, "Fragmenta," bl. Add. ms 6066, dated 1656 (*sic*).

now turn to a consideration of Stratford as archbishop and diocesan, confining our attention fairly strictly to ecclesiastical matters.[27]

On his return from abroad in January 1335 Stratford lost no time in launching a visitation of his cathedral monastery. For this purpose he appeared personally in the chapter house on Friday 3 February. First of all he preached a sermon in the presence of Prior Oxenden and the other monks. Then the formalities began with the reading of the prior and convent's signification that citation had been duly made and the delivery in writing of certain warnings on the archbishop's behalf. These are not specified but would have concerned the monks' behaviour during the process of visitation. To carry out the examination of the brethren Stratford appointed the official of Canterbury, M. Adam Murimuth, and the treasurer of St. Paul's, M. Thomas de Astley. Three notaries were then deputed to copy down the *detecta* and *comperta*[28] with a view to their publication on the following Monday, 6 February. When Monday arrived proceedings were resumed before the archbishop. Details of what had transpired so far were read out, followed by the depositions of the monks and the resulting *comperta*. Certain articles were then abstracted and put to the prior and chapter. On these points Stratford formulated regulations and injunctions, after which there was an adjournment until the following day.

When the monks assembled in their chapter house on the Tuesday the archbishop made some enquiries about Oxenden's election, to which the prior replied verbally and produced letters of Archbishop Mepham in confirmation. Stratford continued to press for further information and caused the relevant register to be read out in order to discover what had happened on former occasions. After some discussion with his clerks Stratford conceded that the prior had indeed been canonically elected.[29] Why the visitor queried Oxenden's election so long after the event (1331) it is hard to say. Possibly it was no more than a legalistic affirmation of archiepiscopal rights of examination and confirmation. Alternatively, and

---

[27] In my view it is perfectly defensible to treat of the more strictly ecclesiastical and the political aspects of Stratford's career separately. To do otherwise would be to fall into a mere chronological catena of events. The archbishop was fully aware of the dichotomy, which nowadays some would discuss in terms of "role play." Unity is provided by the man himself.

[28] Strictly speaking the *detecta* arose from the depositions of those examined while the *comperta* emerged after collation and review by the visitors. The notaries were John de Eccleshale, Nicholas de Ystele, and Simon de Charing.

[29] "Super prefeccione et modo predictis cause cognicionem faciens pleniorem fecit ibidem tunc suum legi registrum ad videndum quid super prefeccione huiusmodi factum fuerat temporibus retroactis." CCL MS A.197.

this is more likely, it could have originated, as the process suggests, in objections raised by some of the monks, who were challenging Oxenden's authority on grounds which are not disclosed. At this stage the hearing was adjourned until the next day, Wednesday 8 February, when for the first time we learn about the underlying conflict within the monastery; a conflict manifested by disobedience to superiors in defiance of a basic tenet of the Benedictine rule. Stratford began the session by delivering a brief homily on the need for charity and obedience, after which Prior Oxenden forgave the monks individually for the rancour generated in the past, provided that henceforth they behaved appropriately towards him. In token of this forgiveness the kiss of peace was exchanged. The prior then read a prepared statement which he claimed had received the assent of all the brethren. In this the monks promised obedience to the prior, subprior and other officers set over them and consented to follow the religious life, subject to penalty should they do otherwise. It was further agreed that notorious delinquents who could not be dealt with by the prior or subprior were to be punished by the archbishop. Stratford then concluded the proceedings by judicially approving the settlement and graciously decreeing that he would take no further action with respect to the *detecta* and *comperta*.[30] From many letters subsequently exchanged between prior and archbishop we can divine that dissension continued to seethe beneath the surface.

It will be appreciated that the relationship between the archbishop and his cathedral priory was a delicate one. In theory they had the strongest of common interests; the well-being of the church of Canterbury and the defence of its rights and prerogatives. One of the priory's *sede vacante* registers is prefaced by a lengthy section devoted to the archbishop's privileges[31] and Prior Oxenden recorded in his memorandum book, mainly devoted to accounts, that at Stratford's request he sent to M. Adam Murimuth copies of papal privileges granted to the metropolitan and of various other muniments.[32] In practice there were areas of recurring friction, notably with respect to the archbishop's rights within the

[30] CCL MS A.197. Simon de Charing's notarial instrument detailing the visitation ends with Stratford's declaration of the validity of Oxenden's election. Reg. Q, fols. 197ʳ-198ʳ (al. 201-202), concludes with the internal settlement reached on the Wednesday.

[31] CCL Reg. G, fols. 1-24.

[32] CCL D.E.3, fol. 25ᵛ. Cf. Churchill, "Table of Canterbury Charters," where the distinction is drawn between the archbishop's own treasury at St. Gregory's, Canterbury, under the seal of the Canterbury chapter, and that of the prior and chapter in Christ Church. Churchill is commenting on an inventory of archiepiscopal charters dated 1330 (PRO E.36/137).

monastery. Prominent among these were the capacity to choose certain obedientiaries by an agreed method, and the power to give and presumably to withhold his assent to the admission of monks.[33]

Prior Oxenden was partially eclipsed by the new, dominant and dynamic archbishop. Their relationship was not a happy one, recalling that between Stratford and Prior Enford at Winchester. Oxenden wisely avoided confrontation, but continued unrest in the convent helped to undermine his position. When in the summer of 1335 Stratford travelled to York, the prior wrote asking solicitously after his health with repeated assurances that all was peace and charity in the community of Christ Church. Subsequent reiteration and the denial of contrary reports argue that all was not so tranquil as the prior claimed.[34] Stratford's long absences from his cathedral city compounded the problems expected to arise in the normal course. One such problem was the degree of jurisdiction to be exercised by the Canterbury chapter over its dependent priory of St. Martin's, Dover; a vexed question for many years. Early in Stratford's archiepiscopate copies of documents covering the case were sent at his instance to the Canterbury official, Murimuth. Both parties agreed to abide by the archbishop's arbitration, but as nothing was done the chapter looked upon its submission as void.[35] In any case the archbishop was an interested party. Christ Church was intent on reviving its claim to appoint the Dover prior (and other officers), despite the fact that in Archbishop Reynolds' time the king's court had decided against the cathedral priory in a suit of advowson. This decision confirmed the archbishops' right to choose the Dover priors, which they proceeded to do throughout the fourteenth century. Stratford's stance in the matter was a foregone conclusion and he too obtained a favourable decision in the royal court.[36]

---

[33] According to CCL Reg. G, fol. 21^r, the archbishop could appoint the subprior, precentor, cellarer, sacrist, chamberlain, and two penitentiaries "cum primo ad capitulum declinaverit ecclesie antedicte." He had the right to depute the keeper of the great gate of the church for life and to appoint the steward of the priory hall. No one was to receive profession without the archbishop's licence.

[34] Lit. Cant. 2, pp. 76 (558), 138-139 (607), 139 (608); ibid., p. 98 (577): "Inter fratres fuit quies seu concordia, benedictus Deus"; 98-99 (578), 99-100 (579), 100-101 (580). See CCL Reg. L, fols. 67^{r}ff., 107^r, 108^v.

[35] CCL D.E.3, fol. 25^v, where the prior notes that the Dover processes were sent to Murimuth with copies of the archbishop's privileges on 23 July 1334. Lit. Cant. 2, pp. 60 (545), 171-172 (641); CCL Reg. L, fol. 36^{r-v}. For Dover material see CCL handwritten index (C.R. Bunce), 4 s.v. Dover, St. Martin's priory.

[36] See Haines, Dover Priory, chap. 2; Dugdale, Monasticon 4, pp. 528-539, esp. p. 531 n. d; CCL Reg. I, fols. 356^v-357^v. The king also had an interest in St. Martin's, Dover, held to be a royal free chapel: Denton, English Royal Free Chapels, pp. 57-66. For Archbishop Islep's ordinance of 1350 see CPR 1348-1350, pp. 508-509.

It was essential for an archbishop to be on hand if he were properly to uphold his rights as titular head, that is abbot, of the cathedral monastery.[37] The established practice when an obedientiary or administrative officer of the priory had to be appointed was for a number of candidates, usually three, to be submitted to the archbishop, so that he could make the final selection. In July 1335 Oxenden complained that the cellarer, Richard de Icham (Ickham), was too infirm to perform his office. The prior did not venture to take the step of removing him. Instead, on the advice of the subprior – himself an appointee of the archbishop's – and of other senior monks, Ickham was suspended temporarily from his duties. Oxenden then pressed Stratford for his authority to remove the cellarer and to appoint someone else. He went further, requesting a general commission which would permit him to remove all the archbishop's obedientiaries and to appoint others as need arose. Stratford's response to these suggestions is not extant, but can be imagined. He would not have wished his rights to be compromised in any way. A general commission of the kind suggested might prove a dangerous precedent and hinder his oversight of individual appointments.[38]

A parallel problem was the admission of those who wished to assume the monastic habit at Christ Church. This could only be effected subject to Stratford's "sight" of the candidates, which in the circumstances was not readily obtainable. The archbishop's remoteness entailed lengthy journeys, which could be dangerous and were invariably expensive. The prior's view was that by ancient custom it was the prior and chapter's privilege to admit suitable clerks to the monastic habit. The archbishop's role was to accept those chosen, either verbally or by letter and without altercation. When in 1337 four monks, already admitted by the prior, were "presented" to him, Stratford complained that their presentor, Br. Thomas de Bourne, did not bring letters properly executed by the prior and chapter; a defect which Oxenden hastened to remedy. Stratford then gave the prior a short lecture on the need to preserve their respective rights and professed himself unwilling to believe that Oxenden would willingly attempt anything to the archbishop's prejudice.[39]

---

[37] This was the case with those other cardinal churches which had monastic chapters: e.g. Carlisle, Augustinian canons regular, and the Benedictine houses of Durham, Coventry, Worcester, Bath, Norwich, Ely, Rochester and Winchester. The claim of a bishop to exercise other than agreed functions within the cathedral precincts would be stoutly resisted. Many *causes célèbres* arose from such claims.

[38] *Lit. Cant.* 2, pp. 106-108 (584), 128-129 (599); ccl. Reg. L, fols. 43ᵛ, 65ᵛ.

[39] *Lit. Cant.* 2, pp. 160-161 (630, 631), 161-162 (632), 162-163 (633), 163-164 (634); ccl. Reg. L, fol. 68ʳ⁻ᵛ.

The correspondence between archbishop and prior reveals a lack of mutual confidence. Oxenden continued to rebut charges made against him to Stratford and claimed that he was not interfering in matters belonging to the archbishop's visitation.[40] Distrust spread to the retinues of the respective parties. In 1336 Oxenden reported on a fracas in which, according to a sworn enquiry held by the archbishop's steward, John de Hampton, various member of Stratford's *familia*, including the keeper of his palace at Canterbury, had been set upon by the prior's men. The latter retorted that the reverse was the truth. Oxenden was at pains to show that in conjunction with Hampton he had done his best to disentangle the conflicting accounts and to bring those culpable to justice.[41]

Violence also erupted in the cathedral church during the week of Pentecost 1337, when a priest was injured. The incident was reported to Stratford with the request that the prior be allowed to secure the services of Bishop Hethe for the necessary reconciliation. The prior's letter unwisely included the plea that unless novices were speedily admitted they might get tired of waiting and take flight. Stratford's rejoinder is remarkable for its rudeness. He expressed displeasure at the pollution of Christ Church and the question of the novices, irritation at the prior's verbosity in explaining the situation,[42] and total rejection of the naïve suggestions put forward for dealing with it. No mass was to be said, no body interred, until reconciliation had been effected, and for that purpose he was sending his commission. He even threatened to abandon affairs of state and to come in person, if no suitable officiant could be found. As to the novices, if they wished to depart for such reasons as the prior advanced, then let them do so and "with God's curse and his own!"[43]

Another occasion of dissension was provided by Oxenden's action in violation of the archbishop's claim to the chattels of felons. The prior had seized a palfrey which, so Stratford alleged, belonged to him by virtue of his lordship of Canterbury. Oxenden preferred a temperate solution. His

---

[40] *Lit. Cant.* 2, pp. 130-131 (601); ccl. Reg. L, fols. 65ᵛ-66ʳ.

[41] *Lit. Cant.* 2, pp. 134-135 (604); ccl. Reg. L, fol. 66ʳ⁻ᵛ, 31 October [1336].

[42] "Displicent nobis multum ea que de pollucione nostre ecclesie et vestris noviciis non cum debita brevitate sed inutili verbositate nobis vestris litteris intimastis." ccl. Reg. L, fol. 67ᵛ.

[43] *HMCR* 9, App. p. 84a; *Lit. Cant.* 2, pp. 153-155 (621) *recte* 19 June 1337, 155-156 (622), 156 (623); ccl. Reg. L, fol. 67ᵛ. The prior's letter had suggested that the novices might tire of waiting and flee. Stratford's response runs: "Si ex dicta causa velint exire ... statim exeant cum malediccione Dei et nostra." This incident was seized upon by Coulton as fuel for his anti-monastic fire. *Five Centuries* 1, p. 329. For him Stratford was acting much like St. Bernard, but more unceremoniously.

offer to surrender the palfrey to the archbishop's steward seems to have settled the dispute.[44]

A more serious secular concern of both archbishop and prior was the military situation in Kent, where the local prelates, such as the bishop of Rochester and the abbot of St. Augustine's, were anxious that able-bodied inhabitants of the county should not be drafted elsewhere, owing to the constant threat of invasion. In this instance Stratford and Oxenden saw eye to eye and local contacts must have ensured that Kentish fears were often made explicit at the level of national government.[45]

Oxenden was to die in the summer of 1338, on 4 August. Foreseeing the likelihood of such an event Stratford, who was at St. Radegund's Abbey by Dover preparatory to embarking for France, empowered his brother, the bishop of Chichester, to act for him. The commission is specific: Bishop Robert was authorized to be present at the election, to carry out a scrutiny of voting procedure, and to install the new prior. It must have come as somewhat of a shock to the appointee, Robert Hathbrand, and presumably to Bishop Robert, when Stratford wrote to object to his brother's admission to the election – a right which belonged solely to the archbishop in person. Stratford's aggrieved letters reached Canterbury on 4 December by the hand of M. Simon de Charing, one of his clerks who was also in the prior's service. Hathbrand, after listening to Charing's exposition of the writer's point of view, wrote a conciliatory reply. With as much tact as he could muster he pointed out that Stratford had issued an enabling commission to the bishop of Chichester. No blame could be attributed to himself, since (as subprior) he had informed the archbishop of Oxenden's death. As late as August of the following year, 1339, Stratford expressed misgivings about the manner of Hathbrand's election. All the same, there was nothing personal in this and he thanked the prior for favours during his absence abroad.[46] It is difficult to make sense of Stratford's behaviour in this business. He could scarcely have

---

[44] *Lit. Cant.* 2, pp. 140 (609), 141 (610); CCL Reg. L, fol. 67[r].

[45] *Lit. Cant.* 2, pp. 158-159 (627): 4 July 1337; CCL Reg. L, fol. 68[r].

[46] The process of Hathbrand's election, including a recension of the commission for Robert Stratford (nobis tunc in remotis agentibus vicarius in spiritualibus generalis, et ad infrascripta noster commissarius specialis) to act in his brother's place is contained in "Littera domini Johannis archiepiscopi super creacione domini Roberti prioris Cant.," dated Canterbury, 10 November 1339. CCL MS C.1300. See also *Lit. Cant.* 2, pp. 192-194 (661), 196-197 (665), 198-199 (667), 199-200 (668), 215 (679); CCL Reg. L, fols. 72[v]-73[r], 86[r], 104[v]. In his letter (no. 679, Reg. L, fol. 86[r]) written from Valenciennes, 26 August 1339, Stratford added: "Vobis insuper ingraciamur de pueris nostris quos vobiscum tenetis." These boys were doubtless choristers from his chapel. Murimuth was at Hathbrand's election and subsequently, 27 October [1338], was asked by the prior to provide details (no. 665, Reg. L, fol. 72[v]).

doubted the *bona fides* of his brother, whom he entrusted regularly with important commissions. Was the objection merely a technical device to discourage repetition of an irregular act? Or was the archbishop just being peevish? Perhaps there was something of both elements in his action. We can be sure that Stratford never let slip an opportunity to emphasize the prerogatives of his see.

Stratford's extended stay on the continent and his political duties perpetuated difficulties which had afflicted Oxenden. In his turn Hathbrand was forced to maintain the strength of the convent – depleted by deaths among the brethren – by the admission of novices. As for the subprior, Hathbrand observed, he preferred to profit from the schools rather than from the cloister. There was a need to replace both him and other obedientiaries.[47] Hathbrand, like his predecessor, was quick to resist Stratford's claim that the admission of monks pertained to the archiepiscopal dignity. From time immemorial, he urged, the prior and chapter had exercised the right without contradiction of the archbishops. The argument continued, but without apparent ill-feeling.[48]

The probability is that Stratford found Hathbrand more congenial than Oxenden. During the troubles of 1340 and 1341 it was at Christ Church with Hathbrand and his monks that Stratford sought sanctuary, eloquently eliciting their prayers and sympathy for his predicament.[49] There is no evidence that the prior was other than consoling at a time when cooperation with the archbishop was certain to entail a measure of unpopularity with the royal government, in fact with the king himself. Both Oxenden and Hathbrand were prodigal of friendly acts. The former, towards the beginning of their relationship, furnished Stratford with horses and grooms for his journey to York (1335), while Hathbrand contributed oak trees for rebuilding the house of Stephen de Scaldeford, said to have been one of the archbishop's clerks. For his part Stratford sent Hathbrand some unspecified medical advice which allegedly proved efficacious against "the worst of fevers."[50] It must have been in the November or very early December of 1339 that Stratford, newly returned

---

[47] *Lit. Cant.* 2, pp. 215-217 (680); CCL Reg. L, fol. 74ᵛ: "De statu suo huiusmodi non contentus ad studium dirigens mentis oculos et affectum in scolis magis proficere creditur quam in claustro." The conduct of the subprior was in effect a criticism of Stratford, who appointed him.

[48] *Lit. Cant.* 2, pp. 246-247 (713); CCL Reg. L, fol. 77ʳ. The prior wished eight persons to be clothed in the monastic habit.

[49] For Stratford's *cri de cœur* see below, "The Crisis of 1341," n. 65; Haines, "Some Sermons at Hereford."

[50] *Lit. Cant.* 2, pp. 95 (573), 95-96 (574), 277 (742), 279 (747); CCL Reg. L, fols. 79ᵛ, 109ʳ.

from the continent, was entertained by Hathbrand at Christ Church. Informed by letter of Stratford's intended arrival,[51] the prior went out to meet him bearing the archiepiscopal cross. A special dinner was prepared and purses costing forty-five shillings, together with seven pounds in money, were distributed among the visitor's *familia*.[52] In March 1343, while staying at his palace in Canterbury hard by the cathedral, Stratford in his turn had Prior Hathbrand as his guest at table on four consecutive occasions.[53]

Prior and archbishop were able to make common cause against the pretensions of the archdeacon of Canterbury. These were of a jurisdictional character. Thus a thirteenth-century archdeacon had claimed authority over St. Martin's, Dover, where we have seen archbishop and cathedral prior themselves in dispute. The archbishop of the day held that Dover priory lay solely within his jurisdiction.[54] But this was only one area of disagreement. At one time or another archdeacons of Canterbury were in conflict with their diocesan over the claiming of criminous clerks from secular justices, the exercise of testamentary jurisdiction, and doubtless other matters as well. The earlier fourteenth century saw many disputes of this type; it is a mistake to assume that all jurisdictional demarcation had been accomplished by the close of the previous century.[55] The precise nature of the archdeacon of Canterbury's claims during Stratford's time eludes us, but in the course of Oxenden's priorate the archbishop let it be known that he would not suffer his archdeacon to encroach on common law rights by any appeal to ancient custom.[56] The archdeacon in question was probably Robert Stratford, but

[51] The messenger carrying Stratford's letters "de adventu suo" was paid two shillings. CCL D.E.3, fol. 41ᵛ. The account is dated Saturday before St. Nicholas [i.e. 4 December] 1339.

[52] Expenses of meeting the archbishop "pro cruce portanda eidem" amounted to 48s 5d; "Item, in bursis emptis et datis familie domini archiepiscopi, vii lib." Ibid.

[53] WAM no. 9222. The prior dined with the archbishop 22-25 March.

[54] *Cant. Admin.* 1, p. 52. This was in Archbishop's Pecham's time.

[55] Ibid., pp. 51-53. The conflict of the bishops of Winchester with the archdeacons of Surrey over a wide range of jurisdiction provides a case in point. See *Lydford*, pp. 134-141 (no. 249), and cf. Winchester Reg. Edyndon 1, fols. 12ʳ-13ᵛ. Lydford's text as printed is extremely corrupt and its editor did not collate it with Reg. Edyndon. E.g. *Lydford*, p. 135 l. 12, "immobilia" [mobilia?]; l. 16, "monia" [omnia?]; ll. 17-18, "iurisdiccionem ecclesiasticam predictam" [ecclesiasticam in archidiaconatu predicto?]; l. 28, "seu deputacione sequenti" [seu deputacione sequestratorum?]; ll. 36-37, "denarios [synodales eciam paschales vocatos et Martinales ac eciam sancti Petri denarios] et quadrantes sancti Swythini vulgariter nuncupatos." For the 1338 agreement between Ralph of Shrewsbury, bishop of Bath and Wells, and Roger de Mortimer, archdeacon of Wells, see *HMCR* 10, App. 3 pt. 1, pp. 538-539.

[56] *Lit. Cant.* 2, p. 81 (564); CCL Reg. L, fol. 39ᵛ. The *ius commune* was, of course, that

it should be appreciated that there was not necessarily anything personal in a dispute of this kind.[57] In itself the upholding of rights pertaining, or thought to pertain, to a particular office or dignity was a commonplace of medieval life. Only when conflicts became prolonged and the spirit of compromise was lacking did acrimony lead to a breakdown of personal relationships.[58] A case in point is provided by the differing experiences of Mepham and Stratford with respect to the second great monastic house in Canterbury, St. Augustine's Abbey.

When in 1329 Archbishop Mepham visited his diocese he "found" that St. Augustine's was in possession of a number of parochial churches appropriated to the monks and for which they claimed exemption from the archbishop's authority. Mepham cited members of the chapter to his audience court so that they could exhibit the privileges they alleged. On their non-appearance he declared them contumacious. Appeal was made to the apostolic see and Mepham in his turn was cited by Itier de Concoreto, the papal judge delegate. Mepham made various unconvincing technical objections to Itier's suitability for hearing the case and then raised the issue in parliament.[59] He claimed that during the parliamentary session Itier had cited him in matters pertaining to the crown rather than to the ecclesiastical forum. Such conduct, contended Mepham, ought to incur the punishment due for contempt and *lèse majesté*. At this certain nobles, egged on by the archbishop if we are to believe the abbey's proctor, declared that Itier should be banished from the realm. It was Stratford and Orleton – then bishops of Winchester and Worcester respectively – who led their colleagues into more peaceable paths. Itier

of the church. For discussion of the archdeacon's powers see Woodcock, *Canterbury Courts*, esp. pp. 19-21.

[57] Robert Stratford was provided to the archdeaconry of Canterbury following the promotion of Simon de Montacute to the see of Worcester in 1333. Vatican Archives, *RA* 45, fol. 387ᵛ; *RV* 106, fol. 284ᵛ; *CPL 1305-1342*, p. 401 (12 June 1334). Somner, *Antiquities*, p. 159, states that he had seen "in archivis consistorii Cant." a plea of Robert Stratford's consisting of many articles and enumerating all the rights and privileges of the archdeaconry.

[58] A number of instances in which such disputes degenerated into violence could be cited. E.g. the conflict between Bishop Orleton and the prior of Hereford (though this was really a political matter) and between the same bishop, then Winchester diocesan, and the archdeacon of Surrey, William Inge. See Haines, *Church and Politics*, pp. 50-51, 67-68; also n. 55 above.

[59] There is confusion here in Thorne's chronology. Apparently it was in the 1331 parliament, rather than that of 1330, that these events took place. This would mean that the fracas at Slindon preceded Mepham's raising the question in parliament. See Thorne, cols. 2043-2045; *Foedera* 2, iii, p. 72; Haines, *Church and Politics*, p. 181 n. 6; Pantin, "Letters of John Mason," pp. 195-197ff.; Lunt, *Financial Relations* 2, pp. 699, 701ff.

was summoned to appear on the following day to explain his conduct. This he did convincingly. Violence attended the attempt of the abbey's proctor and of others to serve a citation on the archbishop as he lay, protesting illness, in his manor of Slindon in Sussex. Eventually the archbishop was pronounced contumacious, his sentences against St. Augustine's were quashed, and he himself condemned to pay a large sum by way of costs. This was where the matter rested when Stratford succeeded Mepham. The monks' view was that their enemies strove to influence the new archbishop against them by interpreting their legal success as subversive of the primatial dignity. But both sides wished to avoid further litigation. An amicable composition was arranged, designed to safeguard the abbey's exemption but allowing to the archbishop his authority to remedy defects in appropriated churches and to ensure the adequacy of their vicarages. At times of visitation the abbey's proctors were to appear with copies of the privileges enjoyed, and to cover their procedures a suitable commission was devised.[60] Stratford did not wish to prolong the unseemly wrangling of his predecessor in a forlorn attempt to impugn well-authenticated immunities.

Stratford's absence from diocesan and metropolitan duties necessitated the appointment from time to time of vicars general to act on his behalf. John Lydford, an ecclesiastical lawyer of a later age, preserved in his notebook[61] a copy of Stratford's commission on one such occasion. It is the only one to survive from his archiepiscopate and is apparently the earliest Canterbury commission to exemplify the powers conferred.[62] Ostensibly it was issued to Bishop Gravesend and others unnamed because of the archbishop's absence abroad.[63] As Gravesend died before

[60] For the whole affair see *Thorne*, cols. 2039-2053, 2068-2071, 2118.

[61] DRO (Exeter) MS 723, now edited by Dorothy M. Owen (*Lydford*). The precise purpose of this memorandum book is difficult to determine. It is not a systematic compilation and probably should not be described in any strict sense as a formulary. It constitutes a somewhat random collection of documents, many of them inaccurately copied. See n. 55 above.

[62] See *Cant. Admin.* 2, pp. 1-10, where the first detailed commission is dated 1375 from Archbishop Sudbury's time.

[63] The initials used for names in Lydford's book are suspect. Thus "J. de B.," Stratford's chancellor, at p. 117 (nos. 212-213) stands for John de Lecch (Northleach). But they are correct in the case of the Chertsey composition. Compare *Lydford*, p. 55 (no. 91) and *Chertsey Cart.*, p. 46. The powers conferred by the commission in *Lydford* (p. 119, no. 219) may be summarized roughly as follows: to perform all things apppropriate to the office of vicar; to enquire into, punish and correct the excesses of the archbishop's subjects; to remove from benefice and office in the city and diocese of Canterbury and in the immediate jurisdictions; to appoint, remove, and to hear the accounts of (rural) deans and other ministers; to appoint penitentiaries; to grant licence to elect prelates in

Stratford's departure in mid-July 1338, this could only date from the archbishop's earlier journeyings in 1334-1335.[64] We know from other sources that M. Nicholas de Tarenta (Tarrant), M. Henry de Iddesworth, and M. Adam Murimuth were vicars general about this time. Murimuth was acting as such in 1334-1335 and in January, February and December of 1336.[65] In this last year Stratford was not outside the realm, but engaged with the king on the Scottish border. During the 1338-1339 vacancy in the see of Worcester it was the official of the Court of Canterbury (Adam Murimuth) who, because the archbishop was *in remotis*,[66] commissioned the prior of Worcester to act as official *sede vacante* in compliance with the composition of 1268.[67] Shortly afterwards, Murimuth – this time entitled vicar general – ordered the sequestration of the goods of the late bishop of Worcester, Thomas Hemenhale, and cited his executors, if any, to appear in London.[68] Robert Stratford was also vicar general at this period; as such he cited opponents of the bishop-elect of Worcester, Prior Wolstan de Bransford, and informed the dean of the province of the date fixed for his consecration.[69] On his brother's behalf he consecrated both Bransford and the new bishop of London, Bintworth, in 1339 and 1338 respectively. It was Robert Stratford, too, who summoned the convocations of 1338 and 1340 and cited the clergy to attend a parliament at Hilary 1339, though this was subsequently postponed.[70] A busy diocesan and royal clerk, who in 1338

---

monasteries of the archbishop's patronage and to examine and confirm, or to quash such elections; to hear appeals and complaints coming to the archbishop's audience, both from his own time and that of his predecessors; to grant licences under the constitution *Cum ex eo*, as well as letters dimissory, and to assent to exchanges of benefices.

[64] Stratford was absent 6 April-5 July 1334 and 24 October 1334-15 January 1335. See below, Appendix 6.

[65] See below, Appendix 2. For Murimuth's grant of probate in accordance with the prerogative jurisdiction see n. 22 above. Murimuth also entitles himself vicar general in his reply to the Canterbury prior's letter about collection of the sexennial tenth, 15 January 1336: CCL Reg. L, fol. 195ʳ. The prior (ibid., fol. 194ᵛ) addresses him as "amice benevole."

[66] WoCL, RSV, fol. 151ʳ: "Cant. archiepiscopo extra regnum Anglie notorie in remotis agente." Churchill (*Cant. Admin.* 1, p. 28) assumes (one suspects rightly) that Murimuth was official of Canterbury at the time, but in her list (ibid. 2, p. 238) he is reported only in 1335.

[67] WoCL, RSV, fol. 151ʳ (pp. 264-265): 29 December 1338.

[68] Ibid., fol. 147ʳ (p. 259). Adam Murimuth's mandate was received at Worcester 7 January 1339. Cf. *Worcester Reg. Bransford*, p. 1 (no. 2).

[69] WoCL, RSV, fols. 147ᵛ-148ʳ (pp. 259-260); WinRO 1, fol. 70ᵛ; *Bath and Wells Reg. Shrewsbury*, p. 348; *Worc. Admin.*, pp. 287-288.

[70] The mandates of the vicar general are dated 21 August 1338 and 15 December 1339 respectively. E.g. *Bath and Wells Reg. Shrewsbury*, pp. 325, 362-365. The parliamentary

had completed a three-year stint as chancellor of Oxford University, Robert must have found it difficult to give adequate attention to the affairs of Canterbury as John's lieutenant.

We catch only an occasional glimpse of Stratford's activities as visitor within Canterbury diocese[71] and the same is true of the province. Apparently it was in 1342 that he first contemplated doing something about the latter obligation.[72] From the apostolic see he sought and obtained a bull which permitted him a greater flexibility than was ordinarily the case; a privilege similar to those which had been secured by some of his recent predecessors. Regardless of whether he had visited his own chapter and diocese he was empowered for a three-year period to pass from one cathedral city or diocese to another for the purpose of visitation and then, should need arise, to return as many times as he wished in order to complete the process. Moreover, he was not obliged to complete the order of visitation begun by his predecessor Mepham, whose efforts to visit Exeter diocese had been met by armed resistance.[73]

Information about one aspect of Stratford's metropolitan visitation comes from Murimuth, who states that immediately after Michaelmas (29 September) 1343 the archbishop attempted to visit Norwich diocese having given due warning of his intention to bishop and cathedral prior. On arrival he was opposed and an appeal to Avignon was launched against the intended procedure. It so happens that in Lydford's note-book

citation is dated 7 December 1338, e.g. WinRO 1, fols. 68ᵛ-69ʳ. For Robert Stratford's consecration of Bintworth as bishop of London: BL Cotton MS Faustina B.v, fol. 82ʳ; *Murimuth*, p. 86. For that of Bransford see *Worcester Reg. Bransford*, pp. xiii, 4-5 (nos. 21, 24); *Murimuth*, p. 87 n. 7 (addition from BL Harleian MS 1729). Mention of Robert as vicar general, 12 January 1339, is in *CCR 1337-1339*, p. 631.

[71] In a mandate to the dean of Lympne, 26 October 1340, Stratford mentions his visitation of Snargate church: CCL A.36 IV, fol. 63ʳ. Ostensibly this refers to a later visitation than that of 1335. Cf. ibid., fol. 28ʳ.

[72] There exists a reply by the prior of Dodnash (Suffolk) to a warning of impending visitation issued by Br. John de Mari D.Th. (for whom see *Biog. Oxon.* s.v.) as visitor on Stratford's behalf (13 May 1336). He expressed himself willing to accept the visitor. But this was a *sede vacante* visitation following the death of Bishop Ayrminne. NNRO, Confirmations and Settlements box, no. 3864.

[73] Both Reynolds and Mepham had bulls of a similar kind. For Mepham's privilege see CCL Reg. I, fols. 427ᵛ-428ʳ. Stratford's bull, Avignon 25 October 1342, is in Vatican Archives, *RV* 155, fol. 217ʳ (cf. *CPL 1342-1362*, p. 86). The archbishop pleads the interruptions of secular affairs: "Sane peticio tua nobis exhibita continebat quod tu qui habes latam provinciam et diffusam propter varietatem negociorum arduorum in regno Anglie et impedimenta frequenter occurrencia non potes in visitacione ipsius provincie ordinem a iure traditum observare." The concession to make "random visitation" was for three years. Grandisson's reactions to Mepham's activities as visitor are in *Exeter Reg. Grandisson*, and see *Murimuth*, p. 65.

there is a copy of the "primary appeal" by an unnamed bishop of Norwich – clearly Anthony Bek – against Archbishop John Stratford's visitation.[74] Murimuth says that the bishop and prior argued that Stratford was not following proper canonical practice. When the archbishop countered by bringing forth the papal indult which overrode any such impediment, it was replied that the bull had been obtained by false pretences – a standard objection in such circumstances. Refusing to admit the metropolitan, those at Norwich saw to it that church, monastery and episcopal palace were put into a state of defence and that lay power was on hand to repel intruders. It was a repetition of Mepham's predicament at Exeter. Stratford's response was similar; he excommunicated bishop and prior and placed the church of Norwich under an interdict. He had to break off the process for a week or so while he hastened south to attend a royal council in London (21-28 November), but as soon as it was over he rejoined the clerks and other members of his *familia* whom he had left behind in Norwich. Understandably local feeling was in favour of the diocesan, who was also honourably received throughout the lands of the earl of Surrey.[75] When Stratford returned it was with the full support of the king for the exercise of his office. Early in 1344 William de Bohun, the earl of Northampton, and Bartholomew Burghersh were directed to act against those who had unlawfully assembled to resist the archbishop and defied the royal proclamations. Writs of *venire facias* were despatched to the sheriff for hauling disturbers of the peace before these commissioners, who were to commend the guilty to prison.[76] But by that time Bek had died. The case was none the less continued in the curia and a decision reached in May of 1344. This did not concern itself with the principal issue of Stratford's right to make visitation despite the unfinished process of his precedessor; it merely quashed his sentences on the grounds that they had been issued following the primary appeal by Bek and the Norwich chapter and before such appeal could be heard.[77]

[74] *Lydford*, p. 117 (no. 211). As the editor remarks, this was not known to Churchill (see *Cant. Admin.* 1, p. 34; 2, p. 149), who has nothing positive to say about metropolitical visitation by Stratford. But both *Murimuth* and *Foedera* could have supplied evidence. So too could the *Continuatio* of the chronicle of the bishops of Norwich (*Anglia Sacra* 1, p. 414) had not Winchelsey's name been erroneously substituted for Stratford's. The archbishop is pictured as expounding his case from a pulpit set up before the doors of the church. He was prevented from finishing by the townsmen. A Norwich MS (see n. 77 below) shows that a second appeal was launched against Stratford.

[75] *Murimuth*, p. 147.

[76] *Foedera* 2, iv, pp. 155-156: 29 November 1343.

[77] NNRO, Confirmations and Settlements box, no. 3856: 8 May 1344. Notarial instrument of process before Sanxius Canale, provost of Agde. "In hiis scriptis diffiniendo

It could be that the diocese of Chichester was visited at about this time, for warning of an intention to do so, issued by an unnamed archbishop, is addressed to "Bishop R.," conceivably Robert Stratford. But this is followed by a series of articles of enquiry for use at times of provincial visitation which conclude with an admonition (monicio) in the name of "Archbishop W." (Walter Reynolds?), so the matter must remain in doubt.[78] We know little more about Stratford's activity in this sphere, except that during vacancies in dioceses he is said to have visited, or threatened to visit, at least one royal chapel which claimed exemption from both archiepiscopal and episcopal authority.[79]

Opportunity for the archbishop to consult his suffragans and other members of the clergy was provided both by parliament and by the periodical meetings of provincial council or convocation, as the clerical assembly is variously described. Anciently there were supposed to be two councils a year throughout the provinces of the church for purposes of correction and the settlement of disputes. A metropolitan who failed to convene even one during the course of a year was liable to canonical penalties.[80] At the Fourth Lateran Council of 1215 the ancient legislation was refurbished. Metropolitans were to hold annual provincial councils for correction and reform. They were also to ensure that in each diocese

pronunciamus, decernimus et declaramus per dominum Anthonium quondam episcopum, priorem et capitulum, ac personas singulas capituli ecclesie Norwicen. et alias personas quascumque eisdem adherentes, tam a prima quam a secunda citacionibus seu mandatis dicti domini archiepiscopi ex causis in libello per partem dictorum episcopi prioris et capituli ecclesie Norwicen. et adherencium eisdem dato conscriptis, ac a processibus et sentenciis excommunicacionis suspencionis et interdicti per dictum dominum archiepiscopum post appellaciones prefatas prolatis et fulminatis bene et legitime fuisse et esse appellatum, predictaque mandata processus et sentencias excommunicacionis suspencionis et interdicti tanquam post et contra dictas appellaciones legitimas latas nullam et nullas fuisse et esse, ac dictos dominum Anthonium ... et eisdem adherentes non fuisse nec esse dictis processibus et sentenciis ligatos."

[78] WSRO Liber E, fol. 264[r-v]. Cf. BL Cotton MS Galba E.iv, fols. 61[r]-65[r].

[79] E.g. Bosham (Exeter Reg. Grandisson, pp. 846-850: provocation against threatened invasion by Stratford as custodian of the Chichester spiritualities sede vacante). In 1323 the bishop of Chichester was cited in the king's court for his actions against the bishop of Exeter (SCKB 4, pp. 111-122, from KB 27/253/Rex m. 18). Bishop Stapeldon had been granted Bosham Chapel in free alms by Edward II (DRO MS no. 1030). See Buck, Walter Stapeldon, pp. 88-90. The visitation by "Archbishop John" of the royal chapels of Derby, Shrewsbury, Penkridge, Bridgnorth, Stafford, Wolverhampton and Tettenhall, apparently refers to John Pecham (1279-1292). See CCL Reg. G, fol. 12[v] (quoted Somner, Antiquities, App. to Supplement, p. 15 no. IVE).

[80] In general see Cant. Admin. 1, chap. 8; Wake, State of the Church; Weske, Convocation of the Clergy; Kemp, Counsel and Consent, esp. pp. 89-112; and for the canonical regulation, Decretum D. 18, cc. 6-7.

there were those who would enquire about defects so that appropriate remedies might be provided at the ensuing council.[81]

In England at this time the summoning of convocations – as distinct from provincial councils – was closely connected with political considerations. While Canterbury metropolitan Stratford convened fourteen provincial assemblies,[82] but on four occasions only did he act without the prompting of a royal writ.[83] Convocations almost invariably coincided with parliaments, thus preventing a duplication of time and expense. But this also entailed a subordination of ecclesiastical to secular concerns, and in this period in particular to urgent consideration of war and national defence.

Each diocesan bishop, unless he were *persona non grata* with the government,[84] could expect to be summoned individually to parliament. His summons usually, but not invariably, incorporated a *premunientes* clause. This required him to secure the personal appearance of the cathedral dean or prior and of the archdeacon or archdeacons, while the chapter was to be represented by one and the clergy by two proctors.[85] In

[81] *Extra* 5, 1, 25 *Sicut olim* (Lateran IV, c. 6). Failure to observe the constitution rendered the offender liable to suspension from office.

[82] See below, Appendix 3. In addition there was what I have called the "quasi-legatine council" of January 1338 (not 1339 as in Weske, *Convocation of the Clergy*, p. 250). This was summoned by Cardinals Gomez and Montfavèz.

[83] For the provincial councils of 19 October 1341, 14 October 1342, and 1 October 1347, as well as for the convocation or provincial assembly of 4 May 1346. How to categorize this last is a difficulty. It has been designated a convocation (e.g. Weske, *Convocation of the Clergy*, p. 252), but in some respects it is closer to the provincial council of this period. The archbishop acted independently of any royal writ, but only bishops were summoned. The lower clergy were regularly summoned to convocation; their presence at provincial councils was not mandatory. The main purpose of the May 1346 assembly was to uphold the privileges of the church against lay encroachment, but the king's demands for anticipation of the tenth were also under discussion. In his appointment of proctors Bishop Trillek refers to it as a convocation, Stratford himself does not give it an appellation. See *Hereford Reg. Trillek*, pp. 15-16, 271-273. Kemp, *Counsel and Consent*, pp. 100-104, stresses Stratford's conscious distinction between convocation and provincial council. Cf. *Exeter Reg. Grandisson*, p. 968 s.a. 1342: "Omnes fere prelati et clerus Cantuariensis provincie ad concilium provinciale, ac eciam ad convocacionem cleri."

[84] As, for instance, in Orleton's case: Haines, *Church and Politics*, pp. 63, 152 n. 83. But Orleton was not kept out of parliament following his elevation to Winchester as long as is suggested there (following Plucknett, "Parliament," p. 94 n. 2). See below, "In the Seat of Power."

[85] E.g. Worcester Reg. Montacute 2, fol. 32^r: writ of summons to parliament at York for 26 May 1335. For the prevalence of the *premunientes* clause see Kemp, *Counsel and Consent*, pp. 90-91ff. Weske, *Convocation of the Clergy*, p. 66 (citing *RDP* 4, pp. 423ff.), pointed out that from the February 1334 parliament the clause became "for all time" an invariable element of the summons to parliament (also Kemp, *Counsel and Consent*, p. 101).

pursuance of this parliamentary summons a "provincial writ" was sent to the metropolitans. On receiving it the archbishop of the southern province ordered the bishop of London, as dean, to enjoin the suffragan bishops to summon their clergy to appear in parliament on the day and at the time named in the king's writ. All the same, there is very little information about the participation of the lower clergy in parliament. Although its presence is discernible for much longer than has been supposed, for all practical purposes this group by the 1340s had focused its attention on convocation.[86] To convoke this purely clerical assembly the archbishop again utilized the dean of the province as intermediary. The dean was to require the personal attendance of the bishops themselves, of priors or deans of cathedral churches, archdeacons, and other "prelates" including heads of regular houses whether exempt or not, while the chapters of these institutions were to be represented by one proctor apiece, the clergy of each diocese by two.[87] For the duration of Stratford's tenure of the archbishopric convocation provided an additional assembly by means of which the government made known its policy and problems. It was there rather than in parliament that the clergy sought to determine questions of financial aid to the government. The canonical provincial council devoted to ecclesiastical reform was by contrast a rare phenomenon.

This is no place to examine the documentary evidence in detail, but there are one or two points worth specific mention. Stratford summoned his first convocation – more correctly convocations – on 12 August 1334. His mandate for the purpose is unusual in its incorporation of two distinct royal writs. The first of these was a summons to parliament at Westminster, with an added instruction that the archbishop reiterate the citation of the clergy already included in the summonses to individual bishops.[88] The second writ, of privy seal, outlined the king's financial

[86] With respect to the "provincial writ" Weske, *Convocation of the Clergy*, pp. 66-67 (citing *RDP* 4, pp. 394, 411ff.), showed how, following the summons for the 16 March 1332 parliament, similar writs were issued until the summons for that of 3 March 1337. They reappeared for the parliaments of 3 February 1339 and of 20 January and 29 March 1340. Thereafter a different type of writ was issued, requiring archbishops to hold convocations to complement the assembly of parliament. Kemp, *Counsel and Consent*, p. 99, remarks on the "concession ... to clerical sensitivities" evinced by the modified form of "provincial writ" issued 3 December 1326 – the objectionable "venire faciatis" was excised. The influence exercised by Stratford and Orleton at the time points to their having had a hand in this.

[87] E.g. Worcester Reg. Montacute 2, fol. 3[r]: royal mandate to summon convocation, which Stratford arranged for 26 September 1334 at St. Paul's. For variations (as reflected in summonses) in the composition of ecclesiastical assemblies during Stratford's archiepiscopate see Weske, *Convocation of the Clergy*, pp. 247-253.

[88] A separate "provincial writ" is omitted. See Kemp, *Counsel and Consent*, p. 101

difficulties as a consequence of disturbances in Scotland and Ireland and ordered Stratford as metropolitan to assemble the bishops and lesser clergy. Stratford prefaced his combined summons with the statement that after discussion with his fellow bishops and other learned men (periti), in order to avoid duplication of expense and labour he proposed to respond to the king's writs by calling an assembly to coincide with parliament,[89] and a further one a week later. Those attending would thus make only one journey.

Stratford's next convocation was summoned from Bamburgh in the far northeast early in 1336. On this occasion too the royal writ was for a parliament. In transmitting it to the dean of the province Stratford, as in 1334, ordered the clergy to assemble at St. Paul's under his presidency or that of his commissary and on the day appointed for parliament's opening at Westminster. Understandably the agenda was concerned with national emergencies rather than with spiritual problems, though we should remember that in any case the clergy was expected to shoulder its full share of the burden of the nation's affairs. Unusual was the holding of a further convocation in the autumn at Leicester. It was called for a week after the great council met at nearby Nottingham.[90] The remaining convocations of the decade, those of 1337 and 1338, were summoned in conjunction with parliaments and because of the financial burden of the war with France.[91] In the 1338 convocation, convened by Robert Stratford in his brother's absence, an anticipation of the dates of payment of the tenth was agreed to on certain conditions, but the lesser clergy refused to follow the lead of the prelates and barons in parliament who had made a grant of wool.[92] By 1340 the archbishop was determined that further support should be given only in return for specific safeguards with

(citing *RDP* 4, pp. 427-430). In effect there were three distinct assemblies, parliament and two convocations. Bishop Montacute excused himself to Stratford for absence from the convocations and to the king for his failure to attend parliament. Worcester Reg. Montacute 2, fol. 4[r]: 16 September 1334. The initial writ (*Cum super diversis et arduis negociis*) is at fol. 3[r]: Reading, 24 July 1334.

[89] E.g. Worcester Reg. Montacute 2, fol. 3[r]: Northampton, 24 July 1334. "Vestris et eorum discriminibus quantum possumus obviare convocacionem huius[modi] ex causis predictis cum minori quo vestro possumus incommodo." See below, Appendix 3.

[90] The council assembled 23 September, convocation on the 30th.

[91] For that of 1337 (St. Paul's, 30 September) see Ely Reg. Montacute, fol. 38[r-v] (cf. *Concilia* 2, p. 623). Details of the 1 October 1338 convocation are in the introduction to *Rochester Reg. Hethe* (pp. xxxvii-xxxix). See below, "In the Seat of Power."

[92] "Clerus provincie Cant. advocacionem vicarii archiepiscopi Cant. comparuit et a consilio regis ad solvendum lanas sicut fecerat populus exacte interpellatus totaliter lanas recusans loco lanarum decimam unam multum invitus clerus dedit et concessit." BL Cotton MS Faustina B.v, fol. 79[v]. Cf. *Murimuth*, p. 85.

respect to the church. The parliamentary statute which Stratford secured with great difficulty (non sine magnis laboribus) was forwarded to the diocesan bishops with the instruction that it was to be preserved in cathedral churches to ensure the church future enjoyment of greater liberty.[93] The instruction was doubtless obeyed, but the abuses complained of – purveyance, misuse of regalian rights of custody and of presentations to livings during vacancies in dioceses, and the waste perpetrated by custodians of episcopal temporalities – were probably little affected in practice.[94]

Stratford resolved that for once he would assemble a provincial council which could give undivided attention to the ecclesiastical purposes for which it had been designed. On 23 July 1341 he issued his mandate for an autumn session and for the first time this did not include the recension of a royal writ. In his preamble the metropolitan bemoaned the neglect of his canonical obligation to hold councils for correction and reform, which he excused on the grounds of his preoccupation with the troubles of the time and pressing affairs of state.[95] The clause citing the heads of religious houses and the lesser clergy did not *require* their attendance. They were to come if they felt it to be in their interest so to do.[96] Murimuth thought this sufficiently newsworthy for quotation.[97] Mandates for two of the three later assemblies which Stratford summoned *motu proprio*, rather than at

[93] *Worcester Reg. Bransford*, pp. 511-512 (no. 323) gives Stratford's accompanying "private letter" (30 May 1340). The charter (16 April), *Sachez qe come en le primer article*, is not in Bransford's register but in WoCL Liber Albus, fol. 164[r-v]. For the Chichester copy see WSRO Liber E, fols. 151[r]-152[v]. See also *Concilia* 2, pp. 655-656 (*Exeter Reg. Grandisson*, pp. 61-63, no. 140); below, "In the Seat of Power," n. 309.

[94] The text is most readily available in *Exeter Reg. Grandisson* and *Concilia* (n. 93 above).

[95] "Quamvis sacris sit canonibus constitutum quod metropolitani archiepiscopi et primates annis singulis, legitimo impedimento cessante, pro excessibus corrigendis et moribus reformandis debeant provinciale concilium celebrare; nos tamen, adversis tribulacionibus temporum et assiduis occupacionibus circa magna aliisque causis variis impediti, quod nostro incumbebat officio in hac parte nequivimus hactenus adimplere. Nunc autem, oportunitate captata quin verius necessitate cogente provinciali coacto concilio adversus excessus in nostra Cant. provincia in dies contingentes medelam appetimus congruam adhiberi." Ely Reg. Montacute, fol. 64[r]; cf. *Exeter Reg. Grandisson*, pp. 968-970.

[96] "Necnon archidiaconos, capitula conventus et collegia universa clerumque cuiuscumque diocesis nostre provincie antedicte qui sua conspexerint interesse premunire curetis"; and below, "si eis expediens videatur" and "si sua crediderint interesse." Ely Reg. Montacute, fol. 64[r]. Athon, *Const. Othonis*, p. 5 ad ver. *Et consensu*, points out that a provincial council "ubi statuenda sunt aliqua, quae tangunt statum provinciae episcopi sunt citandi: & caeteri subditi invitandi, non cogendi."

[97] "Ad quod concilium abbates, priores, clerus, et capitula vocati non fuerant praecise sed causative, videlicet si sua crederent interesse." *Murimuth*, p. 122, and cf. p. 223.

the government's behest, contain similar provisos.[98] The archbishop's purpose was to bring together the bishops and his own expert clerks in order to devise legislation; he was not concerned to have others present unless they felt their particular interests to be at risk. If, in this instance, he expected a large gathering of suffragans, he was to be disappointed. Only eight, two of them from Welsh bishoprics, assembled at St. Paul's on 19 October.[99] Murimuth noted the proceedings with unwonted approval; many matters which touched the liberty of the church and its reform were discussed, even though decisions had to be deferred until a subsequent council.[100] It is probable that to the 1341 council should be attributed the first (draft) series of statutes, which will be discussed in chapter five.

Not surprisingly the archbishop's plans did not run smoothly. In 1342 he was faced with a dilemma. He wished to publish the remedies devised at the previous council and to bring forward more recent developments thought to be detrimental to the church and clergy.[101] At the same time he was in receipt of a writ which proclaimed the king's intention of mounting an expedition against France and enlarged upon the perils of strife on the Scottish border.[102] He resolved the difficulty by issuing two mandates on the same day, one of which convened a convocation for 9 October in obedience to the royal writ, whilst the other ordered a provincial council for 14 October designed to deal exclusively with ecclesiastical affairs. The latter mandate cites no writ and, as we have seen, the lesser clergy was not obliged to attend.[103] As it happened, Stratford was to publish his first set of constitutions as early as 10

---

[98] E.g. the mandate for the council of 14 October 1342, where the words "si utile videatur" are added after "archidiaconi," and the following phrase is inserted: "si sua prospexerint interesse et causas vel negocia habuerint in huiusmodi provinciali concilio tractand." *Worcester Reg. Bransford*, fol. 173^{r-v}, pp. 205-206 (no. 1044). Weske observes (*Convocation of the Clergy*, pp. 94-95) that after Reynolds' summons to a convocation at Leicester in 1327 she did not find a denunciation of absentees until 1346 (*Worcester Reg. Bransford*, p. 131 no. 779, printed *Concilia* 2, pp. 727-728). The 1342 mandate mentioned above does contain a similar penalty clause.

[99] According to *Murimuth*, pp. 122, 223, the bishops were those of London (Ralph Stratford), Chichester (Robert Stratford), Salisbury (Wyville), Ely (Montacute), Bath and Wells (Shrewsbury), Coventry and Lichfield (Northburgh), St. David's (Henry Gower) and Bangor (Matthew de Englefield alias Madoc ap Iorworth). Cf. n. 105 below.

[100] *Murimuth*, p. 122: "multa tractata fuerant pro libertatis ecclesiasticae conservatione et morum reformatione, quae tunc non poterant terminari."

[101] E.g. Worcester Reg. Bransford 1, fol. 173^{r-v}. "Aliisque arduis que in depressionem status ecclesie atque cleri noviter emerserunt."

[102] *Worcester Reg. Bransford*, p. 205 (no. 1043). The writ (Tower, 15 August) is in *Foedera* 2, iv, p. 134.

[103] See below, Appendix 3.

October.[104] The second set apparently followed six days later, when eleven bishops are said to have attended upon Stratford at St. Paul's.[105] It would appear that there was little opportunity for those assembled to do any more than tinker with pre-existent drafts of the constitutions. But, as Bishop Wyville's Salisbury register shows, it was not until 19 May of the following year, 1343, that copies of the second series of constitutions were circulated to the diocesan bishops.[106]

At least part of the business which Stratford had in mind when he wrote of developments threatening the church concerned Exeter diocese, where in August 1342 the irrepressible Bishop Grandisson had ordered the proclamation of sentences of excommunication incurred by those who infringed ecclesiastical freedoms.[107] This was aimed at John de Sodbury and his fellow justices, who were said to have outlawed members of the clerical order and to be proceeding against others. Sodbury, himself parson of Shepton Malet, Hamo de Direworth, and others had been deputed to enquire into "oppressions, extortions, grievances and excesses" inflicted by royal ministers and others in the counties of Devon and Cornwall. Their citation by Bishop Grandisson had been countered by a royal writ prohibiting the bishop from proceeding with the case. Sodbury, Grandisson declared, had behaved in a manner "unheard of in modern times." Under cover of commissions designed for the persecution of the clergy he had had the temerity to outlaw various persons including Paul Brey or Bray, a doctor of civil law, Richard Giffard, the bishop's commissary, John de Pilton, and others – all rectors of churches with cure of souls. Cited for this grievous offence, Sodbury had failed to appear and

<hr>

[104] *Concilia* 2, p. 696; *Concilia, Decreta, Leges*, p. 572.

[105] London (Ralph Stratford), Coventry and Lichfield (Northburgh), Exeter (Grandisson), Salisbury (Wyville), Chichester (Robert Stratford), Hereford (Charlton), Bath and Wells (Shrewsbury), Ely (Montacute), Lincoln (Bek), Worcester (Bransford). The eleventh bishop is named by both Wilkins and Spelman (*Concilia* 2, p. 702; *Concilia, Decreta, Leges*, p. 581) as "David Bangoren," but there is no such bishop at this date. Possibly Dafydd ap Bleddyn, bishop of St. Asaph (1315-1346), was intended. (Alternately it could be a conflation of St. David's and Bangor. Cf. below, p. 398 and n. 99 above.) Both record the date of the council as "Wednesday after the feast of St. Edward." In fact it was 14 October (Monday after the feast of the translation of St. Edward the King). See below, "Provincial Constitutions."

[106] Salisbury Reg. Wyville, fol. 128ʳ (Stratford to Wyville): "vestre fraternitati firmiter iniungentes quatinus congregatis coram vobis personis illis vestre diocesis que de iure in ea parte evocande fuerint infra tempus a canone diffinitum, omnia et singula in dicto concilio acta se eciam diffinita que vobis ut premittitur mittimus plenissime reseretis eisdem ipsaque in illorum deducatis seu deduci faciatis publicam nocionem ac inviolabiliter ut convenit observari." Cf. *Bath and Wells Reg. Shrewsbury*, p. 463; Lincoln Reg. Bek 2 (Reg. 7), fol. 39ʳ.

[107] *Exeter Reg. Grandisson*, pp. 960-961, 964-965.

was declared excommunicate. Grandisson in his turn was cited before the royal justices, but for the time when the October council summoned by Stratford was in session. On the 15th Grandisson is said to have appeared before the great council at Westminster,[108] where under the presidency of the *custos*, the duke of Cornwall, prelates and barons were assembled. The Sodbury business was fully ventilated among the justices and other legal men in attendance, it being concluded that he had not acted rightly or justly in pronouncing outlawry. But the proposal that the outlawed clerks should have letters of remission from the chancellor was objected to by the prelates on the basis that their issue would presuppose guilt. Instead it was agreed that there should be letters of revocation nullifying the whole process, and that others from the area against whom outlawry had not so far been pronounced were to have writs *de supersedendo* until the next full parliament. As his part of the bargain, and out of respect for the king, Grandisson was asked to absolve Sodbury from his sentences. For the purpose Sodbury was summoned before Stratford and his suffragans in the chapel of Our Lady in St. Paul's Cathedral, where he humbly sought pardon. After an appropriate delay, during which Grandisson was urged to comply, absolution was granted on his authority, that of the bishop of London in whose diocese the meeting was being held, and of the whole council. Sodbury swore on the archiepiscopal cross to obey the mandates of the church.[109] The similarity between this case and those in which Stratford was directly involved in 1341 will be obvious. The outcome is strikingly dissimilar; this time those in authority, both clerks and seculars, combined to defuse a potentially dangerous situation. It is almost certainly right to assume that Stratford was prominent among those looking for an accommodation.

Not until 1344 did another assembly meet under Stratford's direction, again at St. Paul's and in response to the king's writ. The main business under discussion by the few bishops who attended seems to have been the grant of a triennial tenth. It was an immense concession, not made without a struggle.[110] In the parliament which met a week later Stratford exacted another "statute" on behalf of the church. This was distributed by the royal chancery to the diocesan bishops under the date 8 July.[111] Seven

---

[108] Summoned for 16 October according to *HBC*, p. 522.

[109] *Exeter Reg. Grandisson*, pp. 965-968. But a note of caution should be sounded here; we have only the clerical side of the story.

[110] *Murimuth*, p. 156; BI. Cotton MS Faustina B.v, fol. 90ᵛ.

[111] E.g. Ely Reg. Montacute, fols. 91ᵛ-92ʳ; Salisbury Reg. Wyville 1, fol. 108ᵛ (livery under great seal by M. William de Alresford). Parliament met 7 June 1344 at Westminster: *HBC*, p. 522.

specific concessions were made involving such contentious matters as the arraignment of bishops before the royal justices, the right of ecclesiastical courts to determine "clergy" and bigamy (as it was understood in medieval times), the free enjoyment of lands acquired under mortmain licence, purveyance, writs of prohibition, the encroachment of secular justices particularly in testamentary cases, and the issue of writs of *fieri facias* for the levying of tenths.[112] Murimuth was understandably sceptical about the king's promises.[113] Stratford seems to have been more sanguine, but in any case was anxious to cooperate with the government at the same time as he resisted inroads on clerical privileges. Thus he strove to secure an anticipation of the dates of payment of the triennial tenth,[114] and ordered the offering of prayers for the success of the king's expedition to France,[115] yet in the preamble to his mandate for assembling the convocation or episcopal council of May 1346 he was particularly outspoken about the invasion by the laity of ecclesiastical rights.[116] In this instance Stratford summoned the bishops alone; there is no mention of the lesser clergy.[117] At the parliament of September 1346 the archbishop was prevailed upon to call an October convocation, which granted the king a biennial tenth.[118] In his summons to what was to prove his final clerical assembly, issued 30 July 1347,[119] Stratford turned again to the correction and reform of excesses and to the preservation of the church's liberties.[120]

[112] See Jones, "Gravamina," p. 230, and below; *Rot. Parl.* 2, pp. 152-153.

[113] "Licet ex parte domini regis multae libertates et bonae conditiones clero et populo promittantur, regales tamen promissiones hujusmodi servare non curant, sed, illis praetermissis, totum quod conceditur plene levatur." *Murimuth*, p. 156.

[114] See, for instance, *Hereford Reg. Trillek*, pp. 267-270, 275-278.

[115] Ibid., pp. 273-274.

[116] "Ignis eciam nostris meditacionibus nos exardescit cotidie dum Anglicanam ecclesiam modernis temporibus per laicorum machinaciones invidas et innatas [*Concilia* has "innitas et minatas"] eis tam contra clericos quam contra libertates, iura et privilegia ecclesiastica dolosas insidias durius solito conspicimus infestari, intollerabilibus lacessiri iniuriis, eiusque iura et libertates undique conculcari." Worcester Reg. Bransford 1, fol. 95ᵛ (printed *Concilia* 2, pp. 727-728); *Bath and Wells Reg. Shrewsbury*, p. 526; *Hereford Reg. Trillek*, p. 271; Winchester Reg. Edyndon 1, fol. 9ʳ.

[117] He instructed the dean of the province, his nephew Ralph, to cite peremptorily "venerabiles fratres nostros coepiscopos electos confirmatos et suffraganeos dicte nostre Cant. ecclesie absenciumque si qui fuerint vicarios generales." See above, n. 83.

[118] The royal writ (under the name of the *custos* of the realm, Lionel) is dated 8 September 1346. Stratford states that he acted "de consensu confratrum nostrorum nostre Cantuariensis ecclesie suffraganeorum in parliamento apud Westmonasterium ... celebrato, nobiscum et cum aliis magnatibus et proceribus regni Anglie presencium convocacionem hujusmodi fore ordinavimus faciendam." *Hereford Reg. Trillek*, p. 285.

[119] Ibid., pp. 306-308.

[120] "Quantum nobis ex alto permittitur adversus excessus qui post ultimum provinciale concilium dudum per nos Londoniis celebratum in detrimentum ecclesie atque cleri

The king, who was abroad at the time, was uneasy about the prospect of further clerical legislation. Certain councillors and judges were deputed to keep an eye on the proceedings; but of this provincial council and hence the possible justification for Edward's fears nothing is known.[121]

And so provincial assemblies provided a forum where Stratford could consult his suffragan bishops, devise and publish legislation, correct and reform excesses, and respond to the requirements of secular government. But the archbishop also maintained contact with his colleagues on the bench by means of an extensive correspondence, both of a formal and informal kind.[122]. Its partial survival permits insight into the relationship with a number of them, from whom we can single out John Grandisson of Exeter, Adam Orleton of Winchester, Hamo de Hethe of Rochester, and his own brother, the bishop of Chichester. As such relationships reflect something of the character and attitude of Stratford, it will be useful to pursue them at this point.

Grandisson's activities are the subject of comment in various parts of this book. Coming from a baronial family, he acted with fearless self-confidence in his dealings with the great men of Devon and Cornwall and with the sheriffs or justices who exercised royal authority there. He regarded himself as a blunt, forthright man, lacking the expertise of such legally trained clerks as Stratford and Orleton, but nevertheless essaying a life of St. Thomas of Canterbury, which he modestly forwarded to the prior of Christ Church for comment and correction.[123] Both in his devotion to St. Thomas and in his manifest concern to maintain ecclesiastical liberty he was at one with Stratford.

emerserunt noviter medelam adhibere congruam desiderantes intense, pro hujusmodi corrigendis excessibus et moribus reformandis provinciale concilium ... fore celebraturum decrevimus." Ibid., p. 306.

[121] PRO S.C.1/39/198. This is printed in Wilkinson, *Chancery*, p. 118 n. 1. "Vous mandoms qe vous facez assembler nostre cher et foial William de Thorp et aucuns autres noz justices et sages de nostre conseil qe ont nostre estat et lestat de nostre dit corone tendrement a cuer et parmy lour avis facez faire prohibicions et mandemantiz tieux come y appartienent a fin qe nulle ordenance ne establissement se face au dit council qe porra sonner en prejudice de nous de nostre corone oue de nos droitures." For the context see below, "Closing Years," n. 159.

[122] It will have been noted that certain matters (such as summonses to convocation or council) were dealt with through the dean of the province, while others were effected directly by the archbishop. The archbishop's more intimate thoughts were conveyed in "littere private" and by means of oral messages.

[123] CCL Reg. L, fol. 91v; *HMCR* 9, App. p. 89. Grandisson described himself as "inutilis cultor ecclesie Exoniensis." For summary biographies see Haines, *DHGE* and *Biog. Oxon.* s.v.

It was in 1328, while Stratford was still bishop of Winchester, that Grandisson wrote to complain of the violence against church property in the southwest, asking his correspondent to provide a copy of the form of general sentence he employed in his diocese.[124] Two years later he again sought the benefit of Stratford's experience in legal matters. Apparently Archbishop Mepham was claiming that Grandisson should reiterate his profession of obedience made to the previous metropolitan, Walter Reynolds.[125] We do not know Stratford's reply, but doubtless it was the same as that of Orleton when pressed on the same point; according to Pope Alexander III's ruling on a similar claim by Archbishop Becket, the initial profession remained binding.[126] Grandisson was reluctant to attend parliament; when summoned to the Westminster assembly of 1330 he asked Stratford, then chancellor, and the bishop of Coventry and Lichfield, Roger Northburgh, to represent him.[127] One cannot doubt that Stratford was sympathetic to Grandisson's complaints about the oppressions and irregularities perpetrated by Robert de Bilkemore as *custos* of the Exeter temporalities *sede vacante* and as sheriff of Cornwall.[128] But when the archbishop intervened on behalf of the Exeter chancellor, M. Walter de Meriet, describing him as "an old and special friend," the bishop was decidedly unresponsive. Grandisson had imposed sequestration on the church of the aging Meriet and relentlessly pursued him for non-residence.[129] In a letter to Stratford he remarked that there was no greater malady than a hostile member of one's *familia* and he expressed the wish that neither he nor the archbishop would be so unfortunate as to have to endure such an experience![130] Stratford's requests for Murimuth to be allowed licence of absence from his duties as precentor of Exeter in order to serve as official of the Court of Canterbury were also received coldly, Grandisson arguing that there must surely be many equally qualified and willing to undertake the task.[131] What Muri-

<hr />

[124] *Exeter Reg. Grandisson*, pp. 172-173. But the list at pp. 960-961 (s.a. 1342) differs from that in WinRS fol. 51ᵛ (s.a. 1330).

[125] *Exeter Reg. Grandisson*, p. 248.

[126] Haines, *Church and Politics*, p. 55.

[127] *Exeter Reg. Grandisson*, p. 250.

[128] Ibid., pp. 251-253.

[129] Ibid., p. 274. In 1338 Meriet was said to be "senio confractus" (ibid., pp. 283 n. 2; 310 n.). Grandisson described him in a letter (ibid., pp. 283-285) as having no king but Caesar (proprium non habere regem nisi Caesarem). See also ibid., pp. 851-852, for a return of the amount of residence performed by him as chancellor of Exeter.

[130] *Exeter Reg. Grandisson*, pp. 278-279, 13 July 1334. "Scimus ... quod non est pejor pestis quam familiaris inimicus." Cf. Boethius, *De Consolatione Philosophiae* 3.5.

[131] Ibid.: "Sunt, enim, per Dei graciam, multi tam scientes quam potentes et volentes,

muth thought of such a remark can be imagined. Despite the conflict of interests in these affairs, and Grandisson's bluntness, the correspondence was conducted in measured terms.

Far more fundamental was the question of the jurisdictional relationship between Exeter diocese and the metropolitan see. We have already had occasion to allude to Mepham's attempt at visitation, which Grandisson countered by inhibiting the dean of his cathedral church from publishing the archiepiscopal mandates. When Mepham arrived none the less, he was met by armed force. The scandal was enormous and Grandisson's condemnation of his superior uninhibited. Various members of the bishop's *familia* who had aided him against "the notorious excesses and personal defects" of Archbishop Mepham were excommunicated and remained so while appeals were under way in the curia. When some of these men sought out Stratford in the north, at Warkworth, he granted them absolution from his predecessor's sentences. Grandisson was indignant; in his opinion this was tantamount to substantiating their guilt. Stratford adopted a mollifying tone, arguing that as the bishop himself would realize he was only carrying out his canonical duty of responding to those who were penitent.[132] On the overall issue Grandisson revealed no lack of skill in debate. He called upon Stratford to remember his own reaction when as bishop of Winchester he anticipated a similar threat to the liberties of *his* see. His response had matched Grandisson's own, as in all honesty he would have to admit.[133] On his side Stratford studiously avoided provocation. He was fully aware of the papal privileges enjoyed by Exeter, whereby neither its bishops nor their officers could be excommunicated by the archbishops or those acting for them.[134] Grandisson naturally wished that privilege to be respected, said Stratford, and as a corollary he should exhibit respect for archiepiscopal rights. He wanted Grandisson to withdraw the mandate which inhibited his subjects from obeying the lawful commands of the Court of Canterbury.[135] The bishop of Exeter was not easily moved; he regarded the court as a thorn in his side. According to him the hate unjustly conceived against him by Mepham had been adopted by its officers, who had issued various threats. But there were other reasons for his antagonism. Stratford must be well

in vestra provincia, dictum officium eque utiliter excercere." See below, "Stratford's *Familia* and Administration."

[132] Ibid., pp. 291-293.

[133] Ibid., p. 291. The special grace granted to Stratford's precursor in the see of Winchester, John de Pontissara, is recorded as an exemplar; ibid., pp. 91-92.

[134] Ibid., pp. 138-139, 140-141; bulls of 20 December 1331 and 30 May 1332.

[135] Ibid., pp. 275-276.

aware, urged Grandisson, that no less than three cases from his diocese had been removed to Canterbury, despite the fact that they involved clear-cut judgments of wilful homicide by a vicar, sortilege, and of dilapidation and fornication.[136]

This lively debate should not blind us to the common ground between the antagonists. We have already observed bishop and primate co-operating against secular intrusion. It was to the archbishop that Grandisson retailed the offensive actions of the new earl of Devon and those of officials during the minority of the king's brother, the earl of Cornwall.[137] It was also under Stratford's aegis that Sodbury's conduct engaged the attention of council and convocation.[138] Moreover, both men shared a background of diplomatic service and Stratford, during his embassies of the 1330s, kept Grandisson apprised of the state of negotiations.[139]

Stratford's relationship with Orleton, bishop of his former see of Winchester, was quite different. Underlying it was a basic conflict not easy to unravel. To some degree this was political in origin, for though both men had been alienated by Edward II's regime, Stratford had continued to cooperate at national level, while Orleton was relegated to the wilderness, unable even to fulfil his diocesan obligations. Both men were to the fore in the deposition of Edward II, but thereafter their paths diverged, Stratford aligning himself with the "Lancastrians," Orleton remaining in obscurity. Following Stratford's emergence as chancellor in 1330, Orleton was permitted only a very limited role in political affairs.[140] The conflict between the two surfaced with Stratford's promotion to Canterbury and Orleton's translation from Worcester to Winchester. The evidence points to Stratford's being at one with the official attitude of the royal government in resisting the promotion. Certainly this was Pope John XXII's impression. He wrote to Stratford with the allegation that under the influence of Orleton's rivals[141] the king was opposing the translation, despite the eminent merits of the man concerned.[142] Much

---

[136] Ibid., pp. 278-279.

[137] Whom he described (ibid., pp. 293-294) as "juvenis ductilis."

[138] Ibid., p. 968.

[139] Ibid., pp. 274, 277.

[140] See Haines, *Church and Politics*, pp. 181ff. But Orleton did take a slightly greater part in affairs than is suggested there. For instance, he was commissioned to explain the king's necessities at the great council of August 1335. *Foedera* 2, iii, p. 132. See below, "In the Seat of Power."

[141] "Quorundam emulorum venerabilis nostri Ade episcopi Winton. dolosis persuasionibus stimulatus."

[142] "Virum litterarum scienciis preditum, fidelitate conspicuum, et probatum fama preclarum et aliis variis ornatum virtutibus."

worse, Stratford himself was believed to have refused recognition of Orleton as a suffragan, to have received income from the Winchester temporalitics under pretext of a royal gift, and to have declined to return the seal of the officiality as well as his own episcopal register and those of his predecessors.[143] The pope's information may not have been wide of the mark. We know that in the mid-summer of 1334 Stratford was granted not only the crops sown in the lands of the see of Canterbury in Mepham's time or during the subsequent voidance, but also all the crops in the Winchester temporalities, without obligation to render anything to the royal custodians. In the normal course the Winchester temporalities would have been restored to Orleton, but this did not take place until towards the end of September (23rd), after the harvest had been gathered.[144] The government gave countenance to a trumped-up appeal to the Roman curia, which attempted to fasten on Orleton responsibility for the more regrettable incidents in the revolution of 1326-1327.[145] This got nowhere, for Pope John already knew whatever was likely to be known about Orleton's participation in those events. Their resurrection at this juncture is surprising, unless it can be explained in terms of an attempt to dissociate Stratford from a past he wished to forget. If so, it was hardly successful, since Orleton's forthright replies were designed to leave no ambiguity about Stratford's implication.[146] Stratford's attitude, as reported in the papal letters, is in marked contrast to that of Grandisson, a man who as bishop fought shy of political entanglements. As one of the executors of the bull in Orleton's favour he was bound to take some action, but he went much further than that. Despite illness he wrote in the warmest terms to the new bishop of Winchester and sent one of the Exeter canons in support of his written sentiments. To Stratford he expounded on the reverence due to God and the Roman church, and the

---

[143] "Ac eciam denegasse dicto episcopo officialitatis sigillum et curie Winton., registro-que tuo et predecessorumque tuorum ...." Lambeth MS 1213, pp. 306-308. See also *CPL 1305-1342*, p. 513 (20 June 1334), from Vatican Archives, *RV* 117, fol. 212^r (which was not available for consultation); *Winch. Chart.*, no. 243b.

[144] *CPR 1330-1334*, pp. 537, 549, 565. Haines, *Church and Politics*, p. 63 and n. 11.

[145] For this see Haines, *Church and Politics*, pp. 62, 189-190. *CPL 1305-1342*, p. 409, gives "John Pebrehave" as the appellant's name, but this is a misreading of "Pebrehare," who is described as "literatus Wintoniensis diocesis." In fact the name is "Prikehare" and a John Prikehare was ordained acolyte 27 March 1316 (*Winchester Reg. Woodlock* 2, p. 877). Cf. Vatican Archives, *RV* 107, fols. 262^v-263^r.

[146] Contained in the *responsiones*, cols. 2763-2768, printed by Twysden, *Historiae Anglicanae Scriptores*, from Lambeth MS 1213, pp. 300-306. Another copy is *Winch. Chart.*, no. 234, the instrument of appeal itself being no. 233 – a transcription of which the writer hopes to have printed shortly.

harm done to that of Winchester, beseeching him "on his knees and with tears in his eyes" to exercise the indulgence he was accustomed to extend "even to sinners." [147]

This unpropitious start should not mislead us into thinking that archbishop and suffragan were perpetually at loggerheads; such was not the case. Orleton was not the vengeful irascible character of his calumniators. He had been helpful in agreeing to the exchange of lands and other matters which facilitated the foundation in 1331 of the Stratford chantry, and even after the new archbishop's unpardonable behaviour over his translation to Winchester, attended Stratford's enthronement at Canterbury. Three days after this event, while still in Canterbury, Orleton agreed to abandon all claims to dilapidations in the manors of Stratford's former bishopric, as well as to pay a thousand pounds for growing crops.[148] On the death in 1339 of Richard Bintworth, the bishop of London, Orleton stepped into his shoes as dean of the province for the time being. This was the prerogative of the Winchester bishops. As dean Orleton executed the mandates of Stratford's vicar general for the summoning of convocation.[149] The following year, when the archbishop tried to appoint a prior of the Augustinian house at Twynham, alias Christchurch, the move was understandably opposed by Orleton, who claimed it to be an infringement of his jurisdiction. An appropriate appeal was launched, but following an exchange of letters and discussion with the respective chancellors, the matter was amicably settled.[150] There can be no question about Orleton's sympathy for Stratford's opposition to unlawful taxation,[151] but the extent of his intervention in the struggle of 1341 between king and archbishop should not be exaggerated. Stratford's attempt to impose a coadjutor on the aging and blind Orleton was successfully parried. The bishop preferred to choose a man of his own liking – William Edington.[152] But in this matter Stratford was acting quite

---

[147] *Exeter Reg. Grandisson*, pp. 281-283.

[148] BL Cotton MS Faustina B.v, fol. 75ᵛ; WinRO 1, fol. 17ʳ. This was possibly advantageous from Stratford's viewpoint. There could have been few growing crops but the liability for dilapidations might have been substantial.

[149] WinRO 1, fols. 83ᵛ-84ʳ. It is noted in the register that Orleton sent mandates to all the bishops of the province with the exception of London (Bintworth ob.) and those of Lincoln (Burghersh) and Hereford (Charlton), who were abroad.

[150] See Haines, *Church and Politics*, pp. 94, 213-214, 255. Lydford thought the case sufficiently interesting to include a number of the relevant documents in his notebook. See *Lydford*, pp. 117-118 (nos. 212-215), where the initials "J. de B." should be "J. de L.," and cf. WinRO 1, fols. 93ʳ-95ᵛ.

[151] Haines, *Church and Politics*, p. 191.

[152] Ibid., pp. 194ff.; 64, 100.

properly in his attempt to remedy a defect. It is an odd coincidence that one of Stratford's last acts was to grant acquittance to the executors of his old rival.[153] One matter left over from Orleton's regime was the long-standing struggle of the Winchester diocesans with the archdeacons of Surrey. In 1348 Stratford was responsible for drawing up a composition between Orleton's successor, William Edington, and the then archdeacon, M. Richard Vaughan.[154]

Hamo de Hethe's relationship with Stratford is a little more difficult to delineate, because the Rochester chronicler is unexpectedly reticent. The diocese of Rochester was not only adjacent to that of Canterbury, it also had a special relationship with the archbishops, who claimed the custody both of spiritualities and temporalities during vacancies.[155] As a consequence an absent archbishop was likely to employ the Rochester diocesan for episcopal functions, as Stratford did in Hethe's case. Although Hethe was reluctant to attend what he considered to be time-wasting sessions of parliament,[156] he was frequently to be found at Canterbury for ecclesiastical functions, notably the consecration of bishops.[157] It was at Stratford's insistence that the bishop of Chichester was allowed to stay in Hethe's London residence, La Place, conveniently close to Lambeth. The arrangement ended in disaster; the visitor's room was burnt down. Somewhat ungraciously Robert Stratford disclaimed any responsibility for the damage, which in his view arose from a defect in the fireplace.[158] In the autumn of the same year, 1340, Stratford joined Hethe at Trottiscliffe for a meal.[159] One wonders whether the archbishop made amends for the damage at La Place, but the chronicler has no comment on this. Cooperation was necessary, also in 1340, when Stratford wrote a letter under his private seal about the abbot of Lesnes, who was said to have committed adultery within the archbishop's jurisdiction of Shoreham in Kent. A jurisdictional wrangle between archbishop and bishop does not seem to have produced excessive friction.

---

[153] *Hereford Reg. Trillek*, p. 135: 6 July 1348.

[154] *Lydford*, pp. 134-141 (no. 249); Winchester Reg. Edyndon 1, fols. 12^r-13^v.

[155] *Cant. Admin.* 1, chap. 5.

[156] Hethe regularly excused himself from attendance. E.g. PRO S.C.10/11/519, 527; 13/619; 17/837, 842; 19/908.

[157] E.g. he was at the consecration of Robert Stratford (Chichester), Bintworth (London), though this was at Lambeth rather than Canterbury, Bransford (Worcester), and of Ralph Stratford (London). BL Cotton MS Faustina B.v, fols. 81^r, 82^r, 88^r. See also *Canterbury Professions*, s.v.

[158] "Non ex culpa sua vel suorum combusta extiterat sed pro defectu cuiusdam scissure in area culpam in alium redundare nitens." BL Cotton MS Faustina B.v, fol. 88^r.

[159] "Cum episcopo buttelam panis cepit." Ibid.

All we know about it comes from the statement of Hethe's case by M. Michael de Berham.[160] In conclusion it may be remarked that while Hethe had been the object of criticism by Mepham following a visitation of 1329, Stratford's attitude, though it could become impatient as in the affair of the pallium, seems in general to have been more accommodating.[161]

It comes as something of a surprise to find that we know comparatively little of the archbishop's dealings with his brother Robert, bishop of Chichester, and even less about those with his nephew Ralph Stratford, bishop of London. In both cases this is largely due to the fact that their episcopal registers are missing.[162] However, something useful can be said about Robert. We have already mentioned the possibility that Archbishop Stratford held a visitation of Chichester diocese. If so, there were no obvious repercussions. Sufficient evidence survives to argue a measure of cooperation between the two brothers. Thus a charter of liberties granted to Bishop Robert and his church in 1338 contains a resounding tribute to his work on the king's behalf and Stratford heads the list of witnesses.[163] Indicative of mutual trust is the arrangement whereby both Bishop Robert and his chapter conceded to the archbishop the right to arbitrate in a dispute over the precise limits of episcopal visitation with respect to the chapter and its jurisdiction in the city and neighbouring vills of Fishbourne and Wick. Bishop and chapter sealed their submissions on the last day of May 1340, on the understanding that Stratford would deliver his arbitration by Michaelmas. Pressure of business prevented the archbishop from doing so in the stipulated time, so a postponement was arranged.[164] Eventually, 11 December 1340, Stratford published the composition at Canterbury, both parties giving assent before the end of the month.[165] To all outward appearance the operation was carried out smoothly, although it has been claimed that in comparison with corresponding settlements elsewhere the Chichester chapter fared rather badly, possibly because of "an unfortunate choice of arbiter." Another

---

[160] Ibid., fol. 90^r.

[161] Mepham's harsh criticisms of Hethe obviously aroused ill-feeling. See ibid., fols. 53^v-55^r.

[162] The first surviving register from Chichester is that of Robert Reade (1396-1415).

[163] WSRO, Liber B, fol. 38^{r-v}; *CChR 1327-1341*, pp. 439-442.

[164] WSRO Liber E, fols. 194^r-196^v. Stratford's excuse for his delay runs (fol. 196^v): "Quia propter multa impedimenta tam ex parte nostra quam vestra contingencia et arduitatem negocii supradicti ipsum festum Sancti Michelis de quo in dictis litteris fit mencio iuxta votum vestrum plene non poterimus expedire."

[165] Ibid., fols. 196^v-197^v. The bishop of Chichester's acceptance is dated 28 December, that of the dean and chapter, 26 December. Ibid, fol. 198^r.

possibility is that decanal authority being less developed at Chichester, the composition entailed no marked departure from previous practice. Had it done so, the dean and chapter's assent would surely not have been given so promptly. A third hypothesis is that Dean Garland was too compliant. Subsequent deans, Walter de Segrave and William de Lynne, are supposed to have appealed – with eventual success – to the apostolic see against Stratford's ruling.[166] Be that as it may, Robert was appointed vicar general by his brother on several occasions and his cooperation in the foundation of the Stratford chantry, as well as in political affairs, speaks well for the brothers' compatability.[167]

Apart from the formal interchange of mandates and the certification of their execution we know little of the contact made by Stratford with most of his other suffragans.[168] What is fairly clear is that most of the bishops were solidly behind their metropolitan in his defence of the church and that Stratford generated little of the friction so widespread in Archbishop Mepham's time. The notable exception to this generalization, as we have seen, was the visitation of Norwich; a dispute cut short by Anthony Bek's death.[169] Stratford's relationship with the northern province and its archbishops, William Melton (1317-1340) and William Zouche (1342-1352), need not detain us, partly because it is peripheral to our present purpose, and partly because the information available is slight and fragmentary. What there is of it is mainly concerned with the long-standing dispute about the elevation of the metropolitical cross, taken to be a sign of jurisdictional authority, by one archbishop when in the territory of the other. As all three archbishops – Stratford, Melton and Zouche – at one time or another held high office in government, they were regularly travelling to councils and parliaments, which were held at this period both in the north and the south. Friction was therefore to be

---

[166] For most of these points see Edwards, *Secular Cathedrals*, p. 131. The documents are summarized in Swainson, *History and Constitution of Chichester Cathedral*, pp. 58-59, 64-66ff. What purports to be an exemplification (18 May 1478) of the process recited in a bull of Innocent vi (19 May 1355) is copied into wsro Cap. 1/12/2 (Swayne's book, "Reg. K"), pp. 171-190 (cf. 213-217). Dean Lynne became bishop in 1362. Stratford's ruling none the less remained in force.

[167] See above and below, "The College of St. Thomas the Martyr, Stratford."

[168] Ralph of Shrewsbury's Bath and Wells register is long, but there seem to be remarkably few personal details. The same is apparently true of Burghersh's Lincoln register, though as a prominent political figure for almost twenty years this bishop's activities and relationships merit attention. The present writer is working on Bishop Montacute of Worcester and Ely, who was apparently well disposed towards Stratford.

[169] 19 December 1343 at Hevingham, Norfolk. *Biog. Oxon.* s.v. (from Blomefield, *Norfolk* 6, p. 375). Cf. below, p. 341 n. 60.

expected. From time to time the king was forced to intervene to ensure that his business did not suffer as a consequence of such ecclesiastical squabbles.[170] It was not until 1353, when Simon Islep was archbishop of Canterbury, that a composition was agreed to and the question of precedence in royal councils and other assemblies carefully defined.[171]

We must turn now more particularly to Stratford's conduct of diocesan affairs at Canterbury. The diocese, with its eleven rural deaneries, a single archdeaconry, and a plethora of exempt parishes,[172] was comparatively small like neighbouring Rochester. But in addition there belonged to the church of Canterbury eight deaneries, which though they lay within the borders of other dioceses were immediately subject to the archbishop.[173] Most extensive were the exempt deaneries in Rochester, Chichester and London dioceses, within which lay some of the most important episcopal manors. A glance at Stratford's itinerary will be enough to show that he was more often out of his diocese than in it, but it should be remembered that the many lacunas may indicate periods when the archbishop was resident. Were his register extant it would certainly help to fill many of those gaps. Naturally Stratford spent a lot of his time at Lambeth (in Winchester diocese) just across the Thames from Westminster, and also at his cathedral city, Canterbury. In fact his longest recorded stay is at the latter, where he resided from the beginning of December 1340 until mid-April 1341. However, the circumstances were exceptional.[174] Charing was roughly in the centre of the diocese. The gate-house of Stratford's palace and substantial remains of the buildings now form part of a farm. It was there that Stratford stayed quite frequently. Every now and then he is recorded as being at Maidstone, Otford, or Croydon; useful staging posts

[170] E.g. *Foedera* 2, iii, p. 82; *CCR 1333-1337*, pp. 316, 481. This protracted struggle deserves examination in the wider context of the perennial question of the relative antiquity and pre-eminence of the metropolitan sees. Stratford does seem to have had a financial relationship with Melton from whom he bought wool and borrowed money. See below, Bibliography, Manuscript Sources, York.
[171] Canterbury Reg. Islep, fol. 99^r-v; Lambeth MS 99, fols. 200^v-202^r.
[172] See *Cant. Admin.* 1, intro. pp. 39ff. For the exempt parishes see ibid., pp. 83ff. They are listed ibid., p. 109 n. 3, from the Black Book of the Archdeacon, which records twenty-eight of them. The rural deaneries are: Canterbury, Westbere, Bridge, Sandwich, Dover, Elham, Lympne, Charing, Sutton, Sittingbourne, and Ospringe. See *Taxatio*, pp. 1-3. Donahue and Gordus, "Archbishop Stratford's Audience Act Book," p. 48 n. 21, are needlessly mystified by references to the "dean of Canterbury." He is simply the dean of Christianity. Cf. *Worc. Admin.*, pp. 62ff.; Lunt, *Papal Revenues* 1, p. 272 (where a dean of Christianity, Peter, occurs s.a. 1278).
[173] *Cant. Admin.* 1, pp. 62ff. The exempt deaneries and the churches within them are listed ibid., p. 63 n. 6.
[174] See below, "The Crisis of 1341" and "Itinerary".

for a journey from Canterbury to London. Maidstone palace lies near the centre of the present town, hard by the church and overlooking the River Medway. By contrast Otford manor is situated in what must have been a somewhat remote area at the foot of the North Downs and in the damp meadows of the Darent valley; not a suitable residence for winter-time. But Stratford liked the place enough to create a new park there, receiving royal licence to alienate thirteen acres of land in Otford with appurtenances in Sevenoaks.[175] Occasionally Stratford is to be found at Wingham between Canterbury and Sandwich, where Archbishop Pecham had founded a collegiate church, at Saltwood castle not far from the Kent coast at Hythe, and at South Malling in Sussex. Towards the end of his life he was often at Lambeth, but it was at Mayfield in Sussex that he died, as Mepham had done before him.

The palace at Canterbury was sadly dilapidated in the later 1340s, as we learn from a report made at Stratford's request by Prior Hathbrand. The great hall required attention to roof, gutterings, windows, timbering, doors and walls, while the ceiling of the chapel was defective. So ruinous was the kitchen serving the chamber that the only recourse was to rebuild it. St. Thomas's hall, next to the lord's chamber, was in much the same state. Two other rooms between the great hall and the great chamber were in need of extensive reparation; the great kitchen was roofless (indiget coopertura). It was the same story in the outbuildings, and throughout the palace stairs, doorways and other features were in need of attention.[176] Quite how matters had been allowed to fall into such a state is not clear, for Canterbury was frequently visited by the archbishops. One wonders whether the fracas of 1336 caused damage to property as well as injury to members of Stratford's *familia*.[177]

It is possible to catch a glimpse of Stratford's household as he moved about the diocese. By great good fortune two of the monthly household rolls from his time have been preserved among the abbey muniments at Westminster. Quite how they came to be there is a mystery. The earlier roll can with a measure of confidence be dated 1343,[178] the other one

[175] Canterbury Reg. Islep, fol. 95ᵛ: 28 January 1348. Cf. Ducarel, "Fragmenta," fols. 76ʳ-77ᵛ. The remains of "Otford Palace" are almost entirely Tudor.

[176] *Lit. Cant.* 2, pp. 282-284 (752); CCL Reg. L, fols. 80ᵛ-81ʳ.

[177] *Lit. Cant.* 2, pp. 134-135 (604); CCL Reg. L, fol. 66ʳ⁻ᵛ.

[178] WAM no. 9222. The possible years (given the days of the week and the dates assigned to them on the recto) are 1337 and 1343. Stratford was almost certainly at the parliament at Winchester 3 March 1337, hence he could not have been at Maidstone. He issued a mandate about the revocation of the sexennial tenth from Lambeth, 21 March 1337, when the account shows him to have been at Charing. On 2 March 1343, at cock-crow, the king landed at Weymouth and reached Westminster by the 4th (*Foedera* 2, iv,

definitely belongs to 1347.[179] The 1343 roll is for the month of March, during which time Stratford travelled from Otford to Maidstone, back to Otford, and then on to Lambeth, where he spent just over a week. After that he journeyed to Canterbury by way of Croydon, Otford, Maidstone and Charing. Spending only four days in his cathedral city, he moved back to Charing and thence to Maidstone and Otford, where we take leave of him on the last day of the month. This account, like the other one, is subdivided to show the expenditure of the various departments: pantry, buttery, kitchen, saucery, poultery, hall, and stables or marshalry. In the ordinary course the kitchen department was responsible for the heaviest expenditure, with the stables next. It seems that the archbishop kept some ninety to a hundred horses, palfreys, and hacks. The total expenditure for March amounted to £169 13s 2³/₄d, at a time when a stipendiary priest would count himself lucky to receive £4 a year. It needs to be remembered though, that not only was the archbishop supporting his own household officers and clerks, but also entertaining a regular stream of visitors who did not arrive unaccompanied. During March his guests at table included William de Clinton, the earl of Huntingdon,[180] various barons – Bartholomew Burghersh,[181] Reginald Cobham,[182] Hugh Neville,[183] and Otto de Grandisson, brother of the bishop of Exeter – as well as the lady Huntingfield,[184] the abbot of Faversham,[185] and John Pulteney,

p. 141), but the roll does not mention any messenger of his. It is curious that dates on the verso (wardrobe account) are appropriate to 1342 (e.g. Wednesday 20th, Friday 22nd, and Monday 25th March). All the same, the grand total for the month on the dorse correctly incorporates the sum on the face of the roll.

[179] WAM no. 9223. The day/date relationship would suit either 1341 or 1347, but an entry of 4 December on the dorse mentions a gift from the executors of the earl of Warenne (Surrey). The earl died 29 June 1347, which settles the matter. Du Boulay, *Lordship of Canterbury*, discusses some features of the rolls (pp. 256-257) but assumes this roll to be from 1341.

[180] Clinton, one of the "new men" who gained Edward III's favour, was created earl in 1337. Stratford was to defend this and other creations of that date. See below, "The Crisis of 1341," and for Huntingdon, *GEC* 6, pp. 648-650.

[181] Brother of Henry, bishop of Lincoln, Bartholomew Burghersh in 1340 was said to be thirty-six and more. He fought at Crécy and died 3 August 1355. *GEC* 2, p. 426.

[182] Of Sterborough in Lingfield, Surrey. Cobham and Burghersh were deputed (29 August 1343) to form part of an impressive embassy to Pope Clement VI. Possibly this was already under discussion with Stratford. See Dugdale, *Baronage* 2, pp. 67-68; *GEC* 3, p. 353; *Foedera* 2, iv, pp. 150-151.

[183] I am unable to trace this Neville in *GEC* 9. He must be the man termed royal councillor in 1344 at the time of his mission to Pope Clement. *Foedera* 2, iv, pp. 169-170; *Murimuth*, pp. 159-160.

[184] Cecily, widow of Roger de Huntingfield and daughter of Sir Walter de Norwich, knight. Dugdale, *Baronage* 2, p. 8; *GEC* 6, pp. 667-668.

[185] In 1340 Stratford had secured a mortmain licence to alienate the advowsons of

a notable London citizen, merchant and money lender, who was a personal friend of Stratford's.[186] As one would expect, influential clerks figured in the list of guests, among them Philip de Weston, Edward III's almoner, confessor, and clerk of his chamber, and M. Simon de Islep, the future archbishop, whom Stratford made official of the Court of Canterbury and who had formerly been vicar general of the bishop of Lincoln.[187] The Canterbury prior, Robert Hathbrand, dined with the archbishop on four occasions, on one of them "with the whole community of the town of Canterbury"[188] a gathering, one supposes, of prominent officers and citizens. On 5 March similar entertainment was provided for a corresponding body from the town of Maidstone. The official of the Court of Canterbury dined on five consecutive occasions, apparently because he attached himself to Stratford's retinue for the journey to London. His presence and that of the dean of Arches suggests that opportunity was taken for a discussion of legal business. Although we are not told this, the officers of the audience court could have been in attendance also.[189]

Like its fellow, the dorse of the 1343 roll is inscribed with the archbishop's wardrobe account for the month, mainly consisting of sundry payments to messengers and other persons encountered during the perambulation of the manors. Many of these disbursements were made at the instance of members of the household or of important clerks. Thus, at John de Eccleshale's request twelve pence were paid to the *garcio* or groom sent by the Stratford chapel warden. A ministrel from Spain who came into the hall was paid 3s 4d on the steward's authority, while John Lacy, on Stratford's order but at Richard Twyverton's instance, was sent

---

Boughton under Blean and Preston-by-Ospringe, both in Kent, to the abbot and convent of Faversham, in exchange for Tring manor, Hertfordshire. CCL Reg. D, fols. 464ᵛ-465ᵛ, MS P.32; *CPR 1338-1340*, pp. 444, 543, 550; *Anglia Sacra* 1, p. 59; *CChR 1327-1341*, p. 472.

[186] Poultney or Pulteney was much involved with Stratford in raising money for the king. See, for instance, *CCR 1333-1337*, p. 547; ibid., *1339-1341*, p. 459; ibid., *1341-1343*, pp. 294, 374; ibid., *1344-1346*, p. 287. For a biographical note see *French Chronicle*, pp. 64-67; also Tout, *Chapters* 5, p. 396 n. 3; Stow, *Survey*, 1 pp. 106, 236, 335; 2 pp. 164-165, 321.

[187] For Weston see Tout, *Chapters* 6, index s.v.; Thompson, "Pluralism," 36 pp. 22-23. Islep is mentioned as Burghersh's vicar general in CCL A.36 IV, fol. 4ʳ, and frequently in Lincoln Reg. Burghersh; his biography is in *Biog. Oxon.* s.v. Islip.

[188] "Et tota communitas ville Cantuar."

[189] From CCL A.36 III and IV (fragments of audience court proceedings in 1334, 1340-1343, and 1347-1348) it is clear that the Court of Audience met at various archiepiscopal manors, but that Stratford's residence so rarely coincided with the sessions that it is specifically noted.

from Lambeth to Oxford for purposes of study at a cost of 6s 8d.[190] Medication (in rebus medicinalibus) for the archbishop cost 18d, and at the marshal of the household's solicitation Stratford gave directions for the payment of twelve pence to a simpleton at the tomb of St. Thomas at Canterbury.[191] The wardrobe expenses for March amounted to £16 17s 3d; the grand total of the whole account being £186 10s 5¾d.

The mutilated 1347 account covers a mere nine days of December, during which period the archbishop was resident at his manor of Croydon. Again there was a considerable influx of visitors, this time including Robert Stratford, the earls of Arundel (Richard FitzAlan), Northampton (William de Bohun) and Huntingdon (William de Clinton), Bartholomew Burghersh, Geoffrey de Say,[192] the lady Margaret Molyns,[193] the clerks Simon Islep and John Carleton, and once again the official of Canterbury.[194] The wardrobe account on the dorse of the roll runs to 15 December, the archbishop by that time having moved to Otford. On the 14th Simon de Worstede was under instruction to make ready gifts for Christmas, while John Paris was already on his way with invitations for the festival, which Stratford planned to celebrate at Maid-

---

[190] "De precepto domini de Lambeth usque ad Oxon. ad scolatizandum ibi nunciante domino Ricardo Twyverton, 6s. 8d." WAM no. 9222 dorse. A John de Lacy had been abroad with Stratford in 1338. *CPR 1338-1340*, p. 98.

[191] "Die veneris xxii die [*sic*, see n. 178 above] Martis apud Cantuar. datum de precepto domini cuidam fatuo existenti ad tumbam sancti Thome nunciante marrescallo domus, xii d." WAM no. 9222 dorse.

[192] Arundel was the son of Edmund FitzAlan, executed in November 1326 during Edward II's overthrow. He was restored to the title in 1330, fought at Crécy, and died 24 January 1376 (*GEC* 1, pp. 242-243). Both Huntingdon and Northampton were creations of 1337 (n. 180 above). Say was a Kentish baron, who had been summoned before Stratford and the council in 1338, and was to play a prominent part in Edward III's campaigns (*CCR 1337-1339*, p. 140; Dugdale, *Baronage* 1, pp. 511-512; *GEC* 11, pp. 475-477).

[193] This lady is difficult to identify. A Margery, daughter and heiress of Edmund Bacon, knight, was wife to William Molyns. William was the son of the notorious John Molyns of Stoke Poges – a particular object of Edward III's wrath in 1340 – and of his wife Egidia or Gill. But Margery is said to have been only fifteen and a half at the time of her marriage "before 12 March 1352." Dugdale's, *Baronage* 2, p. 147; *GEC* 9, pp. 36-40; N. Fryde, "A Medieval Robber Baron."

[194] Islep is mentioned in 1343 (*CPP 1342-1419*, p. 56) as clerk of Edward (later the Black Prince), from whose service he migrated to that of Lionel of Antwerp and then to that of the king (Tout, *Chapters* 5, pp. 23, 378 n. 7). Tout considered Stratford responsible for Islep's advance to royal service. Cf. *Biog. Oxon.* s.v. Islip, and n. 187 above. There are at least two John Carletons at this time, who are said by Emden to have been confused by Tout. This is probably the elder, who died in 1361 after a distinguished career. See Tout, *Chapters* 6, index s.v.; *Biog. Oxon.* s.v. Carleton, John de; cf. Thompson, "Pluralism," 35 pp. 87-90.

stone. Other entries show Stratford to have been in touch with his nephew, the bishop of London, to whom he sent a pipe of wine at the hands of his butler, William Wygheth. Letters were despatched to the bishop of Chichester at Aldingbourne, to John Pulteney at Sutton, and to M. Richard Pulham at Norwich. John de Eccleshale was responsible for the purchase of a silver ewer (cuppa cum aquar' argenti) from Ralph Sporoun of London, for sending to the curia by Carleton's hand. John de Teye, a chaplain who carried letters of M. Richard Vaughan from Avignon, was paid 13s 4d on the authority of Roger Dorkyng; the bishop of Winchester's groom received six pence for delivering the master's letters. On 6 December, the feast of St. Nicholas, two shillings were donated on Stratford's order to the boy-bishop at Croydon. And so we have to leave this tantalizing insight into the day-to-day happenings in the archbishop's household; a glimpse which serves to emphasize what has been lost.[195]

Failing a diocesan register only a piecemeal assessment can be made of Stratford's activities within his see. There are no ordination lists from his time, nor do we know the extent to which he made use of suffragan bishops to execute the tasks for which he himself had inadequate time. His policy for licensing incumbents to be absent for study is likewise unknown, though he is likely to have regarded such requests with sympathy. After his examination of the cathedral priory he would have given some attention in person or by commissary to the remainder of the diocese, but we have to rely on chance allusions for confirmation of this. It is possible that Stratford conducted a subsequent visitation, as was his duty, for in 1340 we learn of his actions on such an occasion in a matrimonial case[196] and with regard to the vicar of Snargate, whom he instructed to pay sums due to the rector for tithes.[197] But the record does not give the date of the visitation or visitations concerned. We do know that Stratford, as at Winchester, was meticulous about the augmentation or establishment of vicarages in appropriated churches. For example, vicarages were ordained in Canterbury at St. Mary's Northgate, Holy Cross Westgate, and St. Dunstan's, all of which churches were appropriat-

---

[195] "Episcopo puerorum sancti Nicholai de Croydon., 2s." WAM no. 9223 dorse. Dorkyng could well be the Roger "Dygge" named steward of Stratford's household in *CPR 1348-1350*, p. 306.

[196] CCl. A.36 IV, fol. 28ʳ (case of Robert Dod of Faversham and his wife Amicia, whom Robert rejected "licet ipse alias in visitacione dicti domini archiepiscopi in dicta diocesi Cant. exercita ad sancta Dei evangelia iuravit ipsam uxorem suam maritali affeccione tractare").

[197] Ibid., fol. 63ʳ ("in visitacione nostre Cant. diocesis," contained in a mandate to the dean of Lympne for enforcing payment).

ed to the Augustinian priory of St. Gregory,[198] in a number of churches belonging to St. Augustine's Abbey, as well as at Croydon in the church of the archiepiscopal manor.[199] To the hospital of Eastbridge, not far from the Westgate in Canterbury, Stratford united the church of St. Nicholas, Harbledown, just to the west of the city.[200] A lengthy series of documents records his proceedings and sentence in the dispute between the vicars of Reculver and Herne and their respective parishioners, notably about burial and other rights claimed by the mother church of Reculvar.[201]

Traces of the archbishop's disciplinary work in his diocese are recoverable from the fragmentary act books of the audience court.[202] Although Stratford occasionally took a part in proceedings, they were in the main conducted by his auditors and commissaries.[203] These men

---

[198] St. Gregory's ordination documents are printed by Somner, *Antiquities*, App. pp. 73-75 (nos. 68-69, 70b).

[199] Croydon already had a vicarage in the late-thirteenth century (*Taxatio*, p. 208). Stratford's ordination, Maidstone 12 June 1348, is in Canterbury Reg. Courtenay (fol. 176^v) as part of the lengthy process of 16 January 1391 (ibid., fols. 175^r-182^v) concerned with the church's appropriation (by virtue of a papal bull) to Bermondsey priory. Ducarel, "Fragmenta," fols. 62^v-66^v, gives a transcript of the ordination. Cf. *Monasticon* 2, p. 90. For the vicarages of Preston-by-Wingham, Chislet, Faversham, Milton, Kennington-by-Ashford, Littlebourne and Northbourne (churches appropriated to St. Augustine's) see *Thorne*, cols. 2081, 2109-2110, 2115-2116, 2091-2094, 2104-2105, 2108, 2111-2113.

[200] CCL Reg. H, fols. 88^v-90^r. From this source it is printed in Somner, *Antiquities*, App. pp. 13-15 (no. 17), and *Lit. Cant.* 2, pp. 251-257.

[201] Ducarel, "Fragmenta," fols. 78^r-86^r: "Exemplification of instruments relating to Reculver and Herne." This is CCL MS R.20, which in part is now difficult to read.

[202] Those which concern Stratford's archiepiscopate are CCL A.36 III (three leaves) and A.36 IV, which though much mutilated constitutes a substantial fragment, notably for 1340-1341 and 1347-1348. The material has been examined by Woodruff, "Notes from an Act-Book," and recently by Donahue and Gordus, "Archbishop Stratford's Audience Act Book," who concentrate mainly on a particular case. I differ somewhat from the authors of the latter in my interpretation of the MS and with respect to points of factual detail. The court did accompany the archbishop on *some* of his travels (cf. ibid., p. 49), but special mention of his presence (e.g. A.36 IV, fols. 24^r, 26^v, 28^v) argues that this was not regular (cf. n. 189 above). The period December 1340 to April 1341 is untypical, since Stratford was static because of the political crisis. There was only *one* archdeacon (of Canterbury) and his official, to whom mandates could be directed (Donahue and Gordus, pp. 45-46). Stratford is unlikely to have been at Merton, hence Laurence Fastolf would not have been "a schoolmate of all the Stratfords" (p. 51). The idea that the MS constitutes a "half completed formulary mixed in with the raw *acta* of Stratford's Audience Court" (p. 49) requires qualification, though the volume is clearly a composite one. The "other categories" of material *are* related to the court proceedings (pp. 45-46). But it is true that the cases are not on the whole "weighty" (nor are those in the contemporary audience proceedings in *Worcester Reg. Bransford*, pp. 504-509).

[203] Principally M. Laurence Fastolf and M. John de Lecch (Loveryng of Northleach), but also M. Richard Vaughan, archdeacon of Surrey, who appears towards the end of the record.

travelled round the archiepiscopal manors holding sessions of the court at regular intervals.[204] The nature of the record is to show clerical indiscipline and immorality, as well as the faults of laymen which fell within the purview of ecclesiastical jurisdiction. Cases came before the court both *ex officio*, by virtue of the archbishop's office, and at the instance of private persons.

Some of the clergy gave an unedifying example to their flocks, though how representative this was cannot be judged. The longest list of charges was brought against William Sare, the vicar of Rainham. According to the indictment he was a frequenter of taverns, especially at night, where he joined in the singing of ribald songs. On St. Sexburga's day[205] he disported himself with shield and buckler in Sheppey and other places.[206] In his own church of Rainham he appeared armed. Even worse, he carried his arms to the high altar, thus setting a deplorable example to the laity! Often and without cause he used shameful words in arguments he provoked with his parishioners. Ignoring the provision made at the establishment of his vicarage, he had failed to find a chaplain for outlying areas of the parish. Many times he had presumed to celebrate mass with the juice of white berries in place of wine, and had used violence against the sacristan of his church, one John Derby.[207] Another case, that of William de Bordenne, rector of Wittersham, was heard before Stratford himself in the church of Saltwood. The rector was accused of having sexual relations with four of his parishioners, one of them a married woman, and this over a number of years.[208] Moreover, he was said to have beaten and kicked a parishioner during mass. Despite the gravity of these allegations Stratford allowed the accused to proceed to purgation, though with a very large number of compurgators – no fewer than thirty-one, all rectors or vicars, are named.[209] Another incumbent, the rector of Blackmanstone, was accused

---

[204] There are regular rubrics which indicate sessions at roughly three-weekly intervals.

[205] The Canterbury calendars give the feast as 6 July. *HD*, p. 61.

[206] "In Scapeya publice cum gladio et parma ludebat." CCL. A.36 IV, fol. 78ʳ. One presumes he was taking part in local games.

[207] "Verbis probosis sepius absque causa contendit"; "Multociens cum sucto uvarum albarum loco vini missam celebrare presumpsit." Ibid. The outcome of the case is not recorded.

[208] With Isabel, wife of Robert Mullere, for five years and more, with Alice Nightynghale for a year, and for some time with Agnes, daughter of Thomas Geffe, and Mabil Filpot, his parishioners.

[209] CCL. A.36 IV, fol. 56ʳ (1342). This would seem to conflict with Stratford's own constitution of the same year restricting the number of compurgators to six for cases of fornication, twelve for those of adultery or major offences, though the thirty-one could have been distributed among the various charges. See *Concilia* 2, p. 700.

of non-residence, illegally farming his church, and concubinage.[210] In the September of 1340 the archbishop's chancellor, John de Lecch, was proceeding against Henry de Southchurch, who was holding the rectory of Newenden, near Tenterden, despite the fact that he was illegitimate and in his youth had adopted the monastic habit at the Cluniac house of Prittlewell, where he had stayed for five years.[211] A more general problem, invariably a preoccupation of reforming diocesans at this time, was the prevalence of non-residence. It would seem that towards the end of Stratford's rule a vigorous attempt was being made by the court to deal with this abuse and the related one of illegally farming deserted benefices.[212] It is unusual, if not unique, to have to rely almost exclusively on a court book, and a fragmentary one at that, for evidence of disciplinary action within a medieval English diocese, but in this instance there is surprisingly little additional information.[213]

One incident, this time involving monastic discipline, has been wrongly reported to Stratford's discredit. The archbishop is said to have "consecrated" prior of Combwell one John Roper, a canon of the Augustinian house of Bilsington. From this position he was allegedly removed for misconduct by the prior of Canterbury during the vacancy following Stratford's death.[214] What the manuscript (*sede vacante* Register Q) actually records is something quite different. Stratford had committed Roper to Combwell priory, another Augustinian house, as a punishment and with the obligation to ·perform penance. This was a means of discipline commonly invoked by bishops at this period.[215] The Bilsington prior and convent, taking advantage of the archbishop's demise, hastened to retrieve their fellow canon and to restore him to his pristine status, an action condemned by the Canterbury prior as scandalous and contemptuous of his authority. Hathbrand then proceeded

[210] CCL A.36 IV, fols. 103ʳ, 108ʳ. The original charge against Rector William was that of non-residence, for which he was cited by Stratford (20 March 1346).
[211] CCL A.36 III (fragments from 1340-1341), m. 1ʳ. The case is continued on m. 3ʳ.
[212] CCL A.36 IV, fol. 101ʳ. "Processus contra non residentes et beneficia sua dimittentes ad firmam" (*Acta* of June 1348 before M. Richard Vaughan).
[213] On the other hand it serves to demonstrate how much of an ordinary's disciplinary work was effected by the routine actions of the courts. Cf. the fragment of audience court proceedings (from 1349) in *Worcester Reg. Bransford*, pp. 504-509. The printed register of Bishop Hethe contains a substantial body of consistory court records and some scattered audience cases. *Rochester Reg. Hethe*, subject index s.v. Courts ecclesiastical.
[214] HMCR 8, App. p. 337a.
[215] Council of Oxford, c. 53 *Hoc quoque volumus* (*Councils and Synods*, p. 213). Cf. Haines, *Church and Politics*, p. 74.

to cite the Bilsington prior and ordered the imposition of an appropriate penance on the errant Roper.[216]

To conclude our study of Stratford as archbishop we must return to a wider sphere, that of the relationship with secular authority. Throughout Stratford's tenure of the primacy there was constant skirmishing, which every now and then, and most remarkably in 1341-1342, erupted into open warfare. Long before the dawn of the fourteenth century an extension of clerical jurisdiction had become unthinkable. The church, it has been cogently remarked, "was forever on the defensive, and it realized it." [217] This fact is underlined by the series of clerical *gravamina* which punctuated the conflict, grievances which were ably and courageously vindicated by some of the more memorable archbishops. In this respect it can be claimed that Stratford was the heir of the redoubtable Robert Winchelsey, whose defence of the church's rights came close to making him a saint.[218] As bishop of Winchester and one of the prime movers of Edward II's overthrow Stratford must surely have been engaged in the formulation of the clerical complaints brought before the parliament of Hilary 1327.[219] As archbishop his long-standing determination to preserve the church's temporalities from secular inroads bore fruit in the statute of 1340 – a "charter of liberties" which Stratford circulated to his suffragans with a justifiable sense of achievement.[220] The conflict of 1340-1341 fathered the *gravamina* of the latter year, giving rise to legislation which was subsequently repudiated by the king.[221] But Stratford was not easily defeated. As we have seen above, in the more relaxed atmosphere of 1344 when the king's necessities dictated compromise, he fostered a further series of grievances, all seven articles of which were incorporated in a statute.[222] The same concerns dictated the content of the third series of the

---

[216] "Nuper bone memorie Johannes Cantuar. archiepiscopus fratrem Willielmum Ropere canonicum prioratus de Bylsingtone pro quibusdam gravibus excessibus per ipsum commissis ad prioratum de Combwell eiusdem diocesis suam factur*um* penitenciam ibidem ex quibusdam causis racionabilibus destinavit." CCL Reg. Q, fol. 222^r-v (al. 218).

[217] Jones, "Gravamina," p. 226.

[218] See, for instance, *Foedera* 2, ii, p. 183; *Oxford Formularies* 1, pp. 58-60; and the panegyric in *Vita Edwardi Secundi*, pp. 40-42. Denton, *Winchelsey*, provides a modern assessment. Wright, *Church and Crown*, pp. 262ff., makes a case for Reynolds' attempt to "work with the crown" and contrasts his attitude with that of Winchelsey.

[219] *Rot. Parl. Inediti*, pp. 106-110, from CCL Reg. I, fols. 416^r-418^v. See Jones, "Gravamina," pp. 225-227.

[220] See nn. 93-94.

[221] Jones, "Gravamina," pp. 227-228, and below, "The Crisis of 1341."

[222] Jones, "Gravamina," pp. 230-231.

archbishop's provincial statutes, published in 1342 and circulated to the Canterbury suffragans in the following year.[223]

The policy of securing statutory or some other form of written and enrolled recognition of the liberties of the church as a whole, or of particular members of it,[224] is manifested by late-medieval cartularies and registers. For example, one of the few remaining medieval manuscripts at Chichester, *Liber E*, is a compilation attributed to William Reed or Rede, who was provided to that see in 1362, some six years or so after Robert Stratford's death. Its contents are a reflection of Archbishop Stratford's own concerns. In its present form it has an introductory section devoted to royal charters confirming clerical privilege.[225] This begins with Henry III's confirmation of Magna Carta as renewed by Edward I, the Charter of the Forest, and the sentences subsequently promulgated against those who infringed their provisions, all of which feature in Stratford's sentences of 1340.[226] Among other later documents are Edward II's "statute" (*Articuli cleri*) "defining those areas in which royal prohibition does not run" [227] and the writ *Circumspecte agatis* (1286).[228] Next comes a lengthy subsection entitled "Articles from divers statutes of Edward III's reign on behalf of the clergy," [229] which incorporates material from Stratford's archiepiscopate and to which is appended his "charter of

[223] Below, "Provincial Constitutions."

[224] Stratford was to the fore, not only in assisting with charters in favour of the bishops of London (Guildhall Library, MS 8762), Chichester (n. 163 above), Winchester (above, "Winchester 1323-1333" nn. 126-127), and Bath and Wells (*SCKB* 6, pp. 121-122; *CChR 1341-1417*, p. 52), but also in securing markets and fairs for his manors at St. Nicholas Thanet, Gillingham, Pinner, Smeeth, Cliffe-by-Lewes, and the newly acquired Tring (*CChR 1327-1341*, pp. 360, 373, 422, 472; ibid. *1341-1417*, p. 38), as well as for the canons of South Malling in Sussex (ibid., p. 24). For the Yorkshire liberty of "Canterburyfee" he secured the view of frankpledge (ibid., p. 53).

[225] At fol. 137ʳ. I use the old foliation in references to this volume. Another of Reed's compilations, Liber D, is now Bodleian Library, MS Ashmole 1146, which contains an invaluable calendar with the terms for the Court of Arches as well as Stratford's ordinances for that court and his constitutions.

[226] WSRO Liber E, fols. 137ʳ: "Carta Magna communium libertatum Anglie per dominum Henricum regem Anglie III concessa et per dominum Edwardum regem Anglie primum eius filium innovata"; 140ʳ: "Explicit Carta Magna de libertatibus Anglie. Incipit carta de Foresta"; 141ᵛ: "Explicit carta de Foresta. Incipit statutum declarans casus in quibus non habet locum regia prohibicio"; 141ᵛ-142ʳ (inserted): "Sentencia lata in contravenientes cartarum predictarum."

[227] Ibid., fols. 141ᵛ-143ᵛ; *Concilia* 2, pp. 460-462: 24 November 1316. For prohibitions see Flahiff, "Use of Prohibitions" and "Writ of Prohibition"; Wright, *Church and Crown*, pp. 177ff, and for the *Articuli cleri*, 187-194.

[228] WSRO Liber E, fol. 144ʳ; Graves, "Circumspecte Agatis."

[229] WSRO Liber E, fol. 144ᵛ: "Articuli diversorum statutorum tempore regis Edwardi tercii pro clero edit."

liberties" (1340).[230] Similarly, documents of fundamental significance for the rights of the church were often copied into episcopal registers – those, for instance, of Stratford's contemporaries Orleton of Winchester and Grandisson of Exeter – and this may perhaps be evidence of the special concern of such men. Clearly Stratford was convinced of the value of explicit muniments, and even if some of them were more honoured in the breach than the observance, it was sound policy to advocate legal right as a defence against arbitrary action.[231]

On many occasions Stratford was personally engaged in contentious incidents involving secular authority. Thus, in 1337 he found himself in the invidious position of receiving Edward III's support on grounds "both of law and custom" [232] against Bishop Orleton, who in the course of his lengthy controversy with Archdeacon Inge,[233] sought the removal of the case from the Court of Canterbury to the papal audience. In his letter of complaint to the pope, Edward III incongruously presented himself as the defender of the rights and honour of Canterbury and stigmatized Orleton as an ingrate who was injuring the metropolitan see despite the favours it had bestowed upon him.[234]

Stratford's charter of 1340 in theory circumscribed the royal practice of filling benefices on the grounds of vacancies in bishoprics. The king promised not to act against those who had held a benefice for a year before the making of the statute, and if in future he failed to present a clerk within three years of a vacancy there would be no obligation on the party concerned to respond to the writ *Quare impedit*.[235] But, as the archbishop soon discovered, inroads continued to be made on his rights of

---

[230] Ibid., fols. 151ʳ-152ᵛ.

[231] It is, of course, a commonplace that muniments were zealously guarded and frequently produced during widespread litigation both in the king's court and in the courts of other jurisdictions. Stratford and Orleton, both lawyers, epitomize in their careers this emphasis on the law and the arbitrary nature of action in contravention of it.

[232] *Foedera* 2, iii, pp. 166-167. "Causae per viam appellacionis, vel querelae, pretextu gravaminum, per suffraganeos Cantuariensis ecclesiae illatorum, ad Cantuariae curiam devolutae, illic tam de jure, quam de consuetudine tractari debeant et finiri." The king's position was that cases should be dealt with in England, while allowing the pope's "plenitudo potestatis." Apparently he is not here directly asserting the "privilege of England" (for which see Wright, *Church and Crown*, pp. 142-154), but supporting the rights of the church of Canterbury with which he claims a special association.

[233] A matter I hope to deal with in detail elsewhere.

[234] "Machinans per commenta callida declinare, in ejusdem matris suae immaculatae opprobrium atque malum, ac si ingrata et injuriosa extiterit, ut non fuit, set potius multos favores, quos non meruit, sibi fecit, sicut veraciter novimus fidedigna relatione multorum." *Foedera* 2, iii, p. 166.

[235] *Concilia* 2, p. 656.

presentation both on this and on other accounts. For instance, in 1343 a writ *Quare non admittit* was served on him as guardian of the Lincoln spiritualities *sede vacante*. Stratford ingeniously temporized by arguing that the writ was wrongly directed against him, since by the terms of a composition with the Lincoln dean and chapter his authority was restricted to choosing an official from among the canons presented to him, so that he exercised "sovereignty" rather than "guardianship." The proceedings were stayed because the same suit was to be brought against the new bishop of Lincoln.[236] Another case arose from the vacancy at Winchester following Orleton's death in 1345, when the archbishop was summoned to answer a plea about the king's claim to present a clerk to Winchester archdeaconry. Stratford rightly argued that the benefice did not become void on Orleton's death, but the jury returned a verdict in Edward's favour. As a result Robert de Burton, a royal clerk, was presented to the archdeaconry, which he was to hold until 1361.[237]

In 1343-1344 the king presented to a prebend in the archbishop's college of Wingham, to the rectory of Wimbledon, and to the archdeaconry of Canterbury; each time on the pretext of Stratford's "unlicensed alienation of the advowson." [238] Again, in 1346, a decision in the court of King's Bench enabled Edward to present to Meopham, though a commission had to be appointed for the arrest of those who hindered the judgment.[239]

There is a notable instance of legal action against Stratford as a consequence of the discordance of secular and ecclesiastical jurisdiction. The archbishop and his principal legal officers were attached at the suit in the king's court of a certain John de Lisle, on the ground that they had proceeded with a tithe case in the ecclesiastical forum in contravention of a royal prohibition. Although pardoned, they were to answer to the aggrieved party, whose case the king did not wish to prejudice.[240]

---

[236] *YB 17 Edward III*, pp. 282-286. For this element in the Lincoln composition see *Cant. Admin.* 2, p. 43.

[237] *CPR 1345-1348*, p. 18. *Le Neve* 4, p. 50, gives John or Jean de Puy Barsac as archdeacon 1328-1343. In 1343 there were two claimants.

[238] *CPR 1343-1345*, pp. 40, 105, 117, 280. The archdeaconry of Canterbury was given to Simon Islep, presumably a beneficiary agreeable to Stratford. The Wimbledon appointment was made allegedly because of a violation of the statute of Carlisle (1307) and that of the last parliament at Westminster by the bringing of bulls into the country. See *Rot. Parl.* 2, p. 145, and for the extension of royal rights of patronage, Deeley, "Papal Provision."

[239] *CPR 1345-1348*, p. 105.

[240] *CPR 1340-1343*, p. 502: 19 August 1342. See cap. 12 of Stratford's third series of constitutions (*Concilia* 2, p. 707), which inveighs against this abuse.

Another type of secular pressure, against which Stratford had inveighed in his constitutions, was the indictment for extortion before the justices of oyer and terminer in Kent of Thomas Mason, his commissary general, presumably for levying pecuniary penalties. The archbishop intervened to secure a pardon for his officer.[241]

Lastly in this connection may be mentioned a chancery case in which the archbishop, following the death of his tenant Nicholas Meynill, sought to enjoy the wardship of his lands in the usual manner. The king's right was alleged, to which Stratford's proctor objected that archiepiscopal lands were excepted both by prescription and by virtue of a "statute" *De prerogativa regis*.[242] An *inspeximus* of the enrolment of the case is among the miscellaneous charters at Lambeth.[243]

In fairness it should be remembered that clerics also made use of the secular courts to coerce their fellows. Thus Stratford's brother, Robert, brought a suit of trespass against M. John de Mitford, a canon of his church of Chichester, and the justices outlawed the canon for non-appearance. The archbishop joined his brother in requesting a pardon for Mitford, who made satisfaction for his trespass.[244]

Whatever conclusion one reaches about Stratford's overall career, it is impossible to overlook his vigorous defence of the rights and duties of Canterbury. Towards the priors of Christ Church he was fatherly, but firm; towards his suffragans he was determined, yet conciliatory; and with respect to secular authority he was ever watchful to resist intrusion.[245] Only four other Canterbury archbishops ruled for roughly comparable periods during the fourteenth century: Robert Winchelsey

---

[241] *CPR 1345-1348*, p. 203: 2 July 1346. It seems likely that Thomas Mason is the same man as Thomas of Canterbury, mentioned as commissary general in the audience court book. There is an earlier mention of him in ibid., *1340-1343*, p. 502: 19 August 1342.

[242] *YB 16 Edward III* pt. 1, pp. 130-134. cf. Wright, *Church and Crown*, pp. 162-163 n. 36. This refers to the entry in *Statutes* 1, pp. 226ff., from BL Cotton MS Claudius D.ii, fol. 222ᵛ, which states that the king is to have custody of all lands held in chief "exceptis feodis archiepiscopi Cant., episcopi Dunolm. inter Tyne et These, et feodis comitum et baronum de marchia." It used to be referred to as a "statute" of 17 Edward II, but is clearly much earlier in origin. See Richardson and Sayles, "The Early Statutes," pp. 564-565.

[243] Owen, *Catalogue*, p. 88 no. 116; Lambeth Cart. Misc. VI 116.

[244] *CPR 1343-1345*, pp. 452, 467-468.

[245] According to the *Annales Paulini* (pp. 363-364) one of Stratford's earliest acts as archbishop was to castigate the mayor of London for removing a criminous Lombard from sanctuary at All Saints, Gracechurch Street, and casting him into Newgate. Stratford hauled mayor and city officers before him in St. Paul's, secured restitution of the Lombard, and imposed penance "pro tam enormi facto."

(1294-1313), Walter Reynolds (1313-1327), Simon Islep (1349-1366) –
whom Stratford is said to have designated as the man most suitable to
succeed him[246] – and William Courtenay (1381-1396). Among them he
can assume an honourable place as a prelate who took his duties seriously
despite the hampering effect of secular office.

STRATFORD'S *FAMILIA* AND ADMINISTRATION

A prevalent feature of medieval life was the close-knit *familia* or group of
laymen and clerks which gathered round prominent men who had
patronage to dispense or influence to exert. Often a core of relatives and
close associates remained with an important figure for virtually the whole
of his career.[1] Loyalty, mutual respect and interest, as well as a feeling of
interdependence kept men in close contact even though the person to
whom they owed "allegiance" advanced from one position to another or
migrated to an entirely different part of the country. Thus familial
solidarity regularly entailed a high degree of mobility, a more pervasive
aspect of medieval society than has been supposed.

As has been remarked in the opening chapter, by 1320 Stratford had
already achieved substantial progress in his career. His prospects were
considerable, if as yet ill-defined. In consequence he had grouped around
himself a number of persons, some of them relatives or fellow-townsmen
from Stratford or neighbouring villages; men who looked to him for
advancement. The list of those granted protection to accompany Archdeacon Stratford abroad in the summer of 1320 illustrates the point. Seven
men are included and the writ of aid was issued in the names of two
more, the archdeacon's brother, Robert Stratford, and Nicholas of
Shottery, a village close to the town of Stratford.[2] Among the seven we

---

[246] *Vitae Arch. Cant.*, p. 41 (Lambeth MS 99, fol. 146ᵛ). Significantly, perhaps, the
author of the *Vitae* allots much space to Islep's biography. After those of Stratford and
Winchelsey (which are exceptional), it is by far the longest.

[1] Stratford and his kinsmen were to secure three sees: Winchester (later Canterbury),
Chichester and London. This can be compared to Orleton and his relatives, the Trilleks,
who were advanced to Hereford (later Worcester and Winchester), Hereford again, and
Rochester. Stratford's "episcopal family" was well established during his lifetime; the
Trillek episcopates belong to the second half of the century. Cf. the section corresponding
to this one in Haines, *Church and Politics*, pp. 81-97.

[2] *CPR 1317-1321*, p. 450: 5 June 1320. Cf. ibid., p. 452.

find the archdeacon's namesake, John de Stratford, rector of Overbury in Worcester diocese. He can be identified as John Geraud or Geroude, whose kinsman – probably brother – Henry de Stratford was the chancery clerk imprisoned during the royal purge of 1340-1341. This Henry was reputedly Archdeacon Stratford's cousin.[3] John Geraud we shall meet later as rector of Stratford and warden of the chantry there.[4] Another possible kinsman is Nicholas de Stratford, seemingly a different man from the Nicholas of Shottery just mentioned.[5] Richard de Ragenhull (Ragnall, Nottinghamshire) was rector of Barnoldby (Lincolnshire) and it is a reasonable assumption that John Stratford encountered him in the course of his duties as archdeacon of Lincoln.[6] This man proved to be a most regular member of his patron's retinue,[7] and was to become one of Stratford's domestic chaplains at Winchester.[8] Also a future chaplain was Walter de Harpham, who secured royal presentation to Stone prebend in Hastings on its vacation by Stratford,[9] but was not as frequent a member of his patron's entourage on missions abroad as was Ragenhull.[10] Finally John de Madeleye, who together with Stratford witnessed the election

[3] *French Chronicle*, pp. 84-85. Henry "de Stratford," priest became rector of Severn Stoke in 1327, at the king's presentation as guardian of the lands of Roger de Clifford. In fact this was an exchange for Berkhampstead, Lincoln diocese. *CPR 1324-1327*, p. 86; *Worcester Reg. Cobham*, fol. 119^v, pp. 212-213, 247. In 1334 (24 June) Henry Geraud, priest, was instituted to Overbury at Worcester priory's presentation (*Worcester Reg. Montacute 1*, fol. 10^v), just prior to an institution to Severn Stoke (ibid.). The rector of Overbury in 1347 is called Henry de Stratford (Stredford). At that time a writ of *levari facias* was issued against him for arrears arising from his custody (with others) of the lands of the abbot of Lyre (*Worcester Reg. Bransford*, p. 327 no. 1031). Overbury was appropriated in 1346, but Henry did not resign until the time of Bishop Barnet (1362-1363). See *Worc. Admin.*, p. 265. Clearly Geraud and Stratford are the same man.

[4] See below, "The College of St. Thomas the Martyr, Stratford."

[5] Alexander de Stratford may also have been a kinsman. He was with Stratford, then bishop, on royal service in 1331 (*CPR 1330-1334*, p. 218) and must be the man whom he, as archbishop, made janitor of the cathedral priory (officium ianitoris prioratus nostre ecclesie) for life. This was no menial office and the appointee presumably had a deputy to discharge the duties. *Lit. Cant.* 2, pp. 217-218 (681-682); CCL Reg. L, fol. 74^v.

[6] Ragenhull acted as substitute proctor (for John Streche) on behalf of William de Estaviaco (rector of Overbury and former archdeacon of Lincoln) in the complex process of exchange described above, "The Making of a Career." See WoCL Liber Albus, fol. 96^v.

[7] Though only until 1325. See *CPR 1321-1324*, pp. 45 (7 December 1321), 182 (18 July 1322), 244 (12 February 1323); ibid. *1324-1327*, p. 129 (6 July 1325).

[8] WinRS, fol. 101^r: at the time of collation of Burghclere rectory (10 March 1327).

[9] Ibid., fol. 93^v. The occasion was the collation of Chilbolton (8 February 1325). At Hastings there was merely an exchange of the prebends of Stone and Wortling. See above, "The Making of a Career," and *CPR 1317-1321*, pp. 133, 150.

[10] *CPR 1324-1327*, pp. 49 (11 November 1324); 94 (12 February 1325), wrongly termed "William"; 129 (6 July 1325).

process at Worcester priory in 1317, accompanied him on two further occasions in the early 1320s but is hard to trace thereafter.[11]

Another grouping of the following year, 1321, delineates the core of the Stratford connection. In this instance we find Robert Stratford, John Geraud, Richard de Ragenhull, and William Mees acknowledging a debt of a hundred and eighty pounds to certain canons of Lincoln.[12] Mees, like Madeleye, knew Stratford because of their mutual affiliation with Worcester diocese, where as an acolyte M. William Mees was instituted to Morton Bagot church (Warwickshire) in the patronage of Kenilworth priory.[13] On Stratford's promotion to Winchester, Mees acts as the bishop's notary.[14] He became rector of North Berkhampstead in Hertfordshire and subsequently of Steeple Mordon in Ely diocese. Between 1321 and 1325 he regularly enjoyed protection as a member of Stratford's retinue embarking for the continent.[15]

Among other clerks and laymen – not readily distinguishable in the records from unbeneficed clerks – associated with Stratford at this period, we may note several from his native diocese of Worcester. William Hatton, a layman, we have already encountered as a Stratford man, member of a family closely related to the Stratfords. He acted as witness to an *inspeximus* of Bishop Maidstone of Worcester's charter for the transfer of land at Ingon by Stratford, which passed eventually to the Stratford chantry. He also accompanied his patron abroad both in 1324 and in 1325.[16] The John de Lacy who was frequently in Stratford's company

[11] Wilson, *Worcester Liber Albus*, p. 165, no. 750. At the time of Prior Bransford's election a Gilbert de Madeleye was subprior. *CPR 1321-1324*, pp. 45 (7 December 1321), 182 (18 July 1322). In 1320 (11 April) at Stratford's request Madeleye was granted custody of a wood "Chaspel" in Kinver Forest. Ibid. *1317-1321*, p. 437. He appears to be the "Madele" mentioned below as taking the grease of the episcopal parks in Winchester diocese. See also *CCR 1327-1330*, p. 93 (13 February 1327) for enrolment of a grant to him by John de Stratton authenticated by Stratford's episcopal seal.

[12] *CCR 1318-1323*, p. 485: 5 August 1321. Cf. ibid. *1330-1333*, p. 278 (29 January 1331), where Stratford, as bishop of Winchester, Robert Stratford, John Geraud and John de Eccleshale acknowledge a debt of six hundred pounds to Italian merchants.

[13] Worcester Reg. Maidstone, fol. 37ᵛ. Cf. ibid. fol. 3ʳ, where he calls himself William Williams (Willelmi) of Mees.

[14] E.g. WinRS, fols. 1ᵛ (1324), 19ʳ (1326), 162ʳ-163ʳ (1326); *responsiones*, cols. 2765-2766 (1327).

[15] *CPR 1321-1324*, pp. 45 (7 December 1321), 182 (18 July 1322), 244 (12 February 1323); ibid. *1324-1327*, pp. 49 (11 November 1324), 94 (12 February 1325), 129 (6 July 1325). The Berkhampstead benefice passed to Henry (Geraud) de Stratford in 1325. Ibid. *1324-1327*, p. 86.

[16] Ibid. *1317-1321*, p. 103; ibid. *1324-1327*, p. 50 (11 December 1324), 94 (12 February 1325), 129 (6 July 1325); and see above, "The Making of a Career."

between 1324 and 1338 may be identifiable as the Stratford parishioner who acted as one of the witnesses for the enquiry preparatory to the appropriation of the parish church to the chantry chapel.[17] If so, he too was a layman. A (younger?) John (de) Lacy was sent in 1343 at Stratford's expense from Lambeth to Oxford to enable him to study.[18] Then there is John de Honnesworthe (Handsworth), rector of Clent, Worcestershire, whom Stratford as bishop of Winchester collated to Bocking. He was abroad with his patron in 1324-1325 and once more in 1331-1332.[19] A man of this name was licensed in 1339 by the Worcester diocesan, Bishop Bransford, to have mass celebrated in his house "Walbrook" within Halesowen parish, which borders Clent.[20] M. William of Ledbury, also confusingly described as "of Worcester," was associated with Oxford University, of which he was a graduate. He accompanied Stratford in 1324 and 1325 and the next year was ordained priest by him and promoted to Baghust rectory in Hampshire. Later he became rector of Avening in Worcester diocese, but exchanged it for the episcopal church of Wonston in that of Winchester.[21]

Two other persons merit remark as frequent companions of Stratford's journeys: Geoffrey Houeles or Howells and Edmund de Shireford. Howells was granted royal protection in 1324, twice in 1325, and again in 1331 and 1332.[22] Shireford is regularly listed with him, except for the 1331 expedition. In 1327, at Stratford's request, he received a royal grant for life of the bailiwick of Baslow, Nottinghamshire.[23]

[17] *CPR 1324-1327*, pp. 50 (11 December 1324), 94 (12 February 1325), 129 (6 July 1325); ibid. *1330-1334*, pp. 218 (28 November 1331), 276 (18 April 1332); ibid. *1338-1340*, p. 98 (1 July 1338). For the enquiry see *Worc. Admin.*, pp. 234, 243; and below, "The College of St. Thomas the Martyr, Stratford."

[18] "... ad scolatizandum ibidem nunciante domino Ricardo Twyverton, 6s 8d." WAM no. 9222 dorse. This may be the same man who accompanied Stratford abroad earlier.

[19] *CPR 1324-1327*, pp. 50 (11 November 1324), 129 (6 July 1325); ibid. *1330-1334*, pp. 218 (28 November 1331), 276 (18 April 1332). Royal ratification of his position as rector of Clent is dated 24 July 1332 (ibid., p. 321), and of Bocking 16 March 1334 (ibid., p. 531). Bishop Orleton licensed him to be absent (2 January 1330) in Stratford's service at the latter's request. *WRO*, no. 305.

[20] Possibly Honnesworthe in retirement since his benefice had passed to others. *Worcester Reg. Bransford*, pp. 5, 447; 45, 360, 437.

[21] *CPR 1324-1327*, pp. 50 (11 November 1324 – termed rector of Botteleye [Botley, Oxford]), 94 (12 February 1325), 129 (6 July 1325). Stratford ordained him priest in February 1326 (WinRS, fol. 143ᵛ). He died in 1337. See *Biog. Oxon.*, s.v. Leobury de Wygornia; *WRO*, nos. 36, 592, 596 (Avening/Wonston exchange). His service with Stratford and some other details are not recorded in *Biog. Oxon.*

[22] *CPR 1324-1327*, pp. 50 (11 November 1324), 94 (12 February 1325), 129 (6 July 1325); ibid. *1330-1334*, p. 218 (28 November 1331), 276 (18 April 1332).

[23] Ibid. *1324-1327*, pp. 50, 94, 129, 276; ibid. *1327-1330*, p. 6 (5 February 1327).

With his advancement to Winchester the need to establish an administration in both the spiritual and temporal spheres vastly increased Stratford's significance as a dispenser of patronage. As we have seen, absences abroad necessitated repeated appointments of vicars general, eleven commissions being issued between the end of 1324 and the beginning of 1333. Robert Stratford was deputed on seven occasions, in conjunction with one or two others. The work was shared with Masters Richard of Chaddesley, Richard of Gloucester, Wybert de Lutulton or Littleton, and on two occasions with the Winchester prior, Alexander Heriard.[24] Chaddesley, whose name points to a Worcestershire origin, was by 1332 a doctor of canon law, possibly of Oxford. Earlier he had become rector of Kempsey, acting as commissary and vicar general for the Worcester diocesan, Maidstone.[25] His entry into Stratford's Winchester administration came in 1324 when, as commissary general, he was given powers over vacant benefices and the goods of intestates, the right to grant probate of wills made by clerks, knights and others,[26] and also that of enquiry, correction and punishment of the bishop's subjects.[27] Another commission gave him authority to deal with cases in the consistory court.[28] It would seem that we can equate this office of commissary or commissary general with that of commissary general or assessor of the diocesan official, in which case Chaddesley was succeeded by M. Hugh Prany[29] before mid-September 1324, and he in his turn by M. John de Lecch, who was possibly active between 1325 and his appointment as official in 1329.[30] Chaddesley soon rose to higher things, being entitled

---

[24] See Appendix 2, List of officers.

[25] *Worc. Admin.*, pp. 90, 102, 131, 324. Like Madeleye and Stratford himself, he had witnessed the 1317 election process at Worcester priory. See n. 11 above. For details of his career see *Biog. Oxon.*, s.v. Chaddesiegh; *Hemingby's Register*, pp. 188-189.

[26] Such wills being considered "more important" were reserved to the bishop or his delegates. But in the archdeaconry of Surrey the right to probate of the wills of laymen other than members of the bishop's *familia* was claimed by the archdeacon. See Winchester Reg. Edyndon 1, fols. 12^r-13^v, and the inaccurate copy in *Lydford*, pp. 134-141 no. 249, also Haines, "Orleton and Winchester," p. 15.

[27] WinRS, fol. 2^r: 19 March 1324.

[28] Ibid. and see above, "Winchester 1323-1333."

[29] Prany was rector of Itchen (Hampshire), ordained priest 23 March 1325, and licensed to be absent for study for two years in 1324 and again in 1326, which would explain why he was superseded in office. WinRS, fols. 92^v, 99^v, 142^r, and cf. fols. 3^v, 8^v. During Orleton's episcopate he appears as official of the archdeacon of Winchester. See Haines, "Orleton and Winchester," pp. 11 n. 4, 20.

[30] See, for instance, WinRS, fols. 4^v-5^r, 7^v, 8^v, 10^r, 11^r, 25^r, 33^v, 40^v, 43^r, 95^r, 162^{r-v}, 171^v-172^r; PRO C.115/K1/6681, fols. 15^r-17^r. Early in 1329, following an appeal by the vicar of Middleton, which alleged Lecch's sequestration of tithes without judicial process at the instance of Robert Stratford (prebendary of Middleton), Ralph de Chiriton and Henry de Bradeweye, the Court of Canterbury issued a prohibition. Ibid., fols. 167^v-168^r.

diocesan chancellor in 1325-1326 and again in 1332-1333.[31] We should expect to find the chancellor acting in the episcopal audience court, which made a circuit of his manors and where technically suits were heard *coram episcopo*. The "Register of Causes" which constitutes a quaternion in Stratford's episcopal register,[32] shows this to have been the case. Both Chaddesley and M. Wybert de Littleton, his successor in office, appear as judges, though apparently not *ex officio* but by virtue of *ad hoc* commissions.[33] Another aspect of episcopal discipline which engaged the judicial attention of Chaddesley was the process of visitation, which has already been described.[34]

The other great judicial office in Winchester diocese was that of official – the officer who presided over the consistory court. Two men successively held this post: M. Richard of Gloucester between 1325 and 1328,[35] and M. John de Lecch from 1329 to 1333, hence presumably to the end of the episcopate.[36] Surprisingly M. Richard does not feature among the known graduates of Oxford or Cambridge. He must have been well qualified in law to have held the offices of vicar general and official, but at present comparatively little is known about him, apart from the fact that he served an apprenticeship as advocate in the Court of Arches, where he acted for the Worcester prior and for Bishops Maidstone and Cobham, from all of whom he received pensions.[37] On the other hand,

[31] E.g. WinRS, fols. 75ʳ, 77ʳ, 93ᵛ, 97ʳ, 133ʳ, 162ʳ-163ʳ, 171ᵛ-172ʳ.

[32] Ibid., fols. 160ʳ-168ʳ.

[33] See, for instance, WinRS, fols. 160ʳff., where cases are sometimes heard before the "chancellor and commissary *ad hoc*" (e.g., fol. 165ᵛ Littleton). Chancellor Littleton's commission (Southwark, 24 November 1326) empowered him to hear and determine cases *coram episcopo* (ibid., fol. 163ʳ). For other notices of Littleton as chancellor see ibid., fols. 19ʳ⁻ᵛ, 69ʳ; *Winch. Chart.*, no. 148. His period of office appears to have stretched between 1326 and 1332. Emden, *Biog. Oxon.*, s.v. Littleton, Wibert, wrongly states that he was appointed chancellor in 1333 (citing WinRS, fol. 74ᵛ). The footnote in WinRS states (after an entry of 30 August 1332) that he left (recessit) and at the top of fol. 75ʳ that Chaddesley arrived (venit). Wybert and his relative (brother?) William (*Biog. Oxon.*, s.v.) were licensed to have divine service celebrated in the chapel of St. James at Littleton in Wellow parish (Somerset), which denotes their place of origin. *Bath and Wells Reg. Shrewsbury*, p. 180, and see *Biog. Oxon.*, s.v. Littleton, William de.

[34] See above, "Winchester 1323-1333."

[35] See, for instance, WinRS, fols. 24ᵛ-25ʳ, 26ʳ⁻ᵛ, 33ᵛ, 35ᵛ, 95ᵛ, 97ʳ, 99ʳ, 101ᵛ, 103ᵛ, 104ᵛ, 164ʳ, 171ᵛ.

[36] E.g. WinRS, fols. 50ʳ (*bis*), 72ᵛ-73ʳ, 121ᵛ; *Winch. Chart.*, nos. 148, 176, 202; PRO C.115/K1/6681, fols. 17ʳ-19ʳ, PRO 31/9/17A, fol. 11ᵛ (*CPL 1305-1342*, p. 373). Emden, *Biog. Oxon.*, s.v. Lecche alias Loveryng, cites fol. 17 of the Llanthony cartulary (PRO C.115 cited above) as evidence of Lecch's being official in 1327; in fact at that date he was commissary general. Cf. WinRS, fols. 25ʳ, 33ʳ. The cartulary does name him official in December 1329 and July 1331.

[37] Worcester Reg. Maidstone, fol. 29ʳ. On 10 April 1328 Worcester Priory granted

there is plenitude of information about Lecch, or John Loveryng of Northleach, as he is more fully described. He was a doctor of canon law by 1338 and of civil law by 1352. In the former year he became chancellor of Oxford University, a position he occupied for a year.[38] His first appearance in Stratford's administration comes in November 1324 as special commissary for enquiry into the excesses of the bishop's subjects and their correction and punishment.[39] Thereafter, as we have already observed, he is to be found acting as commissary general of the official.[40] It appears that he was fleetingly in the service of the bishops of Bath and Wells and Hereford,[41] but this did not involve disruption of more permanent relationships. When Bishop Stratford came to appoint proctors to represent him at Archbishop Mepham's provincial council of September 1332, it was to Chaddesley and Lecch that he turned.[42]

In the absence of both official and commissary general, the consistory court would be served by an acting president. Thus M. John de Shoreham, rector of Walworth (Surrey), was appointed to deal with judicial business there on 30 January 1328.[43] Conceivably one Richard de Shoreham, "le Gladiere," was a connection of his. Richard was incarcerated in Guildford Castle, from which in 1325 the justices of gaol

him a pension of five pounds so long as he continued to plead for them in the Court of Arches. *Liber Albus Calendar*, no. 1131 (fol. 133ʳ). He acted for Cobham in the case of Richard Haukeslowe who claimed to be bailiff of the bishop's liberty of Oswaldslow. *Worcester Reg. Cobham*, fol. 74ʳ⁻ᵛ, pp. 121-122. The bishop granted him an annual pension of two pounds while in his service as advocate. Ibid., fol. 26ʳ, p. 149: 22 April 1323. Cf. ibid., fol. 92ᵛ, p. 164, where he is mentioned as a friend of Thomas de Astley, and fol. 11ʳ, p. 230.

[38] See, for instance, *Biog. Oxon.*, s.v. Lecche alias Loveryng; *Hemingby's Register*, s.v. Lecch, pp. 209-210; Lincoln Reg. Burghersh 1 (Reg. 4), fols. 280ᵛ-281ʳ. For his process (as official) with respect to the claim of Llanthony Priory to the appropriation of Barton Stacey church, see PRO C.115/K1/6681, fols. 17ᵛ-19ʳ (23 July 1331). At the time Masters John de Warblynton, Thomas Mauger and John de Wynterbourn are named as proctors of the consistory, Masters John de Aumbresbury (Amesbury) and Adam de Wamberge as advocates. Lecch, who had died by September 1361, left fifty-seven books to Llanthony. *Biog. Oxon.*, s.v. Lecche alias Loveryng.

[39] WinRS, fol. 7ᵛ: 5 November 1324. By another commission of 2 December 1324 he was to enquire into vacant benefices and to institute and induct suitable persons during Stratford's absence from the diocese (ibid., fol. 93ʳ). At the end of 1329 (1 December) he was appointed to deal with the aftermath of the bishop's visitation in the archdeaconry of Winchester (ibid., fol. 50ʳ).

[40] See above.

[41] In 1328-1329. See *Biog. Oxon.* and *Hemingby's Register* (n. 38 above).

[42] WinRS, fols. 72ᵛ-73ʳ. Lecch was by then official. The date of the proxy is given as 14 Kal. Dec. (18 November) 1332, conceivably an error for 14 Kal. Sept. (19 August).

[43] WinRS, fol. 35ʳ. Shoreham was present in Winchester Cathedral 17 September 1324 and mentioned in the notarial attestation of Walter Wodeland, ibid., fols. 162ᵛ-164ʳ.

delivery refused to release him without sight of his letters of orders. Instead the constable returned him to his fetters. Stratford, incensed by this treatment of "his clerk" (the term is probably used here in a general sense), demanded that he be handed over within six days, failing which the justices were to be cited before the episcopal court. There was no legal obligation, the bishop claimed, to exhibit such letters.[44] A further temporary commission, similar to M. John de Shoreham's, was issued to M. Peter de Wymbourne in the July of 1328.[45]

A less exalted position at Winchester was that of sequestrator or sequestrator general. As implied by the title, this office was concerned with the bishop's control of sequestration, particularly that of benefices, but also with the probate of wills.[46] Stratford's successor in the see, Adam Orleton, seems to have managed with only two sequestrators (general), one each for the archdeaconries of Winchester and Surrey.[47] Stratford's register names four distinct offices. The Isle of Wight, ordinarily comprised within Winchester archdeaconry,[48] received a sequestrator of its own,[49] and there was a sequestrator general whose authority extended to the whole diocese. M. Peter de Wymbourne was appointed diocesan sequestrator in January 1328,[50] but this may have been an exceptional measure, there being no trace of his activity in such capacity after 1328. Nor, it would seem, did he have a successor. The fact that Wymbourne's commission coincides with a grant of custody of Winchester archdeaconry following M. Filippo Sapiti's death may provide the explanation.[51]

Discounting those who did not act – the vicar of Micheldever and M. Richard de Stokele[52] – two sequestrators of Winchester archdeaconry

---

[44] Ibid., fol. 12ʳ.

[45] Ibid., fol. 39ʳ.

[46] Haines, "Adam Orleton and Winchester," pp. 15-16.

[47] Ibid. and Haines, *Church and Politics*, pp. 94-95.

[48] The Isle of Wight, which constituted a separate rural deanery, also had an individual penitentiary. See WinRS, fol. 1ᵛ, for the appointment of Thomas (de Bekford), 29 February 1324.

[49] Nicholas de la Flode, rector of Newchurch, was appointed 10 October 1324 in the same form as that used for the sequestrator in Winchester archdeaconry. Ibid., fol. 7ᵛ, and cf. 28ᵛ, where (in 1327) H. vicar of Godshill acts as such.

[50] Ibid., fol. 34ᵛ: 25 January 1328. He is mentioned also as fols. 35ʳ, 41ᵛ, 42ʳ, 47ᵛ, and with M. Gilbert de Kyrkeby judicially examined the election of the prior of St. Denys, Southampton (ibid., fol. 108ᵛ).

[51] Ibid., fol. 34ᵛ. But it should be noted that M. William of Ledbury was sometimes (loosely?) termed "sequestrator" without limitation. E.g. ibid., fols. 78ʳ, 85ᵛ (a matter concerning the Isle of Wight), 86ʳ⁻ᵛ.

[52] Appointed 7 November 1324, Ibid., fol. 7ᵛ. Stokele, rector of Freefolk (Hampshire) was deputed to proceed against another of the bishop's clerks, Nicholas de Aka, for non-

occur in the records: Thomas (de Bekford), vicar of Alton,[53] and M. William of Ledbury alias "of Worcester," already encountered as companion of Stratford's continental travels.[54] The vicar of Alton, initially deputed to act 29 November 1324,[55] had his commission renewed on 12 June of the following year.[56] In 1328 he received acquittance for money paid during the whole of his time as sequestrator,[57] although we do not find the appointment of his successor, William of Ledbury, until the April of 1330.[58] Ledbury remained active at least until March 1333.[59] The northern archdeaconry of Surrey saw Richard de Rudeham as sequestrator in 1324, but M. Gilbert de Kyrkeby was appointed two years later and reappointed in 1329. The latter appears on several occasions down to August 1333.[60] In the Isle of Wight the rector of Newchurch and the vicar of Godshill successively performed comparable duties.[61] Ordinarily Winchester sequestrators were beneficed locally, which facilitated their task, and were, moreover, native to the diocese. Ledbury, Wymbourne and Kyrkeby are possibly unusual in their closeness to the bishop and his inner circle of clerks.[62]

To complete the administrative picture only the diocesan registrar remains to be mentioned. He was Nicholas de Ystele, an elusive figure, seldom named as registrar in the principal document for which he was responsible.[63] In January 1330 he was admitted to Lingfield rectory as

residence (ibid., fol. 11[r]). See also above, "Winchester 1323-1333." For a brief biography, but only to 1310, see *Biog. Oxon.*, s.v. Stockele.

[53] See above, nn. 48-49.

[54] See above, n. 21.

[55] WinRS, fol. 7[v].

[56] Ibid., fol. 11[v].

[57] Ibid., fol. 33[r]. See also ibid., fol. 25[r-v].

[58] Ibid., fol. 53[v].

[59] Ibid., fols. 59[v], 75[r], 78[r], 85[v], 86[r-v].

[60] Rudeham, rector of Compton-by-Guildford, was appointed 10 October 1324, ibid., fol. 7[v]. Kyrkeby's initial commission is dated 19 July 1326, ibid., fol. 16[r]; the later one, 17 December 1329, ibid., fol. 51[r]. See also fols. 19[r], 65[r], 83[r]. He was rector of Ash (Surrey).

[61] See above, n. 49.

[62] Kyrkeby was to be sequestrator of the Surrey archdeaconry, apparently for a brief time only, at the beginning of Orleton's episcopate. See Haines, "Orleton and Winchester," pp. 15-16. A John de Kyrkeby, rector of Godshill and a royal clerk, is often mentioned in Bishop Woodlock's register (1305-1316): *Winchester Reg. Woodlock*, index s.v. Kirkeby. Gilbert, however, had served Bishop Maidstone at Worcester, where presumably Stratford came into contact with him. See *Worc. Admin.*, index s.v.

[63] I.e. Stratford's episcopal register. But see *Winch. Chart.*, no. 148 (1330); PRO C.115/ K1/6681, fols. 15[r]-17[r], where (in 1329) he is said to be rector of [St. Mary] de Vallibus [Winchester].

Dominus Nicholas de Churchill alias "Ystele." [64] We shall hear more of him at Canterbury.

Chancellor, official, commissary general, sequestrators and registrar comprised the principal officers of Stratford's administration as bishop of Winchester, but many other persons were assiduous in his service. Most prestigious of these, and rather an enigma in certain respects is John le Brabazoun, an Oxford doctor of theology, who was illegitimate and apparently related to Roger le Brabazoun, sometime chief justice of the King's Bench, for whom he acted as executor.[65] His participation in various judicial processes is attested by the diocesan records. It could be indicative of his political persuasion and perhaps part of the reason for his association with Stratford, that in 1331 he was appointed one of the king's envoys to the curia for urging the canonization of Thomas of Lancaster.[66]

In a different category are several clerks who occur from time to time in Stratford's Winchester register and who were obviously close to him. Among them may be numbered William Mees, mentioned above as his notary;[67] John Richards (Ricardi) of Eccleshall, Staffordshire, also a notary, a legatee of Stratford's will, and one of his executors;[68] John of

[64] WinRS, fol. 117ᵛ: 15 January 1330. His full name was not known to Churchill. See *Cant. Admin.* 2, index s.v. Ysteley. The place-name Churchill is widely distributed, there being two examples in Worcestershire.

[65] *Biog. Oxon.*, s.v. le Brabazon; *CPL 1305-1342*, pp. 119, 139, 158, 169, 337. A William Brabazoun accompanied Stratford abroad in 1338 (*CPR 1338-1340*, p. 98). An Isabella Brabazoun is to be found in Wilmcote, Warwickshire, in 1332 (Dugdale Soc. 6, p. 59). But John was from Lincoln diocese where in 1319 a Sir William Brabazoun, knight, received licence for an oratory at Garthorpe. Lincoln Reg. Dalderby 2 (Reg. 3), fol. 422ʳ. Dalderby granted a forty days' indulgence to those praying for the soul of Sir Roger de Brabazon, buried in St. Paul's. Ibid., fol. 376ᵛ. *Biog. Oxon.* does not mention the Stratford connection.

[66] *Foedera* 2, iii, pp. 61-62. Apparently Brabazoun held no specific office, but he was actively engaged with those who did. Thus he was present at the deprivation of the provost of St. Elizabeth's College, for the visitation of the cathedral priory and of Hyde Abbey, and during a case against certain Minorite friars in the audience court. Together with M. Richard Bintworth DCL, the future bishop of London, he acted as Stratford's proctor for the great council at York in July 1328. His participation in diocesan affairs peters out in 1327, when (termed king's clerk) he became treasurer of York. See WinRS, fols. 19ʳ, 39ᵛ, 162ʳ, 171ᵛ-172ʳ; *Biog. Oxon.*, s.v. le Brabazon.

[67] Mees is described as Stratford's "secretary" in 1327. See below, "From Conformist to Revolutionary."

[68] John de Eccleshale is given his full name in *Winch. Chart.*, no. 148, and *Lit. Cant.* 2, pp. 188-189 (658), CCL Reg. L, fol. 72ʳ. A clerk of Coventry and Lichfield diocese, he became rector of Overton (Hampshire) and (by 1338) of Wrotham (Kent). According to *CPL 1305-1342*, p. 372, he was granted provision of a Chichester canonry and prebend in 1332. But Stratford said that nothing came of this and petitioned again on Eccleshale's behalf: "dilectus capellanus suus et antiquus familiaris suus" (PRO 31/9/17A, fol. 87ᵛ, and cf. fol. 90ʳ⁻ᵛ). *Pace Le Neve* 7, p. 56, it is doubtful whether he should be included among

Windsor, who became warden of St. Thomas's hospital, Southwark, and was involved with his patron in acquiring land for its support;[69] M. Hugh de Patrington, one of the bishop's chaplains, who received collation of Avington church and subsequently of Woodhay;[70] William de Harewedon, whom Stratford termed "dilectus clericus noster" and promoted to Crondall;[71] and finally, M. Nicholas de Aka.[72]

Two other clerks should be mentioned, men of much greater distinction than any of those in the previous paragraph. One is Thomas of Evesham, the other M. Thomas de Astley. Evesham, who only on occasion is entitled "magister," [73] was Stratford's clerk in the restricted sense that

the canons of Chichester. He was a canon of London 1343-1357 (ibid. 5, p. 35) and in the 1340s (named as such) was a frequent executor of papal bulls (*CPL 1342-1362*, pp. 182, 199, 201, 217, 236-238, 280). From 1331 he was a regular member of Stratford's entourage abroad: *CPR 1330-1334*, pp. 218 (28 November 1331), 276 (18 April 1332); ibid. *1334-1338*, p. 37 (31 October 1334); ibid., *1338-1340*, p. 98 (1 July 1338). See also, "Beneficiaries of Stratford's Will"; *Bath and Wells Reg. Shrewsbury*, p. 327 no. 1243 (Stratford's letters carried by "M. John de Eccleshale, priest").

[69] WinRS, fol. 12[v]; *CPR 1327-1330*, p. 366. The latter entry (17 February 1329) is a royal *inspeximus* of a grant by Stratford (1 December 1326) to the hospital. See below, "Eastbridge Hospital and Other Benefactions." In a letter to Stratford of 1331 Bishop Hethe described Windsor as "clericus vester ut credimus." *Rochester Reg. Hethe*, p. 390. He was an executor of an earlier Rochester bishop, Thomas Wouldham. In December 1337 Stratford commissioned the Worcester diocesan to exchange Windsor's Wingham canonry for Bishops Cleeve rectory. Worcester Reg. Hemenhale, fols. 12[v], 42[r]. See also WinRS, fol. 66[r]. A person of the same name was a member of Archbishop Reynolds' *familia*. Wright, *Church and Crown*, pp. 62-63.

[70] He received collation of Avington 12 December 1324 and of Woodhay 18 February 1328 (when Avington passed to Aka). With Chaddesley and William Inge he witnessed the creation of a notary in 1324, and with Brabazoun, Littleton and Mees the deprivation of Gorges as provost of St. Elizabeth's College in 1326. WinRS, fols. 10[r], 19[r],   92[v], 113[v].

[71] Ibid., fols. 34[r], 37[r]. His possession was not without disturbance; lands belonging to the church were occupied in defiance of the collation.

[72] He received various benefices in succession: Avington resigned by Patrington (WinRS, fol. 115[r]: 19 February 1329), Brighstone in the Isle of Wight, Bentworth (ibid., fol. 136[r]: 24 October 1333) and Hadleigh (estate confirmed by the king, *CPR 1334-1338*, p. 516: 27 August 1337). In the last reference he is called "Dak." Aka was licensed to leave his cure (e.g. WinRS, fols. 16[r], 40[v]; and for proceedings against him for non-residence, see "Winchester 1323-1333" above). He had been one of Grandisson's clerks and that bishop sent him to Stratford in July 1328 "pro certis negotiis statum suum specialiter tangentibus" (some beneficial matter?). *Exeter Reg. Grandisson*, p. 169. In the early 1330s Aka, as Stratford's attorney, was accounting at the exchequer for his principal's expenses as royal envoy. E.g. PRO E.372/177/40; 179/34. He was granted protection to accompany him 1 July 1338, *CPR* 1338-1340, p. 98. Stratford (as bishop of Winchester) petitioned on his behalf for a canonry and prebend in Romsey (PRO 31/9/17A, fols. 18[v]-19[r]). Aka was granted reservation of a benefice in the gift of Hyde Abbey (*CPL 1305-1342*, p. 372: 5 October 1333). For his association with Hereford diocese (within which lay the parish of Rock or *Aka*) see *Hereford Reg. Orleton*, index s.v.

[73] See *WRO*, no. 367 n. 86.

between 1332 and 1338 he regularly acted as his attorney, usually with Robert Stratford,[74] occasionally with Henry de Bradeweye.[75] A *Dominus* Thomas de Evesham occurs frequently in Worcester sources as a clerk of the prior and chapter who was subsequently in the service of the diocesan, Wolstan de Bransford.[76] If the identification is accurate he could have come from Sedgeberrow in Pershore deanery, a short distance from Evesham, for it was at the instance of a *M.* Thomas de Evesham that Bishop Orleton dedicated the church there in 1331. Evesham may well have been the church's patron and a generous contributor to its fabric. To this day it remains essentially a building of the earlier part of the fourteenth century.[77] For a brief space Evesham had been chancellor of Bishop Grandisson at Exeter,[78] but his importance derives from his employment as one of the greater clerks of chancery between 1332 and 1343. It was he who received the rolls of chancery at the time of the 1340-1341 political crisis. Although he did not retain them for long, this militates against the notion that he was particularly close to Stratford.[79]

The other notable clerk, M. Thomas de Astley, is specifically termed "clericus noster" by Stratford.[80] He was granted protection for travelling abroad with his principal in 1325 and again in 1334.[81] According to one authority he was also in the (arguably incompatible) service of Adam

---

[74] Wilkinson, *Chancery*, pp. 152-153 n. 4, provides a table showing Evesham's employment as attorney for John and Robert Stratford (cf. n. 79 below). See also *CPR 1317-1321*, p. 577 (*inspeximus* of a grant to him by William, abbot of Evesham, 1 May 1320, witnessed by Stratford as dean of Arches and archdeacon of Lincoln); ibid., *1321-1324*, p. 190 (21 July 1322); ibid., p. 245 (12 February 1323); ibid. *1324-1327*, p. 50 (11 November 1324); ibid., p. 84 (12 February 1325); ibid., p. 129 (6 July 1325); ibid., *1327-1330*, p. 30 (8 March 1327 also acting as attorney for Bishop Ayrminne of Norwich); ibid., *1330-1334*, p. 276 (23 April 1332); ibid., *1334-1338*, p. 37 (31 October 1334); *CCR 1337-1339*, pp. 627, 631. Evesham was one of those at Otford for the livery of the great seal, 6 April 1334, to Robert Stratford. *CCR 1333-1337*, p. 309.

[75] E.g. *CPR 1338-1340*, p. 98 (1 July 1338). Also with [John de] Hampton, ibid., p. 387 (19 June 1339).

[76] E.g. *Liber Albus Calendar*, nos. 637, 908, 910, 944, 957, 1230-1231, 1241; *Worcester Reg. Bransford*, index s.v.

[77] *WRO*, no. 367. He alienated land at Badsey to Evesham Abbey for the benefit of sick monks and of his own soul and that of his uncle Robert de Netherton, formerly an inmate. *CPR 1330-1334*, p. 533 (8 March 1334).

[78] *Exeter Reg. Grandisson*, p. 562, where (in 1330) he was given a pension of forty shillings.

[79] Cf. Wilkinson, *Chancery*, pp. 152-153, where the author contends that Evesham "only served members of the same political party at the same time," though putting himself at the disposal of both. See also Tout, *Chapters* 6, index s.v.

[80] WinRS, fol. 4[r].

[81] *CPR 1324-1327*, p. 129 (6 July 1325); ibid., *1334-1338*, p. 37 (31 October 1334).

Orleton. Admittedly that bishop did advance him to a canonry of Hereford, but there seems to be little further justification for the claim.[82] In any case, Astley's subsequent progression was due neither to Orleton, nor even to Stratford, but to the king.[83]

Stratford's translation to Canterbury brought an expected migration of clerks from Winchester, as well as many new faces. In the ordinary course he supplemented his own fund of patronage by securing for members of his *familia* such papal provisions as he could. As archbishop, in an effort further to increase the rewards at his disposal, he lodged special petitions with his curial proctor, M. Andrea Sapiti. In one of these he argued that since his cathedral church had a monastic chapter, he should be permitted to elect individuals (recipi facere ... quas elegerit) to a canonry in each of the other cathedral and collegiate churches of the province and to provide them with a prebend apiece when such fell vacant, even if they already held two or three compatible benefices. A further petition was for a papal faculty to confer benefices the disposal of which had lapsed to the apostolic see.[84]

---

[82] *Biog. Oxon.*, s.v.; *Hereford Reg. Orleton*, s.v.; and cf. Haines, *Church and Politics*, p. 27 n. 3. Astley was almost certainly a member of the Warwickshire family of that name. Sir Thomas Astley in founding the collegiate church at Astley included Archbishop Stratford among those to be commemorated. *VCH Warwicks.* 2, p. 118.

[83] He was sent on various foreign missions from 1324 (*CPR* 1324-1327, p. 49). See *Biog. Oxon.*, s.v.; *Hemingby's Register*, pp. 172-174.

[84] PRO 31/9/17A, fols. 80ʳ-84ʳ. For the relevant papal legislation: Wright, *Church and Crown*, chap. 1. These petitions can be dated after Stratford's receipt of the pallium (he claimed he had not been granted the graces customary at such a time), i.e. post 23 April 1334 but prior to November, the date of one of the papal indults for which he petitioned (*Jean XXII Lettres Communes*, no. 64215; *CPL 1305-1342*, p. 412). The right to promote to canonries in the province and to provide the appointees with prebends was conceded earlier to Archbishop Reynolds (Wright, *Church and Crown*, pp. 59-60ff.), but evidence is lacking for the concession and/or implementation in Stratford's case. Wright, ibid., p. 52, points out that the latter's request to provide to benefices of which the patronage had devolved on the apostolic see recalls an indult granted to the archbishop-elect of Dublin in 1308 (*CPL 1305-1342*, p. 46). The records do not indicate that Stratford was successful in this respect. As bishop of Winchester Stratford through Sapiti (PRO 31/9/17A) petitioned as follows: for John Loveryng (Lecch), a canonry of Salisbury (ibid., fol. 11ᵛ, marked "fiat"; *CPL 1305-1342*, p. 373: 9 March 1332); for M. Ralph Stratford MA, BCL, studying at Bologna, a canonry and prebend of the late Robert de Pickering in Beverley Minster (PRO 31/9/17A, fol. 18ʳ⁻ᵛ); for Nicholas de Aka, a Romsey prebend (above, n. 72); and for Robert Stratford, the archdeaconry of Canterbury (PRO 31/9/17A, fols. 23ᵛ-24ʳ; *CPL 1305-1342*, p. 401, reservation 12 June 1334; *Le Neve* 4, p. 7). Robert had earlier (20 January 1331) been granted provision of the canonry and prebend of Romsey voided by Gilbert de Middleton's death (episcopus Wintoniensis cuius germanus existis nobis super hoc humiliter supplicantes). Vatican Archives, *RA* 38, fols. 469ᵛ-470ʳ; *RV* 97, fol. 38ʳ; *CPL 1305-1342*, p. 325.

Of those who held important office at Winchester, Littleton, Lecch alias Loveryng and Ystele received fresh appointments, Chaddesley[85] and Wymbourne[86] remained, in so far as we have information, as "occasional members" of Stratford's *familia*, while Gloucester disappears from view, though possibly resuming practice as an advocate in the Court of Canterbury. The office of chancellor fell to Wybert de Littleton, but he was to die before the end of August 1335. In any case, as dean of Wells from April 1334 he must have been otherwise occupied.[87] John de Lecch alias Loveryng of Northleach could have been his successor, though the surviving records do not reveal his appointment as chancellor until 24 September 1341.[88] An apparent newcomer to Stratford's service, M. Thomas (Mason?) of Canterbury, became commissary general, an officer whose judicial work, as at Winchester, lay in the consistory court.[89] There

[85] Chaddesley was at York in May 1335 where he witnessed Stratford's recension of crusading bulls (Worcester Reg. Montacute 2, fol. 14ᵛ). But he probably diverted his attention to the affairs of the Salisbury chapter. In 1333 he was granted reservation of a dignity there, Robert Stratford and Astley being two of the executors (*CPL 1305-1342*, p. 375). This proved ineffective, but he secured a prebend by means of an exchange of benefices (*Le Neve* 3, p. 51). With John of Windsor he was appointed proctor of the Canterbury prior for the York parliament of February 1334 (CCL Reg. G, fol. xlviiiᵛ). He also acted as negotiator with France in 1334 and 1337. He had died by August 1348. See *Hemingby's Register*, pp. 188-189; *Biog. Oxon.*, s.v. Chaddeslegh (where the date for his presidency of the consistory court should be 1324, not 1334); *Worcester Reg. Bransford*, pp. 151, 392.

[86] Wymbourne was sent to Bishop Orleton in 1340 as Stratford's personal envoy in connection with the archbishop's attempt to appoint the prior of Twynham (WinRO 1, fol. 94ᵛ; Haines, *Church and Politics*, pp. 213-214). Because of the constitution *Execrabilis* he resigned (conditionally) Broughton church (Salisbury diocese) in 1326 (*Cant. Admin.* 2, pp. 31-32). One presumes he was a relative of M. John de Wymbourne, who took part in the capitular election of Stratford as archbishop (above, "Archbishop of Canterbury 1333-1348") and who wore the prior of Canterbury's livery in the 1330s (as did John of Windsor) and the 1340s (e.g. CCL D.E.3, fols. 13ᵛ, 14ᵛ, 31ʳ). John was official of the archdeacon of Canterbury (CCL A.36 IV, fol. 75ʳ).

[87] See *Biog. Oxon.*, s.v. Littleton, Wibert; *Bath and Wells Reg. Shrewsbury*, pp. xxxvi-xxxviii, 245; *HMCR* 10, App. 3, pp. 231ff. The deanery was disputed. Robert Stratford claimed it by virtue of a provisory bull (*CPL 1305-1342*, p. 402), Chaddesley being one of the executors, but Walter de London became non-resident dean. *Hemingby's Register*, pp. 210-211.

[88] CCL A.36 III, mm. 1ʳ, 3ʳ. Cf. *Lit. Cant.* 2, pp. 220-221 (687); CCL Reg. L, fol. 75ʳ; WinRO 1, fol. 93ᵛ. Auditor of causes during the 1340s (CCL A.36 IV, fol. 5ʳ passim). He was official of the Court of Canterbury between 25 August 1348 (CCL Regs. G, fol. 88ʳ; Q, fol. 200ʳ⁻ᵛ al. 204) and at least 1355. *Biog. Oxon.*, s.v. Lecche alias Loveryng; *Cant. Admin.*, p. 238.

[89] It would seem that the M. Thomas Mason of the patent rolls (*CPR 1340-1343*, p. 502: 19 August 1342; ibid., *1345-1348*, p. 203: 2 July 1346), accused by the justices of "extortion," is the M. Thomas de Cant' of the Canterbury records. Cf. above, "Archbishop of Canterbury," n. 241.

is no mention of anyone else having acted in this capacity during Stratford's time as archbishop.[90]

The principal judge of the Court of Canterbury, not to be confused with the consistory,[91] was the official. M. Henry de Iddesworth (Idsworth, Hampshire) was acting during the vacancy preceding Stratford's promotion,[92] but the new archbishop was bent on securing the services of M. Adam Murimuth, the chronicler, who was based in Exeter diocese. Bishop Grandisson was not cooperative in responding to Stratford's request for a licence to enable Murimuth to be absent from his duties as precentor of Exeter Cathedral, and ribbed the chronicler for his ambition; a nice touch in view of Murimuth's own animadversions on that score.[93] Stratford eventually had his way, at any rate for a while, since not only did Murimuth attend him abroad, but also acted as official in 1334 and 1335 and as vicar general.[94] Meanwhile the archbishop had taken the precaution of petitioning the apostolic see for an indult to enable ten of his clerks, such as officials and auditors of causes and others involved in diocesan and metropolitan jurisdiction, to enjoy the fruits of their benefices even though non-resident. A bull to that effect was secured, but what use was made of it has yet to be ascertained.[95] Apart from Simon Islep, the future archbishop, the only other official who can be found at this time is Loveryng of Northleach, whom Stratford mentions as such in his will.[96]

---

[90] In *Cant. Admin.* 2, p. 229, he is not mentioned and there is a hiatus between 1333 and 1350, when John de Wymbourne acts.

[91] See below, "Ordinances for the Court of Canterbury."

[92] *Cant. Admin.* 2, p. 238 (citing CCL Reg. G, fol. xxxi[r]); *Exeter Reg. Grandisson*, pp. 722-723.

[93] Ibid., pp. 269-271; *Biog. Oxon.*, s.v. Murimouth.

[94] *Exeter Reg. Grandisson*, pp. 276-278, and that bishop's letter to Astley about Murimuth's absence, ibid., pp. 271-272. The Canterbury chapter wrote to Murimuth as official in July [1334] and declined to pay his pension in view of the promotion. *Lit. Cant.* 2, pp. 59-61 (544-545); CCL Reg. L, fol. 36[v]. See also *Exeter Reg. Grandisson*, p. 802; *Cant. Admin.* 2, p. 238; below, Appendix 2.

[95] But it was for six clerks only. PRO 31/9/17A, fol. 81[r-v]; Vatican Archives, *RA* 47, fol. 136[r-v]; *RV* 108, fol. 68[v]; *CPL 1305-1342*, p. 412 (10 November 1334). Cf. Wright, *Church and Crown*, p. 166 n. 13, who argues that the papal indult may be more in use at this time than any customary arrangement for licences "in obsequiis insistendi." I have my doubts about this argument, but the difficulties of more informal arrangements are underlined by the Murimuth case.

[96] Churchill, *Cant. Admin.* 2, p. 238, gives Islep as "temp. Stratford [1333-1349]," citing the Black Book of the Arches. He is hard to find elsewhere, but see Lincoln Reg. Bek 2 (Reg. 7), fol. 131[v] (s.a. 1342) and *CPP 1342-1419*, p. 35 (s.a. 1344). In WAM no. 9222 he appears to be mentioned in addition to the official as a guest at Stratford's table. For Loveryng (Lecch) see CCL W.219.

There is corresponding difficulty in tracing the dean of Arches. Again M. Henry de Iddesworth is named *sede vacante*, being succeeded it would seem by M. John Offord, mentioned between 1333 and 1336.[97] Offord was to have an exceptionally distinguished career until premature death deprived him of the archbishopric of Canterbury.[98] The registrar of the Court of Canterbury was none other than Robert Avesbury, the chronicler,[99] while the scribe of the acts or diocesan registrar was Nicholas de Ystele, transferred from the comparable position at Winchester.[100] Once again Stratford's absences meant that he had to invoke the aid of vicars general. From the analysis of Stratford's Canterbury regimen we already know that, among others, Stephen Gravesend, bishop of London, Robert Stratford and Adam Murimuth were employed in this capacity.[101]

Although, in default of his archiepiscopal register, our overall knowledge of Stratford's Canterbury administration and of the officers engaged in it is comparatively meagre, the partial survival of audience court records for the last eight years or so of the archiepiscopate means that we have much information about the conduct of cases as well as the names of Stratford's auditors and special commissaries.[102] There is also an earlier piece of evidence. The lengthy process involving a dispute between the parishioners of Reculver and Herne incorporates Stratford's commission, dated 21 February 1335, for the appointment as auditors of Astley, Littleton and M. Laurence Fastolf.[103] During the later period the most active judges were Fastolf and the ubiquitous Lecch alias

---

[97] *HMCR* 10, App. 3, Wells 1, p. 237; *Lit. Cant.* 2, pp. 41-42; CCL Reg. L, fol. 27ᵛ; *Biog. Oxon.*, s.v.; CCL D.E.3, fol. 20ʳ names M. J[ohn] Offord as dean (s.a. 1333).

[98] *Biog. Oxon.*, s.v.

[99] *Cant. Admin.* 1, p. 455; ibid. 2, p. 241 (citing Black Book of the Arches, fol. 5ᵛ). Avesbury (BL Harleian MS 200, fol. 76ᵛ), p. 279; Haines, *Church and Politics*, p. 115.

[100] Churchill (alias Ystele) occurs, for instance, in CCL A.36 IV, fols. 24ʳ (1340), 69ʳ (1343); also (early 1337) in Worcester Reg. Montacute 1, fol. 26ᵛ and in London Reg. Gravesend, fol. 101ʳ⁻ᵛ, as Stratford's commissary in Norwich diocese *sede vacante* (following the death of Bishop Ayrminne in 1336: blank in *Cant. Admin.* 2, p. 251). He was notary of Richard Vaughan, archdeacon of Surrey, for the compromise with Bishop Edington of Winchester. *Lydford*, p. 141; Winchester Reg. Edyndon 1, fol. 13ᵛ. Appointed *sede vacante* dean of the jurisdiction of Shoreham 25 August 1348. *Cant. Admin.* 2, p. 231 (citing CCL Reg. G, fol. 29ʳ). He was responsible for *sede vacante* Reg. G, fols. 25ff. (rubric) and is said to have been official of the Canterbury archdeacon 1352-1362 (*Cant. Admin.* 2, p. 229, citing Canterbury Reg. Islep).

[101] See above, "Archbishop of Canterbury 1333-1348"; Rochester Reg. Hethe, p. 1119, where Idsworth (Iddesworth) is recorded to have granted letters dimissory (23 September 1335) as vicar general of Canterbury.

[102] CCL A.36 IV. See above, "Archbishop of Canterbury 1333-1348," n. 202.

[103] CCL R.20; Ducarel, "Fragmenta," fols. 78ʳff.

Loveryng – chancellor from 1341. M. Richard Vaughan also occurs as auditor, but only at the beginning and end of the period covered by the records.[104] Fastolf was brother of the noted legist Thomas Fastolf, a papal chaplain and auditor of causes who became bishop of St. David's in 1352 and who forwarded a petition in the curia for his relative's advancement to a canonry.[105] Vaughan, a doctor of civil law of Oxford, became archdeacon of Surrey in 1347 and five years later was professed as a monk of Christ Church, Canterbury, where he spent the rest of his days.[106]

Other clerks, though not holding specific office (so far as can be ascertained), were patently in the archbishop's confidence. Among these may be numbered no less than five notaries: Mees and Eccleshale, whom we have already come across at Winchester, Richard de Twyverton or Tiverton,[107] Henry called "de Cokham" of Stratford,[108] and Simon of

[104] CCL A.36 IV. Vaughan is named auditor and special commissary in April 1340 (ibid., fol. 4ʳ) and in 1348 conducted the process against non-residents (ibid., fols. 101ʳff.). He was at the curia on royal business in 1346 (*Biog. Oxon.*, s.v.), and Stratford's household roll of 1347 (WAM no. 9223 dorse) shows that letters of his were delivered by John de Teye, chaplain, who was paid 13s 4d for his pains.

[105] *Biog. Cantab.*, s.v., which states that he was an MA "probably of Cambridge" and BCL, but does not mention his relationship to Thomas, for which see *CPP 1342-1419*, pp. 241-242. Occasionally he is discernible at Winchester, e.g. WinRS, fol. 99ʳ, where in July 1326 he is associated with the official, Richard of Gloucester, for enquiry into presentation to Carisbrooke vicarage. In 1340 (23 April) Fastolf and Robert de Tresk were appointed Stratford's proctors at Avignon (CCL A.36 IV, fol. 2ʳ). Sapiti's notebook (PRO 31/9/17A, fols. 101ʳ-103ʳ) records that (in 1336-1337?) Fastolf, as Stratford's proctor, brought a memorandum about the archbishop's unfinished business in the court. The items concern a papal provisor and Cranbrook church, the Mepham-Concoreto case (see Wright, *Church and Crown*, p. 330 n. 63), the claim of Great Malvern Priory to exemption from metropolitical visitation (temp. Reynolds), and an election at Norwich (apparently that of Thomas Hemenhale as bishop in April 1336) – Stratford warned that "contra electum ius regium allegetur pro excusacione domini." See *Foedera* 2, iii, p. 153 (28 October 1336), for Edward's view of this last case. Hemenhale, he alleged, had not secured royal assent to his election but had rushed to the curia for confirmation.

[106] *Biog. Oxon.*, s.v.

[107] He travelled abroad with Stratford in 1338 (*CPR 1338-1340*, p. 98), when rector of Sandhurst, and witnessed the archbishop's letters incorporating papal crusading bulls sent to Bishop Shrewsbury in 1335. *Bath and Wells Reg. Shrewsbury*, pp. 246-247; cf. WinRO 2, fol. 13ᵛ; Worcester Reg. Montacute 2, fol. 14ᵛ. He is mentioned in Stratford's wardrobe account of 1343 (WAM no. 9222 dorse). His position as rector of Adisham and later of Charing (both in the archbishop's collation) received royal ratification (*CPR 1338-1340*, p. 529: 8 June 1340; ibid. *1343-1345*, p. 55: 8 July 1343). He held a mill and rood of land of Stratford's manor at Mayfield (*CPR 1343-1345*, p. 219: 28 February 1344).

[108] One of the notaries at the time of Stratford's publication of crusading bulls, including *Non absque grandi* (Worcester Reg. Montacute 2, fol. 14ᵛ [cf. 1, fol. 10ʳ], and n. 107 above). Perhaps he was more accurately Robert Stratford's clerk. As archdeacon of Canterbury Robert appointed him his proctor for Thomas Hemenhale's enthronement as

Charing – the site of an archiepiscopal manor.[109] The archbishop's close connection with Eccleshall, Staffordshire, is something of a mystery. In his will Stratford was to leave twenty marks for the indigent kin of Peter, rector of the place, and a Peter de Eccleshale was for a time the archbishop's chamberlain.[110] There may well be some tie of kinship which eludes us. Twyverton, like John de Eccleshale, was both Stratford's legatee and one of his executors, though in the event neither acted.[111]

So far we have dealt only with the clerical element in Stratford's *familia*. Among lay members of his household the "Robert le Mareschal of Southwark" mentioned in 1324 could be the same person as the "Robert son of John de Helawe mareschal" of 1338.[112] Certainly the service of William atte Fenne spans much of Stratford's career. As bishop of Winchester Stratford granted him two messuages in Southwark and land in Hayling within Havant manor (Hampshire); a grant which was confirmed by the king in 1332.[113] Fenne, who was with Stratford on the continent in 1334, acted as one of his attorneys four years later.[114] At the time of the archbishop's death he was his domestic chamberlain and as a legacy received the contents of the bedchamber.[115]

Although the recital of such minutiae would be out of place in what is intended as a biography, there exists in Stratford's Winchester register a fairly comprehensive series of appointments to secular offices, which in conjunction with information from the pipe rolls for the lands of the bishopric provides a remarkably full list of the personnel involved with

bishop of Worcester. Worcester Reg. Hemenhale, fol. 10ʳ. In 1348 Cokham appears as chancellor of Chichester diocese. E.g. CCL Reg. Q, fol. 212ʳ⁻ᵛ.

[109] Mentioned by Prior Hathbrand (6 November 1338) as Stratford's clerk (dilectus clericus vester). *Lit. Cant.* 2, pp. 198-200 (667-668); CCL Reg. L, fols. 72ᵛ-73ʳ. He was notary with Stratford at Canterbury during the critical situation of 1341. See Lambeth MS 99, fol. 137ᵛ; *Vitae Arch. Cant.*, pp. 22-23. This by no means exhausts the clerks associated with Stratford. See below, n. 144.

[110] CCL W.219 and see below, "Beneficiaries of Stratford's Will." He is presumably the Peter de Eccleshale who accompanied Stratford abroad in the 1320s, e.g. *CPR 1324-1327*, pp. 94 (12 February 1325), 129 (6 July 1325).

[111] See below, "Beneficiaries of Stratford's Will." A John de Eccleshale of Staffordshire was among the "manucaptors" of William de Shalford, one of Mortimer's agents, indicted (in 1331) for encompassing Edward II's death. Tout, "Captivity and Death of Edward of Carnarvon," p. 188.

[112] *CPR 1324-1327*, p. 50; ibid. *1338-1340*, p. 98. In 1325/6 a John de Thudden is mentioned as Stratford's marshal at Winchester. WinPR 159337, m. 20ʳ, and see WinRS, fol. 15ᵛ.

[113] *CPR 1330-1334*, p. 335 (20 September 1332). Also ibid. *1348-1350*, p. 306, grant to him of liberty of Southwark.

[114] Ibid. *1334-1338*, p. 37 (31 October 1334); ibid. *1338-1340*, p. 98 (30 June 1338).

[115] See below, "Beneficiaries of Stratford's Will."

the temporalities.[116] M. Robert Stratford played a leading role in this sphere, which must strike us as somewhat unclerical. We would expect the steward, or anyone acting in that capacity, to be a prominent layman. However that may be, it was Robert who received the homage of the bishop's tenants, except for those in outlying counties, and who was deputed to oversee the manors and to hold the courts.[117] Walter Wodelok, *vadlet*, was commissioned to survey the episcopal property,[118] and together with John de Madele or Madeleye[119] was assigned to take the grease for the season from the episcopal parks.[120] Thomas de Fulquardeby was made treasurer of Wolvesey, with authority to issue acquittances and tallies on Stratford's behalf.[121] He was certainly a cleric.[122]

Robert Stratford's successor in the steward's office was John de Hampton, knight, who was appointed in 1327.[123] Apart from the steward and the treasurer of Wolvesey the principal officers of the temporal administration were the constables of the castles of Farnham and Taunton together with the bailiffs of the various manors, often grouped in variable combinations.[124] Sometimes the constables also acted as bailiffs of manors other than those associated with their castles. This happened in the case of William Hatton (termed *donzel*), who was first appointed constable of Farnham and bailiff of the manor there, and shortly afterwards bailiff of the manors of Southwark and Esher.[125] Between 1324 and 1332 we have

[116] WinRS, fols. 182ʳ-186ᵛ; WinPR 159336-159345. For their dating see above, "Winchester 1323-1333," n. 46. Cf. Beveridge, "Memoranda," pp. 93-113, esp. p. 113.

[117] WinPR 159336-159337. E.g. 159337 m. 19ᵛ s.v. Farnham: "Et eidem pro expensis partis familie magistri Roberti de Stratford per v dies dum ipse ivit ad dominum [Bishop Stratford] cum festinacione, 5s 4d"; "In expensis magistri Roberti de Stratford senescalli per suos vi adventus, 39s 8d." Although not named steward in his commission to supervise the manors (WinRS, fol. 182ʳ), he is so named in the early pipe rolls. Perhaps it needs to be pointed out that a number of those engaged in Stratford's secular business were clerks.

[118] This was to be done in the presence of constables, bailiffs, reeves, and other ministers. WinRS, fol. 182ʳ⁻ᵛ.

[119] See above, n. 11; *CCR 1327-1330*, p. 93.

[120] WinRS, fol. 182ʳ: 1 August 1324.

[121] Ibid.: 8 July 1324. Fulquardeby was also named attorney to secure episcopal goods and chattels of the manors from the royal custodians (ibid.: 9 August 1324). This commission has the rubric: "Pro empcione instauri."

[122] See *CPL 1305-1342*, p. 161: 8 August 1317, where "Folquardebi" is said to have been dispensed on account of illegitimacy and to be in possession of Calbourne rectory (Isle of Wight).

[123] WinRS, fol. 183ᵛ: 26 October 1327. Hampton was to be made one of the custodians of the Winchester temporalities on Stratford's translation to Canterbury (*CCR 1333-1337*, p. 261). He was still steward in 1331 (WinRS, fol. 65ᵛ).

[124] See below, Appendix 2.

[125] WinRS, fol. 183ᵛ: appointments of 27 May and 27 October respectively.

six appointments of constables of Taunton.[126] The fourth appointee, John de Meere, doubled as bailiff of Downton;[127] the fifth was Thomas (Laurence) de la More, the bishop's "nephew" and an Oxfordshire man.[128] In one instance we find a dovetailing of functions. Thomas de Breilles or Brailles (Brailes, Warwickshire) was made bailiff of Witney and Wargrave in 1324 with authority to maintain the bishop's franchises and to hold the courts of the bailiwick.[129] His colleague, Richard de Longedon, also termed bailiff, was appointed by a commission of the same date to oversee the husbandry of the manors with the help and advice of Breilles.[130] Henry de Bradeweye, whom we have earlier encountered as Stratford's attorney, became bailiff of (Bishops) Sutton and Highclere; subsequently of New Alresford, which lies to the north of Winchester.[131] In 1324 the manors of Waltham and Marwell were placed under the control of Walter de Wodelok as bailiff. Later Marwell, and also the nearby manors of Twyford (Hampshire), Bishopstoke, Merdon and Crawley (Hampshire), were allotted to John de Kyngeston as bailiff.[132]

Only once in the register of the Winchester temporalities is there mention of the episcopal hundred of Hambledon (*Hameldon*),[133] and it is a royal confirmation that has preserved the record of Robert of Chertsey's appointment in 1333 as bailiff for life of the soke of Winchester.[134] There

---

[126] Ibid., fols. 182ʳff.: Adam Bermeyn or Bermayn, William de Sutton, Adam le Brette, John de Meere, Thomas (Laurence) de la More, Richard de Hopton.

[127] WinRS, fol. 183ʳ. Meere was appointed bailiff of Downton 10 July and constable of Taunton 14 July 1326.

[128] Ibid., fol. 183ᵛ (12 July 1329): "Nostre cher et bien aime neofeu Thomas de la More."

[129] Ibid., fol. 182ᵛ: "Pur noz franchises garder et pur noz courts tenir en la dite baillie." Breilles was made coadjutor of the provost of St. Elizabeth's college in 1326 (termed "clericus noster") – he later became provost himself – and was ordained subdeacon 7 March 1327. Ibid., fols. 18ᵛ, 20ʳ, 145ʳ-146ᵛ (Lenten ordination). A Thomas de Brayles, clerk, was commissioned by Bishop Montacute to receive livery of the Worcester temporalities (Worcester Reg. Montacute 1, fol. 2ʳ: 1334). Cf. ibid., fol. 45ʳ, for a Thomas, son of Henry de Brailles, who received letters dimissory to all minor orders not yet received and to all holy orders. Thomas de Packington, lord of Brailes, in his foundation (1334) of Chelmscote chantry (in Brailes parish) included the archbishop of Canterbury among the beneficiaries of the prayers offered. Worcester Reg. Montacute, fol. 19ʳ⁻ᵛ; *Worc. Admin.*, p. 237.

[130] WinRS, fol. 182ᵛ: "Pur noz terres garder et la hosebondre ordenier sur les terres en la dite baillie pur laide et lavisement nostre bien amee Thomas de Breilles."

[131] Ibid., fol. 182ᵛ.

[132] Ibid.: 29 September 1324; ibid., fol. 183ʳ: 4 February 1327.

[133] Ibid., fol. 183ᵛ. Letter testimonial (24 January 1328) concerning a tenant of the hundred.

[134] *CPR 1330-1334*, p. 567. *Inspeximus* (26 July 1334) of the grant made at Wolvesey the Tuesday after All Saints [2 November] 1333. Cf. the appointment in 1305 of a John de Kirkebi as bailiff of the soke. *Winchester Reg. Woodlock*, p. 13.

are two commissions for the custody of debts due to the bishop, the first in favour of Walter Wodelok within the counties of Hampshire and Surrey, the second for John de Basinges within the bishopric as a whole,[135] while John de Rasne was deputed to raise debts due to king or bishop within the episcopal franchise.[136] The commission in Basinges' favour was promptly revoked for undisclosed reasons.[137] Basinges, a local knight of substance, who had been given custody of Porchester Castle at Stratford's nomination, was soon to become *persona non grata* with the bishop. It was in 1330 that Prior Heriard was instructed to enquire into the shameful manner in which he had insulted John de Lecch while that officer was engaged in judicial correction at Alresford and elsewhere.[138]

From the names reviewed it will have been gathered that although, as one might anticipate, many of those who occupied influential positions in Stratford's temporal administration were from local landed families, others such as Robert Stratford, Laurence de la More, Hatton, Breilles, Bradeweye, and possibly Longedon (Longdon, Worcestershire?) were "outsiders" – three of them relatives – whom doubtless the bishop calculated would be likely to give a little more attention to his interests at the same time as their own.

Compared with what is discoverable about Winchester, details of the corresponding Canterbury administration are few. The previous practice of bringing in trusted men from outside is however discernible. Thus Henry de Bradeweye was acting as steward in 1334,[139] and John de Hampton in 1335-1336, when the Canterbury prior described him as "homo valens et prudens." [140] Hampton from time to time resumed the duties of Stratford's attorney, as on occasion did Bradeweye, but it would seem that it was the latter who performed the functions of steward in the later 1330s and perhaps also in the 1340s.[141] The archbishop's treasurer, M. Richard de Longedon or Longdon, another cleric, despite the change

---

[135] WinRS, fols. 182ᵛ, 183ʳ; dated 3 October 1324 and 5 February 1327 respectively.

[136] Ibid., fol. 183ʳ: 28 December 1326. John de Rasne became rector of "Nanfonteyn" [Little Petherick], Exeter diocese, being ordained priest on Holy Saturday 1331 (ibid., fol. 155ᵛ).

[137] Ibid., fol. 183ᵛ: 5 February 1327.

[138] *CPR 1327-1330*, p. 7: 8 February 1327; *Winch. Chart.* no. 130: 10 June 1330.

[139] *Lit. Cant.* 2, pp. 60-63 (546); ccl. Reg. L, fol. 37ʳ. The prior resisted the archbishop's claim that a fee of twenty marks should be paid according to composition directly to the steward. Whatever was due ought to be paid into Stratford's treasury.

[140] *Lit. Cant.* 2, pp. 106-108 (584), 134-135 (604), 141 (610); ccl. Reg. L, fols. 43ᵛ, 66ʳ⁻ᵛ, 67ʳ.

[141] *CCR 1333-1337*, p. 698 (1336); ibid. *1337-1339*, pp. 271, 284, 287-288, 303, 614 (1338); ibid. *1343-1346*, p. 564 (1345): acknowledges debt but not named as steward.

of title could be identical with the overseer of husbandry at Witney and Wargrave.[142] Naturally the *familia* was appreciably expanded as a consequence of Stratford's enhanced responsibilities and prestige. The largest number of persons granted protection to travel with him is to be found in 1338 – his final embassy. Some of these men are well known to us, others mere names.[143] In any case, a more exhaustive search would undoubtedly increase substantially the complement of Stratford's associates.[144]

So far we have tended to assume that an inner group of clerks and laymen served Stratford more or less exclusively. To some extent this is true, but qualification is needed. Many who were close to him also worked for others – fellow bishops, cathedral chapters including that of Canterbury,[145] or the king himself. Most of Stratford's more prominent clerical assistants are at one time or another designated "king's clerk."[146] Obviously men such as Astley and even more particularly Evesham were very much in the king's employment, but what the title indicates in some other cases is a matter which would merit closer examination. Its use, for instance, is almost invariable in royal ratification of collations made by Stratford as archbishop. The allegiance of influential laymen, such as

---

[142] This name is variously spelt, for instance as Longetone and apparently Langdon in CCL. D.E.3, fols. 8^r (1336), 25^r (1334), 41^r (1338?). It could be, therefore, that the name-place is Langdon (Kent) rather than Longdon (Worcestershire). Cf. WinRS, fol. 162^r, where Richard is present (14 September 1326) with Brabazoun, Littleton and Patrington in the audience court of Winchester.

[143] *CPR 1338-1340*, p. 98: 1 July 1338.

[144] Among them the following: Geoffrey de Badyngtone (WinRS, fol. 136^r: dilectus clericus suus; PRO C.115/K1/6681, fols. 15^r-17^r); John Cok or Cook, of Exeter, rector of Cottered, Lincoln diocese, (*CCR 1333-1337*, p. 722; *CPR 1338-1340*, p. 98; apparently the man collated to Saltwood, *CPR 1343-1345*, p. 55); M. John le Cok, not the same as the above (*CPR 1338-1340*, p. 98; CCL. D.E.3, fol. 41^v); Roger de Dorking (WAM no. 9223 dorse; *CPP 1342-1419*, p. 131; CCL. Reg. Q, fol. 197^v), this could be the Roger "Dygge," steward of Stratford's household in 1348, named in *CPR 1348-1350*, p. 306; John de Easebourn (Sussex), who could be a layman and was companion of Stratford's travels in the 1330s (*CPR 1330-1334*, pp. 218, 274, 276, 532; ibid. *1334-1338*, p. 37); and William atte More (PRO C.115/K1/6681, fols. 15^r-17^r). M. John de Wytcherch (Whitchurch) acted as Stratford's commissary general during a vacancy of the see of Ely in 1337. *London Reg. Gravesend*, fols. 101^v, 102^r (pp. 265-266).

[145] Among Stratford's clerks who wore the prior's livery (qui portant robas domini prioris) may be enumerated John of Windsor, John de Wymbourne, Simon of Charing, and Thomas (Mason?) of Canterbury. See CCL. D.E.3, fol. 13^v passim. John de Lecch received a pension of three pounds a year from 1340, Richard Vaughan a corrody nine years later. *Lit. Cant.* 2, pp. 232 (699), 293-294 (769); CCL. Reg. L, fols. 76^r, 82^r.

[146] For instance, Nicholas de Ystele, Richard de Twyverton, Richard of Chaddesley, Richard de Ragenhull, William of Ledbury, John de Eccleshale, as well as both Henry and John Geraud alias "de Stratford."

Hampton or Bradeweye, was expectedly divided between king and archbishop.[147] But when all allowances have been made, there remains at the centre, close to Stratford, a hard core of devoted clerks and laymen. The archbishop was not unmindful of their devotion when the time came to make his will.[148]

---

[147] Thus in 1338 John de Abingdon was called in to act for Bradeweye, Stratford being abroad and Bradeweye himself preoccupied with the safety of the Kentish seaboard. *CCR 1337-1339*, p. 614.

[148] See below, "Beneficiaries of Stratford's Will."

3

Political Involvement

Government concern over the academic conflict at Oxford may well have brought Stratford, who was the university's proctor,[1] to the notice of the authorities. However that may be, it was apparently not until about five years later, in 1317, that he was summoned to a royal council.

The political situation in England at the time was by no means healthy. Thomas of Lancaster, the most powerful noble in the land, had until recently held a commanding position in the nation's affairs. But the country had been wracked by a combination of disasters: famine, Scottish inroads, and widespread lawlessness; calamities accentuated by the ineffectual conduct of the monarch. Even when the internal situation began to ameliorate, failure to act against Scotland hastened the predictable alienation of Lancaster. By 1317 the earl was virtually isolated. Despairing of constitutional means to make himself felt, he withdrew from royal councils and remained on his own lands, sulkily aloof. At the same time there was growing up around the king a group of "courtiers" which profited much from royal favour and patronage.[2] Also close to the king, but credited with a degree of impartiality, was the trusted Aymer de Valence, earl of Pembroke, who for the earlier part of 1317 was absent as leader of an important English delegation to the papal curia at Avignon, one of the covert purposes of which was to secure absolution from Edward ii's oath to observe the baronial Ordinances.[3] Returning in May, Pembroke was captured and imprisoned in the county of Bar, but released the following month subject to payment of a crippling ransom.[4]

---

[1] See above, "The Making of a Career."

[2] For the political background to the events immediately prior to 1317 see Maddicott, *Lancaster*, chap. 5; Phillips, *Pembroke*, chap. 4. For the economic aspects: Lucas, "The European Famine"; Kershaw, "The Great Famine and Agrarian Crisis."

[3] *Vita*, pp. 78-79; Maddicott, *Lancaster*, p. 199; Haines, *Church and Politics*, p. 16.

[4] Phillips, *Pembroke*, pp. 111-117, gives a full account of the incident and its aftermath.

It was in February 1317, shortly after Pembroke's departure for Avignon, that Stratford attended a "colloquium" at the royal manor of Clarendon. There writs were issued for a further meeting at Westminster to which Stratford was summoned, together with six other clerks, for 11 April, the Monday after Easter week.[5] In this group were old acquaintances: M. Gilbert de Middleton, Archbishop Reynolds' councillor, who had been involved in *sede vacante* business at Worcester;[6] M. Andrew de Brugges, Stratford's colleague in Worcester Priory's service; as well as M. Richard de Stanou or Stanhowe, his predecessor as dean of the Arches. Thomas of Lancaster declined to come and not much can be gleaned of the proceedings vitiated by his absence.

While the council was in session news arrived of Pope John XXII's reservation of the see of Hereford, left vacant by Richard Swinfield's death on 15 March, and of his intention to make provision of the king's clerk Adam de Orleton, who for some time had been acting as resident agent at Avignon.[7] The king was furious at what he considered to be Orleton's feathering of his own nest. On 2 May he wrote urgently to Archbishop Reynolds and to Bishop John de Sandale, the chancellor, instructing them to consult with the royal clerks, Masters Gilbert de Middleton, John de Hildesle and Stratford, whom he had entrusted with the task of obstructing Orleton's promotion.[8] Edward had a candidate of his own, a canon of Hereford[9] and member of a rising Shropshire family, M. Thomas de Charlton DCL, whose elder brother became lord of Powys.[10] The chancellor was to issue letters to every member of the Hereford chapter urging them, notwithstanding the papal reservation, to proceed to the election already fixed for 16 May.[11] Here for the first but by no means the last time we see Stratford and Orleton ranged on opposing sides. All the same, it would be unwise to assume at this stage that there

---

[5] *CCR 1313-1318*, p. 455; *Parl. Writs* 2, ii, p. 170-171; *RDP* (App.) 3, pp. 233, 267. For what little is known of these councils see Maddicott, *Lancaster*, pp. 190-191.

[6] For his oath as archiepiscopal councillor (also taken by Richard Stanhowe mentioned below) see *Cant. Admin.* 1, pp. 13-14.

[7] Haines, *Church and Politics*, p. 17. His activities as agent are discussed ibid., chap. 2.

[8] *CChW*, p. 468 (PRO C.81/99/4194).

[9] *CChW*, pp. 469-470 (PRO C.81/100/4221); *Foedera* 2, i, p. 119; *Hereford Reg. Thomas Charlton*, intro., p. i.

[10] John Charlton had been in the household of Prince Edward who, as king, made him chamberlain (1310-1318). For many notices of both John and Thomas see Tout, *Chapters* 6, index s.v.; also Dugdale, *Baronage* 1, pp. 71-72. Ironically John Charlton was under suspicion of disloyalty as early as March 1321 and was with Lancaster at Boroughbridge. See Morgan, "Barony of Powys," pp. 24-25ff.

[11] *CChW*, pp. 469-470 (PRO C.81/100/4221).

was necessarily any personal antipathy. It would have been unthinkable for Stratford to withdraw from a duty expressly imposed by the king. It is pertinent that Stratford's associate, Middleton, seems to have been a friend of Orleton's.[12] As it transpired the king's opposition proved vain; Orleton became bishop of Hereford. The lesson was not lost upon Stratford.

Another summons was sent to Stratford on 1 July 1317, this time for a council at Nottingham on the 18th. The proposed agenda covered a whole range of business: the disturbed state of the realm and the affairs of Wales, Ireland, Scotland and Gascony.[13] Possibly the most pressing problems were the persistence of internal dissension and the insecurity of the northern border. In the hope of bringing peace to Scotland Pope John XXII had despatched two cardinals, Gaucelme d'Eauze and Luca Fieschi, who are reported to have reached Canterbury on 24 June and London four days later.[14] The king's intention was apparently to hold exploratory discussions prior to the cardinals' arrival, but in any case the council's proceedings were delayed by the continued reluctance of Lancaster to put in an appearance.[15] At this juncture there was real danger on the one hand of civil strife, on the other of renewed incursions by the Scots. Lancaster's absence meant that nothing positive could be determined.[16] But before the council broke up the new bishop of Hereford reached Nottingham, where on 23 July writs were issued for the livery of his temporalities. Edward is said to have given Orleton a cordial reception.[17] If this be true, it is to be supposed that the king's overt irritation had been mollified by the cardinals, whose cooperation he was anxious to enlist.

Stratford was in the thick of the political activity which followed the reconciliation at Leake (9 August 1318) between the king and Earl Thomas. In company with other legal clerks and justices he was summoned to the three parliaments which assembled at York in October 1318, May 1319, and January 1320 respectively.[18] The parliament of

---

[12] For Middleton see *Biog. Oxon.* s.v.; Haines, *Church and Politics*, p. 206 and index s.v.

[13] *Foedera* 2, i, p. 129; *Parl. Writs* 2, ii, p. 171; *RDP* (App.) 3, p. 267.

[14] The details are given in what is believed to be a Canterbury chronicle, TCC MS R.5 41, fol. 113ᵛ (cited by Phillips, *Pembroke*, p. 120).

[15] Maddicott, *Lancaster*, pp. 191-192.

[16] His excuses are recorded at length in *Murimuth*, pp. 171-176, and *Bridlington*, pp. 50-52. Maddicott, *Lancaster*, thinks they provide "the best statement of his political case that we have."

[17] This was in the cardinals' presence. *Hereford Reg. Orleton*, p. 16.

[18] *Parl. Writs* 2, ii, pp. 183, 198, 216; *RDP* (App.) 3, pp. 289, 292, 299. They met 20 October-9 December 1318; 6-23 May 1319; 20 January 1320 (duration unknown). *HBC*, p. 516.

1318 was concerned with the implementation of the arrangements agreed upon at Leake; that of 1319 continued the process, but was also marked by Lancaster's attempt to secure for himself the stewardship of the household.[19] Cooperation between king and earl was short-lived. Lancaster is reported to have refused to attend the 1320 parliament, though it has been pointed out that the fact of his witnessing a royal charter during the session suggests that he eventually came.[20] This parliament experienced the reaction of the king's supporters to Lancaster's policies and was followed in the spring by an embassy to Avignon, which apparently secured the long-desired absolution of Edward from his oath to observe the hated Ordinances.[21] By this means the king sought to free his hands for the threatened show-down with Lancaster. Another move to relieve possible external conflict was Edward II's journey to France to perform belated homage to Philip V for Ponthieu and the duchy of Aquitaine, or Gascony as it was more commonly called. On 4 June 1320 Stratford, as a member of the royal contingent, was granted a writ of aid, followed the next day by letters of protection until the feast of the Assumption (15 August).[22] He travelled with an entourage of seven clerks and laymen, presumably in convoy with the main body – a necessary precaution. The king, with Isabella his queen, left the country on 19 June and performed homage at Amiens on the last day of the month.[23] Stratford must have witnessed the ceremony. Presumably too, he attached himself to the royal party on the return trip to Boulogne, where the temporarily rehabilitated bishop of Hereford joined Bishops Salmon of Norwich and Stapeldon of Exeter in consecrating Henry Burghersh, the king's candidate for the see of Lincoln. Back in England, with other councillors he was directed to be at the October parliament at Westminster.[24]

Now designated archdeacon of Lincoln, Stratford was summoned to the exchequer for a council which met in January 1321, as well as to the parliament which assembled at Westminster in mid-July amidst the threat

[19] See, in particular, Maddicott, *Lancaster*, pp. 228-233, 240-244.

[20] Details of this parliament are in Maddicott, *Lancaster*, pp. 253-254.

[21] BL Cotton MS Nero D.x, fol. 110ᵛ (Trivet's continuator); Haines, *Church and Politics*, p. 24 n. 90; Maddicott, *Lancaster*, pp. 255-256.

[22] *CCR 1317-1321*, pp. 449-450, 452.

[23] *Foedera* 2, ii, pp. 3-4; Haines, *Church and Politics*, p. 25; Stuart, "The Interview between Philip V and Edward II." Stuart prints a document (PRO C.47/29/9/25) which suggests that three or four days after the homage (according to *Flores Hist.* 3, p. 193, it was liege homage) some of Philip's councillors suggested that Edward should also swear fealty (tenuz a faire feaute).

[24] BL Cotton MS Faustina B.v, fol. 34ʳ; *Parl. Writs* 2, ii, p. 220; *RDP* (App.) 3, p. 301. Stratford is not specifically mentioned as present at the consecration.

posed by a substantial baronial army. At this parliament, though the prelates stood apart, judgment was given against the king's favourites, the Despensers, who were exiled. Civil war was once again narrowly averted.[25] It was at the very end of the year – protection being granted him on 8 December – that Stratford next went abroad in the king's service.[26] By that date the Marcher barons were in revolt and Edward was moving westwards in an attempt to quell them. In this rebellion Bishop Orleton was to be implicated early in the new year.[27] Such grave matters were to be the subject of representation at Avignon, but initially Stratford's mission stemmed from a vacancy at Lichfield. We have already seen him as a member of the deputation from the Coventry and Lichfield chapters which brought news of Walter Langton's death to the king's officers.[28] Edward was intent on the further advancement of a favourite clerk, Robert Baldock, controller of the wardrobe and since January 1320 keeper of the privy seal.[29] Baldock was archdeacon of Middlesex, as well as a fellow canon of Stratford's at Lichfield. The weight placed on the matter by Edward is indicated by the strength of the embassy which he despatched. This was headed by Rigaud d'Assier, lately provided to the see of Winchester against the royal wish.[30] Assier had been an auditor of the sacred palace and a papal collector in England. With reason he might be thought to have influence at the curia. Travelling with him were two doctors of civil law, William de Weston and Stratford himself.[31] The envoys were also empowered to deal with a further matter affecting Baldock. On 24 December the king addressed a letter to the pope on the topic from Cirencester, where he was celebrating Christmas prior to his military incursion into the Marches. Pope John had asked Edward to refrain from interfering with the process of severing the portion of Milton from the prebendal church of Aylesbury. To such a division the king

[25] BL Cotton MS Faustina B.v, fol. 35ᵛ. In general, see Maddicott, *Lancaster*, pp. 279-289.

[26] *CPR 1321-1324*, p. 41.

[27] Haines, *Church and Politics*, pp. 135ff.; idem., "A Defence Brief for Bishop Adam de Orleton"; Morgan, "The Barony of Powys," pp. 24-25.

[28] *CPR 1321-1324*, p. 33. See above, "The Making of a Career."

[29] There are many notices of Baldock's official career in Tout, *Chapters* 6, index s.v. The combination of the controllership and keepership is commented upon ibid. 5, pp. 2-3. See also *Biog. Oxon.*, s.v. Baldok.

[30] For Assier's promotion in November 1319 see Smith, *Episcopal Appointments*, pp. 33-35.

[31] *Foedera* 2, ii, p. 33. Stratford had grants of protection 7 and 8 December 1321 and safe-conduct for a year. *CPR 1321-1324*, pp. 41, 45. William de Dene, knight, was also one of the party.

objected on the principle that it infringed his rights, but also because he had conferred the Aylesbury prebend on Baldock, who owing to absence was said to be unaware of what was going on. Regardless of this and in defiance of the right of the king's subjects not to be summoned outside the realm in causes of such a kind,[32] Baldock had been cited before one of the papal auditors. The royal case was supported by letters of the same tenor addressed to the cardinals.[33]

Early in January 1322 Edward learned officially that Pope John had already advanced Roger Northburgh to Lichfield,[34] an outcome to which he was not wholly averse in view of the slender chances of Baldock's acceptance at Avignon.[35] It is also true that Northburgh had a claim on royal generosity and that Edward had urged his advancement.[36] In the monarch's eyes the choice was to be justified, at any rate in part, by Northburgh's outwardly uncommitted attitude during the political tension of the final years of the reign. Baldock was not entirely overlooked. As a measure of compensation the king requested that he be given a prebend in Beverley Minster and continued to press his subject's case, and his own, with respect to the Aylesbury prebend.[37]

By late February the king's political position was much improved. The rebellion in the west had collapsed; the Roger Mortimers, uncle and nephew, of Chirk and Wigmore respectively, had given themselves up and were lodged in the Tower.[38] This gave opportunity for a vigorous

---

[32] On this matter of citation outside the realm see Wright, *Church and Crown*, pp. 142-154, esp. p. 153.

[33] *Foedera* 2, ii, pp. 33-34; *Le Neve* 1, pp. 25, 91, 108. Smith, *Episcopal Appointments*, pp. 103-105, "Unlicensed division of a benefice, Aylesbury." Nicholas IV made the division (1290), Clement V gave Milton (1312) to Cardinal Gailhard de la Mothe, while Edward granted Aylesbury to Baldock (June 1320: *CPR 1317-1321*, p. 453), refusing to recognize the separation. Wright, *Church and Crown*, p. 327, no. 47, gives further references.

[34] Royal letter of 4 January 1322 from Worcester. The promotion was said to be "ad nostri instantiam, necnon et ob honorem nostrum, et regni nostri utilitatem." *Foedera* 2, ii, p. 34. Edward wrote the same day to the cardinals on Northburgh's behalf (ibid., p. 35).

[35] Baldock was excommunicated, though the king forbade Archbishop Reynolds to publish the sentences (*CCR 1318-1323*, p. 538). Some clerks were rash enough to disobey the prohibition. See Smith, *Episcopal Appointments*, p. 104 n. 148 (from PRO K.B.27/250/Rex m. 16). There seem to have been whisperings against Baldock, and his responsibility for action against such bishops as Burghersh and Orleton was recognized and disliked at the curia.

[36] Although Tout (*Chapters* 2, pp. 205, 292, 299) regarded him as a nominee of the Ordainers in 1312 and of the supposed "middle party" in 1318 ("the weak king was soon hopelessly in their hands"), he had enjoyed a long career as an administrative clerk.

[37] *Foedera* 2, ii, p. 34.

[38] Haines, *Church and Politics*, p. 134; Maddicott, *Lancaster*, pp. 305-306. The intervention of Sir Gruffyd Llwyd influenced this denouement, but precisely which

restatement at the curia of the king's concerns. Assier, Stratford and Weston received an extended brief.[39] The pope was to be told of the rebels' discomfiture and in particular of Bishop Burghersh's open adherence to the king's enemies.[40] Papal assistance against the Scots was to be sought. With regard to patronage, Baldock was put forward as the royal nominee for the next vacant bishopric, while M. William Ayrminne, "cancellarie nostre secretarius," was warmly commended. There was to be firm resistance to encroachment on the king's prerogative in the matter of the Aylesbury prebend.[41] It was at this moment that Northburgh's bulls arrived in the baggage of an Augustinian friar, M. Robert de Worksop. The king dutifully expressed his thanks.[42]

At some unspecified date Stratford reported back to the authorities in England. He was at York in July 1322[43] and left that city on the 22nd for a further mission to Avignon. Almost a year was to elapse before his return.[44] Piratical attacks by Flemings made the channel crossing more dangerous than usual. Because of this and the urgency of the king's business Robert de Kendale, warden of the Cinque Ports, advised that Archdeacon Stratford should travel in two ships with an armed escort. A third ship was hired to carry twenty horses and their harness.[45]

By the time of this mission affairs at home had altered radically – to the king's benefit. The battle of Boroughbridge (16 March 1322) brought defeat and death to his main opponents, the earls of Hereford and Lancaster.[46] At the parliament which assembled at York in May of 1322, and to which Stratford was summoned as a councillor, the sentence of banishment against the king's close confidants, the Despensers father and son, was nullified, the Ordinances were formally revoked, and the elder Despenser was created earl of Winchester. Everywhere the surviving

castles he captured is variously reported. Morgan, "The Barony of Powys," p. 25, identifies them as Chirk, Welshpool and Clun, correcting Edwards, "Sir Gruffyd Llwyd," p. 592, who (modifying Holinshed) gave them as Mold, Chirk and Holt (substituted for Arundel's castle of Clun). BL Cotton MS Nero D.x, fol. 111ᵛ, none the less appears to read Mold (indistinct), Chirk and Clun.

[39] *Foedera* 2, ii, pp. 38-39: king to pope, Weston Subedge, 25 February 1322.

[40] "Dicto Bartholomeo [Badlesmere] nostro rebelli, totis viribus adhaeret."

[41] Ibid., pp. 38-39.

[42] Ibid., p. 39.

[43] PRO E.101/309/27 m.3.

[44] Ibid. He accounted for 355 days – excluding the last – between 22 July 1322 and 11 July 1323, receiving ten shillings a day, i.e. £177 10s.

[45] Ibid. Forty-four people travelled in his contingent; 14s 8d (2d a head) being charged for customs at Dover and Wissant.

[46] The earl of Hereford was killed in the battle, Lancaster was captured and subsequently executed, 22 March 1322.

rebels, contrariants as they were called, were being rigorously hunted down. Where lives were spared the justices imposed heavy fines.[47] The month of June marked the beginning of the harassment of Orleton, against whose provision to Hereford Stratford had earlier been called upon to protest.[48] Only the Scots remained defiant; to subdue them an expedition was in course of preparation.

From his expense account it transpires that Stratford was under orders to secure four bulls: one for the relaxation of unspecified oaths,[49] another for the legalization of a prospective marriage between unnamed parties, a third for the royal foundation of a Dominican priory at King's Langley in Hertfordshire, where Piers Gaveston lay buried, and the last for the diversion of the papal biennial tenth to Edward.[50] In advance of Stratford's arrival a messenger was despatched on 10 August from Wissant, where the party had landed, to Avignon. This was a fifteen days' journey for which the regular allowance was three pence a day.[51] The bishop of Winchester, Rigaud d'Assier, who had remained abroad, sent another messenger from Montpezat in Gascony to the Roman court and thence to England.[52] It was Bernard, lord of Montpezat, who by his destruction of the *bastide* under construction at Saint-Sardos and the massacre of its inhabitants was to precipitate the sequestration and subsequent military occupation of Gascony by the French monarch, Charles IV.[53]

The temporary upsurge of Edward's domestic fortunes reinforced the demands for the remedying of "gravamina," by which he meant Pope John XXII's encroachment on his rights of patronage. He pointed out[54] that

[47] See, for example, PRO Just. 1/1388. An analysis of the social unrest at this time in the context of the "minor gentry" is given by Waugh, "The Profits of Violence." For Stratford's summons see *Parl. Writs* 2, ii, p. 246; *RDP* (App.) 3, p. 321.

[48] Haines, *Church and Politics*, pp. 140ff.

[49] See below, where these are identified as the oaths of barons and bishops to observe the Ordinances. The cost was seven Florentine florins and sixty-four livres turnois, at 3s 4d to the florin and 3d to the livre, i.e. £1 9s 4d.

[50] *VCH Herts.* 2, pp. 238-240; Lunt, *Financial Relations* 1, pp. 410-412. On 20 April 1322 the English clergy was ordered to pay a tenth for two years beginning 30 May 1322 – for the use of the king in the defence of the realm. Collectors apparently took no further action until January 1323.

[51] PRO E.101/309/27 m.3.

[52] Ibid. The messenger in this instance was Richard de Ragenhull, Robert Stratford's proctor in the exchanges of the benefices in the latter half of 1319. See above, "The Making of a Career" and "Stratford's *Familia* and Administration."

[53] See, *War of Saint-Sardos*, for the background. Two letters from the French king, dated 30 December 1322 and 1 January 1323 were copied into Orleton's Hereford register. *HRO*, pp. 334-337.

[54] *Foedera* 2, ii, pp. 38-39: Newcastle-on-Tyne, 3 August 1322. A chancery warrant of

the Aylesbury prebend had been granted to Baldock after full discussion in his court and in accordance with the law and custom of the realm. There followed a complaint of lack of progress in the business of the Leighton Buzzard prebend in Lincoln Cathedral, likewise conferred on another of his clerks, M. William Ayrminne. Neither claimant had appeared personally in the Roman court, since their presence was urgently required at the king's side and he had actually impeded their going. Even so, their explanations and his supporting letters had been brushed aside.[55] Baldock's opponent, Cardinal Gailhard de la Mothe, was offered another Lincoln prebend, Stoke-by-Newark, released by Bishop Northburgh's elevation and in royal gift by virtue of the Lincoln temporalities. This was by way of compensation for the prebend or portion of Milton Ecclesia – said to be worth only half as much – which the king continued to insist was inseparable from that of Aylesbury. In times past, Edward complained, letters such as he had written would have sufficed to implement his wishes. This was no longer the case; both his clerks had been declared contumacious and placed under sentence of excommunication.[56] The pope's reluctance to accommodate Edward in these matters stemmed principally from his concern at the king's confiscation of the Lincoln temporalities on the grounds of Burghersh's disloyalty. For the remainder of the reign he was to urge the bishop's restoration to favour. As for Burghersh, he did all he could to resist the royal claim to dispose of benefices ordinarily in his collation, without control of which he lacked the means to support his *familia* and hence to govern his diocese effectively.[57]

---

the 4th ordered that letters be made out to the pope, cardinals and others of the king's friends in the curia with regard to royal business and that of M. William Ayrminne. They were to be delivered to Baldock for carrying to the king. *CChW*, p. 53 (PRO C.81/119/6146).

[55] *Foedera* 2, ii, pp. 53-54: Gosford, 8 August 1322. The king had granted Leighton Buzzard to Ayrminne in November 1318. Jean de Puy Barsac claimed it by virtue of a papal expectation. Following Bishop Dalderby's death, Edward re-presented Ayrminne on account of the vacancy. Judgment was given in Ayrminne's favour in the king's court, but the position of Puy Barsac was maintained by the curia and eventually he appears to have been accepted in Edward III's reign. See Deeley, "Papal Provision," pp. 519-522; Smith, *Episcopal Appointments*, pp. 75-76, 125-126; Wright, *Church and Crown*, p. 326 no. 41; *Le Neve* 1, p. 79.

[56] *Foedera* 2, ii, pp. 51-52, 53-54; Smith, *Episcopal Appointments*, pp. 86-88.

[57] *Foedera* 2, ii, p. 183; *Rot. Parl. Inediti*, pp. 169-170; Haines, *Church and Politics*, pp. 155-156. In a letter of 18 March 1325 to Archbishop Reynolds John XXII castigated him (on Burghersh's complaint) for the actions of his court(s) and officers in support of those occupying benefices illegally in Lincoln diocese. "Sane quia venerabilis fratris nostri episcopi Lyncoln. habet gravis conquestio nobis missa quod per cur*iam* [curias?] et offic*iales* tuos ad instanciam et instigacionem quorundam beneficia ecclesiastica et alia

Further recriminatory letters followed in quick succession. The king's agents had supposedly opened his eyes to the injuries suffered with respect to benefices within the realm;[58] not only had *his* rights been prejudiced but also those of the magnates, as their letters had doubtless made plain.[59] For Baldock's enjoyment of the Aylesbury prebend Edward continued to barter Stoke, on the understanding that Cardinal Gailhard ceased his legal proceedings in the curia. Stratford was entrusted with the collation and with explaining the king's mind *viva voce*.[60] Letters reiterating the collation were directed to the pope early in December.[61] John XXII could scarcely concur with Edward's plan, based on his claim to Burghersh's patronage, so he provided John de Grandisson, the future bishop of Exeter, to Stoke, and it was Grandisson whom the Lincoln diocesan, in 1323, ordered his dean and chapter to induct.[62] In the end Edward accepted the situation and while asserting the integrity of the Aylesbury prebend, granted the Milton portion to Cardinal Gailhard for life, of special grace and without prejudice.[63]

Meanwhile, other problems served to emphasize the fundamental weakness of Edward's position. His anxiety to secure aggravatory sentences against the Scots could be countered by the papal claim to an annual tribute. This Edward strove to shelve on account of the expenses he had incurred, and was still incurring, by reason of internal unrest and the expiry of the Scottish truce.[64]

While these exchanges were taking place Stratford was still negotiating for the bulls he had been sent to procure. During his absence the business

iura sue diocesis absque iusto titulo contra Deum ac honestatem et libertatem ecclesiasticam occupancium varia sibi gravamina inferuntur et hactenus sunt illata." PRO S.C.1/50/23 (a copy); cf. *CPL 1305-1342*, p. 468. In June 1325 Burghersh petitioned the king to remove laymen occupying the prebendal church of Leighton Buzzard. PRO S.C.8/237/11806, printed Smith, *Episcopal Appointments*, p. 126.

[58] *Foedera* 2, ii, p. 54: "De injuriis super beneficiis, quae infra regnum nostrum vendicant, aut optinent, sibi factis, prout supradicti nuncii nostri nobis dederunt intelligi."

[59] Ibid., p. 57: "Non solum nos et jura nostra, verum etiam magnates de regno nostro, jura, leges, et consuetudines ejusdem contingit, prout in literis dictorum magnatum, vestrae beatitudini inde directis, credimus contineri."

[60] Ibid., p. 53: Gosford, 8 August 1322.

[61] Ibid., p. 57: York, 4 December 1322. The king also urged his solution on Cardinal Gailhard (ibid., pp. 72-73).

[62] *CPL 1305-1342*, p. 224; Lincoln Reg. Burghersh 1 (Reg. 4), fol. 398ᵛ (a reference I owe to Smith, *Episcopal Appointments*, pp. 86-87); and cf. *Biog. Oxon.*, s.v. Grandisson, where he is thought not to have obtained Stoke.

[63] *Foedera* 2, ii, p. 109; *CPR 1324-1327*, p. 36: 17 September 1324. *Le Neve* 1, pp. 25, 91, concludes that this meant Gailhard was to enjoy both Aylesbury and Milton, but the *Foedera* text only mentions "praedictam portionem de Milton." See also n. 33 above.

[64] E.g. *Foedera* 2, ii, pp. 53-54.

had been left to his subordinate, M. William Mees, a much trusted clerk.[65] By 15 November 1322 negotiations had reached the stage at which it was necessary to seek confirmation or further information from the royal council. Richard de Ragenhull, who had come with Stratford,[66] was sent off on horseback, accompanied by a single servant or groom (garcio). His principal accounted for twenty-three days to cover the journey to York,[67] where the administration must have been in disarray following Edward's unsuccessful strike into Scotland and the retaliatory Scottish raids, one of which forced the king to flee ignominiously from his lodgings at Byland Abbey near Thirsk.[68] In these conditions affairs moved slowly; it was nearly four months before the council found time to digest the messenger's report and to decide on the content of further letters of instruction for the envoys waiting at Avignon.[69] On 21 November the bulls relating to the clerical tenth were ready for despatch from the curia.[70] They were entrusted to another member of Stratford's entourage, John de Madeleye, who in his turn travelled to York, also accompanied by a single servant. Like his predecessor he was kept waiting about, forced to follow the council's migrations. It was not until 1 March that his servant could return to Avignon with the government's response. Before the end of the month a final messenger was on his way back to England with news of the latest developments.[71]

One of the most interesting aspects of Stratford's account for this particular mission concerns the *douceurs* considered appropriate at the Christmas season for officers of the papal court.[72] These included

[65] For whom see above, "Stratford's *Familia* and Administration." Stratford's account claims expenses for Mees for twenty-one weeks and five days from 4 May, i.e. until 3 October 1322. Mees remained in the curia after the departure of the principal negotiators (Stratford, Weston, and Sir William Dene, for whom see n. 31 above), "Antequam dictus Willielmus habuit dictas bullas et antequam dictus archidiaconus [Stratford] rediit ad curiam predictam." PRO E.101/309/27 m. 3.

[66] *CPR 1317-1321*, p. 45. With Mees, Nicholas de Stratford, John de Madeleye and others granted protection for a year, 7 December 1321.

[67] PRO E.101/309/27 m. 3.

[68] Graphically described by one of the chroniclers, who dubs Edward II as a man "qui semper fuerat cordis pavidi et infortunatus in bellis." *Lanercost*, pp. 247-248.

[69] PRO E.101/309/27 m. 3. "Ad dominum regem apud Ebor. et alibi expectando responsum quoad nuncia sua per cv dies per preceptum regis."

[70] Ibid.

[71] Ibid. Fryde, *Tyranny of Edward II*, p. 140, in writing of the hiatus in securing a response (in 1321) about Gascon affairs (Adam Orleton, she thought, "probably did not help"), was apparently unaware that such delays were far from unusual.

[72] PRO E.101/309/27 m. 3. Entitled: "Exhennia et dona pro negociis regis." Cf. Wright, *Church and Crown*, pp. 121-123. *Pace* Wright, I doubt if these were any more than conventional gifts and hence unlikely to affect seriously – if at all – the outcome of any negotiations.

payments to the pope's squires and marshals;[73] to the "nephew" of the vice-chancellor, whose duty it was to lead envoys to the cardinals;[74] to the palace messengers;[75] to the janitors of the first and second portals;[76] to the sergeants of the *soldannus* in charge of temporal awards and the distribution of lodgings;[77] to the cardinals Berengar Frédol, bishop of Porto, and Bertrand de Montfavèz, responsible for diplomatic negotiations with the Scots, as well as their (legal) auditors;[78] to Walter, the clerk of M. Andrea Sapiti, Edward's resident proctor, who had laboured long in royal service;[79] to sundry notaries charged with the execution of the formal documents;[80] and to Pietro de Via, chamberlain and "nephew" of Pope John.[81] In addition there was a final payment to another papal "nephew," Arnaud, "contra festum Pasche." [82] The total expended amounted to £31 6s 8d at the current exchange rate of six Florentine florins to the pound.

By February 1323 Edward was in a position to express gratitude to the pope for benefits already secured at Avignon by Stratford's efforts.[83] But the offences attributed to the bishops of Lincoln and Bath and Wells, Henry Burghersh and John Droxford, still rankled in the king's mind.

---

[73] PRO E.101/309/27 m. 3. Three Florentine florins at the rate of 3s 4d to the florin: 10s.

[74] Vice-chancellor at the time was Cardinal Pierre le Tessier. Baumgarten, *Von der apostolischen Kanzlei*, p. 280; del Re, *La Curia Romana*, p. 290. His nephew's name is given as "Johannes Doun armiger" – who received 13s 4d (PRO E.101/309/27 m. 3).

[75] "Cursoribus domini pape deservientibus in palacio"; three florins: 10s. PRO E.101/309/27 m. 3.

[76] The four janitors at the first portal received five florins: 16s 8d; the janitors at the second one, thirteen florins: £2 3s 4d. Ibid.

[77] "Servientibus unius armigeri vocati *soldannus* qui habet execucionem indiciorum temporalium et eciam liberacionem hospiciorum"; two florins: 6s 8d. Ibid. In 1336 we find legal proceedings taking place in the house of the "soldan" (one Raynaud de Ponte, donzel) at Avignon. Vatican Archives, *RA* 51, fol. 392^{r-v}.

[78] The cardinals received forty florins (£6 13s 4d) on Christmas Eve, their auditors thirty-two florins (£5 6s 8d). PRO E.101/309/27 m. 3.

[79] "Waltero clerico magistri Andree Sapiti qui laboravit in negociis predictis et in eisdem multa scripsit pro labore suo"; six florins: 20s. Ibid.

[80] "Magistro Magoloto et magistro Petro de Castro Bonici notariis'; twenty-four florins: £4. Ibid.

[81] "Petro de Via nepoti et camerario domini pape per consilium nunciorum"; fourteen florins: £2 6s 8d. Ibid.

[82] "Arnaldo nepoti domini pape contra festum Pasche"; twenty florins: £3 6s 8d. Ibid. Possibly Arnaud de Trian, marshal of the curia, though Arnaud Duèse (who succeeded his father Pierre as viscount of Caraman) was another nephew.

[83] *Foedera* 2, ii, pp. 60-61: Newark, 2 February 1323. "Misimus ad pedes beatitudinis vestrae, dilectum clericum nostrum magistrum Johannem de Stratford ... pro certis exponendis negotiis, et gratiis nostro nomine optinendis, quas credimus, ante confectionem praesentium, fore concessas."

Burghersh had made matters worse, for he was reported to have sought the intervention of the king of France at the curia.[84] More immediately, Edward tried to rid himself of the recalcitrant Burghersh by granting him and his *familia* a safe conduct to Avignon, whither he had been summoned by the pope.[85]

Another problem to be committed to Bishop Assier and his fellow-ambassador at Avignon, John Stratford, was the claim of the English king to part of the lands held by a former count of Provence and Forcalquier, one of whose daughters, Eleanor, had married Henry III, another his brother Richard, king of the Romans. Robert, king of Jerusalem and Sicily, descended from the count's fourth daughter, was considered to have usurped Edward's inheritance.[86]

Up to this point, late April 1323, Stratford was secure in royal favour. Despite later aspersions, it is a fair assumption that his diplomatic efforts were receiving the approbation of the home government. Suddenly the whole fabric of a promising career collapsed; on 12 April Rigaud d'Assier died at the curia. Thus not only did the bishopric of Winchester fall vacant but also, because Assier's death occurred at Avignon, the right to fill it was claimed by the apostolic see. This was a rich prize or, as the royal chancery more soberly expressed it, "one of the noblest bishoprics in the kingdom."[87] To Edward the time seemed ripe for the tardy promotion of his familiar clerk Archdeacon Robert Baldock. The news took less than a fortnight to reach the court, from which it elicited a quick response on Baldock's behalf; a response loud in its panegyric.[88] The following day, 27

[84] Ibid. "Quod ipsos, et potissime dictum Lincolniensem (pessimum venenum, de genere proditorum procedens) in regno nostro, absque gravi scandalo et periculo, non poterimus sustinere." M. Robert of Canterbury was sent to the curia with information about Droxford (ibid., p. 65). Edward wrote to King Charles deprecating Burghersh's approach to him: "Quia de nostris fidedignis de Curia Romana, recepimus, quod dictus Henricus, episcopus Lincolniensis, impetravit favorem suum" (ibid., p. 66).

[85] Ibid., p. 61. "Praeterea, pater pie, pro episcopo Lincolniensi praefato (quem ad vestram praesentiam evocandam duxistis) et ipsius episcopi familiaribus, et rebus suis, secum deferendis, literas nostras de conductu fieri fecimus speciales." There is a later papal summons of 21 February [1326] in *CPL 1305-1342*, p. 473. A royal letter of 1 July 1326 requesting that the offending bishops should be translated suggested that the bishop of Orange would be an acceptable alternative to one of them. *Foedera* 2, ii, p. 161.

[86] Ibid., p. 63: Pontefract, 12 and 18 February 1323.

[87] Ibid., p. 70: Thynden, 26 April 1323. Smith, *Episcopal Appointments*, pp. 39-41, gives a brief account of the Winchester affair. However, the pope did *not* claim that Stratford's appointment was made without his knowledge (ibid., p. 40). The lack of knowledge was on the king's part. Natalie Fryde's article, "John Stratford and the Crown," is mainly concerned with this election, but does not examine the charges in detail.

[88] *Foedera* 2, ii, p. 70: "Baldock ... quem virum novimus moribus insignem, literarum

April, a further letter was addressed to the cardinals. It contained the somewhat unbalanced allegation that the bishops had been responsible for the recent disturbances.[89] A day later the king wrote a second time to the pope, complaining of the "indiscretum regimen" of the bishops, a phrase which was to be echoed in the following reign.[90] The implication was that Edward's choice of bishops would ensure political compatibility; an argument not likely to find overmuch favour at the curia, nor for that matter borne out by events. It was essential, Edward insisted, that Winchester should be given to a man preeminently useful in the business of the realm.[91] A supporting letter of the same date was addressed to Cardinal Gailhard de la Mothe, repeating the offer of the prebend of Stoke in order to assuage his feelings against Baldock.[92] As we have seen, this was to prove a futile gesture.

A royal council assembled at Bishopthorpe, near York, in May. It was attended by a group of the most influential magnates, including the Despensers and the earls of Kent, Pembroke and Atholl.[93] Nobles from Ireland and Gascony had also been summoned. The Winchester affair was only a troublesome addition to the main business: settlement of the terms of a thirteen-year truce with Robert Bruce. Proceedings were enlivened by the scarcely concealed opposition of Henry de Beaumont. Exasperated by the turn of events he declined to give counsel and was ordered to leave the assembly. His irritation could have been anticipated. Henry was the brother of Louis de Beaumont, the bishop of Durham; though French-born he had married Alice, the niece and heiress of John Comyn, earl of Buchan, and had much to lose from Robert Bruce's ascendancy. In the next reign, to Edward III's embarrassment, he was to figure strongly among the "disinherited," who strove independently to establish their Scottish claims by military force.[94]

scientia praeditum, in consilio providum, vitae honestate praeclarum, et in agendis quibuslibet circumspectum."

[89] Ibid., pp. 70-71: "... ad turbationes, exortas in dicto regno nostro, ante haec tempora, ex aliquorum desidia seu conniventia praelatorum."

[90] Ibid., p. 72: "Ex quorumdam indiscreto regimine praelatorum, ad memoriam reducentes." Cf. ibid. 2, iii, pp. 4-5 (s.a. 1328): "quae ex quorumdam taciturnitate, immo verius indiscreto regimine praelatorum, creduntur verisimiliter contigisse."

[91] Ibid., p. 72: "Talem profici personam, quae, virtutum donis praemunita, praeesse sciret pariter et prodesse."

[92] Ibid., pp. 72-73.

[93] Ibid., p. 73.

[94] *Scalacronica*, pp. 156, (App.) 294-295; Barrow, *Bruce*, pp. 353ff.; Tout, *PHE* 3, pp. 316-317. See below, "In the Seat of Power."

It was on 7 June 1323, while still at Bishopthorpe, that Edward sent another letter to Avignon. Once more he urged the claims of Baldock and the tranquillity of the realm which he felt his promotion would ensure. Already, he hinted darkly, a "certain rumour" had reached his ears of what was afoot at Avignon.[95] He was well informed. Before his letter could have reached its destination, what the king had feared came to pass. Provisory bulls of 20 June named Stratford as bishop of Winchester; a man worthy by virtue of his learning, conduct, purity of life, honesty of conversation and capacity in both spiritual and temporal affairs.[96]

Edward had no intention of bowing to the inevitable. To the Count of Savoy, who was seeking Winchester for his nephew Thomas, brother of the archbishop of Lyons, he replied in confident tones. Turning the matter over in his mind he had resolved that the person to be appointed should be noteworthy for the gravity of his behaviour and such learning as would enable him to defend the rights of the church, to reform abuses, and to assist the king with counsel and aid in the control of his subjects. Baldock was such a man – one dear to his heart.[97] To the pope Edward made formal complaint; he had not asked for his envoy's promotion to Winchester. On his own initiative Stratford had accepted the see in full knowledge of the royal intention to advance someone else. By so doing he had harmed the king's interests. What is more, his conduct in other matters was to be the subject of investigation.[98] The last point was elaborated in a supporting letter to the cardinals. Stratford, alleged Edward, had spurned his obligation of fealty and allegiance, and had broken his oath to preserve the king's honour with all his might.[99] The same day, 8 July 1323, instructions went out to Edmund, earl of Kent, constable of Dover Castle, to the warden of the Cinque Ports, and to the

---

[95] *Foedera* 2, ii, pp. 76-77.

[96] Vatican Archives, *RV* 75, fols. 26ᵛ-27ʳ; *CPL 1305-1342*, p. 230; *Salisbury Reg. Martival* 2, pp. 431-432 (papal letter to Archbishop Reynolds of same date, 20 June 1323, requiring him to render assistance to Stratford). Pope John warmly recommended his appointee to the king: "Dilectum filium Johannem electum Wyntoniensem archidiaconum Lincolniensem, in sacerdotio constitutum, quem, dono superni numinis, scientia praeditum litterarum, elegantia morum conspicuum, nitidum vitae munditia, conversationis honestate decorum, ac in spiritualibus providum, et in temporalibus circumspectum novimus." *Foedera* 2, ii, p. 77: 19 June 1323.

[97] "Virum utique secundum cor nostrum." *Foedera* 2, ii, pp. 77-78.

[98] Ibid., p. 78.

[99] Ibid.: "Quem ad curiam Romanam, pro negotiis nostris, ibidem procurandis, nuper sub magna confidentia destinavimus, spreto fidelitatis et ligeantiae suae debito, ac juramenti, per ipsum nobis praestiti de honore nostro pro viribus conservando, religione contempta, episcopatum Wyntoniensem ... acceptavit."

appropriate authorities in other maritime towns.[100] They were to seize letters relating to Stratford's promotion, or that of John Eaglescliff as bishop of Llandaff, for he was guilty of the same offence.[101] The request made by the papal vice-chancellor, Cardinal Pierre le Tessier, on behalf of his nephew was brushed aside; so great was the king's anger at receiving letters from the "faithless and ungrateful" Stratford that he was quite unable to respond favourably.[102]

Edward continued to bombard the pope with his views of English prelates whose rule, stemming from the vice of base ingratitude, had brought such notorious misfortunes to the realm. Charge of the more important positions in the land should by no means be entrusted to men of that stamp, particularly in the conditions obtaining at the time.[103] Stratford, sent to the curia on royal business, had knowingly ignored the king's wishes. Indeed, he had acted in such a matter as to circumvent them – that nursling of damnable ingratitude.[104] The provision of Stratford should be revoked and the Winchester chapter permitted to enjoy free election! The king's "dearest friend" Cardinal Napoleone Orsini was asked to bring the royal letters to the pope's attention.[105] A spate of correspondence followed, addressed to cardinals, papal "nephews," and to a citizen of Bordeaux, John Colom, who was sent to Avignon.[106]

Edward's letter of 17 August, directed to the pope and to various members of his *familia*,[107] concentrated its attack on the integrity of Stratford as an ambassador, dubbing him "pseudo-nuncius"; responsibility for the captious delay (morosa dilatio) in the king's business was

---

[100] Ibid.

[101] Ibid. John of Monmouth died 8 April 1323 (*CPR 1317-1321*, p. 810); on 31 May the canons were given licence to elect (*CPR 1321-1324*, p. 293). The king assented to Alexander of Monmouth's election 15 July (ibid., p. 326). Meanwhile, 20 June, Pope John translated Eaglescliff from Connor (*CPL 1305-1342*, p. 232), to which he had recently been translated from Glasgow, against the king's wish. Despite this, on 8 August Archbishop Reynolds instructed Bishop Orleton to examine the process of Alexander's election. This he did at Bromyard 7 September, certifying the archbishop on the 8th. *Hereford Reg. Orleton*, pp. 261-264; and see Smith, *Episcopal Appointments*, pp. 38-39.

[102] *Foedera* 2, ii, p. 79: "Tantus animi rancor et indignatio nos commovit, quod supplicatio pro dicto valetto annuere non possumus ista vice."

[103] Ibid., p. 80.

[104] Ibid.: "veluti dampnandae ingratitudinis alumpnus."

[105] Ibid.

[106] Ibid., pp. 80ff. For Colom see PRO S.C.8/38/25; 48/153 (*War of Saint-Sardos*, p. 90); 50/43, 51; 54/3(iii)7.

[107] Including Pierre, viscount of Caraman, the pope's brother, and Arnaud de Trian (cf. n. 82 above). *Foedera* 2, ii, p. 82.

attributed to his lukewarmness and inactivity.[108] Such neglect of his principal's concerns could be contrasted with the envoy's tireless pursuit of his own ambitions.[109] All these accusations were regurgitated in Stratford's direction, together with the information that his erstwhile colleague, M. Adam Murimuth, was being sent in his place to Avignon to prosecute the affairs he had neglected and to initiate others.[110] Under penalty of all he possessed, Stratford was ordered to surrender to his successor every item of diplomatic material and to inform the king of the current state of negotiations.

Hardly had these two letters issued from the chancery than Pope John's conflicting analysis of Stratford's behaviour was despatched from the curia.[111] Stratford, he claimed, had been chosen as a person who had exhibited much zeal and laboured sedulously in Edward's service; as someone, moreover, who was well equipped with learning, experienced in business, of praiseworthy life, and endowed with remarkable gifts of grace. A native of England, his equable and trustworthy behaviour had made him acceptable to the cardinals.[112] In the circumstances the pope could not retract the promotion, but he did wish the king to know that his initial letters on Baldock's behalf had arrived on 9 May and that Stratford had duly presented them. As God bears witness, he affirmed, the ambassador had acted as a faithful executant of the king's policies before both the pope himself and the cardinals. It was despite his efforts that other counsels prevailed. In the first place, certain things touching Baldock had been related to the cardinals. Stratford was wholly ignorant of this and, the pope added, for good reason he himself forbore to give details in a letter.[113] Secondly, following Assier's death, the cardinals under God's inspiration had come to a discussion of Stratford's suitability

---

[108] Ibid., pp. 82-83: "Pro nostris negotiis ibidem procurandis, nuper destinati, illis neglectis et omissis."

[109] Ibid.: "Ad propriam ambitionem appetitum noxium convertentes."

[110] Ibid. and see *Murimuth*, p. 40.

[111] *Foedera* 2, ii, p. 83.

[112] Ibid.: "Pro arduis et utilibus tuis et regni tui negotiis, denuo fuerat ad nostram praesentiam destinatus; intuentes insuper solicitudinis magnae zelum, vigilis diligentiae studium, sedulosque labores, quibus fideliter, solerter, et utiliter penes nos, et fratres nostros sanctae Romanae ecclesiae cardinales, regia negotia promovebat; considerantes etiam, quod vir est litterarum scientia praeditus, in rebus agendis expertus, vitae laudabilis, et multis gratiarum dotibus insignitus, et de regno Angliae oriundus, et quod, per ejus conversationem placidam et honestam, quam in Romana curia nobiscum, et cum eisdem fratribus plurimum reddebatur acceptus."

[113] Ibid.: "Sed tunc propter aliqua de persona dicti Roberti, nobis, et dictis fratribus, querelose relata, dicto Johanne id penitus ignorante, quae ex causa praesentibus subtacemus."

and found themselves unable to acquiesce in the king's desire.[114] In a subsequent communication[115] Pope John repudiated the allegation of Stratford's negligence. It was his own multifarious occupations which had slowed down business; in such unrewarding conditions he could only commend the persistence of the royal envoy.[116] As for Edward's claim to a portion of Provence, the pope professed to lack precise information as well as opportunity to communicate with King Robert of Sicily.[117]

Predictably the papal apologia fell on unresponsive ears; all the more so because of another wholly disconnected event. The escape of the younger Roger Mortimer from the Tower, most appropriately on the feast of St. Peter ad Vincula (1 August), had heightened Edward's determination to harry those who opposed him.[118] His agents were becoming jumpy. A note of explanation and apology had to be sent to Avignon when clerks of Cardinal Raymond de *Ruffi* [Roux] were arrested at Dover and unceremoniously gaoled. It was not, apologized Edward, Archbishop Reynolds' doing, as some had maliciously averred. Surely the pope was not unaware that sedition was rife in England? Absconders from prison were joining other malcontents on the continent and hatching conspiracies. He had done what he could. Once the clerks had been brought before him he had secured their release. He trusted that the pope would consider the archbishop fully exonerated.[119] Such arguments might help to explain; they could hardly excuse such an untoward incident. For his part the pope waited for the royal anger against his nominee to subside. In a letter of 13 September 1323 commending the new bishop of Winchester to his reluctant master, he explained that he had been obliged to retain Stratford at the curia because of business for which his help was essential.[120]

---

[114] Ibid.: "Tum etiam, quia statum, post ejusdem Rigaldi decessum, inspirante Domino, firmiter deliberavimus de persona dicti Johannis praeficienda ecclesiae memoratae."

[115] Ibid., p. 84: 13 September 1323.

[116] Ibid.: "Quapropter eum, super mora prolixa, quam in curia contraxisse noscitur, excusantes: et de diligentia, quam in praedictis prudenter adhibuit, multipliciter commendantes."

[117] Ibid., p. 84.

[118] Haines, *Church and Politics*, pp. 108-109, 143-144.

[119] *Foedera* 2, ii, p. 85.

[120] Vatican Archives, *RV* 112, fol. 184[r] [40[r] in *CPL*]: "Propter occupaciones tamen multiplices quibus anxiamur continue supra vires ipsum nequivimus cicius expedire." Cf. *CPL 1305-1342*, p. 455; *Foedera* 2, ii, p. 84. In another letter, 29 December, the pope declared that he accepted Edward's arguments in Baldock's favour, whom he was now prepared to receive into his grace. Vatican Archives, *RV* 112, fol. 186[r] [42[r] in *CPL*]; *CPL 1305-1342*, p. 456. By a strange error the MS has "Johannes Escorforden" as the new bishop of Winchester, hence the confusion in *CPL*: "John, bishop of Hereford, whom the

It was against this background that towards the end of November the king commenced his quasi-judicial attack on the former ambassador. On entering London Stratford had been intercepted on the king's warrant by the city officers, and the bulls he was carrying seized.[121] As soon as Edward heard the news he sent the younger Despenser, his chamberlain, Geoffrey le Scrope, justice of the Bench, and M. Robert de Ayleston, keeper of the privy seal, collectively described as trusted "secretaries," with instructions to elicit an exposition of the state of English negotiations at the curia. Stratford is said to have declined to respond in their presence, thereby incurring a charge of contempt.[122] Consequently, he was summoned to appear before Hervy de Staunton and his associate justices on 25 November 1323.[123] The writ was delivered to Stratford in the Carmelite cloister at Nottingham by one of the king's sergeants-at-arms.[124] But Stratford failed to appear on the appointed day to make his excuses, thereby compounding his contempt. He did present himself on the 28th, when he returned the writ. At that stage he was ordered to bring into court the indenture which set out the nature of the king's business entrusted jointly to him and to Assier, the late bishop of Winchester.[125]

Stratford obediently produced the indenture, handing it to M. Robert de Ayleston. The document listed nine items, some of which help to fill in our knowledge of curial transactions. The first four concern themselves with Scotland. The envoys were instructed to secure an intensification of the ecclesiastical sentences against the rebellious Scots, whose imperviousness to the church's censures smacked of heresy.[126] The remaining three Scottish items pertain to the episcopate. The king had no wish to see Scotsmen as bishops; they fostered political unrest. The mooted translation out of Scotland of the Englishman John Eaglescliff, bishop of Glasgow, would be prejudicial to royal interests, as Stratford was said to

pope has translated to ... Winchester." Adam Orleton was, of course, the Hereford diocesan.

[121] *Cal. PMR*, pp. 3-4.

[122] *CChW*, p. 546 (PRO C.81/125/6744). There was an administrative confusion since the king directed that Stratford should be summoned before the justices rather than the chancellor, but two days later (24 November) Edward's inspection of a transcript of the chancellor's writ revealed that it contained no date for appearance – the most important element! Ibid. (PRO C.81/128/7022). See also *CCR 1323-1327*, pp. 1, 147. The use of the word "secretarius" is considered by Tout, *Chapters* 2, p. 19.

[123] *Foedera* 2, ii, p. 89: s.a. 1324, *recte* 1323.

[124] Ibid., ii, p. 90: s.a. 1324.

[125] Ibid.

[126] This, of course, was a commonplace in such circumstances – failure to obey ecclesiastical mandates.

be in a position to demonstrate. Lastly, the king insisted that when bishops were appointed to Scottish sees, application for livery of the temporalities should be made to the English king and to no one else. This, he asserted, was the usual practice.[127]

Stratford had no difficulty in responding to these particular items, and in such a way as to make the king's councillors at home look rather foolish, as well as guilty of double-dealing. The pope, he declared, had instructed Cardinals Frédol and Montfavèz to resume the processes against the Scots and to "aggravate" them if necessary. At great expense of time and money he had reduced an unwieldy process of vast complexity to manageable order. Following Assier's death he had presented the case to the cardinals. It was only when they were apprised of the king's accommodation with the Scots, accompanied by a copy of the truce arranged for thirteen years on 30 May 1323, that this policy was abandoned. Peace then became the primary objective. In any case, one article of the truce specifically declared that with Edward's consent such sentences might be relaxed. In the event of absolution all that he, Stratford, could do, was to press the pope to maintain royal rights and to minimize damage to the English church.[128] As for the remaining Scottish articles, the pope had replied that since no Englishman could enter Scotland in safety, souls would be imperilled if the king's premise were to be upheld. The bishopric of Glasgow exemplified the point; the pope declined to entertain such requests. Temporalities were a different matter; here the pope claimed to have written regularly to the king for their livery in the accustomed manner.

The remaining five articles touched Edward more nearly. The Ordinances had already been abrogated in the York parliament of 1322, while the king had seemingly been absolved from his personal oath to respect them as long before as 1320. What remained were the oaths undertaken by the prelates and magnates in derogation, so Edward alleged, of royal rights and of the crown. This matter, Stratford answered, was to prove difficult, though eventually the pope was prevailed upon to accede to the request. Bulls were being sent to Archbishop Reynolds to enable him to accomplish whatever might seem expedient for the king's honour and that of the realm.

[127] This indenture and subsequent process provide a rare insight into the way in which envoys worked and the limitations imposed upon them. An individual negotiator's success or failure seems to have depended upon skilful tactics rather than on strategy, which was predetermined. For Eaglescliff see above, n. 101.

[128] For this and what follows see Stratford's "Responsio domini papae": *Foedera* 2, ii, pp. 90ff.

Two of the articles relate to the prebends of Aylesbury and Leighton Buzzard and the rejection of the *excusaciones* advanced on behalf of Baldock and Ayrminne, the royal clerks. Pope John deftly side-stepped the issue by pronouncing his complete support for royal rights of presentation and collation, but castigating the inordinate greed of certain clerks who showed no consideration for the king's honour. It would be improper for him to intervene, he added, since the cases were *sub judice*. By the same token, the "excuses" of the parties having been set forth in the ablest manner by Stratford, papal intervention could only prejudice the outcome. Despite the envoy's insistence that the clerks in question were urgently required at the king's side, the pope would add nothing to what he had already said.

The last two articles, eight and nine, are enigmatic and Stratford's responses equally so. One has to do with "certain prelates," presumably those accused of rebellious activities; the other has reference to a secret message about the creation of cardinals which had been confided to Stratford on his return. The former gave rise to a bull entrusted to M. Robert of Canterbury, the latter to an expression of the king's thanks. It would appear that the man whom Edward had in mind for the cardinalate was Roger Northburgh, bishop of Coventry and Lichfield.[129] In the long run nothing came of this.

Other articles ranging beyond the scope of the indenture had been entrusted subsequently to Assier and Stratford; for these too the latter was called upon to answer. The chief item was the biennial tenth to be raised from the English clergy, which Edward wished to divert to his own purposes. In responding to his interrogators Stratford stressed the considerable difficulty he had encountered before the required bulls could be carried by his own donzel to the king.[130] The procedure had been complicated by the pope's intention to reserve a fourth part of the tenth for himself. This manoeuvre Stratford had circumvented by refusing to carry the requisite bulls to England. Instead he consented to take back others which could give the king opportunity to discuss the matter with his council.[131] In Stratford's opinion the lack of information about the problems discussed at York (presumably the king's urgent financial

---

[129] Edward had written on his behalf to pope and cardinals in 1320 and 1321, prior to his promotion as bishop. See *Foedera* 2, ii, pp. 7-8, 22.

[130] Ibid., p. 91.

[131] Ibid.: "Papa voluit sibi tradidisse bullas ... pro exactione quartae memoratae: quas portare recusavit, eo quod tendebant in dampnum domini nostri regis."

requirements), and the non-payment of papal tribute, had seriously hampered the progress of royal affairs at the curia.[132]

The remaining business "outside the indenture" was speedily dispensed with. In his defence Stratford merely drew attention to the executive action taken. Two bulls were obtained for the Dominican friars, doubtless in connection with the royal plans for King's Langley; another was intended to facilitate Edward's confession. On the subject of the king's claims in Provence the pope was sending a "bulla clausa," and for the Cistercian monks of Thame authority to appropriate Chalgrove church.[133]

At least to his own satisfaction, Stratford had decisively demonstrated his effectiveness as an advocate. He had also managed to give more than a hint of the shortcomings of the authorities at home. The case was adjourned until 20 January 1324, to give the justices time to consider Stratford's replies. In the meantime a writ dated 26 November 1323 from Ravensdale, prior to the session before Staunton, required the envoy to present himself *coram rege* on the morrow of St. Nicholas, that is 7 December.[134] He complied, but having already been assigned a day he was not called upon to make further response. When he did reappear before Staunton in January it was at Hereford. There the justice was heading a commission for the examination of alleged contrariants, including Bishop Orleton.[135] The question of the Aylesbury and Leighton Buzzard prebends was singled out for further investigation. In a sense this reveals the narrowness of the scope of the enquiry and its personal bias. The beneficial concerns of royal clerks stood paramount; broad issues affecting the country's policy and fundamental interests were not reopened. But we need to remember that behind the concerns of the moment lay the principle of unfettered exercise of the *ius regale* with respect to ecclesiastical appointments in vacant sees or, as in this case, in those in which the temporalities were in the king's hand for punitive reasons.[136] Pope and king were certain to be equally adamant over such an issue.

---

[132] Ibid.: "Et certe non solutio census; et pro eo quod non fuerit dicta praelocuta, fuit maximum impedimentum negotiorum regiorum in curia Romana."

[133] *CPL 1305-1342*, pp. 200, 221. The second of these bulls, concerning Chalgrove, is dated 29 May 1322.

[134] *Foedera* 2, ii, p. 91. From another source we know that the king himself was at Ravensdale at this time: BL Add. MS 35114, fol. 7r.

[135] PRO Just. 1/1388; K.B.27/254/Rex mm. 38r-39r: summarizes proceedings against Stratford until his summons to the February 1324 parliament – the source of the *Foedera* entry. For Orleton see Haines, *Church and Politics*, pp. 144-145ff.; idem., "Defence Brief."

[136] On this point see Wright, *Church and Crown*, pp. 155-157ff., and in general, Howell, *Regalian Right*.

Stratford continued by demonstrating his appointment as Baldock's proctor for arranging a settlement with Cardinal Gailhard. Finding that there was no hope of a successful outcome on that basis, he submitted both himself and Baldock to the arbitration of Cardinal Bertrand de Montfavèz, whom the pope deputed for the purpose. In doing so he had been careful to make reservation of royal rights. But before the case could proceed he was obliged to provide surety of two thousand marks. This done, Cardinal Bertrand made his award, a copy of which remained in Stratford's possession in London. From this instrument it could be verified that the *ius regale* was duly safeguarded. If anything had been done contrary to or in addition to his commission, which he did not believe to be the case, it could only be to his own loss. Stratford then proceeded in similar fashion to deal with the corresponding conflict between William Ayrminne and Jean de Puy Barsac with respect to Leighton Buzzard. The examination concluded at this point with the justices' direction that Stratford make a further appearance on 9 February. This he did, only to be informed of a royal writ transferring the case to the parliament summoned to meet at Westminster on 23 February 1324. We do not know how he fared there.[137]

The attack on Stratford – it can be described in no other way – finds a striking parallel in that conducted simultaneously against Orleton. Since both bishops were of Pope John's creation the coincidence merits closer examination. The king's animus against Orleton was rekindled by Roger Mortimer's escape, an event which could have determined Edward to move with equal vigour against Stratford. Orleton too appeared before Staunton at Hereford (three days after Stratford) and subsequently (at about the same time) before the February 1324 parliament. It may be indicative of the different responses of the two men that Orleton's defiant stance impressed certain of the chroniclers, while Stratford's judicial appearance merited no comment. The manner of citation, to which Orleton was to take exception, suggests the intervention of those close to the monarch. Indeed, it is tempting to see the royal hand behind both prosecutions.[138]

Following his trial, if such it can be called, Stratford was to spend some months in limbo. He could do little about his diocesan responsibilities

---

[137] The king's writ is dated from Worcester, 15 January 1324. *Foedera* 2, ii, p. 91; *Parl. Writs* 2, ii, p. 241; *CCR 1318-1323*, p. 154. Justice Hervy de Staunton was directed to assign a day for Stratford to appear. Quite when his case came up is uncertain. Orleton appeared on the second day of the parliament, as mentioned below.

[138] See above, n. 135.

until his temporalities were restored. This was not the only financial restraint imposed upon him. It was not until February 1325 that he was permitted to submit an account for the recovery of his expenses at Avignon. The initial allowance of £200 had been far exceeded and Stratford was left to bear the deficit himself.[139] The king continued to resist any papal provision to the prebends he had wished to confer on his own clerks, on the grounds that this would be to his disinheritance.[140] But before long Edward's attitude towards Stratford began to soften. In a letter sent to the curia, probably towards the end of March 1324, Bishop Cobham of Worcester expressed his views about the predicament of those bishops who remained under the cloud of Edward's displeasure – Orleton, Stratford and Burghersh. Orleton's situation remained as before, but that of Stratford and Burghersh was promising. Cobham had approached the king on Stratford's behalf and received a favourable reply.[141] In any case, Stratford's anomalous position did not preclude his cooperation with the other bishops. On 1 June 1324 he joined with Archbishop Reynolds and eight other diocesans of the Canterbury province in a letter to the pope bemoaning the unfortunate effects likely to arise from a war that appeared imminent and asking him to do whatever he could to secure a lasting peace.[142]

Eventually, on 28 June, writs were issued for the livery by the royal custodians of the Winchester temporalities.[143] Even at this stage Stratford

---

[139] The total expenditure came to £268 4s 9d. The writ of 13 February permitted Stratford to submit his account up to 12 July 1323: "quo die electus fuit in episcopum Wynton." See PRO E.101/309/27 m. 3; *CCR 1323-1327*, p. 256. In 1323 the sheriffs of London had been instructed to take Stratford's goods and chattels left as surety for wardrobe payments. The sheriff of Warwickshire, the bishops of Lincoln, Chichester and Coventry and Lichfield, and later the dean and chapter of Lincoln, were directed to sequestrate other property of his. *CFR 1319-1327*, pp. 221, 238-239. This process was not reversed until 28 June 1324. See n. 143 below.

[140] *Foedera* 2, ii, p. 100: Westminster, 6 June 1324: "Cum absque exhaeredationis periculo sustinere utique non possumus, quod provisio fieret de dicta praebenda."

[141] *Worcester Reg. Cobham*, fols. 94ᵛ-95ʳ, pp. 168-170; Haines, *Church and Politics*, p. 151.

[142] *Rochester Reg. Hethe*, pp. 339-341.

[143] *Foedera* 2, ii, p. 101; PRO S.C.8/139/6903 (Stratford's undated petition for livery). Richard Ayrminne and William de Pillaunde were the custodians. Stratford had to concede "se velle temporalia episcopatus praedicti recipere ex nostra liberatione et gratia speciali." The *Historia Roffensis* records (BL Cotton MS Faustina B.v, fol. 43ᵛ) that after sustaining many persecutions at the instigation of Chancellor Baldock, Stratford was reconciled to the king on the feast of St. John the Baptist (his nativity, 24 June?) at Tonbridge. Certainly it was at Tonbridge that the writs for restitution were dated, including one for goods and chattels impounded since the summer of 1323. *CCR 1323-1327*, p. 117, and see n. 139 above.

was not to be excused, but was summoned to appear in the king's palace at Westminster. There, at the royal command conveyed by Chancellor Baldock,[144] who was present for the proceedings, Sir Roger Beler, baron of the exchequer, read out a formal protestation on the subject of the papal provision to Winchester.[145] Somewhat ingenuously this professed to set out the traditional method of appointing archbishops and bishops in the English realm.[146] Until King John's reign right of appointment was said to have belonged to the monarchs. John, by counsel and consent of the barons, granted freedom of election, saving to the king and his successors the custody of vacant churches.[147] Under this system, before proceeding to election the electors were to secure royal licence, then to present the elect for the king's assent, which might be refused for good reason (ex causa racionabili). Following royal assent the elect had to seek his temporalities from the monarch. And so, it was concluded, the grace conceded to Stratford out of reverence for Pope John was by no means to be taken as a precedent.[148]

Stratford was called upon to accede to the protestation. At the same time he expressly renounced any right by virtue of his provision to administer the temporalities, as well as anything else contained in the papal letters deemed prejudicial to the king or crown. Such oaths had been enforced against provisors since the late-thirteenth century.[149] Having consented to receive the temporalities as an act of the king's special grace, Stratford was permitted to take the oath of fealty in the presence of Walter Stapeldon, bishop of Exeter and royal treasurer, and of the two chief justices, Geoffrey le Scrope of the King's Bench and William Bereford of the Common Pleas.[150]

This was not all. Stratford was subjected to a severe financial penalty; one which made a lasting inroad on the temporalities of his see. He was

---

[144] Baldock became chancellor 20 August 1323. *HBC*, p. 84.

[145] *Foedera* 2, ii, p. 101: 30 June 1324; PRO S.C.7/56/17 (attached document). For Beler see Buck, *Walter Stapeldon*, index s.v.

[146] A similar declaration had been made at the time of Orleton's promotion to Hereford in 1317. Haines, *Church and Politics*, p. 30 n. 17. In this instance the ecclesiastical part of the process, e.g. papal and metropolitan confirmation, is omitted.

[147] *Councils and Synods*, pp. 38-41 (s.a. 1214).

[148] Eaglescliff also had to acknowledge that he received his temporalities of royal grace and to pay a thousand marks. *CPR 1324-1327*, p. 11.

[149] Wright, *Church and Crown*, pp. 157-163. For Bishop Gainsburgh of Worcester's submission: *Worc. Admin.*, p. 76.

[150] *Foedera* 2, ii, p. 101. Stratford's obligations may be summarized as follows 1. Acceptance of the royal protestation; 2. Renunciation of rights to temporalities by virtue of provision; 3. Necessity to petition for temporalities "de gracia speciali"; 4. Recognition that he received them only by the king's special grace.

forced to enter into a recognizance with the king for the crippling sum of £10,000; £2,000 of which was payable on demand, the remainder being held over as a bond for the bishop's good behaviour. This means of bringing the bishop to subservience was later to be laid at Baldock's door; the king himself was in 1326 to disclaim any intention of exacting the full amount.[151] It represents an extension to the ecclesiastical sphere of a practice common among the laity. Faced with a similar demand, Orleton rejected as unlawful so manifest a subjugation of his bishopric to lay power. Rather than prejudice his position he chose to subsist without his temporalities.[152] Stratford's later petition (of 1327?) to the king and council urged that in view of the losses sustained at the hands of royal custodians the cathedral chapter might in future be permitted to administer the temporalities at times of vacancy. He was speaking from personal experience.[153] In 1324, regardless of the inroads made by the custodians, the new diocesan was called upon to pay a sum little short of £2,500 for growing crops.[154]

Before long Edward was able to explain to the papal envoy, M. Hugh d'Angoulême, and to Henry de Sully who accompanied him, why his position towards Stratford had softened. The reasons are set out in a letter sent to the pope from Porchester on 10 July 1324. Pope John, said Edward, had shown him much favour: he had managed to restrain the Scots, though they were in fact dissemblers secretly persisting in their stubbornness; he had endeavoured to arrange peace with France; above all he had taken back Baldock into his grace. The king went on to assure the pope that the "suggestions" made against his trusted clerk in the curia were without foundation and thanked him for recalling the Aylesbury case to his own audience – a most deferential concession.[155]

---

[151] Ibid., pp. 174-175; *CCR 1323-1327*, p. 198; ibid., *1327-1330*, p. 24; *CMRE*, nos. 521-522, 911, 1488. Fryde, "John Stratford and the Crown," pp. 160-161, provides a useful table of the "Financial transactions of John Stratford with the royal government 1322-1330."

[152] Haines, *Church and Politics*, p. 150 n. 77, where the note summarizes Orleton's feelings on the matter expressed in a damaged copy of his letter: BL Cotton MS Vitellius E.iv 9.

[153] PRO S.C.8/15/719: "Comme nostre seint piere le pape lui dona levesche laquele le dit Johan troua ut destruite en maisons, en boys, en viners, en parkes et en autres choses et auxint troua ses gentz molt damagees par les gardeins le piere le dit nostre seignur le Roi qi dieux assoill." Endorsed "Coram magno consilio," with the instruction that the treasurer and barons of the exchequer search the rolls and remembrances for information about earlier vacancies. The chancellor summoned the treasurer and others of the king's council to have a charter drawn up in accordance with the petition.

[154] *Foedera* 2, ii, p. 174; *CCR 1323-1327*, p. 203. The unpaid portion of the £2,460 5s 10d was remitted in 1327: *CMRE*, no. 333.

[155] *Foedera* 2, ii, p. 104. Baldock was not in practice fully rehabilitated. John XXII was

The change of front can be otherwise accounted for. Edward had urgent need of papal assistance. The situation in Aquitaine had been badly mishandled. Having agreed to surrender Montpezat whose lord, together with the seneschal of Gascony, had been responsible for the destruction of the Saint-Sardos *bastide*, the English ambassadors reversed their decision.[156] At the same time they sought to postpone Edward's overdue homage.[157] The French king, Charles iv, promptly confiscated Gascony and Ponthieu. Invasion followed, and with the capitulation of La Réole on 22 September most of Gascony submitted to Charles.[158] It was a virtual repetition of what had happened under Philip the Fair in the 1290s.[159]

At home preparation for an expedition to Aquitaine, for maritime defence against French invasion,[160] and for a definitive peace with the Scots, gave way to more panicky measures which were certain to bring reprisals or were themselves intended as such: the arrest of all Frenchmen,[161] seizure of the lands of alien priories and those of Queen Isabella,[162]

to point out in 1326 that his absolution from excommunication was to enable him to receive a benefice, not to recover the Aylesbury prebend from Cardinal Gailhard (*CPL 1305-1342*, p. 252). Despite Edward's strenuous efforts he was not permitted to become bishop of Norwich, though he acted as bishop elect and confirmed from 29 August 1325 (NNRO, Reg. 1/2/ fol. 1ʳ). It has been suggested (Smith, *Episcopal Appointments*, pp. 42-43, citing *Foedera* (R.C.) 2, p. 560, i.e. *Foedera* 2, ii, p. 104) that a possible reason for Stratford's acceptance was Edward's anxiety to improve Baldock's chances at Norwich. This is to mistake the year; the see did not fall vacant until early July 1325.

[156] *War of Saint-Sardos*, p. 188 n. 1, where an extract from PRO C.47/30/6/17 sums up the conditions accepted by Edmund, earl of Kent, and Archbishop Bicknor.

[157] For the ambassadors' letters of credence and detailed instructions, see *War of Saint-Sardos*, pp. 181-188.

[158] Ibid., pp. 189-190ff.; Perroy. *Hundred Years' War*, pp. 64-66.

[159] Fryde, "Financial Resources of Edward i and Some Comparisons with Edward iii." More generally, Déprez, *Les préliminaires*, chap. 1; Chaplais, "English Arguments concerning Aquitaine"; idem., "Le Duché-Pairie de Guyenne."

[160] *Foedera* 2, ii, pp. 104ff. As bishop of Winchester Stratford was ordered (4 August 1324) to take the oaths of those deputed to guard the ports in the county of Hampshire and the Isle of Wight. Commissioners of array were appointed (6 August); Archbishop Reynolds and most of the bishops (including Droxford and Burghersh, but excluding Orleton) were called upon to assist: "Mandavimus enim praefatis custodibus per se, et praefatis arraiatoribus per se, quod ad vos, pro informatione in praemissis habenda, quotiens opus fuerit, accedant, et ea faciant quae per vos, et ipsos, super hoc contigerit ordinari."

[161] Envoys to negotiate a "final peace" with Bruce were appointed 15 July 1324 (*Foedera* 2, ii, p. 104); orders for the arrest of Frenchmen were issued on the 21st, Charles iv having given instructions on 24 June to impede the passage of Englishmen at the ports. A further writ of 18 September barred exception for members of the king's household or that of the queen. See ibid., pp. 105, 111; *War of Saint-Sardos*, pp. 190-191. These measures caused many inconveniences, for instance to the queen, Hugh d'Angoulême the papal nuncio, and to John of Brittany (Jean de Bretagne), earl of

as well as of benefices held by foreigners.[163] But more constructive counsel was to prevail. About the end of September 1324 it was proposed that the English case against France should be placed before the papal curia and that Stratford, with the aid of two or three clerks from the king's council, should review the agreements reached in Edward I's time, together with subsequent developments. By such means it would be possible to establish Edward II's innocence of any infringements – or so it was thought.[164]

The idea was readily adopted. Pope John, eager to emulate the peace-making activities of his predecessors Boniface VIII and Clement V in the time of Edward I and Philip the Fair, was already planning to send as his emissaries William, archbishop of Vienne, and Hugh, bishop of Orange. The Pauline annalist seems to be correct in his statement that they arrived on 8 November and departed on the 21st,[165] for on both the 11th and the 20th they dined with Edward in the Tower, and at their leave-taking on the 21st received presents from his treasure stored there.[166] Less agreeable to the king were other aspects of the emissaries' instructions; to take up the cases of the bishops of Hereford and Lincoln, still languishing without their temporalities,[167] and to press for payment of arrears of tribute and of a portion of the biennial tenth.[168] A letter sent to the pope at this time by Bishop Cobham of Worcester, reveals the temper of those bishops who

Richmond. They embarrassed the English envoys in France (*War of Saint-Sardos*, pp. 128, 130-131).

[162] *Foedera* 2, ii, pp. 110, 114-115. In Isabella's case the view has been advanced (e.g. Tout, *Chapters* 5, pp. 274-275) that this was not really a punitive measure engineered by the Despensers, as some chroniclers would have us believe. E.g. *Vita*, pp. 135, 142. It is doubtful whether the queen herself would have agreed. See, for instance, McKisack, *Fourteenth Century*, p. 81; Blackley, "Isabella," pp. 225-226; Fryde, *Tyranny of Edward II*, p. 146; Buck, *Walter Stapeldon*, pp. 151-152, 175. That Bishop Stapeldon had a prominent hand in the affair must in retrospect have seemed particularly galling.

[163] *Foedera* 2, ii, p. 115. Here individual exceptions had soon to be made for the cardinals, whose interests in English benefices are tabled by Wright, *Church and Crown*, App. 3, pp. 285-308.

[164] *War of Saint-Sardos*, pp. 68-69 (from PRO C.47/27/12/50).

[165] *Annales Paulini*, p. 308. This is close to the 6-21 November of Bishop Cobham's letter (n. 169 below). See also *Foedera* 2, ii, pp. 109, 118, 120; *Treaty Rolls* 1 (from PRO C.76/10), pp. 246-248 (no. 638).

[166] BL Egerton MS 2814; PRO E.101/381/4. I owe both these references to *War of Saint-Sardos*, p. 192 n. 1.

[167] *Foedera* 2, ii, p. 120: 19 November 1324. Only the bishop of Lincoln is specifically mentioned here, followed by "et alios," but see the later instruction in *Lettres secrètes Jean XXII*, no. 2508; *CPL 1305-1342*, pp. 465-466 (Haines, *Church and Politics*, p. 152 n. 85, where "had earlier" should read "were later").

[168] *Foedera* 2, ii, p. 120.

owed their sees to papal provision. Four of them, Bishops Stratford of Winchester, Burghersh of Lincoln, Eaglescliff of Llandaff,[169] and Cobham himself, are said to have escorted the papal envoys to their lodgings and on the following morning to the royal palace of Westminster. It was a demonstration of solidarity; only Cobham's promotion had been effected without conflict.[170] Somewhat arcane phrases in a much damaged copy of one of Orleton's letters suggest that he too may have wished to be a member of the reception committee, or at any rate to have converse with the envoys, but was prevented by threats of violence.[171]

The main outcome of the discussions was the decision to send an embassy to treat with King Charles. It comprised John Salmon, bishop of Norwich, Stratford as the second bishop, John of Brittany, earl of Richmond, and the Henry de Beaumont who had been angered by Edward's accommodation with the Scots.[172] In the ambassadors' letter of credence Edward wrote of the papal envoys' intervention in the cause of peace and besought Charles to have a concern for the Holy Land and the harmony of Christendom.[173] A few days later he thanked the pope for the successful intervention of his emissaries.[174] The new policy had enabled Stratford to reestablish himself as a diplomat; this was to be the first of four missions to the continent undertaken in quick succession. As a bishop he was elevated to a far higher level in the diplomatic hierarchy; nothing could be decided at Paris unless one or other of the bishops was party to the arrangement.

The ambassadors were empowered to treat for peace, to arrange a meeting between Edward and Charles, to repossess Aquitaine and Ponthieu and to take the oath of fealty for them in the king's name, as well as to settle the multifarious conflicts arising from the warlike dissensions

---

[169] Originally I accepted (*Church and Politics*, p. 152) Pearce's transcription as "London" (*Worcester Reg. Cobham*, p. 173). In fact the MS register (fol. 96ʳ) reads "Landaven," which is better sense. The four are described as "Episcopi qui sunt prout noscis de sede apostolica procreati" [Gravesend was not "provided"]. Lower down, the papal envoys are said to have been entertained for fifteen days.

[170] The "hospicium" is taken by Pearce to be the Worcester bishops' house in the Strand. Smith, *Episcopal Appointments*, pp. 26-27, suggests (without evidence) that Cobham had been in disfavour since his candidature for the see of Canterbury in 1313. For the other promotions see ibid., s.v.

[171] BL Cotton MS Vitellius E.iv 9; Haines, *Church and Politics*, pp. 150-151, n. 77; 152 n. 85.

[172] *Foedera* 2, ii, pp. 118-119: 15 November 1324; *War of Saint-Sardos*, p. 192.

[173] *War of Saint-Sardos*, p. 192.

[174] *Foedera* 2, ii, p. 120 (19 November 1324): "Digna laudum praeconia et uberes gratiarum actiones vestrae referimus sanctitati."

between the English and French monarchs.[175] We know that Stratford
was still at Canterbury on 8 December, because on that day he despatched
one of his messengers (nuntii), Adam,[176] to secure last-minute instructions
from the king and his councillors at Nottingham. It was three days later
that he and his entourage, numbering eighty-three persons, were ready to
make the crossing from Dover in a ship provided by William de Shephey
(Sheppey) at a cost of £3; two further ships, one supplied by Shephey, the
other by William Gyles, served to carry the fifty-four horses and their
harness and equipment. Arrived at Wissant, the bishop was escorted to
the house of James the goldsmith, where he lodged. From there he sent a
courier (cursor) to contact the archbishop of Vienne and the bishop of
Orange, who were already in Paris. The date of Stratford's arrival in the
capital is not known. The first mention of his being there is on 26
December, the feast of St. Stephen, when his man Adam came from
Nottingham with the king's reply to the points raised before Stratford left
England.[177]

The negotiations hung fire. Stratford was later to report that the French
were prevaricating and keeping the English envoys waiting about.[178]
About the second week of January 1325 the bishop left Paris for the coast.
There a fierce channel storm was raging. Twice the bishop's party – now
reduced to eighty persons – and the horses were loaded into barges and
taken out to the ships waiting off Wissant. Twice they were brought back
again. Only at the third attempt did it prove possible to set sail. Special
gifts were given to the sailors and other helpers at Wissant who performed
the tedious task of repeated loading and unloading. Even then, it would
seem, a shift in the wind meant that a number of Stratford's household
and all the horses had to remain in port for a further ten days.[179]

Stratford reached Dover on 13 January 1325, bearing with him the
papal envoys' suggestions for a settlement and the statement for delivery
to the king's council agreed upon by the royal ambassadors.[180] During his

[175] Ibid., pp. 118-119; *Treaty Rolls* 1, pp. 248-253 (nos. 639-647). Stratford's letters of
protection, dated 11 November 1324, are in *CPR 1324-1327*, p. 49. The detailed
instructions (La credence les ditz messages) are in *War of Saint-Sardos*, pp. 192-194.
[176] This may well be the Adam de Stevynton or Styvinton granted protection in *CPR
1324-1327*, p. 49; also ibid., pp. 94, 129.
[177] PRO E.101/309/27 m. 1.
[178] *Foedera* 2, ii, p. 132. In a letter from Edward to the pope, 8 March 1325.
[179] PRO E.101/309/27 m. 1: "Item in donacione facta nautis et aliis adiuvantibus ad
Whitsand. ad ponendum in navi et extrahendum dictos liiii equos per tres vices, vi s: pro
qualibet vice ii s."
[180] Ibid. The account is for the period until 13 ("17" crossed out) January 1325: "Quo
die transivit mare de partibus illis." Thomas de Astley travelled back with Stratford. *War*

absence the English government had been hard at work pursuing schemes of alliance and retaliation against the French.[181] The earl marshal, Thomas of Brotherton, and a host of others, were directed to assemble at Portsmouth by mid-Lent Sunday (17 March) when it was proposed to send reinforcements to Edmund, earl of Kent, the king's lieutenant in Gascony.[182] Plans were to be concerted by barons, bishops and other prelates at an assembly summoned to Winchester for 3 March.[183] The date of the army's departure was soon postponed for two months, until 17 May, that of the assembly until 14 April, with its venue changed to Westminster.[184] Lesser expeditions, each comprising some two thousand footsoldiers with men-at-arms, under the command of the earl of Surrey, did set sail and reached Bordeaux on 10 and 11 May.[185] Envoys were hurriedly accredited to Castile in an attempt to arrange a match between Alfonso XI, a minor, and Eleanor, Edward II's seven-year-old daughter, on the one hand, and between Edward's eldest son, of the same name, and Eleanor, sister of the Castilian monarch, on the other. This dynastic alliance was to be linked to a promise of military assistance.[186] Another embassy embarked for Aragon with orders to propose marriage between the eldest son of the Infante, Alfonso, and the English Eleanor's younger sister, Joan "of the Tower." Because the English chancery was uncertain whether the aged monarch, James II, was still alive, alternative letters were made out in the name of his son as king of Aragon![187] James proved to be very much alive, but he had his own reasons for not provoking a

---

of Saint-Sardos, p. 195 n. 1. For the pourparlers with which he returned see ibid., p. 195; and for the credence of the bishop of Norwich and the earl of Richmond given to Stratford for the king's information, ibid., pp. 129-132; Chaplais, Diplomatic Practice 2, pl. 14. Astley was promptly sent back to France with various conditions from the English side, one of them being that Mortimer "and the other traitors and enemies of the king" should leave France before the queen arrived. See War of Saint-Sardos, pp. 195-196, and n. 189 below.

[181] Divers alliances (or projected alliances) in Spain (Castile), Aragon, Hainault and elsewhere against the crown of France were deprecated by the French king, "la quele chose il tient auxi come crime de lese majeste." War of Saint-Sardos, p. 130.

[182] Foedera 2, ii, pp. 121-122: Nottingham, 21 December 1324.

[183] Ibid., p. 123: Nottingham 30 December 1324; War of Saint-Sardos, p. 134.

[184] Foedera 2, ii, p. 129: Westminster, 20 February 1325; War of Saint-Sardos, p. 134.

[185] Ibid., pp. 173, 209-211, esp. p. 210 n. 1 (from PRO S.C.1/49/61), 220-226.

[186] Foedera 2, ii, pp. 124-126. For the negotiations see War of Saint-Sardos, pp. 214-217 (from BL Cotton MS Vespasian C.xiii, fol. 60ʳ⁻ᵛ).

[187] Foedera 2, ii, pp. 128-129: 19 February 1325; CPR 1324-1327, p. 104; War of Saint-Sardos, pp. 230-231. Another marriage proposal had earlier, October 1324, been made by Archbishop Bicknor, Edmund earl of Kent, and others, but it was found "nullatenus complacere." Foedera 2, ii, pp. 113-114. See also Acta Aragonensia 1, pp. 499-500; War of Saint-Sardos, p. 275.

quarrel with France. He responded that in view of the dissension between the English and French kings he could not countenance an alliance of the kind advocated.[188]

During the brief interval of about a month which Stratford spent in England he was busy discussing the flagging French negotiations with the king and his councillors. Charles's position was that were Edward to cease his harassment and to acknowledge the fact of Gascony's resumption by the king of France, appropriate response would be forthcoming. The papal envoys counselled that if Edward surrendered the Agenais and Ponthieu, acknowledging them to be held of the French king, they could be restored subject only to the performance of homage. Lastly, those closest to Charles had given Stratford to understand that if the young prince Edward and his mother, Isabella, were allowed to travel to France, it was likely that the truces would be extended and, following homage, Edward's continental lands given back. That the prince should be sent proved unacceptable to the English councillors, but M. Thomas de Astley was hastily despatched to France in case the queen's coming alone might be sufficient to ensure the success of the negotiations.[189]

On 12 February 1325 Stratford was granted protection until Midsummer, together with a large number of others who were to accompany him abroad.[190] In addition to Stratford himself, the leaders of the embassy were once again Bishop Salmon of Norwich and the earl of Richmond, both of whom had remained in France. The purpose of their mission was stated to be the securing of an alliance with John, duke of Brittany, and of peace with the king of France.[191] Stratford carried with him letters addressed to the papal negotiators and to his fellow ambassadors, in which Edward declared that he had decided to adopt their suggestions for peace and the successful outcome of his affairs. As a result, Queen Isabella was already on her way to the coast.[192] This time the returning envoy sailed from Dover with a somewhat smaller complement of seventy persons and forty horses. After landing in France on 18 February he seems to have spent most of his time in Paris and nearby St. Germain. Messengers plied to and fro between the bishop and Edward's court, wherever it happened

---

[188] He informed King Charles what had happened. See *War of Saint-Sardos*, pp. 276-277.

[189] Ibid., pp. 195-196. Astley was to say that Bishop Stratford was close on his heels. See also *Foedera* 2, ii, pp. 132, 135, for résumés of what happened, incorporated in subsequent letters of Edward to the pope.

[190] *CPR 1324-1327*, pp. 84, 87-88, 94.

[191] *Foedera* 2, ii, p. 126; *CPR 1324-1327*, p. 87.

[192] *War of Saint-Sardos*, pp. 197-198.

to be, and regular contact was maintained with the other two ambassadors.[193] These were mere preliminaries; decision waited upon the queen's coming.

A great deal of misunderstanding about Isabella's journey to France has arisen from the prejudice or credulity of chroniclers. The notion that Bishop Orleton was somehow responsible for the scheme is one of the mischievous inventions of Geoffrey le Baker.[194] The so-called Lanercost chronicler gives an intriguing but probably apocryphal story to the effect that Isabella's anxiety to leave England arose from a plan of the younger Despenser to send Thomas de Dunheved and Robert Baldock to obtain from the pope a divorce between her and the king.[195] It is safe to say that neither King Charles, the papal envoys, nor Stratford had the slightest inkling of the extraordinary outcome of the policy they were advocating. Only in retrospect could the more imaginative discern an overall scheme and the hands of its manipulators. Stratford, we know, urged the queen's visit to her brother as a means of escape from a diplomatic impasse, but in so doing he was not motivated by some far-ranging plot to destroy his master or to serve the interests of Isabella. Whoever initiated the idea, perhaps Charles or one of his councillors, perhaps the papal envoys, it was readily adopted as a viable proposition by all concerned. Early in March Pope John sent letters to Stratford and his fellow ambassadors, praising their efforts for a harmonious resolution of the disputes, as well as to Isabella herself, whom he conventionally described as an "angel of peace." Stratford, the pope supposed, would not have returned to England (in January) unless peace had been well on the way; he was urged to keep the curia informed by letter of the further progress in negotiations.[196]

The queen landed at Wissant in the Pas-de-Calais on 9 March 1325. She made a leisurely journey towards Paris, arriving at her brother's palace at Poissy by the 21st. There she had discussions with Stratford, Bishop Salmon and the earl of Richmond, who dined with her daily

---

[193] PRO E.101/309/27 m. 1. He left London 14 February 1325 and made the return crossing 10 April.

[194] *Chronicon*, pp. 17-18. See Haines, *Church and Politics*, pp. 104-105, 154.

[195] *Lanercost*, p. 254. For this reason, urges the chronicler, Despenser wanted the queen to cross to France. Cf. *Annales Paulini*, p. 337.

[196] *Lettres secrètes Jean XXII*, nos. 2407-2409; *CPL 1305-1342*, p. 468: 5 March 1325. On 18 March John XXII wrote of the promising situation to Reynolds: "Et venerabilis frater noster ... Winton. episcopus cum grato responso ad collegas suos pro pace destinatos predicta iter suum iam arripuerit redeundi rumores placitos nunciantes." PRO S.C.1/50/23; *Lettres secrètes Jean XXII*, no. 2427; *CPL 1305-1342*, p. 468. Isabella can be seen earlier (April 1324) taking a hand in negotiations: *War of Saint-Sardos*, pp. 42-43 (PRO S.C.1/60/126, draft). Cf. Fryde, *Tyranny of Edward II*, p. 146.

between the 22nd and 24th. The two bishops were again entertained by the queen on the 30th. The following day Isabella, the king of France's negotiators and the papal envoys drew up formal letters embodying the state of the negotiations. Somewhat later, 3 April, Isabella arrived at Bois-de-Vincennes, where she stayed for five days. Oddly enough, Stratford's own expense account gives no hint of contact with Isabella.[197]

On taking leave of the queen Stratford was given letters for delivery to her husband. These outlined the slow progress in the discussions between the English and French representatives and their conclusion with an agreement to extend the truce between the two sides from 14 April until 9 June.[198] Stratford recrossed the channel to Dover on 10 April. Both he and William Ayrminne, whom the king had sent in Isabella's company, reported to Edward at Beaulieu in Hampshire.[199] Shortly afterwards, at the beginning of May, representatives from the three groups of negotiators – Stratford, Henry de Sully, and the bishop of Orange – appeared before the king's council at Winchester.[200] From the English standpoint their news was a disappointment, for reasons which are summed up by Edward in a letter to the pope of 14 May. No definitive peace had been secured, merely a few weeks' extension of the truce. He was being called upon to surrender his possessions on the continent to the king of France and to do homage, after which their restoration was promised. But certain occupied territories were to remain in Charles's hand pending judgment in his court. As though this was not bad enough, his envoys had been permitted only one month after Easter (7 April) to return with their answer to the proposals. Three weeks had elapsed before these had even reached him.[201] His hastily summoned councillors found themselves on the horns of a dilemma; acceptance of the terms outlined could bring disinheritance with subsequent war, while rejection would entail immediate conflict. On such weighty matters they feared to give advice except in a parliament summoned for the purpose.[202] None the less,

---

[197] Hunter, "Journal of Queen Isabella," pp. 245ff.; *War of Saint-Sardos*, App. 3, pp. 267-279 (itinerary of Isabella, 9 March-14 November 1325). For Stratford's movements see PRO E.101/309/27 m. 1ᵛ.

[198] *Foedera* 2, ii, p. 135; *War of Saint-Sardos*, pp. 199-205, where documents illustrating the stages of negotiation are printed.

[199] PRO E.101/309/27 m. 1ᵛ; *War of Saint-Sardos*, p. 199. Stratford reached London 14 April and his register shows him to have been at Beaulieu on the 14th. WinRS, fol. 10ᵛ.

[200] *War of Saint-Sardos*, pp. 205-207 (from PRO C.47/32/3 m. 11). And see *Vita*, pp. 135-138 for some other happenings at Winchester.

[201] *Foedera* 2, ii, pp. 135-136.

[202] Ibid.: "Non audebant, in tam arduo et periculoso negotio, nobis dare consilium."

Edward expressed himself willing to perform homage, at a suitable place and time, even though King Charles ought first to return the lands he had occupied.[203]

While at Winchester, on 6 May, Stratford and his former colleagues, with the addition of Ayrminne, were appointed to resume the French negotiations.[204] What happened to Stratford on this occasion is not at all clear. For some reason he did not set out with Ayrminne to join the others. There is no expense account of his for any journey at this time. In the agreement concluded at Paris on 31 May 1325 it is Bishop Salmon, John of Brittany, and William Ayrminne who are named "messages et procureurs" of the English king. The treaty set out the conditions under which the lands of Edward would be kept for the time being by his brother of France, named Beauvais on 15 August for the performance of homage, and made provision for judicial settlement with compensatory damages in the case of disputed areas.[205] During the month of June the outstanding details were being thrashed out in Paris; the truce was extended once again and the homage postponed until 29 August.[206]

On 5 July 1325, the day before Bishop Salmon's death, Stratford was deputed, in company with the earl of Richmond and William Ayrminne, to treat of the transfer of Aquitaine to Edward's son.[207] A similar document authorized the two secular clerks to act by themselves, or Stratford alone.[208] The same arrangements were made with respect to the suggested performance of homage by the young prince.[209] A further proposal, entrusted to all three ambassadors, was for the marriage of the son of Charles, count of Valois, with Edward's daughter, Joan.[210] Stratford himself was commissioned as special envoy to promise money to those who rendered assistance to Edward, with authority to borrow funds on the king's behalf.[211] This third diplomatic visit to France began

[203] Ibid.

[204] Ibid., p. 134; *Treaty Rolls* 1, pp. 253-236 (nos. 648-653).

[205] *Foedera* 2, ii, pp. 137-138; Chaplais, *Diplomatic Practice* 2, pl. 15-16; *Foedera* (*R.C.*) 2, p. 604.

[206] *Foedera* 2, ii, pp. 138ff.

[207] *Treaty Rolls* 1, pp. 256-257 (no. 654). Protection was granted on 6 July to Stratford, M. Thomas de Astley, and to a large contingent going with the bishop. *CPR 1324-1327*, p. 129.

[208] *Treaty Rolls* 1, p. 257 (no. 655).

[209] Ibid. 1, pp. 257-258 (nos. 656-657).

[210] Ibid. 1, pp. 258-259 (no. 659). In 1322 a marriage had been mooted between Edward's son, Edward, and a daughter of Charles of Valois. Chaplais, *Diplomatic Practice* 2, pl. 12b.

[211] *Treaty Rolls* 1, p. 258 (no. 658).

on 13 July. The bishop was to account for ninety-two days' absence until 12 October – by far his longest stay in the country. His party was a large one, comprising eighty people and forty-six horses. Initially he established himself at Orleans, close to Queen Isabella's residence at Châteauneuf-sur-Loire;[212] subsequently at Paris, which was between two and three days' journey from the queen.[213] On 2 September the bishop made a personal visit to Châteauneuf,[214] the reason for which is not hard to imagine. To outward appearances there had been a surprising last-minute turn of events. Edward was staying with his friend the abbot of Langdon, near Dover, preparatory to leaving England for Beauvais. Just over a week before the day appointed for the ceremony Edward had written to excuse himself on the grounds of ill-health – the last of a series of postponements. To make his excuses, and if need be to swear to their validity, he deputed Stratford and M. John de Bruton, canon of Exeter.[215]

The royal illness, genuine or feigned, was followed closely by the *volte face* foreshadowed in the envoys' instructions of the beginning of July. Edward surrendered to his young son, the earl of Chester, first the county of Ponthieu and Montreuil in the Pas-de-Calais and then, just over a week later, the duchy of Aquitaine. It is noted that the charter granting the duchy was drawn up in accordance with information supplied by the bishop of Winchester.[216] King Charles, who stood to gain substantial financial advantage from the transfer, could neither have been aggrieved nor particularly surprised. We surmise that he learned of the latest developments at Châteauneuf, where he visited his sister on 4 September, a couple of days after Stratford's reception there. In his turn, Edward stood relieved of the tiresome obligation to acknowledge himself a vassal of the king of France and to undertake a potentially dangerous journey.

---

[212] PRO E.101/39/27 m. 2ʳ; *War of Saint-Sardos*, pp. 268-269.

[213] PRO E.101/39/27 m. 2ʳ.

[214] Hunter, "Journal of Queen Isabella," p. 250; *War of Saint-Sardos*, p. 269: "Isto die comederunt cum regina episcopus Wynton. et quedam pars familie sue."

[215] *Foedera* 2, ii, p. 141: Langdon, 21 August 1325. The *Historia Roffensis* describes fears allegedly expressed at the time: "De transitu ipsius [regis] tractatum fuit atque dictum quod si transiret prope Whissant insidias paratas esse ad capiendum eum et ducendum extra regnum, et si ad regem Francie transiret, paratos inveniret ad offerendum sibi bellum" (BL Cotton MS Faustina B.v, fol. 45ᵛ). Cf. *Murimuth*, p. 44, who emphasizes the Despensers' anxiety for their own safety; *Vita*, pp. 38-39, 40, where the magnates and prelates are said to have felt that the king should go to avoid disinheritance, and where the author has much the same view of the Despensers.

[216] *CPR 1324-1327*, pp. 173-174; *Foedera* 2, ii, pp. 141-142: Dover, 10 September 1325. "Ista carta facta fuit secundum notam missam per episcopum Wyntoniensem." For the signification of Edward's intentions to Charles, dated the same day, see *War of Saint-Sardos*, p. 241.

Public explanation of the policy was given by Archbishop Reynolds in a letter of 22 September 1325 for distribution to the province. In this he states that advice was given by the queen, the papal nuncios, and by Stratford and the earl of Richmond – the king's envoys abroad – that it would be better for Edward to remain in England governing his people in peace and justice, and to send his son instead. The archbishop proceeded to grant a forty days' indulgence for those who prayed for the safe return of the queen and her son, the tenderness of whose age had not exonerated him from exposure to the dangers of land and sea in obedience to his father's commands.[217]

Meanwhile, on 12 September, the young duke embarked at Dover. Two days later Stratford, Stapeldon and Henry de Beaumont were appointed his guardians.[218] Homage was performed at Bois-de-Vincennes, where the queen had been staying, on 24 September.[219] In the notarial instrument recording the proceedings it is the bishop of Winchester who heads the list of the English representatives.[220] His task was now completed. Shortly afterwards, 12 October, he took ship for Dover. Seemingly he reached the king's palace at Sheen by the 15th, where Edward was lamenting the outcome of his affairs as we know from letters to the archbishop of Vienne and the bishop of Orange.[221] He had performed all that he had promised: sent his consort to France, surrendered his French possessions to Charles, and then transferred his rights in them to his son, who had performed homage. Despite such compliance, the French monarch declined to return the Agenais and certain other lands. What is more, both from the papal envoys' own letters and from the bishop of Winchester's *viva voce* account of affairs, he was

---

[217] Letters of King Charles (*Foedera* 2, ii, pp. 141-142) are dated 4 September from Châteauneuf, though Isabella's itinerary does not mention a visit from her brother. For Reynolds' mandate see *Rochester Reg. Hethe*, pp. 356-358, and in general, Déprez, *Les préliminaires*, pp. 20-21.

[218] *CPR 1324-1327*, p. 174; *War of Saint-Sardos*, p. 269. The queen, Stratford, Stapeldon and Beaumont were to advise the young prince as to the appointment of a seneschal of Gascony. Just before the prince's departure the kings had mutually "laid aside their rancour." *Foedera* (*R.C.*) 2, p. 608.

[219] *War of Saint-Sardos*, pp. 241-242 (Dispensation by Charles for homage to be performed by Edward, earl of Chester, despite his minority); 269: "Isto die [24 September] comedit regina cum rege Francie quo die filius regis Anglie fecit homagium suum pro Vasconia."

[220] Ibid., pp. 243-245.

[221] *Foedera* 2, ii, p. 144; in which the king mentions Stratford's "relatio" of events. The *Historia Roffensis* also laments the homage: "Quod et factum est ad regis et regni desolacionem non modicam et confusionem. Nam regina cum filio tanquam derelicti multo tempore in Francia permanserunt" (BL Cotton MS Faustina B.v, fol. 45ᵛ).

dismayed to learn that they had left the French king's side before the completion of negotiations, thus remaining ignorant of the outcome. He looked for their help to secure final restitution of his territory to the earl of Chester.[222]

It was fortunate for Stratford that he had been absent from the later stages of the diplomatic exchanges which culminated in the treaty of 31 May 1325. William Ayrminne, who seems to have stepped into his shoes at this point, was to be blamed for Charles's failure to return the Agenais and La Réole – the source of the conflagration. It is true, though, that following Bishop Salmon's death Ayrminne had accepted provision to the see of Norwich, thus laying himself open to the same charge of selfish ambition with which Edward had pursued Stratford.[223] Another prelate to experience the king's virulent verbal onslaught as a consequence of the débâcle in Gascony was Alexander Bicknor, archbishop of Dublin, who was alleged to have counselled the earl of Kent to surrender La Réole in the first place.[224] Edward's failure to provide adequate reinforcements made its eventual capture inevitable.

Stratford's fourth and final mission of the reign was also his shortest. It occupied a mere twenty-two days. His entourage was correspondingly attenuated, being only forty strong – about half the usual size.[225] Letters patent of 20 October 1325 had empowered him, with the earl of Richmond, to extend the truce with John, duke of Brittany, for a year from All Saints (1 November). The document, accompanied by more personal letters close on an undisclosed topic, were given to John de Molyns for delivery to the bishop.[226] Molyns must have reached him well before his departure from Dover on the 28th.[227] From other sources we know that Stratford's main task was one of exceptional delicacy, to

---

[222] *Foedera* 2, ii, p. 144; *Vita*, pp. 141-142.

[223] For a defence of Ayrminne see Grassi, "William Airmyn." See also *Foedera* 2, ii, p. 152; *Lettres secrètes Jean XXII*, no. 2544 (and cf. no. 2535); and for the most circumstantial chronicle account, *Vita*, pp. 140-141. Also below, "From Conformist to Revolutionary."

[224] *Foedera* 2, ii, pp. 136-137: 28 May 1325. This is the king's indictment of Bicknor in a letter to John XXII. See also Haines, *Church and Politics*, p. 157. It is noteworthy that on 1 October 1324, after the fall of La Réole (22 September 1324: PRO C.47/29/10(1)), though possibly before full details reached Edward, Bicknor was one of those appointed to negotiate an alliance with Aragon. *Foedera* 2, ii, pp. 113-114.

[225] PRO E.101/309/27 m. 2ᵛ. The account is for the period 28 October-18 November 1325, counting both extreme days. Stratford was paid five marks a day, the total of the account being £73 6s 8d.

[226] *Foedera* 2, ii, p. 147; *CPR 1324-1327*, p. 183.

[227] Blackley, "Isabella," p. 232, incorrectly assumed that Stratford was abroad as early as 20 October. See n. 225 above.

persuade the queen to return with her son to England. According to the king's subsequent account of this surprising affair contained in a letter to his errant wife, he had asked her to return both before and after her son's homage, in other words, as early as mid-September. She had pleaded pressure of business. Later on Stratford had told him that Isabella's declared reason for not returning was fear of the younger Hugh le Despenser.[228] But, the king argued, in view of her warm leave-taking of Despenser and the friendliness of her subsequent letters to him, it was difficult to credit such an assertion. He himself had always treated her kindly and only once, due to her own fault, had he administered any words of reproof, and these were in private. He urged her to return speedily and to bring their son with her.[229]

Stratford's expense account[230] indicates that he was in regular contact with the queen by letter, but gives no indication of an opportunity for a personal interview until they both reached Paris. Isabella had left the capital with her son on a minor progress to Rheims, where she arrived on 30 October, the eve of the feast of All Saints. Two messengers were sent to her there by Stratford. She returned to Paris on 12 November, apparently in advance of the bishop, for he sent his man John Faulk to the capital with letters from Amiens and Senlis. As Stratford reembarked for England on the 18th, that did not leave much time for discussion. The return journey was not without incident, six of his horses being carried by contrary winds into Sandwich. The envoy must have hastened to report at Westminster, where what was to prove the last "regular" parliament of the reign was in session.[231]

---

[228] *Foedera* 2, ii, p. 148: 1 December 1325. Similar letters were sent by Edward to the king of France, whose own letters (ibid., pp. 147-148) had earlier been delivered by Stratford, presumably about 18 November (see n. 225 above). A letter of 2 December was directed to Prince Edward, instructing him to return (ibid., p. 148). Cf. ibid., p. 158 (cedula) and *Vita*, pp. 135, 142-144, 144-145 (transcript of a letter said to have been sent by the bishops to the queen).

[229] *Foedera* 2, ii, p. 148. The king assured his wife that she would not be kept short of anything – a reference to her alleged impecunious state while abroad.

[230] PRO E.101/309/27 m. 2^v. This can be compared with Isabella's itinerary in *War of Saint-Sardos*, pp. 267-270, and the account in Hunter, "Journal of Queen Isabella."

[231] Blackley, "Isabella," p. 230 (and n. 58) assumes that Stapeldon left Paris "on or about 31 October." This seems to be somewhat late. His expense account for 12 September-31 October (PRO E.101/309/31) must include a number of days travelling on French soil, so 27 October, or thereabouts, is nearer the mark. This account mentions payments made on Stratford's advice to advocates in the court of the French king "pro salario." On his departure the bishop left money to Stratford for the same purpose. Buck, *Walter Stapeldon*, p. 156 n. 204, says that Stratford never accounted for this at the exchequer.

Stratford may also have had something to say to the king about the
circumstances of Bishop Stapeldon's ignominious departure from France.
Stapeldon, though entrusted with the guardianship of the young Edward,
had seized the chance provided by Isabella's journey to Rheims to escape
from a situation in which he felt his life to be at risk – or so he claimed.
The queen castigated him for leaving without her permission or that of
her husband the king, and regardless of his obligation to the prince. It was
also rudeness to her brother, King Charles. To Isabella's disgust Stapeldon
had failed to provide her with money for household expenses. She
scorned his fears, claiming that she could have given him all the
protection he needed. With a final thrust she accused him of being one of
Despenser's minions, which is a pointer to the underlying cause of her
angry outburst.[232] Of course, Stapeldon had already given his own version
of the story. It is even possible that he found time to relate it to Stratford,
whom he could have encountered as he fled northwards to the channel.[233]
It will be noticed that up to this point there has been no mention of Roger
Mortimer, who had sought refuge in France after his sensational escape
from the Tower in early August 1323. It seems that he is not reliably
mentioned as one of the queen's associates until 18 March 1326 in a letter
from Edward to King Charles.[234] It may be assumed, one supposes, that
Edward's information was based upon reports of a liaison already well
established.

On this note of developing crisis ended Stratford's work as a diplomatic
envoy to Avignon and France in the service of Edward II. It would be
unwise to attribute to him the initiation or determination of particular
policies, although his reports or even advocacy must have influenced
in some degree the decisions arrived at by the king's "most secret
councillors." Throughout the French negotiations he gives the appearance
of having been scrupulously loyal to his master. No blame fell upon him
as a consequence of royal dissatisfaction with the aftermath of the French
treaty. Above all, there is no evidence that he had a treasonable understanding with Isabella, or much personal contact with her. Such contact as
he did have arose from his diplomatic duties. Of course we cannot be sure

[232] This interesting letter (PRO S.C.1/49/118) is reproduced and transcribed by
Blackley, "Isabella," pp. 230-231.
[233] Stratford proceeded to Paris by slow stages by way of Montreuil-sur-Mer, Amiens,
Noyon, and Senlis, sending messengers and letters to the queen en route. PRO E.101/309/
27 m. 2ᵛ. The queen was progressing from Rheims to Paris. Stapeldon allegedly fled
incognito, in the guise of a pilgrim (*Vita*, p. 142). See Buck, *Walter Stapeldon*, pp. 156-
159, 228-229.
[234] *Foedera* 2, ii, p. 153.

that under the influence of later events he did not come to sympathize with Isabella's cause, that is before her return with an army; a cause with which he must have become familiar – insofar as it was formulated at that time – during his last hectic mission to France.[235]

Ostensibly he returned to England and his see of Winchester to perform the ecclesiastical and secular functions which his position required. From the king's point of view, and from that of Baldock and Despenser, his loyalty was in any case assured by the recognizances imposed upon him; a financial sword of Damocles kept suspended above his head for the rest of Edward II's reign.[236]

FROM CONFORMIST TO REVOLUTIONARY 1326-1327

The situation arising from Queen Isabella's refusal to return from France, made more serious by her son's detention there, was further exacerbated by credible reports of her intimate association with the fugitive rebel, Roger Mortimer.[1] At a time when negotiations were under way for the marriage of the duke of Aquitaine to a sister of the king of Spain, rumour reached Castile that the prince was to be married "in partibus Franciae"; a rumour that was denied with a vehemence born of uncertainty.[2] In a mood of peevish recrimination Edward turned self-pityingly to the pope as his sole refuge (singulare refugium) in this sea of troubles. It was, he claimed, on the advice of the papal nuncios that he had sent his wife and son to France. There the acts of Isabella had been regulated by alien counsel, his own councillors having returned in despair to England. He urged the pope not to grant permission for any marriage which lacked his assent.[3]

---

[235] It will be shown shortly that Stratford was rather slow to shift his allegiance following Isabella's landing.

[236] The unscrupulous manner in which financial pressure was put on Stratford can be seen from the table in Fryde, "Stratford and the Crown," pp. 160-161. Cf. n. 151 above.

[1] Edward mentions the fact in a letter to the king of France, Lichfield, 18 March 1325. *Foedera* 2, ii, p. 153. Like Blackley ("Isabella," pp. 221ff.) I am dubious about a much earlier intimate association between Isabella and Mortimer.

[2] Negotiations were for a double marriage (see above, "Councillor and Diplomatic Envoy"). The youthful Alfonso was to marry Eleanor of Woodstock (*Foedera* 2, ii, pp. 124-125, 144-145), who in fact married Count Reginald II of Guelders in 1332. Discussions with Aragon about the marriage of the Infante's son to Joan "of the Tower" were to prove equally futile. As we shall see (below "Lancastrian Spokesman") she in fact married David Bruce. *Foedera* 2, ii, pp. 127-128; *CPR 1324-1327*, p. 104.

[3] *Foedera* 2, ii, p. 150: 3 January 1326.

In his exasperation Edward vented his wrath on William Ayrminne, newly provided by the pope to the see of Norwich. He was alleged to have given the approval of his seal to an agreement whereby the French king was enabled to retain certain lands after Prince Edward's homage.[4] The Rochester chronicler, William Dene, contended that by virtue of his position as proctor of the English king Ayrminne had legitimized King Charles's encroachments.[5] His impression of the subsequent parliament[6] is that discussion ranged round three points. Should the proxy be repudiated? Should the action taken be confirmed? Or should the king cross the sea to do homage? The first suggestion was ruled unworthy of consideration; the third was adopted and the parliament dissolved.[7] Ayrminne, wrote Dene spitefully, received Norwich as a reward for his services to the king of France and to Queen Isabella.[8] The younger Despenser, continued Dene, boasted in a private conversation with Bishop Hethe that but for the discord aroused by Ayrminne and his accomplices the king of England would have been unmatched in wealth.[9] This is a boast which accords well with what we now know about Edward's

---

[4] Ibid., p. 152: Leicester, 6 March 1326. Ayrminne, originally bishop elect and confirmed of Carlisle, lost the see to the papal provisee John de Ros, an auditor in the curia. Later in the same year, 20 July 1325, John XXII informed the king that he had appointed Ayrminne to Norwich two days after hearing of Salmon's death at Folkestone on 6 July (not 2nd as in Smith, citing the original Le Neve, *Fasti Ecclesiae Anglicanae* 2, p. 463). Both Isabella and Edward supported Ayrminne's candidature for Carlisle, but Baldock was the royal nominee for Norwich. See Smith, *Episcopal Appointments*, pp. 41-45; above, "Councillor and Diplomatic Envoy," n. 223.

[5] BL Cotton MS Faustina B.v, fols. 44ᵛ-45ʳ. In 1329, at the Westminster parliament, Dene suggests an unlikely verbal exchange between Ayrminne and Queen Isabella on the question of responsibility for what happened (ibid., fol. 55ᵛ). The chronicler assumes that Bishops Stratford, Salmon and Stapeldon were associated with Ayrminne, but imputes no blame to them. It was John of Brittany and Bishop Salmon who, together with Ayrminne, sealed the treaty.

[6] Which met 25 June 1325 at Westminster to discuss the affairs of the kingdom and of Gascony. Parry, *Parliaments*, p. 90; *HBC*, p. 517. Dene (BL Cotton MS Faustina B.v, fol. 44ᵛ) says that it met on the Translation of St. Thomas (7 July), and the regnal year "19" (which would mean 1326) is in the margin of the MS.

[7] BL Cotton MS Faustina B.v, fol. 45ʳ. Cf. *Vita*, pp. 138-139.

[8] BL Cotton MS Faustina B.v, fol. 45ʳ: "Rex siquidem Francie et regina Anglie considerantes bonum servicium domini W. de Ermyne predicti quod fecerat pro rege Francie contra regem Anglie." Much the same story, differently expressed, is in *Vita*, pp. 140-141.

[9] BL Cotton MS Faustina B.v, fol. 46ᵛ: "Quod regem tradiderat Anglie et ideo factus est episcopus, asserens quod rex Anglie non habuisset parem in diviciis si regina et episcopus Norwycen. et eorum complices discordiam inter reges non suscitassent." Cf. *Vita*, p. 136, where Edward is shown (in 1325) to have preferred to keep his money than to pay the soldiers he had mobilized.

success in amassing treasure, at great cost to his subjects.[10] Despenser's indictment was not disinterested; by making the new bishop a scapegoat he sought to divert attention from his own culpability.[11]

By mid-March 1326 an invasion of England was felt in many quarters to be imminent. The sheriffs received instructions to seize persons carrying suspect letters into the realm as well as to examine suspicious characters entering or leaving it.[12] Perhaps the situation in France was other than it appeared: Charles IV was not planning a military intervention on Isabella's behalf. Indeed, it would be helpful to know precisely what he thought of his sister's misconduct and the continued presence of the English exiles.[13] His hand was forced by Edward, who in his anxiety to mitigate the harm engendered by the duke of Aquitaine's removal from his control, resumed the English continental possessions in the guise of "governor and administrator." Charles's reaction was swift; he reoccupied parts of Gascony from which he was in process of withdrawing.[14] It has been assumed that throughout this time of tension Stratford was in France actively forwarding Queen Isabella's insidious preparations.[15] As we have seen, the contrary was the case. The bishop had returned to England and was attending to his neglected diocesan duties; to all outward appearances loyally cooperating with the government, which on the eve of the September invasion was accepting his advice on the appointment of commissioners of array for some of the southern and southwestern counties.[16]

---

[10] Fryde, *Tyranny of Edward II*, esp. chaps. 7 and 8.

[11] It is a tenable hypothesis that Despenser and his supporters conceived the plan (they certainly sanctioned it) and that when it misfired they blamed the vulnerable Ayrminne.

[12] *Foedera* 2, ii, pp. 153-154: Lichfield, 18 March 1326. Cf. *Lanercost*, p. 254: "Interim factus est rumor publicus in Anglia quod regina Angliae, cum filio suo duce et exercitu Franciae, intraret Angliam in navibus."

[13] Perroy, *Hundred Years War*, pp. 75-76, argued that Charles was disgusted with his sister's behaviour and increasingly embarrassed by the exiles. Lucas, *Low Countries*, p. 52, felt "her continued sojourn in Paris impolitic for her brother ... who found it impossible to aid the aggrieved queen." The *Vita* (p. 143) records Charles's unwillingness, despite English representations, to expel her.

[14] *Foedera* 2, ii, pp. 160-161: Westminster, 27 June 1326. Edward justified his action by the terms of the agreement with Charles under Stratford's seal – the bishop having been present.

[15] Justification is lacking for Tout's statement (*PHE* 3, p. 298) that Stratford and Ayrminne "united themselves with the queen and fugitive Marcher." McKisack likewise remarks (*Fourteenth Century*, p. 82) that in the spring of 1326 "what seems to have been anticipated was a joint invasion of the king of France and the queen of England, supported by the influential group of exiles then in Paris – Kent, Richmond, Beaumont, Stratford of Winchester, Ayrminne of Norwich, and, above all, Roger Mortimer of Wigmore."

[16] *CPR 1324-1327*, pp. 268 (10 May 1326), 303 (28 July 1326). The substitutes for the earl of Winchester (the elder Despenser) nominated by Stratford (ibid., p. 303) were John

In April 1326 Edward was again writing to the pope,[17] this time to acquaint him with the contents of letters he had sent to King Charles and to the duke of Aquitaine. Indignantly he repudiated the notion prevalent in France that he had banished his son – who in any case was of such tender years that no offence could be imputed to him. Such rumours were not so easily scotched. Their currency in England is vouched for by the chroniclers[18] and by the fact that on 25 April Reynolds was induced to issue a directive from his Otford manor-house for the denunciation of those particular "fictitious assertions," and also of another to the effect that the papal nuncios would be unable to come to England without danger of life, limb, and personal possessions.[19] In a circular to the Canterbury metropolitan and to the other bishops (including Burghersh and Droxford, but excluding Orleton) Edward stressed the obligation of all inhabitants to defend the realm; more particularly the bishops, for they had greater possessions! They were to certify the king as to the number of their familiars and the strength of their retinues in horsemen and footsoldiers.[20] Despite elaborate precautions, letters and people were infiltrating into the country. The Thames estuary was particularly vulnerable and John de Weston, constable of the Tower, was ordered to supervise the reach of river between London and Gravesend.[21]

By June 1326 the papal nuncios were back in England.[22] The topics under their consideration and that of the king's councillors had already been exhaustively discussed time and time again. To questions about the status of his wife, Isabella, the king responded orally in French, his replies

de St. John and Ralph Camoys, the barons who had attended his enthronement. There appears to be nothing sinister in this.

[17] *Foedera* 2, ii, p. 155: Kenilworth, 15 April 1326.

[18] E.g. Brut (ccc ms 174), fol. 139ᵛ: "But boþe were exiled þo moder and hire sone"; *Historia Roffensis* (BL Cotton ms Faustina B.v), fol. 46ᵛ: "Ad tractandum de reditu regine filii regis et comitis Cancie exulancium sicut vulgariter dicebatur." And see Perroy, *Hundred Years War*, p. 67.

[19] E.g. *Hereford Reg. Orleton*, pp. 359-361: Otford, 25 April, and Fulham, 6 May – mandate of Bishop Gravesend as dean of the province. For other references see Wright, *Church and Crown*, p. 358 n. 73.

[20] *Foedera* 2, ii, p. 156: Gloucester, 12 May 1326; *Rochester Reg. Hethe*, pp. 303, 374-377, 380. There was to be a muster at Canterbury on 4 August. Hethe worried about the threat to ecclesiastical privilege, but Reynolds argued the exceptional nature of the circumstances.

[21] *Foedera* 2, ii, pp. 156-157: Gloucester, 12 May 1326.

[22] Granted safe-conduct 18 May 1326 (*Foedera* 2, ii, p. 157); Edward wrote to the pope of matters under discussion (ibid., p. 158, Sturry, 10 June). He rode to Canterbury and then to the archbishop's castle at Saltwood for consultations. A meeting between nuncios, Reynolds, and other bishops of the royal council (but not seemingly Stratford) took place in Christ Church chapter house at Canterbury on 9 June. TCC R.5 41, fol. 120ᵛ.

being translated subsequently into Latin for transmission with the pope's letter. The younger Despenser was also present to rebut the accusations directed against him. All of which goes to support Dene's statement that one of the purposes of the nuncios' mission was to seek appropriate guarantees for the safe return of the queen and her son, together with the king's half-brother, the earl of Kent. If so, this was a futile quest, for Isabella was certain to reject any arrangement which did not include the removal of the younger Despenser from the king's intimate counsels.[23] According to one chronicler, she swore by God and his saints that she would not return to England until her enemies – traitors to king and kingdom – were removed from her husband's side.[24] Other matters which came up for discussion with the envoys had engaged Stratford's attention in 1322-1323: the continued non-payment of tribute and the papal demand for a portion of the clerical tenth. They could scarcely have offered more than polite attention to the renewed tirade against the "recalcitrant" bishops – Orleton, Burghersh, Ayrminne and Bicknor – all of whom continued in the confidence of the pope. The king stressed that legal proceedings involving their baronies had been undertaken in accordance with the law and custom of the realm. Although Baldock was one of those behind the king's policy in this respect, Edward urged Pope John to disregard sinister insinuations of the envious and once again to restore his clerk to favour.[25] Edward had an additional piece of galling intelligence of which to complain to the envoys and hence to the pope. The queen, not content with admitting the traitor Mortimer into her confidence, had allowed him to wear the duke of Aquitaine's livery and to appear publicly in his entourage – before the whole of Paris – during the celebrations for the coronation on the feast of Pentecost (11 May).[26]

---

[23] BL Cotton MS Faustina B.v, fol. 46ᵛ: "Rex itaque archiepiscopo Vien. et episcopo Auriacen. domini pape ac regine Anglie nunciis occurrit ad tractandum de reditu regine .... Deinde H[ugo] de Spenser filius episcopo inter alia retulit quod archiepiscopus et episcopus nuncii supradicti petierunt ex parte regine securitatem ad regem redeundi cum filio et comite antedictis, quibus responsum fuit quod securitatem exigere non oporteret sed secure et salvo redire possent."

[24] TCC MS R.5 41, fol. 120ʳ: "Regina Anglie votum vovit Deo et sanctis eius quod nunquam in Angliam veniret donec inimici eius proditores regis et regni a societate domini sui regis Anglie penitus ammoverentur et vindicta eis fieret iuxta exigenciam delictorum." For Isabella's message to Stratford of 5 February 1326 to much the same effect, but naming the younger Despenser, see responsiones, cols. 2767-2768; from which, Froissart (ed. Lettenhove) 18, pp. 9-10.

[25] Foedera 2, ii, p. 158: "Sinistris aemulorum relatibus (si qui fiant forsitan contra ipsos) obauditis penitus rejectis." See above, "Councillor and Diplomatic Envoy," n. 155.

[26] Foedera 2, ii, p. 158: "Qui portavit sectam dicti filii nostri et in ipsius comitiva, publice, coram tota gente Parisius in solempnitate coronationis ... in magnum

As the summer wore on Edward's councillors did their best to secure Isabella's removal from France,[27] both by diplomatic means and by the less respectable one of bribery and, so it was alleged, of attempted murder.[28] Dene tells us of a plot, incongruously attributed to John of Brittany, for the capture of the queen and her removal to England by force.[29] Warned of her danger by the queen of France, so the tale runs, Isabella took a bold course. On the Nativity of Our Lady (8 September) she summoned the earl to her presence and questioned him about the date of his return to England. When he answered that it would be about Michaelmas (29 September), she decided on immediate action. Gathering together a few companions, she rode through the night to seek refuge in Hainault. The French chronicler, Jean le Bel, takes up the story at this point. In conventional chivalric terms he describes how the gentle knight Jean de Hainault, in the flower of his manhood, wept for pity at the queen's plight.[30] From Isabella's point of view it was a providential encounter, for the gallant Jean conducted her to Valenciennes for a meeting with his elder brother, Guillaume, count of Hainault.[31] It was not long before the enterprise was set on foot which culminated in a successful landing on the English coast.[32]

In England, meanwhile, the government tried to mobilize the church in an endeavour to explain policy, dispel rumours, and to gain support. This

contemptum et vituperium nostri et omnium nostrorum." I suspect this does *not* mean that Mortimer carried the prince's train, as has been commonly said.

[27] E.g. Brut (ccc ms 174), fol. 140^{r-v}. According to this story one Arnold of Spain a "broker of London" was captured with a cargo of silver intended as a bribe for the "twelve peers of France" and taken to Jean of Hainault.

[28] Fryde, *Tyranny of Edward II*, p. 181, says that Isabella went to Hainault "probably early in 1326," while Lucas, *Low Countries*, p. 54 (citing *Istore et croniques* 1, p. 334) suggests the "early summer of 1326." In a letter of 12 August to Archbishop Reynolds Edward speaks of King Charles still detaining his wife and son and this is reiterated in a mandate of 4 September to Bayonne for the harassment of the French. *Foedera* 2, ii, pp. 163, 165. Cf. *Rochester Reg. Hethe*, pp. 306-307 and n.

[29] BL Cotton ms Faustina B.v, fol. 47^r (cf. *Walsingham* 1, p. 179). John of Britanny was long associated with Edward II, having been his attendant in 1307 when he was Prince of Wales. Captured by the Scots at Byland in 1322 (*Lanercost*, p. 247), Edward tried to raise money in parliament for his ransom. On his release and following a mission to Flanders he was summoned before the king's court and his lands confiscated. They were not returned until Edward II's detention. *Foedera* 2, ii, pp. 152, 158, 162-163; *GEC* 10, pp. 814-818; Lyubimenko, *Jean de Bretagne*, chap. 4 (1307-1334), pp. 104ff., and on his accord with Isabella, p. 115.

[30] *Jean le Bel* 1, pp. 14-15ff.

[31] Guillaume I (1304-1337), the son of Jean (II) of Avesnes.

[32] BL Cotton ms Faustina B.v, fol. 47^r: "Mox ad portum maris in Holandia Wlp se dederunt et conductis navibus naves ascendentes...."

was to be effected by means of the pulpit[33] and by the offering of prayers and works of piety on behalf of king and country.[34] On the advice of the archbishop of Vienne and his fellow nuncio, the bishop of Orange, as well as of certain English prelates, a provincial convocation was summoned to meet at St. Paul's on 13 October.[35] But this clashed with the meeting of a royal council at Stamford; so at the king's request it was postponed until 3 November.[36]

By the beginning of September urgent naval dispositions were being made. All sizeable vessels (pondus triginta doliorum et ultra portantes) from the Thames' mouth to the north[37] were to assemble "at Orwell" on St. Matthew's day (21 September) armed and victualled for a month.[38] This timely mobilization proved ineffective. Only three days after it was due to take place Isabella and her small army were anxiously contemplating the dawn from somewhere near the mouth of the River Orwell.[39] No hostile onslaught materialized. The French Chronicle supplies a reason; the sailors refused to fight out of antagonism towards Despenser.[40] But this could be hindsight; the king's "most secret councillor" was to be blamed indiscriminately for most of the misfortunes of the latter part of the reign.

Once she had landed the queen circularized the bishops and other prominent men with the instruction to hasten to her presence for the good of the kingdom.[41] Despite some too ready assumptions, we remain largely

[33] "Ut series gestarum rerum universis et singulis nota fiat."

[34] Foedera 2, ii, p. 163: Clarendon, 12 August 1326.

[35] This mandate, dated 20 July 1326 from Lambeth, was circulated by the dean of the province, Bishop Gravesend, from Stepney the following day. Hereford Reg. Orleton, pp. 368-369; Concilia 2, pp. 552-553.

[36] Parry, Parliaments, p. 91; HBC, p. 555; Concilia 2, pp. 532-533; Foedera (R.C.) 2, p. 642. But see below.

[37] The ports of Harwich, Colchester, Manningtree, Maldon, Salcott, Tollesbury, Mersea, Fingringhoe, St. Osyth and Foulness, all in Essex, are enumerated.

[38] Foedera 2, ii, pp. 164-165: Porchester, 3 September 1326.

[39] BL Cotton MS Faustina B.v, fol. 47ʳ: "Die Mercurii ante festum sancti Michelis [i.e. 24 September] in aurora ad portum de Orewelle applicuerunt." Cf. Annales Paulini, p. 313: "Applicuit in portu de Arewelle et cepit terram vocatur Colvasse"; Lanercost, p. 255: "Apud portum de Herwyke." Round, "Landing of Isabella," suggested Walton-by-Felixstowe to the north of the Orwell rather than Walton-on-the-Naze (R. G. Marsden, "The Mythical Town of Orwell," agreed). Though not widely adopted this alternative makes better sense of the subsequent itinerary via Bury-St.-Edmunds and Cambridge (Annales Paulini, p. 314).

[40] French Chronicle, p. 51: "Pur le graunt errour q'ils avoyent vers sire Hughe le Despenser." They are said to have carried out a piratical attack on the coast of Normandy instead.

[41] "Receperunt episcopus Roffensis sicut ceteri prelati et maiores regni litteras regine ut ad eam pro utilitate regni acceleraret. Tales literas quando applicuit omnibus misit." BL

ignorant of the number of prelates that responded.[42] We do know that Stratford was not one of them. The evidence points in the other direction. His initial reaction seems to have been to rally to the king. Joining forces with Archbishop Reynolds, Bishop Stephen Gravesend, and the abbots of Westminster and Waltham, he presented himself at St. Paul's. There, on 30 September, a bull of excommunication originally aimed at the Scots – the one which Orleton had carried from Avignon early in 1320[43] – was brought forth and read aloud by the archbishop's clerk, Thomas de Stowe, as though it were directed against Isabella and her followers. The Londoners were hostile and not taken in by the adventitious document. The stratagem failed. Shortly thereafter the king fled from London, never to return. His supporters were left to fend for themselves.[44]

Even then Stratford showed no inclination to join the queen. For the moment he sought to temporize. The Canterbury convocation had been summoned in far different circumstances for 13 October, and it was on that day at Lambeth, rather than St. Paul's, that a rump of bishops assembled. Present, in addition to Stratford, were the primate, Reynolds, and Bishops Stapeldon of Exeter, Cobham of Worcester, Gravesend of London, and Hethe of Rochester.[45] The composition of the group is worth examination. Reynolds, despite occasional kicking against the pricks of royal policy, was a loyal cooperator in Edward's government. Stapeldon, with a measure of justice, comes down to us as a grasping and unpopular ex-treasurer.[46] Cobham, a great scholar and sometime candidate for the

---

Cotton MS Faustina B.v, fol. 47ᵛ; cf; Baker, *Chronicon*, p. 21. Letters were sent to London on 29 September and 6 October: *French Chronicle*, pp. 51-52; *Great Chronicle*, pp. 29-30; *Chronicle of London*, pp. 50, 152-153 n. K. On 28 September the king required that all such letters be intercepted and sent to him unopened. *Foedera* 2, ii, p. 167.

[42] See Haines, *Church and Politics*, p. 160.

[43] Ibid., p. 22 and n.; PRO E.159/93/77. According to TCC MS R.5 41, fol. 121ᵛ, the bull dated from the first year of John xxii's consecration (1316-1317).

[44] *Annales Paulini*, p. 315. For the state of affairs in the capital see Williams, *Medieval London*, pp. 295-299, and in general: M. Weinbaum, *London unter Eduard I und II*. Tout's "rough itinerary" of the chancery, hence probably of Edward (who appears to have left London on 2 October), is in *Chapters* 3, p. 2 n. 3 (cf. *Parl. Writs* 2, i, pp. 449ff.). This can be supplemented from the chamber account of 20 Edward II (SA MS 122, fols. 43ᵛ-45ᵛ). The six days afloat, 19-25 October, between Chepstow and Cardiff – for lack of wind – seem to support Baker (*Chronicon*, pp. 22-23), who suggests the royal destination was Lundy Island.

[45] BL Cotton MS Faustina B.v, fol. 47ᵛ.

[46] Wright, *Church and Crown*, pp. 243-274, makes the best possible defence of Reynolds' life and policy. *Vita*, p. 139, describes Stapeldon as "ultra modum cupidus." See now Buck, *Walter Stapeldon*, chap. 9.

primacy, was gravely ill and reluctant to accept the logic of events.[47] Gravesend, as his subsequent conduct serves to illustrate, was loyal to the king even long after Edward's death, while Hethe seems to have been on good terms both with the monarch and with Despenser.[48] Without question Stratford was for the time being acting in concert with that section of the episcopate ready to make some sort of stand for Edward. It was a lost cause almost from the outset.[49]

The *Historia Roffensis* tells of the preliminaries to the Lambeth assembly and provides an arresting account of what happened there. The Rochester diocesan, a cautious man much frightened by the violence in London, expressed reluctance to cross the Thames for the meeting arranged at St. Paul's. In his opinion the people's hearts were alienated from the episcopate; an alienation which had turned to hatred. His analysis of the situation was down to earth; men loved the queen and hated the king.[50] The archbishop then suggested that those already assembled should adjourn to the Augustinian priory of St. Mary Overy in Southwark. Here they would be south of the river – in fact within Stratford's diocese – but within a stone's throw of St. Paul's. As Stapeldon and Hethe sat in the canons' chapter house discussing the inconstancy of the world (de varietate seculi confabulantes), a large dog is said to have entered. After approaching Hethe in friendly fashion it turned its attention to Stapeldon, at whose feet it settled down. The bishop of Exeter's squires interpreted this as a bad omen, as indeed it proved to be to be only a few days later.[51] From Southwark the bishops retreated to Lambeth, as we have seen. There, on 14 October, they set about the task of selecting two of their number willing to mediate between the king and his queen.

---

[47] Haines, *Church and Politics*, pp. 163-164. Cobham's illuminating letter, probably written in the latter half of October, is in *Worcester Reg. Cobham*, fol. 116ᵛ, pp. 204-205.

[48] Dene (BL Cotton MS Faustina B.v, fols. 46ᵛ-47ʳ) records what purports to be Hethe's final conversation with the king and the younger Despenser. "Rex dixit episcopo: 'Quando vis petere aliquid a me? Multa fecisti pro me et domino Hugone et nunquam retribui tibi. Multa feci pro hiis qui ingrati sunt michi quos promovi ad statum magnum et facti sunt michi hostes in capite. Et ideo domine Hugo precipio tibi quod si episcopus Roffensis quicquam habeat facere fiat.' Ad quod dictus H[ugo], 'Domine libentissime quia bene meruit'."

[49] The clearest picture of what was happening is provided by Dene (BL Cotton MS Faustina B.v, fols. 47ᵛ-48ʳ). Bishop Hethe is said to have explained to Archbishop Reynolds: "Quod corda tocius populi ab episcopis aversa fuerunt, et omnes episcopos oderunt, quia totum malum quod contingit in Anglia pigriscie, fatuitati et ignorancie episcoporum fuit imputatum." The basis for so forthright a denunciation is not revealed.

[50] Ibid., fol. 47ᵛ: "Et omnes reginam dilexerunt et regem oderunt." And cf. previous note.

[51] Ibid. Dene is not a regular retailer of superstitious stories.

Stratford expressed himself willing to undertake this onerous mission, provided that someone agreed to accompany him. The rest of the bishops demurred, but eventually they combined to ask Hethe whether he would consent to go. Although Reynolds, Gravesend and Stapeldon continued to press the point, Hethe pleaded inadequacy and emphatically refused. Instead he sought the archbishop's licence to return to his own diocese, but was prevailed upon to postpone his departure until the following day, Wednesday 15 October. Stratford rose early on the 15th and privately entreated Hethe to accompany him to the queen – the king is not mentioned. It could be that by this stage Stratford had resolved to throw in his lot with Isabella. But the bishop of Rochester was not so readily persuaded. He asked for time to consider the proposal, promising to give his reply in the evening (hora vesperarum).[52]

While Rochester was endeavouring to make up his mind a terrible tragedy occurred. Dene gives us a full and circumstantial account of what happened.[53] An insurrection took place in London where a large crowd, comprising men both of the greater and meaner sort, assembled at the Guildhall. There they are said to have taken counsel as to how best they might capture and kill the bishops of London and Exeter and others of the king's justices who were gathered in the house of the Dominican friars. Another of their supposed objectives was the sacking of property belonging to city merchants. Their cause was Isabella's, but the gain they sought was their own; those unwilling to join the queen were to be taken for traitors. Some of the more bloodthirsty set an ambush for Bishop Stapeldon, whom they forcibly removed from the porch of St. Paul's Cathedral, whither he had gone for sanctuary. They then dragged him to the great cross at Cheap and there beheaded him. After this atrocity the rioters rampaged round the city on the lookout for friends of the king or of the Despensers. The royal justice, Geoffrey le Scrope, escaped across the Thames and made off with one of the archbishop's horses. Bishop Hethe was alerted by the commotion as he sat at table in his room. When he looked for means of escape it was to find that Archbishop Reynolds had

[52] Ibid., fol. 48[r]: "Wynton. [Stratford] ire concessit si socium haberet. Ceteris ire negantibus tandem omnes episcopi Roffen. rogaverunt ut cum eo iret. Qui ipsius insufficienciam licet ab archiepiscopo episcopis London. et Exon. plurimum fuisset excitatus, ad eundem exponens ad id faciendum totaliter se excusavit.... Die Mercurii, videlicet in crastino summo mane, venit Wynton. et Roffens. intime rogans ut versus reginam eum sociaret. Cui Roffen. respondit se velle super hoc deliberare et hora vesperarum ipsum certificare."

[53] Ibid. Cf. *French Chronicle*, pp. 51-55; *Annales Paulini*, pp. 315-317; TCC MS R.5 41, fols. 121[v]-122[r] (recte 122-123); *Walsingham* 1, p. 182.

already departed for Kent with all the horses but without a word of warning.[54] He was compelled to follow on foot as best he could. With this unseemly débâcle all hope of episcopal mediation vanished for ever.

On the day of Stapeldon's brutal murder[55] Isabella was at Wallingford in pursuit of her husband, who was moving in the direction of Gloucester. There, according to the hostile Geoffrey le Baker, the bishop's head was to be brought to her like an offering to Diana.[56] It was at Wallingford that Isabella published a proclamation defining her intentions.[57] Whether Stratford arrived while the queen was still there is uncertain. We do find him at Bristol on 26 October with those bishops who had joined the insurgents at an earlier stage: Archbishop Bicknor of Dublin, Hothum of Ely, Burghersh of Lincoln, Orleton of Hereford, and Ayrminne of Norwich. With the possible exception of Hothum[58] all these men had been regarded as the enemies of the king and of the younger Despenser. As such they had been prevented from leading a normal existence in their bishoprics. The assembly of clerical and lay magnates at Bristol proceeded to declare that the king and Despenser had left the country bereft of government, and for that reason the duke of Aquitaine was named *custos* of the realm.[59] In all probability Stratford accompanied the queen's army to Hereford. It was there he received the first fruits of his cooperation; on 6 November he was named deputy-treasurer. William Melton the treasurer, who was also archbishop of York, was said to be engaged in business in the north. Doubtless this was so, but his sympathy for Edward ii was common knowledge. Stratford's writ of appointment was issued in the king's name but under the seal of his son as *custos*. He

---

[54] TCC MS R.5 41, fol. 122ʳ, states that Reynolds, frightened for his own skin (timens pelli sui) – a favourite phrase of this chronicler – fled to Croydon, thence to Otford and Maidstone. Canterbury being for the queen was prepared to receive the archbishop only on conditions.

[55] 15 October. The "15 August" in Haines, *Church and Politics*, p. 163 (second paragraph) is a slip. For details of Stapeldon's murder see Buck, *Walter Stapeldon*, chap. 10.

[56] *Chronicon*, p. 23: "Capud vero episcopi regine apud Gloverniam suo exercitui incubanti sicut sacrificium Deane bene placitum, optulerunt." But the classical allusion is scarcely apt!

[57] *Responsiones*, cols. 2764-2765; *Foedera* 2, ii, p. 169; cf. BL Royal MS 12 D.xi, fol. 30ʳ. The document is dated 15 October from Wallingford. Orleton expounded its contents at Oxford in the same month, and there (according to Baker, *Chronicon*, p. 23) preached a public sermon on the text "Capud meum doleo" (4 Kings 4.19).

[58] The indictment of the younger Despenser alleges that Hothum's temporalities were encroached upon. But this bishop made a show of cooperation with the government and his fall from grace is somewhat of a mystery. Haines, *Church and Politics*, pp. 158-159; Taylor, "The Judgment on Hugh Despenser," pp. 70, 75.

[59] *Foedera* 2, ii, p. 169.

brought it to the exchequer in London on the 14th. Stratford arrived in style, escorted by Mayor Hamo de Chigwell and a large crowd of Londoners. There followed some administrative formalities concerning the transfer of the treasurer's keys. In Melton's absence Walter of Norwich had been acting as his lieutenant, and throughout that time the royal clerk William de Feriby had done duty as custodian. He duly produced the keys for Stratford's inspection, whereupon the new lieutenant handed them back. Feriby was next sent to find the seal of absence, used at times when the king was abroad. This was handed to Stratford and by virtue of a mandate he brought with him, he despatched it to the queen and the young prince for use during Edward II's technical absence "extra regnum." [60] On the following Monday, 17 November, Stratford first officiated in the treasury of receipt. One of his initial tasks was the drawing up of an indenture between himself and Melton's representative, Feriby, with respect to the contents of the royal treasury.[61]

Meanwhile, Archbishop Reynolds had still not overtly declared his intentions; he had a facility for not making up his mind.[62] As late as 7 December he is reported to have been at his palace of Maidstone. Bishop Hethe was also there. Twice the reluctant bishop was urged by letter and then by word of mouth to join the queen at Wallingford,[63] to which place she had returned following the king's capture and the destruction of her chief opponents. To all such demands Hethe remained adamant, but he had made his excuses to the queen while she was at Gloucester through the agency of John de Hethe, a Franciscan friar. In his turn he advised Archbishop Reynolds not to attend the parliament in London with those who were excommunicate, but instead to withdraw to Canterbury where the great men of the realm could consult him. This unrealistic advice fell on deaf ears. Reynolds was not cast in a heroic mould; his fear of the

[60] *CMRE*, no. 832. Davies, *Baronial Opposition*, p. 568, no. 49, gives a transcript of Stratford's appointment as "locum tenens" from PRO E.403/220. From another source we learn that the seal was delivered to Stratford 15 November 1326. Years later, 20 May 1329, he was asked to produce it because Edward III was about to go abroad. He replied that he had sent it to Hereford. *WinRS*, fol. 211^v; see Appendix 1.

[61] *CMRE*, no. 832.

[62] According to Wright, *Crown and Politics*, p. 274, "Indecision is perhaps the strongest charge we can lay to Reynolds." The anonymous of Canterbury states that he made an unsolicited offer to Edward II of armed men, but though by failing to keep his promise he lost the king's favour, he did not gain that of the queen. TCC MS R.5 41, fol. 121^v.

[63] BL Cotton MS Faustina B.v, fol. 49^r. In *Church and Politics*, p. 164 n. 13, I wrongly attributed the urging to Reynolds. The archbishop was with Hethe at the time but pressure on the bishop apparently came from an emissary sent by the queen. Reynolds, though, was clearly wavering.

earthly queen outweighed his fear of the king of heaven.[64] In any case, the time for heroics had largely passed.

As we have seen, Stratford reached Westminster on 14 November, a fact which precludes his having been at Hereford for the arraignment of Robert Baldock on the 24th.[65] The former chancellor was to be brought to the capital and imprisoned in the bishop of Hereford's house, Montalt or Mounthaw, from which he was violently abstracted and thrust into Newgate gaol. There he suffered a lingering death as a consequence of sustained ill-treatment.[66] According to Bishop Orleton, admittedly defending himself against the charge of conniving at Baldock's death, it was at the insistence of Stratford that Edward's former chancellor was taken to London to answer at the Canterbury convocation for his manifold offences against the church.[67] Both Stratford and Orleton had suffered at Baldock's hands, but it would go beyond the evidence to conclude that either of them deliberately sought his physical harm, let alone his death.

Stratford brought various directives from the queen to London. At her command Hamo de Chigwell was removed from the office of mayor. His unpardonable fault was to have been on the panel of judges responsible for Mortimer's condemnation to death. Richard de Betoyne (Béthune) was elected in his stead and associated with John de Gisors as custodian of the Tower. Both men are thought to have connived at Mortimer's escape. The tables had indeed been turned. When Stratford presented himself at the Guildhall he swore to maintain the city's liberties. It may be assumed also that he took part in the ceremonies at Westminster on 17 November, the day the new mayor arrived on horseback with a fine retinue to take the customary oath.[68] Early in December, in his capacity as deputy-treasurer,

---

[64] BL Cotton MS Faustina B.v, fol. 49: "Plus enim timuit quam regem celi."

[65] According to the *Annales Paulini* (pp. 319-320) Baldock was brought before the same justices as the younger Despenser immediately after the latter's condemnation, i.e. 24 November. Evidence for Orleton's involvement in Baldock's death is examined in Haines, *Church and Politics*, pp. 111-112. A Canterbury source gives the date of the Despenser judgment as 1 November (All Saints) 1326. CCL Reg. I, fols. 414r-415v.

[66] *Annales Paulini*, pp. 320-321, 334. He died 28 May.

[67] *Responsiones*, col. 2763: "De praecepto domini regis et reginae matris suae, excitante et procurante potissime venerabili patre domino J[ohanne] tunc Wyntoniensi episcopo et Angliae thesaurario."

[68] But Chigwell bounced back as mayor in the following year. See *Great Chronicle*, pp. 31-32. The principal narrative accounts are: *French Chronicle*, pp. 55-56; *Annales Paulini*, pp. 318, 321-322. The London to which Stratford returned was in a state of violent unrest, it being difficult to conduct everyday business or to resume regular work in the courts. For the implication of Betoyne and Gisors in Mortimer's escape see *Parl. Writs* 2, ii, pp. 249, 288; *Annales Paulini*, pp. 305-306.

Stratford delivered to Queen Isabella's wardrobe the jewels and other precious objects which the younger Despenser had stored in the Tower.[69]

Isabella returned to Wallingford for Christmas. She rejoiced in the knowledge that her cause was well on the way to fruition; now was the time to plan her future campaign. Present for the festivities and more serious matters were Stratford, Reynolds the new recruit,[70] William Ayrminne acting-keeper of the great seal, and the earls of Lancaster and Kent. Here again the testimony is Orleton's: in order to safeguard the queen's reputation he was directed to proclaim the reasons for Isabella's refusal to return to her husband – depicted as having homicidal tendencies. He claimed to have acted in strict accordance with the letter of the instructions given to him in the presence of the archbishop, Bishop Stratford, and of the others mentioned.[71] Another source records Stratford's presence in London at Christmastide, together with that of Sir Thomas Wake, Henry of Lancaster's son-in-law. The bishop is stated to have volunteered to supply lead for the roof of the Guildhall chapel, and Wake to have offered the necessary timber.[72]

Meanwhile, on 10 December, the papal envoys William, archbishop of Vienne, and M. John Grandisson, archdeacon of Nottingham, the future bishop of Exeter, arrived in England. They had been granted letters of safe-conduct on 30 November and were under instructions to bring peace between England and France, particularly in Gascony. Their appearance was inopportune, so they were kept waiting at Canterbury. Not until 4 January did they enter London, by which time the queen and her son had arrived and also a number of magnates. The bishop of London summoned a convocation to St. Paul's for the 16th – from which Stratford excused himself – in a vain attempt to raise a subsidy for use against the emperor, Louis of Bavaria. As the envoys did not recross the channel until 26 January they must have learned of the extraordinary happenings in London.[73]

---

[69] *CPR 1324-1327*, pp. 339-340: Woodstock, 6 December 1326. This by the hand of M. John de Brunham, wardrobe official. In mid-December Stratford paid certain sums on the queen's behalf, and on the advice of the earl of Kent, for ten horses, one of which died en route. BL Harleian Ch. 43 I 40.

[70] The precise date of his accession is unknown, but it must have been shortly after 7 December. See above and BL Cotton MS Faustina B.v, fol. 49ʳ.

[71] *Responsiones*, cols. 2766-2767.

[72] *Calendar of Letter Books* E, p. 215.

[73] *Exeter Reg. Grandisson* 1, pp. 315-323, esp. 320-321; Lincoln Reg. Burghersh 2 (Reg. 5), fol. 390ʳ (*Concilia* 2, p. 534); WinRS, fol. 21ʳ. The bishop of London issued his mandate 20 December, reciting that of Reynolds dated 20 July, issued on the advice of the archbishop of Vienne and the bishop of Orange. According to *Annales Paulini*, p. 324, the papal envoys left the city "quasi timorati" three days after the St. Paul's "council." The

Writs for a parliament had been issued in the king's name on 28
October 1326. The assembly was originally scheduled for 14 December,
but then postponed until 7 January in the new year. At the opening of
parliament Edward was still nominally king; long before its dissolution
his son had replaced him.[74] The means by which this political revolution
was effected, and the motives of those involved, have been the subject of
minute investigation. Here we are concerned almost exclusively to
determine Stratford's participation in these momentous events. For this
purpose it will be useful to review the narratives of four chroniclers who
throw particular light on the matter: Geoffrey le Baker, the anonymous
author of what is called the Lanercost Chronicle, William Dene, and
another anonymous writer associated with Canterbury.

Geoffrey le Baker was an otherwise insignificant secular clerk from
Swinbrook in Oxfordshire. We know little about him apart from the fact
that he was somehow connected with Osney Abbey and that he was in a
position to gain some eye-witness testimony from Stratford's "nephew"
Sir Thomas (Laurence) de la More, a local knight.[75] One initially baffling
aspect of Baker's *Chronicon* is that despite Stratford's close concern with
Gascon and French affairs, the furore aroused by his provision to
Winchester, his advocacy of Isabella's journey to France, and his
advancement to office by the queen on her return, no mention is made
of him until January 1327. So conspicuous a series of omissions is
explicable, at least in part, if we interpret Baker's version of Edward II's
fall as a propaganda document. He was determined above all to find
scapegoats for the political revolution once it had begun to turn sour.[76]
Pride of place in his invective was reserved for Isabella; that vindictive
female, that merciless virago. But her satellites (punningly the *alumpni
Jesabele*),[77] in Baker's opinion the manipulators of the whole nasty
business, were none other than the much persecuted bishops of Hereford
and Lincoln, Orleton and Burghersh – more particularly Orleton. It was
no part of Baker's scheme to cast a jaundiced eye on Stratford's doings.
It is arguable, with only slight reservation, that Baker was favourably
disposed towards our subject,[78] despite his close involvement in Edward's

date of Isabella's arrival in London "with great solemnity" is given as 4 January 1327 in
TCC MS R.5 41, fol. 124^r.

[74] Parry, *Parliaments*, p. 91; *HBC*, p. 518.

[75] See Maunde Thompson's introduction to the *Chronicon*; Haines, *Church and
Politics*, pp. 102ff.

[76] Haines, *Church and Politics*, p. 106.

[77] *Chronicon*, p. 21.

[78] Under the year 1334 he describes Stratford (*Chronicon*, p. 55) as: "Vir magne
sapiencie et doctor egregius utriusque iuris."

displacement; an outcome manifestly distasteful to the chronicler.[79] The overt bias of Baker's *Chronicon*, which in its earlier part is mainly an expansion of the sober and circumspect account of a much more distinguished clerk, Adam Murimuth, has not prevented its acceptance as an important first-hand source for Edward's reign, especially its final moments.

But before dealing with Baker's version it is necessary to sketch the overall picture emerging from the various accounts of happenings at the 1327 parliament. It seems that there were two missions to King Edward, at the time imprisoned in Kenilworth Castle under the surveillance of Henry of Lancaster. The first of these was to secure the king's attendance, so that he might be given the opportunity (in theory at least) of being heard in his own defence. The second constituted a formal delegation charged with securing his renunciation of the kingship in conformity with what had been determined in parliament. With respect to the parliamentary proceedings, we are given the impression that certain bishops were given the task of political persuasion.

Baker does not record two journeys to Kenilworth, only the principal one (admittedly in two parts), nor does he mention the preliminary perorations. He begins his account of the parliamentary sessions in close reliance on Murimuth, from whom he copies the composition of the delegation to Kenilworth. After that he inserts a lengthy passage of his own to show what happened when the delegation reached its destination. Stratford, Orleton and Burghersh are named as the chief negotiators (college principales negocii tractandi). He claims to know because his mentor and patron, Thomas de la More, having been in the entourage of Bishop Stratford, saw what occurred and subsequently recorded his impressions in French.[80] Stratford and Burghersh were sent on ahead of the main party to induce the king, with the aid of Henry of Lancaster, to resign the crown in favour of his son. The three persuaders grouped themselves round Edward and assured him that after his deposition he would be held in no less esteem than formerly. With some adulteration of the truth (adulterantes verbum veritatis) they urged that the course they were advocating would carry merit with God, promote peace among the

[79] Who writes of the former monarch (*Chronicon*, p. 28) as: "Generosus dominus Edwardus, quondam rex."

[80] Ibid., p. 27. The so-called "Pipewell chronicle" records (BL Cotton MS Julius A.i, fol. 56^(r-v)) a preliminary mission of the bishops of Hereford (Orleton) and London (Gravesend) and a representative delegation which included the bishops of London, Winchester (Stratford) and Hereford. This is followed (ibid., fols. 60^r-62^r) by details of the coronation. Cf. PRO C.49/roll 11 (dorse).

king's subjects, and provide the sole means open to Edward for the future. In acting thus, Baker balefully observed, the bishops were prophesying in the manner of Caïphas – who gave advice to the Jews that it was expedient for one man to die for the people.[81] After the bishops had plied him for some time with these and other blandishments the king, not without much sobbing and sighing, bowed to their admonitions. Secure in the knowledge that a good pastor lays down his life for his sheep,[82] he chose to end his life for Christ rather than live to witness the disinheritance of his children and the further disturbance of his realm. According to this exposition, by the time the body of the delegation arrived Stratford and Burghersh had achieved their purpose. It was left to Orleton to arrange the delegates in order of precedence within the royal chamber. On emerging from his private room Edward was overcome by what he saw and fainted. It was Stratford and Henry of Lancaster who sprang to his aid, lifting him to his feet in a state of semi-consciousness. Orleton, whom Baker stigmatizes as the king's worst enemy, explained the purpose of those assembled and appended a threat similar to the one already made by Stratford and his companion: if Edward failed to surrender the crown to his son, whoever appeared most suited to rule would be chosen instead.[83] On the following morning homage was renounced through William Trussell, acting on behalf of the whole realm, while the steward of the king's household, Thomas le Blount, broke his staff of office. Their mission accomplished, the group made its way back to parliament.

For Stratford's biographer this is a significant chronicle because it gives the bishop of Winchester one of the two leading roles in the king's dethronement. The other main part was played allegedly by Bishop Burghersh, though in fact his involvement is suspect and possibly to be explained in terms of Baker's thesis that with Orleton he was a prime mover in the calamitous finale of Edward II's reign. Other major, and indeed minor, chroniclers do not mention Burghersh as a member of the second mission to Kenilworth, or even of the first. Incongruously, in view of Baker's calculated besmirching of Orleton, that bishop was relegated to a minor, more honorific position, though admittedly there is countervailing emphasis on his callousness in confronting the swooning Edward. It

---

[81] John 18.14.

[82] John 10.11.

[83] *Chronicon*, p. 28: "Quod eligerent in regem quemcumque visum ipsis apciorem pro regni tutela." Cf. ibid., p. 27: "Filiis quoque suis repudiatis, alium in regem exaltarent quam de sanguine regali."

must be allowed that Stratford is somewhat of a *deus ex machina*, for Baker, as we have shown, has given no earlier hint of his career despite its relevance to his theme. What is more he barely mentions him subsequently, even when in other accounts Stratford is portrayed as holding the centre of the stage.[84]

William Dene was a secular clerk of more elevated status than Baker. As archdeacon of Rochester – within easy reach of the capital – he was clearly close to many of the events he describes and much concerned with the everyday life of his diocesan, Hamo de Hethe, who took a negative part in national affairs. Unlike Baker he begins by telling us what went on in "the parliament of the queen regent" (regina regnans).[85] On the first day of the assembly, 7 January, all the prelates, earls, barons, and the people in great number, came together at Westminster.[86] Bishop Orleton, by what authority we are not told, thereupon proceeded to explain that were the queen to return to her husband she would be killed by him. He ended by posing the crucial question. Did they wish Edward or his son to rule over them? All were then sent away until the following morning, when the question was put a second time. After much vacillation, those present chose the son as with a single voice. Homage was then done to the new king, who was led into Westminster Hall with the cry, "Behold your king." Reynolds was next to speak, taking the demagogic theme, "The voice of the people is the voice of God." [87] Stratford followed him with an exegesis of the text, "If the head is weak, the other members suffer." [88] Orleton concluded with what, in view of the duke of Aquitaine's youth, might be thought an ambiguous topic, "Woe to the land whose king is a

[84] See, for instance, *Chronicon*, pp. 48, 53, 54-55, 61.

[85] BL Cotton MS Faustina B.v, fol. 49[r]. Dene received papal provision to the archdeaconry 15 September 1323, when it became vacant by the promotion of the cardinal bishop of Palestrina, Pierre des Préz, to York archdeaconry. The executors were Bishop Stratford, the abbot of Langdon and M. John de Lescapon, archdeacon of Dublin. Vatican Archives, *RV* 76, fol. 22[r-v]; *CPL 1305-1342*, p. 234.

[86] BL Cotton MS Faustina B.v, fol. 49[r]: "Omnes prelati, comites, barones, atque populus in multitudine magna et precipue cives London."

[87] "Vox populi vox Dei." Wilks, *Problem of Sovereignty*, p. 190, notes the coronation in 1328 of Louis IV of Bavaria "by the Roman people" and draws attention (ibid., n. 4) to the text used by Reynolds. He also quotes from Stanley, *Westminster Abbey*, p. 57, that a medal was struck to commemorate Edward III's coronation with the motto "Populi dat iura voluntas." Stanley adds that a hand was outstretched to save the falling crown with the words "Non rapit sed accipit." The original authority he did not know. The same story, but with the motto "Populo dat iura volenti," is in Carte, *General History* 2, p. 383. R. W. Southern, *Western Society and the Church in the Middle Ages*, p. 51, asserts that the "people" here means the magnates. However, the overall details of Edward II's deposition clearly argue a wider constituency.

[88] "Cuius capud infirmum cetera membra dolent."

boy!"[89] But in fact he appears to have been referring to Edward II's puerilities rather than to his son's tender years.[90] Understandably a degree of confusion followed these inflammatory addresses. When Thomas Wake had restored order there came a shout of "Ave rex" in recognition of the new monarch, and the bishops' fealty was taken by the justices. Archbishop Melton of York and Bishops Hethe of Rochester, Gravesend of London and Ross of Carlisle declined to take the oath. It was at this juncture, says Dene, that Bishops Gravesend, Hothum of Ely,[91] and Orleton were despatched with representatives of the laity to Kenilworth in order to renounce the homage of the realm.[92] In view of Gravesend's refusal to take the oath his inclusion is suspect; of Stratford we hear nothing. On the bishops' arrival the king pleaded abjectly for his life: to such entreaties, we are told, Orleton returned a cruel answer.[93] From this sketch it will be clear that Dene's version lays much more stress than Baker's on the parliamentary proceedings. He gives only a brief summary of what occurred at Kenilworth and allots to Stratford a subordinate part in the whole affair.

Internal evidence argues that it was a Franciscan friar (from Carlisle) rather than a canon of Lanercost Priory who was basically responsible for the "Lanercost Chronicle," behind which lies a lost Minorite original. All the same, the title has become accepted and will be used here.[94] Whoever the author was, he makes a clear distinction between a first and a second mission to Kenilworth.[95] The first comprised Stratford and Orleton, whose ostensible purpose was to persuade the king to come to parliament, there in conjunction with his liegemen to arrange what would be just and

[89] "Vae terre cuius rex puer est." Eccles. 10.16.

[90] Cf. *Lanercost*, p. 257, where Orleton is allotted a different text (Ecclus. 10.3): "Et multum ponderavit insipientes et fatuitates regis et facta sua puerilia, si puerilia dici debent."

[91] BL Cotton MS Faustina B.v, fol. 49ᵛ, and see Haines, *Church and Politics*, pp. 174, 214. According to the Brut (CCC MS 174), fol. 145ʳ, the bishop of Ely yielded fealty and homage (*sic*) for all the archbishops and bishops of England. The same source (fol. 144ʳ) names Hothum as one of the guardians of the king at Kenilworth.

[92] BL Cotton MS Faustina B.v, fol. 49ᵛ. The Brut (CCC MS 174), fol. 145ʳ, gives a more schematic account: Bishop Hothum acted for the clergy, the earl of Surrey for the earls, and William Trussell for the knights and sergeantry. For another recension of Trussell's revocation of homage see CCL Reg. I, fol. 415ᵛ.

[93] BL Cotton MS Faustina B.v, fol. 49ᵛ: "Cui Herefordensis penitenti et veniam petenti severum durum et crudelem inrespondendo se ostendit."

[94] For discussion of the authorship see Little, *Franciscan Papers*, pp. 42-54; idem, *EHR* 31 (1916), pp. 269-279; ibid. 32 (1917), pp. 48-49. Galbraith discusses the common relationship of the Lanercost and Anonimalle chronicles to a lost Minorite source: *Anonimalle Chronicle*, pp. xxiv-xxx and App., xlvi-xlix.

[95] *Lanercost*, pp. 257-258.

appropriate for the crown of England. Despite the chronicler's categorical statement, the two bishops could hardly have travelled to Kenilworth and back in the five days of the parliamentary session before 12 January. On that day they are stated to have entered Westminster Hall, where parliament was sitting, and to have declaimed the king's negative response "before all the clergy and people." [96] It was on the 13th that the bishops are supposed to have begun their addresses – one at a time – each on a separate day. Orleton took a verse of Ecclesiasticus for his theme: "A foolish king destroys his people." [97] His concluding words were greeted with a shout: "We do not wish him to reign over us any longer." The next day it was Stratford's turn. Taking as his text "My head is sick," [98] he proceeded to demonstrate that for many years England had suffered from the weakness of its ruler. Archbishop Reynolds spoke last, on the 15th, taking as his starting point: "The voice of the people is the voice of God." Having completed his peroration he informed his hearers that by the unanimous consent of all the earls and barons, archbishops and bishops, and of the whole clergy and people, Edward was to succeed his father. That done the magnates, with the consent of the community, sent delegates (solemnes nuncios) to the king at Kenilworth to renounce their homage and to declare his deposition. The chronicler names two bishops, Stratford and Orleton, among the contingent of twenty-four persons. In this recital of what happened Stratford is seen to have played a role at least equal in importance to that of his colleague of Hereford. On the two occasions where the bishops are mentioned together, Stratford is placed first. Moreover, it is arguable that in this narrative the order of speaking – Orleton, Stratford, Reynolds – is one of inverse importance; matters reached a climax with the primate's definitive pronouncement. [99]

From elsewhere we learn that Orleton himself was very willing to cede pride of place to Stratford, though admittedly in his own defence. So he claimed that the bishop of Winchester was responsible for the drawing up of the articles of deposition, which were incorporated in a public instrument by his secretary, William Mees. [100] And there are other places

---

[96] Ibid., p. 257: "Intraverunt magnam aulam Westmonasterii, ubi tenebatur parliamentum predictum, responsum durum coram toto clero et populo publice recitantes."

[97] "Rex insipiens perdet populum suum." Ecclus. 10.3. Cf. n. 90 above.

[98] "Caput meum doleo." 4 Kings 4.19.

[99] This is the basis of the statement in Haines, *Church and Politics*, p. 175, which perhaps goes a little too far, that the Lanercost chronicler "gives him [Stratford] even greater prominence than Orleton in the proceedings of the January 1327 parliamentary assembly."

[100] *Responsiones*, col. 2765: "Ea autem quae de consilio et assensu omnium praelatorum, comitum et baronum et tocius communitatis dicti regni concordata et ordinata

where it is recorded that these or similar articles were published by Archbishop Reynolds.[101]

The articles, though interesting from the point of view of the rationalization of the military coup, are not particularly remarkable, except perhaps for the comparative moderation of their tone and the total lack of rhetoric. They constitute a six-point indictment of Edward. The king had demonstrated his inadequacy for government by allowing himself to be badly counselled, to his own dishonour, the destruction of Holy Church, and to the detriment of his people. Instead of availing himself of wise counsel and exercising sound government, he had engaged in unsuitable occupations, without consideration for the business of the realm. By his default Scotland had been lost, as well as other lands in Gascony and Ireland, even though his father had left him in peace and amity with the king of France. By his haughty behaviour and as a consequence of evil advice he had damaged Holy Church, imprisoning some of its members and leaving others in distress. Great men of the land had been put to death, imprisoned, exiled and disinherited. Although by his oath he should have done right to all men, Edward had sought his own benefit and that of evil councillors close to him. He had abandoned his realm and people; his cruelty and the defects of his person had rendered him incorrigible without hope of reform.[102]

There remains the anonymous Canterbury-based chronicler responsible for the seemingly independent account in a Trinity College, Cambridge, manuscript.[103] With respect to chronology the author or compiler is refreshingly precise about the opening of parliament on 7 January and the deposition of Edward II on the 13th; thereafter no dates are inserted. Allusion to a mission to Kenilworth comes immediately after the deposition, but only as a part of Orleton's explanation of events to "the

---

fuerunt contra dictum regem et amotionem suam a regimine regni, contenta sunt in instrumentis publicis reverendo patre domino J[ohanne] Dei gratia nunc Cantuariensi electo tunc Wyntoniensi episcopo et Anglie thesaurario conceptis et dictatis, et manu magistri Willelmi de Mees clerici sui secretarii et publici notarii conscriptis et in publicam formam redactis."

[101] E.g. *French Chronicle*, p. 57, where articles are said to have been published 13 January.

[102] *Responsiones*, col. 2766.

[103] TCC MS R.5 41. Although for Edward II's reign this chronicle may prove to be largely independent, Stubbs in his introduction to the *Chronicles of Edward I and II* 2, pp. x-xi, pointed out that both it and College of Arms MS Arundel 20 (Chronicle of John of London) come from Christ Church, Canterbury (cf. n. 22 above), and "contain much common material." The "fifty dolia of wine" given by Reynolds as a sop to the Londoners (TCC MS R.5 41, fol. 124ʳ) is also recorded in BL Cotton MS Faustina B.v, fol. 50ʳ, and in the *Annales Paulini*, p. 323.

people." Further mention follows Edward III's coronation and the transfer of his father to Berkeley Castle; a separation of events which suggests that the passage was borrowed from some other source.[104] On the later occasion we are told the composition of the Kenilworth delegation, which included three unnamed bishops.[105] The remarkable feature of this chronicle is its directness in laying bare the nature of the political revolution. It actually names Roger Mortimer, who is not mentioned in the other sources we have examined, nor it seems elsewhere. Parliament, we are informed, commenced in the presence of the queen and of her son, but in the king's absence. It was the magnates and prelates who assembled in Westminster Hall, and it was the magnates who urged Roger Mortimer to declare to the people what had been determined. Mortimer initially demurred on the basis that he ought not to be held legally responsible (non debere culpari de iure) for what had been enjoined on him by common assent (communi omnium assensu). He then declared that the magnates had agreed that the king should no longer govern since he was inadequate, a destroyer of church and realm in violation of his oath and of the crown, and had adopted evil counsel. If the people agreed, the duke of Aquitaine was to reign in his stead. Thomas Wake then shouted that so far as he was concerned the king should reign no longer (dico pro me numquam regnabit). Only then do the prelates emerge to justify the action taken. Orleton, taking a texts from Proverbs, "Where there is no ruler, the people fall," [106] proceeded to explain the manner of the king's response at Kenilworth to him and to the magnates. As for Stratford, his participation would appear to have arisen from his own initiative (cupiens alloqui populum). His text is given as "My head is sick," as in the Lanercost Chronicle, but he is made to continue with the tag, "Where the head is weak the other members suffer," the theme allotted to him by the Rochester chronicler. Finally he declared that the king's son should reign, provided the people concurred with this decision of prelates and barons (si huic ordinacioni consentiret). When this question was put to those assembled, the reply was vociferously affirmative.[107] Last to speak was Archbishop Reynolds on the explosive theme: "The voice of the people is the voice of God." [108] Immediately he finished there was a threefold shout

---

[104] TCC MS R.5 41, fol. 125ᵛ.

[105] As well as two earls, two barons, two abbots and two justices. Ibid.

[106] Prov. 11.14.

[107] Thomas Wake put the question with arms extended and hands gesticulating; it was acclaimed "voce clamosa."

[108] As in *Lanercost* and the *Historia Roffensis*. Cf. n. 87 above. Here the chronicler states that Reynolds spoke to the people "in gallico" (rather than "in vulgari"). His

of "Fiat" followed by "Amen." It will be observed that the order of speaking duplicates that of the Lanercost Chronicle, but that the impression given of Stratford's political significance is different. Without question the Canterbury chronicler rates Stratford's involvement as comparatively minor. This is at one with his general lack of interest in the bishop's career.[109]

Complete reconciliation of these divergent historical impressions would be an impossible task,[110] but so far as Stratford is concerned they combine to furnish abundant evidence of his involvement in the process of justification of the political revolution and in the creation of a quasi-legal basis for it. To achieve these purposes he was working with an equally well-qualified lawyer, his episcopal colleague Orleton. But if we are to judge from subsequent events this must have been an uneasy alliance; both men were strong characters and their objectives, though sometimes difficult to determine with precision, were clearly not always the same. Although the reality of power lay elsewhere, its manipulation lay mainly with Stratford and Orleton, who from the ecclesiastical viewpoint dominated the scene for the duration of the political change-over.

It was during the parliamentary sessions, on the feast of St. Hilary (13 January 1327),[111] that a large concourse of laymen and clerics came before the mayor and aldermen of London and took an oath to support Isabella and her son Edward in their cause against the younger Despenser and Robert Baldock, to give good counsel, to safeguard the city's liberties, and to maintain what had been accomplished so far in the "quarrel," as well as to observe the ordinances made, or to be made, in the current parliament.[112] Apart from the metropolitans of Canterbury and Dublin,

---

argument was that they had appealed to God for remedy and this had been granted by the action of the barons, subject to the people's assent (si unanimiter consentitis).

[109] He has no mention of Stratford's promotion to Winchester or Canterbury, or of his death. Of course, chroniclers were often uneven in their treatment of people or events. Orleton is important as the spokesman of the Kenilworth delegation. It will be observed that in this narrative the king is made to agree to the substitution of his son prior to the parliamentary speeches. Most of the relevant part of the chronicle is printed (with a number of errors and oddly paragraphed) by Fryde, *Tyranny of Edward II*, pp. 233-235.

[110] Wilkinson, "Deposition of Richard II," pp. 223-230, essayed the task, but only for certain chroniclers. See Haines, *Church and Politics*, pp. 168-169ff.

[111] Generally regarded by the chroniclers as the day of Edward's deposition. E.g. *French Chronicle*, p. 57; Bodl. Lib. Bodley MS 956, pp. 205-206; TCC MS R.5 41, fol. 124[r] (recte 125[r]). According to BL Cotton MS Galba E.iv, fol. 183[v], the day of the king's renunciation was 24 January "et eodem die rex Edwardus filius eius tercius post Conquestum incepit regnare."

[112] *Cal. PMR*, pp. 12-14. Cf. *Annales Paulini*, pp. 322-323, where the text of the oath really belongs to a later occasion – 20 January (*Cal. PMR*, p. 11 n. 2; *French Chronicle*,

twelve diocesan bishops took the oath, Stratford as bishop of Winchester and acting-treasurer heading the list, Orleton bringing up the rear. Melton of York and Bishops Ross of Carlisle, Berkeley of Exeter (elected on 5 December but as yet unconsecrated),[113] Gravesend of London and Beaumont of Durham – clearly occupied elsewhere – were the only diocesans whose names are missing. From Dene we learn that Melton, Gravesend and Ross actually refused the oath. And so, he added, an immense crowd came to witness the fatuity of the bishops as they made their sacrifice to Mahomet.[114] Another oath, in which the young Edward is styled king, is said to have been taken on 20 January by Archbishop Reynolds and seven other bishops.[115]

Shortly after this, 28 January 1327, Stratford relinquished his office at the treasury. He was not to hold a government position again until 1330,[116] when Edward III assumed personal rule. It is customary to interpret this as a shift of political power, but Orleton who succeeded as treasurer, himself acted for a mere two months, although credited with being a confidant of Isabella and Mortimer. It almost looks as though, their function performed, the bishops were jettisoned; but it could be that their skill was more urgently required abroad. It was not long before both bishops resumed their diplomatic activities as representatives of the new government; Stratford at the court of France, Orleton at the papal curia in Avignon.

Meanwhile preparations had been made for the coronation of the duke of Aquitaine as Edward III. Jean de Hainault knighted him; the queen judiciously absented herself to Eltham for three days. The coronation ceremony took place in Westminster Abbey on the Sunday before Candlemas, 1 February 1327. Archbishop Reynolds crowned and anointed the new king assisted by Stratford and – so it is said – Gravesend, who on account of Edward's tender years supported the crown on his head. To avoid the crush of people the king was given a seat high up in the

p. 58). In TCC MS R.5 41, fol. 124ʳ, the taking of the oaths is not dated but comes at the beginning of the account of parliament.

[113] Le Neve 9, p. 1. Cf. BL Cotton MS Faustina B.v, fol. 50ᵛ, where the bishops of Chichester and Rochester are said to have attended the consecration, 22 March 1327.

[114] Cal. PMR, p. 13; BL Cotton MS Faustina B. V, fol. 50ʳ: "In presencia comitis Canc. et multitudinis immense qui ad videndum fatuitatem episcoporum quomodo machumeto sacrificabant confluxerunt."

[115] Cal. PMR, p. 11; French Chronicle, p. 58; Annales Paulini, pp. 322-323. See n. 112 above.

[116] CPR 1327-1330, p. 1. Appointment of Orleton as treasurer (28 January 1327) with mandates in pursuance to Archbishop Melton, late treasurer, and John Stratford, former deputy-treasurer.

monastic choir.[117] At this point the Brut adds some interesting information not found in other chroniclers.[118] Because Edward was so young and his father had been misled by false councillors, it was ordained at the coronation[119] that he was to be governed by twelve great lords of the land, without whom nothing should be done. The episcopate provided one third of this advisory council. In addition to Stratford we find the archbishops of Canterbury and York and Orleton. Melton's inclusion is noteworthy, for he had been extremely reluctant to accept the change of king. From the laity came four earls, those of Lancaster, Norfolk (the earl marshal), Kent and Surrey, and an equivalent number of barons, Thomas Wake, Henry Percy, Oliver Ingham and John Ros. These men were to counsel the king truly and to give details of their governance every year in parliament.[120] Elsewhere it is claimed that nothing was to be effected without the oversight of four members of the council: a bishop, an earl, and two barons.[121] Presumably this body was not initiated without Mortimer's acquiescence but, laments the author of the Brut, it soon lapsed and all was determined by Isabella and Roger Mortimer alone.[122] The plaint is echoed by the royalist Dene who remarked that for a period of some four years after the coronation Mortimer reigned and the queen ruled.[123] It was an outcome bitterly disappointing for Stratford.

Following the coronation, parliament resumed its sitting and was flooded with petitions for the redress of grievances suffered under Edward II's rule.[124] Already on 9 February Stratford had secured the

---

[117] BL Cotton MS Faustina B.v, fol. 50ʳ; cf. Foedera 2, ii, p. 172. The latter "official account" does not record Gravesend's attendance, nor that of Hethe, whom Dene describes as taking a prominent part in the ceremony. See Haines, Church and Politics, p. 178. The Annales Paulini, pp. 324-325, record the participation of Gravesend and Stratford.

[118] CCC MS 174, fols. 152ᵛ-153ʳ.

[119] Although the council's composition suggests formation prior to Hothum's appointment as chancellor, 28 January 1327.

[120] Brut (CCC MS 174), fol. 153ʳ: "Alle þese were sore treuliche forto conceile þe king and þey shulde ensuere every ȝere in þe parlement of þat shulde be done in þe tyme of þat governayle" (continued in n. 122 below).

[121] Knighton, p. 454; Rot. Parl. 2, p. 52.

[122] Brut (CCC MS 174), fol. 153ʳ (see n. 120 above): "But þat ordynaunce was sone owen done and þat was muche lost and harme to al Engelond for þe king and al þe lordes þat shulde governe him were governed and reuled after þe kinges moder dame Isabel and by sire Roger þe Mortymer and as þey wolde al þing was done boþe amonge hey and amonge lowe."

[123] BL Cotton MS Faustina B.v, fol. 50ᵛ: "Regnavit sic Rogerus de Mortuo Mary et regina imperavit circiter quatuor annis."

[124] Ibid., fol. 50ʳ⁻ᵛ: "In crastino omnes ad parliamentum convenientes multi et magni de regno sperantes de novo rege petitiones a tempore Johannis regis dependentes fuisse expeditas." Cf. Foedera 2, ii, p. 172; Rot. Parl. Inediti, pp. 99-179; Rot. Parl. 2, pp. 3-12.

cancellation of the heavy recognizances which had been demanded from him by the former king.[125] He proceeded to petition for the restitution of four hundred marks which the royal custodians had levied upon the churches of East Meon and Hambledon, which formed part of the spiritualities of his bishopric.[126] On a broader front Stratford endeavoured to avoid future depredations by petitioning that at times of vacancy the cathedral chapter should be allowed to administer the temporalities on payment of an appropriate sum to the exchequer.[127] Stratford's temporary position of influence is reflected in a number of concessions made at his instigation and recorded on the patent rolls.[128]

Parliament was still in session on 22 February 1327 when an embassy was formed to negotiate a truce with King Charles of France. Apart from Stratford its members consisted of Bishop Ayrminne of Norwich, John of Brittany, Jean de Hainault and Hugh Audley. Safe-conduct was issued on 7 March and, the following day, protection until Michaelmas.[129] It was also on the 8th that Stratford went in person to the exchequer and there received £166 13s 4d towards the expenses of his mission.[130] Two days before this, a number of persons who may be described as constituting the ruling group in the country witnessed the City of London's charter of liberties.[131] This group, somewhat smaller than the standing council, comprised four bishops – the primate Reynolds, Chancellor Hothum, Ayrminne and Orleton – as well as the earls of Norfolk, Lancaster and Kent, and three barons – Mortimer himself, Wake and Ross.[132] As Stratford was in the capital at the time his omission might indicate a falling-off in political influence. Perhaps this was the case; we cannot be

[125] *Foedera* 2, ii, pp. 174-175. As late as 13 September 1326 at Porchester Stratford acknowledged a debt of £2,000 payable to the younger Despenser, which was cancelled 1 Edward III. *CCR 1323-1327*, p. 647. See above, "Councillor and Diplomatic Envoy."

[126] *Rot. Parl. Inediti*, p. 173. See above, "Winchester 1323-1333," n. 123.

[127] PRO S.C.8/15/719. See above, "Winchester 1323-1333," n. 122.

[128] E.g. on behalf of Edmund de Shireford and John de Basinges. See above, "Stratford's *Familia* and Administration." At his request Thomas de la More was exempted for life from being put on assizes or appointed sheriff etc. against his will. *CPR 1327-1330*, p. 184.

[129] *Foedera* 2, ii, p. 180; *CPR 1327-1330*, p. 16: Westminster 22 February 1327; ibid., pp. 30-31.

[130] Under writ of privy seal issued on 7 March. PRO E.372/172/8; E.101/309/40.

[131] This is prefaced by a pardon (28 February 1327) for all homicides, robberies and other crimes committed between the date of Isabella's landing (24 September 1326) and the coronation. *Annales Paulini*, pp. 325-332.

[132] *Annales Paulini*, p. 332. Orleton was treasurer. Ayrminne until Hothum's appointment (28 January 1327) had been keeper of the great seal. *HBC*, p. 84; Tout, *Chapters* 6, pp. 10-11.

sure. Certainly there were no obvious signs of any diminution in his status. Leaving London on 9 March he crossed from Dover with a larger complement than on any previous occasion. Into three ships and a barge were loaded sixty-three horses and ninety-five men. In mid-channel the wind dropped and an extra boat had to be chartered to bring the bishop ashore at Wissant. Arrived in port he sent his messenger Adam[133] to Paris with news of his intentions and at Beauvais welcomed him back. From Paris Adam was despatched to Peterborough and the courier (cursor) John to Nottingham, as necessitated by the migration of the English court. John returned to Stratford at Clermont, not far north of the French capital. The bishop appears to have been either there or at Paris for the remainder of his stay abroad.[134] The number of messages which he despatched was considerable.[135] Bishop Ayrminne was contacted at Dover in late April, the count of Boulogne at Wissant, the archbishop of Vienne at Lisieux (Lusarch') , the papal curia at Avignon, and the English government at a variety of places from York to Wargrave.[136] At last, on 31 March, Stratford's efforts and those of the other ambassadors resulted in the sealing of an agreement at Paris. By this the lands in Aquitaine were to be restored, the English king was to pay a substantial sum of fifty-thousand marks, and there was to be an arrangement whereby men of each side could return to their own lands.[137] For the writing of various letters of safe-conduct and for the engrossing of the peace agreement Stratford paid £7 13s 4d to M. Peter de Pretis and a further twenty-five shillings to his clerk. The treaty concluded, Stratford remained in France – mainly at Paris – for another two months before recrossing the channel. Reaching Canterbury on 1 June, he despatched the courier Adam to the king at York with news of his return.[138]

The state of affairs at home was disturbed, as Dene and other chroniclers affirm. At the time of James de Berkeley's consecration as bishop of Exeter on mid-Lent Sunday the inhabitants of Canterbury are said to have emulated those of London in their unruliness. In every city, town or vill, claimed Dene, malefactors were in control. After Trinity,

---

[133] Adam [de Stivynton or Stevinton?] himself was at a later stage (June 1327?) of the negotiations to have an escort of five men to ensure his safe passage from Dover to Wissant.

[134] The various journeys made by *nuncii* on the bishop's behalf are itemized in Stratford's original account, PRO E.101/39/40.

[135] Ibid.

[136] Ibid.

[137] *Foedera* 2, ii, pp. 185-186.

[138] PRO E.101/39/40.

within a few days of Stratford's return, a Rochester mob broke down the cathedral doors and beseiged the monks for a whole night. It was at the Lincoln parliament, so we are told, that on 22 September 1327 Thomas Gurney, that "satellite of Satan," informed the queen of her husband's death.[139] Stratford had been summoned to the assembly but excused himself on the grounds that he was too busy about the affairs of his church to attend in person.[140] Edward II's protégé, Archbishop Reynolds, had died on 16 November at his manor of Mortlake. Eleven days afterwards he was buried at Canterbury with Stratford and the Rochester diocesan, Hethe, in attendance.[141] The passing of Edward of Carnarvon and of Reynolds marks the end of an era in political affairs and provides a convenient place at which to pause. The brief period of Stratford's influence as one of the principal manipulators of the revolution had passed.

"LANCASTRIAN SPOKESMAN" 1328-1330

The revolution achieved by a temporary coalition of alienated groups, including the greater part of the baronage, a portion of the episcopal bench, and the City of London, had been skilfully manipulated by able but often incompatible men, notably Stratford and Orleton, both of whom entertained a lawyer's respect for appropriate procedure and due form. Ostensibly, and by design, it appeared to command wide "popular" support. But no sooner was the primary objective achieved than a political struggle ensued between, on the one hand, the supporters of Queen Isabella and of Roger Mortimer who retained custody of the king, and on the other, those of Henry of Lancaster in alliance with men who were

---

[139] BL Cotton MS Faustina B.v, fol. 51[r]. Cf. *French Chronicle*, p. 60; *Knighton* 1, p. 446. This date is probably that of Gurney's departure from Berkeley. Cf. Smyth, *Lives* 1, pp. 296-297, where Gurney is said to have carried the news to Nottingham. The king is believed to have died 21 September. This date, the feast of St. Matthew, was observed for his annual commemoration, e.g. by Croxden Abbey, *Foedera* 2, ii, p. 198, and by Canterbury Cathedral Priory, BL Cotton MS Galba E.iv, fol. 183[v]. It is the date recorded in official documents, e.g. Moore, "Documents relating to Edward II," p. 223 (Chancellor's roll, 1 Edward III). But see below, "Lancastrian Spokesman."

[140] The writ in Stratford's register is dated 7 August 1327 and the assembly described in the margin as a council. It was summoned for the morrow of the Exaltation, i.e. 15 September. WinRS, fols. 29[r-v], 203[r].

[141] BL Cotton MS Faustina B.v, fol. 51[r]: "Die sancti Edmundi confessoris obiit Walterus archiepiscopus Cant. apud Mortelake et sepultus est in ecclesia Cant. die Veneris proxima post festum sancte Katerine cuius sepulture affuerunt Wynton. et Roff. episcopi." Cf. CCL Reg. Q, fol. 123[r] (al. cviii).

anxious to keep green the memory of the dispossessed monarch. Despite the widely-held view that he was a staunch adherent of Mortimer, Orleton chose this moment to retire from internal politics, though continuing to cooperate with the government to the extent of acting as envoy to France and Avignon. Stratford was soon forced to adopt a different course. Deliberately excluded from all hope of office at home or of employment abroad – as he was later to point out with some bitterness[1] – he determined to make himself felt in opposition.

How Stratford came to be associated with the "Lancastrian cause" is obscure. As we have seen, he emerged into political prominence only with his promotion to Winchester in 1323, the year after Thomas of Lancaster's death following the battle of Boroughbridge. Prior to that time he had been one of a group of lesser councillors with excellent opportunities for observing political processes at first hand. His close contact with Thomas's brother, Henry of Lancaster, seemingly dates from the time of his mission to the king at Kenilworth early in 1327, when the earl was acting as Edward II's custodian. It was towards the end of that year, when the Canterbury convocation met at Leicester, that Stratford, Chancellor Hothum and Earl Henry are said to have promised to secure the implementation of certain conditions attached to the grant of a clerical tenth towards the cost of operations against the Scots. Such conditions were in fact ignored.[2] What we can be sure about is that Stratford was not a relative of Earl Henry's, as is suggested by an entry in the *Calendar of Papal Letters*.[3]

The "Lancastrian cause" was a strong one, which its supporters strove to dignify by urging on the pope the canonization both of Thomas of Lancaster and of Archbishop Robert Winchelsey, who had taken his stand alongside the magnates against Edward II's favourite, Piers Gave-

---

[1] *Vitae Arch. Cant.*, p. 29 (Lambeth MS 99, fol. 140ᵛ): "Quia tunc de regiis negociis non intromisimus quovis modo, sed in curia regia, qua de causa novit Deus, omnibus fuimus odiosi." Exactly when this ostracism began is hard to tell. Presumably it came after his return from France at the end of May 1327.

[2] *Annales Paulini*, p. 348; cf. p. 338. The information is given in connection with the refusal of the clergy to grant a subsidy at the Lambeth convocation of 1330 (for which see below).

[3] *CPL 1305-1342*, p. 313. Cf. Vatican Archives, *RA* 36, fols. 393ᵛ-4ʳ; *RV* 94, fol. 154ʳ. This is a licence for Stratford when bishop of Winchester to appoint two notaries, issued at the petition of the earl of Lancaster and dated 30 June 1330. It is in the usual form and the relevant passage (in which the editor apparently took "fraternitas" to mean "consanguineus") is as follows (from *RA*): "Hinc est quod nos dilecti filii nobilis viri Henrici comitis Lancastrie et Leicestrie devotis supplicacionibus inclinati, fraternitati tue de qua fiduciam gerimus...."

ston.[4] At a more mundane level the struggle for power seethed below the surface, so that the details are obscured. But it is apparent that Henry of Lancaster was gradually edged out of the commanding position which he appears to have occupied early in 1327. The chroniclers explain this in terms of the increasing dominance of Isabella and Mortimer and their "accroachment" of royal power.[5]

The rift between the two groups is exemplified by the government's Scottish policy. In 1323 Edward II had concluded a thirteen-year truce with Robert Bruce which, though ill-kept on both sides,[6] served to ameliorate the previous condition of chronic warfare and devastating border incursions. Edward III's accession had been marked by an opportunist Scottish attack on Berwick, which was followed by the ignominious skirmish at Stanhope Park, when James Douglas in a commando-like exercise led a party of armed men into the English encampment and all but captured the young king as he lay asleep.[7] Some chroniclers affected to believe that this could only have been engineered

---

[4] E.g. *Foedera* 2, ii, pp. 181, 183. In general, for the archbishop's repute see Denton, *Winchelsey*, pp. 15-33. Meanwhile alms were being collected for the chapel under construction on the hill outside Pontefract where Earl Thomas was beheaded. *Foedera* 2, ii, p. 190 (cf. ibid. 2, ii, p. 4). Maddicott, *Lancaster*, p. 319, suggests that the earl was on "close personal terms only with Warwick and possibly Archbishop Winchelsey," whose canonization he tried to secure and whom, according to Davies, *Baronial Opposition*, p. 108, he is alleged to have regarded as a "pillar of baronial opposition." See also ibid., p. 62; *Lit. Cant.* 1, pp. 50-53. For the veneration of "Seint" Thomas as a martyr before the tablet he had erected in St. Paul's see *French Chronicle*, pp. 46, 54. Maddicott, *Lancaster*, pp. 329-330, summarizes the earl's posthumous reputation. The longest chronicle account of his miracles is probably that in the Brut (ccc ms 174), fols. 136ʳ-138ʳ; and see for the "office of St. Thomas of Lancaster," Wright, *Political Songs*, pp. 268-272; *Documents Illustrating the History of St. Paul's Cathedral*, pp. 11-14.

[5] E.g. bl Cotton ms Faustina B.v, fol. 50ᵛ (where Isabella and Mortimer are assumed to have determined affairs from the beginning of the reign); Brut (ccc ms 174), fols. 149ʳ, 152ʳff. (which gives one of the fullest accounts of the early years of the reign); *French Chronicle*, pp. 61-62 (La royne dame Isabele et sire Roger Mortimer achrocherent à eux real poair des plousours grauntz d'Engeltere et de Gales); *Knighton* 1, p. 447 (Appropriaverunt sibi regalem potestatem in multis et regni thesaurum, et subpeditaverunt regem).

[6] The truce concluded 30 May 1323 at Bishopthorpe (*Foedera* 2, ii, pp. 73-75) contained a clause to the effect that Edward would not hinder the Scots in their quest for absolution from papal penalties. Yet, as we have seen ("Councillor and Diplomatic Envoy") Stratford was upbraided for failing to do just that. *The Bruce* (p. 471) claims that the English destroyed Scottish ships despite the truce. See Barrow, *Bruce*, pp. 353-354ff.

[7] There is a lengthy account in *The Bruce*, pp. 482-488. See also *Lanercost*, pp. 259-260; Brut (ccc ms 174), fols. 150ʳ-151ʳ; *French Chronicle*, p. 60; *Knighton* 1, p. 445. It was from Stanhope that the king summoned the Lincoln assembly for 15 September; the writ mentions the skirmish in the park. See above, "From Conformist to Revolutionary."

with English connivance, Mortimer being the obvious scapegoat.[8] Lancaster is thought to have favoured an offensive policy;[9] Isabella and Mortimer were determined to conclude a permanent peace – doubtless swayed by the insecurity of their position at home, but also mindful of continental problems. Scottish representatives were invited to the parliament which met at York in February 1328, and to which Stratford came. It was there on 1 March that the English king, acting as a mouthpiece of the ruling group, acknowledged Scotland to be a separate kingdom. The understanding was to be sealed by the marriage of Edward III's sister, Joan "of the Tower," and Bruce's son David. Significantly it was on the other side of the border, at Edinburgh, that the arrangements were hastily concluded just over a fortnight later.[10] The Edinburgh treaty was ratified at the Northampton parliament on 4 May.[11] Modern opinion tends to regard the treaty as essentially reasonable and long overdue. Not surprisingly, in 1328 many Englishmen held the view that long-fought-for interests and rights had been wantonly sacrificed on the altar of political expediency. Geoffrey le Baker waxed vociferous on the subject of the "turpis pax," placing the blame on Isabella and Mortimer, to whose names he gratuitously added that of Bishop Orleton.[12]

During and after the session of parliament at Northampton there occurred a government reshuffle. The treasurer, Bishop Burghersh, one of

---

[8] E.g. *French Chronicle*, p. 60: "Par assent des ascuns treitres"; *Bridlington*, p. 97: "Non fecisset nisi cum quibusdam Anglicis conspirasset"; Baker, *Chronicon*, p. 35: "Permissione quorumdam magnorum prodiciose cum ipsis confederatorum." The Brut (CCC MS 174), fols. 150v-151r, 155v, 163v, is certain that Mortimer was the guilty party and that by his connivance the Scots escaped unmolested. The charge was to figure in Mortimer's indictment. See n. 14 below.

[9] Brut (CCC MS 174), fol. 150v.

[10] Barrow, *Bruce*, pp. 360-369; Stones, "The English Mission to Edinburgh," gives details of the expenses and itineraries of the leaders of the English delegation; idem, "The Treaty of Northampton"; Nicholson, *Edward III and the Scots*, chap. 4. For the documents: *Foedera* (R.C.) 2, pp. 730, 734-735.

[11] Barrow, *Bruce*, p. 364: "The peace was concluded after a bare week of final discussion on March 17th."

[12] *Chronicon*, p. 41; cf. *Murimuth*, p. 57. The blaming of Orleton is an interpolation in a passage taken from Murimuth. Haines, *Church and Politics*, pp. 109-110. The Brut (CCC MS 174), fol. 154r, speaks of the "accursed day" that the Northampton parliament was ordained and of the "false disinheritance" of the English king. See also *Lanercost*, p. 261, which records that the treaty arose from the evil counsel of the queen mother and of Mortimer, "Qui erant ductores praecipui regis." Cf. *Knighton* 1, p. 444, for whom the treaty arose "Propter quandam conventionem inter illos [Scotos] et matrem regis Isabellam, et Edmundum comitem Cantiae, et Rogerum de Mortuo Mari dum starent in transmarinis contra coronam Angliae." Dene asserts (BL Cotton MS Faustina B.v, fols. 61v-62r) that peace was made "Absque concensu prelatorum et parium regni vel saltim sanioris partis eorundem."

the negotiators at Edinburgh, became chancellor, while Bishop Charlton succeeded him in his former office. John de Wysham was made steward and Sir Thomas Wake chamberlain. The last two had strong Lancastrian sympathies, but those present in St. Andrew's priory, Northampton, for the transfer of the great seal to Burghersh were predominantly of the Mortimer persuasion.[13] It is said that Lancaster was allotted the influential task of acting as councillor in permanent attendance on the youthful monarch, but this claim was advanced later by his opponents in their anxiety to prove his dereliction of duty. The Lancastrian interpretation of the matter was that Earl Henry was denied access to the king.[14]

At Northampton the pacific withdrawal of claims to Scotland was paralleled by the militant decision to assert kingship in another quarter. It cannot be that the two were unconnected.[15] The death of Charles le Bel and the coronation of Philip vi of Valois in his stead elicited a protest which was carried to Paris by Bishops Orleton and Northburgh. Stratford was later to single out this policy of asserting Edward iii's right to the French crown as the precipitating factor in the conflict known to us as the Hundred Years' War.[16] At the time the protagonists of the idea claimed that Lancaster was a consenting party.[17]

[13] *Annales Paulini*, pp. 339-340; *Cal. PMR*, p. 79; *CCR 1327-1330*, p. 387. The Pauline annalist states that the bishop of Norwich (Ayrminne) became chancellor and that of Chester (Northburgh) treasurer. Norwich is an error, but Northburgh though appointed 2 March 1328, apparently did not act. Tout, *Chapters* 3, pp. 16-18; 6, pp. 11, 21; *HBC*, pp. 84, 101.

[14] *Cal. PMR*, p. 79; Brut (ccc ms 174), fol. 153ʳ; *French Chronicle*, p. 62: "Henry counte de Lancaster, qe estoit fait gardein du roy a comensement de son couronement par commun assent de tut le realme, ne poeit a luy approcher ne conseiller." The first article of the indictment of Mortimer asserts his responsibility. For this indictment see *Knighton* 1, pp. 454-458; *Rot. Parl.* 2, pp. 52-53.

[15] As the author of *Lanercost* (p. 262) thought: "Erat quia nisi rex prius fecisset pacem cum Scottis non potuisset Francos, qui eum exheredaverant, impugnasse, quin Scotti Angliam invasissent." The treaty of Corbeil (April 1326) involved an undertaking by Scotland and France to assist each other against the English king. *APS* 12, pp. 5-6.

[16] *Vitae Arch. Cant.*, p. 29 (Lambeth ms 99, fol. 140ᵛ): "Qui [Bishops Orleton and Northburgh] juxta ordinationem hujusmodi eis legationem injunctam tunc assumentes, gressus suos versus Franciam direxerunt: quae quidem legatio maximam guerrae praesentis materiam ministravit." Cf. *Foedera* 2, iii, p. 13: 16 May 1328. Dene (bl Cotton ms Faustina B.v, fol. 79ᵛ) states: "Et quando rex Anglie Adam Wygorn. et Rogerum Lychefeldensem episcopos ad coronacionem regis Francie miserat ad contradicendum predicti regis coronacionem et ostendendum ius regis Anglie, iste Robertus de Artoys respondit pro rege et omnibus aliis de regno Francie quod rex Anglie ius nullum habuit ad coronam Francie et episcopos comminabatur ut recederent et sic metu recesserunt." Philip was more concerned with Flanders, and the English protest was disregarded. See Perroy, *Hundred Years War*, pp. 81-82; Déprez, *Les préliminaires*, p. 36 (where "Chichester" should read "Chester").

[17] *Cal. PMR*, p. 78.

During the summer of 1328 the internal situation deteriorated markedly. Lancaster is reported to have attended the king's court at Warwick as well as a council which met at Worcester in June, but to have been unwilling to approve the despatch of forces to Gascony until a larger assembly had been given opportunity to discuss the proposal. When parliament did meet at York in July the earl excused himself from attendance. In any case, as Stratford pointed out in returning the summons, the time available was insufficient for him to execute the writ. So a further assembly was summoned to Salisbury for October. On the way south, at Barlings near Lincoln, the king's entourage encountered the earl and his armed retinue. We are told that Edward – then in his sixteenth year – orally demanded that Lancaster attend the forthcoming parliament.[18]

The omens were inauspicious. Lancaster was intent on mustering support for opposition to what, for want of a better name, we may call the court party. As early as 12 August the Londoners were in guarded correspondence with the earls of Kent and Lancaster, Stratford, and Thomas Wake, whom they thanked for past favours. In mid-September Stratford and Wake appeared in the city where they are said to have publicized the opinion that the king lacked good counsel and the means to support his own household – allegations that according to the government were maliciously spread abroad at Avignon and the French court by foreigners who abounded in London.[19] Archbishop Mepham arrived on 25 September from Norfolk, where he had done fealty to the king at Lynn. His stated purpose was to visit his dying brother, M. Edmund, though in the light of his later commitment one may surmise that he had other business as well.[20] The court did not remain inactive. Oliver Ingham and Bartholomew Burghersh were sent to elicit from the city authorities an explanation of the activities of Stratford and Wake. Their written response to the enquiry is dated 27 September. When the king paused at Cambridge on his way south news reached him of the mobilization of men-at-arms by Earl Henry at Higham Ferrers in Northamptonshire. It comes as no surprise to find that Stratford was there on the 11th. For

---

[18] Ibid., p. 79; for Stratford's return to the writ of summons: WinRS, fols. 38^v-39^r. The York parliament met 31 July - 6 August 1328, that at Salisbury 16-31 October, being adjourned to Westminster. Parry, *Parliaments*, p. 93; *HBC*, p. 518.

[19] *Cal. PMR*, pp. 66, 68-69. Stratford and Wake addressed the citizens in the Guildhall on 17 September.

[20] *Annales Paulini*, p. 342.

safety's sake the royal party joined forces with the queen mother and they travelled as a unit to Salisbury.[21]

Parliament began to assemble on 16 October, Bishop Burghersh and M. Walter Hervy, archdeacon of Salisbury, having been delegated to open the proceedings. The Lancastrian sympathizers mustered in some number. Among them may perhaps be counted the king's uncles, Thomas of Brotherton and Edmund of Woodstock, earls respectively of Norfolk and Kent,[22] and certainly the archbishop of Canterbury, whom Dene pungently dismisses as a political ignoramus.[23] There were some conspicuous absentees. Lancaster's excuses for not being present were conveyed by his proctors, but many people supposedly found them less than satisfactory. The bishops were too cautious to voice their opinion, preferring – according to one source – to await the bishop of Winchester's arrival. When Stratford eventually put in an appearance it was to claim that the reason for the earl's absence was his dispute with Mortimer. To this the bishop added an item of hearsay; Mortimer had concluded the Scottish treaty in order to free his hands for an attack on Lancaster. But, Stratford concluded, all might still be well if an arrangement could be made between the contending parties.[24]

Against these aspersions Mortimer, about this time created earl of March,[25] defended himself in the king's presence. He did so, it is claimed, to the satisfaction of the prelates and of others. He then ostentatiously took

[21] *Cal. PMR*, pp. 68-69, 79-80; WinRS, fol. 110ʳ. Letters of credence for Ingham and Burghersh were issued 22 September from Horsford (north of Norwich). The city authorities replied with a summary of the Lancastrian grievances: 1. The king should live of his own and have sufficient treasure to enable him to deal with his enemies; 2. It had been laid down at the Westminster parliament (1327) that the king should havs prelates and barons around him to give counsel; 3. Peace should be maintained in the realm. Cf. Brut (CCC MS 174), fol. 155ʳ. The citizens' response was that amendment should be effected in parliament.

[22] Holmes, "Rebellion of Lancaster," p. 85, regards the earls as "among the more disinterested," but Kent's wife, Margaret, was sister and heiress of Lord Wake. Dugdale, *Baronage* 1, p. 541; *Annales Paulini*, p. 310.

[23] *Foedera* 2, iii, p. 20; BL Cotton MS Faustina B.v, fol. 51ᵛ: "In festo omnium sanctorum [1 November] tentum est parliamentum apud Sar. ubi archiepiscopus novus modum et mores hominum totaliter ignorans comitibus Kancie et Lancastrie et eorum sequele qui contra reginam et Rogerum de Mortuo Mari regnantes sub colore utilitatis regni se partem facientes cepit adherere."

[24] *Cal. PMR*, p. 80.

[25] The date of his elevation is usually given as 16 X 31 October – the term of the parliament. One chronicler says he was made earl "quodam die Dominico" (16, 23 and 30 October were Sundays in 1328). As the Sunday in question was supposedly the day of Stratford's flight, the 30th is the most likely date. *Vitae Arch. Cant.*, p. 19 (Lambeth MS 99, fol. 136ʳ). The Pauline annalist reports (pp. 342-343): "Et talis comitatus nunquam prius fuit nominatus in regno Angliae."

an oath on the cross of the archbishop to the effect that he intended no harm to the earl of Lancaster or his people. This done, Stratford and Stephen Gravesend, the bishop of London whose sympathies lay very much with the dispossessed king, were delegated to report the parliamentary happenings to Lancaster and to urge him to come to Salisbury, though without Sir Henry Beaumont, one of his more objectionable supporters.[26] The mission proved fruitless, though it did extract a statement of the earl's position. Henry claimed to be acting not from selfish motives, but in the interests of the church, the king, and of the realm. Certain abuses called out for remedy: the king should live of his own without oppressing his people; the queen likewise should be permitted to enjoy her dowry without charge to others. Peers of the realm who had been appointed councillors at the coronation ought to answer for their conduct at the next parliament. Lastly, the earl expressed himself willing to come to Salisbury to discuss these matters, but not without an armed force, which was necessary solely to protect himself. If the king considered that he was bound to come without such force, then he would require letters of safe-conduct.[27]

Doubtless it was Mortimer himself who parried the earl's complaints on the king's behalf. It was no difficult task. Lancaster had laid himself open to criticism by failing to attend councils and parliaments – his brother had done the same before him. On the face of it this constituted an abandonment of his obligation, indeed of the very policy he advocated. As for the proposed safe-conduct, it was argued that this could be issued only in terms which reserved the king's obligations to do justice to all men in accordance with Magna Carta. On such terms Earl Henry forbore to come and the last day of October saw the parliament adjourned to Westminster. Civil war came one step nearer.[28]

With Mortimer in arms at Salisbury, Lancaster proceeded to occupy Winchester with a force to which the Londoners had surreptitiously supplied a contingent.[29] Proceedings at the parliament suffered in consequence of this confrontation. The ill-concealed hostility of the Mortimer faction persuaded Stratford of the wisdom of slipping away

---

[26] *Cal. PMR*, pp. 80-81. And for Gravesend's former unpopularity with the Londoners because of his loyalty to Edward II, ibid., p. 36.

[27] Ibid., p. 81.

[28] Ibid., pp. 81-82.

[29] Ibid., pp. xxxiv, 73-74. On 18 November the authorities denied that any armed men had gone to Winchester with their knowledge or consent. The Brut (CCC MS 174), fol. 156ᵛ, says that the Londoners sent six hundred men.

early; an action for which he was to be called to account.[30] His efforts to reach safety are vividly recounted by the anonymous author of the lives of the archbishops.[31] During parliament's session Stratford had lodged with the nuns at Wilton to the northwest of Salisbury. Allegedly Mortimer's agents were bent on his destruction. Warned of the danger, the bishop escaped under cover of darkness and spent the night in the open fields. The following morning he took refuge at his manor of Downton,[32] where he remained for what was left of the parliament. On the same day that Roger Mortimer was made earl of March – a much criticized promotion – Stratford was forced to flee from a new threat, this time to his own cathedral city, Winchester. There his familiars, presumably following Lancaster's evacuation of the city on 3 November, were afraid to receive him, so he moved on to another of his manors, Bishops Waltham. Even there he did not feel secure, judging it prudent to hide out in nearby "Hordereswode."[33] So ends a circumstantial tale for which there is scant corroboration elsewhere, though it could be substantially true for all that.[34]

While Stratford was fleeing for his life the sheriff of Hampshire received instructions to go to Winchester and there arrest all carrying arms contrary to the recent statute of Northampton.[35] This seems to have had no immediate effect. When (about 3 November) the royal forces reached Winchester, Lancaster and his men moved off without hostile incident but in full view of members of the royal household.[36] Little credence should perhaps be given to the findings of an enquiry held by the city authorities at Winchester on 28 November. These were to the effect that Henry of Lancaster, Thomas Wake, Hugh Audley and Roger de Grey, while en route for Salisbury, stopped on 30 October at Winchester

[30] *CCR 1327-1330*, p. 420; *Foedera (R.C.)* 2, p. 753; PRO K.B.27/275/Rex m.1ʳ. And see below.

[31] *Vitae Arch. Cant.*, p. 19 (Lambeth MS 99, fol. 136ʳ).

[32] In Wharton's edition (above n. 31) this place is given as "Honiton," the MS has "Dounton."

[33] This is Waltham Chase, the park belonging to the episcopal manor. *VCH Sussex* 3, p. 278. *Cal. Inqu. Misc.*, no. 1039 (PRO C.145/109/7) gives Lancaster's stay in Winchester as 30 October - 3 November.

[34] Of the confusion in which the parliament broke up there is, of course, no doubt. "Sed in magna discordia archiepiscopi et episcopi et fere omnes alii inde recesserunt." *Annales Paulini*, p. 342.

[35] *Cal. PMR*, pp. 82-83.

[36] Ibid., p. 83; *Cal. Inqu. Misc.*, no. 1039. The royal forces were apparently at Winchester 3-6 November. See Holmes, "Rebellion of Lancaster," p. 84.

with their household, but unarmed! There they remained until the following Thursday without doing harm to anyone.[37]

From Winchester the king, accompanied by Philippa of Hainault his queen, by Isabella the queen mother, and by the new earl of March, travelled in a body to London. One chronicler's impression is that they arrived about the feast of St. Nicholas (6 December) and remained for a week.[38] By report the whole city welcomed them with gifts; a demonstration calculated to conceal the Londoners' real sympathies.[39] No sooner had the king's supporters evacuated the place than the Lancastrians arrived in their turn. There are signs of a pre-arranged plan. Dene states that Bishop Hethe, on 30 November while at his favourite manor of Trottiscliffe in Kent, received a summons to the capital for what appears to be 17 December.[40] Possibly Stratford, undeterred by recent experiences, was behind the citation which ran in the names of the earls of Norfolk and Kent. This urged bishops, and presumably others, to foregather in London just before Christmas.[41] The king, it was alleged, was riding about the countryside, devastating it, and in violation of his coronation oath and of Magna Carta seizing the goods of churches and of lay inhabitants and destroying the nobles of the realm.[42] In reply to the summons Bishop Hethe pleaded illness. By nature a cautious man, he fought shy of political entanglements. The archbishop, irritated, insisted that he come and render all the help of which he was capable. When Hethe replied with a copy of his excuse to the earls, Mepham indignantly denounced his pusillanimity. One of his familiars quipped that the bishop of Rochester wanted to be a letter "A" all on his own. The comment stung Hethe into making an

[37] *Cal. Inqu. Misc.*, no. 1039. The sheriff held a similar enquiry.

[38] *Annales Paulini*, p. 343. Holmes, "Rebellion of Lancaster," p. 84, suggests an earlier arrival, giving Westminster dates as 21 November - 1 December.

[39] *Annales Paulini*, p. 343: "Cui tota civitas occurrit, et misit magna exennia."

[40] BL Cotton MS Faustina B.v, fol. 51ᵛ: "Ibidem [Trottiscliffe] in festo sancti Andree moram faciens et contra Natale Domini necessaria preparans, per [?] octo dies ante festum Natale predictum litteras comitum Kancie et Mareschalli recepit continentes quod omnibus aliis pretermissis Lond. veniret ad tractandum cum eis et prelatis super magnis periculis eminentibus regi et regno." Stubbs, *Chronicles Edward I and II* 1, p. cxviii (citing Dene), says that the writs were issued "that day" (i.e. 18 December). Cf. Holmes, "Rebellion of Lancaster," p. 85 n. 7.

[41] BL Cotton MS Faustina B.v, fol. 51ᵛ and cf. *Annales Paulini*, p. 343, where Mepham is said to have arrived on the 18th, possibly the date in the citation. See n. 40. For Stratford's movements see below, "Itinerary."

[42] BL Cotton MS Faustina B.v, fol. 51ᵛ: "Eo quod rex in multitudine armatorum innumerosa equitabat, patriam devastando, res et bona ecclesie et regnicolarum contra magnam cartam et iuramentum in coronacione ipsius dirripiendo et capiendo, necnon et fideles suos regni pares destruendo."

uncharacteristically forthright rejoinder, though this was probably intended for his own immediate circle. He would rather be an isolated "A," he retorted, than be strung together in syllables with those other letters, the prelates gathered in London.[43] It was past belief that in the depths of winter the archbishop should find it necessary to travel from a remote place where preparations for the Christmas festival were in train merely to bandy words on far-fetched matters with juveniles and with the feckless and unskilled, and to organize meetings behind the king's back.[44]

We do not know the number of bishops who braved the wintry conditions and governmental disapproval in order to be in London for the dissident assembly. They could not have been numerous and may have comprised no more than the archbishop of Canterbury and the bishops of Winchester and London, who alone figure in the records, so far as is known.[45] If the chroniclers are a true guide, Stratford did not take the leading part that might have been expected. Whether this arose from distrust of the way things were going or because he was overreached by the impetuous Mepham or by Gravesend, it is hard to determine. The proceedings opened at St. Paul's as scheduled on the Sunday before Christmas. After the procession from the choir Archbishop Mepham preached to the congregation in the nave. We may venture to assume that this was a political address designed to defend the Lancastrian course of action. On the days which followed bishops and magnates discussed the state of the realm and the means of amendment.[46]

In the meantime Isabella and Mortimer had withdrawn to the west of England. This shortened their lines of communication with Mortimer's territory in the Marcher country. In the king's name a letter was sent from Gloucester to the mayor and sheriffs of London.[47] Its purpose was to deter the citizens from rendering assistance to the dissident faction. Accompanying it was a rejoinder to the criticisms of the government's conduct voiced by Lancaster. It is couched in the form of a résumé of events from the time of the treaty of Northampton, with palliatory interpolations.[48]

---

[43] Ibid., fols. 51^v-52^r: "Episcopus Roffensis vult esse 'A' per sey per se solitarius.... Respondit episcopus, 'Malo esse "A" per sey quam litteris aliis, hoc est prelatis London. congregatis sillabicari'."

[44] Ibid., fol. 52^r: "Archiepiscopus London. ire disposuit cum iuvenibus et improvidis ac imperitis super causis colorati [sic] exquisitis et archiepiscopum latentibus retro regem conventicula faciendo tractaturus."

[45] E.g. *Annales Paulini*, p. 343. Of course, we need to know more about the itineraries of individual bishops at this time.

[46] Ibid.

[47] *Cal. PMR*, pp. 77-78.

[48] Ibid., pp. 78-83.

This *pièce justificative* was obediently published at the Guildhall on the feast of St. Thomas, 21 December, in the presence of the Lancastrian lords Thomas Wake, William Trussell and Thomas Roscelyn, who explained that Earl Henry could not respond until he had taken counsel with his peers. For its part the city was careful to tender assurances of its continued loyalty.[49] Alarmed at the threatening aspect of events, Mepham two days later despatched the archdeacon of Essex with a letter for delivery to the court, which the messenger found at Worcester. This embodies a "petition of prelates, earls, barons and of the whole community of London" said to have been drawn up on St. Thomas's day, presumably as a riposte to the government statement. It was urged that it had been agreed at Salisbury that no proceedings were to be taken against the magnates until parliament reconvened at Westminster.[50] By the terms of Magna Carta the king ought to proceed against such persons only by judgment of their peers and due process of law. It was well known to Edward's advisers that councils held by various prelates of the land had placed disturbers of the peace under sentence of excommunication. Mepham pleaded that Edward, who by common knowledge was moving against certain peers with an army, should desist pending discussion of the problem in parliament.[51]

Lancaster, who earlier had been covering the royal forces from the neighbourhood of Kenilworth,[52] spent the Christmas festival at Waltham in Essex. On the first day of the new year he journeyed to London with a substantial following and joined in the meeting at St. Paul's with the other magnates and prelates. From there he went to the house of the Dominican friars for a reconciliation with Thomas of Brotherton, the earl marshal. The two are said to have been estranged chiefly because of the killing of Robert Holland by the over-zealous Sir Thomas Wither, intent on avenging Robert's betrayal of Thomas of Lancaster in his hour of need.[53] The following day, 2 January, the confederates assembled once more at St. Paul's and determined on ordinances which they deemed beneficial for

---

[49] Ibid., pp. 83-84.

[50] Parliament eventually reconvened there on 9 February 1329. *Foedera* (R.C.) 2, p. 756.

[51] *Cal. PMR*, p. 84. The text is in *Lit. Cant.* 3, pp. 414-416 (from cci. Reg. I, fol. 427^{r-v}). The part omitted in *Lit. Cant.* at the turn of the page is supplied by Holmes, "Rebellion of Lancaster," p. 87 n. 9.

[52] *Cal. PMR*, p. 77; Holmes, "Rebellion of Lancaster," p. 88 (from pro C.49/file 6/13: ordinance for seizure of Lancaster's lands).

[53] *Annales Paulini*, pp. 343-344. The Brut (ccc ms 174), fols. 154^v-155^r, suggests that on his release from prison Robert Holland was "wonder privy" with Isabella and Mortimer and that the former was angry at his death, hence Lancaster's embarrassment.

both king and realm, binding themselves together by oath.[54] It all has a familiar ring. Stratford was present, the Pauline annalist informs us, but this is almost the last chronicle reference to him during the abortive insurrection. His register shows that he returned to his diocese before 8 January,[55] apparently having washed his hands of the affair. Leadership of the clerical group was now being exercised by the politically inept archbishop, Simon Mepham.

While the Lancastrians were organizing themselves in London, Mortimer and the queen mother felt sufficiently confident to take the initiative. A writ of privy seal, dated 29 December from Worcester and addressed to the authorities in the capital, was accompanied by a proclamation of the king's intentions. His forces would advance to Warwick on New Year's day and were expected to be in Leicester on the feast of the Epiphany – 6 January.[56] If those in arms against him submitted before the 7th an amnesty would be granted, saving the lords Beaumont, Roscelyn, Wither and Trussell.[57] Mortimer proved as good as the word he put into the king's mouth, proceeding to ravage the Lancastrian lands as he advanced[58] and reaching Northampton by the middle of January. The author of a continuation of the Brut chronicle writes of a twenty-four-mile journey by night in the direction of Bedford, during which Queen Isabella rode by her son's side clad in armour like a knight.[59]

In London the dissident group selected Archbishop Mepham, Bishop Gravesend and the earls of Kent and Norfolk as emissaries. Their task was to precede the army with the intention of dissuading the king from "riding" against the confederates and from taking prizes from church and

---

[54] *Annales Paulini*, p. 344: "Et confoederati super quibusdam ordinationibus ad commodum regis et regni Angliae."

[55] Ibid. and WinRS, fol. 41ᵛ. Apart from Stratford the annalist mentions the archbishop of Canterbury, bishop of London, the earls of Lancaster, Norfolk and Kent, Thomas Wake "et alii plures magnates." But cf. *Knighton* (next note).

[56] According to *Knighton* 1, p. 450, Mortimer's forces in fact arrived on 4 January and stayed in the area eight days devastating it: "nihil in ecclesiis inventum vel alibi relinquendo, ac si esset in tempore guerrae inter regna." Knighton is not too precise. At this time, he states, Lancaster was coming from the south with a great force, accompanied by Kent and Norfolk, Bishops Stratford and Gravesend, Wake, Beaumont, Audley and Roscelyn. He does not mention events in London meanwhile.

[57] *Cal. PMR*, pp. 85-86. Cf. Brut (ccc ms 174), fol. 156ᵛ; bl. Cotton ms Faustina B.v, fol. 52ʳ. Sir Thomas Roscelyn of Edgfield and Walcott in Norfolk is among those mentioned as supporters of the queen in 1326 (*Knighton* 1, pp. 431-432).

[58] *Knighton* 1, p. 450. This chronicler is not of course an unbiased reporter. Cf. n. 56 above.

[59] ccc ms 174, fol. 156ᵛ.

people.[60] In the event of the king's failure to respond to this plea they were to express their intention to resist by armed force.[61] Mepham, so we are told, insisted on forging ahead of the other emissaries, his cross and banner held defiantly erect. Alas!, comments Dene, he had neither the spiritual force nor the moral worth of Elias – certainly not his success.[62] Arriving in the vicinity of the royal army somewhere near Bedford, the archbishop asked an attendant, Thomas de Aledon,[63] whether he ought to go forward and greet the king. Thomas replied in the affirmative, adding a warning that he should say nothing about his mission. Were he to reveal the slightest inkling of his purpose the royal council would readily divine the whole truth. And so it turned out, the Rochester chronicler ruefully observed. Having greeted the king, the queen, and their attendant councillors, Mepham drank with them and fatigued by the journey and his labours waxed talkative. Soon all was revealed to his astute listeners, who proceeded to justify their actions. Mepham was won over by their arguments and confirmed his new affiliation with an oath. He was then sent back to his former companions with the promise that if they submitted all but four would be received back into the king's grace. Dene claims that the archbishop made a fool of himself, but he is a notably unsympathetic commentator and we possess no means of checking his account. As for the earls, they humbly approached Edward on foot and prostrating themselves in the mire implored his grace.[64] This was granted

---

[60] *Annales Paulini*, p. 344; BL Cotton MS Faustina B.v, fol. 52ʳ: "Ad dissuadendum regi ne sic equitaret et a prisis ecclesie et populi desisteret."

[61] BL Cotton MS Faustina B.v, fol. 52ʳ: "Alioquin dicti comites et eorum adherentes in vi armata regi occurrere, resistere et eum vi comprimere se velle asserebant."

[62] Ibid.: "Non tamen in spiritu et virtute Elye." Cf. Mal. 4.5; 2 Kings 1.8ff.

[63] This could well be the Thomas de Aldon from Kent mentioned s.a. 1327 as an adherent of Badlesmere at the siege of Leeds (1321), but subsequently pardoned. *CCR 1327-1330*, pp. 50-51, and cf. ibid., p. 593.

[64] BL Cotton MS Faustina B.v, fol. 52ʳ⁻ᵛ: "Et factum est quod omnes qui de adventu archiepiscopi spem habuerunt firmam de pace facienda et de eius adventu plurimum gaudebant, postea in ridiculum habentes et in fabulam prothdolor ei male dicebant. ... Comites vero Lancastrie Kancie et ceteri eis adherentes confusi expectabant adventum regis apud Bedeford. ubi regi equitanti pedites occurrerunt et omnes in luto profundo genibus provolutis prostrati gracie regis se submiserunt." *Knighton* 1, p. 450, asserts that the uncles of the king left Lancaster in the lurch and incriminated him: "Reliquerunt comitem, et se dederunt matri regis et Rogero Mortymer, procurantes comiti Lancastriae malum seditionis in quantum poterant." He is kinder to the archbishop (ibid., p. 451), whom he credits with taking part with other bishops and magnates in an agreement: "Quod omnes errores emendarentur in proximo parliamento sequenti; et hoc ne forte omnes surgerent communes in hac communi causa cum comite." *Murimuth*, p. 58, is also not critical of Mepham.

on terms which included a heavy ransom.[65] The date of this submission is uncertain, but it was probably on or about 19 January 1329.[66] On the 21st the mayor and twenty-four men of the City of London were summoned to St. Albans to answer for the assistance given to Lancaster at Winchester and Bedford.[67] Thus a civil war was circumvented, but only at the cost of the unchallenged supremacy of Isabella and Mortimer.

In the circumstances Stratford was not going to be allowed to forget his contumelious flight from Salisbury. As early as 11 November a writ had been issued to the sheriff of Hampshire for the bishop's appearance before the King's Bench in Hilary term on a charge of contempt. He failed to appear, was declared to be "in mercy," and instructions were given to the sheriff to enforce distraint against him. Cited again for the octave of the Purification (9 February 1329), the king's advocate, Adam de Fincham, argued his transgression and contempt; the defendant, again absent, was declared "in mercy" for various faults and subject to a penalty of a thousand pounds. Stratford eventually presented himself in the Easter term (during May) and conducted his own case. His defence, hitherto unnoticed, foreshadows that which he was to adopt in 1341. As a peer of the realm and a prelate of Holy Church it was for him to come to the king's parliament when the king chose to summon him. If he or his fellows in parliament were to be at fault vis-à-vis the king, then it was in parliament that correction should be undertaken rather than in any lesser

[65] The Brut (CCC MS 174), fol. 156ᵛ, gives Lancaster's ranson as £11,000; the "official" figure is £30,000, though this was never paid. The names of those who made recognizances after Bedford and the sums involved are in CCR 1327-1330, pp. 528-531. From Wallingford on 10 April 1329 a writ was directed to the sheriff of Bedfordshire with a schedule of those "who came with armed power against the king at Bedford." He returned that the men were not to be found in his bailiwick. Commissioners were appointed to hold an enquiry. PRO K.B.27/276/Rex. m.24ʳ. Fryde, Tyranny of Edward II, pp. 218-223, deals with Lancaster's revolt and states (without specific reference) that Orleton was "a more surprising episcopal recruit to Lancaster's camp" than others including Stratford. Orleton's itinerary does not help here and I await confirmation of the statement. See also Redstone, "Some Mercenaries of Lancaster."

[66] TCC MS R.5 41, fol. 127ᵛ (recte 128) gives 17 January. An itinerary of the chancery between 2 November 1328 and 20 January 1329, which is probably roughly coincident with the king's movements, is given by Holmes, "Rebellion of Lancaster," p. 84. On 15 January Chancellor Burghersh was at Northampton, where he temporarily relinquished the seal for safe custody in the wardrobe. In the presence of William de Montacute, Richard de Bury, and of other councillors close to the king, he received it back on Thursday 19 January in Newnham Priory by Bedford. Foedera 2, iii, pp. 20-21. It is Burghersh who is supposed to have received the submission at Bedford of the confederates "sub certa forma arta et dura" (BL Cotton MS Faustina B.v, fol. 52ᵛ). Cf. Maunde Thompson, Chronicon, notes p. 220, following Stubbs, Chronicles of Edward I and II 1, p. cxxi; Holmes, "Rebellion of Lancaster," p. 87.

[67] Annales London., pp. 241ff.

court. The king would not wish him to respond other than in parliament.[68] When the case was resumed in Michaelmas term Stratford again appeared in person. For the king it was argued that he could bring delinquents into whatever court he thought fit. Stratford reiterated his contention and the case dragged on from term to term throughout 1330 without result.[69]

Meanwhile, in the still seething atmosphere following the Bedford fiasco, Mepham was enthroned in his cathedral at Canterbury on the feast of St. Vincent, 22 January 1329.[70] Many people are said to have been present, but few magnates.[71] As for prelates, Dene mentions only the bishops of London and Rochester and the abbot of Glastonbury.[72] Five days later the archbishop presided over his first provincial council.[73] Stratford's register records the summons and his implementation of it, but no commission for proctors. This and the fact that he was at Southwark at the time of the meeting imply his presence.[74] Dene is scathing about the lack of attention to the church's *gravamina*, a notable series of which was submitted by Bishop Grandisson, but it is quite wrong to suggest that nothing was done.[75] The bishop of Norwich celebrated a mass for peace

[68] *Foedera (R.C.)* 2, p. 753; PRO K.B.27/275/Rex m.1ʳ; 276/Rex m.9ᵛ.

[69] PRO K.B.27/276/Rex m.9ᵛ. One presumes that after Michaelmas 1330 the case was dropped.

[70] *Annales Paulini*, p. 344. "Sunday *after* the Conversion of St. Paul" is the date given in BL Cotton MS Faustina B.v, fol. 52ᵛ. But "post" must be an error for "ante," which would give the right date.

[71] BL Cotton MS Faustina B.v, fol. 52ᵛ: "Ubi populus multus sed ex magnatibus pauci."

[72] Ibid. Bishop Grandisson claimed that Mepham had not informed him of the enthronement. *Exeter Reg. Grandisson*, p. 449.

[73] Which sat 27 January - 10 February at St. Paul's. *HBC*, p. 555; *Concilia* 2, p. 548; WinRS, fol. 43ʳ. The mandate speaks of the "carbonibus odii inter proceres reaccensis" and the injustices inflicted on the church and ecclesiastics: "ipsos viros ecclesiasticos mutilare, trucidare aut hostiliter capere non formidant."

[74] WinRS, fol. 43ʳ, and see below, "Itinerary." In accordance with Mepham's injunction to hold preliminary discussion with the clergy "De gravaminibus et defectibus dicti concilii studio reformandis," Stratford directed M. John de Lecch to summon them for the second juridical day after the Epiphany (probably Monday 9 January).

[75] BL Cotton MS Faustina B.v, fol. 52ᵛ: "In concilio antedicto nulla fuerunt expedita sed sicuti prelati et clerus in magnis sumptibus ad concilium venerunt ita vacui sine reparacione gravaminum ecclesie recesserunt." Baker, *Chronicon*, p. 43, declares that Mepham "ordinavit aliqua ponderanda" and itemizes the proper observance of Good Friday and All Souls Day – with freedom from servile labour – and of the Conception of Our Lady (8 December). He is close to *Murimuth*, pp. 59-60. A fuller account of proceedings is in *Annales Paulini*, pp. 344-345. A minor series of provincial constitutions resulted. Lyndwood, *Constitutiones Provinciales*, pp. 41-43; *Concilia* 2, pp. 552-554. For Grandisson's *gravamina* and admonitory letter to the archbishop, and his certifying of Mepham and (significantly?) of Bishops Stratford (Winchester), Orleton (Worcester) and Gravesend (London), see *Exeter Reg. Grandisson*, pp. 446-452; *Concilia* 2, pp. 549-551. Grandisson, however, did not attend.

and after the gospel sentences of excommunication were solemnly pronounced against the murderers of Bishop Stapeldon, as well as against those who had burned the abbey of St. Edmund and that of Abingdon and carried off goods belonging to them.[76] Even in this matter the clergy was not entirely of one mind, for Bishop Gravesend was to give honourable lodging to the former mayor of London, Hamo de Chigwell, whom the king's justices had imprisoned for complicity in the abduction of the abbot of St. Edmund's but who claimed benefit of clergy and successfully proceeded to purgation.[77]

With the rebels cowed and the justices in session at the Guildhall,[78] the parliament so hastily adjourned from Salisbury was able to reassemble as arranged at Westminster on 9 February 1329.[79] This, as we have seen, was the date assigned to Stratford for appearance before the King's Bench. Attendance at parliament possibly accounts for his failure to respond.[80]

French affairs were now a matter of urgency. Following the assertion of Edward III's right to the throne of France, Isabella and Mortimer had played for time.[81] By 1329 Philip VI's position was unassailable and he was pressing for the homage of his vassal, the English king. The government was forced to bow to the inevitable. Edward crossed to France on 26 May. Granted letters of protection to accompany him were three bishops, including Chancellor Burghersh, and a reliable body of clerks and laymen with known Mortimer affiliations.[82] On 6 June the sixteen-year-old Edward performed homage to Philip in the choir of Amiens cathedral, but with a protestation by Burghersh to the effect that this entailed no renunciation of rights in Gascony and was not to be construed as modifying the *status quo*.[83] On the feast of Pentecost (11 June) the royal party returned to Dover.[84] In changed conditions, when

---

[76] *Annales Paulini*, pp. 344-345. For what happened at Bury see Lobel, "The Rising at Bury St. Edmund's," pp. 215-231.

[77] *Annales Paulini*, pp. 346-347; Lobel, "The Rising at Bury St. Edmund's," pp. 215-231; *French Chronicle*, p. 55, and for various notices of Chigwell, ibid. index s.v.; *Annales London.*, pp. 246-247.

[78] *Annales London.*, pp. 242-243ff.; *Foedera* (*R.C.*) 2, p. 755.

[79] *Foedera* (*R.C.*) 2, p. 756.

[80] See above.

[81] Déprez, *Les préliminaires*, p. 40. Today, perhaps, we could not say that Isabella's evasive replies were "en manière de femme!"

[82] *Foedera* 2, iii, p. 27.

[83] Déprez, *Les préliminaires*, pp. 42-46, where the implications are discussed. The homage, he concludes, was not liege, and there were reservations about the return of lands seized by Charles IV.

[84] *Foedera* 2, iii, p. 27. According to *Knighton* 1, pp. 451-452, Philip VI was plotting to arrest Edward; so the return was a hurried one. Prompt evasory action is said to have been taken by Bishop Burghersh, described as the king's "ductor et gubernator."

Edward tried to enforce his claim to France, this act of homage was to be held against him.[85]

Mortimer was to strike one more blow against his opponents at home. The manner in which he did so constitutes an element of the most bizarre incident in the history of Edward II, whose influence on events was to continue well beyond the grave. The case for believing that Edward of Carnarvon was murdered at Berkeley on or about 21 September 1327 has been ably presented by T. F. Tout in a memorable article, which even now requires only a few amendments. Recently the whole issued has been reopened, notably by Professor Cuttino, who has contributed little new information but who has placed the events in a detailed chronological framework and with the aid of his co-author dismissed some widely inexact iconographical attributions.[86] This is no place to review the evidence in detail, but the matter is sufficiently germane to the present enquiry to warrant a recapitulation of the salient points. The argument for Edward's survival after the generally accepted date of his death rests principally on a copy of what purports to be a letter sent by Manuele Fieschi, a papal notary,[87] to Edward III, coupled with a tradition about an English medieval king attached to certain places in Italy identifiable as those referred to by Fieschi.[88] According to the contents of this letter – allegedly derived from Edward of Carnarvon's own confession[89] – he escaped from Berkeley and later from Corfe and then travelled widely in Europe, visiting Pope John XXII at Avignon and finally withdrawing to a hermitage in Lombardy. At the time of his escape from Berkeley Edward is said to have killed the porter and it was the latter's body which was in fact buried in Gloucester Abbey.[90]

[85] The more so because on 9 March 1331 at St. Germain-en-Laye it was agreed that this should be interpreted as liege homage – an agreement ratified by Edward III on 30 March. Perroy, *Hundred Years War*, pp. 83-84, 93; Déprez, *Les préliminaires*, pp. 72-73, 227-229; and below, "In the Seat of Power."

[86] Tout, "Captivity and Death of Edward of Carnarvon"; Cuttino and Lyman, "Where is Edward II ?"; Fryde, *Tyranny of Edward II*, chap. 14.

[87] Stubbs, *Chronicles of Edward I and II* 2, pp. ciii-cviii; Tout, "Captivity and Death of Edward of Carnarvon," pp. 178-179; Cuttino, "Where is Edward II ?," pp. 526-527, 537-538, provides a revised translation and transcription. Cf. Fryde, *Tyranny of Edward II*, pp. 204-205: one presumes this part of the book was written before Cuttino and Lyman's article apeared, though their article figures in the footnotes.

[88] The family came from Genoa and Manuele was bishop of Vercelli, not so far away, from 1343. Melazzo d'Acqui and the abbey of Sant' Alberto di Butrio – where Edward of Carnarvon allegedly sought solace – are both near Vercelli.

[89] The propriety of this revelation has rarely been questioned.

[90] The killing of a gatekeeper was a feature of the Lancastrian Robert Walkfere's escape from Corfe in 1326 (*Annales Paulini*, p. 311) and of the attempted escape by the Dominican, Thomas Dunheved, from Pontefract Castle in 1327. Dunheved, who was

The principal argument against the genuineness of the letter, apart from the inherent improbability of its contents, is the weight of evidence to the contrary. The circumstantial account of Edward's last moments given by Baker has been regarded with justifiable suspicion, but the essential features are duplicated in the Brut.[91] In each case the intention is to demonstrate that Edward's body could appear unmarked even though he had been murdered. Need we doubt that such concealment would have been in the murderers' minds? One of the most laconic of chroniclers, Adam Murimuth, is emphatic that many people had opportunity to view the royal corpse, in fact were encouraged to do so.[92] At least some of the onlookers must have been familiar with Edward's features, for he had been to Gloucester often enough. That, in Murimuth's opinion, they saw the corpse only "superficially" implies, one suspects, nothing more than an inability to get close enough to inspect it for visible wounds or contusions – Edward was a healthy man in the prime of life who officially died of natural causes.[93] Because of the evisceration of the body and the removal of the heart prior to embalming, doubt has been thrown on the commonly expressed contemporary opinion that the naked body was exhibited in the hope of allaying suspicion of foul play.[94] There may indeed be some confusion between what happened shortly after death and the subsequent "lying in state" behind the protection of wooden crush-

with Edward II on his flight into Wales, had conspired to release him from custody (ibid., p. 337). Cf. *Lanercost*, p. 260; Brut (CCC MS 174), fol. 149ᵛ. For modern accounts: Tout, "Captivity and Death of Edward of Carnarvon," pp. 157-158; Tanquerey, "Conspiracy of Thomas Dunheved."

[91] CCC MS 174, fol. 152ʳ; *Chronicon*, pp. 33-34. The same basic story is in *Knighton* 1, p. 446; cf. TCC MS R.5 41, fol. 125ᵛ (recte 126).

[92] *Murimuth*, pp. 53-54: "Et licet multi abbates, priores, milites, burgenses de Bristolla et Gloucestria ad videndum corpus suum integrum fuissent vocati, et tale superficialiter conspexissent, dictum tamen fuit vulgariter quod per ordinationem dominorum J[ohannis] Mautravers et T[homae] de Gorneye fuit per cautelam occisus." The identical passage is in *Historia Eduardi*, p. 390. Cf. *Knighton* 1, p. 446: "Ne exterius plaga aliqua cuiquam intuenti locum daret, dicentes, non mortem naturalem sed subitam ei evenisse." Would not the murdered porter's body have shown signs of the manner of his death?

[93] The Lanercost chronicler wrote cautiously (*Lanercost*, p. 260): "Mortuus est, vel morte propria naturali vel ab aliis violenter inflicta." The *French Chronicle* (p. 60) states that he was "tretousement murdriz." The account of Edward's final days and death in Corpus Christi College Oxford's version of the Brut (MS 78, fols. 169ʳ-170ᵛ) has elements akin to those found in Baker. See Galbraith, "Extracts," pp. 216-217.

[94] Fryde, *Tyranny of Edward II*, pp. 202-203: "This again is part of the legend." If so it was a contemporary one. The woman who performed the evisceration was conducted to Isabella at Worcester by a clerk, Hugh de Glanville. The omission of this item from the roll of particulars when Glanville claimed expenses has been regarded with suspicion. See Moore, "Documents Relating to Edward II," pp. 215-226, esp. pp. 218-219, 226; Cuttino and Lyman, "Where is Edward II ?," p. 525 n. 18.

barriers.[95] But the point involved is the manner of death rather than the identity of the corpse. Had the body been other than the king's, unbeknown to the authorities, there was ample opportunity for uncovering the deception; burial did not take place until 20 December.[96] In Tout's words: "A public exhibition of almost excessive respect seems to have been thought the most desirable policy."[97] But we can be tolerably certain that Isabella took the precaution of having her husband's body identified. Clearly she considered the heart to be her husband's for she had it placed in her coffin, conjecturally out of a belated feeling of remorse.[98] Substitution of the porter's body in the way suggested by the putative confession would have involved the connivance of a number of persons. In view of the certain consequences of such deceit and the likelihood of almost immediate discovery, it would have been foolhardy – much more dangerous than having to admit the prisoner's escape.[99] If, on the other hand, it be argued that the authorities, having learned of the deception, none the less decided to proceed as though nothing had happened, we are left with the difficulty of the lengthy exposure of the unkingly corpse and later official encouragement of the rumour that Edward of Carnarvon was still alive. Such encouragement is credible only if we assume that those behind it knew that Edward was in fact dead.

There is no doubt that the difficulty in assessing the validity of the Fieschi letter is compounded by the fact that Mortimer, who was still perturbed by the degree of opposition to his regime and that of Isabella, sought to isolate the friends of the former king from their Lancastrian allies by taking advantage of a story that Edward was alive.[100] Lancaster

---

[95] See Fryde, *Tyranny of Edward II*, pp. 203, 269 n. 29; Tout, "Captivity and Death of Edward of Carnarvon," p. 170 n. 2; also PRO E.101/624/14. The body was at Berkeley for a month before being moved to Gloucester. Tout, "Captivity and Death of Edward of Carnarvon," p. 168; Moore, "Documents Relating to Edward II," esp. pp. 224-226 (Glanville's account).

[96] *Annales Paulini*, p. 338: "Domino Edwardo rege primogenito et aliis magnatibus terrae praesentibus." Fryde, *Tyranny of Edward II*, p. 203, gives the date of the funeral as the 21st.

[97] "Captivity and Death of Edward of Carnarvon," p. 170.

[98] Ibid., p. 169 (it was removed before the body went to Gloucester); Fryde, *Tyranny of Edward II*, pp. 202-203, 269 nn. 28-29.

[99] That Edward did in fact escape is shown by the letter of John Walwayn, the younger (PRO S.C.1/35/207; printed by Tanquerey, "Conspiracy of Thomas Dunheved"). At least one more attempt was planned in Wales (Tout, "Captivity and Death of Edward of Carnarvon," App. 1, pp. 182-189). Fryde, *Tyranny of Edward II*, p. 202, mentions an attempt organized in Buckinghamshire.

[100] E.g. BL Cotton MS Faustina B.v, fol. 55ᵛ: "Ad cuius vite assercionem per reginam et Rogerum de Mortuo Mari ut dicebatur quidam procurati fuerunt ad denunciandum Edmundo comiti Kancie quod frater eius viveret, similiter archiepiscopo Eboracen.,

had been deputed to take part in the continued negotiations with France and so might be held to be actively cooperating with the court – at least for the moment.[101] The time was opportune for the incrimination of those who still nourished the memory of Edward of Carnarvon and were prepared to believe in his continued existence. Such wishful-thinkers, egged on by Mortimer's *agents provocateurs*, were all too easily implicated in a misconceived plot to secure Edward's release from the castle in which he was supposedly held. The unwary earl of Kent fell into the trap.[102]

The fullest account of this sad affair is given by the continuator of the Brut.[103] According to him the earl visited the pope in order to press the claim to canonization of Thomas of Lancaster. When the pope parried the request by stating that he would first need reliable confirmation of Thomas's suitability from the local ecclesiastical authorities, the earl changed the subject. He confided to the pope his belief that the former king, his brother, was still living and asked what course of action he should follow in these circumstances.[104] Pope John is alleged to have urged him to secure Edward's release by every means in his power, absolving the earl and his companions *a pena et a culpa*. Back in England Kent was approached by some Dominican friars – an order much favoured by Edward – who persuaded him that his brother was imprisoned in Corfe Castle.[105] The earl hastened to Corfe, which lies in the

London. episcopo et aliis benevolis regis patris datum fuit intelligi in dolo quod rex esset vivus." Cf. n. 102 below.

[101] *Foedera* 2, iii, pp. 31-32. Protection granted 12 September 1329.

[102] *Annales Paulini*, p. 349: "Fuerunt hiis diebus quidam pessimi exploratores, qui asserebant hominibus per totum regnum Anglie regem, nuper mortuum, in transmarinis partibus vivere et in brevi supervenisse, si habuerit assensum et auxilium procerum regni; et multi credebant hoc esse verum." Cf. *Bridlington*, p. 100; *Historia Roffensis* in n. 100 above; *Murimuth*, p. 60; *Rot. Parl.* 2, p. 52: an article of Mortimer's condemnation asserts his responsibility for the fabrication. Baker, *Chronicon*, pp. 43-44, has a somewhat embroidered story and explains that the earl was unpopular because of the prizes he levied on the countryside. Cf. *Historia Eduardi*, p. 395. *Lanercost*, p. 264, makes Thomas de Dunheved the instigator of the story – having raised the devil (cf. *Foedera* 2, iii, p. 40). But Dunheved himself had died in the meantime.

[103] CCC MS 174, fols. 158[r]-161[r].

[104] The Brut has sometimes been overlooked and hence the explanation as to how John XXII was supposed to have known about Edward's "survival." Papal involvement is alleged in Kent's confession: *Murimuth*, pp. 253, 255 (from BL Cotton MS Claudius E.viii). The Mortimer-Isabella government suggested to the pope that Kent was conspiring abroad for the introduction of an invading force by way of Scotland (*Foedera* 2, iii, pp. 40-41). The pope discredited Kent's story. He had believed no such thing and in any case would not have dealt with any individual noble in such a matter. The funeral was public; no deception was possible (*CPL 1305-1342*, p. 499).

[105] The "absolution *a pena et a culpa*" is also in Bodl. Lib. Bodley MS 956 (Lichfield

extreme south of Dorset close to the sea. There he urged the constable, Sir
John Deverel or Deverill, as he is variously called, to lead him to the
former king. Naturally Sir John showed reluctance, which he explained
on the grounds that his instructions forbade him to let anyone see the
prisoner. Thereupon Kent prepared a letter for his brother in which he
promised not only his own support but also that of others who had bound
themselves by oath. Deverel promptly delivered the treasonable document
to Mortimer, who used it to stage-manage the earl's condemnation at
Winchester, where a parliament was in session with Stratford in
attendance.[106] Isabella is reputed to have been furious at what she termed
the earl's treachery and to have been instrumental in hastening his death
for fear the young king should insist on pardoning him. Kent was
beheaded outside the gates of Winchester Castle after a delay occasioned
by the fact that for some time no one could be found to carry out so
impious a task.[107] Following the earl's apprehension some of Edward of
Carnarvon's known sympathizers were implicated in Kent's acknowledged treason.[108] Among those named were Archbishop Melton of York,
Bishop Gravesend, the abbot of Langdon, whom Edward II had once put
forward as an episcopal candidate, as well as the provincials of the
Dominican and Carmelite friars.[109]

chronicle), p. 208. Edward was at Corfe at some stage of his captivity. E.g. Galbraith,
"Extracts," pp. 216-217 (CCC Oxford MS 78, fols. 169r-170v). Another version of the Brut
(CCC MS 174, fol. 152r) mistakenly claims that he died there. *Murimuth* (p. 52) has: "Et quia
timuerunt [i.e. Thomas de Berkeley and John Maltravers] aliquorum adventum ad ipsum
liberandum, de loco predicto [Berkeley] fuit deductus de nocte ad loca diversa, videlicet ad
Corf et aliqua alia loca secreta; sed finaliter reduxerunt eum ad Berkeley, ita quod vix sciri
potuit ubi fuit." Cf. *Historia Eduardi*, p. 388.

[106] This met 11 March and dispersed on the 21st. *HBC*, p. 518. A marginal note in
Exeter Reg. Grandisson, p. 43, says that Grandisson was there and that Kent was
beheaded.

[107] *Knighton* 1, p. 452, claims that he was condemned "absque communi consensu"
and that he was beheaded on St. Cuthbert's eve (19 March) by a "ribaldus sceleratus de
Marchalsia."

[108] For his confession see *Murimuth*, pp. 253-257; *Walsingham* 2, pp. 351-352.

[109] Baker, *Chronicon*, p. 44, names the provincials of the Preaching and Carmelite (the
scholarly John Baconthorpe) friars, Bishop Gravesend, Robert de Taunton (Archbishop
Melton's clerk), and Richard Bliton (Despenser's confessor, a Carmelite friar and one of
those adrift with him in the Severn estuary 19-25 October 1326: SA MS 122, fol. 45v). Dene
(BL Cotton MS Faustina B.v, fol. 56v) mentions Melton (for whose confession see
Peterborough Chronicle, p. 165: BL Cotton MS Claudius A.v, fol. 41v), Gravesend and the
abbot of Langdon. Cf. *Murimuth*, p. 60, one version of which (ibid., p. 11) adds William la
Zouche to the bishop of London and Robert de Taunton (Tauton). The fullest list is in
Kent's confession (*Murimuth*, pp. 253-257), which implicates several others not
mentioned above, including the exiles, Beaumont and Roscelyn, then in Paris. For
government measures against the credulous after Kent's death see *Foedera* (*R.C.*) 2,
p. 787; for Tauton see Buck, *Walter Stapeldon*, pp. 58-59.

The relationship of these events to the Fieschi letter, which itself mentions Kent's death, is self-evident. Assuming for the moment that the document is genuine, then incidents in Manuele Fieschi's career and internal evidence combine to suggest a date about 1336-1338, and in any case before 6 July 1343, when Fieschi became bishop of Vercelli.[110] This is just the period when Edward III was attempting to inveigle Louis of Bavaria into taking part in hostilities against France; a policy repeatedly condemned by the papacy. Could it be that the original document was a carefully contrived forgery designed to embarrass the English king at a crucial period?[111] Neither imposters nor kings who returned from the dead are rare.[112]

Stratford had never been closely linked with the group that can be labelled "Edward of Carnarvon's friends," so not surprisingly there is no mention of him in connection with the affair. If any one knew the truth, surely he did. In any case he was certainly not a gullible man, nor one likely to adopt a subterfuge of that kind as a prop to political dissent. After the Lancastrian collapse at Bedford he seems to have avoided overt political entanglement, preferring to wait in patience for a favourable turn of events. It was not to be long in coming.

Shortly after the Winchester parliament had dispersed, a convocation assembled at Lambeth.[113] There, if Dene is to be trusted, it was the bishop

---

[110] So runs the argument in Cuttino and Lyman, "Where is Edward II ?" But although Fieschi had letters nominating attorneys in England for two years, 8 June 1335 (*CPR 1334-1338*, p. 116), he was already abroad in September 1333, when the Salisbury chapter wrote to him at Avignon. See *Hemingby's Register*, pp. 85, 198-199; a source overlooked by Cuttino and Lyman. He could have returned in the interval, but the chapter's letters state that he was "staying beyond the seas."

[111] *Pace* Stubbs *inter alios* there is a factual slip in the document. Edward would have had to be in hiding for two and a half not one and a half years in order to leave Corfe after Kent's death. I.e. ca. 21 September 1327 - ca. 21 March 1330.

[112] For resurrected kings see Cohn, *Pursuit of the Millenium*, chap. 6. TCC MS R.5 41, fol. 111ᵛ (recte 112) writes s.a. 1312 of "quidam scriptor nomine Johannes" with his familiar spirit (murilegum sibi familiarem), who at Oxford publicly declared himself the true heir to the throne. Brought before the king at Northampton, he was convicted of lying and hanged. This is the same case as in *Annales Paulini*, pp. 282-283, s.a. 1318. A William le Galeys was arrested at Cologne in 1338 "qui asserit se patrem domini regis" and was escorted by Francis Lumbard to Edward III at Coblence, where the king met Louis of Bavaria. Another custodian brought him back to the royal base at Antwerp (should the "December" of the MS read "September"?). PRO E.36/203/fols. 88ᵛ-89ʳ, al. pp. 178-179. I owe the reference to Cuttino and Lyman, "Where is Edward II ?," p. 530 n. 43.

[113] It met 16 April 1330. *HBC*, p. 535; *Annales Paulini*, p. 348; BL Cotton MS Faustina B.v, fol. 56ʳ; *Concilia* 2, pp. 558-559.

of Rochester who alone dared to oppose a grant to the king.[114] Hethe, always loyal to Edward II, was at the same time not one to be snared into plotting on his behalf. But he was not easily silenced, particularly when it came to taxation, for his was a poor diocese. But at last Mortimer's luck was running out. It was neither the Lancastrians nor Edward of Carnarvon's friends who contrived his overthrow, but a small group within Edward III's intimate circle led by the young William de Montacute. On 19 October the earl of March, his paramour Queen Isabella, and their faithful collaborator Bishop Burghersh, were surprised in Nottingham Castle where they were lodging during a session of parliament.[115] Mortimer was executed on 29 November following his condemnation unheard at the parliament hastily summoned for the purpose to Westminster.[116] Stratford, who had not been at Nottingham, came up to London. The day before Mortimer's death he was appointed chancellor;[117] clearly his capacity was not lost on the now liberated king. His years in the political wilderness were over.

In the Seat of Power 1330-1340

John Stratford's tardy assumption of ministerial responsibility came at a difficult time, though it was some years before this became fully apparent. In the decade from 1330 the Scottish policy epitomized by the treaty of Northampton, disliked by Edward as much as by his subjects, was abandoned, war with France was launched – a conflict destined to last more than mid-way through the following century – and a heavy burden

---

[114] BL Cotton MS Faustina B.v, fol. 56ʳ: "Omnes excepto Roffen. episcopo ad contribuendum consenserunt."

[115] See Crump, "The Arrest of Roger Mortimer." The longest chronicle account of the final days of Mortimer's regimen appears to be that of the Brut (CCC MS 174), fols. 161ʳ-164ʳ. As he had done at the time of the "Kent crisis," Pope John wrote to Stratford (among others) about the state of affairs, asking him to use his influence for clemency. CPL 1305-1342, pp. 491-492, 498-499. For a recent estimate of the period 1327-1330 see Fryde, Tyranny of Edward II, chap. 15. For the suggestion that Mortimer and Isabella "launched an unusually serious executive effort to improve the state of peace" see Kaeuper, "Commissions of Oyer and Terminer," p. 745 passim; Cam, "General Eyres of 1329-30," p. 243.

[116] This parliament was summoned 23 October for 26 November – only thirty-one days' notice. Parry, Parliaments, p. 95; HBC, p. 519.

[117] BL Cotton MS Faustina B.v, fol. 57ʳ: "In illo parliamento archiepiscopus Ebor. thesaurarius, episcopus Wynton. cancellarius regis facti fuerunt." Stratford was to be chancellor 28 November 1330 - 28 September 1334. See Tout, Chapters 6, p. 11; HBC, p. 84.

of taxation was laid upon a reluctant population. It would be no easy task for a royal chancellor, who was also a bishop with a debt of gratitude to Avignon, to steer a course between the Scylla of papal policy, dedicated to peace at home and the furtherance of a crusade in the east, and the Charybdis of Edward III's martial yearnings, stimulated by adventure-loving knights clamouring for a chivalric conflict calculated to expunge the memory of Edward of Carnarvon's inglorious days.[1] That the decade closed with a deadly feud with his master, the king, was not an outcome of Stratford's choosing, but of an increasing divergence of aims, or perhaps more accurately, of means to achieve aims that were not as divergent as has sometimes been supposed. In 1330, however, such disturbing events could scarcely have been envisaged even by the most acute political observers. The king's personal rule began on a quiet and distinctly accommodating note.

The November parliament in which Mortimer had been condemned was predictably concerned with the rehabilitation of those who had been in arms at Bedford, notably Henry of Lancaster and the exiled lords Thomas Wake, Henry de Beaumont and Thomas Roscelyn, as well as with the cancellation of recognizances exacted for their good behaviour almost two years previously.[2] Among the recognizances discharged was Stratford's own for £2,000, half of which was said to have been exacted by Queen Isabella in the king's name "at the instance of those who wished him ill."[3] At Westminster past events were brought vividly to mind, not only as a consequence of Mortimer's indictment[4] which left many wondering whether they too might be implicated,[5] but also of the judicial examination "coram rege in pleno parliamento" of Thomas de Berkeley in connection with the murder of the king's father, Edward II. Surprisingly, it would seem to us, he claimed to be unaware of the fact that the former

---

[1] MacKisack, *Fourteenth Century*, pp. 125-126, summarizes the temper of the times (1336). Cf. Déprez, *Les préliminaires*, pp. 225-226 (apropos the "Vow of the Heron," for which see below). Parliament, it would seem, on the whole exhibited a more circumspect and practical attitude.

[2] *Rot. Parl.* 2, pp. 31ff.; *Foedera* 2, iii, p. 53.

[3] *Rot. Parl.* 2, p. 60.

[4] For which see *Rot. Parl.* 2, pp. 52-53; *Knighton* 1, pp. 454-458; and cf. Brut (CCC MS 174), fol. 163ᵛ; *Chronicon*, pp. 47-48; *Melsa*, pp. 360-361.

[5] E.g. *Historia Roffensis* (BL Cotton MS Faustina B.v), fol. 57ʳ⁻ᵛ. This rousing passage begins: "Tunc conturbati sunt principes Edom robustos Moab optinuit tremor obriguerunt habitatores philistini pro morte principis sediciosi et fautoris omnium predonum malefactorum et rifliatorum London. et ceterorum in regno qui se in adventu regine coniunxerant...."

king had died from other than natural causes.[6] A jury of knights[7] acquitted him of the major charges, but it was not until 16 March 1337 that he was exonerated entirely.[8] Berkeley's subordinates, Thomas Gurney and William Ockley, were convicted of the crime, his brother-in-law and fellow-custodian, John Maltravers, of encompassing the death of Edward III's uncle, the earl of Kent. All three escaped abroad. Gurney was vigorously pursued, dying in captivity (under somewhat suspicious circumstances) before he could be brought back to face punishment. Ockley vanishes from view. Maltravers alone was eventually pardoned.[9] It has been felt by some that Edward, while energetically tracking down the underlings, let the principals go free.[10] But who were these principals? Mortimer was hanged at Tyburn, one of the charges being that he had consented to Edward of Carnarvon's suffocation.[11] With him died two henchmen, Simon de Bereford and John Deverel, Kent's deceiver. Geoffrey le Baker claimed that these men could have made public confession of Edward's death had not those who feared the truth prevented them.[12] Queen Isabella was allowed to spend the remainder of her life in honourable semi-retirement, well provided for and visited by her son. Edward could scarcely have taken punitive measures against her even in the retributive atmosphere of 1330, although the pope deemed it prudent to counsel the emancipated monarch to treat Isabella kindly.[13] If

[6] What he allegedly said was (*Rot. Parl.* 2, p. 52): "Nec unquam de morte sua usque in presenti parliamento isto." In view of the well advertized funeral and the implication of treason involved, he cannot have meant that he did not know the king was dead (*pace* Fryde, *Tyranny of Edward II*, p. 203), but that he knew *nothing about* his death. The indictment of Mortimer declared it to be notorious that he was responsible for Edward of Carnarvon's demise (*Rot. Parl.* 2, p. 57). See also, *Knighton* 1, pp. 454-455.

[7] *Rot. Parl.* 2, p. 57. Parry, *Parliaments*, p. 95 n. "v," says the jury of knights was anomalous – the peers had protested against being called upon to judge Simon de Bereford, since he was not their peer.

[8] The story is told by Tout, "Captivity and Death of Edward of Carnarvon," pp. 174-175. See also *Rot. Parl.* 2, pp. 57, 62; *Foedera* 2, iii, pp. 160-161; Smyth, *Lives* 1, pp. 292-297.

[9] Tout, "Captivity and Death of Edward of Carnarvon," pp. 101-102; Hunter, "Apprehension of Thomas de Gournay"; *Acta Aragonensia* 3, pp. 747-748. One version of the Brut associates Maltravers with Gurney in the king's murder and says both fled to Compostella: Galbraith, "Extracts," pp. 216-217 (cf. *Historia Eduardi*, p. 390).

[10] E.g. McKisack, *Fourteenth Century*, pp. 94-95, echoing Tout, "Captivity and Death of Edward of Carnarvon," p. 178; cf. idem, *Chapters* 3, pp. 33-34; Cuttino and Lyman, "Where is Edward II ?," pp. 529-530.

[11] *Murimuth*, p. 63: "Fuit consentiens quod pater regis ... fuerat suffocatus."

[12] *Chronicon*, p. 48: "Libenter fecisse[n ?]t pupplicam confessionem de morte crudelissima et modo moriendi patris regis, si non per emulos iusticie et veritatis fuisset sibi tempus denegatum."

[13] *CPL 1305-1342*, p. 498; *Foedera* 2, iii, p. 71.

Berkeley's plea of ignorance and his alibi of being critically ill at Bradley at the crucial moment of Edward of Carnarvon's death be taken seriously, this leaves Maltravers, for whom pardon (on another count) came only a quarter of a century later after praiseworthy service and grave financial loss in Flanders.[14] But the story of Edward of Carnarvon's survival well beyond 1327 dies hard. It has been suggested that the change in attitude towards Berkeley and Maltravers might be accounted for by the revelations in Edward's supposed confession, which has been examined in the previous section. They could no longer be held responsible for the death of a man who had escaped unharmed![15] So intriguing a speculation would cast a different light on Maltravers' involvement in the earl of Kent's death; he was not officially accused of that of Edward of Carnarvon.[16] But all of this is speculation and far from convincing. What does seem fairly clear is that the men in power after Mortimer's arrest were not anxious to go too far in settling old scores. Even the younger Despenser's bones were collected up from the various towns in which they had been exposed as a warning to traitors, so that they could be given a decent burial.[17] The time also appeared opportune for renewing the plea for the canonization of Despenser's chief political opponent, Thomas of Lancaster, although there were unhelpful stories at the curia that he had connived at Gilbert de Middleton's attack on the cardinals near Durham in September 1317.[18] Such politically inspired sanctity was not taken too seriously at Avignon.

Stratford's personal initiative in these affairs must remain a matter of conjecture, though we know enough of his sympathies to guess his reactions. He received livery of the great seal on 28 November 1330, two

[14] Smyth, *Lives* 1, pp. 296-297; Tout, "Captivity and Death of Edward of Carnarvon," pp. 177-178, gives details of Maltravers' later life. Cf. Dugdale, *Baronage* 2, p. 102; Bellamy, *Law of Treason*, pp. 82-83.

[15] See Cuttino and Lyman, "Where is Edward II?," pp. 529-530. I do not understand the statement in Fryde, *Tyranny of Edward II*, p. 206, that "Nobody was ever convicted of the king's murder." Several persons were judged guilty of that crime in 1330. See *Rot. Parl.* 2, p. 53; Tout, "Captivity and Death of Edward of Carnarvon," pp. 173ff.

[16] Had Edward II been alive in 1330 Kent's treason would have been real enough. *Pace* Fryde, *Tyranny of Edward II*, p. 206, it was only of Kent's death that Maltravers stood accused. See below, "Closing Years."

[17] *Foedera* 2, iii, p. 55: Westminster 15 December 1330. Hugh le Despenser, his son, was pardoned. *Rot. Parl.* 2, p. 61. The son of the executed earl of Arundel was rehabilitated, but there were to be no reprisals. Ibid., pp. 55-56, and for the earl's confrontation with John Charlton involved in the capture of his father, p. 60.

[18] *Foedera* 2, iii, pp. 61-62. Even before the coup d'état in March 1330, Walter Burley and John Thoresby, the future archbishop of York, had gone to Avignon on behalf of Lancaster, described as: "Nobilis Christi miles et athleta." Ibid. 2, iii, p. 39.

days after parliament was scheduled to assemble, so he must have been in the closest touch with the king and his most influential councillors.[19] It was to him as chancellor, in pursuance of what was described as a decision of 4 December in parliament, that instructions were given to issue letters of pardon and release to those who had appeared in arms against the king at Winchester and Bedford – as alleged by his "late enemy" Mortimer.[20]

Domestic readjustments were not the only concern of parliament. Relations with France constituted the most urgent external problem with which the government was faced, though the condition of both Ireland and Scotland demanded attention as well. In the case of France the attitude of Philip of Valois looked menacing and Edward, uncertain about stability at home, was afraid that failure to accede to the French king's insistence on liege homage in place of the ill-defined undertaking of 1329, might entail loss of his continental possessions. He was in no position to offer adequate resistance should they be declared confiscate. According to Froissart,[21] towards the end of 1330 the French court sent various ambassadors to London to press Edward to agree to liege homage. The English council instructed two skilled civil lawyers, John Schordich and Thomas Sampson, to study all the documents bearing on Guienne, so that they could give parliament their opinion of what might be done.[22] We know nothing of any parliamentary debate on the issues, but towards the end of January 1331 an embassy comprising the bishops of Worcester and Norwich – Adam Orleton and William Ayrminne – Schordich, Sampson and two barons, Henry Percy and Hugh Audley, set out from London. With surprising alacrity, considering the complexity of the problems involved, a convention was sealed at Paris on 9 March.[23] Déprez attributed this outcome to Edward III's duplicity; he was anxious to

---

[19] *Foedera* 2, iii, p. 52. He received livery in the palace of Westminster. "Qui praestito sacramento de officio cancellariatus fideliter exercendo, ut est moris, dictum magnum sigillum a praefato domino rege recepit, et illud secum ad hospitium suum in Suthwerk deferri, et die crastina brevia de cursu apud Westmonasterium ad lapidem marmoreum consignari fecit." On 26 November a staunch supporter of Edward II, Archbishop Melton, was appointed treasurer, but he only acted for a few months. Tout, *Chapters* 6, p. 21.

[20] *CCR 1327-1330*, pp. 528-531.

[21] *Chroniques*, ed. Luce, 1, pp. 96-97; *Foedera* 2, iii, p. 36.

[22] Déprez, *Les préliminaires*, p. 71 (from PRO S.C.1/37/161). For the background see Chaplais, "English Arguments concerning Aquitaine," and idem, "Le Duché-Pairie de Guyenne."

[23] *Foedera* 2, iii, p. 56; PRO E.101/310/6. See Haines, *Church and Politics*, pp. 33-34 (where the day of Orleton's crossing should be 28 January – not February); Déprez, *Les préliminaires*, pp. 71-73.

temporize even at the price of humiliation.[24] A mutually acceptable formula for homage was devised and later ratified by Edward at Eltham on 30 March. The sole difference from that used at Amiens in 1329, wrote Déprez, was the addition of the word "liege."[25] Ten years afterwards responsibility for the oath was to be laid at Stratford's door and the well-disposed chronicler Baker, who clearly regarded this as the crucial point in the attack on the former minister, states that Stratford had not intended to act to the king's prejudice or in order to appease King Philip, but solely because he felt it to be for the welfare of the realm.[26] That was far in the future; the immediate outcome of the Paris agreement was Edward's surreptitious journey to France. The last-minute nature of the plan is demonstrated by the fact that parliament was due to meet on 15 April, an arrangement cancelled as late as 23 March.[27] Stratford as chancellor, William de Montacute, and some fifteen knights are said to have constituted Edward's exiguous retinue.[28] Murimuth tells us that the king travelled in the guise of a merchant and caused it to be spread abroad in London that his purpose was pilgrimage.[29] On leaving his episcopal manor of Southwark Stratford entrusted the great seal to his brother Robert, the king's brother John of Eltham being designated *custos* of the realm. Stratford with others of the royal group embarked at Dover in the early morning of 4 April, landing at Wissant the same day.[30] They journeyed to Pont-Sainte-Maxence, not far from Senlis, and remained there from 12 to 16 April.[31] During this period Philip is known to have been staying at Saint-Christophe close by.[32] This must mark the stage at which the meeting or meetings of the monarchs took place. In the opinion

[24] *Les préliminaires*, p. 73: "Il fallait donc gagner du temps, fût-ce au prix d'une humiliation, dissimuler et attendre."

[25] Ibid., p. 73 n. 3; *Foedera* 2, iii, p. 61.

[26] *Chronicon*, p. 75 (s.a. 1342). Cf. the document from the Winchester cartulary printed by Harriss, *King, Parliament and Public Finance*, pp. 521-522.

[27] Parry, *Parliaments*, p. 96 (from *RDP* [App.] 4, p. 402).

[28] *Foedera* 2, iii, p. 62.

[29] *Murimuth*, p. 63. Cf. *Chronicon*, p. 48; *Foedera* 2, iii, p. 62 (pro implendo quodam voto); *CCR 1330-1333*, p. 299; Déprez, *Les préliminaires*, p. 74 n. 5. The Rochester chronicler has an interesting comment: "Eodem tempore rex cum paucis videlicet undecim equitibus cum malis retro sellas absque consilio vel consensu parium et communitatis regni occulte mare transiens ad regem Francie, honorifice est receptus, sed ab omnibus regnicolis Francie et Anglie pro modo et periculo eundi plurimum vituperatus." BL Cotton MS Faustina B.v, fol. 57ᵛ.

[30] *Foedera* 2, iii, p. 62.

[31] The royal itinerary, hence one supposes that of Stratford, is given by Déprez, *Les préliminaires*, pp. 75-76: 4 April, Dover-Wissant; 7th, Saint-Just-en-Chaussée; 12th-16th, Pont-Sainte-Maxence.

[32] Ibid., p. 76.

of Déprez (who in this is supported by Clement VI) there was no repetition
of the actual ceremony, the formal act sealed by the vassal being sufficient
for a retrospective interpretation of what had happened at Amiens.[33] Other
matters called for resolution: the French occupation of Saintes and the
subsequent burning of the castle in which the English defenders were
holding out. Philip denied responsibility but agreed to compensation and
the castle's restoration to the seneschal of Gascony. He also consented to
an amnesty for those banished from France who had been granted asylum
in English territory.[34] Such concessions helped to mask Edward's
humiliation. No time was lost before re-embarkation at Dover on 20
April, the king's party spending the subsequent night at Wingham near
Canterbury.[35]

This effort to secure a peaceful solution to the question of the English
continental possessions was endorsed at the parliament which gathered at
Westminster on 30 September 1331. Stratford, as chancellor, declared the
purpose of the assembly. Was there to be a treaty with France, or war?
The way of peace was considered preferable and Stratford was among
those named by the king to treat of his affairs with Philip of France.[36]
Almost as pressing was the problem of Ireland. English authority had
never fully recovered from the military successes, temporary though these
were, of the brothers Edward and Robert Bruce.[37] But the Scots proved
even more unpopular than the English, so on the death of Edward Bruce
after a struggle in which the justiciar Roger Mortimer played an effective
part, the situation returned to a turbulent norm. Now the royal presence
was urgently required, as well as reforms in government, but first of all
adequate forces would have to be sent to prepare the ground.[38] One
suspects that another matter which received attention was the prospective
alliance with Guelders. Edward and his councillors felt it prudent to
extend the good relationship with the Low Countries already established
by the royal union with Philippa of Hainault.[39] It was in pursuance of this

[33] Ibid., p. 77: "L'acte signé par le vassal, qui se disait lige, suffisait à préciser la forme de l'hommage"; Murimuth, p. 148.

[34] Déprez, Les préliminaires, pp. 77-78.

[35] Foedera 2, iii, p. 65. Shortly afterwards the king held a tournament at nearby Dartford. Murimuth, p. 63; BL Cotton MS Faustina B.v, fol. 57ᵛ.

[36] Rot. Parl. 2, pp. 60-61; Parry, Parliaments, p. 96.

[37] McKisack, Fourteenth Century, pp. 41-45, summarizes the affairs of Ireland during Edward II's reign. See also Curtis, Medieval Ireland, pp. 178-201; Orpen, Ireland under the Normans 4, pp. 160-206; and most recently, R. Frame, English Lordship in Ireland 1318-1361.

[38] Rot. Parl. 2, p. 61; Foedera 2, iii, p. 71.

[39] Stratford was not at York in time for the marriage ceremony on 24 January 1328 (HBC, p. 36; BL Cotton MS Galba E.iv, fol. 183ᵛ; Knighton 1, pp. 446-447, has 25th – the

policy that on 20 October plenipotentiaries – headed by Stratford and the treasurer, Bishop Ayrminne – drew up the agreement for the marriage of Reginald II, count of Guelders, with Edward's sister Eleanor, who not so long before had been put forward as a possible bride for Philip of Valois' eldest son, John.[40] In a letter five days later the king outlined to Pope John the various difficulties which beset him and the measures he proposed to adopt. To France he was sending his chancellor, Stratford, accompanied by a royal kinsman, Henry de Beaumont, and by William de Montacute and Antonio di Pessagno. They were authorized to arrange a union between his infant son Edward, born 15 June 1330, and King Philip's daughter, as well as to plan the mooted crusade and to settle outstanding problems concerning Aquitaine. The embassy was scheduled to reach the French court by 15 November.[41] There were unexpected delays; Stratford did not leave England until much later, 2 December in fact. On that day in company with the experienced civil lawyer Schordich he travelled from London to Dover, from where he crossed the channel to Wissant. Shortly thereafter he had an interview with King Philip at Bois-de-Vincennes.[42] Mid-January 1332 saw him back in England. Leaving Schordich to follow a few days later he reported to Edward at Bramford in Suffolk on the 15th.[43] Nothing tangible emerged from the embassy, but Anglo-French relations seemed outwardly more cordial than they had been for a long time.[44]

An assembly of prelates and magnates took place at Westminster in January of 1332, at which time a parliament was summoned for 16

---

date adopted by Lucas, *Low Countries*, p. 72). He was occupied with diocesan visitation, so his absence may not indicate political isolation (see below, "Itinerary"). Orleton was there (to make peace with the court for accepting the see of Worcester) and the Pauline annalist (pp. 338-339) says that Philippa came to London with him (he was returning from abroad). For events leading up to the union see Lucas, *Low Countries*, chap. 2, esp. pp. 70-73.

[40] *Foedera* 2, iii, pp. 70-71, 73-76; and cf. ibid., pp. 28, 35, 42. See Lucas, *Low Countries*, pp. 98-101. Orleton was among those appointed to accompany Eleanor to the continent. Dene (BL Cotton MS Faustina B.v, fol. 63ᵛ) is critical of the value of this alliance and blames the abbot of Langdon (an old friend of Edward II's) for it: "Ad cuius nupcias multi nobiles et iuvenes de Anglia venientes, credentes comitem fuisse potentem, magnum et valentem, sed contrarium invenientes et regis sororem esse deceptam immo perditam dolendo sunt reversi. Fuit abbas de Langedon nuncius illius maritagii atque patrator unde non inmerito ab omnibus culpatus fuit."

[41] *Foedera* 2, iii, p. 71.

[42] PRO E.372/176/67.

[43] Ibid. Stratford was paid at the rate of five marks a day for forty-five days, a total of £150. The crossing Dover-Wissant cost £19 0s 5d, and Wissant-Dover £19 10s 6½d. Messengers were allowed £5 12s 8d for their expenses. The grand total was £194 3s 7½d.

[44] Déprez, *Les préliminaires*, pp. 81-82.

March at the same place. The writs specifically excluded the appointment of proxies on account of the urgency of the business under consideration – the crusade.[45] Proclamations were made against the carrying of arms in the city of London or in the neighbourhood of the palace of Westminster, as well as against the playing of games by children and others during the parliamentary sitting.[46] The preliminaries over, Stratford introduced the main business "en fourme de predication." The king of France would be going to the Holy Land some two years hence and wished Edward to accompany him.[47] One of the chroniclers is more communicative on the topic. According to him, after discussion of Philip's proposal it was decided that the English king should commend the plan. As for Edward's part in it, once peace was assured in England, Scotland and Ireland, and there were no other hindrances, he would set out not in the king of France's company but with a separate army of his own. Clergy, prelates and people are said to have declined to associate themselves with this reply because of the subsidy it might entail.[48] A matter closer to home was worrying the government; a band of outlaws ensconced in the inaccessible mountain and forest area of Derbyshire. Their leader sported the title "King of the Peak," appointing his own justices and other officers. A crowning stroke of insolence was the capture of a future chief justice of the King's Bench, Richard Willoughby, who was "fined" a thousand marks (in fact thirteen hundred).[49] At the end of the parliament the form of commission for keepers of the peace was adopted and – in the chronicler's view – the more vigorous action against malefactors which this presaged determined the outlaws of the Peak to seek refuge with the Scots.[50]

[45] Parry, *Parliaments*, p. 97; *Foedera* 2, iii, p. 73.

[46] *Rot. Parl.* 2, p. 64. The proclamation was to be made regularly at subsequent assemblies. Stratford was probably there for the first day, but the archbishop and some others had not yet arrived.

[47] Ibid., no. 4.

[48] BL Cotton MS Faustina B.v, fol. 60ᵛ.

[49] Ibid., fol. 60ʳ. Cf. TCC MS R.5 41, fol. 129ᵛ (recte 130), where the ransom is given (correctly it seems) as 1,300 marks. Willoughby was captured 14 January 1332. *Knighton* 1, pp. 460-461, attributes the number of outlaws to the courts of "trailbaston" (as they were nicknamed) and gives Richard de Folville as the captor of Willoughby. See Keen, *Outlaws of Medieval England*, pp. 197-200; Stones, "Folvilles of Ashby-Folville," p. 122.

[50] BL Cotton MS Faustina B.v, fol. 60ʳ; *Rot. Parl.* 2, p. 65, no. 12; Stones, "Folvilles of Ashby-Folville," pp. 125-126; Putnam, "Transformation of Keepers of the Peace"; idem, *Proceedings before Justices of the Peace*, esp. pp. xxxviii-xxxix. Putnam (in the last work) shows that Scrope, the man behind the policy adopted in the 1332 parliament, was an exponent of the system of afforcing the commissions with magnates who were given wide powers.

Barely a month after parliament's dismissal arrangements were complete for a new approach to the French court. The embassy was an impressive one. Stratford on this occasion was accompanied, not by Ayrminne, who had recently ceased to be treasurer,[51] but by Orleton, the bishop of Worcester, a man of considerable diplomatic experience. Three items were to form the basis of discussion: the crusade, a personal meeting of the two monarchs to arrange a permanent alliance, and a marriage between Edward's son and Philip's daughter, Joan.[52] Stratford, as the account later presented by his attorney Nicholas de Aka shows, set out from London on 27 April. Crossing by the regular Dover to Wissant route he arrived at Amiens. From there he despatched a messenger with an accompanying squire to the French king, who was at St. Germain-en-Laye. The ambassadors then moved south and took part in a conference with Philip and his councillors at Bois-de-Vincennes.[53] Behind the scenes John XXII, anxious to launch the crusade, was making every effort to mollify Philip and to bring him to a cooperative frame of mind. There were some discordant notes. Letters followed hard on the heels of the departing ambassadors with complaints about the despoiling of London merchants in Saintonge and in Britanny, and of the imposition of a *maltôte* on Gascon wine. By the end of May discussions were concluded. The English ambassadors returned to the coast and after an absence of forty-one days appeared on 6 June before King Edward at Woodstock.[54] Again there was no obvious outcome.

Not long after Stratford's return, 23 June 1332, Antonio di Pessagno, one of his fellow ambassadors in 1331, came before the exchequer at Westminster. There, in a room where the king's council commonly met, he delivered a writ addressed to the keepers of the great seal. They were to entrust the seal to the person nominated by the chancellor, who was said to be busy about the king's affairs. Pessagno also brought Stratford's

---

[51] Appointed 1 April 1331. His successor, Robert Ayleston, was commissioned 29 March 1332. Tout, *Chapters* 6, p. 22. According to Dene (BL Cotton MS Faustina B.v, fol. 60ʳ) this was decided at the "council of January 1332," and Hethe could have had the office but would not offer money for it. "In quo concilio episcopus Roffen. licet absens tamen vocatus, si pecuniam effudisset regis thesaurarius fieri potuisset, sed nullam optulit."

[52] *Foedera* 2, iii, pp. 77-78; Haines, *Church and Politics*, pp. 34-35; Déprez, *Les préliminaires*, p. 84 nn. 4-6.

[53] Déprez, *Les préliminaires*, pp. 84-87; PRO E.372/177/40.

[54] *Foedera* 2, iii, pp. 77-78; PRO E.372/177/40. Personal expenses amounted to £136 13s 4d at five marks a day. The passage Dover-Wissant cost £18 17s 6¹/₄d; the return trip Wissant-Dover, £13 13s 2¹/₂d. The messengers' expenses were £6 6s 4d. The total was £175 10s 5¹/₄d, which left £75 10s 5¹/₄d to be recovered by Stratford.

letters nominating his brother Robert as temporary keeper.[55] The particular royal business supposedly engaging the chancellor's attention is not revealed, but it is known that he snatched the chance of giving some overdue consideration to his diocese. He did make a quick journey to Northampton early in September, possibly in connection with the forthcoming parliament. On the way, at Witney, he wrote to Archbishop Mepham, excusing himself from personal attendance at the council summoned to St. Paul's for the reform of abuses in the province. This met on 4 September and on the 7th the meeting was enlivened by Bishop Orleton who, as the ringleader of those who objected to certain of Mepham's proceedings, appealed to the Roman curia on the grounds of *gravamina* in the summons and the fact that it was harvest time.[56]

When parliament reassembled at Westminster on Wednesday of the second week in September, Stratford was on hand to declare the purpose of the summons. It was Irish and Scottish rather than crusading affairs which demanded immediate action. Prelates, barons and commons deliberated separately; their discussions made more urgent by the frequent arrival of alarming reports from Scotland. In these circumstances a grant was conceded to Edward, who feeling that the time for talking was over, left parliament and its unfinished business for the battle front.[57] Stratford, the burden of office removed from his shoulders, slipped back to his diocese.

However much the king's imagination might linger on chivalric deeds in distant lands, he was drawn inexorably to the reality of everyday political life, above all to the question of Scotland. We have seen that the "turpis pax" of Northampton, or more properly of Edinburgh, had left that country an independent kingdom with Robert Bruce's four-year-old son married to Edward III's sister, Joan.[58] Between the death of King Robert on 7 June 1329 and his own death on 20 July 1332 Thomas Randolph, earl of Moray, ruled the kingdom as regent. Moray's departure from the scene opened the way for the "disinherited," men like Henry de

---

[55] *Foedera* 2, iii, p. 79. For Pessagno see Fryde, "Antonio Pessagno of Genoa."

[56] WinRS, fols. 72ᵛ, 74ʳ. Of those present, only the bishops of Rochester (Hethe) and Salisbury (Wyville) did not put their names to the appeal (fol. 72ᵛ margin). The real reason for the protest was Mepham's activities as metropolitan visitor. See *Murimuth*, p. 68; *Annales Paulini*, pp. 356-357.

[57] *Rot. Parl.* 2, pp. 66-67; Parry, *Parliaments*, p. 98. Of this parliament Dene writes (BL. Cotton ᴍs Faustina B.v, fol. 63ᵛ): "Ubi in summa tractatum fuit de subsidio faciendo regi pro rebellione quorundam in Hibernia propulsanda et Scotorum comminancium marchiam Anglie et Scocie devastare, et fuit concessa a laicis quintadecima et collecta."

[58] See above, "Lancastrian Spokesman."

Beaumont, who claimed the earldom of Buchan through his wife,[59] his young relative Gilbert de Umfraville, *soi-disant* earl of Angus, David de Strathbogie, earl of Atholl, and Thomas lord Wake. Many others joined them, including the redoubtable Ralph Stafford and the Hainaulter, Walter Manny. Edward III adopted a policy of duplicity. He had allowed Edward Balliol, claimant to the Scottish throne, to come to England in 1330 under the aegis of Beaumont.[60] He gave no official countenance to him or his associates, but he was privy to what was on foot.[61] At the end of July Balliol and a small army of adventurers, which the continuator of the Brut put at five hundred men-at-arms and two thousand archers and footsoldiers, set sail from Ravenspurn, landing just short of a week later at Kinghorn in Fife. On 12 August they won a momentous victory at Dupplin Moor over a much larger force led by Donald, earl of Mar, the new regent. The following month Balliol was crowned king of Scots at Scone.[62] Edward was not slow to reveal his true feelings. In November by the treaty of Roxburgh Balliol acknowledged the English king's overlordship and undertook to cede Berwick to him. Balliol's triumph was short-lived. Defeated in a surprise attack by the new earl of Moray, he was forced to flee in ignominious haste to Carlisle where, the Lanercost chronicler tells us, he was well received on account of the havoc he had earlier wreaked among the Scots.[63]

Parliament was summoned to York for 4 December 1332. As the king was unable to come until later the archbishop of York, William Melton, together with Robert de Stratford and Geoffrey le Scrope were deputed to open the proceedings. Robert acted as his brother's proctor, for Stratford had expressed himself too ill to come and was temporarily immobilized at his manor of Farnham.[64] Arrangements were made to treat with the Scots

---

[59] Beaumont was considered to be a Frenchmen. His responsibility for bringing Balliol from France is alleged in the Brut (CCC MS 174), fol. 165^{r-v}. A list of his companions is given in *Bridlington*, pp. 103-104; cf. *Melsa*, p. 362.

[60] Probably the best short account of these events is by Tout, *PHE* 3, pp. 315-324. See also Balfour-Melville, *Edward III and David II*, which contains a brief bibliography, though not including the Brut; Campbell, "England, Scotland and the Hundred Years War."

[61] According to *Lanercost*, p. 267, Balliol set off for Scotland, "habito prius cum rege Angliae consilio privato." Cf. Brut (CCC MS 174), fol. 165^v, where a speech declining permission for Balliol to pass through his lands is put into the English king's mouth. Cf. *Murimuth*, p. 66 ; *Chronicon*, p. 49; *Knighton* 1, p. 461: "non tamen eos aperte juvare potuit"; *Melsa*, pp. 362-363: "prohibuit ne per terram Anglie profiscentes."

[62] Brut (CCC MS 174), fols. 166^{r}ff. Long accounts are in *Knighton* 1, pp. 461-465; *Bridlington*, pp. 102-109, and the related *Melsa*, pp. 362-365ff. Some chroniclers, e.g. *Lanercost*, p. 267, point out that the earl of Mar had earlier given countenance to Balliol.

[63] *Lanercost*, p. 271. He was received by the Minorites there.

[64] *Foedera* 2, iii, p. 85; WinRS, fol. 156^r; PRO S.C.10/17/813 (Stratford's proxy dated from Farnham, 18 November 1332).

and on 15 December Edward, having arrived at York, wrote to the pope with an explanation of the northern situation.[65] For a time he gave the appearance of deciding between Balliol on the one hand and King David II, supported by representatives of King Philip, on the other. In reality the choice was unambiguous, for only by reinstating Balliol could the English king gain Berwick and a dependent vassal. For the whole of this period negotiations were in process at the French court. Orleton was the principal member of an embassy which left London for Paris on 11 November 1332. He remained there until 22 February of the following year, when he left for Avignon, doubtless under orders to persuade the pope and cardinals of his master's good intentions.[66] Edward's position was a delicate one. He must avoid stampeding Philip into a military alliance with Scotland or compromising the still unresolved problems of Aquitaine. Philip too had to tread with care for, as Déprez has pointed out, he had an interest in preserving the docility of a potentially dangerous vassal.[67] Edward was also aware of the danger from the Flemings, whose ships could be and allegedly were being used for succouring the Scots with men, money and arms. In June 1333 an embassy to the count of Flanders was to be at pains to mitigate this nuisance.[68]

Meanwhile, Stratford was able to take his customary part in the parliament which reconvened on 20 January 1333. According to the rolls, the December session had been adjourned because in the absence of certain prelates and other magnates – Stratford among them, though he is not specifically mentioned – those remaining felt themselves unable to respond to the royal request for the accustomed service or its equivalent.[69] Deliberation on the king's affairs is said to have been conducted in three groups: the first comprised the archbishop of York (Melton), the bishop of Ely (Hothum), Winchester (Stratford), Lincoln (Burghersh), Chester (Northburgh) and Norwich (Ayrminne), the earls of Surrey and Warwick, and the lords Percy, Beaumont, Courtenay and Clinton – apparently those most closely concerned with political matters; the second group was made

[65] Foedera 2, iii, p. 86.

[66] Haines, Church and Politics, p. 35; Déprez, Les préliminaires, p. 88, who remarks: "Les négociations de 1333 n'eurent aucun résultat."

[67] Ibid., p. 91: "Fallait-il abandonner les Écossais ou, au contraire, les soutenir et rompre du même coup avec un vassal maintenant si docile?"

[68] Foedera 2, iii, p. 94. Sent to Louis I, count of Flanders and Nevers (1322-1346) were M. John de Hildesle, William de la Pole and Robert de Kelleseye (Kilsby). See Lucas, Low Countries, pp. 142-145.

[69] Rot. Parl. 2, pp. 67-69; Parry, Parliaments, pp. 99-100. The parliament which assembled 4 December 1332 at York was prorogued until 20 January 1333 and dissolved on the 27th.

up of the rest of the prelates, earls and barons; while the third consisted
of the knights of the shire and others of the commons.[70] Stratford
pronounced the result of these separate deliberations, which were
apparently inconclusive, though it was suggested that further consultation
should take place with the pope and the king of France. He then added
that it was the king's wish that wardens of the march be appointed and
that a special group of councillors be in close attendance on him.[71] Dene
has a more specific impression of what took place. It was decided, he says,
that the king should go to the defence of the Scottish march and that the
disinherited should pass into Scotland in search of their enemies.[72] And so
it transpired. Balliol and the army he had collected resumed hostilities in
March by investing Berwick. The strength of the fortifications raised by
Edward's grandfather ensured that the seige would be protracted.[73] April
saw the English king ready to intervene on Balliol's behalf; thus reversing
the policy imposed upon him when under tutelage. Writing from
Newcastle on the 23rd he requested Archbishop Mepham to organize
prayers and pious exercises for the success of his forces.[74] The seige
dragged on into June. On the 20th, when acknowledging Stratford's
letters and those of the king of France, Edward transmitted his council's
advice that in responding to Philip the chancellor should be circumspect
about Scottish affairs.[75]

Edward's preoccupation in the north brought disquiet elsewhere.
Following celebration of mass at the royal foundation of Battle Abbey on
the summer festival of St. Martin (4 July) Bishop Hethe took occasion to
voice his anxiety, which was doubtless reflected in the minds of others all
along the south coast. The gathering after dinner in his chamber included
many from the maritime towns. He stressed the king's youth and the
influence which might be exercised by those around him who were well
disposed towards the French.[76] King Philip, he warned, was preparing

[70] *Rot. Parl.* 2, p. 69.

[71] Ibid., no. 7.

[72] BL. Cotton MS Faustina B.v, fol. 64ᵛ: "Et Anglici exheredati cum novo rege Scocie
Scociam penetrarent hostes suos quesituri." Cf. *Bridlington*, pp. 110-111.

[73] BL. Cotton MS Faustina B.v, fol. 65ʳ; *Bridlington*, p. 111; *Lanercost*, p. 272. However,
Colvin, *King's Works* 2, pp. 563-571, suggests that the castle's siting was defective and
that much of Edward I's rebuilding had been in timber rather than stone. Cf. *Lanercost*,
p. 214 (s.a. 1309): "Berwicum, quam villam rex Angliae muro forti et alto et fossa fecerat
circumcingi."

[74] *Foedera* 2, iii, p. 91; *Murimuth*, p. 67; *Chronicon*, p. 50. Murimuth (expanded by
Baker) argues that the king was formerly bound by the traitor Mortimer's counsel "contra
consilium matris suae [Isabella]."

[75] Déprez, *Les préliminaires*, p. 91 n. 5 (transcript of PRO C.81/200/6429).

[76] Beaumont, for instance. See n. 59 above and *Lanercost*, p. 267.

attacks on the English realm and gathering a fleet to assist the Scots. Now that King Edward was outside the country it was bereft of defence and wide open to invasion. The inhabitants of the ports would have to prepare ships and men. The well-meaning bishop was preaching to the converted. The reply came that spies had already been sent into France and also messengers to warn King Edward of the dangers which threatened. The king's response had been that they should guard the sea and that he had instructed the Kentish knights to keep watch on the coast with an armed force.[77] Shortly afterwards (16 July) and doubtless influenced by warnings such as these, Edward told Stratford of the measures he wished to be adopted. The ports were to be put into a state of military preparedness; William de Clinton was to be commissioned as admiral in those parts and also as *custos* of the county of Kent. But the king did not wish English seamen to harm the French, provided that they did no injury to his own subjects. It was vital that no occasion for war should be given.[78]

Circumstances soon altered beyond recognition. On 19 July, the eve of St. Margaret, came the longed-for day on which the rebellion of the Scots and their pride and obstinacy were put down – as the Rochester chronicler chauvinistically expressed it.[79] He was referring to the victory of Halidon Hill, won by the combined forces of Edward and Balliol, using much the same tactics as had proved so effective at Dupplin Moor. The surrender of Berwick followed the next day and the French ambassadors, detained at Newcastle by the mayor, returned home with the unwelcome news.[80] A couple of days later Archbishop Mepham was directed to offer prayers for the victory and a general thanksgiving was ordered.[81]

In the autumn of 1333 occurred an event which was to modify profoundly Stratford's career: Archbishop Mepham died on 12 October. As we have seen already,[82] the prior and chapter postulated Stratford as his successor, the king warmly concurred, and Pope John xxii translated him without reference to either. The vacancy thus created at Winchester

[77] BL. Cotton MS Faustina B.v, fol. 65^{r-v}.

[78] Déprez, *Les préliminaires*, pp. 90-91 n. 4 (transcript of PRO C.81/200/6464).

[79] BL. Cotton MS Faustina B.v, fol. 65^v: "Venit dies desideratissimus ... in quo Scotorum rebellio et superbia fraus et obstinacia iusto Dei iudicio puniuntur et Anglorum miseria in qua per triginta quinque annos Anglici detenti fuerant."

[80] Ibid., fol. 66^r. Cf. Brut (CCC MS 174), fols. 170^r-173^r; *Lanercost*, pp. 272-274; *Murimuth*, p. 68; *Knighton* 1, pp. 466-470; *Bridlington*, pp. 114-118.

[81] *Foedera* 2, iii, p. 97: Berwick, 22 July 1333; *Bridlington*, pp. 116-118. The king went to Canterbury on pilgrimage. "Ipse vero rex Anglie cum modica familia in magna humilitate regionem peragrans nullos de suis populum gravare permittens Cantuar. cum summa devocione sanctum Thomam visitavit." BL. Cotton MS Faustina B.v, fol. 66^r.

[82] Above, "Archbishop of Canterbury."

was expeditiously filled by another translation – that of Orleton from Worcester. Orleton was at Avignon at the time and the circumstances of his provision are strikingly similar to those of Stratford himself in 1323. In view of this fact the metropolitan-elect could be regarded as ungenerous in opposing his colleague's promotion. Edward's unfavourable reaction to Orleton's further advancement stemmed in the main from his desire for the elevation of Simon de Montacute, brother of the William de Montacute who had been to the fore in Mortimer's overthrow. Montacute was indeed provided to a bishopric at this time, but it was the less desirable see of Worcester, whence he later migrated to Ely. According to some unfriendly observers, notably Baker but also his exemplar Murimuth, Orleton's translation resulted from the intervention of the king of France – after all he had been long in Paris and it could be alleged (spitefully and without foundation) that the ambassador had served Philip better than his master, himself best of all! Possibly Philip did have a good word for an able diplomat at his court; if so, in the jingoistic mood of the day that was unfortunate for Orleton's standing at home but constituted flimsy ground for such bitter condemnation.[83] Another more general consideration weighed with Edward; he wished to be master in his own house, and that included the episcopate. There had been too many instances of opportunism of this kind. Stratford's position in all this was a difficult one. As chancellor he was the king's mouthpiece and bound to oppose Orleton, at least officially, whatever his private feelings might be. He owed a debt of gratitude to Edward for unstinted support in his own case. However that may be, his reaping of financial advantage from Orleton's predicament is indefensible.[84] Stratford's other loyalty was, of course, to the pope; he knew perfectly well that in translating Orleton John XXII was exercising an established canonical right, from which he himself had benefited.

But there was another quite different and highly unusual facet of the affair; the still current debate about the responsibility for the deposition and subsequent fate of Edward II. An attempt to fasten guilt on Orleton for the revolutionary changes of 1326-1327 has as its counterpart an exoneration of Stratford. That Stratford was personally involved in Orleton's harassment is suggested both by the nature of the appeal to the apostolic see against the new bishop of Winchester – coupled with the answers it elicited – and by the pope's allegations made shortly after-

---

[83] See Haines, *Church and Politics*, pp. 36-38.
[84] For this aspect of his actions at the time see above, "Archbishop of Canterbury."

wards.[85] The appeal was published on 2 April 1334 in Winchester Cathedral. Present for the sensational event was a strong official element including the sheriff of Hampshire and the noted diplomat John de Schordich, who broke his journey to the coast for the purpose, doubtless on instructions from the royal council. The nominal appellant was an obscure clerk of the diocese.[86] Allegedly Orleton was convicted by public notoriety[87] on three counts, and was thereby disqualified from office. The first charge concerned the violent death of Robert Baldock in January 1327 at the hands of the Londoners. It was Stratford as treasurer, retorted Orleton, who had been chiefly responsible for Baldock's transfer from Hereford to London, not himself.[88] The second charge was that as a consequence of a sermon delivered by Orleton the hearts of Edward II's subjects had been alienated, whereupon some of them imprisoned the king. Orleton's riposte was to posit his version of events. Stratford, he said, was the man responsible for the articles of deposition and it was his clerk who had drawn them up.[89] The final charge – that Orleton had been instrumental in the breakdown of Queen Isabella's marriage by implanting a spurious fear of her husband – was parried by an answer which likewise implicated Stratford. The address given by Orleton, which formed the basis of this allegation, followed from a decision of a council in which the then bishop of Winchester had participated. Orleton claimed to have been a mouthpiece, no more.[90] The new bishop of Winchester felt that the best form of defence was attack; he had no doubt about the direction in which he should aim.

Another possible pointer towards Stratford's involvement in the attack on Orleton is the opposition to the latter of M. William Inge, the archdeacon of Surrey. Inge seems to have been a trusted confidant of

[85] Ibid., n. 143.

[86] Ibid., n. 145.

[87] "Et adhuc laborat publica vox et fama, quodque notoria per totam Angliam communiter reputantur." *Responsiones*, col. 2768 (Lambeth MS 1213, p. 306).

[88] "Excitante et procurante potissime venerabili patre domino J[ohanne] tunc Wyntoniensi episcopo et Angliae thesaurario." *Responsiones*, col. 2763.

[89] "Contenta sunt in instrumentis publicis reverendo patre domino J[ohanne] Dei gratia nunc Cantuariensi electo tunc Wyntoniensi episcopo et Angliae thesaurario conceptis et dictatis, et manu magistri Willelmi de Mees clerici sui secretarii et publici notarii conscriptis." *Responsiones*, col. 2765.

[90] "Deliberato consilio cum reverendis patribus bonae memoriae Waltero tunc Cantuariensi archiepiscopo ac Johanne tunc Wyntoniensi nunc vero Cantuariensi electo.... Quod juxta informacionem mihi super hoc factam, in praesencia domini Cantuariensis et nobilium praedictorum feci, nichil addens de proprio vel minuens de injuncto." *Responsiones*, cols. 2766-2767.

Stratford's, for in 1324 the bishop had chosen him to conduct his enthronement and subsequently made use of him in other ways.[91] Throughout Orleton's episcopate Inge was a thorn in his flesh and there is good reason to suspect that this is not explicable solely in terms of jurisdictional conflict, some evidence of which is also to be found during Stratford's tenure of Winchester.[92] But as primate Stratford could not prolong a personal (or could it be political?) vendetta of this kind without harm to his own reputation. Murimuth informs us that when Orleton's temporalities were restored on 23 September 1334 it was at the intercession in parliament of Stratford and his fellow bishops. Baker in recording the same incident had his own reasons for omitting mention of Stratford.[93] It has been thought that royal anger against Orleton was so great as to exclude him from parliament until 1336.[94] This is an exaggeration. In reality he was summoned (by writ of 22 February 1335) to the parliament or great council at Nottingham,[95] subsequently to the York parliament of 26 May 1335, and then in the following August to the London parliament or council, where he even served as one of the presidents, Stratford being too busy to come.[96] Whether Stratford arrived at a more amicable relationship with his rival can only be a matter of conjecture, but we shall see one last flare up between the two.[97] However, we must return to the impact of Scottish affairs in the earlier 1330s.

The movement of the centre of political gravity to York occasioned by Edward's continued preoccupation with Scotland, coupled with the assumption of the duties of metropolitan, made it impossible for Stratford personally to attend to the whole range of his duties as chancellor. From 17 December 1332 until 8 January of the following year the great seal was placed in the custody of two chancery clerks, Henry Cliff and Henry

[91] See above, "Winchester 1323-1333," nn. 15, 51.

[92] See Haines, *Church and Politics*, index s.v. Inge.

[93] *Murimuth*, p. 70; *Chronicon*, p. 55. Comparison of the two entries is interesting. Murimuth writes: "Quo die archiepiscopus et ceteri episcopi in parliamento Londoniis rogaverunt pro ipso, ita quod, causa cognita, mandavit sua temporalia sibi reddi"; while Baker has: "ad preces episcoporum in parliamento Londoniis, graciose refudit."

[94] E.g. Haines, *Church and Politics*, pp. 37-38, misled by Plucknett, "Parliament," p. 94 n. 2.

[95] WinRO 1, fol. 132ʳ (al. 4); *RDP* (App.) 4, p. 441.

[96] Writs of 1 April from Nottingham and of 7 August from Perth respectively, summoned the York and London assemblies. WinRO 1, fols. 132ᵛ (al. 4), 135ʳ⁻ᵛ (al. 7); *RDP* (App.) 4, pp. 443-444 (Winchester not cited), 453. Orleton was associated in the presidency with Bishop Gravesend (London) and M. Laurence Fastolf. *Foedera* 2, iii, p. 132. For the London assembly (met 25 August) see *Cal. PMR*, pp. 92-93 and below, n. 155.

[97] See below, "The Crisis of 1341."

Edwinstow, who were succeeded for the period 10 August 1333 until 13 January 1334 by William Melton, the archbishop of York.[98] Tout was of the opinion that these men, and others who preceded or followed them, were essentially Stratford's "friends" and that by control of the chancery "Lancastrian and baronial influence prevailed for practically ten years in the highest administrative office." [99] This is too sweeping a claim. In the context of the oppressive and grasping rule of Isabella and Mortimer, which had induced the opposition of a recognizable group of prelates and barons, Stratford had certainly identified himself with those principles which have been labelled "Lancastrian." Now that Edward III was of age the pressures under which these principles became explicit were for the time being less in evidence. It would be hard in these circumstances to distinguish in practice between Stratford and what Tout categorized as the "curialist" elements in Edward's administration. Certainly Stratford, his relatives and appointees exercised an influence on government, but this cannot be defined with precision. As we shall see, independence of mind only becomes discernible again at a time of crisis precipitated partly by external events and partly by the ill-considered actions of the king, some of them blatantly unlawful.[100]

The year 1334 was to prove an arduous one for the new archbishop. Having spent Christmas at Wallingford Edward travelled north to a parliament summoned for 21 February at York. Before setting out for the same destination Stratford spent some time in Winchester diocese, which he had yet to vacate.[101] For much of the time he was at Farnham Castle. On the Saturday in Embertide, 18 December 1333, he held his final ordination ceremony at the parish church in the town.[102] The following day he travelled north to Chertsey Abbey, where he consecrated the new bishop of Durham, Richard de Bury.[103] Bury's provision to Durham is a striking illustration of the king's real attitude to capitular election and also, it would seem, of a chapter's determination to follow an independent line without due regard for the inevitable repercussions. Robert Graystanes, a monk of the cathedral priory trained in theology, had been elected by the chapter, confirmed by the amenable Melton as York metropolitan,

---

[98] Tout, *Chapters* 6, p. 12; *CCR 1330-1333*, pp. 594, 619; ibid. *1333-1337*, pp. 129-130, 188, 296.

[99] *Chapters* 3, pp. 42-43.

[100] Below, "The Crisis of 1341."

[101] WinRS, fol. 139ᵛ.

[102] Ibid., fols. 157ᵛ-159ʳ.

[103] *Murimuth*, p. 71; *Graystanes*, p. 763. Murimuth wrongly states that the consecration took place immediately after Christmas.

consecrated by him in his archiepiscopal chapel, and installed as bishop in
the church of St. Cuthbert. Edward, however, had other ideas for
Durham and would not assent to the election. On the contrary, he had
already written to the chapter on behalf of Bury, his early mentor and
close confidant. Learning of the papal provision of his candidate, for
which he had asked, Edward expressed his unwillingness to offend the
pope. On this occasion both were working in concert, but to the detriment
of capitular election.[104]

Edward Balliol was summoned as king of Scots to the York parliament,
but disturbances in the Scottish islands prevented his personal attendance.[105] The Scottish situation was complicated by the active intervention
of Philip of France, who in May was to provide the means which enabled
David II to escape with his wife and then, with an escort of ten vessels out
of Dieppe, to reach France, where by an ironic twist he was housed in
Richard I's great fortification of Château-Gaillard.[106] This created a
potentially dangerous situation, made more so by Edward III's foolishness
in inflicting such hard terms on his puppet, Balliol, that he stood no
chance of maintaining his position against a resurgent Scottish nationalism.[107]

It was to France that Edward now turned his attention. On 26 March
1334 ambassadors were appointed to continue the endless legal processes
of Périgueux, Agen and Montreuil.[108] Four days later a high-powered
embassy was named. It was led by Stratford, the sole prelate. Accompanying him were two barons very close to the king – William
Montacute and William de Clinton – as well as the justice Geoffrey le
Scrope and the inevitable John de Schordich. Apart from the perennial
questions concerning Gascony the envoys were empowered to make
plans for the crusade and to negotiate a match between John, the four-
year-old son of Edmund earl of Kent, and a daughter of one of the nobles
of France.[109] A day later, 31 March, the same persons, with the exception

[104] The business of Robert de Graystanes' election and his supersession by Bury is
given at length in *Graystanes*, pp. 762-763ff. (*Historiae Dunelmensis Scriptores Tres*,
pp. 120-122ff.). *Le Neve* 6, pp. 107-108, has most of the essential references. See also
Denholm-Young, "Richard de Bury," pp. 11-12; *Biog. Oxon.*, s.v. Bury, Graystanes.
Melton had to seek the king's pardon for his consecration of Graystanes.

[105] *Murimuth*, p. 72; BL Cotton MS Faustina B.v, fol. 75ʳ.

[106] Déprez, *Les préliminaires*, p. 119 n. 4; *Anonimalle Chronicle*, p. 2.

[107] See, for example, *Historia Roffensis* (BL Cotton MS Faustina B.v), fol. 75ʳ;
Anonimalle Chronicle, p. 2.

[108] *Foedera* 2, iii, pp. 108-110.

[109] Ibid., p. 111. The necessary quorum was two, of whom Stratford was to be one.

of Montacute, were directed to oversee the state of the county of Ponthieu, of which Bartholomew Burghersh had been made seneschal.[110] An additional duty imposed on Stratford, in conjunction with Scrope, was to receive the fealty for his English lands of the duke of Britanny, Jean de Bretagne, and to look into the matter of his homage.[111]

Stratford left the archiepiscopal manor of Charing in Kent on 6 April and set sail from Dover on the 8th for Wissant and Le Crotoy, where he disembarked. Further letters of instruction, dated 9 April from Huntingdon, followed him. In these he was associated with William de Cusancia for arranging a marriage between the king's brother John of Eltham, earl of Cornwall, and Marie, daughter of the count of Blois.[112] Stratford and his party proceeded by way of Rue in Ponthieu, where Bishop Hethe arrived with the pallium,[113] and reached Saint-Louis about 8 May.[114] It was there that he appears to have met Philip VI and his negotiators: Ralph count of Eu,[115] Pierre Roger, archbishop of Rouen and future Pope Clement VI, and the marshal of France, Mathieu de Trie.[116] Little or nothing is known of the progress made towards solution of the major problems under discussion, but from a letter sent by Stratford to the prior of Canterbury[117] and the fact that a further embassy was planned for the autumn, we can deduce that the signs were encouraging.

During May Stratford was writing to his brother Robert and other custodians of the great seal[118] about two commissions for the expedition of Gascon matters, drafts of which he was sending. He asked for sealed commissions to be sent as soon as possible.[119] Somewhat earlier in the

---

[110] Ibid.

[111] Ibid., p. 110.

[112] PRO E.101/311/6 (bis); Foedera 2, iii, p. 112. Stratford is said to have transferred the great seal at Otford on the same day (6 April) that he was at Charing: CCR 1333-1337, p. 309.

[113] See above, "Archbishop of Canterbury," n. 14.

[114] Senliz, which Déprez (Les préliminaires, p. 97 n. 1) identifies as a hamlet of Egreville, arr. Fontainebleau (Seine-et-Marne). But see n. 119 below.

[115] In 1333 negotiations were in train for the marriage of his daughter Joan to John of Eltham, earl of Cornwall. Foedera 2, iii, pp. 89-90.

[116] The French negotiators are named by Déprez, Les préliminaires, p. 97.

[117] Lit. Cant. 2, p. 56 (539); CCL Reg. L, fol. 36ʳ.

[118] "Robert de Stretford et aliis custodibus." Robert Stratford does not appear in Tout's list (Chapters 6, p. 12) at this point. Edwinstow, Bamburgh and St. Pol are given as acting until 17 February 1334, after which there is a gap until Bishop Bury's appointment as chancellor in September.

[119] PRO S.C.1/39/57. The document is much damaged on the right-hand side, where it is partly illegible. It is dated 23 May 13[3]4 from Silvanectum (Senlis). There is a virtually complete transcript in Déprez, Les préliminaires, p. 110 n. 7, where it is dated from Senlis, 23 March 1335 (sic).

month he had informed his brother and the chancery that he had duly received the duke of Brittany's fealty on the 8th at Saint-Louis, but had respited the homage temporarily, now that he was in possession of all the relevant documents. Writs were to be issued to the escheators and custodians for livery of the duke's lands.[120] Another project which prospered at last was that of finding a wife for John of Eltham. Earlier plans for marriage with Joan daughter of the count of Eu, Marie daughter of the count of Blois, and with another Marie, daughter of the lord of Coucy, had all come to nothing.[121] The successful candidate was Marie daughter of Ferdinand of Spain, lord of Lara. Ferdinand having died the marriage agreement was drawn up between Blanche, countess of Savoy, and the English ambassadors.[122] But it was not until the end of September that the formal arrangements were sealed, King Philip promising a dower of 30,000 *livres petits turnois*.[123] Meanwhile, in mid-June at his manor of Wingham, Stratford summarized the results of his mission in a letter to Bishop Grandisson. Things had gone better than he expected and he now knew more about the intentions of the king of France than he had ever done before.[124]

Stratford had returned by way of Le Crotoy and Dover in the first week of June 1334, and not without difficulty. It can only have been bad weather that forced various members of his *familia* to land at Winchelsea and Hythe rather than at Dover.[125] From the coast Stratford seems to have travelled by way of Wingham and Lambeth before continuing north-wards.[126] A royal mandate of 12 June forbade the metropolitan of York to obstruct Stratford on the pretext that he might be raising his primatial cross in the northern province, since he was on the king's urgent business.[127] It was on that date, at Newcastle, that Edward Balliol ceded Berwick and other marcher towns and castles to the English king.[128] Stratford was too late for the ceremony; his expense account ends on 5 July at Doncaster.[129]

[120] PRO S.C.1/39/56: *Seint Liz*, 16 May 1334. The letter is addressed "a noz bien amez maistre Robert de Stretford nostre trescher frere et a autres gardeins du graunt seal."

[121] *Foedera* 2, iii, pp. 89-90, 112, 117.

[122] Déprez, *Les préliminaires*, p. 96 n. 3.

[123] *Foedera* 2, iii, pp. 118-119; Déprez, *Les préliminaires*, p. 96 n. 3.

[124] *Exeter Reg. Grandisson*, p. 274.

[125] "Item in portagio familie et hernas. eorundem de navibus usque ad terram apud Hethe et Wynchelse et Dovorr." PRO E.101/311/6.

[126] *Exeter Reg. Grandisson*, pp. 274-276.

[127] *Foedera* 2, iii, pp. 114-115.

[128] Ibid., p. 11. See also above, n. 107.

[129] PRO E.101/311/6. The total of expenses claimed for this embassy amounts to £500 0s 8d. Stratford received £100 at the exchequer 9 March 1334 and £85 at Paris from the

Roughly at this point, following his account of the fortunes of the pallium, the Rochester chronicler has an intriguing incident to relate, the precise date of which is uncertain. The king is said to have returned from Scotland to Canterbury with a few companions and then moved on to London for discussion with Stratford about a meeting held at Coventry in the presence of Isabella the queen mother.[130] This has a sinister ring. Could it be that Isabella was angling for support against the king's Scottish policy or fostering some plot or other? The entry can be made to bear a less sensational interpretation. Isabella was in dispute with the local prior about their respective rights in the manor and town of Coventry. The matter became important enough to merit the compilation of a lengthy roll in connection with proceedings before the council in 1336.[131] But if this is what Dene referred to, why was it worthy of mention among national events, and why did Edward travel from Scotland – if indeed he did – on such business? The restitution to Isabella in September 1334 of the counties of Ponthieu and Montreuil suggests that if anything had aroused the king's concern, it was soon dismissed from his mind.[132]

The instability of the Scottish situation was soon apparent to Balliol's overlord. News of the capture of Richard Talbot and other English knights, as also of Balliol's enforced flight to the shelter of Berwick, was brought to the parliament which assembled at Westminster on 19 September. Retaliatory measures were needed. For these the king's presence was required in the north and a tenth and fifteenth were granted for that purpose. It was agreed that Edward should go on crusade in five years, or as most chroniclers thought, at some indefinite time in the future.[133] With respect to France, a further embassy was to be sent to

merchants of the Bardi. The number of days involved was ninety-one at £5 a day for personal expenses (£455). The costs of transport on the outward journey were £13 2s 9d, for the return, £24 19s 8d. In the latter case the ships came from Dover to Wissant and then to Le Crotoy in Ponthieu. The cost of sending messengers to various parts – Normandy, France and England – amounted to £6 18s 3d. Cf. PRO E.372/179/34.

[130] "De Scocia rediens cum paucis Cant. venit et deinde London. tractans cum archiepiscopo de quadam congregacione facta sive conventiculo apud Coventr. in presencia regine matris." BL Cotton MS Faustina B.v, fol. 76ᵛ.

[131] *Rot. Parl. Inediti*, pp. 240-266 (mid-Lent parliament of 1336).

[132] *Foedera* 2, iii, p. 118.

[133] There is a similarity between the passages in the *Historia Roffensis* (BL Cotton MS Faustina B.v, fols. 75ᵛ-76ʳ) and in *Murimuth* (pp. 72-73). The first runs: "Rex post quinquennium versus terram sanctam iter irripuit cessante impedimento quod per solempnes nuncios videlicet archiepiscopum Cant. [Stratford] et alios nobiles regi Francie extitit denunciatum"; the second: "In dicto parliamento dominus rex concessit quod iret in terram sanctam propriis sumptibus, sed tempus certum inchoandi itineris non expressit; sed ordinavit mittere archiepiscopum Cantuariensem ad papam et ad regem Franciae ut

secure the restoration of Gascon lands, though one chronicler declared
this to be a lost cause – already the king must have spent some twelve
thousand pounds on such embassies! [134] Within a week of the conclusion
of parliamentary business, on 28 September, the new bishop of Durham,
Richard of Bury, was appointed chancellor in Stratford's place, an office
he was to occupy until 6 June 1335, when the archbishop was reinstated.
We do not need to read anything more into this than appears on the
surface. Reynolds had likewise resigned the chancellorship following his
elevation to Canterbury.[135] From Edward's viewpoint Bury was Stratford's obvious successor.[136]

Relieved momentarily of the burden of secular employment, Stratford
busied himself with preparations for his enthronement, which took place
at Canterbury on 9 October.[137] From Canterbury he withdrew to Charing
preparatory to setting off for Dover and a return sea-passage to Le Crotoy,
which he reached on 26 October.[138] Associated with him on this occasion
were the abbot of Dore and William de Clinton. The same problems
remained on the agenda, notably Aquitaine and the crusade.[139] By 20
November, if not before, Stratford reached Paris, where he was able to
confer with a most experienced English envoy, one John Piers or Peters,
who was on his way back to England after a six-month stay at Avignon.[140] It had crossed Edward's mind that Stratford and his fellow

possent de tempore concordare." See also *Chronicon*, pp. 53-54, and for the Scottish
aspect, *Anonimalle Chronicle*, pp. 2-3.

[134] BL Cotton MS Faustina B.v, fol. 75ᵛ. This must have been a fairly conservative
estimate. In 1334 Stratford himself accounted for more than £1,000. PRO E.101/311/6;
E.372/179/34.

[135] As Wright, *Church and Crown* (p. 258) points out, Reynolds was the first man
since Hubert Walter in the reign of King John to serve as chancellor while archbishop.
Stratford was to combine the offices for much longer than did Reynolds.

[136] Tout, *Chapters* 6, p. 12. That Bury was Edward's tutor in the 1320s is upheld by
Denholm-Young against Tout. Bury's subsequent career in public office is summarized by
the former. See "Richard de Bury," pp. 4, 8-12.

[137] BL Cotton MS Faustina B.v, fol. 75ᵛ; *Murimuth*, p. 73: "Cantuariae, ubi solempne
convivium more solito celebravit." For details see above, "Archbishop of Canterbury."

[138] PRO E.101/311/6; E.372/179/34. Stratford was at Charing 24 October and
accounted for eighty-four days until 15 January 1335. The passage out was in four ships
and a barge, costing £35 7s 4¹/₂d; the return Paris to Wissant and hence to Dover in five
ships cost £25 8s 8d. Messengers added £6 8s to the bill, and the archbishop's personal
allowance at £5 a day came to £420, a total of £507 4s 0¹/₂d. The Bardi paid £400 to Stratford, half in London, the other half in Paris. £20 was allocated (17 July 1335) in the
exchequer for the *custuma* exacted on behalf of the countess of Boulogne "by convention"
at the time Stratford received the pallium (i.e. on the earlier trip).

[139] *Foedera* 2, iii, pp. 119-120.

[140] Déprez, *Les préliminaires*, pp. 100-101. For Piers see *Hemingby's Register*, pp. 218-
220; *Biog. Oxon.*, s.v. and also ibid. 3 App., s.v. Petri, John.

envoys might continue to the curia, but other advice prevailed.[141] This is hardly surprising if Baker's story of what transpired at the French capital can be accepted, and he could well have been in a position to receive a report from Stratford himself, whom he portrays as having a tête-à-tête with the French king. On meeting Philip, so Baker tells us, Archbishop Stratford presented Edward III's case. His master looked for continued amity with his brother of France, but required the restoration of those cities and castles which Philip continued to occupy in Gascony and a declaration of neutrality with respect to Scotland. On such conditions Edward would be prepared to depart with Philip on crusade. But, Baker continues, the "tyrant calling himself king of France" regarded the English king as unworthy of his friendship so long as he continued to wage war against the Scots, who in his view were just men prepared to render obedience. As for the restoration of Gascon territory, the French king replied that he first expected payment of the expenses incurred by his father, Charles of Valois, on account of military operations in Aquitaine. He then returned to the question of the Scots, reading Stratford a lecture on the purity of his motives. He was, he claimed, the friend of law and common justice. Neither on grounds of affinity nor friendship would he stray from the path of justice, which he dearly loved. By every means he knew he would endeavour to restrain those who disturbed the peace of the Scottish realm. Finally he ventured a prophecy: "There would never be perfect peace among Christians until the king of France from within the heart of England exercised justice as ruler over the combined realms of France, England and Scotland." [142] It was pointless to contemplate further discussion; Stratford indignantly withdrew.[143] Despite the embroidery, there may be a degree of truth in this episode, on the face of it derived from an eye-witness account. None the less, it does not appear to have vitiated further negotiation. We know that in December Edward was concerned for the early arrival of a French embassy.[144]

[141] PRO C.81/219/8335, 8354. Edward in a letter from Roxburgh (23 December 1334) asked the advice of Chancellor Bury and Treasurer Burghersh on this matter. Both documents are printed by Déprez, Les préliminaires, pp. 103 n. 1 (8354), 408 (8335).

[142] Chronicon, pp. 55-56. It should be pointed out that a similar dictum is attributed to Philip in William of Norwich's letters of credence of late 1340. Vatican Archives, RV 135, fols. 112v-114r; Registres de Benoît XII, no. 2981. Also printed in Déprez, Les préliminaires, pp. 423-426. See below, "The Crisis of 1341," n. 153.

[143] Chronicon, p. 56: "Isti prophecie, quam prophetavit, cum esset rex anni illius, non adiecit loqui set indignanter se subtraxit nuncius ad alia profecturus."

[144] Foedera 2, iii, p. 122; Déprez, Les préliminaires, p. 104 n. 2 (which has a transcript of PRO C.81/219/8339).

Before quitting Paris Stratford had sent a messenger to Château-Gaillard, presumably with some communication for the exiled David II. By the time the returning messenger caught up with him the archbishop was in Ponthieu, though it was not until the first week of January 1335 that he recrossed the channel from Wissant to Dover.[145] Already Stratford must have learned of the death of his benefactor John XXII, which took place at Avignon on 4 December. Pope John reached the age of ninety, but he died a disappointed man: his interpretation of the beatific vision stood condemned – he recanted on his deathbed; he had failed to bring amity between Philip and Edward, who were steadily slipping towards war; his plan for a crusade had not materialized; and he had been unable to impose his will on the emperor Louis of Bavaria. All of these problems, save the first, provided an unenviable legacy for his successor, Benedict XII, who on 9 January 1335 wrote to inform Edward III of his election.[146]

Stratford's immediate task on his return was to give attention to his responsibilities as Canterbury diocesan. On 15 January he was at his castle of Saltwood and shortly thereafter reached his cathedral city.[147] The primary visitation of the Canterbury chapter and diocese had to be put in train; a whole range of matters awaited discussion with the cathedral prior, always ready to proffer advice to new incumbents of the see. None the less, it was impossible to shelve political problems for long. Stratford and his fellow metropolitan of York were both summoned to a council at Nottingham for 26 March. There envoys from the French and Scots came to examine proposals for a truce, which was arranged until the feast of St. John (24 June).[148] Negotiations continued, but at the parliament which came together at York at the end of May it was decided that an English army should go to Scotland.[149] From Newcastle-on-Tyne, shortly before the expiry of the truce, Edward wrote to the archbishop asking prayers for the success of his forces and their safe return.[150]

[145] PRO E.101/311/6; E.372/179/34.

[146] See Déprez, Les préliminaires, p. 103; Mollat, Popes at Avignon; Foedera 2, iii, p. 122.

[147] PRO E.101/311/6.

[148] Parry, Parliaments p. 101; Murimuth, p. 75; BL Cotton MS Faustina B.v, fol. 77ʳ. Knighton 1, p. 472, writes of the Nottingham "secret council": "Responsum est Francis et Scotis mere et plane regem Edwardum nolle concordare in illa parte cum eis."

[149] Murimuth, p. 75. Dene (BL Cotton MS Faustina B.v, fol. 77ʳ) writes: "Quo facto rex et eius consilium versus Ebor. ibant et in septimana Pentecost. parliamentum tenens ad congrediendum contra Scotos in manu forti se paravit et sic usque ad Novum Castrum in festo sancti Johannis Baptiste talem exercitum congregavit qualem antea nullus rex Anglie sic bene dispositum et ordinatum ac bene provisum fertur habuisse." Stratford attended the parliament.

[150] Foedera 2, iii, p. 129; Anonimalle Chronicle, pp. 3-4.

The king was reluctant to lose Stratford's services.[151] On 6 June – shortly after the York parliament dispersed – the archbishop was re-appointed chancellor, an office he was to hold until 24 March 1337, when Robert Stratford stepped into his shoes.[152] It is likely that Stratford was prevailed upon to spend much more time than he would have wished in the north, where on 24 July and again on 11 and 31 August councils were held at York.[153] Meanwhile the parliament which met in London on the morrow of St. Bartholomew (25 August), opened with Stephen Gravesend, bishop of London, Orleton and M. Laurence Fastolf[154] acting as royal commissioners. Their function was to explain the king's policy in the light of the grave dangers of invasion both by land and sea.[155] Edward's alarm is reflected in the hasty transfer of his son's household to Nottingham Castle, close to the centre of the kingdom, in his instructions to William de Clinton to destroy an invasion flotilla believed to be assembling at Calais, and in his mandate to the seneschal of Gascony, Oliver Ingham, for the equipping of ships to repel "the malice of the enemies of the king of Scots." [156] Some assistance came from Edward's continental allies. The marquis of Juliers rode in Edward's army and the youthful count of Namur, Guy de Dampierre, was granted four hundred marks a year for his service in the royal retinue.[157] But Guy's arrival in Scotland was ill timed. In attempting to overtake the English army he was cut off in Edinburgh, ignominiously chased through the streets, and captured.[158] Edward himself met with little resistance. When he returned

---

[151] E.g. *Murimuth*, p. 76 (s.a. 1335): "Rex autem non permisit Johannem archiepisco-pum Cantuariensem ab ipso longe distare."

[152] Tout, *Chapters* 6, p. 12; *CCR 1333-1337*, p. 493.

[153] Parry, *Parliaments*, p. 102.

[154] See above, n. 96.

[155] *Foedera* 2, iii, p. 132. Doubtless those assembled also heard of some royal successes in Scotland and of the earl of Atholl's submission (*Bridlington*, pp. 123-124). According to *Cal. PMR*, pp. 92-93, there was intelligence that at the parlement of Paris (said to have met 29 July) Philip declared his wish to aid the Scots with a thousand men-at-arms as well as escort vessels. He alleged a perpetual alliance between the kingdoms (cf. Philip's letter, dated 7 July, suggesting papal arbitration, and Edward's reply of 22 August rejecting that course, in *Bridlington*, pp. 124-126). To facilitate discussion of these matters Chancellor Stratford (who had remained at York) and other councillors are said to have divided the realm into three parts: north of Trent, south of Trent, and the Welsh marches. Within each area meetings to inform the people were to be held by prelates and nobles. For other more ambitious French plans see Campbell, "England, Scotland and the Hundred Years War," pp. 189-190.

[156] *Foedera* 2, iii, pp. 129, 131, 133.

[157] Ibid., pp. 129-130, 133-135.

[158] See, for instance, BL Cotton MS Faustina B.v, fol. 77ʳ; *Bridlington*, p. 123; *Anonimalle Chronicle*, p. 4. The chivalric count merited a section in *Jean le Bel* (1, p. 113,

to England after a successful campaigning season there seemed little chance that the Scots would be able to gather an army large enough to oppose him. He had no sooner turned his back than the earl of Atholl, newly returned to Edward's allegiance, was killed in the forest of Kilblene.[159]

Warlike operations did nothing to diminish the intensity of diplomatic activity. An embassy was formed in mid-July 1335 to continue the legal processes in which the French and English were interminably engaged, and further to debate the rapidly receding prospect of an expedition to the holy land.[160] At the same time it was planned to extend the system of continental alliances by the marriage of Frederick, eldest son of Otto duke of Austria, to Edward's infant daughter Joan "of the Tower," and by arrangements with the archbishop of Cologne and sundry counts of the Low Countries.[161] As for the papacy, Benedict resumed his predecessor's policy of working for peace in the west to enable Christendom to wage war in the east. In September, from Edinburgh, Edward gave instructions for the safe conduct of the papal envoys Hugh Aimery, bishop of St. Paul-Trois-Châteaux, and Roland d'Asti, canon of Lodi.[162] Before the close of November a truce between the English and Scots had been arranged until Christmas. In the interval the papal nuncios were to go to Newcastle for discussions with a deputation of Scots loyal to David II, envoys sent by King Philip, and Edward's own commissaries. The papal collector, Bernard Sistre, also took part.[163] Just before Christmas the truce was extended, a process repeated a month later, 22 January 1336.[164] Finally the resumption of hostilities was staved off until a fortnight after Easter – 14 April.[165] The immediate object of papal interventions had been

cap. xxiv): "Comment le jeune counte de Namur et son frère passèrent en Angleterre et furent pris."

[159] *Murimuth*, pp. 75-76; BL Cotton MS Faustina B.v, fol. 77ʳ; *Knighton* 1, pp. 473-475; *Anonimalle Chronicle*, p. 5. The terms of the agreement with the Scots (18 August 1335) are given in *Avesbury*, pp. 298-302.

[160] The fortunes of the crusading project are traced by Déprez, *Les préliminaires*, pp. 105-109. More broadly see Atiya, *Crusade in the Later Middle Ages*; Luttrell, "Crusade in the Fourteenth Century"; and from the viewpoint of papal taxation, Lunt, *Financial Relations* 2, pp. 88-94. Edward wrote from York, 13 December 1335, to Leo king of Armenia, promising to go on crusade after he had settled his own problems. Papal envoys, an Armenian embassy, French plenipotentiaries and Scottish representatives were all in England during the early part of 1335. See *Foedera* 2, iii, pp. 123-125, 139-140.

[161] *Foedera* 2, iii, pp. 131, 140; Lucas, *Low Countries*, pp. 185-186.

[162] *Foedera* 2, iii, p. 136.

[163] Ibid., pp. 138-139ff.; *Anonimalle Chronicle*, p. 6.

[164] *Foedera* 2, iii, pp. 140-141.

[165] Ibid., p. 142. For all these negotiations and successive prolongations of the truce see Déprez, *Les préliminaires*, pp. 116-119. He sums up Philip's position as follows (p. 116):

achieved. The crusade was another matter; Benedict despaired of its ever taking place. When Philip, in company with the duke of Normandy and the kings of Navarre and Majorca paid a visit to Avignon in March, he opened his mind on the subject. In view of the disturbances in Europe – Scotland, Germany, Lombardy and elsewhere – it would be foolhardy to set out as arranged on 1 August. Benedict therefore released the French king, designated captain-general of the crusading enterprise, from his vow.[166] Stratford would have been closely associated with these developments, but his individual opinion of persons and policies can only be imagined. Inevitably the papal nuncios counted on his support for their peace-making overtures,[167] yet he cannot have stood aside from the popular military policy in the north.

Despite the temporary halt in campaigning, the year 1336 progressed ominously. The numerous meetings of councils and parliaments only served to heighten the tension and to dispel any real hope of lasting peace, whether between the Scots and English, or much more alarmingly, the English and French. The mid-Lent parliament at Westminster provides a case in point. There, according to one account, the various envoys came to work out an acceptable compromise. David Bruce, it was suggested, should enjoy all those lands in England which his father had held and should remain there. Edward Balliol was to have the Scottish realm for life; thereafter David and his heirs would hold it in chief of the English king.[168] In practice, the chronicler ruefully concluded, things degenerated into the usual discord.[169] Shortly after parliament's dissolution the young Henry of Lancaster, destined to have such a distinguished career in the Hundred Years' War, was appointed to command the army against the

---

"Philippe VI négociait sans grand enthousiasme; il souhaitait que le conflit anglo-écossais fût de longue durée." Cf. Campbell, "England, Scotland and the Hundred Years War," pp. 188-191, who argues that Edward was equally anxious to play for time – to crush the Scots.

[166] Déprez, Les préliminaires, pp. 122-124. The pope's reasons for "shelving" the crusade are given in a letter of 13 March 1336 to Philip (Vatican Archives, RV 131, fols. 11ʳ-12ʳ; printed Déprez, Les préliminaires, pp. 410-413). Luttrell argues that Benedict had come to realize that Philip's objectives "were primarily financial" and that his prerequisite of peace became an excuse for inactivity. "Crusade in the Fourteenth Century," pp. 133-134.

[167] E.g. Vatican Archives, RV 131, fols. 87ᵛ-88ʳ: Avignon 29 November 1336. Cf. CPL 1305-1342, p. 562. The pope urged Stratford to receive his envoy M. Peter de Cambarlhaco, "eum dirigere ac ut memorato regi secrete que sibi explicanda imposuimus plene referre valeat, idemque rex nostris salubribus exhortacionibus acquiescat...."

[168] BL Cotton MS Faustina B.v, fol. 77ᵛ.

[169] Ibid.: "Set sine profectu versa est in pristinam ac solitam discordiam."

Scots, in association with Balliol.[170] Threatened invasion was countered by instructions to the sheriffs to arm every able-bodied male between sixteen and sixty years of age.[171]

From Newcastle Edward's letters patent nominated Stratford, the treasurer Henry Burghersh, and the earl of Cornwall to open the council convened at Northampton for 25 June. To this assembly came a large number of merchants in connection with the royal policy of manipulating the sale of wool. But the king did not linger for their deliberations; he left hurriedly for the scene of action in the north, reaching Perth with only a handful of companions. The Rochester chronicler offered thanks that no misfortune had attended so rash an act.[172] One result of this council was the despatch of another embassy to France. It was to be the veteran diplomat Orleton's last mission. He was accompanied by William Trussel and M. Richard Bintworth; the latter a lawyer by training who would shortly become bishop of London. The agenda was much as before, but with the addition of powers to treat with David Bruce.[173] The outcome (foreseeably) was disappointing. Edward's interpretation of the negotiations was that Philip openly affirmed his intention of assisting the Scots in every way possible. For that purpose he was actively collecting galleys and ships, as well as armed men.[174]

Stratford, it seems, was fated never to elude completely the shadow of Edward II's reign. During the year two incidents from that time occupied his attention as chancellor; one involved the younger Despenser's piracy, the other the supposed misappropriation of Edward of Carnarvon's jewels and other treasure, which he was believed to have taken with him on his flight into Wales. To Despenser was ascribed the plundering of a Genoese vessel carrying precious articles and oriental merchandise. The king denied that either he or his father had knowledge of the piracy, but he agreed to pay 8,000 marks as compensation. This was a measure of his anxiety to gain the good-will of the ship-building Genoese. Negotiations in this and other matters were undertaken by Niccolino Fieschi, styled "cardinal of Genoa," whom Edward made a member of his council at an

---

[170] *Foedera* 2, iii, p. 146: Waltham, 7 April 1336. For his career see Fowler, *The King's Lieutenant.*

[171] *Foedera* 2, iii, pp. 142-143. This was in accordance with the statute of Winchester (1285).

[172] Parry, *Parliaments*, pp. 102-103; *Foedera* 2, iii, p. 148; BL Cotton MS Faustina B.v, fol. 78^r.

[173] *Foedera* 2, iii, p. 149. See Haines, *Church and Politics*, pp. 38-39.

[174] *Foedera* 2, iii, p. 150: Perth, 24 August 1336.

annual retaining fee of twenty pounds and the customary robes.[175] The second matter, the whereabouts of royal treasure estimated to be worth £60,000, prompted a commission of enquiry. William la Zouche, lord of Glamorgan and Morgannou, who had married Despenser's widow, Eleanor,[176] was instructed to empanel a jury for the purpose.

In the autumn of 1336 there was a parliament or great council at Nottingham,[177] followed a few days later by a convocation of Canterbury province at the abbey of St. Mary-in-the-Meadows, Leicester.[178] The main object of these assemblies was to secure financial aid for the Scottish campaign and to explain the threats to the realm from other quarters.[179] The discussions concluded, Stratford journeyed northwards to York, as did the king. There the chancery and other offices of state were concentrated in temporary lodgings. The chancery was in the church of St. Mary's abbey, the chancellor and clerks residing within the abbey precincts; hardly an arrangement conducive to monastic discipline.[180]

Stratford was seemingly in the north for the Christmas festival, but early in January 1337, or possibly just a little before, he travelled back to London. The occasion was a council over which the archbishop, in association with others, was to preside.[181] The Rochester chronicler says nothing about this particular meeting but much about another which – ac-

[175] Ibid., pp. 148-149, 152. Despenser's plundering of the Genoese ship and the slaughter of its crew are recorded s.a. 1321 by a contemporary chronicler. *Vita*, pp. 115-116.

[176] *Foedera* 2, iii, p. 147. William la Zouche (Mortimer) had been implicated as a friend of Edmund earl of Kent. The lands in Wales formerly belonged to Eleanor, but Mortimer earl of March had deprived her of them. See Dugdale, *Baronage* 1, pp. 153-154.

[177] Summoned 24 August, it met 23 September. *HBC*, p. 519; Parry, *Parliaments*, p. 103. The writ is printed, for instance, in *Exeter Reg. Grandisson*, pp. 53-54. Cf. *Foedera* 2, iii, p. 150.

[178] *Concilia* 2, pp. 582-583.

[179] Ibid.; *Foedera* 2, iii, p. 150. As usual Rochester was reluctant to go: "Miserat episcopus [Roffen.] apud Leycestriam et apud Notyngham excusatorem ad excusandum se eo quod non venit ad consilium regis. In quo concilio clerus concessit regi decimam et laici quindenam pro repulsione Scotorum." BL Cotton MS Faustina B.v, fol. 79r.

[180] BL Cotton MS Faustina B.v, fol. 79r: "Direxit tunc rex gressus suos versus Scociam et archiepiscopus Cant. cum cancellaria versus Eboracum, ubi tunc omnes curie regis residebant, ibidem moras suas per totam hiemem ordinando." For details of chancery migration see Tout, *Chapters* 3, p. 57 n. 2, and for Stratford's arrangements in York, ibid., pp. 59-60.

[181] *Foedera* 2, iii, pp. 155-156. The royal writ addressed to those coming to London for the assembly of 3 January 1337 appointed Stratford, Bishop Gravesend of London, the earl of Surrey, Henry of Lancaster, and the constable of Dover, William de Clinton, to act for the absent king. Either four, three or two could act, but Stratford had to be one of them.

cording to him – was summoned by the king, who had himself returned to the capital.[182] The royal instructions were that prelates and other important men (magni) should assemble at the Tower on 23 January.[183] Explanation was made of the king's right to the throne of France, Philip's detention of Gascony, and the ways and means so far adopted for the resolution of such grievances.[184] A fundamental question presented itself. Within what time should Edward, now in his twenty-fifth year, either claim or abandon his inheritance? This, it was argued, belonged to him on the death of his uncle Charles; for the son of a sister (Isabella) was a more direct heir than the son of an uncle. Legally the inheritance of the kingdom of France should be by "descent" rather than by "ascent." [185] Then again, should the king cultivate friends on the continent so that he could resist the French monarch? Such problems are said to have nonplussed those present; they were so momentous as to defy resolution. Deliberating apart the prelates and *magni* eventually concluded that a solemn embassy should be sent to King Philip to seek peace and that meanwhile the English king should strengthen his fleet and secure aid from friends against the unjust occupation of the realm of France.[186] This was the policy adopted. If we ask where Stratford stood on these issues, the answer is suggested by the *libellus famosus* and the archbishop's response to it. Only reluctantly did he accept the inevitability of war; it was not his decision but a common one arrived at because of the stubborn refusal of Philip to come to terms.[187]

---

[182] BL Cotton MS Faustina B.v, fol. 79[r]. Immediately after the Epiphany (6 January), he says, king and archbishop came from the north and in the octave of St. Hilary (i.e. 20 January) at Westminster "Rex prelatos et magnos conveniri fecit."

[183] The king does seem to have been at the Tower about this time and a number of naval appointments was made. E.g. *Foedera* 2, iii, pp. 157-159. See n. 187 below.

[184] BL Cotton MS Faustina B.v, fol. 79[r]: "Quibus die Jovis proximo post predictas octavas [i.e. 23 January] in turri London. congregatis fuit expositum de iure quod rex Anglie habet ad coronam Francie et de detencione Vasconie ac de modis et viis oblatis regi Francie."

[185] Ibid. "Nam propinquior heres est filius sororis quam filius avunculi et hereditas regni descendere de iure pocius debet quam ascendere."

[186] Ibid., fol. 79[r-v]. "Prelati tamen et magni traxerunt se in partem et deliberaverunt quod rex deberet mittere solempnes nuncios ad regem Francie pro pace inquirenda, et habita responsione regis Francie quod rex faceret fortem se in mari et adquireret sibi amicos in auxilium contra regem Francie iniuste occupantem regnum. Et sic predicto die Jovis in turri London. consilium est solutum."

[187] See the discussion of the *libellus* and of Stratford's *excusaciones* below, "The Crisis of 1341." It will be noticed that the major issues which the *Historia Roffensis* assigns to the council of 23 January (apparently not commented upon elsewhere) are those which are held to have been decided in the Lent parliament of 1337. Is this a confusion on Dene's part or did the parliament merely endorse decisions already taken? See n. 183 above.

It was in January 1337 that Stratford as archbishop presided over a sad occasion, the burial in Westminster Abbey of the earl of Cornwall, the king's brother, John of Eltham. Only just twenty years of age he had died the previous September while campaigning in Scotland.[188] Stratford celebrated requiem mass, the treasurer Bishop Burghersh read the gospel, Bishop Charlton of Hereford the epistle. Dene reprovingly observed that they read with their mitres on their heads; a sight never seen before except in the church of Lyons, where all the canons wear mitres. And so, by revelling in such novelties they never grow old![189]

After sundry prorogations and changes of venue parliament eventually convened at Westminster on 3 March 1337.[190] The bishop of Rochester was of the opinion that the session was a waste of time. After spending a whole day with eight other bishops "looking at the walls" he left in disgust for one of his manor houses.[191] But Hethe's outlook was jaundiced, not to say incredibly insouciant. Stratford was later to affirm that this parliament gave its assent to war against Philip for the recovery of Edward's right to France and also to the policy of the German and

[188] The young earl's death is a mystery. See Balfour-Melville, *Edward III and David II*, pp. 10-11. The *Scotichronicon* (4, p. 1029), claims that he was killed by his brother the king in a fit of exasperation. *Murimuth*, p. 78 and n. 12, says that he died in October; in fact it was September (BL Cotton MS Cleopatra A.xvi gives the 13th as in *HBC*, p. 422), since Grandisson ordered sequestration of his goods on the 30th (*Exeter Reg. Grandisson*, pp. 827-828). MS Cleopatra A.xvi, fol. 149ʳ, gives the date of burial as the eve [of Epiphany], i.e. 5 January; *Annales Paulini*, p. 365, has 13th; BL Cotton MS Faustina B.v, fol. 79ᵛ, has 27th. Cf. Tait, *Chronica Johannis de Reading*, pp. 81-82. Eltham is referred to in no. 15 of the "Stratford sermons." HCL MS P.5 XII, fol. 80ᵛ; Haines, "Some Sermons at Hereford." For the earl's effigy: Stothard, *Monumental Effigies*, pp. 92-93, pl. 55-56; Gough, *Monuments* 1 ii, pp. 94-95, pl. 31-33.

[189] BL Cotton MS Faustina B.v, fol. 79ᵛ: "In sepultura comitis Cornubie Johannes Cantuariensis missam celebravit, Henricus Lyncolniensis evangelium et Thomas Herefordensis episcopi epistolam cum mitris indutis legerunt, quod nunquam ante visum fuit nisi in ecclesia Lugdun. ubi omnes canonici portant mitras super capita, et ideo in novitatibus semper delectantes novo semper sensu habundant et non veterescunt." (Cf. *Annales Paulini*, p. 365, where masses are said to have been celebrated at St. Paul's on Sunday 12th prior to burial at Westminster the following day.) This is an early mention of the Lyons mitres not hitherto noticed. See Moille, "The Liturgy of Lyons," pp. 402-408, esp. 405-406; King, *Liturgies of the Primatial Sees*, p. 37. The burial of the earl was in the chapel of St. Thomas [St. Thomas and St. Edmund]: MS Cleopatra A.xvi (n. 188 above).

[190] Summoned 29 November 1336 to York for 13 January 1337; prorogued 10 December for 9 February at the same place; prorogued 14 January to Westminster. *HBC*, p. 520; Parry, *Parliaments*, pp. 103-104.

[191] BL Cotton MS Faustina B.v, fol. 79ᵛ: "Quo die adveniente episcopus Roffen. in concilio se presentavit et per unum diem cum aliis octo episcopis muros respiciendo ibi moram traxit, et videns quod ibi nichil profuit rediit apud Bromlegh."

other continental alliances.[192] This provides a convincing context for the
unprecedented number of promotions to the higher ranks of the peerage.
The king's elder son[193] was made duke of Cornwall, Henry of Lancaster
(Grosmont) earl of Derby, while William Bohun, William Montacute,
Hugh Audley, William Clinton and Robert Offord became respectively
earls of Northampton, Salisbury, Gloucester, Huntingdon and Suffolk.
The promotions were supported by generous grants. In this way Edward
gathered round him a group of men whose earlier loyalty was rewarded
and to whom he could look for support in the future.[194] Stratford, on
whom blame for this largesse was to be cast, retrospectively defended the
action on the grounds of the excellent service rendered by the nobles
concerned.[195] Another item considered at this parliament brought a
further spectral echo from the previous reign; the exoneration of Thomas
lord Berkeley from anything other than a slight degree of negligence with
respect to Edward of Carnarvon's death.[196] Murimuth comments on the
statutes which prohibited the export of wool but sought to encourage
cloth manufacture in England, and also clothworkers, regardless of their
place of origin. No one was to use cloth worked outside the realm save the
king, the queen and their children. These measures, summed up the
chronicler, were of no effect – except that things became worse than
before. Modern opinion, however, is that Edward was more concerned
with the diplomatic effect of such legislation.[197]

A month after parliament dispersed Bishop Burghersh and the newly
created earls of Huntingdon and Salisbury were deputed to treat with
"Philip of Valois." Being doubtful of Philip's peaceful intentions they are
said to have turned aside to Hainault, where they were approached by
envoys from France. The envoys are supposed to have stated emphatically
that their master had no desire for peace with the king of England.[198]

---

[192] See below, "The Crisis of 1341." Cf. Harriss, *King, Parliament and Public Finance*,
p. 234.

[193] The second son, William of Hatfield, was born in 1336, but died in boyhood. *HBC*,
p. 36.

[194] *Murimuth*, pp. 78-79; BL Cotton MS Faustina B.v, fols. 79ᵛ-80ʳ; *Anonimalle
Chronicle*, p. 9, which tells of the advantage taken by the Scots of the absence in London
of the English nobles.

[195] See below, "The Crisis of 1341."

[196] *Foedera* 2, iii, p. 160.

[197] *Murimuth*, p. 79: "Immo circa praemissa error posterior pejor fuit priore"; Lucas,
Low Countries, p. 203.

[198] *Foedera* 2, iii, p. 165; BL Cotton MS Faustina B.v, fol. 80ʳ: "Sed quia cum rege
Francie pacem habere dubitarunt versus eum viam deserentes ad comitem de Henaud
sunt profecti ubi in presencia multorum amicorum regis Anglie suos nuncios destinavit
rex Francie respondendo expresse se nolle pacem habere cum rege Anglie."

Philip's intransigence, particularly with respect to Gascony, is regarded by Déprez as presaging a declaration of war.[199] By this time there was a further source of irritation for Philip. Edward had given asylum to Robert d'Artois, indicted as a forger, poisoner, abettor of assassins, and traitor to his overlord the king of France.[200] This move was denounced by the pope in a series of letters dated November 1336, one of which was directed to Stratford.[201] An opinion commonly held in France – one that provided the basis for the *Vœu du Héron* – was that Robert egged on his host to recover his French inheritance by military force.[202] Bearing in mind Robert's recent relationship with Philip, he may well have done so; but no instigator is needed to account for Edward's choice of war. Burghersh and the other English ambassadors were making feverish attempts to weave a pattern of offensive alliances with the rulers on the Empire's northwest frontier and with the emperor himself – Louis of Bavaria. By the summer there were agreements with, among others, John duke of Lorraine, Brabant and Limbourg, Rupert count palatine of the Rhine, William marquis of Juliers, and the counts of Guelders, Hainault, Zeeland, Berg, Clèves and La March.[203] In Flanders the English representatives were unsuccessful. Louis de Nevers was not to be suborned from allegiance to his overlord Philip. In April an English embassy was urging his consent to the union of his eldest son with Joan "of the Tower," Edward's daughter previously offered as a bride to the son of the duke of Austria.[204] All this was wasted effort, though the commercial interests of the Flemish towns determined that there would be no overt breach with the English.[205]

---

[199] *Les préliminaires*, pp. 162-163.

[200] BL Cotton MS Faustina B.v, fol. 79ᵛ. For Artois see Lucas, *Low Countries*, pp. 113-114, 176-181. Lucas (p. 179) considers that Robert's flight to Edward III's court took place about Easter 1334. The most recent discussion is that of Diller, "Robert d'Artois et l'historicité des Chroniques de Froissart."

[201] Vatican Archives, *RV* 131, fols. 87ᵛ-88ʳ; *Registres de Benoît XII*, nos. 1155-1157. Cf. *CPL 1305-1342*, pp. 561-562.

[202] Déprez, *Les préliminaires*, pp. 224-226. He concludes (p. 226): "Le *Vœu du Héron* n'est qu'une agréable fiction et l'anecdote relative à Robert d'Artois est sans doute controuvée. Il est du moins hors de doute qu'en 1338 et en 1339, Édouard est bien décidé à envahir la France pour déloger les Valois." Cf. Lucas, *Low Countries*, pp. 180-181. In any case, Whiting, "The Vows of the Heron," pp. 261-278, has argued with effect that the poem is intended to ridicule chivalric attitudes.

[203] *Foedera* 2, iii, pp. 165ff.; *Anonimalle Chronicle*, p. 12; Déprez, *Les préliminaires*, pp. 152-154; Lucas, *Low Countries*, chap. 7. The countess of Hainault, sister of Philip VI, made a last effort to avert the threatened danger to France by trying to persuade her brother to treat with the English envoys at Valenciennes.

[204] *Foedera* 2, iii, pp. 164-165; Lucas, *Low Countries*, pp. 240ff.

[205] See Lucas, *Low Countries*, chap. 8.

Overall, Burghersh and his colleagues achieved substantial diplomatic success, but only at immense cost in money, arms and commercial concessions. It was the road to financial insolvency; that it was followed is to some degree Stratford's responsibility.

The approaches made to the emperor posed problems which were different in kind. For Stratford they involved a conflict of loyalties. Benedict XII was aware of the deplorable drift of events. It could have been no surprise to him that M. Paul de Montefiori, Edward's trusted clerk, arrived at Avignon with a request that he permit a confederacy with the excommunicated Louis. As might be expected, the papal response of 20 July 1337 was a resounding denunciation of the emperor and all his works, not least among them the creation and support of that "hypocrite of devilish presumption" the anti-pope Br. Pietro de Corbaria. Stratford was enjoined to add his voice to the papal arguments and injunctions. Benedict had no intention of countenancing a course which he considered detrimental to Edward's honour and certain to involve him in the severest ecclesiastical penalties.[206] His exhortations fell on unresponsive ears. An alliance with the emperor was concluded on 26 August, but at the enormous cost of 300,000 florins. In return Louis agreed to assist the English king with two thousand men by 30 November.[207] Already, three months before the conclusion of this agreement, the French ruler's action in confiscating Gascony and Ponthieu (24 May) had made war only a matter of time.[208] Neither England nor Gascony was unprepared[209] and the frenetic diplomatic efforts of Edward's agents had erected an impressive though flimsy structure of alliances.[210]

Although in the March of 1337 Stratford had given way as chancellor to his brother Robert,[211] he was still very much engaged in the business of various councils held during the year, as well as with preparations for

---

[206] Vatican Archives, *RV* 132, fol. 52^{r-v} (a letter of the same tenor addressed to the king is at fols. 51^r-52^r). See *Registres de Benoît XII*, nos. 1418-1422; Déprez, *Les préliminaires*, pp. 415-417.

[207] *Foedera* 2, iii, pp. 184-185; Déprez, *Les préliminaires*, pp. 151-152. For much material concerning the continental alliances see *Das deutsch-englische Bündnis* 1, Quellen.

[208] Déprez, *Les préliminaires*, p. 154 n. 1. In this lengthy note is much information from French sources about the immediate results of this confiscation.

[209] Ibid., pp. 155-156ff.

[210] *Foedera* 2, iii, p. 186, gives a list of the arrangements concluded at Valenciennes, Mons, Brussels, Cologne and elsewhere by Burghersh, Montacute and Clinton; arrangements confirmed 26 August 1337 at Westminster.

[211] Robert, then archdeacon of Canterbury, was chancellor from 24 March 1337 until 6 July 1338. Tout, *Chapters* 6, p. 12; *CCR 1337-1339*, p. 117.

the country's defence. The king summoned one such council – of prelates and barons -- to Stamford for the end of May, subsequently ordering Stratford and other councillors to remain there until they received further instructions.[212] Later the archbishop was authorized, together with the new treasurer William la Zouche and others, to hold an additional session at Stamford in mid-June for deliberations with certain wool merchants.[213] On the 28th Bishop Bury, William la Zouche, the earl of Warwick, the lords Henry Percy and Ralph Neville, and Geoffrey le Scrope were instructed to expound the decisions of the Stamford council to those due to assemble at York on 12 July. It was from Stamford also that a mandate emanated for the provision of a naval escort for the ambassadors returning from the continent.[214] From Lincolnshire Stratford travelled to London where he is to be found with the king on 25 July. On that day in a chamber of the Tower he and his brother were among those who witnessed the renunciation by Thomas de Hemenhale, the newly provided bishop of Worcester, of any portion of his bulls which might be considered prejudicial to the king.[215]

Edward relied on the administrative structure of the church as a means of broadcasting the government's view of the political crisis. On 21 August the archbishops were directed to make the appropriate arrangements by allotting specific times and places for this purpose. The conflict between England and France, urged the king, was none of his making. He had always desired peace. It was Philip who kept back lands in Aquitaine and spurned offers of a dynastic alliance; it was he who even at that moment was preparing large-scale war.[216] In the county of Kent Stratford and William de Clinton, warden of the Cinque Ports, were to make known these *pièces justificatives* and also additional matters which the

---

[212] Parry, *Parliaments*, p. 104; *CCR 1337-1339*, pp. 129, 131; PRO S.C.1/45/229: writ of privy seal dated from *Clyve* (Kingscliffe) 1 June 1337 addressed to the archbishop, the bishops of Durham (Bury) and Chester (Northburgh) "et as autres grauntz assemblez a cesti nostre conseil a Estannford."

[213] Parry, *Parliaments*, p. 105. It was at Stamford, Stratford was to declare, that agreements were entered into by merchants: "Pro vestris vero et vestrorum stipendiis in hac parte solvendis in concilio quodam apud Staunford tunc propterea convocato cum certis mercatoribus terrae vestrae nobis praesentibus conventiones certae factae fuerunt" (*Vitae Arch. Cant.*, p. 30). The indenture of a general agreement with leading merchants is dated 26 July, the day after the opening of another *colloquium speciale* at Westminster (*HBC*, p. 520 n. 3). See Lloyd, *English Wool Trade*, pp. 144, 146; Fryde, "Edward III's Wool Monopoly," p. 13; idem, *Wool Accounts of Pole*, p. 5 n. 16.

[214] *Foedera* 2, iii, pp. 171-172, 175.

[215] Ibid., p. 182. Among others present was M. Richard Bintworth. See n. 217 below.

[216] *Foedera* 2, iii, p. 183. The writ in Ely Reg. Montacute, fol. 69[r-v], is dated 28 August. The schedule of *pièces justificatives* is also registered.

archbishop and others had been considering at the recent Westminster council.[217]

Among the defensive preparations was the drafting of a thousand Welsh footsoldiers into Stratford's cathedral city, where the priory church had only recently been reconciled by Bishop Hethe – the archbishop being busy elsewhere.[218] Stratford presumably played his part in devising political propaganda and in promulgating official justifications of the current situation, casting the blame on the French and on their Scottish allies. It was contended that despite the truce conceded by the English the Scots had killed the earl of Atholl.[219] The French king was responsible for rejection of a long-term peace. Under cover of preparation for the crusade he had mobilized and armed a fleet, captured English ships, massacred those on board, and plundered the Channel Islands and south coast towns. His crowning infamies had been a refusal to receive Edward's envoys and the armed occupation of Gascony.[220]

Parliament met in the last week of September 1337, followed by the Canterbury convocation in St. Paul's on the 30th.[221] The cause of the king's financial need was explained and a triennial tenth was granted by the clergy, a fifteenth by the barons and knights. This was an unprecedented concession.[222] Urgent measures followed for the collection of wool, corn, cheese, fish and dues of every kind.[223] Immediately after the parliament an embassy headed by Bishop Burghersh and the earls of Northampton and Suffolk, together with the steward of the household John Darcy, set out for the continent. Their overt instructions would appear to signify a last-ditch attempt to come to terms with the French.[224]

---

[217] *Foedera* 2, iii, pp. 183-184, 187, and cf. BL Cotton MS Faustina B.v, fols. 80ᵛ-81ʳ. The council met 21 July (*HBC*, p. 520) and Stratford returned from Stamford to be present (see, for instance, *CCR 1337-1339*, pp. 139-140).

[218] *Foedera* 2, iii, pp. 186-187. Bishop Hethe reconciled the cathedral church on 4 July 1337. *Lit. Cant.* 2, pp. 157-158 (625); CCL Reg. L, fol. 68ʳ.

[219] See n. 159 above.

[220] *Foedera* 2, iii, pp. 187-188.

[221] Parry, *Parliaments*, pp. 105-106; *CCR 1337-1339*, pp. 241-242; *HBC*, p. 520.

[222] BL Cotton MS Faustina B.v, fol. 80ᵛ. *Murimuth* (p. 80) is more detailed. Dene tells us of the attempt to raise an extra-parliamentary subsidy, the results of which were disappointing and from which the clergy excused themselves because they were to pay a tenth. On this matter see Willard, "Edward III's Negotiations for a Grant in 1337"; Bryant, "Financial Dealings of Edward III with County Communities," esp. pp. 766-768.

[223] BL Cotton MS Faustina B.v, fol. 80ᵛ: "Interim omnes lanas per totum regnum in manibus mercatorum et aliorum, necnon frumentum, caseum, pisses, et alii diversi generis vectigalia in numero copioso fecit congregare. Mercatores quosque in regno et precipue London. posuit ad faciendum redempcionem bonorum suorum. Omnes tunc mercatores famosi de regno fecerunt finem."

[224] *Foedera* 2, iii, p. 190: Westminster, 3 October 1337.

This was nothing more than window-dressing. Dene regarded the embassy as a means of strengthening the confederacy and making preparations for the king's arrival. The envoys took with them ten thousand sacks of wool to defray their own expenses and as payment to the new-found allies of their master.[225] Further efforts were made to win over the count of Flanders by the reiterated offer of a marriage alliance, but he was not to be persuaded. Instead negotiations were resumed for a match between Edward's daughter, Joan "of the Tower," and the eldest son of Otto, duke of Austria.[226] On 7 October the duke of Brabant, the marquis of Juliers and the earl of Northampton were appointed Edward's proctors and lieutenants to claim his "lawful inheritance" of France and to exercise his rights there.[227] It must have been about this time that Bishop Burghersh made his dramatic appearance in Paris – as recounted by Frois- sart – to repudiate the homage taken by Edward in his adolescence and to exhort Philip to renounce the kingship.[228]

Benedict XII, now poised to step between the combatants, despatched Cardinals Pedro Gomez and Bertrand de Montfavèz to England for talks. A safe conduct was issued to them on 15 October. Two days later a letter setting out the English case was sealed at Westminster.[229] Stratford's brother Robert, elected bishop of Chichester in August, was consecrated at Canterbury on St. Andrew's day, 30 November. The same day he made his profession before the high altar of Christ Church in the presence of Bishops Orleton, Wyville and Hethe.[230] It would appear that the arch- bishop was not there, though known to have been at Wingham two days previously awaiting news of the cardinals' expected landfall at Dover.[231] The cardinals journeyed by way of Rochester, where the diocesan was too ill to greet them but sent presents as a token of goodwill.[232] Stratford and

---

[225] BL Cotton MS Faustina B.v, fol. 81^r; *CCR 1337-1339*, p. 228. Apparently Dene is the only chronicler to give the correct number of sacks. See Lucas, *Low Countries*, p. 241.

[226] *Foedera* 2, iii, pp. 190-191, 193. The Austrian marriage alliance had been broached in July 1335 (ibid., p. 131).

[227] Ibid., pp. 192-193. A "coup de théâtre," writes Déprez of Edward's action (*Les préliminaires*, p. 171).

[228] Déprez, *Les préliminaires*, p. 172, citing *Froissart* (ed. Luce) 1, p. ccxxx.

[229] *Foedera* 2, iii, pp. 194, 195-196. Earlier, 7 October, letters of credence had been addressed to the cardinals with respect to Bishop Burghersh and his companions. Ibid., p. 193.

[230] BL Cotton MS Faustina B.v, fol. 81^r; *Canterbury Professions*, p. 100 no. 283. Once again one notes Orleton's presence at an occasion involving the Stratford family.

[231] PRO S.C.1/39/199.

[232] BL Cotton MS Faustina B.v, fol. 81^r. According to *Vitae Arch. Cant.* (Lambeth MS 99, fol. 136^v) the cardinals arrived 2 December 1337 (printed text, p. 20, has 1327) and departed 11 July of 1338 (1328 in printed text). 2 December is also given in BL Royal MS 12

his fellow bishops Orleton,[233] Hothum, Northburgh and the newly consecrated Robert escorted the travellers from Shooters Hill by way of Blackheath to the capital.[234] The king welcomed the nuncios at the entrance to the smaller hall of Westminster Palace and then escorted them into the painted chamber. Opportunity was then given for an exposition of their mission. After this writs were issued for a parliament at Westminster on 3 February 1338, the king promising not to undertake offensive action meanwhile.[235] The *Historia Roffensis* has something to say about the cardinals' determined efforts to win over the bishops of the Canterbury province to the papal viewpoint. The latter were summoned to appear in the house of the Carmelite friars, where an attempt was made to induce them to sway the king in favour of a truce. Each was asked individually to respond to the arguments advanced. The bishops were not to be cajoled, or intimidated. They claimed that it was not in their power to act without the consent of the peers of the realm.[236] At that juncture they trooped over to Westminster for the parliament, where the cardinals' views cut equally little ice. It was pointed out that peace had been offered to Philip, who had refused it.[237] Baker goes further. The king is supposed to have likened Philip's conduct towards the English to that practised against Jews or the enemies of Christ: expulsion, killing, deprivation and imprisonment.[238] All the same, Edward diplomatically conceded that it was out of reverence for the pope and at the cardinals' urging that he agreed to an extension of the truce until 24 June.[239] Those assembled then turned to practical matters; a discussion of the king's crossing to the continent and the means of financing it. Half the wool crop of the realm, estimated at a round figure of 20,000 sacks, was to be offered for sale at a moderate

D.xi, fol. 18ʳ. Lunt, *Financial Relations* 2, p. 624, adopts a later date, 18-20 December, citing *Annales Paulini*, p. 367; *Knighton* 2, p. 2.

[233] Cf. Haines, *Church and Politics* (Itinerary), p. 250, which shows Orleton conveniently located at Southwark 3-19 December.

[234] *Murimuth*, p. 81.

[235] Ibid.; *Foedera* 2, iii, pp. 197-198, 200. The "invasion of France" was put off until 1 March. Lucas, *Low Countries*, p. 239.

[236] BL Cotton MS Faustina B.v, fol. 81ᵛ.

[237] Ibid.: "Vie pacis oblate regi Francie et per eum recusate erant ostense."

[238] *Chronicon*, p. 60: "Tanquam Iudeos aut inimicos Christi, expellendo, trucidando, spoliando, et incarcerando."

[239] *Foedera* 2, iii, pp. 198, 200; iv, pp. 3-4. The king's contention was that although in parliament it had appeared dangerous to grant further delay, he had done so because of his desire to follow any reasonable road to peace, out of regard for the pope and at the cardinals' persuasion.

price.[240] In fact this merely continued an arrangement of the previous summer between the king and the merchant community for the borrowing of 30,000 sacks.[241] One version of Murimuth's chronicle states that the prelates as a whole had never given assent to such a levy but that the king had extorted it from them none the less.[242]

From Berwick on 28 March 1338 the king wrote to Stratford as archbishop, announcing his warlike intentions with a biblical flourish. Stratford, like Moses, was to pray continually for the royal triumph.[243] The truce was revoked on 6 May on the pretext that Philip had failed to observe it.[244] Efforts to confirm the Low Countries in Edward's cause went on apace; the king's son, the duke of Cornwall, was offered as husband for a daughter of the duke of Brabant.[245] As part of the arrangements preliminary to Edward's departure the now bishop of Chichester, Robert Stratford, on 6 July surrendered the great seal at Walton-by-Orwell. The king handed it to Richard Bintworth, bishop-elect of London, who set out for Lambeth and his consecration six days later.[246] Stratford made his own preparations for departure in the company of the cardinals and that of Richard de Bury, bishop of Durham.[247] Baker's

[240] BL Cotton MS Faustina B.v, fol. 81ᵛ; *Murimuth*, p. 82 and ibid., n. 11 (a much longer passage from BL Harleian MS 1729, fol. 136ʳ⁻ᵛ).

[241] As Lloyd, *English Wool Trade*, p. 151, emphasizes. The contemporary Dene is equally explicit, declaring that since the king had only received 10,000 sacks, "rogavit maiores regni ut de residuo colligendo ut numerus impleretur ordinarent." He adds: "Manebat tamen illa ordinacio in suspenso usque post transitum regis sicut inferius patebit." BL Cotton MS Faustina B.v, fol. 81ᵛ. See above, n. 213.

[242] *Murimuth*, p. 82 n. 11; BL Harleian MS 1729, fol. 136ʳ: "Et licet clerici ad hoc non fuerunt vocati exceptis paucis prelatis qui clerum ab iniuriis defendere non curarunt, tamen rex a clero lanas exegit et pro magna parte postea vi e[x]torsit." This version is scathing about the whole affair: "Et attende diligenter quam mirabiliter, vel pocius miserabiliter ista extorsio lanarum excogita fuerit et perfecta." Cf. *Historia Eduardi*, pp. 416-418. In 1337 Stratford loaned Edward forty-nine sacks, eight cloves of wool from Kent, valued abroad at £436 4s 11d and thought to represent the bulk of the yield of the estates there: Du Boulay, *Lordship of Canterbury*, p. 214 (citing PRO E.101/457/30; E.159/115/m.27; references supplied by E. B. Fryde).

[243] *Foedera* 2, iv, p. 10. A similar instruction to the archbishop of York follows, ibid., pp. 10-11.

[244] Ibid., pp. 16-17.

[245] Ibid., pp. 18-19.

[246] Ibid., p. 27. The old seal was sent to John de St. Pol, chancery clerk, at Bramford-by-Ipswich, thence to the *Christopher* in the port of Orwell, where the king handed it to William Kilsby. Ibid., p. 28.

[247] Ibid., pp. 24-25. Their letters of authority are dated from Walton 21 June 1338. For various sums paid to Stratford, and by him on the king's behalf, in the early part of 1338, see *CCR 1337-1339*, pp. 191, 303-305, 322. On 7 June, for his faithful services, Edward rescinded all Stratford's debts to the crown. *CPR 1338-1340*, p. 88.

impression was that the cardinals took ship with a light heart, confident that Edward was prepared to compromise and that the war was as good as over. If he is right, they were foolishly oversanguine. Baker it should be remembered was seeking to accentuate his presentation of Philip as an obstinate tyrant.[248] But there is another point; Stratford and Bury were allegedly determined to press the policy of peace.[249]

Stratford embarked at Dover for Wissant on 11 July. He did not return until the second week of October in the following year, 1339. This total of four hundred and fifty-six days constituted by far his longest absence from his native country in royal service. The archbishop departed with a princely retinue. Four ships and a barge were necessary to transport a hundred and eighty-nine persons and ninety-seven horses. Stratford's detailed expense account is a remarkable document for it shows that not only did he act openly as a diplomat but also secretly as the director of an espionage network.[250]

Officially there remained a loophole for peace. Stratford and the cardinals were destined initially for Paris. En route, at Amiens, Stratford sent an agent, Robert de Fécamp, on a mission to Rouen to take note of the ships there. Robert reported to the archbishop at Paris, from where he was sent to reconnoitre Dieppe and the coast of Normandy. He had instructions to observe the shipping and to pump the sailors for information. Stratford's stay in Paris was cut short before the end of July 1338 by letters from the king, then at Antwerp, revoking his authority to treat with Philip.[251] He made his way to Arras, from which vantage point he despatched Peter de St. Omer to Amiens to estimate the size of the French army assembling there and to discover what plans were afoot for its deployment. The information gleaned was duly retailed to Edward. Another spy, Bernard de Vaus, was sent to procure intelligence of ships on the coast of Flanders and in the ports of Wissant and Calais. From Amiens Stratford despatched letters to the king at Cologne. The town was on Edward's route to Coblence for the impressive ceremony which took place in mid-September in the emperor's presence. Louis solemnly declared the forfeiture of the kingdom of France and presented the

---

[248] *Chronicon*, p. 61: "Cum ista responsione leti recesserunt cardinales, estimantes guerram iam finiri." Cf. the more convincing *Historia Eduardi*, p. 415, which gives the date of the cardinals' departure (11 July 1338): "frustrati totaliter de intentione."

[249] PRO C.49/46/8: undated letters of credence [1338-1339] for explaining continental developments to the duke of Cornwall and the home council. See below, n. 272.

[250] PRO E.101/311/35; E.372/184/42; *CPR 1338-1340*, pp. 93, 98, 101.

[251] PRO E.101/311/35; E.372/184/42; *Foedera* 2, iv, pp. 28-29; *CPR 1338-1340*, p. 190.

English king with a gold wand as insignia of the vicariate of the empire,[252] an office which he had been exercising prior to the ceremony.[253] Meanwhile Stratford sent Bernard de Vaus to Paris in an attempt to probe the secrets of Philip's council, while Peter Assamari kept an eye on the coast between Dieppe and Calais. Peter de St. Omer was similarly engaged in surveying shipping between Dieppe and the ports of Le Crotoy and Boulogne. Another stipendiary in the archbishop's service was a merchant, Gregory of Florence. Riding with a companion, two grooms and two horses this man was able to visit the cities of Ghent, Bruges, Sluys and Ypres, in fact to wander throughout Flanders and Brabant testing the dispositions of the rulers of those regions. This was only the first of four such journeys. In due course Gregory was in a position to report a favourable shift towards the English.[254] From Arras Bernard de Vaus set out for Amiens to reconnoitre the French troops there, and later for Douai and Tournai, where the king of Navarre's men were mustering.[255] The information garnered by Bernard was relayed to Antwerp from Compiègne, to which place Stratford must have travelled for further talks with Philip.[256] After that the archbishop can be traced at Valenciennes prior to his return to Arras for renewed discussion with the cardinals.[257] From Arras there was an interchange of letters with Edward at Antwerp and Brussels.[258] Another operation for which Stratford

[252] PRO E.101/311/35. Déprez, *Les préliminaires*, pp. 195-198, gives a lengthy account of Edward's meeting with the emperor. Possibly the most informative chronicler is *Knighton* (2, pp. 5-7), but BL Cotton MS Nero D.x, fol. 118ʳ (quoted *Murimuth*, pp. 84-85 n. 16) is also detailed and gives the date of the anglo-imperial agreement as 15 September. Cf. PRO E.36/203/fols. 88ᵛ-89ʳ.

[253] Offler, "England and Germany," pp. 608-631, esp. 610-611.

[254] PRO E.101/311/35. Payment was made: "Ad explorandum voluntates communitatum illarum parcium que tunc primo se convertebant ad benevolenciam regis."

[255] Ibid.: "Eidem [Bernard de Vaus] equitanti ut supra de Arraz usque Douwy et Tourneye ad explorandum connivenciam regis Navarre et hominum suorum ad arma ibidem congregatorum."

[256] Ibid.: "Johanni Taverner equitanti per se in negociis regis de Andwerp usque Compyne et de ibidem usque Valenciens per convencionem factam cum eodem, xviiis. Eidem equitanti cum litteris domini archiepiscopi de Compyne usque Andwerp ad certificandum regem et consilium suum de rebus ... exploratis." Stratford and Bury are said to have been at Compiègne for a parlement. *Knighton* 2, p. 7. See also Déprez, *Les préliminaires*, pp. 208-210.

[257] PRO E.101/311/35. Cf. *Anonimalle Chronicle*, p. 14: "Et apres, en la ville de Attrabatum tanqe al mois de Novembre, ensemblement demurreount et del acorde treteount. Mes al darrein saunz pees avoir ou espoir de pees ... les evesques al roi Dengleterre, adonqes en Braban esteaunt, repaireount." Baker, *Chronicon*, p. 62, says that Stratford, Bury and the cardinals awaited Edward's arrival at Arras, but this is not borne out by the account. See also *Knighton* 2, p. 7.

[258] PRO E.101/311/35.

claimed allowances was the fostering of support for Robert d'Artois in the county of Arras and various parts of Picardy – lands of which he had been deprived by Philip of Valois.[259]

Stratford's extensive efforts did not prevent the capture at Sluys of five of the king's ships, including the *Christopher*, which were subsequently taken to Normandy, or the sack of Southampton.[260] The situation was a serious one, possibly more serious than the English suspected at the time. The duke of Normandy was preparing an invasion fleet and with excessive optimism imagined himself repeating the events of 1066 even to the point of assuming the title of king of England. It was to prove a harmless phantasy, but only in retrospect.[261]

In following Stratford's activities by means of his expense account we have progressed too far and must retrace our steps to mid-June of 1338 – immediately prior to his departure for the continent. At that time there seems to have been an attempt by the king to win Stratford's gratitude and to acquire much-needed ready money by granting him for life the castle and manor of Leeds, Kent, in return for a thousand pounds. Robert Stratford later came into chancery as his brother's vicar general and vicegerent and in the chancellor's presence declined to accept the concession or to pay the thousand pounds; instead he sought cancellation of the enrolment.[262] It was as vicar general that Robert presided over the convocation which was summoned to St. Bride's church in London on 1 October. His task was to respond to the king's further demand for wool and to secure an anticipation of the dates of payment of the biennial tenth. The clergy proved critical of the intolerable burdens and *gravamina* heaped on the church, the exaction of jewels and other ornaments,[263] and the extortion practised by royal officials with respect to purveyance. None the less, provided the king issued letters forbidding the seizure of wool, a tenth for a third year would be granted by those who did not contribute wool. Those who had promised wool at Northampton would not be liable

[259] Ibid.

[260] BL Cotton MS Faustina B.v, fol. 82ᵛ; Baker, *Chronicon*, p. 62 (who says they were unladen); *Murimuth*, p. 87.

[261] Dated Bois-de-Vincennes, 23 March 1339, and said to have been discovered at Caen some seven years later, when it was published by Stratford (see below, "Closing Years"). *Avesbury*, pp. 363-367; *Murimuth*, pp. 205-211; *Froissart* (ed. Lettenhove) 18, pp. 67-73 no. 24. See Déprez, *Les préliminaires*, p. 202 where (n. 1) it is dated 1338 and hence inserted in the wrong portion of the author's narrative.

[262] *CChR 1327-1341*, pp. 447-448, 454-455. Cf. n. 247 above for other concessions to Stratford.

[263] *Foedera* 2, iv, p. 26.

for the tenth. Subject to these conditions it was agreed to advance the terms for payment of the tenth already conceded.[264]

In mid-November 1338 Benedict XII was preparing to salvage something from the imminent wreck of his attempts at mediation. Denouncing the anti-pope Nicholas V and his arch-supporter the *soi-disant* emperor, he scolded Edward both for accepting the office of vicar and for wielding his ill-based authority to the detriment of ecclesiastics. The pope defended himself from accusations of partiality. He claimed that he had not paid an immense sum from the camera to Philip, or permitted him to exercise patronage over all the churches in France. As for the concession to the French king of the proceeds of the crusading tenth, this was not to finance action hostile to Edward but to meet the threat from continental adherents of the false emperor. To err is human; perseverance in error must be accounted diabolical. The English king was warned not to continue to injure the rights of the apostolic see by his activities in Germany; exercise of the vicariate rendered him excommunicate under the ruling of Pope John XXII. In response Edward so far modified his stance as to agree to Stratford's resumption of negotiations with the cardinals and with the envoys of Philip – but only as Philip of Valois, not as king of France.[265]

Major military operations were at a standstill. The impact on Edward's finances was catastrophic. So much so that he was forced to pawn his crown to Baldwin, archbishop of Trèves.[266] Bitterly he complained of the lack of the long-awaited wool and parliamentary subsidies. Nothing had reached him, he was compelled to have recourse to usurers.[267] At Antwerp on 10 May 1339 Stratford, Bishops Bury and Burghersh, four earls, and others including William Kilsby, agreed to stand surety for 140,000 florins loaned by a merchant of Lucca, Niccolo Bartholomei.[268] In June an agreement drawn up at Brussels for the marriage of Margaret, daughter of the duke of Lorraine, to Edward's son contained a penalty

---

[264] *Rochester Reg. Hethe*, pp. xxxvii-xxxix; WinRO 1, fol. 65^{r-v}; *Murimuth*, p. 85; BL Cotton MS Faustina B.v, fol. 82^v.

[265] Vatican Archives, *RV* 133, fols. 120^r-123^r; *CPL 1305-1342*, pp. 569-570; *Foedera* 2, iv, pp. 37-39ff.; *CPR 1338-1340*, pp. 194, 196. John XXII had excommunicated Louis in 1324; the subsequent process against the emperor at the time of his Italian expedition in 1327 was published by Stratford as Winchester diocesan (WinRS, fols. 30^r-32^r).

[266] *Foedera* 2, iv, pp. 42-43; Lucas, *Low Countries*, pp. 303, 380.

[267] *Foedera* 2, iv, pp. 45-46: Antwerp, 6 May 1339.

[268] Ibid., p. 46. The earls were those of Derby, Northampton, Salisbury and Suffolk. For other arrangements in which Stratford acted as guarantor see *CPR 1338-1340*, pp. 371-372, 384-385.

clause for non-observance. Once again it was Stratford who headed the list of guarantors.[269]

As late as 1 July 1339 peace feelers were being extended by Edward at the cardinal's prompting. Stratford, Bishops Bury and Burghersh, various earls, and a group of clerical experts were empowered to reach agreement on the points at issue between Philip and the English king, to arrange mutual compensation for injuries suffered on land and sea, and to bring about perpetual peace.[270] Talks of some kind did take place at Arras. As we have seen from his expense account, Stratford was either present or in close contact by messenger with the king and his council at Antwerp.[271] In fact an undated letter of credence issued to the earl of Suffolk and M. Nicholas Canteloue (Cantilupe) required them to inform the duke of Cornwall and the council in England that the archbishop and bishop of Durham had stayed close to the king and pressed their advice that only by the cardinals' mediation could an honourable and profitable peace be achieved. At the same time, they are said to have argued that unless some tactical sortie were made in the near future the king would suffer dishonour.[272] With some justification but singularly little tact the cardinals are reported to have expressed their opinion that Edward had no chance against the might of France and would be unable to set a foot in that country. In the latter part of September 1339 the king's destructive sweep into Cambrai, Vermandois and other areas proved them wrong – much to the elation of the English.[273] The campaign of Thiérache, as it has been called, did something for Edward's damaged self-esteem, but little else came of it. Chronic shortage of money and supplies continued to plague the king and his councillors. Yet in England itself a chronicler could complain with bitterness of the "unaccustomed and unheard of burdens

[269] *Foedera* 2, iv, pp. 47-48: Brussels, 22 June 1339.
[270] Ibid., p. 49.
[271] See above; also PRO E.101/311/35 and *Wardrobe Book*, p. 404.
[272] PRO C.49/file 46/8. "Primerement ils deivent dire coment ... lercevesque et levesque de Duresme sont venue au roi et ont bien dit qe par mediacion des cardinaux nen autre manere ils ne trouent pees ne treue honurable ne prof[it]able pur le roi, par quoi ils demorent entour le roi mettant lour conseil de iour en autre coment le roi poet estre eidez a chivaucher a plus en hast q[i]l poet."
[273] Déprez, *Les préliminaires*, chap. 7. Baker, *Chronicon*, pp. 64-65 has one such story about the cardinals' discomfiture, which is retailed by Déprez (*Les préliminaires*, p. 257). The *Historia Roffensis* (BL Cotton MS Faustina B.v, fol. 83ᵛ) has another. In mid-August the home government was circulating a request to Stratford and other bishops for prayers on behalf of the royal expedition into France. *Foedera* 2, iv, p. 50. A subsequent newsletter from Brussels, 1 November 1339, addressed to Stratford and others of the royal council is printed in *Avesbury*, pp. 304-308.

and exactions made on the king's behalf." [274] Edward considered that his campaign had been brought to a standstill by unwarranted economic deprivation. His high hopes of military glory had been dashed. He determined to send Stratford, Bishop Bury and the merchant-financier William de la Pole to make his necessities known at home and to apply the requisite remedies.[275] Stratford made ready for departure. On 10 October 1339 he sailed from Wissant with five ships and a "hekboat." His mission had cost almost two and a half thousand pounds. Its achievements were not so obvious. The archbishop must have been well aware that his next task would be even more exacting.

In one way Stratford had been fortunate in his absence from England at a time when the main concerns of the home council deputed to advise the juvenile *custos* were the defence of the realm and the raising of burdensome taxation to palliate the insatiable thirst of Edward's continental allies, whose continued adhesion in any case depended upon speedy military success. Stratford returned as principal councillor, though the precise implications of this term are difficult to determine. His appointment has been viewed as "a shrewd move" on the king's part, designed to counteract "papal pressure on Stratford to use his influence for mediation" and to short-circuit "the domestic opposition, in whose eyes the archbishop was the traditional defender of popular liberties of the realm (and home council) against the *curiales*." Edward, it is argued, sought both to "buy Stratford with the grant of office" and to "buy out the opposition with limited reforms" carried out under the archbishop's direction.[276] Such a pragmatic view begs a number of questions, examination of which must be deferred until the end of this section. For

[274] BL Cotton MS Faustina B.v, fol. 83[r]: "Insolita et inaudita onera, exacciones per partem regis sunt petita, sed quia dominus rex parum vel nichil profuit ultra mare immorando petita omnia sunt negata."

[275] *Foedera* 2, iv, p. 51: Marcoing "within the march of France," 26 September 1339. Stratford, Bury, Chancellor Bintworth, the earls of Arundel and Huntingdon, Henry Percy, Ralph Neville and William de la Pole – at the earl of Salisbury's request – were empowered to pardon small debts (under £10) owed to the exchequer, escapes from prison and other matters.

[276] Harriss, *King, Parliament and Public Finance*, pp. 253-254. Baldwin, *King's Council*, comments (p. 369) that William of Valence in Henry III's reign and Thomas of Lancaster in 1316 had titles similar to the one enjoyed by Stratford. In 1377 William of Wykeham was to be styled "capitalis secreti consilii ac gubernator magni consilii." At their deaths in 1340 Geoffrey le Scrope and Bishop Burghersh are termed respectively "principalis justiciarius et consiliarius" and "principalis consiliarius regis." *Murimuth*, p. 120.

the moment we must consider what happened at the parliament summoned to Westminster for 13 October 1339.[277]

Parliament was presented with three matters for consideration: the safeguarding of peace within the realm, the defence of the Scottish march, and naval defence against foreign incursion. Stratford then expounded the king's difficulties on the continent, provided an explanation for the lack of offensive action, and showed that Edward's expenses and the cost of maintaining his allies had mounted to £300,000. To save the king's honour a large sum would have to be raised. Stratford and the prelates[278] then joined the earls and barons for discussion of the best means to raise the money required, being aided in this by members of the royal council who had close knowledge of the king's affairs. The archbishop opportunely revealed the contents of letters patent authorizing him to make certain concessions to both barons and commons. It was decided that a two-year tenth (similar to that ordinarily given by the church) should be granted, and the barons proceeded to offer this so far as they were concerned, though with the addition of certain demands for redress in parliament.[279] For their part the commons acknowledged the king's necessities, but stated that they would have to consult with the commons in their localities (les communes de lour pais) before answering in the next parliament. They did respond to the three points of the parliamentary agenda by urging afforcement of the commissions of the peace,[280] the appointment of wardens of the Scottish march, and the adoption of various suggestions for improving coastal defence. Finally, they put forward six articles for which they sought remedy.[281] It was a remarkable demonstration of independence. As Stubbs remarked, at this parliament "the first symptoms appeared of a disposition to make conditions before consenting to a grant." [282] And so the principal business was postponed

---

[277] Parry, *Parliaments*, p. 108; *HBC*, p. 521; *Rot. Parl.* 2, pp. 103-106. Summoned on 25 August, it met 13 October, ending about 3 November.

[278] Nine diocesan bishops were there: Durham (Bury), Chester (Northburgh), Exeter (Grandisson), Ely (Montacute), Carlisle (Kirkby), London (Bintworth), Bath and Wells (Shrewsbury), Salisbury (Wyville), Chichester (Robert Stratford).

[279] *Rot. Parl.* 2, pp. 103-104. For the concessions see above, n. 275; *Foedera* 2, iv, pp. 51-52. The schedule includes something which Stratford had been urging – the payment of a fixed "fine" at ecclesiastical voidances. Fryde, "Parliament and the French War," who has much to say about this parliament, regards (p. 265) the concessions as inadequate, as indeed they proved to be. See also Harriss, *King, Parliament and Public Finance*, chaps. x-xi, for the financial aspects.

[280] *Rot. Parl.* 2, p. 104; also above, n. 50.

[281] *Rot. Parl.* 2, pp. 104-105.

[282] *Constitutional History* 2, p. 381.

until a further parliament scheduled for 20 January 1340. Stratford's personal attendance was required and he was further instructed to arrange for a Canterbury convocation at St. Paul's a week later.[283] Added stimulus to action was provided in parliament by Thomas Ughtred's arrival to explain the loss of Perth.[284]

On the continent the king continued his parade of largesse. Steps were taken to provide a marriage portion for Edward's seven-year-old daughter Isabella as the prospective wife of the eldest son of Louis de Nevers, count of Flanders,[285] who was reluctantly being impelled towards the English confederacy – a trend of which Stratford had learned through his spies. This was a welcome diplomatic success, though an ephemeral one.[286] The marquis of Juliers, largely responsible for Edward's entente with the emperor, was made a member of the royal council and promised 20,000 gold florins for the losses he had sustained in the fighting. The duke of Lorraine was also rewarded with a substantial sum.[287]

During the night of 7-8 December Chancellor Bintworth died in Bishop Orleton's house at Southwark. At dawn the great seal was delivered to Stratford at his manor of Lambeth a little further up the Thames. From there it was taken back to the City where the royal council was in session at the Carmelites' friary in Fleet Street. Stratford was in attendance with the treasurer M. William la Zouche, dean of York.[288] But he did not at that point assume the seal himself. The duke of Cornwall as *custos* gave formal assent – he was only nine at the time – to its transfer to three chancery clerks. Bintworth's death also meant a vacancy in the episcopate. This gave opportunity for the election of Ralph Stratford as bishop of London. One cannot but see the archbishop's hand behind this and the rapid confirmation by the king of the canons' choice.[289] Stratford's mandate for

[283] *Foedera* 2, iv, pp. 56-57. The *custos* was unable to attend the parliament and on 19 January a writ entrusted Stratford, M. William la Zouche (the treasurer), Richard de Willoughby and John de Stonore (justices), and John de St. Pol with opening it. Ibid., p. 63.

[284] Ibid., p. 54.

[285] Ibid., pp. 55-56, 62. An embassy was deputed 15 November 1339 to negotiate with the count. For details see Lucas, *Low Countries*, pp. 358-359, 361.

[286] The count fled to Paris, but the arrangements with Flanders went ahead notwithstanding. Lucas, *Low Countries*, pp. 360-367; Viard, "Le siège de Calais," pp. 160, 161 n. 149.

[287] *Foedera* 2, iv, pp. 57-58, 60.

[288] Ibid., pp. 58-59.

[289] Ralph was elected 26 January. Signification of royal assent came on the 29th and the temporalities were restored 13 February. *CPR 1338-1340*, pp. 412, 429; *Murimuth*, p. 103 (who is a week out with the consecration date). *Le Neve* 5, p. 2.

his nephew's consecration is dated 13 February 1340 and the ceremony took place at Canterbury on the second Sunday in Lent (12 March). This was somewhat of a family affair, for both the archbishop and his brother Robert took part.[290]

Parliamentary business at Westminster in the new year was postponed for four days on account of bad weather, which delayed the arrival of many who were summoned to attend, among them merchants and ships' masters. Thus it was not until 24 January 1340 that the object of the summons was declared: to grant an appropriate aid as promised in the last parliament for the security of the realm and its inhabitants, and for safeguarding the sea, the Scottish march, Gascony, and the Channel Islands. With God's help, the exhortation ran, a reply pleasing to the king and his council would be given. But the commons were not so over-whelmed by threats to king and country as to relieve such necessities un-conditionally. They postponed their answer until 19 February, the last day of the parliament, when they offered an aid of 30,000 sacks of wool subject to conditions set out in indentures. These conditions were felt to touch the king so nearly that they would have to sent for his consideration and that of the "secret council" attendant on him (son secrez counseil pres de lui).[291] On the same day the barons granted a tenth in conformity with their earlier proposal. Reading between the lines of the formal record we can divine that Stratford played an influential part in this parliament, which with Treasurer Zouche and some others he had been deputed to open and conduct. Much of the business pertained to military matters: the array for the Scottish march, the victualling and munitioning of towns and castles, the strengthening of defensive arrangements in the Isle of Wight and the Channel Islands. To avoid the evils of purveyance it was specifically stated that payment for supplies should come from the aid to be granted to the king.[292] Two items concern remedies for encroachments on the liberties of the church. The first of these was prompted by Robert de Tauton's action as keeper of the privy seal[293] which had allegedly resulted in the taking into the king's hand of the temporalities of the provostship of Wells, to the detriment of the vicars choral and of others;

---

[290] *Canterbury Professions*, pp. 101-102, no. 286; BL Cotton MS Faustina B.v, fol. 88ʳ. The other bishops present were Hethe (Rochester) and Wyville (Salisbury). Prominent laymen were the earl of Huntingdon and Reginald de Cobham.

[291] *Rot. Parl.* 2, p. 107.

[292] E.g. *Rot. Parl.* 2, p. 109, nos. 25, 26. Purveyance was, of course, a perennial evil and had been the subject of resentment in recent parliaments. See Fryde, "Parliament and the French War."

[293] He had been keeper 1334-1335. *HBC*, p. 91.

the second involved waste and dilapidations believed to have been perpetrated by those administering the property of alien monasteries.[294] Satisfaction of the king's urgent financial requircments was shelved pending his arrival, though in response to the argument that money would have to be borrowed to equip an armed fleet or dire consequences would result, the commons did offer 2,500 sacks of wool as surety, to be deducted from the 30,000 if their conditions were accepted, otherwise to be treated as a gift.[295]

Edward, who while at Ghent had laid formal claim to the throne of France, arrived in the Orwell on 21 February. The same day he addressed a letter to Stratford under his newly-adopted style as king of France.[296] With him came the man who was possibly his closest adviser, Bishop Burghersh, and also the earls of Derby and Northampton, men well qualified to elaborate on the military situation and its exigencies. Having kissed the soil of his native land, Edward hastened to visit his mother and the shrines of the saints before setting out for London.[297]

Parliament assembled at Westminster on 29 March. Present was a strong contingent of ten bishops, including the three Stratfords.[298] What the members had earlier failed to do they now accomplished in the king's presence; lords and commons granted a ninth of grain, fleeces and lambs, but only on conditions comprised in a series of petitions.[299] Thereupon a joint committee was formed headed by Stratford and Bishops Bury and Northburgh and including Thomas de la More, the archbishop's nephew.[300] Their task was to cast the petitions in the form of statutes. From Stratford's viewpoint the second and fourth of these were of special significance. The second was regarded by Stubbs as a milestone in

---

[294] *Rot. Parl.* 2, pp. 108-109 no. 33, 111 no. 44.

[295] Ibid., p. 108 no. 9. For discussion of this parliament see Stubbs, *Constitutional History* 2, pp. 382-383; Tout, *Chapters* 3, p. 104; Harriss, *King, Parliament and Public Finance*, chap. xi.

[296] For this claim and the document incorporating it see *Avesbury*, pp. 308-310; *Hemingburgh* 2, pp. 336-340; *Foedera* 2, iv, pp. 66-67. The mandate to Stratford was for another session of parliament. The pope wrote to dissuade Edward from using the style and title: "stuporis et admirationis magnam nobis materiam ministrarunt." Vatican Archives, *RV* 135, fols. 92ʳ-93ʳ; *CPL 1305-1342*, pp. 579-580; *Foedera* 2, iv, p. 70.

[297] BL Cotton MS Faustina B.v, fol. 84ʳ; *Foedera* 2, iv, p. 69.

[298] The other bishops were Lincoln (Burghersh), Durham (Bury), Chester (Northburgh), Salisbury (Wyville), Ely (Montacute), Norwich (Bek), Carlisle (Kirkby), making ten in all with the Stratford group.

[299] *Rot. Parl.* 2, pp. 112-113.

[300] Ibid., p. 113. More was returned as a member for Oxfordshire in the parliaments of February and July 1338, January and March 1340, April 1343, and of February 1351. See Williams, *Parliamentary History of Oxford; Return of Members of Parliament* 1.

constitutional development: "perhaps ... the most distinct step of progress taken in the reign."[301] It declared that the current subsidy should not be taken as a precedent; in future aid was to be granted only in parliament and by the common assent of prelates, earls and barons, other great men, and of the commons. Moreover, the yield of the ninth and other profits of the realm were specifically earmarked for the expenses of war, thus limiting the king's financial control.[302] The fourth and last statute was designed to eradicate some longstanding clerical *gravamina*: abuses of purveyance, of royal presentation to benefices by reason of vacant sees, and of custodianship of bishoprics.[303] During the session various persons were assigned to deal with specific matters. Stratford was named as a member of several committees, dealing respectively with the pledge undertaken by the king at Brussels, English merchants, and the affairs of Gascony.[304] Most important, he headed a powerful commission for the audit of the accounts of William de la Pole, who had conducted major financial operations on the king's behalf.[305] The continental policy received recognition with the creation of the marquis of Juliers as earl of Cambridge.[306] It was arranged that the duke of Cornwall should act as *custos* of the realm during the king's absence. Stratford and the earls of Lancaster, Warenne (Surrey), and Huntingdon were to attend on him, with authority to co-opt such justices and other skilled persons as they might think fit.[307] Almost at the end of the record of this parliament is a memorandum to the effect that Stratford and Huntingdon were to be

---

[301] *Constitutional History* 2, p. 383; *Statutes* 1, pp. 281-294. The petitions are printed by Harriss, *King, Parliament and Public Finance*, App. A, pp. 518-520 (from the Winchester cartulary, no. 297), where they constitute five articles (discussed ibid., pp. 259-260ff.). The date prefacing the petitions, "Die mercurii proxima post primam dominicam quadragesime," gives 8 March rather than 29 March 1340, which suggests that "primam" is a scribal error for "quartam." Harriss reasonably infers that petitions sent to the king in February 1340 were close to those of March (*King, Parliament and Public Finance*, p. 260 n. 1 and idem, "The Commons Petitions of 1340"), but Fryde, "Parliament and the French War," p. 268, regards this view as mistaken and the earlier grievances to be irrecoverable.

[302] *Statutes* 1, pp. 289-292.

[303] Ibid., pp. 293-294. There can be little doubt, in the light of his previous concerns and actions, that the hand of Stratford lay behind this statute. Harriss, *King, Parliament and Public Finance*, p. 260, points out that cap. 1 of the March petitions went so far as to ask for the redress of infringements of ecclesiastical liberties in parliament at the plaintiff's suit. Cf. cap. 5 of Statute 1 (*Statutes* 1, p. 282).

[304] *Rot. Parl.* 2, p. 113 nos. 14, 15, 18.

[305] Ibid., p. 114 n. 22; *CPR 1340-1343*, p. 87; Harriss, *King, Parliament and Public Finance*, p. 263 n. 1.

[306] *Rot. Parl.* 2, p. 114 no. 35.

[307] Ibid., p. 114 no. 36.

commissioned as principal councillors for the business of the realm, while Bishop Burghersh was to counsel the king abroad.[308] Parliament dispersed on 10 May; the immediate crisis was over, the repercussions were still to come.

The same reticence about unrestricted grants for war purposes had been evidenced at the Canterbury convocation which met in London on 27 January 1340 and continued in session until after mid-February. Stratford exhibited his anxiety about the pressures on ecclesiastical liberty, a concomitant of the efforts of royal officials to raise money and supplies. From Lambeth on 30 May he sent a private letter to his provincial bishops accompanied by a copy of the "charter of liberties" conceded by the king to the English church. The document, he suggested, should be carefully preserved. On examination it turns out to be none other than the fourth statute of the recent parliament.[309] Stratford's letter also gave disturbing information about the royal intention to take the cardinals' procurations as a loan from the collectors, by force if need be. He advised the bishops to retain sufficient of the royal tenth to allow of repayment; a concession he had apparently wrung from the king.[310]

If Edward's intention had been to bribe Stratford into becoming an advocate of his war policy with authority to throw a sop to the "opposition," he was soon to be disappointed. Indeed, if such was the case Edward both misjudged his man and the strength of the opposition to taxation and its concomitants. As long before as the March of 1339 Stratford's attitude to the malpractices engendered by financial exigency was made clear in a letter written at Antwerp and preserved in at least two episcopal registers.[311] He denounced the manner in which mandates from the chancery entailed unlawful levying of taxes from ecclesiastics and enjoined his fellow prelates to attend parliament so as to ensure proper defence of the church's liberties.[312] In May of the same year he urged the

[308] Ibid., p. 116 no. 55.

[309] *Worcester Reg. Bransford*, pp. 67-68, 511-512. See above, "Archbishop of Canterbury," n. 93, and Tout, *Chapters* 3, p. 105 n. 4. A carefully written copy is in LAO A/2/12 (portion of Norwich register temp. Bishop Bek), fols. 1r-2v; also PRO C.115/K1/6681 (Llanthony cartulary), fols. 238r-239r, and elsewhere.

[310] *Worcester Reg. Bransford*, pp. 67-68, 511-512. This letter is not noted in Lunt's otherwise very full account of the levying of these procurations and of the royal seizures, *Financial Relations* 2, pp. 632-633.

[311] WinRO 2, fols. 30r-31v; *Bath and Wells Reg. Shrewsbury*, pp. 357-358. Cf. Tout, *Chapters* 3, p. 88.

[312] The letter is worth closer study than it has been given. Stratford maintained that it was the custom for subsidies to the king to be granted in convocations of the province, for which writs should be directed to the archbishop or his vicar. No response ought to be

denunciation of those who illegally abstracted grain or other goods from ecclesiastical houses or closes – a direct attack on purveyance and other forms of financial coercion.[313] It was inevitable that once in power Stratford would pursue the same line of policy. Although fully appreciative of the necessity to defend the realm, and even of the "justice" of the king's claim to the throne of France, he could not bring himself to allow that financial expediency condoned illegal acts or encroachment on ecclesiastical liberty. One detects a note of triumph in his distribution of the fourth statute. As a lawyer he felt that he had safeguarded the future; as a politician he was naïve if he failed to consider the possibility that Edward might renege on his commitment.

There were other elements in the situation which compounded Stratford's difficulties. His removal from the aegis of the peace-seeking cardinals did not insulate him from papal influence. Edward's assumption of the vicariate and his action against the bishop of Cambrai had merited excommunication.[314] The alliance with Jacob van Artevelde and the Flemings, whose count had eventually fled to Paris, contributed to the pope's exacerbation. Benedict was not prepared to admit the contention that as Edward was now the "rightful king of France" the withdrawal of Flemish allegiance from Philip was a logical step which ought not to invoke ecclesiastical or other penalties.[315] To these sources of friction, was added another in England, the disputed election at York following

given to the king – particularly "in arduis" – save by the counsel and assent of the prelates and of all the clergy. He lamented the fact that bishops were being approached individually for the convoking of diocesan clergy to grant subsidies. By virtue of such chancery writs clerical goods were being seized. A prelate should actively preserve ecclesiastical liberty and be a defender of justice. It was his responsibility to attend parliaments and to give counsel for the public weal. See *Bath and Wells Reg. Shrewsbury*, p. 237, for a writ of privy seal (Windsor, 5 September [1338]) asking the diocesan to summon his clergy and, in view of the royal needs, to speed the payment of tenths.

[313] Salisbury Reg. Wyville 1, fol. 53ᵛ; *Bath and Wells Reg. Shrewsbury*, p. 358; *Exeter Reg. Grandisson*, pp. 914-915. This mandate (received by Wyville as late as 11 July) invoked Mepham's canon (Council of London, 1328), which reiterated earlier legislation. *Concilia* 2, pp. 552-553.

[314] Vatican Archives, *RV* 134, fols. 124ᵛ-126ʳ; *CPL 1305-1342*, p. 577; *Foedera* 2, iv, pp. 53-54. The arguments are rehearsed in a bull to Stratford, *RV* 134, fols. 126ʳ-127ᵛ: 12 October 1339. Edward's justification of his policy (16 July 1339) to pope and cardinals is in *Murimuth*, pp. 91-100; *Hemingburgh* 2, pp. 316-326; *Walsingham* 1, pp. 201-208; and see *Knighton* 2, pp. 6-7.

[315] Vatican Archives, *RV* 135, fols. 93ᵛ-94ʳ; *CPL 1305-1342*, p. 580; Lucas, *Low Countries*, pp. 363-364, 371-373; also above, n. 286. BL Cotton MS Faustina B.v, fol. 84ʳ, comments on the great sum to be paid to the Roman curia should the Flemings rise against the king of France. Cf. *Knighton* 2, p. 14.

Archbishop Melton's death.[316] Edward wanted to promote his keeper of the privy seal, William Kilsby, but was forestalled by William la Zouche, dean of York, who obtained first capitular election and then papal provision.[317] Stratford is reported to have recommended Zouche to the pope and thereby to have incurred the bitter enmity of the disappointed candidate.[318] Towards the end of April 1340 Edward was writing to the absentee dean of Salisbury, Cardinal Raymond de Farges, with a request to counteract the rumours current at Avignon that he was an oppressor of ecclesiastics; this was a calumny, for he had always held them in great favour.[319] At this juncture Stratford was reappointed to the office of chancellor. The formal ceremony took place on 28 April, shortly before parliament's dismissal. The great seal was surrendered to the king in the white chamber at Westminster Palace and he, after withdrawing to the small chamber which led off on the south side, delivered it to Stratford, who took the customary oath and carried the seal back to Lambeth.[320]

The chancellor's office was not one to be lightly assumed at this time. Despite the supposition that he was an ambitious man, Stratford's subsequent actions may indicate that on this occasion he was somewhat reluctant to accept responsibility. He had already experienced a foretaste of the problems he would assuredly encounter. One could even hypothesize that Stratford only agreed to serve because by doing so he might mitigate the harm which threatened the church and the liberties of other sections of the population.

In the forefront of the chancellor's concerns was the burden of royal debts. Edward showed no inclination to practise economies, which he considered prejudicial to his honour and dignity. The new earl of

[316] For this conflict see Tout, *Chapters* 3, pp. 108 n. 1, 116-118; 6, p. 125 (corrigenda for p. 117 n. 1).

[317] Zouche was elected 2 May 1340. Edward tried to stop him going to the curia. Kilsby was prebendary of Wilton in York chapter. Déprez, *Les préliminaires*, p. 363, makes the point that the pope considered Kilsby to be the architect of the detested anglo-imperial alliance. The king did not mince his words about Zouche's behaviour in a letter to the pope: *Foedera* 2, iv, p. 71, 14 March 1340 [*sic*]. Benedict instructed Stratford to use excommunication against those who impeded Zouche's journey to Avignon. The elect was provided to the see 26 June 1342; not until 19 September were the temporalities restored. *CPL 1305-1342*, p. 549; *Le Neve* 6, p. 3; *HBC*, p. 264.

[318] BL Cotton MS Julius B.iii, fol. 23ʳ⁻ᵛ. "Et quia Johannes Cant. archiepiscopus pro dicto Willelmo eidem pape litteras commendaticias scripserat W. Kyllesey alter coelectus tunc portitor privati sigilli regis erga archiepiscopum Cant. graviter offensus, regem adversus ipsum nequiter excitavit adeo quod ipse dictum Cant. per brevia regia super prodicione quasi per totam Angliam defamavit."

[319] Déprez, *Les préliminaires*, p. 420 (from PRO C.70/743 m.3).

[320] *Foedera* 2, iv, pp. 72-73.

Cambridge was to be supported by an annual assignment of six hundred pounds from the customs and a further four hundred from the exchequer.[321] Assignments were made on the ninth for the redemption of Edward's crown, that of Queen Philippa, as well as of a third smaller crown.[322] Stratford himself was promised the expenses of his recent mission out of the proceeds of the same tax in the county of Kent.[323] In fact assignments flowed thick and fast, particularly in favour of creditors in the Low Countries.[324] Towards the end of May Edward was making arrangements for his departure – by the advice and assent of the prelates, earls, barons, and of the community of the realm. Stratford and the earl of Huntingdon were nominated to the council, together with the lords Henry Percy, Thomas Wake, and Ralph Neville.[325] Clearly this predominantly lay council was intended to be a strong one militarily; a well-warranted precaution.[326]

If it is argued that Stratford was a grasping man, then it has to be admitted that reimbursement of the cardinals' procurations and the assignment for his own massive outlay in the king's service abroad proved insufficient to convince him of the wisdom of Edward's proceedings. He travelled to Orwell Haven, where he found the king aboard the cog *Thomas*. His purpose was to dissuade Edward from leaving. The proposed journey was dangerous; Philip had collected a great force of armed ships to prevent his entering the Swin river. It would be wiser, pleaded Stratford, for the king to wait until he had gathered a stronger force to protect himself. The impetuous young monarch brushed aside these warnings, declaring his determination to sail whatever the danger. At this point, states the chronicler Avesbury, Stratford put himself outside the council and after receiving licence to withdraw surrendered the great seal.[327] The king then summoned his admiral Sir Robert Morley and a

[321] *Foedera* 2, iv, p. 74. PRO C.47/30/8 (3-9) is a file of documents surrendered by William, duke of Juliers, concerning grants made by Edward III to his father.

[322] *Foedera* 2, iv, pp. 74-75; *CPR 1338-1340*, p. 534.

[323] *Foedera* 2, iv, pp. 76-77; *CPR 1338-1340*, pp. 534, 546; ibid. *1340-1343*, p. 1. Stratford was to receive £3,333 6s 8d "pro vadiis suis de tempore quo stetit in obsequio nostro in partibus transmarinis ... ac aliis expensis per ipsum in dicto servitio nostro factis, prout per compotum ipsius archiepiscopi ... plenius poterit apparere."

[324] E.g. *Foedera* 2, iv, pp. 74-75ff.; *CPR 1338-1340*, p. 534.

[325] *Foedera* 2, iv, p. 75: Westminster, 28 May 1340. Cf. ibid., p. 76, for the powers of the *custos* during the king's absence. Those named were to accompany the *custos* "et eidem consiliis et auxiliis assistere." Cf. nn. 307-308 above.

[326] Percy and Neville were to be prominent in the battle of Neville's Cross (1346). E.g. *Murimuth*, p. 218; *Anonimalle Chronicle*, pp. 26-27.

[327] For the royal letter sent to Stratford and all the bishops for the recovery of the cardinals' procuration from the clerical tenth, see *Foedera* 2, iv, p. 76: Shotley, 18 June

skilled but unscrupulous commander, John Crabbe, who boasted an intimate knowledge of the continental coastline. To Edward's disgust they are supposed to have confirmed Stratford's opinion. To outward appearances this was a conspiracy to prevent his departure. With considerable irritation Edward is said to have expostulated: "I shall cross the sea without your approval. You who are afraid, where there is nothing to fear, can stay at home." [328] Morley and Crabbe reaffirmed the existence of the danger under oath, but volunteered to precede the king even to their own death. Edward, who had seemingly smelt subversion, was mollified by this. Avesbury's version of the outcome is that he recalled Stratford and handed him back the seal.[329] We know this to be untrue. The official record states that Stratford pleaded illness as his reason for giving up the chancellorship. The seal itself was broken up and another made subsequently. This new seal was placed in the custody of the chancery clerks until such time as Robert Stratford, the new chancellor, could retrieve it. The handover took place on 12 July in the painted chamber at Westminster. The archbishop was there, as were the treasurer Bishop Northburgh and other members of the council.[330]

Stratford's not unreasonable fears for the king's safety were submerged in the jubilation which followed the naval victory off Sluys on 24 June; a victory to which Morley and Crabbe contributed in full measure, but which also owed much to the incompetence of the French commanders.[331] Rumours of the successful engagement were current in London the following day.[332] They were confirmed by letters issued by the duke of

1340. Stratford surrendered the seal on the 20th in "La Cogge Thomas" anchored in the port of Orwell where the fleet lay ready to depart. Two bishops (Burghersh and Northburgh) were present, four earls, and others including Kilsby. Ibid., p. 78. The elaborate story of Stratford's caution is in *Avesbury*, pp. 310-312, who adds that in fact the king sought to assemble a larger fleet. But we know he sailed on 22 June, a mere two days after Stratford's surrender of the seal. *Foedera* 2, iv, p. 79. The *Historia Roffensis* (Bl. Cotton MS Faustina B.v, fol. 84ᵛ) employs allegory: "Ante transitum regis duo animalia cornuta regi varium consilium dederunt more Achitofel et Chusi. Achitofel vero ut rex cum paucis, Chusi vero cum multis consul[u]erunt transfretaret, et licet consilium Achitofel pluribus innotuerit non tamen omnibus fuit denudatum sed manet semper impunitum in regni grande detrimentum et periculum."

[328] *Avesbury*, p. 311: "Vos et archiepiscopus confoederati estis in uno praemeditato sermone."

[329] Ibid.: "Blandis sermonibus sibi loquens, retradidit sibi sigillum cancellariae."

[330] *Foedera* 2, iv, p. 78: "Praetendens se, propter infirmitatem et impotentiam corporis sui, non posse diutius in dicto cancellarii officio laborare."

[331] See Lucas, *Low Countries*, pp. 395-403.

[332] *Avesbury*, p. 312. Colourfully described as the "communis vox populi, quae vox Dei dicitur."

Cornwall dated the 28th from Waltham Holy Cross. Stratford received his copy, coupled with a request for the offering of a general thanksgiving. To some it might seem that an over-protective dotard had been made to look foolish by a confident young warrior.[333] Flushed with triumph Edward, who had been slightly wounded in the fray, wrote eagerly of his plans to invest Tournai and of Robert d'Artois' intention to attack St. Omer. The king's need, as always, was for money. A deputation, bearing the royal letter, was sent to explain the situation at the renewed session of the Westminster parliament in July.[334] Without immediate financial relief Edward feared that some of his soldiers would desert and that his allies might change sides.[335] The ninth was already virtually bespoken for the first year. What more could be done? Recourse was made once again to the wool crop. Members of the council led by Archbishop Stratford, his brother Robert and his nephew Ralph, offered to lend their own wool. Prompted by this example the commons agreed to a loan of 20,000 sacks repayable from the instalment of the ninth due in 1341, but only on stringent conditions.[336] Arrangements were made for the king to purchase the wool at fixed prices and to sell it to merchants for one mark (13s 4d) less. After adding the duty of forty shillings a sack the merchants were to pay what they owed to the king's representatives in the Low Countries.[337] The grant was actually made on 24 July[338] and the details were widely circulated.[339] When the parliament had dispersed merchants came before the council and contracted by indenture for specific amounts of wool, but the number of sacks accounted for fell far short of expectations. The council was constrained to arrange loans with William de la Pole, whose earlier operations had attracted investigation, and with, among others, the merchant houses of the Bardi and Peruzzi. Such creditors were to be repaid by assignments on the ninth and on the clerical tenth.[340] The wool transactions proved a disaster. In the words of a recent writer: "The loan of 1340 turned out to be the most unsuccessful of all the attempts to raise

---

[333] Ibid., pp. 312-314; *Foedera* 2, iv, p. 79.

[334] *Foedera* 2, iv, pp. 79-80; *Rot. Parl.* 2, p. 118 no. 6.

[335] *Foedera* 2, iv, p. 80. Cf. Jacques van Artevelde's plea (11 January 1340) that money should be sent so that the Flemish archers could be fed. Déprez, *Les préliminaires*, pp. 419-420 (from PRO S.C.1/41/166).

[336] *Rot. Parl.* 2, pp. 118-119.

[337] For a full discussion see Lloyd, *English Wool Trade*, chap. 5, esp. pp. 155-159, 166ff.

[338] *Rot. Parl.* 2, p. 122 (Monday the eve of St. James).

[339] Orleton's registrar entered the arrangement under the rubric: "Littera regis testimonialis patens de xx mill. saccis lane." WinRO 1, fol. 167ᵛ.

[340] *Rot. Parl.* 2, pp. 120-121.

wool for the king's use and neither English merchants nor royal creditors laid their hands on very much." [341] Defending himself in 1341, Stratford blamed those who had failed to carry out their obligations, but in recent times the principal reason suggested has been widespread resistance of the local population.[342] The ninth of grain, fleeces and lambs also proved very difficult to collect and yielded far less than had been expected.[343] The government was to do what it could to enforce payment, but in vain. Economic trends were adverse, buyers could not be found. Recent good harvests, particularly those of 1337 and 1338, had depressed prices, a tendency accentuated by heavy taxation and chronic shortage of money.[344]

Although meeting the royal needs was the primary problem considered in the parliament of July 1340, many other matters received attention. Prominent among these were the defence of Scotland, to which various revenues were assigned from the York temporalities owing to the vacancy following Melton's death, as well as that of Carisbrooke and the Isle of Wight. We may descry Stratford's concern in agreements for the avoidance of double taxation by the clergy under the terms of the clerical tenth and of the ninth, for relief from the latter in the case of alien priors and others who were being forced to pay a farm to the king for their lands, and for a similar quittance of tax in favour of hospitals founded for the poor and sick.[345] A letter of 30 July under the names of Stratford, his brother the chancellor, Treasurer Northburgh, the earl of Arundel and Thomas Wake, summed up the parliament's sensitivity to the king's exposure to danger and his necessities and reassured him that there was no intention of entrusting the current aid to those who had previously

[341] Lloyd, *English Wool Trade*, pp. 157-158.

[342] *Vitae Arch. Cant.*, p. 30 (Lambeth MS 99, fol. 141ʳ): "Si ergo infortunium aliquod propter defectum pecuniae contigerit, quod nos taedet; hoc illis qui dictas conventiones fregerunt et dicta subsidia male expenderunt et dilapidaverunt." Cf. Lloyd, *English Wool Trade*, p. 158: "The main reason for the lack of success was probably the sheer resistance of the population."

[343] Fryde, "Edward III's Removal of Ministers," p. 152, argues that the ninth yielded only £15,000 by the end of 1340, against Edward's assignments prior to his departure in June of more than £190,000. The most detailed examination of financial arrangements and problems is that of E. B. Fryde, "Financial Resources of Edward I and Comparisons with Edward III 1337-1340," *Revue Belge* 40, 45, who gives at (45) pp. 1194-1216 tables A-D itemizing the loans raised and their recipients. Cf. Harriss, *King, Parliament and Public Finance*, pp. 277-278.

[344] See *inter alios* Harriss, *King, Parliament and Public Finance*, pp. 250-251; Fryde, "Parliament and the French War," pp. 264-265; Kershaw, "Great Famine and Agrarian Crisis"; Ames, "The Sterling Crisis of 1337-1339"; Titow, "Winchester Yields."

[345] *Rot. Parl.* 2, p. 119 no. 17.

mishandled wool on his behalf.[346] A further letter of 13 August from London[347] specified the grant, full details of which and also of other matters dealt with by parliament and council were being sent to Edward under seal by the hand of William Trussel.[348]

The interval between the August letter, with its ring of hope, and the truce of Espléchin, reluctantly concluded on 25 September because of Edward's lack of resources, was a mere six weeks. Almost as damaging to Edward's pride was the capture of the earls of Salisbury and Suffolk, who were taken to Paris,[349] and the necessity to leave his commanders, the earls of Derby, Northampton and Warwick, as pledges for the repayment of his debts.[350] With increasing vehemence the hostility of those who were physically close to the king, both soldiers and members of the council in the Low Countries, was directed towards the home government and more particularly Stratford. An obvious but none the less important question demands some sort of answer, however inadequate. To what extent was Stratford responsible for the state of affairs which reached crisis proportions by the last quarter of 1340? One thinks not merely of technical responsibility, but also of the degree to which his actions might have ameliorated the crisis, or alternatively served to exacerbate it. But first something must be said of the nature of the authority he exercised.

The Walton Ordinances of July 1338, though by no means entirely novel, were designed to make provision for a divided administration during the king's absence abroad.[351] They were intended above all to subordinate the chancery and the exchequer to direct royal control by developing the system of warrants under the privy seal[352] and at the same time decentralizing certain aspects of government by requiring the

---

[346] Ibid., pp. 121-122.

[347] Though his itinerary shows that by that time Stratford had migrated to Kent.

[348] Rot. Parl. 2, p. 122.

[349] Foedera 2, iv, pp. 83-84. The earls were taken prisoner while inadvisedly attacking Lille. It is alleged that Philip wanted to kill them but was dissuaded by the king of Bohemia. Murimuth, pp. 104-105; cf. French Chronicle, pp. 73-74; Anonimalle Chronicle, p. 15; Lucas, Low Countries, p. 386.

[350] Foedera 2, iv, pp. 57-58. Warwick replaced the captive Suffolk. Salisbury himself, marshal of England, was originally named as co-hostage with the earl of Derby.

[351] They are printed by Tout, Chapters 3, pp. 143-150, and commented upon ibid., pp. 69ff. See also Hughes, A Study of Edward III, chap. 4.

[352] William Kilsby was keeper between July 1338 and June 1342 (HBC, p. 91). He is believed by many either to have been the author of the ordinances or one of those reponsible (e.g. Hughes, A Study of Edward III, p. 58 ; Harriss, King, Parliament and Public Finance, p. 246). See also Stones, "Geoffrey le Scrope," p. 7.

election locally of sheriffs and other officials.[353] The offices of treasurer of the exchequer[354] and of keeper of the privy seal were crucial to the system envisaged by the compilers of the ordinances. Tout looked upon them as "the clearest exposition of the high curialist party, whose policy always was to subject central and local administration, the administration of the king's non-English lands,[355] and the administration of the financial side of war, to the strict control of special agents of the crown." [356] For our purposes another noteworthy aspect of the ordinances is the recognition of a divided council, each section having a "principal councillor." [357]

These ordinances were sent to Chancellor Bintworth on 12 July 1338, the day after Stratford's departure on his mission to Paris and the Low Countries, and six days after Robert Stratford's surrender of the great seal.[358] The making of a more impressive seal for the new keeper, William Kilsby, and of a second great seal – of absence – epitomized the new arrangements. For Tout the scheme marked the triumph of the curialists[359] over the "Lancastrians" who, with Robert Stratford's withdrawal, were left without a representative in the higher reaches of government.[360] Perhaps this goes too far in its premature assumption of factional infighting. At their inception the ordinances were a necessary administrative expedient for the government of a country whose head was to be

[353] Tout, *Chapters* 3, pp. 71-72; Hughes, *A Study of Edward III*, p. 54; Wilkinson, *Chancery*, p. xxv (for a summary of the chancellor's powers). Of the local elections Tout remarks (*Chapters* 3, p. 75): "The object was not to conciliate local opinion so much as to give the crown additional power. So far from being considered dangerous to prerogative, such interference was intended to enable the king the more easily to get his own way."

[354] Robert Woodhouse was acting as treasurer in March 1338; William la Zouche assumed office on 31 December. Robert Sadyngton succeeded him 5 May 1340 and on 26 June Northburgh assumed office, acting until his dismissal on 1 December. *HBC*, p. 101.

[355] On this topic see Brown, "Gascon Subsidies and the Finances of the English Dominions."

[356] Tout, *Chapters* 3, p. 77.

[357] Ibid., pp. 71, 145: "Celi ou ceux, qi serra ou serront gouernors et chiefs des ditz conseilx." Cf. ibid., p. 146: "Et les ditz chefs gouernors des auant ditz conselx."

[358] Ibid., pp. 69, 81 n. 3. Tout regarded (p. 81) the addition to the chancellor's oath of a clause for the exercise of the office "iuxta quendam ordinacionem" as significant of a shift of political power away from Stratford. Hughes, *A Study of Edward III*, p. 59, contends that Robert Stratford "was anxious to resign the chancellorship" and that Bintworth "shared the administrative view of the royal advisers and was willing at least to attempt to apply them." Certainly some of the writs issued under his aegis irritated Stratford. See above, n. 312.

[359] *Foedera* 2, iv, pp. 27-28, 69, 78; Tout, *Chapters* 3, pp. 80-81.

[360] Tout, *Chapters* 3, p. 81: "The alarm of the Lancastrians was shown when Robert Stratford, their only important representative left in high office, realized that the policy adopted was incompatible with his retaining his post." Cf. above, n. 358.

heavily engaged abroad. At the same time there is no need to deny that in practice the new arrangements meant a shift of power to certain individuals at the monarch's side, particularly Kilsby. One aspect of Robert Stratford's surrender of secular office has been overlooked; to his duties as bishop of Chichester were added those of vicar general of his archiepiscopal brother.[361] Though a man of industry and talent he could hardly cope with all three responsibilities at once. It is legitimate to question the assumption that the archbishop was ousted from government. Scheduled for an important if ambivalent task, that of peacemaker with the cardinals and spy for the English king, he was, so to speak, at the focus of action. There is no indication of his having been forced out by some curialist coup d'état, nor is there reason to believe that initially he was hostile to the logical administrative plan adopted.[362] There is likewise no evidence that in the early stages he reacted unfavourably to the king or his policies, dangerous though they might appear. Naturally he preferred the papal road of peace, but not at any price, certainly not that of English interests. What he did object to subsequently was what he considered to be unlawful acts perpetrated by Chancellor Bintworth and royal officials against the church's liberties.[363] There was nothing novel about rising to the defence of the church, even in a national emergency; such action need not be interpreted as a deliberate attempt to impede royal policy.[364]

Only from October 1339, on his return to England, was Stratford in a position to grapple with the problems of government at home. Thus his period of responsibility for the shortfall in aid is of relatively short duration. Already Edward's profligacy must have been beyond redemption. The king's claim, in a letter to Benedict XII, that Stratford had encouraged him to return to the continent (in June 1340) with inadequate

---

[361] I would regard McKisack's conclusion (*Fourteenth Century*, p. 158) as nearer the mark than Tout's. "The motive force behind the Walton Ordinances and the promotion of Bentworth and Kilsby was the desire for greater speed and efficiency, particularly in the raising of supplies for the war. Some personal animosities may have played their part but, if so, it was a minor one. Edward III was seeking neither to eliminate the magnates from his counsels nor to follow the example of his father in surrounding himself with courtiers and favourites of inferior rank."

[362] For Robert as vicar general see above, "Archbishop of Canterbury." The archbishop's own activities as diplomat and spy are dealt with earlier in this section.

[363] See above, nn. 312-313.

[364] Much of Stratford's activity at the level of central government has been interpreted too narrowly in terms of political opposition. It might be fairer to regard Stratford as a man who was anxious to support the king, but not at the expense of legality and privilege. The word "privilege" now often bears a derogatory meaning; it would not have done so in the fourteenth century when it was often used as a virtual synonym for "liberty." Cf. Harding, "Political Liberty," pp. 441-444.

resources but with a promise that money would be sent within a few days is a palpable fiction.[365] Stratford was as reluctant to see the king depart as to continue in office. Tout saw the incident from an administrative aspect: "The king had fled from England, leaving Stratford to rule in his place." No longer were there two ministries, he declared, "for the court was dependent on the home government." [366] Others would date the abandonment of the double ministries to Michaelmas 1339, when Stratford was named principal councillor. In this view Stratford's role was that of "a strong man at the helm," a man calculated to provide impetus for the home government.[367] Associated with this kind of interpretation is the idea that as a result of the petitions of 1340 the council at home "had received plenary power." Stratford, in short, had taken advantage of the discontents of council and commons "to re-establish his own position against the king's *familiares*." [368] Such analysis reveals the archbishop as the champion of council and commons against interference from those at the king's ear in the Low Countries.[369] Obviously there are elements of truth in most of these suggestions, but it may be more accurate to look upon Stratford after June 1340 as a reluctant councillor, one who was none the less determined to make the most of an impossible situation. His earlier career shows him to have been sympathetic towards elements of the commons' petitions, but this does not mean that he was directing some opposition programme. The petitions were not of his making (though the statutes were); they arose as a reaction to expedients for raising more and yet more money, expedients which predated Stratford's later ministerial responsibility. They were prefigured, for instance, in petitions of 1339.[370]

[365] Vatican Archives, *RV* 135, fol. 113ᵛ; *Registres de Benoît xii*, no. 2981. "Qui de consilio suorum sibi pro tunc assistencium et principaliter domini Cantuariensis predicti subito se paravit ... absque provisione pecunie vel equorum sub confidencia principali dicti domini Cantuariensis, qui infra certos et paucos dies pecuniam sibi sufficientem promiserat destinare."

[366] *Chapters* 3, p. 115. An opinion endorsed by Harriss, *King, Parliament and Public Finance*, p. 275.

[367] McKisack, *Fourteenth Century*, p. 160. But she adds (p. 161): "It is just possible that the archbishop was beginning to be troubled by scruples as to the propriety of the king's methods, if not of his ultimate aims." Cf. Tout, *Chapters* 3, p. 102, who comments that in September 1339 "Stratford had at last won back more than his ancient authority."

[368] Harriss, *King, Parliament and Public Finance*, p. 273.

[369] Ibid., p. 274: "In defending this settlement [of 1340], Stratford could count on the support of those who had secured it – the home council and the Commons."

[370] *Rot. Parl. Inediti*, pp. 267-272, and esp. petitions 5 and 7. There is some doubt about their date. Fryde, "Parliament and the French War," pp. 250 n. 1, 256 n. 34, would prefer to assign them to March 1337. Cf. Harriss, *King, Parliament and Public Finance*, p. 248 n. 2.

As principal councillor Stratford bears responsibility for orders of July 1340 prohibiting collection of the ninth from those who had not been summoned to parliament and had therefore not given their assent. This again was a matter of legality and of ecclesiastical liberty.[371] We shall see that Stratford stuck to his point. As late as the last day of October Edward had written to the members of the home council reiterating his plight and that of his men but specifically exonerating them from blame.[372] Within two weeks or so his attitude had changed entirely. We can only surmise that the increasing helplessness and frustration of his position turned him to anger and irrational courses. There would have to be sacrificial victims; his position dictated that Stratford would be among them.

Naturally Stratford could have acted differently and in theory much more effectively. It has been suggested that he ought to have lowered the prices set for the sale of produce levied for the ninth, that he blundered in resorting to a loan of wool in June 1340, and that he showed "a tendency to let matters drift" in the latter part of 1340.[373] Thus, it was not until 27 November 1340 that collectors of the ninth were ordered to deliver receipts directly to William Edington, regardless of any assignments.[374] Then too, the peculation and dishonesty of customs officials was crying out for radical reform.[375] But one has to bear in mind the restricted space for manoeuvre in the short term and the context of deflationary economic conditions. It could be contended that the scheme devised in 1336 for raising ready money from wool was one of considerable originality, but like most promising schemes, it had subsequently been pushed too far. It

---

[371] *CCR 1339-1341*, p. 613. Note, however, the concession to Bishop Grandisson on 5 February 1340, made because he had not been present and therefore not consulted, and bearing in mind that the amount of wool from his diocese was not great. *Exeter Reg. Grandisson*, pp. 60-61.

[372] Déprez, *Les préliminaires*, pp. 355-357 (from PRO C.81/270/13498): Ghent, 31 October. It was sent in response to a letter from the home council, and contains the phrase: "Ne pur quant nous ne susmettons nulle defaute a vous ne a nul de vous."

[373] McKisack, *Fourteenth Century*, p. 167. The arguments are derived from E. B. Fryde's doctoral thesis (Oxford D.Phil. 1947, "Edward III's War Finance 1337-1341"), material from which is to be found in his "Financial Resources of Edward I and Comparisons with Edward III." *Vide* summary in "Wool Monopoly of 1337," pp. 8-24.

[374] *CCR 1339-1341*, p. 55. See Harriss, *King, Parliament and Public Finance*, pp. 282-283.

[375] See Baker, *The English Customs Service*, esp. pp. 33ff. ("The Failure of the Customs Service, 1336-1343), and p. 50: "There is good reason to believe that Edward III's advisers had concluded by 1340, if not earlier, that the problem of finding trustworthy controllers was insoluble"; Fryde, "English Farmers of the Customs," esp. pp. 16-17. Harriss, *King, Parliament and Public Finance*, p. 246, n. 2, insists on "the more substantial fact that Edward's plans foundered on deeper political conflicts."

is more realistic to look at the king's unprecedented and chimerical demands as the substantive cause of the crisis which erupted with Edward's return to England at the end of November 1340.

THE CRISIS OF 1341

Details of the violent but not unheralded conflict provoked by Edward III's return to England towards the end of 1340 have often been recounted.[1] The affair has been subjected to minute analysis by historians concerned to subordinate the temporary but none the less keen personal antagonism between the king and his archbishop to broader considerations of a political, constitutional, legal or fiscal character.[2] At the risk of some repetition we must here review the factual details, placing particular emphasis on Stratford's involvement and the light which this throws on his character, motives, and underlying policy or preconceptions.

Undoubtedly Edward was highly incensed by the financial embarrassment which forced him to conclude the truce of Esplèchin at the very moment that the bombardment of Tournai, coupled with the bloody defeat of a large-scale sortie and the increasing dearth of water and food within the city, promised an early surrender and the prospect of considerable loot.[3] The king's anger was slow to come to the boil, but

---

[1] My emphasis in what follows will be on Stratford's personal position, attitudes and responses, as illustrated more particularly by the exchange of *libelli* with the king.

[2] Possibly the lengthiest account from Stratford's standpoint is that of Hook, *Lives* 4, pp. 33-67. Stubbs, *Constitutional History* 2, pp. 384-392, puts the matter firmly in a constitutional context, as do (much later) Lapsley, "Archbishop Stratford," and Wilkinson, "The Protest of the Earls." Hughes in a pioneer work, *A Study of Edward III*, devotes chap. 7 ("The Crisis of 1340") and chap. 8 ("The Constitutional Struggle") to the conflict between king and archbishop, as well as part of chap. 9, but she is understandably not concerned with Stratford as an individual. Tout's discussion, *Chapters* 3, constitutes a long section entitled "Administrative and Constitutional Crisis, 1338-1343" (cf. idem, *PHE* 3, pp. 349-351). Recently the events have been reviewed in a fiscal context as part of a series of political crises over taxation: Harriss, *King, Parliament and Public Finance*, chaps. XII-XIII. See also Pike, *Constitutional History of the Lords*, pp. 186-198; Vernon Harcourt, *His Grace the Steward*, pp. 338-345; Baldwin, *King's Council*, pp. 99, 351-352; Fryde, "Edward III's Removal of Ministers," who is notably unsympathetic to Stratford; and Jones, "*Rex et Ministri*," who somewhat offhandedly remarks (p. 2) that Stratford retired to Canterbury "where he spent the next several months fantasizing about the martyrdom which to him seemed increasingly imminent." It was, I suspect, more a case of "reculer pour mieux sauter." The principal chronicle is the anonymous *Vitae Arch. Cant.* ("Birchington"). The *French Chronicle* has useful details; *Murimuth* gives a summary of events; and most of the documents are in *Hemingburgh*.

[3] *French Chronicle*, pp. 77-79, sums up the progress of the siege: the bombardment, the diversion of the water supply and the famine – all contrasted with the allegedly comfortable conditions of the besiegers – and the capture of a messenger sent to Philip of

when it did his intemperate actions recalled some of the more unfortunate characteristics of his father. But unlike Edward of Carnarvon his son exhibited a capacity for not allowing his emotions permanently to cloud his judgment or to impede his long-term interests and plans.

Following the unlooked-for truce, the king retired to Ghent. From there, the French Chronicle tells us, he reiterated letters to the home government with complaints of its failure to remit the proceeds of taxation. The councillors left in England are depicted as "faus treitres," but we also learn that one of them secretly supplied the king with damning information about the conduct of government, with the hint that were Edward to come without warning to the Tower he would find treasure for all his needs.[4] This somewhat sensationalized story of a hostile informer can be corroborated in essentials. Among the muniments at Westminster is a copy of a letter in French, sent by one of the home councillors[5] to someone at the king's side, though possibly not Bishop Burghersh.[6] This man, as he tells us himself, was also in contact with William Kilsby. The letter must have been written after 8 September 1340, by which date the Bardi and Peruzzi were supposed to have discharged certain of the king's debts,[7] and prior to 2 October, for which day a council was projected, allegedly to punish "false ministers" as an example to others.[8] The letter writer paints a gloomy picture of home affairs. He despaired of a speedy realization of funds by the sale of wool, as of other business touching the king, and suggested that the latter should make new appointments of officials for the better serving of his interests and those of the people. Should the necessary mandates fail to arrive in

---

Valois to give intelligence of the city's plight. The terms of the treaty are given, for example, in BL Cotton MS Faustina B.v, fols. 86^v-87^r; *Avesbury*, pp. 317-323; *Foedera* 2, iv, pp. 83-84.

[4] *French Chronicle*, pp. 82-83: "Un de eux q'estoit jurée au roi mientz voilant à luy qe nul des autres, et savoit touz lour privetés et contractes."

[5] WAM no. 12195. The writer records how, after his correspondent's departure, Br. Richard de Winkley and M. Robert de Askeby came to England with letters addressed to the archbishop, the treasurer, "et a nous et as autres grauntz du conseil."

[6] Fryde, "Edward III's Removal of Ministers," p. 154, assumes that it was. But the form of address used is "Trescher sire" and "Trescher piere." Were the letter to a bishop we would expect "piere en Dieu" or "reverent piere," though this is not perhaps conclusive.

[7] He writes of the Nativity of Our Lady last past. The date could perhaps be narrowed to 14 September (see n. 8).

[8] "Ou serra ordinez a leide de Dieu punissement de faux ministres pur doner example as autres." This appears to militate against the notion of an autonomous home council. The summons for the meeting is dated 14 September: *CCR 1339-1341*, p. 624; Parry, *Parliaments*, p. 112.

time he would exert his influence to redress the matter.[9] Echoing these sentiments are those of the king himself expressed in a letter written aboard his ship while at sea.[10] The departing Edward was reassuring the townsmen of Ghent that he would soon put matters to rights and so be able to fulfil his agreements.[11]

Whoever was the recipient of the home councillor's letter,[12] it may be right to single out the relatively junior William Kilsby, keeper of the privy seal, as the king's *éminence grise*. Kilsby's record points to his having been an unprincipalled man, not above employing strong-arm methods to advance his concerns. His failure to secure the archbishopric of York – for which he was eminently unsuited – against the canons' election of Dean Zouche, was still very much a live issue.[13] While journeying to the apostolic see to further his candidature the elect and his party were set upon in the neighbourhood of Geneva.[14] Their release was made conditional upon Zouche's undertaking not to reveal the names of his captors; an oath which the pope promptly declared invalid.[15] Tout regarded Zouche, who had been treasurer in the archbishop's administration as being, so far as the king was concerned, "too strongly with the party of Stratford."[16] That presupposes some clear-cut "Stratford interest," which may be going a little too far. But, as we have seen, there is indication that Stratford favoured Zouche for the northern archbishopric,

---

[9] "Pur ordiner et mettre les places issint qe le roi et le people soient serviz nemie eant regard a nully persone de quelle condicion qil soit et en cas qe les mandementz ne veignent par temps nous mettroms nostre poair devers ceux qe sont de conseil per decea de faire les redresces."

[10] "Don en le meer": 28 November 1340.

[11] PRO 31/8/142, fol. 303^{r-v}. I owe the reference to Fryde, "Edward III's Removal of Ministers," p. 154, who quotes some passages in translation.

[12] Ibid. (see previous note).

[13] The author of the *Vitae Arch. Cant.*, p. 22 (Lambeth MS 99, fol. 137^v) dubs him "principalis incentor discordiae." At the time he appeared to have a bright political future. See Tout, *Chapters* 6, index s.v.

[14] "Aliquibus ex eisdem familiaribus vulneratis et atritis graviter captivarunt violenter et miserabiliter sicque captivos et aflictos multis atrocibus iniuriis et offensis extra viam publicam ad quendam locum solitarium ultra lacum de Lausan. in Teira."

[15] Vatican Archives, *RV* 135, fol. 81^{r-v}; *CPL 1305-1342*, pp. 547-548, 578. Is there a case for seeing Kilsby's hand in the affair? He could be unscrupulous. Both William and his brother Robert were accused by the papal auditor William de Cerzeto of having procured the imprisonment of a curial messenger on a trumped-up homicide charge. The bishops of Winchester (Orleton), Chichester (Robert Stratford) and Durham (Bury) were directed to cite the brothers to appear in the curia. The king repudiated the charge and asked for them to be excused. *RV* 136, fols. 113^v, 114^{r-v} (7 July 1341); *Foedera* 2, iv, pp. 85-86 (18 October 1340 [*sic*]).

[16] *Chapters* 3, p. 116.

and it is indisputable that Zouche preferred the security of York to the vagaries of royal service.[17] In view of Edward's opposition he had to fall back on papal provision. In Benedict's eyes Kilsby, being associated with the anglo-imperial alliance, was not a viable candidate.[18]

William Kilsby was by no means the only member of the council abroad to harbour ill-feeling against Stratford. "Birchington," the archbishop's biographer, claims that two of Edward's most venerable and trusted advisers, Geoffrey le Scrope[19] and Bishop Burghersh, both of whom were to die within a week of the royal departure from Ghent for London, should be considered Stratford's "enemies in chief," actively plotting against him.[20] However that may be, the lineaments of the royal case against the archbishop are to be found in the exposition of policy prepared for Pope Benedict in mid-November 1340,[21] a fact which has not been accorded sufficient emphasis.

Once Edward had decided on a course of action it was carried out with military precision, regardless of the political repercussions or of personal hazards. Accompanied by a diminutive band of knights and clerks[22] he embarked on a sea-crossing, the unusually tempestuous nature of which was attributed by a chronicler to the devilish conjurations of the French,[23] and eventually tied up at Tower Steps at about midnight on the feast of St. Andrew, 30 November.[24] Disembarking by torchlight he made a precipitate entry into the fortress to find that the constable, Sir Nicholas Beche, who also had custody of the young prince, was absent from his

---

[17] He was eventually consecrated at Avignon 6 or 7 July 1342 and enthroned 8 December. *Le Neve* 6, p. 3. See above, "In the Seat of Power," nn. 316-318.

[18] See above, "In the Seat of Power," n. 317.

[19] Scrope had been one of those sent to bring Stratford before the king in 1323. *CChW*, p. 546 (PRO C.81/125/6744). For him see Stones, "Sir Geoffrey le Scrope."

[20] They died 2 and 4 December respectively according to *Vitae Arch. Cant.*, p. 21 (Lambeth MS 99, fol. 137ʳ): "Qui ipsius archiepiscopi facti sunt hostes in capite, [et] multa illicita ordinarunt, ut creditur, contra eum."

[21] Vatican Archives, *RV* 135, fols. 111ᵛ-116ᵛ; *CPL 1305-1342*, pp. 583-585; Déprez, *Les préliminaires*, pp. 423-426 (from PRO C.81/270/13351).

[22] *Chronicon*, p. 72. Baker says he had eight men with him, but names only seven: the earl of Northampton (Bohun), the knights Nicholas de Cantilupe, Reginald de Cobham, Giles and John de Beauchamp, and the clerks William de Kilsby and Philip de Weston (almoner and confessor to the king: Tout, *Chapters* 3, p. 120). He omits John Darcy (the son) and Walter Manny, the Hainaulter. Both are in his exemplar *Murimuth*, pp. 116-117. Cf. *Foedera* 2, iv, p. 87; Tout, *Chapters* 3, pp. 120-121.

[23] *French Chronicle*, p. 84.

[24] Ibid., pp. 83-84, has "la nuit prochein après le jour seint Andreu"; *Vitae Arch. Cant.*, p. 20 (Lambeth MS 99, fol. 136ᵛ), "in vigilia sancti Andreae apostoli ... latenter circa mediam noctem." Cf. *Foedera* 2, iv, p. 87 (St. Andrew "circiter mediam noctem").

post.[25] Attended by Beche's deputy the impatient king insisted on an immediate inspection of the premises. Ignoring the lateness of the hour he summoned the mayor of London, Andrew Aubrey, who on pain of life and limb was commanded to bring various justices and royal clerks to the Tower. Those that were unlucky enough to be found were aroused from their beds and on arrival at the fortress confined in separate chambers. Among the chancery clerks arrested was Henry Stratford, the archbishop's cousin,[26] who was later confined to Corfe Castle.[27]

At first light on 1 December the chancellor, Stratford's brother Robert, arrived at the Tower, where he was peremptorily relieved of his seal. It was handed to the triumphant Kilsby, who placed it with the other great seal formerly used for the king's business abroad.[28] Orders were given for the apprehension of the absentee constable and of a chancery official, John Molyns, a man steeped in peculation and later shown to have secreted a substantial quantity of questionably-acquired treasure in St. Albans Abbey. This the king forcibly appropriated without pretence of legal process. Molyns prudently hid himself from the king's wrathful pursuit.[29] Despite widespread charges of corruption Molyns, who has been stigmatized as a "medieval robber baron," survived to continue his malpractices. It is claimed that no other magnate "terrorized his part of the world for such a length of time."[30] This suggests that Edward, his righteous anger notwithstanding, had no greater success than Stratford in eradicating corruption.

[25] The under-constable, on his knees, admitted that his principal was "hors de vile." *French Chronicle*, p. 84. For his instructions of 6 June 1340 see PRO C.81/270/13159 (cited Fryde, "Edward III's Removal of Ministers," p. 149).

[26] One of the "clerici cancellarii majores" (*Murimuth*, p. 117). See above, "Stratford's *Familia* and Administration."

[27] *French Chronicle*, p. 85. The incarcerations were said to have been ordered "par le conseil sire William de Killesby." Beche, the negligent constable, was taken to Tickhill, John de Stonor to Nottingham, John de Pulteney (Stratford's friend) to Somerton, William de la Pole to Devizes, Richard de Willoughby to Corfe, William de Shareshull to Caerphilly, M. Michael de Wathe and Sir Thomas Ferrers to Windsor, and John de Shardelow, M. John de St. Pol and John de Thorp to the Tower of London. For the action against the judges – Stonor, Willoughby, Shareshull and Shardelow – see Putnam, *Shareshull*, pp. 138-140; Fryde, "Edward III's Removal of Ministers," p. 157.

[28] *Foedera* 2, iv, p. 87. All the chancery documents in the house of the *custos* of the rolls, John de St. Pol, were delivered into Kilsby's custody in the Tower.

[29] *French Chronicle*, pp. 84-85 and n. 27 above. However justified his suspicions of Molyns may have been, the king behaved in an outrageously illegal manner. He broke into Molyns' private "safe" in the abbey of St. Albans and proceeded to ravage his properties at Stoke Poges and Ditton. Ibid., pp. 86-87. For this man and his subsequent career, see Tout, *Chapters* 3, p. 123 n. 3; 6, index, s.v.; Fryde, "A Medieval Robber Baron."

[30] Fryde, "A Medieval Robber Baron," p. 207.

While Edward could imprison lesser clerks with impunity, at any rate in the short term, he found the bishops resistant to such summary treatment. Both Robert Stratford and the displaced treasurer, Bishop Northburgh, stood on their rights and thus retained their freedom.[31] Robert was summoned before the king and council but refused to recognize such a tribunal. Subsequently he declined to respond to repeated summonses and the ineffective sheriff of Sussex was imprisoned in the Tower for failing to execute his commissions.[32] Paradoxically this was as well for the king; the forcible detention of bishops could only have redounded to his discredit. As for the archbishop himself, there was every intention of including him in the round-up of those suspected of malpractice. The king's emissaries anticipated that he would be at Lambeth, across the Thames from Westminster, but sought him there in vain. In fact he was at his Kentish manor of Charing to the northwest of Ashford, close by Canterbury.[33] News of the violent happenings in London must have reached him within twenty-four hours of the king's landfall. In the circumstances discretion seemed the most prudent course and on 2 December Stratford sought refuge in the cathedral monastery at Canterbury, where in any case, his biographer suggests, he was expected for the profession of some of the novices.[34] By coincidence it was the festival of St. Thomas of Canterbury's return from exile – a usage which Pope John xxii had recently (1333) extended to the rest of the western church.[35] Round about Vespers on the very same day the king's messenger, Sir Nicholas Cantilupe, rode into the cathedral city and sought out the archbishop in the prior's chamber, where the number of people present suggests that his arrival was not unheralded.[36] With a notary public John Faringdon as witness, Cantilupe produced his credentials and proceeded to address Stratford. "My lord archbishop," he said, "you well know that you are under obligation to the merchants of Louvain for a

---

[31] *Pace* Hook, *Lives* 4, p. 37, there is no reliable evidence that the bishops were imprisoned. *Vitae Arch. Cant.*, p. 21 (Lambeth MS 99, fol. 137ʳ) states specifically "dictis episcopis duntaxat exceptis." But cf. the garbled statement in *Chronica Johannis de Reading* (BL Cotton MS Cleopatra A.xvi, fol. 152ʳ). Fryde, "Edward iii's Removal of Ministers," pp. 159-160, elaborates on the refusal of Robert Stratford to plead before the king and council. To the references given there may be added PRO C.49/file 46/11 (mutilated fragment); Lambeth MS 99 (Brute), fol. 50ᵛ.

[32] Fryde, "Edward iii's Removal of Ministers," p. 160 (from PRO C.81/270/14083).

[33] *Vitae Arch. Cant.*, p. 20 (Lambeth MS 99, fols. 136ᵛ-137ʳ), where (in both) "Septembris" is an error for "Decembris."

[34] Ibid., p. 21 (Lambeth MS 99, fol. 137ʳ).

[35] *HD*, p. 62 n. 2.

[36] "Astantibus ibidem multis."

sum of money which has to be paid on the king's behalf. On his authority I order you to make ready to cross the sea and meanwhile to appear before the king in London next Sunday to receive what is your due." [37] Stratford replied that such matters were too complex and weighty for an immediate answer; he would require time for deliberation. Some days later the archbishop's response was delivered to Edward, who found it little to his liking. The letter is no longer extant, but the author of the *Vitae* gives us the gist of its contents. Stratford, according to him, urged the king to maintain peace, as enjoined by his oath, and explained that he himself could not leave Canterbury for London because of the danger of death at the hands of some who were close to the monarch. [38] The archbishop was not yet prepared to risk a martyr's crown, but conscious of his responsibilities as St. Thomas's successor he was determined to remind Edward of his ancestor's folly and the foolishness of his own behaviour.

Murimuth states that Kilsby publicly accused the archbishop in the London Guildhall. If so, this marked the prelude to the more formal charges which had yet to be drawn up. [39] The occasion for Stratford's counter-attack was provided by the commemoration of the passion of St. Thomas, [40] which fell on Friday 29 December shortly after the carefree festivities of Christmas. After the offertory Stratford, who spoke in English so that the ordinary people could understand him, took as his text a passage from Ecclesiasticus: "In his time he did not fear the prince." [41] As he commended the life of his patron the contrast with his own became increasingly apparent. Towards the end of his address Stratford spoke specifically of his personal record. With sorrow he admitted that from the time of his elevation to the archiepiscopate he had been immersed in the secular affairs of king and kingdom; affairs which involved the oppression of the clergy and of the community of England and the raising of tenths for royal purposes. He humbly acknowledged his error and, like many an English bishop both before and after his time, lamented the consequent neglect of his spiritual functions. With tears in his eyes Stratford entreated

[37] Stratford acted as guarantor on a number of occasions, as did the other councillors, e.g. *Foedera* 2, iv, pp. 46-48; *CPR 1338-1340*, pp. 371-372, 384-385. See also Lucas, *Low Countries*, pp. 355, 426, 430.

[38] *Vitae Arch. Cant.*, pp. 21, 26 (Lambeth MS 99, fols. 137ʳ, 139ʳ). Stratford's letters are described as "responsales et exhortatorie."

[39] *Murimuth*, pp. 117-118.

[40] *Vitae Arch. Cant.*, p. 21 (Lambeth MS 99, fol. 137ʳ) where this is termed simply the "festum passionis."

[41] Ecclus. 48.13. This continues defiantly: "nor could anyone bring him into subjection."

his hearers for their forgiveness. It was his wish, he declared, to protect the rights and liberties of the church and of ecclesiastics and to assist the clergy and the whole community in parliament. In future he would devote himself exclusively to such matters and to the exercise of his pastoral office. To all outward appearances this was a radical change of heart fully in tune with that of St. Thomas, his illustrious predecessor on the throne of St. Augustine. But, continued Stratford on a more ominous note, there were men at the king's side who hated him,[42] who had arrested chancery clerks, justices and knights in defiance of Magna Carta, and had even been guilty of defaming him of treason. Whatever happened he intended to rise up against all such presumptuous persons. At this point a climax was reached. The archbishop, standing in his sacred vestments amidst the clergy of the city, with lighted candles in his hands and his cross held high, solemnly pronounced sentences of greater excommunication. One can imagine the awed hush which ensued as the candles were extinguished by being thrown to the ground as a sign of perdition.[43]

The sentences comprised six categories of offender: those who in any way diminished the liberties and customs of the church of Canterbury;[44] those who disturbed the peace of the realm;[45] those responsible for charters and statutes which infringed the provisions of Magna Carta that a free man should not be detained, imprisoned, deprived of his lands, or outlawed, or which contravened other charters of liberty or of the forest;[46]

---

[42] "Et quia in odium capitis dicti archiepiscopi quidam juxta latus regis sibi malevoli existentes quosdam clericos cancellarii regis ac etiam justiciarios et milites contra Magnam Cartam indebite arrestando, ac ipsum archiepiscopum de proditione nequiter diffamando."

[43] *Vitae Arch. Cant.*, pp. 21-22 (Lambeth MS 99, fol. 137^{r-v}). Excommunication could be "in genere," the offenders being unknown, or at any rate unnamed, or "nominatim." See *Worc. Admin.*, pp. 186-192, and in general, Logan, *Excommunication and the Secular Arm*.

[44] In the notes which follow details of the sentences are derived from *Vitae Arch. Cant.*, p. 22 (Lambeth MS 99, fol. 137^v) – an abbreviated and somewhat inaccurate summary – and the archiepiscopal mandate of 31 December 1340, *Sacrosancta ecclesia*, in WinRO 1, fols. 99^v-100^r. There are printed versions in, for example, *Hemingburgh* 2, pp. 375-380; *Walsingham* 1, pp. 237-240. The latter is collated with the Rochester entry by Charles Johnson, *Rochester Reg. Hethe*, pp. 653-655. At this point the reference is to "Omnes et singulos illos qui ecclesias suo iure privare," Oxford (1222), cap. 1; Reading (1279), cap. 11; Lambeth (1281), cap. 10. See *Councils and Synods*, pp. 106, 848-849, 906-907.

[45] "Illos qui pacem et tranquillitatem regis aut regni": Oxford (1222), cap. 2; Reading (1279), cap. 11 ii; Lambeth (1281), cap. 10 ii. See *Councils and Synods*, pp. 106-107, 849, 906.

[46] "Cum in Magna Carta Henrici ... quod nullus liber homo." See *Councils and Synods*, pp. 51, 137-138, 477-478. The "Age of Charters," in the sense of formal

those who laid hands on ecclesiastical property;[47] who imprisoned clerks and prevented their release;[48] and those who were guilty of defamation, more particularly of the greater clergy.[49]

As might be expected, there is nothing novel about these sentences. They are derived principally from the Council of Oxford (1222) as reiterated and expanded by Archbishop Pecham at the councils of Reading (1279) and Lambeth (1281).[50] Pecham, himself involved in a conflict with secular authority, had ordered the clergy to expound his sentences to their flocks on the Sunday after each rural chapter;[51] a measure, which if effective, would have made them very widely known indeed.[52] Another element, the confirmation of the charters, also had a remote ancestry. From the copy of the sentences distributed to the bishops of the province[53] it is clear that Stratford was referring to Henry III's reissue of Magna Carta and of the Charter of the Forest in 1225 (renewed by Edward I),[54] and he quotes verbatim from the sentence of excommunication against violators which was reluctantly accepted by the same king in 1253 and confirmed by Pope Innocent IV in the following year.[55] This particular sentence was republished by Archbishop Kilwardby in 1273 and is subsequently alluded to both by Pecham and Winchelsey.[56] It

confirmations, may have passed as Harriss (*King, Parliament and Public Finance*, p. 261) has remarked, but such documents remained extremely important in Stratford's thinking.

[47] "Omnes et singulos qui de domibus maneriis, grangiis aut locis aliis ad archiepiscopos, episcopos...": Reading (1279), cap. 11 ix; Lambeth (1281), cap. 10 ix. See *Councils and Synods*, pp. 849, 907.

[48] "Quia temporis malicia clericis laicos tradit infestos adeo quod ipsos capiunt et detine[n]t invitos." Cf. *Sext* 3, 23, 3: "Clericis laicos infestos oppido tradit antiquitas." The word "oppido" is in *Vitae Arch. Cant.* but not in WinRO 1, fol. 100ʳ. *Clericis laicos* (1296) was directed against the taxation of the clergy without papal authority. Stratford could have cited Archbishop Boniface's constitution *Contingit* (Lambeth 1261, cap. 9: *Councils and Synods*, p. 677), which refers to the excommunications of the earlier council of Oxford. Lyndwood glosses the pertinent point: "An laicus detinens clericum invitum sit excommunicatus" (*Const. Prov.*, p. 92 ad ver. *Contingit aliquando*). He concludes guardedly that excommunication might not lie in certain circumstances.

[49] "Cum omnes et singuli qui in nostra Cant. provincia alicui vel aliquibus crimen falso ex odii fomite maliciose imponunt": Oxford (1222), cap. 5; Reading (1279), cap. 11 v; Lambeth (1281), cap. 10 v. See *Councils and Synods*, pp. 107, 849, 906.

[50] See above, nn. 47-49.

[51] *Councils and Synods*, p. 848.

[52] Even before fourteenth-century regulations for promulgation. See Wright, *Church and Crown*, pp. 197-200ff.

[53] WinRO 1, fols. 99ᵛ-100ʳ, and see above, n. 44.

[54] *Councils and Synods*, pp. 137-138; *Statutes* 1, pp. 114ff.; WSRO Liber E, fols. 137ʳ-140ʳ. For Winchelsey's struggle to obtain the *Confirmatio cartarum* (1297) see Denton, *Robert Winchelsey*, pp. 136-176.

[55] *Councils and Synods*, pp. 474-479.

[56] Ibid., pp. 473 n. 3, 850.

features in William of Pagula's manual for priests, the *Oculus sacerdotis*, and its derivatives, and can be found in many manuscript collections of the statutes.[57] For Stratford it was an excellent weapon, having behind it the force not only of ecclesiastical authority, but of secular sanction as well. Another of the archbishop's denunciations – against those who defamed clerks – opens with words close to those of the incipit of Pope Boniface VIII's controversial canon *Clericis laicos* incorporated in the recent canonical collection known as *Sext*.[58]

There are several additional points worth making. Stratford was merely pronouncing sentences which had already been incurred *ipso facto*, that is as a direct consequence of specific infringements of canon law.[59] He deliberately avoided naming individuals,[60] thereby technically circumventing the charge of defamation, though this was to be brought against him none the less. With respect to the contravention of the charters, a fifteen-day respite was allowed so that offenders could make their peace with the ecclesiastical authorities.[61] Furthermore, Stratford was careful to attribute malpractice to the king's councillors rather than to Edward himself, who was expressly exempted from the excommunications.[62] Despite such conventional subterfuges, both parties were fully aware that this was to be a personal contest. What riled the king was Stratford's sweeping condemnation of his recent measures, coupled with the obvious pertinence of the sentences.

While at Canterbury Stratford sought the consolation and spiritual help of the brethren of his cathedral priory. At Hereford there exists a collection of sermons mainly devoted to such episcopal functions as the reconciliation of churches, visitation, ordination, and the assembly of prelates, but also with the commemoration of St. Thomas of Canterbury. These sermons, with their allusions to the troubled times of Edward II and Edward III, have been attributed to Stratford,[63] but not all of them are

---

[57] Ibid., pp. 474-475.

[58] *Sext* 3, 23, 3. See above, n. 48.

[59] See above, n. 43.

[60] "Quibus neminem diffamavimus cum nullum nominaverimus in eisdem." *Vitae Arch. Cant.*, p. 34 (Lambeth MS 99, fol. 143r).

[61] Ibid., p. 22 (Lambeth MS 99, fol. 137v), has "monuit, ut ea emendarent sub pena excommunicacionis majoris." Cf. WinRO 1, fol. 100r.

[62] This, of course, was regular practice and in accordance with papal privilege granted to the king. E.g. PRO S.C.7/11/20.

[63] Macray, "Sermons," pp. 85-86. "The period is found to be that of the reign of Edward III, and the internal evidence afforded by a sermon respecting the preacher's own trials ... points to the authorship of archbishop Stratford."

his.[64] Among those which strongly suggest Stratford's composition is one which must surely have been delivered during his "exile" in Canterbury. It constitutes a plea for help in time of trouble and persecution addressed to a monastic community. Taking his text from St. Paul's epistle to the Romans, "Help me by praying to God for me," [65] the preacher proceeds to give apposite advice to his congregation, reinforcing it with analogies to his own predicament. The applicability of these analogies to the archbishop's situation in late 1340 and the early months of 1341 is inescapable.[66]

Fortified by firm belief in the justice of his cause and relying on the sympathetic support of his cathedral monastery, Stratford formally joined battle with the sealing on 31 December of his letter *Sacrosancta ecclesia* in which the sentences of excommunication are prefaced by a spirited preamble in defence of ecclesiastical liberties. The archbishop's nephew, Ralph Stratford, in his capacity as dean of the province proceeded to circulate the letter to the comprovincial bishops. So expeditious was he that one bishop at least had his copy by 8 January.[67] For his part Edward had had enough of clerical ministers whom he was unable to discipline in the way he considered appropriate. He is said to have sworn that he would not have a cleric as chancellor or treasurer, or in any other high office, but only such men who, if they played him false, he could draw,

---

[64] As Bishop Kemp points out ("History and Action," p. 349), one of the Hereford sermons (on the text "Cecidit coronam capitis") assigned to the feast of St. Thomas the Martyr (MS P.5 XII, fols. 99ᵛff.) very probably dates from 29 December 1314, i.e. shortly before Piers Gaveston's burial at Langley, 2 January 1315 (BL Cotton MS Cleopatra D.iii, fol. 56ᵛ). The rubric (and end-note) to another copy of the sermon (Lambeth MS 61, fols. 143ʳ-147ᵛ) ascribes its delivery at Oxford to "M. Henry de Herclay." Harclay was a D.Th. and chancellor of Oxford (1312-1317). See *Biog. Oxon.*, s.v. Harkeley. Stratford as the university's proctor (above, "The Making of a Career") must have known him well; he could even have heard the sermon, which was preached "sollempniter in universitate Oxon." For a discussion about which of the Hereford sermons might be ascribed to Stratford see Kemp, "History and Action"; Haines, "Some Sermons at Hereford."

[65] Rom. 15.30.

[66] HCL MS P.5 XII, fols. 90ᵛ-92ᵛ: "Ad impetrandum subsidium oracionum in tribulacionibus et persecucionibus." Near the end he quotes from St. John's gospel (8.32), "Cognoscetis veritatem et veritas liberabit vos," a text used in his *excusaciones*, asking for the hearers' prayers "Ut pastoris officium quod ante hec tempora male dereliqui ... valeam sic assumere et exercere quod sit ad honorem Dei et salvacionem animarum." This sermon is now printed in Haines, "Some Sermons at Hereford." Its similarity to that of 29 December commented upon by the archbishop's biographer is clear, but the themes are different and there are fewer political allusions in the Hereford sermon than one might expect.

[67] WinRO 1, fol. 99ᵛ. See also *Exeter Reg. Grandisson*, pp. 933-935, where the bishop's executory mandates are dated 25 January.

hang or execute.[68] In the more sober words of Professor Tout, Edward wished to make his ministers "justiciable in the king's courts." [69] In pursuance of the new policy Sir Robert Bourchier was appointed chancellor[70] and the former chief justice of the king's bench, Sir Robert Parving, became treasurer.[71] In the case of the treasurership the king's anticlerical resolution lasted only for some nine months.[72]

News of the archbishop's attempt to win "popular support" at Canterbury and of his measures to resist what he rightly felt to be an incursion on ecclesiastical and other liberties must soon have reached the king. In any case, Stratford wrote to Edward on the first day of the new year. It is the letter of an elder statesman to a wayward young monarch. "In the multitude of councillors," he quoted, "there is safety," [73] and proceeded to give the well-worn example of Rehoboam, "who left the good counsel of his father and of the aged and wise men that had been with his father, and did according to the counsel of young men who would fain please him and who knew little." [74] Stratford then drew a risky parallel with Edward II's reign, reminding the king of the consequences of evil counsel and adding ominously: "What happened to him for that cause you, sire, do know." In his turn, alleged the archbishop, the king was acting against the law and the great charter "abetted by certain people of this land which are not so wise as were needful, and by others which seek rather their own profit than your honour or the safety of the land." Specifically, he was seizing clerks and others contrary to the charter. Reminding Edward of his coronation oath, Stratford advised him to reject such as "now make themselves governors and counsellors, more than their estate doth warrant," and to take instead "the great and the wise" of the country, conducting his affairs "by them and their counsels." Those near to the king who have charged their archbishop with treason are *ipso facto*

---

[68] *French Chronicle*, p. 86.

[69] *Chapters* 3, p. 124.

[70] Kilsby handed over the seal to him on appointment, 14 December 1340: *Foedera* (R.C.) 2, p. 1142. Parving succeeded Bourchier 28 October 1341. Tout, *Chapters* 6, pp. 13-14; *HBC*, p. 84. Of Offord's promotion to chancellor in 1345 *Murimuth* (p. 177) remarks: "Sicque officium cancellariae ad clericos quod prius per milites fere per septennium regebatur."

[71] Appointed 15 December 1340, admitted 16 January 1341. Tout, *Chapters* 6, p. 23; *HBC*, p. 101.

[72] William Cusance was appointed 28 October 1341: Tout, *Chapters* 3, p. 161; 6, p. 23. For Edward III's supposed anticlericalism, see ibid. 3, pp. 151ff., where the difficulties encountered by lay officials are discussed; also Wilkinson, *Chancery*, pp. 184-188.

[73] Prov. 24.6.

[74] 3 Kings 12.6-8.

excommunicate. Should it please the king to summon the prelates, great men and peers of the realm enquiry could be made as to what happened to the wool and other taxes raised on the king's behalf. Those guilty of any offence might then be punished according to the law. Saving the estate of Holy Church and of his order, Stratford expressed willingness to stand by the judgment of his peers. He asked the king not to countenance the evil things alleged against him: if people "shall be judged without answer judgment of the good and the evil shall be all one." The letter closed on a more conciliatory note. Given a common purpose the king's difficult undertakings could be successfully accomplished. It was as primate and as the king's spiritual father that he was moved to tell the truth about the whole situation.[75]

This pastoral letter, which some might consider self-important if not impertinent, fell on deaf ears. Edward determined to send another envoy to his "insubordinate" archbishop. This time it was Ralph Stafford, steward of the royal household, who reached Canterbury on 4 January 1341.[76] Having presented his credentials he requested details of the articles of excommunication. Stratford turned the question by pointing out that the articles were not of his devising. He had merely promulgated sentences already determined by the canons and constitutions of the holy fathers and of the church. Stafford then formally cited the archbishop to appear in London to answer to the king for his conduct of the business of the realm.[77] Stratford's reply was already extant in both his sermon and his letters – he would answer only in full parliament.[78] According to the archbishop's version of the incident the envoy brought no safe-conduct. All that he had to rely upon was Stafford's unsupported word that he

---

[75] *Hemingburgh* 2, pp. 363-367; *Walsingham* 1, pp. 231-234; *Avesbury*, pp. 324-327; *Foedera* (R.C.) 2, p. 1143 (from BL Cotton MS Claudius E.viii, fol. 252ʳ).

[76] *Vitae Arch. Cant.*, p. 22 (Lambeth MS 99, fol. 137ᵛ). According to Tout, *Chapters* 4, p. 108, Stafford's expense account (20s a day for six days) indicates that he engaged in two missions.

[77] *Vitae Arch. Cant.*, pp. 22, 26 (Lambeth MS 99, fols. 137ᵛ, 139ʳ). Dene (BL Cotton MS Faustina B.v, fol. 88ᵛ) declares that about St. Hilary (13 January) Edward summoned Stratford to his council in London: "Qui venire se excusans propter pericula que metuebat, asserens se libenter velle ad parliamentum regis sed non ad consilia venire."

[78] The precise meaning of the term "plenum parliamentum" is discussed at length by Wilkinson, *Studies*, chap. 1. He concludes (p. 4): "It seems probable, therefore, we must assume, that a 'plenum parliamentum' was normally an assembly including the prelates and lords. On no occasion was it merely the council, unless the term council can be used without qualification to indicate an assembly of parliament including ... the general body of magnates." This commonsense dictum accords with Stratford's own use of the terms. See previous note and *Vitae Arch. Cant.*, p. 31 (Lambeth MS 99, fol. 141ᵛ).

would not be molested if he made his way to London.[79] Edward
thereupon issued a safe-conduct which instructed royal officers to ensure
the archbishop's security on both the outgoing and return journeys.[80]

The safe-conduct could scarcely have arrived when Stratford made his
next move. This was to send a letter (dated 28 January) to the new lay
chancellor, Bourchier, setting out the terms under which the hard-pressed
clergy had agreed to the levying of an additional tenth and subsequently of
a ninth for two years.[81] The ninth, Stratford stressed, was not payable by
those liable for the tenth. Conversely, those from whom the ninth was
exacted – ecclesiastics holding by barony and regularly summoned to
parliament – were not under obligation to pay the tenth.[82] The business
was further complicated by the concurrent attempts to raise the cardinals'
procurations, "borrowed" by the king but after Stratford's protest in 1340
being recouped from the proceeds of the tenth.[83]

The Bourchier letter was followed by a similar one addressed to Stratford's fellow bishops. It was sent directly rather than through the usual
channel of the dean of the province.[84] The archbishop made much of the
sanctity of agreements freely entered into and of the ingratitude of those
who received favours.[85] If the illegalities of the collectors were permitted
to continue great damage and prejudice would accrue to the church from
the abuse of lay power; the faith itself would be subverted. In the event of
tenths or ninths being exacted other than in accordance with the terms of
their concession, those offending were to be compelled by ecclesiastical
censures. Should they not respond, collection of the residue of the tenth

---

[79] *Vitae Arch. Cant.*, p. 32 (Lambeth MS 99, fol. 142[r]): "nobis dixerat nudo verbo sic."
[80] *Foedera* 2, iv, p. 89; *CPR 1340-1343*, p. 124: 26 January 1341.
[81] *Hemingburgh* 2, pp. 367-369; *Walsingham* 1, pp. 234-235. See above, "In the Seat
of Power." Under Stratford's leadership the council in July 1340 had suspended collection
of the ninth other than from those summoned to parliament (*CCR 1339-1341*, p. 613).
The policy was reversed in January 1341. This "outrage on the church's liberty" brought a
protest to Stratford from the cathedral priory and other religious houses in Winchester
diocese. Roger Brian was sent to discuss the matter. *Winch. Chart.*, nos. 522-523.
[82] See previous note and for the letter to the bishops in the same terms below, n. 84.
[83] The royal writ to the bishops and to the collectors of the biennial tenth, permitting
once more the repayment of the sums withheld, is dated 20 March 1341 and entered, for
instance, in WinRO 2, fols. 171[v]-172[r]. See also *Worcester Reg. Bransford*, pp. 3, 67-68,
291, 311-312.
[84] See, for instance, WinRO 1, fols. 101[v], 101[r] (entry interrupted by other material);
Salisbury Reg. Wyville 1, fol. 61[r-v]; *Concilia* 2, pp. 659-660 (*Exeter Reg. Grandisson*,
pp. 937-938): *Cum animosa guerrarum.*
[85] "Cum igitur nichil magis congruat humane fidei quam ea que placuerunt inter
partes fideliter custodiri." WinRO 1, fol. 101[r]; *Concilia* 2, p. 660.

was to be suspended forthwith. The bishops were to certify what they had done by 1 May.[86]

Yet another letter was despatched by Stratford on 30 January, once again to the bishops.[87] Its language is equally uncompromising. The church, declared the metropolitan, ought to be free; in practice it was burdened with numerous exactions, levies and infamous tallages, some of them not agreed to by the clergy. The path of law has been abandoned, continued Stratford, truth has fallen before power, hate has driven out justice. Those engaged in impieties of this kind should be warned that the bishops – in the last resort the archbishop himself – bear the responsibility for their souls. Suffragans were to exhort their subjects to treat churches and ecclesiastical persons with due honour and to desist from inflicting injuries upon them. The letter concludes with a clarion call for the bishops to join their archbishop in the protection of the rights and liberties of church and realm – a process to which he himself had already given considerable impetus.[88]

In all this the archbishop was going no further than taking a firm stand against illegalities, the responsibility for which he placed firmly on the royal officers.[89] But by this time the new government had prepared a counter-attack. It could not afford the unpopularity that the archbishop's proceedings were certain to engender. A writ, dated 10 February, prohibited the episcopate from acting upon Stratford's instructions to excommunicate royal collectors who overstepped their functions.[90] At the same time a wide-ranging denunciation of Stratford's official career was circulated among the bishops and other prelates in an attempt to undermine his authority. This document has come down to us as the "libellus famosus," because Stratford dubbed it such in his reply.[91] In reality the term is a generic one, in regular use for pamphlets of a scurrilous, unpleasant or contentious nature.[92] Its authorship has often

---

[86] Ibid.

[87] See, for instance, WinRO 1, fol. 100ᵛ; *Concilia* 2, p. 660 (*Exeter Reg. Grandisson*, pp. 938-939): *Christi legacione fungentes.*

[88] "Vestros eciam subditos exhortacionibus efficacibus similiter inducentes ut ecclesias ecclesiasticasque personas plus solito habeant in honore et ab eorum iniuriis colentes iusticiam omnino desistant, necnon pro libertatibus et iuribus ecclesie et regni per nos ut speramus utiliter inchoata cum Dei adiutorio manutenere protegere et tueri ... Deus vos dirigat in agendis."

[89] E.g. in his letter to the bishops of the province mentioned above: "Absque dicti domini regis, ut credimus, conniventia." WinRO 1, fol. 101ʳ; *Concilia* 2, p. 660.

[90] E.g. WinRO 1, fol. 171ᵛ (al. 43ᵛ); *Foedera* 2, iv, p. 90.

[91] It is usually found in the plural form.

[92] It occurs, for instance, in contemporary papal registers.

been attributed to Bishop Orleton, on the grounds of his supposed scurrility and of his former antipathy to the archbishop, for which he had some justification stemming from the time when Stratford opposed his promotion to Winchester.[93] Despite Avesbury's assertion to the contrary, Orleton is unlikely to have been the author. At most he injected some criticism about the conduct of foreign affairs and the onset of the war with France, for both Orleton and Stratford had been engaged for many years in diplomatic service at the French court.[94]

Ancient histories have shown, the *libellus* begins, and they have been confirmed by modern experience, that many who have benefited from the kindness of kings have given way to pride. When King Edward was an adolescent he desired to be directed by wise counsel and thinking that Stratford, then bishop of Winchester, was pre-eminent in virtue and discretion, he determined to be guided by him both in matters concerning his soul's salvation and those involving the good estate of the realm. The archbishop was accepted into such close contact with the king as to be entitled "our father" and revered by all as second only to Edward himself.[95] When the kingdom of France devolved on Edward by right of succession, it being notoriously occupied *de facto* by Philip of Valois, the archbishop pressed him to ally with the princes of Germany and with others against Philip and thus to expose himself to the expenses of war, promising to raise the necessary money from the issues of the royal lands and by means of subsidies. He had further suggested that the king would be assisted by a people vigorous and experienced in war. Fortified by these promises the king crossed the sea and, as was appropriate, incurred large expenses for warlike preparation and undertook to pay substantial sums of money to his allies, confident of the promised aid from home. But how he was misled! He had relied on a staff that turned out to be a broken reed, which when leaned upon merely pierced the skin of the hand which held it.[96] Hopes of subsidy were dashed, not without suspicion of fraud. As a result the king was obliged to contract heavy debts at such high rates of interest as to be virtually insupportable. His original plan abandoned,

---

[93] See Haines, *Church and Politics*, pp. 61-63, 194-197.

[94] For Orleton's diplomatic activity, ibid., chap. 2.

[95] "Ac illam in se humanitatem expertus; ut pater noster vocaretur, et adoraretur ab omnibus post regem secundus." The *libellus famosus* is most readily available in *Vitae Arch. Cant.*, pp. 23-27 (Lambeth MS 99, fols. 138ʳ-139ᵛ) – from which I quote in the notes which follow; *Concilia* 2, pp. 661-663 (from Parker, *De Antiquitate*); *Foedera* 2, iv, pp. 90-91 (copy addressed to Bishop Ralph Stratford). ECL MS no. 2227 (cited *HMCR*, Var. Coll. IV, p. 75) is an original. Copies are dated 10 or 12 February.

[96] Is. 36.6.

he was forced to return to England,[97] where he explained his predicament to the archbishop and summoned a parliament, which granted a ninth.[98] Some have considered that had the ninth and the previously conceded tenth been collected faithfully they might well have sufficed for the royal needs. At any rate, trusting in the archbishop's renewed promises to raise the money effectively, the king sailed to Flanders.[99] After gaining a great naval victory at Sluys,[100] he began the siege of Tournai in silent expectation of the promised assistance from England. Frustrated of this hope, he had been compelled to accept a truce at the very moment of his triumph. For despite the fact that the royal needs had been made known to the archbishop and to the councillors around him, Stratford had fobbed off the king with frivolous excuses. On his return to Flanders lack of money forced the king to resort once more to the whirlpool of usury in order to pay those fighting in his service. At length, after discussing the impasse with his faithful friends, comrades of his pilgrimage and its hardships, it became clear that blame, inactivity, not to say malice, were attributable to the archbishop, the person entrusted with the government of the realm. All agreed that it was an intolerable situation and that if appropriate remedy were not forthcoming they would withdraw from the royal service and resile from the truce, to the subversion of the realm, the king's perpetual ignominy, and the everlasting reproach of the English nation. Thereupon the king turned his attention to the correction and discipline of the officials he had removed from office, men who there was reason to believe were guilty of maladministration, subversion of justice, oppression of his subjects, corruption, and other serious offences. He had proceeded to imprison both these and lesser offenders to ensure that justice would be done and proper enquiry made as to the truth. It was particularly important, in view of the concealment practised by the archbishop, to consult him as the person exercising the highest position in the land.

Having thus outlined the basic case against the archbishop, the *libellus* proceeds to give details of the unsuccessful attempts of Cantilupe and Stafford to persuade him to come before the king in London. The author is withering in his scorn. That the archbishop – so tumescent in

[97] The king was absent in the Low Countries 16 July 1338 - 21 February 1340. For what follows cf. above, "In the Seat of Power."

[98] Parliament was summoned on the day of Edward's return and met 29 March 1340.

[99] He sailed 22 June 1340, two days after Stratford's surrender of the great seal.

[100] 24 June 1340.

prosperity, so timorous in adversity[101] – should have trembled for his life
is made to seem ludicrous. Nothing of the kind crossed the king's mind or
was considered by those around him, even though the archbishop had
made himself hateful by his ill-will towards clergy and people. Naturally,
the *libellus* argues, the king desired the safety of all those summoned
before him, whether by letter or by messenger. The archbishop, a man
accorded great honour by the king, behaved like a father so long as his
every wish was granted, then suddenly changed into a heavy stepfather,
ungrateful and arrogant. In the words of the proverb he was to his host:
"Mus in pera, serpens in gremio, ignis in sinu." The king, in the exercise
of government by hereditary right and by God's grace, has always
endeavoured to rule his subjects with appropriate justice and in peace.

Regardless of this fact, the archbishop has brought into question the
king's good faith and that of his ministers by preaching and publishing in
various places his view that nowadays the people are unjustly oppressed,
the clergy thrown into confusion, and the church weighed down by
numerous exactions. Never, asserts the *libellus*, has the archbishop borne
the title of "good shepherd." Far from it, he has himself confessed to being
a "hireling." [102] With fox-like cunning he has simulated zeal for the
church's liberation.[103] Yet, if any such vexations have been suffered by
church or clergy, they ought more truthfully to be ascribed to the neglect
or sly invention of the archbishop and his misguided counsel. His
sentences of excommunication insult the king's reputation, defame his
ministers, incite sedition among the people, and serve to withdraw the
magnates from their devotion to the royal majesty. Contrary to the
practice laid down in provincial council, certain articles have been
published in prominent places by means of archiepiscopal letters.[104] This
has compelled the king to speak out in defence of his reputation and
integrity in an effort to circumscribe the archbishop's malice and to evade
the snares prepared for himself and his ministers. For the present he

[101] "Ipse vero semper tumidus in prosperis, et timidus in adversis, trepidans timore,
ubi non est timor."
[102] John 10.14. As we have seen, in his sermon of 29 December Stratford bemoaned
his preoccupation with secular affairs. See above, n. 66.
[103] "Fucatum zelum vulpinae calliditatis fuco perizomate palliatum." It may be noted
that the proverbial language in which this particular part of the attack is couched finds an
echo in Edward ii's denunciation of Orleton to the pope in 1325: "Ignem in sinu portare et
in gremio fovere serpentem." *Foedera* 2, iv, p. 137. See below, n. 135.
[104] "Specificatis nonnullis articulis praeter et contra solitum modum in concilio
provinciali traditum mandavit, per suas literas in pluribus locis insignibus publicari." I am
uncertain of the purport of this allegation. It seems to imply that Stratford acted
improperly by operating directly rather than through his suffragans.

intends to remain silent about many of the archbishop's misdeeds, but to bring others to public notice.

At this point the *libellus* breaks off its interpretation of recent events to make additional accusations of malpractice. It was, it alleges, the archbishop's improvident counsel, the king being a minor, that had prompted so many gifts and unlawful alienations as to exhaust the treasury and greatly diminish the royal revenues. Corrupted by gifts, Stratford remitted debts without reasonable cause and applied to his own purposes, or those of his friends, profits and income which should have been retained for the king's necessities. Not only was he an accepter of gifts, but also an accepter of persons.[105] In contravention of his oath of fealty he had removed worthy men from office and substituted others who were unsuitable, to the detriment of the king's estate and of the royal dignity, to the people's harm, and in abuse of the power he was exercising. If he continues in such obstinacy and rebelliousness, the *libellus* threateningly concludes, the king will deal with him openly at a suitable time and place. Such was the indictment, in many respects an obvious travesty of fact, sometimes abusive, and at a number of points vague, there being a reluctance to quote specific instances. It elicited from Stratford a reply, the main criticism of which must be its rather pedestrian quality and excessive length, though the latter fault is partly due to the accepted practice of repeating the accusations individually before proceeding to their refutation.[106]

Stratford's *excusaciones* open with a statement of political philosophy on traditional lines, unaffected by current theories of a less stereotyped kind.[107] The world, he declares, is ruled principally by two authorities: sacred pontifical authority and royal power ordained [of God]. The authority of priests is the more important and exalted of these, as is to be seen from the fact that it is they who have to render account of kings at the last judgment.[108] The king's highness must be aware that it is he who

---

[105] This is one of a number of examples of a play on words to be found in the *libellus*. "Qui etiam nedum munerum sed et personarum acceptor contra votum nostrum."

[106] Orleton, in his reply (*responsiones*) to accusations made against him in 1334 used the same method which, of course, was common practice in the return of mandates of all kinds.

[107] On the continent a pamphlet war was being waged between the supporters of Louis of Bavaria and those of the pope – William of Ockham being a participant. Current theories are examined by Wilks, *The Problem of Sovereignty*, but Stratford, like Orleton, appears to have been singularly uninfluenced by "modern concepts." Both men were trained in canon law and looked in that direction for their authority.

[108] "Sacra pontificalis auctoritas et regalis ordinata potestas, in quibus est pondus tanto gravius et sublimius sacerdotum." This is the Gelasian dictum incorporated in Gratian,

relies on their judgment rather than they who are under direction of the royal will. Who can doubt, the archbishop asks, that the priests of Christ are to be considered as the fathers and mentors of kings, princes, and of all the faithful? [109] Surely it would be foolish if a son were to attempt to subjugate his father or a student his master? Canonical writings testify that bishops have often sentenced kings and princes. Thus Pope Innocent excommunicated the emperor Arcadius for permitting John Chrysostom to be violently expelled from his see, [110] while Bishop Ambrose of Milan took similar action against the emperor Theodosius, who earned absolution only after rendering condign satisfaction. [111] A good prince, asserts Stratford, should restore damaged churches, build new ones, and protect and honour the priests of God. For instance, when the question of the position of clerks was put to Constantine, he replied: "You cannot be judged by anyone." [112] This follows the apostle's dictum: "He that is spiritual is judged of no man." [113] Consider, resumes Stratford in a paternal tone which could only have irritated the king, how great is the penalty whether by human or divine law for a son who should defame an innocent father to whom he owes reverence and honour. Even pagan princes rendered honour to the priests of their temples, whom they called "Flamines." [114] How much greater, he asks, should be the reverence of Christian rulers for the ministers of Christ and for bishops? For shame! The honour due to the archbishop as a father by virtue of his dignity, however unworthy, is turned into reproach, devotion into blasphemy, and reverence into contempt. All this by reason of the king's letters patent, more correctly *libelli famosi*, concocted and written by the archbishop's enemies and those envious of him, which attribute to him various crimes and enormities and require that they be published by his suffragans of the Canterbury province; a move calculated to render lukewarm the devotion of his subjects and to turn obedience into contempt. One can learn from

Decretum D.96, c. 10. For discussion of this functional distinction see Ullman, *Papal Government*, pp. 20-21ff.; Wilks, *The Problem of Sovereignty*, pp. 266-267ff.

[109] This is derived from *Decretum* D.96, c. 9: letter from Pope Gregory VII to the bishop of Metz.

[110] The two cases are cited from *Decretum* D.96, c. 10. Chrysostom was expelled from his see of Constantinople by the agency of the empress Eudoxia.

[111] Ambrose, a fourth century bishop of Milan, rebuked the emperor for his massacre of the rebellious Thessalonians.

[112] *Decretum* C.11, qu. 1, c. 41: "Dignum non est quod nos iudicemus deos." See Rufinus's rendering of Eusebius cited in Haines, "Defence Brief," p. 238; Ullman, *Papal Government*, pp. 39-40.

[113] 1 Cor. 2.15. Cf. *Extrav. Commun.* 1, 8, 1.

[114] There were fifteen *Flamines* attached to particular deities in Rome.

the wise monarch Solomon that power comes from the Lord and virtue is infused from on high.[115] To judge God in the persons of his ministers and priests is to act in opposition to divine and human law, as well as human reason.[116] The archbishop, the king's spiritual father, the principal peer of the land (par terre maior), has been condemned unheard – neither summoned, nor convicted "per recordum vestrum," as the saying goes. Such conduct redounds to the peril of the king's soul and to the manifest prejudice and pernicious example of all the peers of the realm.

It should not be assumed, cautions Stratford, that consciousness of guilt caused him to adopt a subterfuge for avoiding the king's enquiries. There was no one he would rather see than the king, both to advise him with respect to the perils of the realm and to inform him of the adulation of his people. He suspects, too, that on seeing his face the king will be reminded of the labours he has performed in his service. But most of all he is anxious to restore his good fame – so cruelly lacerated by the *libellus* – in the sight of the king, the prelates, and the peers of the realm. What prevented him were the threats of death uttered by some of the king's chief councillors, acting not as Joseph in Egypt but as the many kings who sat on the ground while one who had never been considered bore the diadem.[117] Neither pride nor disobedience held him back from Edward's presence, solely a well-founded fear of the consequences. He was every ready to obey the king's majesty in all things, saving the honour of God, the status of Holy Church, and his own order. But while the "tyrants" continue to exercise authority he must establish his innocence by responding to the allegations in the *libellus* one by one.

First, as to his responsibility for affairs during the early years of the king's reign, while Edward was still under age, the facts are so notorious that they require little explanation from him. At the time he was bishop of Winchester the whole kingdom is aware by whose counsel the king was ruled.[118] When the question of the realm of France arose following the death [February 1328] of King Charles, brother of the queen mother [Isabella], the issue came before the Northampton parliament.[119] There it was determined that France had devolved on the English monarch by hereditary right, whereupon the bishops of Worcester [Orleton] and of Coventry and Lichfield [Northburgh] were commissioned to vindicate the

---

[115] Sap. 6.2-4.
[116] Cf. *Decretum* C.11, qu. 1, c. 41.
[117] Ecclus. 11.5.
[118] The king at that time was under the aegis of Roger Mortimer and Queen Isabella.
[119] This met 24 April 1328. See above, "Lancastrian Spokesman."

claim and to impede the coronation of the new king. According to this instruction they turned their steps towards France. It was their embassy that provided the principal occasion for the present war.[120] As for himself, Stratford argues, he could not have adopted any specific attitude towards the king during his adolescence, for he took no part in royal business, being considered odious to all those at court, for what reason God alone knows. Later, in changed circumstances, it pleased the king that he should take part in royal affairs with the other secretaries in an endeavour to secure peace between England and France and thus to obviate dangers to body and soul posed by the threatened war. He had laboured long in this cause, crossing the sea many times, encountering danger, hard work, and great expense in his endeavours to secure personal audience with Philip of Valois. Every effort was made for peace but Philip, asp-like, refused to listen. Two special envoys were therefore sent, the bishops of Durham [Bury] and Winchester [Orleton],[121] and then again the bishop of Lincoln [Burghersh], William de Montacute and William de Clinton, now earls of Salisbury and Huntingdon respectively.[122] But these men could neither secure peace nor delay the war. In fact, while the envoys were still abroad, Philip gave instructions to destroy the men and ships of England and to invade Gascony.[123] Thus it was not the king of England's fault but Philip's that the war began. Moreover, claims Stratford, it was not his own doing but a consequence of the deliberation and assent of parliament at Westminster,[124] and because of Philip's continued obstinacy, that the policy of alliance with the Germans was begun.

Stratford then turned to the question of supply. It was the council of Stamford that saw the drawing up in his presence of agreements with certain merchants, the form of which could be examined in chancery.[125] Had these been honoured, as was his wish and that of all the other royal councillors, they would have sufficed, in conjunction with other subsidies and customs dues, for the whole war. The king's majesty should know that he did not violate or change these agreements, nor did any part of such subsidies come into his hands. If misfortune has stemmed from shortage of money, he regrets this, but the cause should be attributed to those who breached the agreements and either spent or squandered the subsidies, rather than to himself who has borne the burden and heat of the

---

[120] Ibid., n. 16.
[121] This refers to the embassy of July 1336. See Haines, *Church and Politics*, pp. 38-39.
[122] In April 1337. See *Foedera* 2, iii, p. 165; also above, "In the Seat of Power."
[123] Philip confiscated the duchy 24 May 1337. See Déprez, *Les préliminaires*, p. 154.
[124] A reference to the parliament of March 1337. See above, "In the Seat of Power."
[125] This met in late May and June. See above, "In the Seat of Power," nn. 212-213.

day. In any case, after the king's first crossing [in 1338] he, Stratford, did not in fact stay in the country, but journeyed with the cardinals and the bishop of Durham to the king, then in Brabant, coming and going on a number of occasions. Peace being despaired of, and finally abandoned, together with other prelates and barons he undertook heavy obligations with respect to the large sums contracted at usury on the king's behalf. Far from being a broken reed, he should rather be compared with that strong staff by which Jacob crossed the Jordan.[126]

Then there was the question of the king's lack of resources at Tournai, which forced his return to England. The king should know, argues Stratford, that before the second crossing to the continent the whole of that part of the ninth to be collected in the first year had been assigned to royal creditors, both by his own consent and that of his council, a fact which could be ascertained from the assignments themselves. Thus when the siege was undertaken – and he, Stratford, did not know of its commencement[127] – nothing could be transmitted to the king, nor had anything been promised.[128] Delay in the payment of the subsidy could not possibly be attributed to him; the terms had been arranged in full parliament. On that account he and other councillors had informed Edward that without his presence they could not provide assistance. It was not a matter of false councillors but of truthful servants. In the words of the evangelist: "You shall know the truth and the truth shall make you free." [129] And so it would turn out, God willing! Very little if any of the subsidy had been paid before the king's second return,[130] but everything would soon be in the hands of the present councillors. Hopefully they would dispense it in the future to the king's honour! As for the claim that following the siege and the king's return to Flanders the dearth of money was due to the failure of his ministers, Stratford insists that he made no promises, hence he could not be accused of fraud or negligence on that account. As in the past he had faithfully executed royal mandates – "God himself will not require more of a man than he can manage." [131] With respect to the

[126] "Non in illusoris baculo arundineo spem vestram nostris consideratis operibus posuistis ... sed in baculo firmissimo illi simili in quo Jacob Jordanem transivit." Cf. Is. 36.6.

[127] "Cujus etiam obsidionis initium ignoravimus." This is an interesting assertion. It appears that news of the royal action was first brought to the July 1340 parliament. *Rot. Parl.* 2, p. 118 no. 8.

[128] "Nihil Deo teste transmittere potuimus nec promisimus destinare."

[129] John 8.32.

[130] On 30 November 1340.

[131] "Ultra posse viri non vult Deus ulla requiri."

demand of the king's friends for appropriate remedy, Stratford declares himself to have been given the impression that those guilty of faults would be punished. In practice, clerks exempt from secular power as well as free men have suffered arrest in violation of the laws and customs of the realm and have been detained against their will. Whatever their offences, the king cannot be ignorant of the peril to souls arising from such action, for not only are these matters made plain in the holy constitutions, they have also been published throughout the province of Canterbury. It is to be feared that such processes will turn the hearts of the people from the king.

Stratford then addressed himself to the demands made upon him by the king's messengers. They could not be kept secret, having been recorded by notaries and made known to large numbers of people. The peremptory summons by Nicholas de Cantilupe to be in Brabant within eight days and the bald words of Ralph Stafford, "I cite you to take yourself before the king," were contradictory: a requirement to be in Brabant and simultaneously to remain in England![132] With due respect, it might appear at first glance that the royal letters of safe-conduct would be adequate, that is had he been summoned as a member of the royal council, but such was not the case. Yet, on the very same day a writ of *venire facias* was addressed to the sheriff of Kent to secure his appearance before the council in London to respond to a charge of contempt. God knows what zeal for justice had conceived such a plan! On the one hand the safe-conduct permitted him to return, on the other the nature of the writ imposed on him the necessity of remaining in the hands of his enemies. This ill became the king's majesty. None the less, Stratford concludes, he would always be prepared to answer before the prelates, magnates and peers of the realm and to obey the judgment of the peers in all things, saving his status and order. But those who endeavoured to prevent the meeting of parliament were merely avoiding the truth: "For everyone that doeth evil hateth the light."[133]

The archbishop then directed his attention to the charge of ingratitude. This he attributes to the odiousness of the author of the *libellus* rather than to its sender. He launches his argument with a text from St. Mark's gospel: "There is no man who hath left on my account father and mother, wife or children, house or lands, who shall not receive back an hundredfold and possess eternal life." From the time that he became engaged spiritually in the royal service he worked for the king's honour and the safety of the

[132] "Videbantur cuique circumspecto repugnantia continere, in Brabantiam videlicet divertere et in Anglia pro informationibus hujusmodi obtinendis jugiter permanere."
[133] John 3.20.

realm to the best of the ability given to him by God. Not only did he give up his father, family and wife – that is the church – his spiritual children and the care and improvement of his lands, but by day and night he journeyed sleeplessly, both at home and abroad, and so depleted his temporal goods that he resembled a pauper.[134] Are these the doings of a stepfather? Let God judge! In reality he has been a good father to the king, but on his account a burdensome stepfather to his spiritual children. As for being a *mus in pera*, he has gnawed his own things rather than the king's. It is the prudence of the serpent he has shown, not the malice of venom in the lap. The fire he is said to have kindled in the king's breast is the fire of divine law and of charity. The return he has rendered for royal benefits and honours cannot be diminished before the Most High despite the malice of the author of the *libellus*. In future he will not benefit from the collation or procuration of secular princes but from God's liberality, "Who giveth to all men liberally and upbraideth not." [135] Far from impugning the king's innocence or the actions of those of his councillors and officers who have proceeded justly, he has ever been zealous in preserving the king's good name and diligent in requiring the prayers of the royal subjects for his safety and the favourable outcome of his affairs. Yet, by the damnable presumption of some of the royal officers, but without Edward's knowledge, the people are oppressed contrary to justice and both clergy and people are burdened by numerous taxes. For now things are exacted from the clergy which they have never conceded. The people are ruled by new and unaccustomed laws; scarcely able to afford food they will be reduced to abject poverty – to the king's disgrace. As for those responsible, the archbishop has named no one and has therefore harmed no one. He has acted from no perverse intention, but to enable his royal majesty to provide appropriate remedy and to prevent the devotion of the people from being adversely affected by unlawful *gravamina*

At this juncture Stratford turned to rebut some of the more scurrilous imputations of the *libellus*, commencing with the cheap jibe that on his own admission he was no "good shepherd" but a "hireling." This, he argues, is a matter of scriptural exegesis. God alone is the good shepherd. In preaching that he was not a good shepherd he was following the Saviour's own teaching: "I am the good shepherd" and "There is none good but one, that is, God." [136] While not presuming to usurp the title of

[134] "Bona nostra temporalia expendendo quasi pauperes facti sumus." See below, n. 141.
[135] James 1.5. "Mus in pera, ignis in sinu, serpens in gremio": *Decretum* C.13, qu. 1, c. 1 (pars 3, para 11).
[136] John 10.11; Mat. 19.17.

"good shepherd" he rejects the imputation of vulpine cunning. Whatever he may be, he has always worked for the relief of the king's necessities and the utility of the realm. He has procured many subsidies towards the repulsion of enemies of the realm and of the church – a heavy burden laid upon the clergy. Stratford then alluded to the charge of treachery arising out of his publication of sentences of excommunication. There could be no question of his being tried before a secular court, for no king or temporal lord was competent to act as judge. He wishes to make public protestation that no words of his, present or future, are to be taken as prejudicing his status in this respect. However, extrajudicially he is prepared to assert his innocence. His sentences were published with exception of the king and his family and since he mentioned no names he defamed no one. *Pace* the author of the *libellus* he has not thereby traitorously aroused sedition.[137]

The archbishop next sought to refute the accusations tacked on to the end of the *libellus*. To suggest that when the king was young he had encouraged him in alienations to the exhaustion of his treasury and in abuse of his office, that he had accepted bribes and engaged in peculation contrary to his oath of fealty, was tantamount to a charge of perjury *per viam criminis*. In such a matter the king could not be his judge. But to general statements he would respond generally. He has always served the king faithfully and given wise counsel in accordance with the discretion God has given him. He denies giving assent to prodigal gifts, prohibited alienations, or remission of debts without reasonable cause, and being corrupted by favours. On the contrary, he has opposed many such gifts and received little thanks for so doing. The only substantial ones he can recall – of which he had knowledge and for which he was present – involved the recent creation of earls with the consent of parliament in the royal palace of Westminster, which he believed then, and still believes, to have been for the king's good and honour rather then to his prejudice.[138] Experience has shown how much the recipients have

---

[137] "Nec per hoc in populo, salva dictantis reverentia, seditionem proditorie procuravimus." Bellamy, *Law of Treason*, pp. 66-67, suggests that the charge in the *libellus* "sounds very much akin to accroaching" (on royal power), but that Stratford chose to interpret it as an accusation of treason. Moreover, because no formal indictment exists, we do not know the construction put on the archbishop's deeds by Edward. Cf. Haines, "Defence Brief."

[138] Parry, *Parliaments*, p. 104 n. q, who points out that the parliament (of March 1337) merely concurred in the creations. Tout, *Chapters* 3, pp. 36-39, comments: "Similar marks of royal favour were extended in every direction. Hereditary offices and jurisdictions were scattered in a way hardly compatible with the interests of the crown, or with sound finance." But, we may ask, can Stratford be held responsible for this? Hughes,

suffered and continue to suffer for the king. Likewise, he cannot on the spur of the moment recall excessive remissions, unless it be of the debts of the whole English parliament assembled at Westminster, at the time the ninth was granted. The community of the realm would not consent to the grant under any other conditions.[139] As to the charge of misappropriation, continues Stratford, he has done nothing of the kind. On royal business he has crossed the sea thirty-two times as well as journeying to Scotland on numerous occasions. From the beginning of the war until the present he has received only three hundred pounds towards his expenses. "O that my grief were thoroughly weighed, and my calamity laid in the balance together!"[140] Never has he been an accepter of persons. The king's purpose has always been given precedence; worthy persons have been appointed to office, and he has not received bribes.

Thus, Stratford sums up, a sufficient reply has been given to the *libellus famosus*, and would that for the king's honour it had never been issued! At first glance the document might seem to cast doubt on his own reputation, but when properly considered it will show that those who have concocted it, or given counsel or consent with respect to it, are themselves not without stain of treachery to the king and kingdom.

The archbishop's reply is a formidable document hard to fault on points of factual detail, though obviously these are made to bear his own particular interpretation. For the most part the *libellus* had tossed out ill-defined allegations. Stratford's tactic was either to deny them in the same general terms, or alternatively to counter them with specific instance. On a broader front the archbishop was careful to distinguish the accusations which could be reduced to charges of treason or perjury. On neither of these counts could he, or would he, submit to a secular judge. He was prepared to defend his administrative record, but only in "full parliament." It was in this forum, he insisted, that all the political decisions complained of had been made: to claim the French crown, to build up a German alliance and, of course, to make grants of taxation and

---

A Study of Edward III, argued (pp. 126-127) from the number of grants on the charter rolls that concessions were more lavish (on average) for the period 1330-1337, than for 1338-1344, which she viewed as a time when Edward was asserting his personal authority in such matters. One would need to examine the nature of the grants and to be somewhat chary about laying them at Stratford's door on the grounds that he was chancellor or a prominent councillor. Other evidence demonstrates Edward's profligacy in economic matters.

[139] "Nec alio modo consentire voluit dicta communitas ad nonae predictae subsidium faciendum." *Statutes* 1, p. 281 (14 Edward III, stat. 1, cap. 3); also above, "In the Seat of Power."

[140] Job 6.2.

to fix their dates of payment. Here we have a clear statement of collective responsibility.[141]

Copies of the *libellus famosus* were dated either 10 or 12 February 1341.[142] Within a week or so they were widely distributed among bishops and other prelates.[143] It was on Sunday the 18th that William Kilsby arrived in person at Canterbury accompanied by merchants from Brabant. According to Prior Hathbrand they were ostensibly on pilgrimage, so he offered them refreshment. The merchants claimed to represent the duke of Brabant and on reaching the cathedral priory craved audience with the archbishop. Stratford, suspicious of their intentions, sent Thomas de Brochull one of his knights, together with the notary Simon of Charing. They gave permission for the merchants to have an interview with their master, but objected to one of the accompanying notaries, Geoffrey Baron, who on account of his connection with St. Augustine's Abbey was deemed *persona non grata*. Eventually the merchants withdrew for consultation with Kilsby. What followed is regarded by Stratford's biographer as quite unprecedented. Though they had no royal mandate, Kilsby and his associates proclaimed to those whom they had caused to assemble at the cross outside the priory gate that because of his obligation for the debts of the English king, the archbishop should go to Flanders and remain there until these had been discharged. Kilsby and his companions then hastily withdrew from the city.[144] The cathedral prior's account, contained in a letter asking help of the earl of Huntingdon, is rather different. He was more anxious about a pronouncement that he had failed to receive a royal messenger carrying letters addressed to him. This was merely a trick, but Hathbrand did not want to be branded as disobedient. On Stratford's advice a counter-declaration was made, this too at the cross outside the priory, to the effect that no such messenger had sought audience of the prior.[145]

---

[141] Some caveats have been entered against Stratford's presentation. Fryde, "Edward III's Removal of Ministers," p. 158, argues that Stratford, like Molyns, "was quickly repaid any debts the king owed him, even in difficult times when other magnates were more accommodating." Hughes, *A Study of Edward III*, p. 135, was not convinced that the first year of the ninth was pledged to creditors by advice of the whole council and further contended that Stratford "glossed over" non-payment of creditors. She aknowledged his dexterity (ibid., p. 136).

[142] See Tout, *Chapters* 3, p. 128 n. 1; also above, n. 95.

[143] It was clearly available in Canterbury by 21 February. *Vitae Arch. Cant.*, p. 23 (Lambeth MS 99, fol. 138[r]).

[144] Ibid., pp. 22-23 (Lambeth MS 99, fols. 137[v]-138[r]). The chronicler's account accords fairly well with the Canterbury prior's relation of the incident in a letter to the earl of Huntingdon. *Lit. Cant.* 2, pp. 226-230 (696); CCL Liber L, fol. 76[r]. But see below.

[145] *Lit. Cant.* 2, pp. 226-230 (696) (see previous note).

Three days later, Ash Wednesday, Stratford preached in the cathedral on the text: "Turn unto Me with your whole heart," [146] calling upon the people to confess their sins during the following week, with promise of a twenty days' indulgence for those who did so. On completing his sermon the archbishop announced the arrival of certain letters patent – the *libellus famosus* – which were directed to the prior with the order to publish them. They were read article by article in English, after which Stratford asserted his innocence and replied to them seriatim. At the end of this lengthy process he asked those present to pray for the king, the queen, and their children, with promise of a forty days' indulgence for those who complied, being duly penitent, and also for those who listened to his sermon. The hostile action of the abbot of the neighbouring Augustinian house on receiving his copy of the *libellus*[147] was allegedly due to personal antipathy for Stratford, though it more likely stemmed from jurisdictional conflict between the abbey and the metropolitans.[148] The abbot published and commented upon the *libellus* but ignored Stratford's version of what had happened.[149] Copies of the *libellus* were accompanied or closely followed by a writ *Cum vos et ceteri prelati*, which alleged that bishops had inhibited religious and other persons, under threat of excommunication, from paying the ninth and the king's servants from collecting it. Edward forbade the publication of sentences against his officers, but conceded that it was not his intention that clergy who paid the ninth should be compelled also to render the tenth.[150] This writ was, of course, a riposte to the mandate Stratford had issued to his suffragans in January.[151]

The king now determined to reinforce his case against the archbishop at the curia. This he did in a letter reiterating the arguments of the *libellus*, which he despatched with M. John Walwayn and Brother Thomas de Lisle, prior of the Dominican friars at Winchester. These envoys were instructed to liaise with William of Norwich (de Norwyco), dean of Lincoln, who was already in Avignon.[152] The case originally presented to the pope and cardinals in November 1340 by the royal agents – William of Norwich, Archdeacon John de Offord and John de Thoresby – anticipated much of the argument of the *libellus*, but there are additional

---

[146] Joel 2.13.

[147] *Vitae Arch. Cant.*, p. 23 (Lambeth MS 99, fol. 138r).

[148] For which see *Thorne*, cols. 2039ff., 2068ff.

[149] *Vitae Arch. Cant.*, p. 23 (Lambeth MS 99, fol. 138r): "Idem abbas singula contenta in his literis regiis populo astanti exposuit ac publicavit in odium dicti archiepiscopi."

[150] *Foedera* 2, iv, p. 90: 10 February 1341; WinRO 1, fol. 171v (al. 43).

[151] *Cum animosa guerrarum pericula*. See above, n. 84.

[152] *Foedera* 2, iv, p. 95: Langley, 14 March 1341; *Concilia* 2, pp. 671-672.

elements. For instance, King Philip is said to have replied to Edward's proposals for a settlement: "All will not be well until a single king rules over both France and England." [153] The theme was allegedly adopted with enthusiasm by Stratford in a sermon preached in London before a large congregation of prelates, earls, barons and people. This, the story goes, prompted the king, who had come of age, to call a parliament. [154] There, by the counsel of all, but especially of Stratford, it was determined that as peace was unobtainable by moderate means (per viam humilitatis), Edward's right should be asserted, if necessary by force of arms. On the death of his uncle Charles, the throne of France devolved on him as the next male heir; such was the view sustained by doctors and advocates of the Roman curia and of the universities of Paris and Oxford, as well as by all the most distinguished and learned prelates of England. [155] To implement Edward's right more effectively Archbishop Stratford, the bishops of Lincoln (Burghersh), London (Stephen Gravesend), Salisbury (Wyville) and Lichfield (Northburgh), together with other prelates, earls and barons, swore an oath on the archiepiscopal cross. Among other measures adopted was the formation of alliances in Germany, Bishop Burghersh being the chief negotiator. [156]

Although no dates are quoted, the presentation appears to have kaleidoscoped events, [157] but it agrees with Stratford's contention that the crucial decisions were taken in parliament, which can only be that of March 1337. It continues by asserting that Edward, in his anger and frustration at the lack of money for the siege of Tournai blurted out: "I honestly believe that the archbishop wishes to bring about my downfall and death by means of a shortage of money." [158] There follows an even more sinister suggestion; that Stratford had spoken such things to the king about his wife, and vice versa, that if taken seriously would have opened a

---

[153] See above, n. 21. "Nunquam bene erit quousque unus fuerit rex utriusque regni tam Francie quam Anglie." Vatican Archives, *RV* 135, fol. 113^{r-v} (Déprez, *Les préliminaires*, p. 424). Cf. "In the Seat of Power," n. 142.

[154] Which met in March 1337. See above, "In the Seat of Power."

[155] Vatican Archives, *RV* 135, fol. 113^v. For a modern discussion see Giesey, *Juristic Basis of Dynastic Right to the French Throne*.

[156] See above, "In the Seat of Power," n. 207.

[157] The king assumed personal rule in 1330, in November of which year he was eighteen. Initially, as we have seen, the policy was to conciliate Philip; a policy which in 1341 was attributed to Stratford – to his discredit. The period 1337-1340 – not very profitable from Edward's point of view – is passed over.

[158] "Vere credo quod archiepiscopus voluit quod propter defectum pecunie perditus fuissem et interfectus." Vatican Archives, *RV* 135, fol. 114^r (Déprez, *Les préliminaires*, p. 425).

permanent rift between them.[159] The pernicious allegation recalls the similar charge against Bishop Orleton with respect to Edward II and his wife, Isabella. The parallel must have been obvious to all.[160] The presentation ends with William of Norwich's declaration that what he had reported came from the king's own mouth, together with instructions to tell all to Pope Benedict but with the request to keep secret the fact that Edward had consented to the truce for lack of money and also the revelations about Archbishop Stratford.[161]

The tense situation in England was not assisted by the actions of Bishop Grandisson of Exeter. He was well connected; member of a baronial family and brother-in-law to William Montacute, earl of Salisbury, whose younger brother Simon was successively bishop of Worcester and Ely.[162] A man of wealth, he was a lavish spender on his cathedral church and on the collegiate foundation of Ottery St. Mary. Although he seems to have deferred to Orleton and Stratford in legal matters, he did have some training in civil law, but then studied theology at Paris under Jacques Fournier (later Benedict XII). He eschewed personal pomp and was more concerned with diocesan than with political affairs.[163] When Hugh de Courtenay (who had recently received livery of the earldom of Devon)[164] and his fellow justices attempted to hold sessions at Exeter on the first Monday in Lent, the bishop sent them a copy of Stratford's excommunications and forbade them to administer oaths during the penitential season. He also called upon them to publish his letters, which he closed with the promise of an indulgence for all who dutifully listened to them and who acted accordingly.[165] The bishop's intransigence could have been construed as political, since the justices were charged with executing the royal policy of examining ministers thought to have been guilty of

[159] "Talia eciam alias dixit michi seorsum de uxore mea, et econtra talia dixit uxori mee seorsum de me, propter que si fuisset exauditus ad tantam nos iram mutuam provocasset quod perpetua inter nos fuisset divisio." Ibid.

[160] *Responsiones*, cols. 2766-2767.

[161] "Ista, pater sanctissime, videlicet quod propter defectum pecunie dominus rex treugis consenserat ineundis et ea que dominum archiepiscopum tangunt si placet teneantur secreta, cetera omnia poterunt propalari." Vatican Archives, *RV* 135, fol. 114ʳ.

[162] BL Harleian MS 1729, fol. 131ʳ, has an interesting biographical note (*Murimuth*, pp. 55-56, n. 6).

[163] See, for instance, Oliver, *Lives of the Bishops of Exeter*, esp. pp. 75-89; Dalton, *The Collegiate Church of Ottery St. Mary*; Haines, *DHGE*, s.v.; *Biog. Oxon.*, s.v.; also above, "Archbishop of Canterbury," for his relations with Stratford. Carved heads of the bishop and of his sister, the countess of Salisbury, are in Ottery St. Mary.

[164] On 11 January 1341. *HBC*, p. 425.

[165] *Concilia* 2, pp. 669-670: Chudleigh, 24 February 1341 (*Exeter Reg. Grandisson*, pp. 943-945).

misconduct, and it was regular practice for diocesans to grant dispensations to enable sessions to be held during Lent.

The response from the king's new administration was immediate and unequivocal. Grandisson's action was condemned as highly prejudicial to the crown and royal dignity. The bishop was accused of deliberately holding up the process of enquiry into malpractices, regardless of the fact that the king's impending departure necessitated a speedy conclusion. He was warned that if he failed to withdraw his denunciation he would be regarded as an enemy of the king, a rebel, and a disturber of the peace.[166] Attempted intimidation of this kind only strengthened Grandisson's resolve to defend ecclesiastical liberties. Scarcely had he digested the contents of the royal mandate than he issued another of his own, this time addressed to the dean of his cathedral church, to the archdeacons of Cornwall and Barnstaple, to the official of the absent archdeacon of Exeter, and to his own commissary.[167] This reiterated the sentences of excommunication and condemned without reservation those who brought injury upon churches and ecclesiastical persons. Did not the Lord himself say, "Touch not mine anointed"?[168] The cathedral dignitaries were colourfully enjoined to "Cry aloud without ceasing and to lift up their voice like a trumpet."[169] The sentences were to be pronounced on the very next sunday – Mid-Lent Sunday – and on the following ones up to and including Easter. Absolution of any who incurred such sentences was reserved to the bishop and no one defamed or suspect was to be admitted to the sacraments.

It must have been during the latter part of February or early March that Stratford put the final touches to his *excusaciones* in the form of a letter to the king. Apparently the precise date is unknown, but on 10 March 1341 the archbishop circulated a letter to his suffragans, outlining in general terms the charges of the *libellus*, protesting his innocence, emphasizing his efforts to establish it before the king in parliament, and deploring the fact that his arrest had been contemplated in defiance of the liberties of the church.[170] Should the royal mandate for the circulation of the *libellus* have

[166] *Foedera* 2, iv, p. 94: Westminster, 6 March 1341.

[167] *Concilia* 2, pp. 672-673: Chudleigh, 16 March 1341 (*Exeter Reg. Grandisson*, pp. 945-946). The diocese consisted of the four archdeaconries of Exeter, Barnstaple, Cornwall and Totton, the bishop's commissary being deputed to act in the last.

[168] 1 Chron. 16.22.

[169] Is. 58.1.

[170] WinRO 1, fol. 102^{r-v}: *Purioris nitore luminis*; Salisbury Reg. Wyville 1, fol. 67^{r-v} (al. 63). An abbreviated text is in *Concilia* 2, pp. 670-671 (cf. *Bath and Wells Reg. Shrewsbury*, p. 432). "Et utinam toti mundo constaret liquide quid de nostri corporis capcione fuerat ordinatum in status episcopalis ecclesie sancte clerique preiudicium et

been published,[171] it was to be superseded, since not only the authors of the *libellus*, but also those publicizing it in derogation of their spiritual fathers standing in place of the apostles, would incur the heaviest penalties whether by civil or by canon law.[172] It could be that Stratford did not distribute copies of the *excusaciones* themselves, since they do not seem to have found their way into episcopal registers.[173] At the same time the archbishop was determined to maintain pressure for the release of the imprisoned ecclesiastics. His mandate of 14 March to the bishops named four chancery clerks – John de St. Pol, Michael de Wath, M. Robert de Chigwell, Henry de Stratford – and the exchequer clerk, John de Thorp, as being still under illegal detention. The diocesan bishops were to order their release within ten days, failing which those responsible were to be declared excommunicate, in general terms if their identity was unknown, otherwise by name.[174]

As for the king, he was already taking steps to mitigate some of the illegalities perpetrated on his behalf. On 6 March he issued instructions to the sheriffs about the liability of clerks with respect to the ninth and the tenth.[175] The same day a writ was issued for the denial of rumours that he proposed to rescind the statutes of 1340 and the pardon of debts made at that time.[176] On the 11th, acknowledging his diversion of the cardinals' procurations, Edward authorized the receiver of the tenth in the province

futurorum perniciosum exemplum." Lapsley, "Archbishop Stratford," pp. 15-16, thought that the archbishop was arrested 26 January. In fact no such arrest seems to have taken place. McKisack, *Fourteenth Century*, p. 170 n. 2, draws the parallel with Becket and the then sheriff of Kent (FitzStephen, *Vita Sancti Thome*, p. 51).

[171] "Si ad publicacionem mandati regii vobis si quod fuerit super hiis directi per vos aut alios auctoritate vestra processum extiterit in hac parte, quod tamen vos fecisse in nostri opprobrium credere non valemus, nostras excusaciones huiusmodi in genere si conceptas ... publicetis." Wyville returned that he had stayed publication of the king's writ "ex causa" and would therefore deal likewise with the archbishop's mandate. WinRO 1, fol. 102ᵛ; Salisbury Reg. Wyville 1, fol. 67ᵛ; also previous note.

[172] "Non solum dictatores et scriptores libellorum huiusmodi famosorum sed eciam recitantes et publicantes eosdem contra patres spirituales loca apostolorum tenentes." WinRO 1, fol. 102ᵛ.

[173] *Pace* my suggestion in *Church and Politics*, p. 196, n. 94. What Stratford seems to be requiring in *Purioris nitore luminis* is the publication of his arguments in general terms. He uses the word *excusaciones* (see n. 171 above), but this does not, I think, refer specifically to the document so named.

[174] WinRO 1, fol. 103ʳ⁻ᵛ; Salisbury Reg. Wyville 1, fols. 64ʳ⁻ᵛ (al. 60), 68ʳ (al. 64). Orleton responded that he knew of no such imprisoned clerks within his diocese. Wyville returned that by public report Henry [Stratford] was in Corfe Castle under the custody of the constable, whom he had been unable to cite. The denunciations had been made. Cf. above, n. 27.

[175] *Foedera* 2, iv, p. 94.

[176] Ibid.

of York to put their collectors in possession of the amount that had been "loaned." [177] Other relaxations followed.[178] But there was no slackening of the onslaught on Stratford. On the contrary, a further outburst was incorporated in another, much briefer *libellus*, *Cicatrix cordium superbia*.[179] This constituted a somewhat feeble counterblast to Stratford's telling *excusaciones*, his sermons, and the instructions issued to the comprovincial bishops. The archbishop was accused of pride, which for remedies generates disease and from the means of healing, sickness. To his original offence he is said to have added others by impugning the king's truthful explanations. Ignoring the well-established custom of popes, cardinals and lesser prelates, he had not received the royal letters with a good grace, but had denigrated them as *libelli famosi* and issued others of his own which defame the king of falsehood. A man responsible for the public welfare, prepared to prove the crimes of which he has written, provided that good faith prompted the accusations, is to be praised rather than blamed. Stratford, however, has not followed others in showing respect for their princes, but has heaped abuse on his king. What is worse, he has dragged others into his sin and by his words has fanned irreverence and contempt among his suffragans and other faithful subjects.

In God's eyes, continues the *libellus*, it is not status but a better life that earns approbation. The archbishop, exalting in his own elevated position, has demanded reverence as Christ's legate, yet has failed to render what is due to the king. Both the archbishop and other prelates who have livery of their temporalities at the king's hand by their oath of fealty render loyalty, honour and reverence. Stratford alone has rendered perfidy for loyalty, contumely for honour, and contempt in place of reverence. The king is always ready to show respect for spiritual fathers, but not to overlook their offences. On account of the crimes with which he was charged in royal letters, the archbishop claims to have been condemned unheard and *in absentia*, as though there had been some judicial process. That is a mere

[177] Ibid.
[178] Ibid., p. 96; WinRO 1, fols. 171ᵛ-172ʳ (al. 43). Cf. WinRO 1, fols. 165ʳ-169ᵛ; *Worcester Reg. Bransford*, pp. 3, 67-68, 289, 291, 511-512. Certain heads of religious houses, including the abbot of St. Augustine's, Bristol, complained that although they had not previously been summoned to parliament, they were being held liable for the wool granted to the king at Northampton (1338). Measures against them were relaxed. E.g. *Worcester Reg. Bransford*, pp. 280-281; *Bath and Wells Reg. Shrewsbury*, pp. 381-382; *Foedera* 2, iv, pp. 98-99.
[179] *Vitae Arch. Cant.*, pp. 36-38 (Lambeth MS 99, fols. 144ʳ-145ʳ); *Foedera* 2, iv, pp. 96-97.

312

THE CRISIS OF 1341

pretence. The king did only what was necessary to preserve his good name. It is appropriate that this should redound on Stratford's own head, for he had maliciously imputed oppression and grievous faults to the king and his councillors. He who judges another, while committing the same offence, condemns himself. As for Stratford's "devotion," this has been directed towards the satisfaction of his own greed rather than for the king's profit. In the archbishop's own words, he has worn himself out with work and is fearful that by so doing he has incurred the censure of God and man. He has good reason to fear, being like a man who gives instruction in language so as to promote falsehood, or one who labours for the purpose of doing evil.[180] To keep the matter brief, says the author, the king will not trouble to confute Stratford's other inventions. The bishops must publish the royal letters [the *libellus famosus*] regardless of any archiepiscopal mandate to the contrary issued in derogation of the king's honour or of his rights, and in breach of Stratford's oath of fealty. At the same time, they are forbidden to publish further prejudicial letters at the metropolitan's behest. If they have published any such already they are to revoke them forthwith.

This minor *libellus*, much given to personal abuse, is dated 31 March, and marks the close of the pamphlet war.[181] The next stage was to be at a more personal level and in the context of the parliament already summoned (3 March) to Westminster for 23 April.[182] The main chronicle source for the events is again Stratford's biographer, whose account can be supplemented by the somewhat variant "official version" of the rolls of parliament.[183] At last the time had arrived for the archbishop to emerge from his self-imposed seclusion. Leaving Canterbury on 17 or 18 April, he travelled towards London in easy stages, staying at his manors en route. He reached Lambeth on the first day of the parliament – 23 April, the feast of St. George. The following day he crossed the Thames to Westminster, supported by his relatives the bishops of London and Chichester and by a substantial group of clerks and squires. On reaching the entrance

---

[180] "Et hoc juste timere poterit, cum in illorum forte censeatur, qui juxta propheticum improperium docuerunt linguas suas loqui mendacium; et ut inique agerent, laborarunt."
[181] See above, n. 107.
[182] *HBC*, p. 522; *Rot. Parl.* 2, p. 126. Due to a slip this date is given in *Church and Politics*, p. 196, as 17 April (according to the *Vitae* the last day of Stratford's sojourn in Canterbury). Before setting out the archbishop received his summons together with a safe-conduct for the journey to and from Westminster. *Vitae Arch. Cant.*, p. 38 (Lambeth MS 99, fol. 145r).
[183] *Vitae Arch. Cant.*, pp. 38-41 (Lambeth MS 99, fols. 145r-146v); *Rot. Parl.* 2, pp. 126-134.

to the great hall of the royal palace Stratford's party was confronted by
Ralph Stafford, steward of the king's household, by John Darcy, the royal
chamberlain, and by the serjeants-at-arms. They brought a message from
Edward to the effect that before entering parliament Stratford should
respond to certain matters in the exchequer.[184] The archbishop replied that
no day had been assigned to him for that purpose, but only one in which
he was to be present in parliament with the peers of the realm.[185] There
was a specific matter for which the archbishop had been summoned to the
exchequer – the alleged non-payment of forty-five sacks and fifty-seven
pounds of wool. Stratford, through his attorney Elias de Waddeworth,
had denied liability, but was unable to produce the necessary evidence on
the spot. The case was then adjourned from session to session without
result. It used to be thought that Stratford had been negligent about his
obligations; it is more likely that the claim was merely a device to
embarrass him.[186] But there was more to the charges than a supposed
negligence in paying taxes. When Stratford to accommodate the king
agreed to enter the exchequer, he was promptly presented with a series of
articles.[187] Requesting time to deliberate, he betook himself to the painted
chamber, where the bishops were assembled on their own. He took his
seat[188] in company with his relatives Robert and Ralph Stratford and with
the bishops of Lichfield (Northburgh) and of St. David's (Henry
Gower).[189] His purpose in coming was explained in a formal statement. It
was, he said, for the honour, rights and liberties of the English church; for
the public welfare and the well-being of the realm and people; for the

[184] Tout, *PHE* 3, p. 350, wrote that the king ordered Stratford "to answer in the
exchequer the complaints brought against him." Of course, as Vernon Harcourt pointed
out (*His Grace the Steward*, p. 339) there was no question of the primate's trial for treason
there. Did Tout mean that? The *Vitae Arch. Cant.* is quite clear: "Quod objicienda sibi
primo in scaccario regis respondere deberet, antequam parliamentum intraret." See also
Pike, *YB 15 Edward III*, p. xliv.

[185] *Vitae Arch. Cant.*, p. 38 (Lambeth MS 99, fol. 145ʳ).

[186] Compare Vernon Harcourt, *His Grace the Steward*, p. 340 (who accepts Stratford's
negligence and makes it worse by correcting Pike's misreading, *Constitutional History of
the House of Lords*, p. 191, of the memoranda roll) and Fryde, "Edward III's Removal of
Ministers," p. 160, who calls the proceeding "quite unjust."

[187] "Ad placendum regi, intravit scaccarium; et articulis sibi expositis, dixit se velle
deliberare super ipsis." *Vitae Arch. Cant.*, p. 38.

[188] "Et ibi in loco parliamenti assignato sedebat." Ibid.

[189] *Rot. Parl.* 2, p. 126, gives the following bishops as present on 26 April when the
reasons for the parliamentary summons were declared: Winchester (Orleton), Durham
(Bury), Ely (Montacute), Chester (Northburgh), Exeter (Grandisson), Hereford (Charlton),
St. David's (Gower), Bath and Wells (Shrewsbury), Salisbury (Wyville) – nine in all.
London (Ralph Stratford) and Chichester (Robert Stratford) are first mentioned on 3 May.
Ibid., p. 127, but cf. below, n. 192.

honour of the king and the good of the queen; in order to purge himself in full parliament of the charges (crimina) brought against him; and because when summoned to parliament by the king's writ he was obliged to do what was incumbent upon him. Then, it being the ninth hour, Chancellor Bourchier adjourned the proceedings until the following day (25 April) and the bishops retired to their lodgings. On that day, the feast of St. Mark, the archbishop returned to Westminster from Lambeth and once again joined his fellow bishops in the painted chamber. The king did not put in an appearance, so nothing was done. The following day, Thursday 26 April, Stratford paid a further visit to the exchequer, his purpose being to respond to the articles presented to him earlier in the week. Nothing else was done on that day.[190]

The pattern of events for Friday 27 April was somewhat different. This time the archbishop approached the entrance to the great hall of the palace, only to encounter a knot of seculars – John Darcy, Giles Beauchamp and Ralph Neville[191] – intent on blocking his entry. They tried to insist that he return once more to the exchequer. Stratford was not to be fobbed off. It was, he said, to parliament that he had been summoned, and to parliament he wished to go and not, on this occasion, to the exchequer. All the same, he had no option but to retire to the painted chamber, where he sat down with eight other bishops.[192] The king still did not come.[193] Instead he sent the bishop of Winchester, Adam Orleton, Chancellor Bourchier and John Darcy. This is the first mention of Orleton in this account of the proceedings. He was now old and blind, or nearly so, but his advice had seemingly been sought for dealing with so formidable a man as the archbishop, who in the past had opposed his

[190] "Nil aliud faciens illo die." *Vitae Arch. Cant.*, p. 38. Using this source Wilkinson, "Protest of the Earls," pp. 192-193, provides a handy summary of events.

[191] John Darcy, senior, was seemingly the king's chamberlain, who had been abroad with Edward 1338-1340. For the confusion about the Darcys, father and son, see Tout, *Chapters* 3, p. 89 n. 1. Giles Beauchamp, earlier mentioned as knight of the chamber, was also mentioned as a member of Edward's council in the Low Countries, ibid. 3, pp. 89-90. Tout speaks of "an organised and exclusive court party" (ibid. 3, p. 90) with the king. Ralph Neville of Raby was steward of the household 1330-1336, an office which Darcy held 1337-1340. His activities are much less well known. See ibid. 4, pp. 81-82.

[192] Those of London, Chichester, Ely, Coventry and Lichfield, Bath and Wells, Hereford, Salisbury and St. David's. The editor (Wharton) of *Vitae Arch. Cant.* wrongly extended the ms "R" for Northburgh as "Robert." These names can be compared with the list in *Rot. Parl.*; above, n. 189. Missing are Winchester (Orleton), Durham (Bury) and Exeter (Grandisson). The absence of the first two merits no comment; one would have expected Exeter to have been with his colleagues.

[193] "Ad quos rex non curavit venire." *Vitae Arch. Cant.*, p. 39 (Lambeth MS 99, fol. 145ʳ).

interests.[194] The emissaries tried to inveigle the archbishop into submission by delivering a royal message to the effect that he should humble
himself and obey the king, in the assurance of finding grace. Stratford
replied evasively. He was and always would be obedient to the king,
saving his order and status. An interesting incident then took place.
Orleton, possibly somewhat embarrassed by his position of isolation from
his episcopal colleagues, volunteered the information that he was not
responsible for the *libellus famosus*. The claim was met by stony silence
on Stratford's part.

When the archbishop arrived at Westminster on Saturday 28 April
he was met by two serjeants-at-arms, who with an outward show of
politeness told him that they were forbidden to allow him to enter the
painted chamber in which the king was holding his parliament.[195] Their
tone elicited a courteous reply, though Stratford declared that his
summons was to parliament where he ought to have the first voice after
that of the king. What was more, as upholder of the rights of the church
of Canterbury he expected to be granted access.[196] The serjeants declined
to let him pass or the bishops of London and Chichester, who were
standing with their superior. The archbishop stood firm. Grasping his
primatial cross he refused to leave the spot until he should hear otherwise
from the king. His intransigent attitude must have been relayed to
Edward, for after an interval a group of knights – the two John Darcys,
Giles de Beauchamp and Thomas de Medham – arrived on the scene. In
an angry voice the elder Darcy demanded to know what Stratford was
doing there.[197] The archbishop reiterated the fact of his summons, the
need to vindicate the rights of his church, and his resolve to stay where he
was. Darcy, by now even angrier, declared that he wished the archbishop
would remain there for ever. Stratford interpreted this as a physical threat.
His body was ready, he ostentatiously announced; Darcy could do what
he wished. He hoped to give back his soul to the Creator. The heroics,

---

[194] This matter is discussed in Haines, *Church and Politics*, pp. 180-198. *Rot. Parl.* 2,
p. 126, mentions Orleton's presence on the 26th. See above, n. 189.

[195] "Inhibitum est nobis, ne vos cameram depictam regis, ubi rex parliamentum suum
tenet, ingredi permittamus." *Vitae Arch. Cant.*, p. 39 (Lambeth MS 99, fol. 145ᵛ).

[196] "Amici mei, dominus meus rex me Johannem archiepiscopum ad hoc parliamentum per breve suum vocavit, et ego major post regem primam vocem habere debens,
jura ecclesiae meae Cantuariensis vendico, et ideo ingressum istius camerae peto." Ibid.
Despite the editor's rubric citing Parker, *De Antiquitate*, this passage is in the Lambeth MS.

[197] "En quid facis hic?" *Vitae Arch. Cant.*, p. 39 (Lambeth MS 99, fol. 145ᵛ) and see
above, n. 191.

though genuine, were perhaps misplaced.[198] Darcy sneeringly retorted
that neither was the archbishop sufficiently worthy nor himself so foolish
as to give occasion for martyrdom. But, he added, Stratford was guilty of
disobedience to his liege lord. This the archbishop denied. He was
obedient, he claimed, and came humbly with his cross in his hands,
prepared to endure death for the right of his church. Darcy irritably
commented that Stratford was worthy neither of his cross nor of entry to
parliament. He had served the king unfaithfully and his suggestion that
Edward was no longer advised by experienced councillors was a lie;[199] a
lie which would be proved, if need be, on the body of anyone who uttered
it, but not on that of the archbishop, because of his honour and dignity.
Beauchamp then took up the verbal onslaught. The archbishop, to his
mind, was born in an evil hour, for he had impeded the noblest prince in
the world and the business of the French kingdom. Stratford made an
attempt to turn the tables by uttering a curse in the name of God, the
Virgin Mary and St. Thomas, as well as of himself, on any who impeded
the king. The riposte which this elicited was childish in its rudeness. Such
a curse could fall only on the archbishop's own head. Stratford spurned
such shameful words and, according to the sympathetic chronicler, the
knights retired amidst the indignation of those within earshot.[200]

The archbishop's party continued its vigil at the entrance to the
chamber, while particulars of this latest exchange were reported to the
councillors and doubtless to the king himself. Some time later the earls of
Northampton and Salisbury, William de Bohun and William de
Montacute, emerged.[201] The archbishop spoke to them of his summons to
parliament and of his being refused entry, and asked them to request the
king to allow him to exercise the right of his church of Canterbury.[202]

[198] Stratford's initial response was: "Ego ex brevi regis ad hoc parliamentum vocatus,
pro jure ecclesiae meae vindicandae hic sto et stabo ad ingrediendum parliamentum." To
this Darcy "malefico vultu" retorted: "Utinam ibi stes perpetuo, et nunquam recedas."
Stratford "malitiam eorum considerans" replied: "Hic est corpus paratum, de quo facere
poteris, quod volueris. Animam meam spero reddere Creatori." Ibid.

[199] "Et quicumque dixerit, quod dominus rex non sit seniori ductus consilio, quam fuit
tempore tuo; mentitur per os suum." Ibid. Stratford's claim here is perhaps not so much
about the youth of the councillors but their length of service and "weight."

[200] The archbishop's curse ran: "Maledictio Dei et Beatae Mariae et S. Thomae, et mea,
qui dictum regem impedierunt taliter, sit super eorum capita nunc et semper, Amen." His
reply to the taunt "Tunc illa maledictio super caput tuum veniet" was: "De verbis tuis
probrosis non curo."

[201] Both earls were created in 1337.

[202] "Rogo vos dominos, quod hoc domino regi intimare velitis; ex parte mea ipsum
rogantes, quod jus ecclesiae Cantuariensis dignetur servare." *Vitae Arch. Cant.*, p. 40
(Lambeth MS 99, fol. 145ᵛ).

While awaiting a reply the bishops were joined by the bishop of Ely, Salisbury's brother, who took up the archbishop's cross and preceded him to the small hall of the palace of Westminster, where Stratford remained for some time in the company of the other bishops. Eventually, escorted by prelates and peers,[203] Stratford entered the painted and white chambers.[204] Discussion took place with the view to a peaceful settlement, at which point the king withdrew.[205] The process must have involved considerable mutual recrimination. Orleton, whom the Canterbury biographer considered to be a "lover of discord," was said to have been caught out in a lie[206] in that he claimed that Stratford, when a royal councillor, had contrived the wording of the declaration of homage to the French king out of his own head, without appropriate consultation. Some of those present interjected that Orleton, being absent on the continent with Ayrminne, then bishop of Norwich, the count of Hainault, Henry Percy and John de Schordich, could not have known what was taking place. The argument must refer to the revised oath of liege homage agreed to in 1331, but is not convincing. Orleton did go abroad at that time, but the date of his return, prior to Stratford's own departure, would have provided ample opportunity for discovering how the oath had been determined.[207] As the king did not return to the chamber, Stratford withdrew.

Sunday 29 April was spent quietly by Stratford at Lambeth. Kilsby and Darcy were less peaceably occupied. They called a meeting in the chapter house at Westminster Abbey, close to the palace. There, in the presence of the mayor, aldermen and community of London these "fomenters of discord" strove maliciously to rouse the people against the archbishop, concocting accusatory articles which the following day, 30 April, they republished in parliament with the intention of damning Stratford in the eyes of the "community of the realm." [208] Nothing else happened at West-

---

[203] "Cum ipsis prelatis et paribus." Ibid.

[204] These were separate chambers of some size used for parliaments. It is recorded that in the parliament of April 1343 the prelates and magnates "debated" in the white chamber, the knights and commons in the painted chamber. *Rot. Parl.* 2, pp. 135-136ff.; Parry, *Parliaments*, pp. 114-115.

[205] "Ubi tractatu pacis habito ab eodem archiepiscopo rex Angliae se retraxavit." *Vitae Arch. Cant.*, p. 40 (Lambeth MS 99, fols. 145ᵛ-146ʳ).

[206] "Convictus fuit super eo, quod falso imponebatur dicto archiepiscopo." Ibid. (fol. 146ʳ).

[207] For this incident see Haines, *Church and Politics*, pp. 196-197.

[208] "Simili modo communitati Angliae hujusmodi articuli per conspirationem, ut premittitur, fabricati, fuerant publicati." *Vitae Arch. Cant.*, p. 40 (Lambeth MS 99, fol. 146ʳ).

minster that day, according to the chronicler, but on 1 May the archbishop arrived early and offered to purge himself of the allegations against
him in full parliament. Twelve peers are said to have been chosen to
investigate the matter and to advise the king as to what else should be
done. The elect comprised four bishops and an equal number of earls and
of barons. The bishops were those of London (Ralph Stratford), Hereford
(Thomas Charlton), Bath (Ralph of Shrewsbury) and Exeter (John
Grandisson); a group on the whole favourable to Stratford.[209] On
Wednesday 2 May the archbishop came before the king in the white
chamber and renewed his offer to purge himself. The councillors are said
to have refused to hear him.[210] Possibly they feared to allow the archbishop further opportunity for argument. In any case, according to this
particular chronicler, the long-drawn-out drama ended the next day,
3 May, when ten bishops,[211] various earls,[212] a number of abbots and
barons, John Darcy the chamberlain, the mayor of London, the barons of
the Cinque Ports, as well as others, interceded with the king on Stratford's
behalf. He was admitted to the king's grace and exonerated from the
crimes of which he was accused.[213]

For the sake of continuity it has been found convenient to follow the
parliamentary story through the eyes of a single chronicler. At this point
some other accounts will have to be considered. The French Chronicle,
which is fairly economical in its treatment of events, undergoes a sudden
expansion to include an incident not recorded elsewhere. This incident
has attracted much interest and no little speculation.[214] But first the

---

[209] The earls were Arundel (his wife Eleanor was daughter of Henry, earl of
Lancaster), Salisbury (Montacute), Huntingdon (Clinton, to whom the Canterbury prior
had complained of Kilsby's behaviour and who was a colleague in the 1340 council), and
Suffolk (Ufford). The barons were Wake, Stratford's long political associate, Ralph Basset,
Henry Percy and Ralph Neville. Wake, Percy and Neville had been members of the 1340
home council.

[210] "Sed dicti regis consiliarii nolebant ipsum audire." *Vitae Arch. Cant.*, p. 40
(Lambeth MS 99, fol. 146ʳ).

[211] London, Chichester, Salisbury, Bath and Wells, Coventry and Lichfield, Hereford,
Exeter, St. David's, Durham and Carlisle. Ely (Montacute) is not mentioned and Carlisle
(Kirkby) is not recorded in *Rot. Parl.* as having been at the parliament. Cf. above, nn. 189,
192.

[212] Arundel, Salisbury, Huntingdon, Exeter (Devon), St. David's (*Meneven.* [sic] a
confusion with the bishopric), Pembroke, Suffolk and Angus.

[213] "Rex idem archiepiscopum ad suam admisit gratiam, et ipsum super criminibus
sibi impositis excusatum habuit undequaque." *Vitae Arch. Cant.*, p. 41 (Lambeth MS 99,
fol. 146ᵛ).

[214] See in particular, Wilkinson, "Protest of the Earls"; Lapsley, "Archbishop Stratford," pp. 195-196.

chronicler states that apart from the archbishop two bishops – said to be Chichester and Chester – were excluded from parliament for the whole of the first week of the session (23-28 April). In fact Roger Northburgh (Chester), the former treasurer, was not associated in the archbishop's exclusion, but there is no mention here of Stratford's relative the bishop of London, who certainly was. In the second week, the chronicler continues, the earl of Surrey (Warenne), a man of the archbishop's own generation, came into parliament when the king was present. Finding there Robert Parving, Ralph Stafford, William Kilsby and John Darcy, he was moved to make a pointed observation on the changed aspect of the assembly.[215] Those who should be principals were excluded, while others who had no right to be there were present – rather than the peers of the land alone, men in a position to assist and make provision for the king.[216] This looks like a statement of the "Lancastrian" position that the monarch should be guided only by those of appropriate status.[217] Made conspicuous by Surrey's remarks, Kilsby and Darcy, men at the heart of the opposition to Stratford, discreetly slipped away. It was the earl of Arundel's turn next; a much younger man.[218] Rising from his seat he advanced the suggestion that the archbishop be allowed to come before the king. Should he fail to respond satisfactorily to the matters put to him, they could further deliberate on what was to be done. The king acceded to the earl's proposal and a schedule of thirty-two articles was compiled. Stratford promptly rejected all the allegations it contained.[219]

With a certain amount of adjustment it is possible to accommodate part of this account to the day-to-day version of the Canterbury chronicler. The thirty-two articles can be equated with those attributed to Kilsby and Darcy, which were first published on 29 April and again the following

---

[215] The *Vitae Arch. Cant.* suggests that the most likely date for the incident recounted in the *French Chronicle* (p. 90) would be 28 April – Saturday the close of the first week of parliament. Lapsley adopts this date ("Archbishop Stratford," p. 195), which is regarded as probable by Wilkinson ("Protest of the Earls," p. 180). The latter regards the earl of Surrey's intervention as a contribution to the debate of 28 April, in which Orleton took part.

[216] *French Chronicle*, p. 90.

[217] See, for instance, the arguments put forward in 1328; above, "Lancastrian Spokesman."

[218] Richard FitzAlan was born ca. 1310. His father was executed in 1326 following Queen Isabella's return to England. The earldom was restored to him 12 December 1330. One would not expect him to be well disposed towards Stratford. *GEC* 1, pp. 242-243.

[219] "Et furent mis en escripture xxxii articles encontre luy, et l'ercheveske les denia touz, et dit q'il n'estoit de rien coupable de nul poynt qe l'em luy mist sure." *French Chronicle*, p. 90. Harriss, *King, Parliament and Public Finance*, p. 295, misread this as "twenty-two articles."

day in parliament. In which case, as has been pointed out,[220] the action of the earls may be assigned more convincingly to 28 than 30 April – the commencement of parliament's second week – in other words to the day Stratford is supposed to have been admitted tardily to the painted chamber.[221] As the records make plain, this was not a "full" session of parliament but a meeting of a more restricted character.[222] We are left to speculate as to the nature of Stratford's submission and reconciliation to the king. His desire to justify himself *in pleno parliamento* was circumvented. It would have led to damaging recriminations and interminable wrangles, to the detriment of Edward's underlying purpose, the raising of money for a speedy return to the continent. Some ecclesiastics thought that Stratford underwent the familiar process of purgation under oath.[223] On the other hand, the Canterbury chronicler denies this. For him what happened, and *in pleno parliamento*, constituted an intervention on Stratford's behalf of a group ranging from earls and prelates to knights of the shire and the mayor of London; in fact a cross-section of parliament. One explanation of this massive intervention – even John Darcy is included – is that Stratford had won a substantial victory for his "party." [224] The truth is probably somewhat different. Stratford's firm stance had inconvenienced the royal ministers; so much so that the status of some of them had been questioned. It was impossible "constitutionally" to debar the archbishop from parliament or the king's counsels. Had such a precedent been established, it could have redounded to the disadvantage of many others. What may have developed was not so much a marked increase in support for the archbishop as an individual, as a general anxiety to resolve an irritating problem in order to leave the way clear for consideration of broader issues of common concern. This is made clearer by the rolls of parliament, in which the Stratford affair appears as a side-issue.

The version of events recorded on the rolls of parliament differs markedly from the impressively detailed story of the Canterbury

---

[220] Wilkinson, "Protest of the Earls," p. 180.

[221] See above, n. 215.

[222] See above, n. 78.

[223] BL Cotton MS Faustina B.v, fol. 89ᵛ: "Vocatus est tunc archiepiscopus ad parliamentum regis et ibi de multis sibi obiectis per regem iuramento super crucem se purgavit. Et sic regi est reconciliatus."

[224] E.g. Stubbs, *Constitutional History* 2, p. 389: "Stratford had not only won a personal victory, but the peers, acting at his instigation, had secured for their order a real privilege [trial by their peers], which the events of the last reign, and of the early years of the present, had shown to be necessary."

chronicler. A committee of twelve (naming the bishop of Chichester in place of his colleague of Hereford) is recorded to have been appointed, not on 1 May but on the 3rd, and to have been concerned, not with Stratford, but with a fairly radical petition of the lords for the trial of peers in parliament.[225] This committee reported on 7 May, advocating a modified version of the lords' petition coupled with proposals for what looks uncommonly like a claim for the parliamentary control of ministers,[226] as well as for the observance of ecclesiastical privileges, the country's laws and charters, and sundry liberties enjoyed by the City of London and other privileged elements in the realm.[227] Petitions on these lines were submitted by the lords, the clergy, the lords and commons, and by the commons themselves.[228] It was at this point, according to the rolls, that the archbishop appeared before the king in the painted chamber with other prelates, magnates and the commons. The penitent Stratford is said to have humbled himself before Edward and to have requested reinstatement in his good lordship and beneficence.[229] The statement is broadly compatible with the more expansive one in the Canterbury chronicle, though there it comes four days earlier, or so it would seem. However, an attempt has been made to square the two accounts in this respect by suggesting that the phrase "Et meisme cesti jour" in the rolls in fact refers back to 3 May and that the report of the committee on the 7th is an interpolation.[230] This is certainly an atttractive idea, the more so since it makes the rolls internally consistent. The king's reply to the petitions of the lords and commons was given on 9 May. This was found to be unsatisfactory. A new committee was struck in which the bishops of Durham (Bury), Ely (Montacute), and Salisbury (Wyville), replaced those of Chichester (Robert Stratford), Bath (Ralph of Shrewsbury), and Exeter (John Grandisson). Among the earls, Northampton took Suffolk's place. To what extent, if any, this represented a shift of political emphasis it is

---

[225] *Rot. Parl.* 2, p. 127 no. 6. The composition of the committee is the same as that given in the *Vitae*, except that *Rot. Parl.* has Chichester (Robert Stratford) in place of Hereford (Charlton). See above, text and n. 209.

[226] *Rot. Parl.* 2, p. 127 no. 7. See Lapsley, "Archbishop Stratford," p. 197.

[227] *Rot. Parl.* 2, p. 127 no. 7.

[228] Ibid., pp. 128-131; Stubbs, *Constitutional History* 2, pp. 389-390.

[229] "Et le dit Ercevesqe se humilia a nostre seignur le roi, enquerant sa bone seignurie et sa bienvolliance; et nostre seignur le roi lui resceut a sa bone seignurie: dont les prelatz et autres grantz lui mercierent tant come ils savoient ou purroient." *Rot. Parl.* 2, p. 127 no. 8.

[230] Wilkinson, "Protest of the Earls," p. 184 n. 2. Another point which favours the rehabilitation taking place on 3 May is the fact that Robert and Ralph Stratford were made members of the committee formed on that day (above, n. 225).

hard to say. Grandisson was assuredly an outspoken supporter of Stratford, while Montacute, the archbishop's crucifer at the height of the crisis,
seems also to have been sympathetic. Chichester was obviously an
unmitigated loss. Although Northampton was one of those who landed
with the king at Tower Steps, he was also one of the earls whose creation
in 1337 Stratford had defended. Orleton, it will be noticed, figured in
neither committee.[231] More significant was the addition of a group of
royal officers, including the chancellor, the treasurer, and others with
legal training.[232] The royal answers to the clergy's petitions, now
presented by Stratford and the other bishops, were reported to parliament
on Friday 11 May. In the ensuing debate they were adjudged inadequate.
Eventually, when the magnates had made amendments, agreement was
reached.[233] On the Saturday Edward's response to the petitions of lords
and commons was delivered.[234] The various replies were drafted in
statutory form, a concession which was the condition of a grant of 30,000
sacks of wool as compensation for the second year of the ninth.[235] But
when the chancellor, treasurer and other royal officers were called upon
to swear on the primatial cross to maintain the statutes, they protested
their inability to do so in the case of such as were contrary to the laws and
customs of the realm, which they were already sworn to observe.[236] As
for Stratford himself, one matter remained unresolved; his long-sustained
claim to a parliamentary hearing. The outward reconciliation of early
May had signalled a cessation of conflict, but the charges had only been
shelved. And so, on 26 May, a committee of two bishops, Durham and
Salisbury, and four earls, Arundel, Salisbury, Warwick and Northampton, was deputed to hear the metropolitan's replies to the allegations
against him. Were the king and council to find them insufficient they
could be debated in the next parliament and judgment given there. But
Stratford was not to have his way. He declared himself ready, but the earls
demurred; they were unable to deal with the business at that time. It was
unobtrusively dropped.[237] A second more formal reconciliation is
recorded in the Winchester cartulary. This is said to have taken place on

[231] *Rot. Parl.* 2, pp. 127, 129 no. 17.

[232] *Rot. Parl.* 2, p. 129 no. 17; Lapsley, "Archbishop Stratford," pp. 199-200; Vernon
Harcourt, *His Grace the Steward*, pp. 342-343.

[233] *Rot. Parl.* 2, pp. 129-130 no. 26; Lapsley, "Archbishop Stratford," p. 200.

[234] *Rot. Parl.* 2, p. 130 nos. 34-41.

[235] Ibid., p. 131 no. 42. Lloyd, *English Wool Trade*, pp. 159ff., discusses this, pointing
out that it was not a loan but a tax, and not additional to the ninth, for this was cancelled.

[236] *Rot. Parl.* 2, p. 131 no. 42.

[237] Ibid., no. 44; *Murimuth*, p. 120 (who gives the committee but omits Arundel);
Vernon Harcourt, *His Grace the Steward*, p. 345.

23 October in the great hall at Westminster. Arrayed in the trappings of royalty the king was seated on a dais, with the archbishop and other prelates who had been summoned to a council standing at a lower level. The hall was packed with barons and others, among them the earl of Derby who was acting as mediator. Stratford delivered a prepared statement in which he thanked the king for allowing him to come into his presence, offered obedience saving his status and dignity, and repeated his request to be allowed to reply to the articles of accusation before such prelates and nobles as the king might appoint. He then responded to the two most damaging articles; one concerning the declaration of homage, the other a remission of a large sum said to have been due from the king of France.[238] He swore that he had not sealed or consented to the sealing of such letters with malicious or seditious intent. But he also made it plain that in responding he was not recognizing the king as his judge. He then swore not to take action against those of the council, or other officers of the king, on account of the articles or actions taken against him since he incurred the royal indignation. Lastly he swore to uphold the king's honour and royal estate, saving that of the church and of himself.[239] Even then the matter was not laid to rest. It was at the Easter parliament of 1343 that Edward ordered the annulment of the "arraignment" of the archbishop on the grounds that it was untrue and contrary to reason. The documents in the case, presumably comprising the thirty-two articles, were to be brought into parliament by M. John Offord for destruction. Offord had in June 1342 succeeded Kilsby as keeper of the privy seal and was to become chancellor and momentarily, on Stratford's death, archbishop of Canterbury.[240] As late as 3 June 1346 it was considered necessary "for the greater security of the archbishop and considering the good place he has held and holds" to issue letters patent to the effect that Edward accounted Stratford blameless of the articles with which he had been charged and "deservedly excused." [241]

---

[238] This seems to refer back to the events of 1331. See text above and n. 207.

[239] This document is printed from the Winchester cartulary (no. 518) by Harriss, *King, Parliament and Public Finance*, App. A, pp. 521-522. The transcription is misleading. For instance, on p. 521, for "quia" the ms has "quasi," for "ecclesiam," "culpam," and for "milium," "militum" [*sic*]; while on p. 522 "dictaxat" should be "dumtaxat"; "prosequeretur," "persequeretur"; "illium," "illum"; "regi," "regis"; and "benevolenciam," "benivolenciam."

[240] *Rot. Parl.* 2, p. 139 no. 22; Tout, *Chapters* 6, pp. 14, 52; *HBC*, pp. 84, 91. Offord was provided to Canterbury 24 September 1348, received the temporalities 14 December, and died 20 May in the following (plague) year. See *Biog. Oxon.*, s.v.

[241] *CPR 1345-1348*, pp. 121-122. This shows the scope of the articles: disherison of the king and his crown, annulling of the law of the realm, hindering of the king's quarrel

As presaged by the ministerial protestation, the statutes of 1341 had a brief life. By letters close of 1 October 1341 Edward instructed the sheriffs to publish the repeal of the "pretended statutes" as contrary to the law of England and his own prerogative, except in so far as they conformed to what had been approved by his predecessors. He confessed that he had dissembled to avoid the breakup of parliament; his assent had not been freely given. Simultaneously Stratford was prohibited from promulgating anything in his forthcoming provincial council in support of the "so-called statutes." At the parliament of 1343 the commons petitioned for their reinstatement. The king answered that they would be examined and such parts as were appropriate observed. In the event they were repealed, but the royal promise to re-enact the inoffensive portions was evaded.[242] Edward's conduct in 1341 has been variously interpreted. Stubbs remarked that "under an appearance of gracious magnanimity or careless generosity, he conceded all the privileges which his people demanded, and then by a clever manœuvre, a piece of atrocious duplicity, he nullified the concession." [243] Lapsley is more accommodating. He believed the king to have been "quite right to repeal the statute" and that "it was done in a regular way by an ordinance based on the judges' protest and confirmed by parliament." For him the reprehensible aspect was the failure to grant a new statute, though this was "a comprehensible if not an excusable" wrong. Richardson and Sayles, having sketched in the legal context, point out that the 1341 revocation was by no means without precedent, while Galbraith warned (in discussing "statutes" of the previous century) of the danger of drawing constitutional precedents from crises "when the kings made promises to their subjects under duress." [244] But when all is said, Edward must have been fully aware of the dangers of repeating such a *volte face*.

How are we to interpret Stratford's behaviour in all this? To what extent, we may enquire, was the archbishop responsible for the change in emphasis from a defence of his own position and of the illegally imprisoned clerks to what looks like a well-organized parliamentary

and sedition, contempt and vituperation, pardoning of royal debts, alienating of crown lands and of treasure, custodies etc. Chronologically the accusations went back to his days as a diplomatic envoy for Edward II.

[242] *Foedera* 2, iv, p. 12; *CCR 1341-1343*, p. 335; *Rot. Parl.* 2, pp. 139 no. 23, 139-140 no. 27; *Statutes* 1, pp. 295-298.

[243] *Constitutional History* 2, p. 391.

[244] Lapsley, "Archbishop Stratford," pp. 203-204; Richardson and Sayles, "The Early Statutes," pp. 551-552ff.; Galbraith, "Statutes of Edward I," pp. 176-191 (esp. his conclusion).

"coalition" for effecting constitutional and administrative reforms? Is it possible to identify the primate as the moving spirit of a reforming movement, if that is an appropriate designation? Can he be looked upon as the champion of clerical liberties, or even perhaps of the liberties of the country as a whole? To most of these questions it is hard to give satisfactory answers; the records are not sufficiently explicit. On the one hand is the fact that the demands made in 1341 by lords, clergy and commons had a long-standing history; on the other there is the striking similarity between what Stratford was advocating in his personal defence and the petitions which preceded the statute. As we have seen, the Canterbury chronicler understandably makes Stratford the centre of his narrative. He does not even mention the petitions or the statutes to which they gave rise. By contrast the rolls of parliament take little account of Stratford's personal predicament, but make much of the statutes and the prelude to them. Professor McKisack suggests that "before parliament met, Stratford had provided each of the estates with a cause to champion."[245] We may take the liberty of expanding her list somewhat. For the clergy there were the arrests of clerks, lay encroachment on church courts, and the unlawful levying of taxes. The magnates, recollecting all too vividly the rough justice of Edward II's reign, looked for a trial by their peers (as did Stratford), the appointment of ministers in parliament and the taking of oaths there before the lords. For the commons and the City of London there was the defence of the charters, of common law, and the maintenance of franchises and customs, as well as the relaxation of debts due to the crown. For both peers and commons there was the audit of accounts.[246] But McKisack did not feel that Stratford had any genuine concern for these matters, except perhaps for the rights of the clergy.[247] According to her analysis, Stratford's "main object in stirring up so many hornets' nests was to clear his own reputation and to effect a reconciliation with the king."[248] It seems to me that this interpretation does much less than justice to the archbishop.

It is all too easy to dismiss medieval statesmen-bishops as selfish, ambitious careerists, with no underlying convictions at all, or at best a few which they were prepared to jettison as necessity dictated. In Stratford's case this would be an over-simplification. That he had the church's

---

[245] *Fourteenth Century*, p. 174.

[246] Ibid.

[247] Ibid.: "The archbishop himself must be credited with some genuine concern for the interests of the clergy; but his subsequent conduct strongly suggests that for the rest he cared little."

[248] Ibid.

interests at heart is manifested by his whole career and by the manner and matter of his legislation in provincial council, which will be dealt with later. His concern for what have been termed "Lancastrian" principles is evident from his actions in 1326-1327 and in 1328. The concepts that the king should live of his own, that he should be advised by a council of magnates, clerical and lay, and that corruption arose from inadequate or inappropriate ministers, were all in evidence at those times, and in 1328 there can be no doubt that Stratford was hazarding his future career, indeed his life. The question remains as to why he accepted Edward's *volte face*, which in 1341 turned a victory for the estates of parliament into one for the monarch himself.[249] We may surmise that he was influenced by the obvious reluctance of the barons to repeat the confrontations of 1311, 1321-1322, 1326-1327 and 1328-1329. Even so, a degree of complaisance is discernible. In Stratford's defence it could be argued that the substantive points had been made and that although Edward refused to have his hands tied by specific statutes, he had learned so valuable a lesson that his future actions were to give no cause for any comparable crisis of confidence in his ability to rule with justice and common sense – qualities markedly lacking in his father.[250] Stratford, as we shall see, continued to show independence of mind, but it was principally in the more restricted sphere of clerical affairs.

It would be hard to substantiate the notion of Stratford's leadership of a "reforming movement." It is more credible to suppose that he provided a timely instance of resistance to illegalities stemming from Edward's anger at having his over-ambitious schemes thwarted and his determination to lay the blame on anyone but himself. Edward's intention of speedily crushing Stratford proved a gross miscalculation. Momentum was given to an already deep-seated sense of grievance,[251] indeed of fear of the repetition of happenings fresh in the memory of all the participants – at which the archbishop more than hinted during the course of his

[249] Tout, *PHE* 3, p. 351, writes: "Thus the fallen minister brought the estates to the greatest triumph over the prerogative won during Edward's reign."

[250] McKisack concludes, *Fourteenth Century*, pp. 179-180: "Edward's extravagance and unwisdom had opened the way for Stratford to raise dangerous issues; but the king never repeated the mistakes of his early years and for a generation after the crisis these issues lay dormant."

[251] This, of course, was manifested particularly in the petitions and statutes of 1340, but goes right back to the beginning of the reign (see above, "Lancastrian Spokesman"). The *Speculum regis Edwardi* is now thought to date from 1331 and to be the work of William of Pagula. See Boyle, "William of Pagula"; Haines, *Church and Politics*, p. 107 n. 24. In which case, *pace* Harriss, *King, Parliament and Public Finance*, p. 179, it may have some specific reference.

defence.[252] Stratford's stand, it may be hazarded, assisted the temporary success of the estates, but he was not in any strict sense their leader, still less the leader of some concerted baronial opposition. In fact, it has been suggested that the nature of baronial action at this time is by no means to be compared with that of 1311, or, one might add, of 1328.[253] At the same time it needs to be remembered that the repudiated statutes of 1341, with their emphasis on the liberties of the church, the observance of the charters,[254] the trial of officers in parliament, do largely reflect the points which Stratford had raised in a personal context.

Kilsby himself, memorably described by Tout as the "stormy petrel of curiality"[255] deserves a postscript, because in this affair personalities are highly significant. His attack on Stratford had badly misfired; his policy of confrontation lay in ruins. He had been worsted in the pamphlet war and derided by some of the magnates. But he was not to be spared the humiliation of reconciliation with his more able opponent. Following the king's own public reconciliation with Stratford, Kilsby at Edward's command accompanied a deputation to the archbishop's manor of Otford. After a suitable show of reluctance on the archbishop's part the former adversaries are said to have embraced and then to have sat down amicably round the dinner table with the rest of the company.[256] It was a bitter denouement. From high hopes of political and ecclesiastical advancement the disappointed but versatile and still energetic curialist turned to martial pursuits. In fulfilment of a vow he set out with the king's blessing in the spring of 1343 on a visit to the Holy Sepulchre. Surviving this perilous ordeal, he took part in the Crécy campaign and apparently died before the walls of Calais in the autumn of 1346, two years before Stratford himself.[257]

---

[252] Notably in his letter of 1 January 1341. E.g. *Foedera* (*R.C.*) 2, p. 1143.

[253] Wilkinson, "Protest of the Earls," p. 191.

[254] Which remained fundamental to Stratford's mind.

[255] *Chapters* 3, p. 161.

[256] Harriss, *King, Parliament and Public Finance*, pp. 520-521 gives the text (from the Winchester cartulary, no. 517) of a letter sent by a member of Stratford's *familia* to an unnamed person. It is dated 3 November [1341] from "Mansfeld" [recte Mayfield].

[257] *Chapters* 3, pp. 161-163; ibid. 6, index s.v.

4

Closing Years 1342-1348

It must be confessed that compared with the earlier period of Stratford's political life, the six years which had still to run before his death constitute a distinct anticlimax and are sparsely documented in the chronicles[1] and elsewhere. To some degree this is compensated for by our knowledge of his activities as metropolitan, which have already been examined.[2]

Following Stratford's formal reconciliation to Edward III in 1341,[3] his further rehabilitation was somewhat delayed. Indeed, it could be that it was never complete. That the destruction in 1343 of the articles alleged against the archbishop was followed some three years later by letters patent attesting his innocence and declaring that he owed nothing to the royal exchequer save the current obligations for chattels and fines with respect to his church of Canterbury, argues an element of insecurity, perhaps engendered by some backbiting on the part of the envious.[4] Possibly it was just a sensible precaution to prevent confiscation of assets after his death. At the same time, our sources suggest that Stratford did receive a substantial measure of the king's confidence and that he dutifully cooperated by giving such counsel as was expected of the primate and of a man of great experience in national affairs. In fact the anonymous Canterbury biographer states that Edward first restored him to the council – he being the wisest and most prudent man in the kingdom – and then, in 1342, made him principal councillor.[5] He is regularly grouped

---

[1] The "continuation" of Murimuth's chronicle provides an exception. Compared with the others it is remarkably full. At this period the chronicler was in his late 60s and early 70s, but kept a close eye on affairs.

[2] See above, "Archbishop of Canterbury," and below, "Ordinances for the Court of Canterbury," and "Provincial Constitutions."

[3] See above, "The Crisis of 1341."

[4] *CPR 1345-1348*, pp. 121-122: Porchester, 3 June 1346.

[5] *Vitae Arch. Cant.*, p. 41 (Lambeth MS 99, fol. 146ᵛ): "Reassumpsit eundem archiepiscopum, tanquam prudentiorem et sagaciorem totius regni Angliae, ad suum privatum concilium; et factus est ei principalis consiliarius in agendis, anno domini

with the chancellor and treasurer, and at such times is afforded pride of place.[6] But there was a change in the nature and extent of the authority or influence which Stratford exercised. Neither he nor his close relatives, the bishops of Chichester and London, held specific office in the government. Such office conferred powers which though incapable of strict definition were none the less considerable.[7] It could be that Stratford was not altogether dismayed by this turn of events. Without the day-by-day grind of secular administration he was able to turn his mind to matters more befitting an archbishop; matters which he had shelved for too long. But there were areas of decision in which Stratford did retain his prominence: those which concerned the king's relationship with the curia and with the church at home. Whether the archbishop became the king's pliant instrument in these matters, or whether he retained a measure of his old independence and determination to defend ecclesiastical liberties is a question about which one ought not to be too dogmatic. It will become clear though that Stratford, by this time an elderly man, had no intention of ending his days in violent dispute with royal authority. The emphasis was to be on cooperation rather than conflict. We still find indications of royal coercion of clerics, but these give rise to no crisis at the national level. Moreover, in the king's dealings with papal emissaries, Stratford's attitude – so far as it can be divined – would seem to be that much as he desired peace, war with France was inevitable while Philip remained obdurate.

For his part Edward had learned more than one salutary lesson. However necessary they might appear as a springboard for action against France foreign alliances, founded and maintained by expensive borrowing, were futile and unstable, as the pope had cautioned.[8] It was also dangerous to give occasion for dissension in parliament, for this might

---

MCCCXLII [apud] Hogges in Normannia." This is a dittography. "Apud Hogges in Normannia" occurs a little later (three lines below in the printed text). Edward, of course, was not there in 1342. BL Cotton MS Julius B.iii, fol. 38ᵛ, is no help, for the text there omits the whole passage about royal activities (possibly an insertion from another source) and runs: "... principalis consiliarius. Post hec circa regimen cure pastoralis...."

   [6] E.g. the six privy seal writs printed in the appendix to *Jean le Bel* 2, nos. 15, 17, 19, 21, 24, 25, all of which date from 1347.

   [7] See Wilkinson, *Chancery*, intro. pp. xxiv-xxxi, for a summary of the powers and authority of the fourteenth-century chancellor. Wilkinson cautiously argues that he possessed "only a limited influence in political affairs" and that "it is to misunderstand his true position entirely to assume that by virtue of his office alone he could dominate the great political councils of the reign of Edward III" (ibid., p. xxvii).

   [8] Vatican Archives, *RV* 132, fol. 52ʳ; *CPL 1305-1342*, p. 564; Pope Benedict XII's letter of 20 July 1337.

serve to foster "popular discontent." Edward was unwilling to contemplate the sacrifice of his warlike ambitions, but outstanding military success and a sounder financial policy, coupled with a growing acceptance of the need for regular taxation to maintain the king's rights abroad and the defence of the realm at home, helped to preserve political stability.[9] No small part of Edward's success can be attributed to greater political maturity. His bullying tactics had proved ineffective against Stratford's reliance on fundamental principles. The king had no stomach for another encounter of the kind and, in any case, Stratford was the last of a line of archbishops prepared to defend clerical liberties *à outrance*. For about thirty years the realm was to enjoy a remarkable freedom from internal political strife.[10]

According to Murimuth the feast of the Assumption (15 August) 1342 was marked by the marriage in the Tower of London of the king's third son, Lionel of Antwerp, to the daughter of the earl of Ulster. There arrived three Dominican friars seeking letters of safe-conduct for Cardinals Pierre des Préz and Annibale di Ceccano, who were anxious to urge the cause of peace in England on behalf of the newly elected Clement VI. Stratford was summoned to Edward's side for consultation. After two days of discussion the king somewhat jauntily replied to the proctors' request. It was not his wish, he declared, to put the cardinals to the expense of crossing the channel. He was prepared to meet them in France, for which he would be sailing in a few days.[11] Already by the writ *Terribilis in iudiciis* Edward had asked Stratford and the other bishops and prelates to petition God, in the manner of Moses, for the success of the expeditions he was planning to despatch to Scotland and to the continent.[12] As it turned out, his departure was delayed and it was not until the end of October that he disembarked at Brest on the Atlantic coast of Brittany.[13]

---

[9] See the discussion in Harriss, *King, Parliament and Public Finance*, chap. 14, and (for 1341) Prestwich, "English Armies," pp. 110-111.

[10] For the "crisis of 1371," which Edward III was unable to manage, see Wilkinson, *Chancery*, pp. 123-127. Highfield, "English Hierarchy," p. 138, suggests that the archbishops' loyalty became "less critical" particularly after 1349, and he concludes: "In the march towards the state-controlled church there was a long and decisive step forward in the reign of Edward III."

[11] *Murimuth*, pp. 125-126, 227. The accepted date for the marriage is the morrow of the Nativity of Our Lady – 9 September. E.g. *HBC*, pp. 36, 464.

[12] *Foedera* 2, iv, p. 134, where it is dated 20 August. The date in *Hemingburgh* 2, pp. 393-394, is 12 August and agrees with that in copies of the mandate sent to the dean of the province by Stratford. E.g. *Worcester Reg. Bransford*, pp. 206, 296; nos. 1045, 1171.

[13] *Murimuth*, p. 128.

Edward's intervention in Brittany was occasioned by the death of Duke John III "Le bon" on the last day of April 1341. This meant a disputed succession and an opportunity too good to miss for embarrassing the French king. Edward determined to support John de Montfort, whose claim (incongruously) was roughly analogous to that of Philip to the throne of France, and conferred on him the honour of Richmond. As was to be expected, Philip supported the rival candidate, his nephew Charles of Blois. But Montfort was soon captured by John duke of Normandy, Charles's cousin, and forced to leave his courageous wife, Joan of Flanders, to carry on the struggle.[14] She was besieged at Hennebont, which was relieved in the nick of time by Sir Walter Manny. Edward himself had some success and eventually settled down to the siege of Vannes, a city second only in importance to Nantes. Philip VI moved his army into the vicinity, but neither king being willing to hazard a battle the ubiquitous cardinals were able to arrange the truce of Malestroit, sealed in the local priory on 19 January 1343. This was to last until Michaelmas and meanwhile – by 24 June – ambassadors from the contending kings were to be sent to Avignon.[15] The English army returned home, the victim of tempestuous weather which occasioned some loss of life. Edward showed himself a devoted son of the church, going on foot as a pilgrim to Canterbury and then on horseback to Gloucester[16] and Walsingham.[17]

Parliament assembled at Westminster on 28 April 1343.[18] It was to prove an arduous session, relieved only by the creation as Prince of Wales of the king's eldest son. Stratford was there on the first day, when such spiritual and temporal lords as had already arrived came together in the white chamber of the royal palace. The following day, Tuesday, the king appeared and the by then customary proclamation against disturbers of

[14] *Jean le Bel* 1, pp. 244-272; *Froissart* (ed. Luce) 2, *sommaire* pp. xxxii-xliv, 86-115. Jean le Bel describes Joan thus: "laquelle avoit bien cuer d'omme et de lyon" (p. 248; cf. *Froissart*, p. 114). *Murimuth*, p. 121, says that the Bretons sought the English king's help against Philip of Valois, who would not admit the rightful heir. Invasion plans of 1341 may have been a major reason for Edward's anxiety to come to terms with Stratford. See Prestwich, "English Armies."

[15] *Murimuth*, pp. 125, 127-135; *Avesbury*, pp. 339-352; *Jean le Bel* 1, pp. 297-342; *Froissart* (ed. Luce) 3, pp. 1-22; Déprez, "La conférence d'Avignon," pp. 301-302. The text of the truce is given in Latin by Murimuth, in French by Avesbury.

[16] This visit to the tomb of his father is worth noting in view of the suggestions that he was not in fact buried there.

[17] *Murimuth*, p. 135.

[18] *HBC*, p. 522: summoned 24 February 1343, writs for expenses 20 May. *Rot. Parl.* 2, pp. 135-145.

the peace was read. Not until the last day of April did Stratford and the king, together with nine bishops (including Robert but not Ralph Stratford), sundry earls and barons, as well as the commons, gather to hear the reasons for the summons. The initial business was to be the truce concluded with France in Brittany, details of which were expounded by Bartholomew Burghersh. It was stated that since the war had been launched by the common assent of prelates, barons and commons, the king wished that decisions about peace should likewise receive their approval. The prelates and barons were then charged to consider the matter in the white chamber, the commons in the painted chamber. Both were to report back on the Thursday (1 May). They did so by commending the truce as honourable, adding that the pope should be approached as peacemaker in the role of a friend rather than that of an adjudicator.[19]

While negotiations preliminary to papal arbitration were under way the king and his advisers decided to rely once again on the sale of wool to finance in part the expected military operations. Recently the amount exported had fallen substantially, with consequent loss of revenue. The immediate task was to devise an arrangement acceptable to the merchants. Minimum prices for the commodity were raised and the commons conceded a subsidy of forty shillings as an addition to the ancient custom. The management of the customs was entrusted by indenture to a "company" of thirty-three merchants, probably acting for the merchant community as a whole. This was an exceptional disposition; previously such revenue had been absorbed mainly by assignment to creditors.[20] Stratford was only too well aware of the difficulties inherent in such arrangements. In his opinion, it will be remembered, the failure of the merchants to meet their obligations had been at the root of the financial crisis of 1340. He was no less aware of the tediousness of the diplomatic negotiations which were being planned.[21]

The commons submitted a sheaf of petitions, the first of which was by then traditional – that the rights and privileges of the church be maintained inviolate. As we have seen, one of the petitions sought the reinstatement of the statutes of 1341, held to have been conceded in return

---

[19] *Rot. Parl.* 2, pp. 135-136. The bishops present were Durham, Chester, St. David's, Salisbury, Ely, Norwich, Exeter, Chichester and Carlisle.

[20] *Murimuth*, p. 136: "Et de pretio certo statuendo super ipsis, secundum diversas partes regni apponendo pretium majus et minus." See Lloyd, *English Wool Trade*, pp. 193-199, for a full discussion of the 1343 arrangements.

[21] See above, "The Crisis of 1341."

for the ninth and 30,000 sacks of wool. Another urged that the chancellor and treasurer should be of sufficiently elevated status; to which the king responded that he would appoint such ministers as he pleased, as his ancestors had done. There is surely more than an echo here of Stratford's contention in 1341. Some petitions touched the church adversely, such as the commons' demand that no one should be impleaded in Court Christian for tithes of brushwood (silva cedua), the church's right to which Stratford had upheld in his provincial statutes of the previous year.[22] Complaint was also made that deans and officials of ecclesiastical courts were taking cognizance of pleas belonging to the crown.[23] It was to be expected that aliens occupying English benefices would be a target for attack on the grounds that many of them were allegedly enemies of the realm who transferred money abroad. Singled out for special condemnation was Cardinal Talleyrand de Périgord, "the bitterest enemy imaginable in the curia." But undoubtedly the petition which raised the most disquiet in Stratford's mind was that which demanded the prohibition of bulls of reservation and provision, as well as of the papacy's levying of first fruits (annates) and tenths.[24] This threatened to undermine curial authority and the fiscal system so carefully created. In the commons' eyes it was a matter of preserving legitimate English interests against outsiders – nonresident aliens. The argument used was well worn; it had provided the basis of a petition at the parliament of Carlisle in 1307, a fact which points to some careful preparation by clerks well acquainted with the precedents. Neither Stratford nor his colleagues on the episcopal bench could openly countenance any such restriction of papal power, although many diocesans were adversely affected by curial inroads on the fund of patronage so essential for the support of their familial clerks.[25] Murimuth informs us that Stratford and the York metropolitan, William la Zouche, wished to withdraw with the other bishops, but were prevented from doing so by Edward's prohibition.[26] Those concerned – the earls, secular lords, knights, burgesses and others of the commons (populares) –

---

[22] *Rot. Parl.* 2, pp. 139-145. See also below, "Provincial Constitutions."

[23] *Rot. Parl.* 2, pp. 142-143 no. 56.

[24] Ibid., pp. 143-144, no. 59. See below for Schordich's expostulation about Talleyrand.

[25] For a recent analysis of papal provision, its effect on English benefices, and the manner in which it could be manipulated for local interests, see Wright, *Church and Crown*, pt. 1, pp. 1-97 (and for the complaints at Carlisle, ibid., pp. 97, 133).

[26] *Murimuth*, p. 138: "Archiepiscopis et episcopis non audentibus adhaerere dictae querelae, immo recedere nitentibus; sed per praeceptum regis compulsi fuerant remanere."

embodied their grievances in the form of a petition for redress to the pope,
dated 18 May 1343. Following a respectful exordium the petition argues
that benefices, whether abbeys, collegiate or parish churches, were
endowed by the ancestors of kings, nobles and others for the honour and
increase of the Christian faith in the land, the maintenance of hospitality
and almsgiving, and to enable those in charge of them to give teaching and
instruction in the native tongue by confession and other means. Yet, by
papal reservation and provision which – as was rightly asserted – had
greatly increased in Clement's time, such benefices were being entrusted
to aliens, some of them the king's enemies. The practice served to
controvert all the pious intentions of the founders; God's service was
destroyed, souls were being imperilled, church fabric was in decay,
scholars lacked support, and treasure was being shipped out of the
country. As remedy the impetrants sought the revocation of all such
provisions and their abandonment for the future.[27]

This plea on behalf of the particular interests of the *Ecclesia Anglicana*
was backed up in September 1343 by a letter from the king himself. He
complained to Pope Clement about what he regarded as encroachment on
his rights and those of his realm. The "fatter" benefices, he argued, had
been given to aliens, often suspected persons, who did not reside, had no
knowledge of their flocks, could not speak the native tongue, and who like
mercenaries sought only their own profit. The letter closed with a strong
condemnation of the papal practice of inhibiting elections effected by
chapters of the greater churches.[28]

A timely incident high-lighted the arguments of the English laity.
Murimuth, a caustic critic of the financial policy of the papacy as it
affected the English church, relates the story at length. Two of the pope's
"nephews," Cardinal Adhémar Robert and the general of the Dominicans,
Cardinal Gérard de Garde, had been allocated the income from vacant
benefices in the provinces of Canterbury and York respectively, to the
tune of a thousand marks each. Their proctors were hailed before the
royal chancellor and members of the council and questioned about the
authority for their actions. Naturally they claimed papal sanction; their
purpose being to prosecute the lawful affairs of their principals. The
explanation was adjudged inadequate and they were consigned to the
custody of the sheriff of London pending their expulsion. In the city
proclamation was made to the effect that no aliens were to attempt to

---

[27] *Murimuth*, pp. 138-142, gives the text in French (the editor adds a translation); cf.
Avesbury, pp. 353-355.
[28] *Foedera* 2, iv, p. 152: 10 September 1343. Cf. ibid., p. 155: 29 November 1343.

secure benefices in England.[29] Writs of 20 July 1343 authorized by king and council were despatched to all bishops forbidding the admission of aliens to benefices or the promulgation of ecclesiastical sentences against those who resisted such men.[30] Instructions were given to sheriffs – in accordance with the determination of the last parliament – to prohibit anyone from executing graces in favour of aliens and to scrutinize all bulls coming into the country.[31]

Clement's reaction was prompt. On 4 August he wrote to Bishop Orleton of Winchester. The choice is significant. Orleton was known to be a defender of papal authority and to have enjoyed a close relationship with Pope John xxii. Moreover his nephews, the Trillek brothers, were actually at the curia, so that messages could be exchanged by word of mouth.[32] The pope adjured Orleton to remain constant in resisting the novelties introduced at the whim of evil men to the dishonour of the Roman church and to join with others in erecting a defensive wall against such intrusions.[33]

Stratford's position was unenviable. Clearly he could not approve the measures to which the king was giving countenance. At the same time he was known to be one of Edward's inner circle of councillors. Some were even suggesting to Pope Clement that both the action against the cardinals' proctors[34] and the policy of excluding aliens from benefices should be laid to his charge. On the first count the king wrote warmly in his defence, though the argument is somewhat equivocal. The archbishop, he urged, had always been a zealous defender of ecclesiastical liberty. The pope should not withdraw his favour, for Stratford was a faithful and useful director of the king's council.[35] The pope himself expressed reluctance to

[29] *Murimuth*, pp. 142-143. See below.

[30] E.g. *Worcester Reg. Bransford*, p. 302. The writ is dated 22 July 1343 in Ely Reg. Montacute, fol. 89ᵛ, and in the margin a face has been drawn with the words "Nota mirabilia."

[31] *Foedera* 2, iv, p. 149: Clarendon, 23 July 1343.

[32] Vatican Archives, *RV* 137, fol. 71ᵛ; *CPL 1342-1362*, p. 2: 4 August 1343.

[33] "Rogamus attencius et hortamur quatinus te constanter tenens in illis super quibusdam novitatibus quas aliquibus malis hominibus procurantibus contra honorem eiusdem sancte Romane ecclesie displicenter audivimus in illis partibus hiis diebus preteritis attemptatas, te pro eadem ecclesia una cum prelatis aliis ipsius ecclesie fidelibus murum defensionis opponens ut a talibus et similibus cessetur penitus." *RV* 137, fol. 71ᵛ.

[34] *Foedera* 2, iv, p. 151: "Et quia sanctitati vestrae (ut dicitur) est suggestum quod ... Cantuariensis archiepiscopus, totius Angliae primas, querelarum et clamorum hujusmodi auctor extitit, vel dederat causam illis, seu quod captionis vel detentionis, quae facta fore praetenditur de nunciis domini cardinalis de Garda, verbo vel opere fautor fuerat et promotor."

[35] "Consilii nostri fidelis et utilis ductor." Ibid.

believe that Stratford was a Judas. It was inconceivable that the archbishop, who owed so much to the church, was now a changed man and
acting to its detriment. He begged Stratford to work for the revocation of
new-fangled measures, so harmful to the church. One of his auditors of
causes, M. William of Norwich, a protagonist of the archbishop's, was
coming to England. He trusted that Stratford would give him every
assistance in these and other matters.[36]

Both the royal letter of September 1343,[37] which expanded the case
against curial policy, and the petition from parliament are said by
Murimuth to have been presented to the pope at Avignon by the veteran
diplomat John Schordich. One version of the chronicle gives a lively and
seemingly authentic account of the interview. Clement received the
emissary seated in a private room surrounded by the cardinals. Schordich
then withdrew to the more public audience chamber while the pope read
the letters he had brought. On Schordich's return some harsh words were
directed towards him, the pope retorting that he had provided only two
aliens to [English] benefices. The emissary was unable to contain himself.
He angrily blurted out: "Holy Father, you *did* provide the lord of Périgord
[Cardinal Talleyrand], whom the English king and all the magnates
consider a major enemy of both king and kingdom." To this Clement
responded: "We know that you did not compose these letters, but there is
one that pricks us and we shall punish him. We know all about this
matter." [38] We are left to guess the object of this threat. We would not
expect Stratford to be implicated, although there can be no question that
his reputation at the curia was much tarnished.

The air was full of rumour and speculation. In January 1344 a royal
letter to Clement recounts an incident which reveals considerable hostility
towards Stratford's brother, the bishop of Chichester. On the way to his
cathedral Bishop Robert's party had been set upon and his baggage
pillaged. Among other items, he was carrying letters addressed to the dean
and chapter requesting their prayers for the success of Edward's
forthcoming expedition. Some of those implicated were alleging in the
curia that the bishop had litigated against them in the royal court to the

---

[36] Ibid., fol. 172v: 13 January 1344. This important letter is obscured by the composite
entry in *CPL 1342-1362*, p. 5.

[37] Dated 10 September in *Foedera* 2, iv, p. 152. The copy in *Murimuth*, pp. 143-146,
has 26 September. The argument, like that of the letter sent by the laity from parliament,
reiterates the line adopted in the preface to the statute of Carlisle (1307). Cf. the preface to
the statute of Provisors (1351). *Statutes* 1, pp. 150, 316.

[38] *Murimuth*, pp. 229-230 (from BL Cotton MS D.x, fols. 131v-132r). Cf. ibid., pp. 143-
146, 149.

prejudice of ecclesiastical jurisdiction. What actually happened, the royal letter contends, was that the bishop took action in a secular court because armed force had been used in violation of the king's peace. The pope was requested not to summon Bishop Robert to the curia, for he was blameless and fully prepared to obey papal mandates.[39] Conflicts of this kind about spheres of jurisdiction and clerks seeking remedy in secular courts were not uncommon,[40] but the fact that Stratford's brother was concerned may indicate something more particular. Much more mysterious is the report said to have been circulating in the curia that Richard FitzAlan, earl of Arundel, had made some (unspecified) aspersions against the archbishop. Clement reassured Edward that to the best of his knowledge the earl had written nothing either in Stratford's favour or to his discredit.[41]

Can it be that Clement was attempting to sow seeds of disharmony in the heart of the royal council? If so, the plan met with little success. It is more likely that he was concerned merely to maintain a steady pressure on English churchmen to rise in defence of papal authority and established practice.[42] But the die was already cast. The earlier measures were fortified by a proclamation against provisors issued at the end of January 1344 and the formulation of writs suitable for its implementation.[43] A letter brought from Avignon in July by Andrew Offord produced an uncanny echo of the sentiments so vigorously expressed by Stratford in 1341. The royal councillors, Clement thundered, had incurred divine and canonical penalties, edicts had been promulgated in derogation

[39] *Foedera* 2, iv, pp. 157-158: 3 January 1344.

[40] See, for instance, in a somewhat earlier period, Flahiff, "Use of Prohibitions," and "Writ of Prohibition."

[41] Vatican Archives, *RV* 138, fols. 1^v-2^r: 19 May 1344. "Nos ne veritatis claritas mendaciorum tenebris super hiis obfuscetur excellenciam regiam volumus non latere quod prefatus comes nec contra prefatum archiepiscopum, nec pro ipso aliqua que nostra teneat memoria nobis scripsit." Arundel, it will be remembered, was the noble who intervened on Stratford's behalf in 1341 (above, "The Crisis of 1341"). But his father was put to death in 1326, when the then bishop of Winchester became a supporter of Isabella.

[42] Mollat, *The Popes at Avignon*, pp. 263-264 (following Schordich's mission): "Knowing full well the power of court intrigues he began secret discussions and hampered the execution of the king's will by means of the insidious schemes he fostered among members of the king's entourage." One would welcome chapter and verse for this statement. Mollat continued by arguing that by such means Clement was able to prevent the implementation of the measures introduced in parliament. But was it ever Edward's intention to implement them, other than selectively?

[43] The writ prohibiting provisions, addressed to the archbishops, bishops and other clergy, is dated 20 [recte 30] January 1344 in *Murimuth*, pp. 153-154, 233. In the appendix to *Murimuth* (from BL. Cotton MS Nero D.x, fols. 133^r-135^r) are printed the king's letter to the Prince of Wales on the subject (dated 30 January) and three forms of writ for execution by sheriffs (pp. 233-242). Cf. *Foedera* (*R.C.*) 3, pp. 2-3.

of ecclesiastical liberties, churchmen had been imprisoned and papal letters intercepted. Edward was enjoined to remedy all this and to conduct himself as a catholic prince.[44] In October 1344 a further letter to Stratford inveighed against the policy of the English government. By such novelties, warned Clement, the divine majesty was affronted, the liberty of the church infringed, the honour and good name of the king and of the whole of the clergy and people brought into disrepute, and men's souls placed in the gravest jeopardy. The archbishop, a man who held the foremost place among the English prelates, the successor of the St. Thomas who had assumed the crown of martyrdom in defence of the church, and a close councillor of the king, should urge Edward to abandon such paths.[45]

Meanwhile, the archbishop was having other troubles of a more domestic kind. Towards the end of August 1343 he was granted royal protection to go to Canterbury on the king's business and his own. Because threats had been made against him, he was authorized to travel with such armed men as might be necessary for his defence.[46] What lay behind this writ is uncertain. There is no corroboration of Stratford's presence at Canterbury at this time, but undoubtedly he would have wished to deliberate with the chapter and to consult the muniments preparatory to his attempt immediately after Michaelmas to visit the see of Norwich. Resistance may well have been anticipated, but possibly not the stubbornness of Bishop Bek, who was nearing the end of his life, and of his cathedral chapter. Appeals to Avignon were made against Stratford.[47] The king was almost too eager in rallying to the support of his archbishop and councillor, but in any case the visitation had to be broken off owing to an urgent summons to a council in London. What happened there will be discussed in a moment in connection with the further negotiations for peace with France.

The diplomatic activity subsequent to the truce of Malestroit need not concern us here, except insofar as it directly involves Stratford. The ebb and flow of the negotiations at the curia have been minutely examined by

[44] Vatican Archives, *RV* 138, fols. 40ᵛ-41ᵛ; *CPL 1342-1362*, p. 9: 11 July 1344.

[45] Vatican Archives, *RV* 138, fol. 100ʳ; *CPL 1342-1362*, p. 11: 8 October 1344. "Ut tu frater qui locum maiorem inter prelatos Anglie obtines, et illius gloriosi martiris beati Thome videlicet qui pro tuendis ecclesie libertatibus coronam martirii est adeptus in archiepiscopali sede successor esse dinosceris, ac carissimi in Christo filii nostri Edwardi regis Anglie illustris assistis lateri super revocandis eiusdem novitatibus efficaciter curares interponere partes tuas."

[46] *CPR 1343-1345*, p. 115: 26 August 1343.

[47] For details of the dispute see above, "Archbishop of Canterbury."

Eugène Déprez in his "La conférence d'Avignon." We have already observed that the English vigorously pursued two divergent issues – the war and papal provision. It was in the March of 1343 that Stratford's old enemy, William Kilsby, who had taken part in the fighting in Brittany, embarked on a pilgrimage to the Holy Land by way of Avignon. He carried the warmest recommendations from Edward as one who had served him well and whom he continued to hold in the highest esteem.[48] On 29 August a substantial embassy headed by the earls of Derby, Warwick and Suffolk, but from which bishops were conspicuously absent, was deputed to appear before the pope in his private capacity.[49] Negotiations were also in train for a marriage treaty with Alfonso, king of Castile, and for an alliance with the neighbouring king of Aragon.[50] Other envoys were busy in Flanders and Brabant – where a double marriage was proposed.[51] Eventually even the duke of Bavaria and his father the emperor were approached, despite the less than satisfactory outcome of earlier arrangements.[52] To the king of Armenia's pleas for help against the "infidels" Edward could express only sympathy, coupled with the promise that he would do what he could when his own difficulties were overcome.[53] The efforts to build alliances, however ephemeral, and the firm attitude towards the exercise of certain aspects of papal authority in England were calculated to strengthen the hands of Edward's negotiators, but effectively diminished the prospect of peace.

Stratford, as we have just noticed, had to relinquish his visitation of Norwich to attend the royal council held in London during the week 21-

[48] *Foedera* 2, iv, pp. 141-143. The king took Kilsby's many benefices under royal protection.

[49] Ibid., pp. 150-151. The embassy included a strong contingent of lawyer-clerks: William (Bateman) of Norwich, dean of Lincoln, the brothers John and Andrew Offord or Ufford (alias le Moigne), and Robert Hereward, archdeacon of Taunton.

[50] E.g. *Foedera* 2, iv, pp. 151-152, 161, 165-167, 170, 180-181.

[51] Ibid., pp. 147, 169, 174; Déprez, "La conférence d'Avignon," p. 313 n. 1. Lucas, *Low Countries*, chap. 13: "The Total Collapse of King Edward's Alliances (1343-1345)." discusses the complexities of the situation in the north. The young count of Hainault, William II, abandoned the policy of his father and in 1343 sought accommodation with Philip VI. Edward's staunch ally Reginald, duke of Guelders, died unexpectedly on 12 October 1343, while Duke John of Brabant, the marriage of his daughter to Edward's son blocked by papal reluctance to grant dispensation, moved towards reconciliation with the exiled Louis of Flanders and with King Philip.

[52] *Foedera* 2, iv, p. 178: 6 July 1345. The vicariate granted to Edward had been revoked in June 1341 because of the emperor's *rapprochement* with Philip of France. *Foedera* 2, iv, pp. 105-106; Lucas, *Low Countries*, p. 437.

[53] *Foedera* 2, iv, p. 152: 22 September 1343: "Turbat quidem nos intime gravis infidelium persecutio, cui regnum vestrum subicitur, hiis diebus." Cf. "In the Seat of Power," n. 159 (the similar response of 1335).

28 November 1343. Andrew Offord, newly returned from the Roman curia was present to report on his mission. The English envoys had urged that an essential preliminary to negotiation was the release of John de Montfort in compliance with the terms of Malestroit. This matter, according to Murimuth's remarkably full account, which would appear to anticipate subsequent negotiations, was shelved by the pope and the French in favour of the principal business. While not giving way on this issue the English turned to a declaration of Edward's claim to the French crown on the grounds that he was the nearest lawful heir of Charles IV.[54] The pope then advanced counter-arguments on behalf of King Philip. How, he asked, could the English monarch maintain such a claim when he was excluded from the French throne on three counts? First, because there were other survivors of lawful blood in the masculine line. Secondly, because the mother of the English king was incapable of succeeding to the realm of France, despite her relationship to Charles.[55] Lastly, because Edward had actually performed homage to Philip of Valois as king of France and then by his letters acknowledged this to be liege homage. This last argument was an embarrassing one for Stratford, who was held to have been the councillor chiefly responsible.[56] What happened next, according to Andrew Offord, was that the English envoys offered to respond to these points, but that the pope did not wish to hear them at that stage, preferring to deliberate instead about the duchy of Aquitaine, which was considered to be the direct cause of the war. As the envoys lacked authority to do this they sought leave to withdraw; a request which the pope was reluctant to concede lest the truce be breached.[57]

The council over, Offord returned to Avignon to secure safe-conducts for the members of an important mission, the chief object of which was to prolong the truce.[58] The king's letter to Clement announcing this

---

[54] *Murimuth*, pp. 147-149.

[55] Ibid.: "licet sit soror dicti regis Karoli ex utroque parente." Isabella was the "first-born" of Philip le Bel, Charles (IV) the youngest son. Isabella, even the English admitted, "juxta consuetudinem et statutum praedicta in dicto regno succedere non potest." The statute was alleged to have embodied custom and to have been enacted in Charles IV's reign. See ibid., pp. 100-101, where Edward's claim is set out and the objections made to it. For a modern summary see Perroy, *Hundred Years War*, pp. 69-76; and, at length, Giesey, *Juristic Basis of Dynastic Right to the French Throne*.

[56] See above, "The Crisis of 1341." It was argued on the English side that when Edward performed homage he was a minor, even on the second occasion: "pubet tamen, et adhuc minor existens declaravit per literas suas authenticas illud homagium fore ligium." *Murimuth*, p. 101.

[57] *Murimuth*, p. 148: "Ne treuga videretur infringi."

[58] Ibid., pp. 152-153. Cf. *Foedera* 2, iv, p. 155.

development blamed the French for infractions of the truce and on the subject of provisions denied that royal policy embodied novelties; he was only following the practice of his progenitors, in particular that of his grandfather, Edward I.[59] The death of Bishop Bek of Norwich on the night of 18-19 December 1343[60] provided a test case for the government's resolution with regard to papal provision. William Bateman alias "of Norwich," dean of Lincoln, a distinguished lawyer, papal chaplain and auditor of the sacred palace, was elected by the canons acting on "divine inspiration."[61] This man, who came from an urban background comparable to Stratford's own, was almost certainly personally congenial to the archbishop. But Clement, ignoring the chapter's procedures, claimed the reservation of the see and on 23 January 1344 issued provisory bulls in Bateman's favour.[62] The bishop-elect, who was at the papal court as one of Edward's negotiators, returned to London about the beginning of February. If Murimuth speaks the truth, he persuaded the royal council of his potential usefulness in Avignon[63] and by that means secured the speedy livery of his temporalities. Edward sent him to Stratford, who was at his manor of Otford in Kent. With Bateman came knights and clerks of the king's inner council,[64] accompanied by the keeper of the privy seal, John Offord. The intention was to prepare letters for the pope with the archbishop's assistance. Bateman shortly returned to the curia at the head of an embassy. It was only at this point, argues Déprez, that Edward finally agreed to accept papal arbitration. Once at the curia Bateman was consecrated and then secured a bull to reimburse himself for the expenses of his journey in both directions and for his stay in Avignon. Execution of this bull was entrusted to Stratford and to the dean of St. Paul's, who levied a halfpenny in the mark on ecclesiastical benefices. Such astuteness did not commend itself to Murimuth who uncharitably concluded that Bateman effected no business but served his own interest. He did help to secure his former deanery of Lincoln for

[59] *Foedera* 2, iv, p. 155: 29 November 1343. The embassy included the earls of Derby, Warwick, Suffolk, and Huntingdon, barons Bartholomew Burghersh and Thomas de Bradeston, and the clerks M. William of Norwich and M. John Offord.

[60] Norwich Reg. Anthony Bek, fol. 73ᵛ.

[61] *Murimuth*, pp. 156-157; Vatican Archives, *RV* 138, fols. 40ᵛ-41ᵛ; *CPL 1342-1362*, p. 9.

[62] Norwich Reg. Bateman, fol. 41ʳ.

[63] *Murimuth*, p. 157: "Veniens circa Purificationem [2 February] ad regem, qui tunc fuit Londoniis cum concilio suo, quibus se facturum erga papam multa promisit."

[64] "Idem dominus rex misit eum ad archiepiscopum Cantuariensem apud Ortefordiam cum quibusdam militibus et clericis secretioribus sui concilii." Ibid., p. 157.

another of Edward's negotiators, John Offord, Stratford's short-lived successor at Canterbury.[65]

Talk of peace at Avignon was accompanied in England by financial preparations for war. Following commissions of 5 February 1344 Stratford must have been busy examining the accounts of the Bardi and Peruzzi, as well as those of Paul de Montefiori.[66] He would also have been at the council which met at Westminster on 18 April, to which the bishops and other prelates were summoned. There, we are told, it was decided that royal business could not be carried out without parliament and convocation.[67] But the convocation of 31 May was ill attended; apart from Stratford only the bishops of London, Chichester, Ely (Montacute) and the bishop-elect of Hereford (John Trillek) put in an appearance to debate the prospective taxation for the king's needs. This angered Edward, who directed Stratford to take measures against those who had not responded to the summons.[68] There was a similar lack of attendance during the first few days of the parliament which followed convocation on 7 June. Only on the 10th was it possible to declare the reasons for the meeting, by which time there was a respectable quorum of some ten bishops, including Stratford.[69] The provisions of the truce were outlined and then the violations of it attributed to the French king. As for the Scots, the abettors of Philip, the statement alleged their open declaration to break the truce as soon as they were given the word by their ally.[70] In response the clergy made an exceptional grant of a triennial tenth, but not without considerable concessions on the king's behalf made in response to clerical petitions. These were embodied in letters under the royal seal dated 8 July 1344 and were commonly regarded by the clergy as a statute.[71] The

---

[65] Ibid.; Salisbury Reg. Wyville 1, fols. 121^r-123^r (al. 142-143); Lunt, *Financial Relations* 2, pp. 638-639; *Biog. Cantab.*, s.v. Bateman, William alias Norwich (de Northwico, de Norwico). A farthing in the pound of Stratford's levy was for earlier procurations. See also Déprez, "La conférence d'Avignon," pp. 304-305, and for documentation of the arbitration process (including a number of letters to Stratford), *Froissart* (ed. Lettenhove) 18, pp. 205-206 nos. 57-58.

[66] Among others. *CPR 1343-1345*, pp. 274, 276, 284.

[67] *Rot. Parl.* 2, p. 146 no. 1.

[68] Ibid.; *Murimuth*, p. 156.

[69] *Rot. Parl.* 2, pp. 146 no. 1, 147 no. 6.

[70] Ibid., p. 147 no. 7.

[71] E.g. Ely Reg. Montacute, fols. 91^v-92^r, where the rubric runs: "Statutum domini regis factum prelatis et aliis personis ecclesiasticis in subsidium libertatis ecclesie." For the grant see *Rot. Parl.* 2, p. 148 no. 9; for the clerical petitions and responses to them, ibid., pp. 151-152; for the clerical charter of 8 July, ibid., pp. 152-153, and cf. *Statutes* 1, pp. 302-303.

contents have already been outlined in the discussion of convocation.[72] Here it may be remarked that the first petition, against the arraignment of archbishops or bishops before the justices in criminal cases – they being subject in such matters solely to the pope – was closely related to Stratford's own experience. Although the king's reaction was disarmingly positive, the caveat "unless by our special order" effectively nullified the concession.[73] The tactic employed in this parliament is reminiscent of that used in 1340, when Stratford secured his "charter of liberties." As Murimuth ruefully observed, although the king promised much to clergy and people, royal promises were ill kept.[74]

Other developments in parliament were by no means to Stratford's liking. Commons' petitions, additional to those which conditioned their financial grant to the king, were designed to consolidate the anti-papal measures of the parliament of 1343. There were demands for the punishment of those who attempted to upset decisions of the royal court by appeals to Avignon, for the enforcement of the ordinance against persons who since that parliament had accepted benefices by papal process, together with the request that ordinances made at that time should be given the permanence of statute. Other petitions set out arrangements for filling benefices vacated by those who occupied them by virtue of papal reservation or provision, demanded the acceptance of bishoprics by election rather than by papal provision and the diversion to the defence of the realm of the profits of benefices held by aliens resident in enemy territory.[75] If Stratford was ever given to reliance on "popular" support in his efforts to protect the rights of the church, he was now in a difficult position. There was clearly a limit to what could be endured even under the pressures of preparation for war.

It was about the beginning of July 1344 that Henry "of Grosmont," earl of Derby, returned to England from Avignon. He had conversed with the pope, particularly about the crusade, an idea restored to life by Clement's enthusiasm.[76] This was the occasion for the summoning of a council to meet in London on 11 August.[77] Whether Stratford was there or not we

[72] See above, "Archbishop of Canterbury."
[73] *Rot. Parl.* 2, p. 152: "Si le roi ne le comande especialment."
[74] *Murimuth*, p. 156: "Licet ex parte domini regis multae libertates et bonae conditiones clero et populo promittantur, regales tamen promissiones hujusmodi servare non curant, sed, illis praetermissis, totum quod conceditur plene levatur."
[75] *Rot. Parl.* 2, pp. 153-154.
[76] Luttrell, "Crusade in the Fourteenth Century," p. 134.
[77] *Murimuth*, pp. 158-159. The chronicler confessed he did not know what news the earl brought, though he suspected it was displeasing. Cf. Clement's letter of 21 July 1345 and its mention of Derby (ibid., p. 183).

are not told, but as the meeting was a prelude to sending further envoys to the pope his presence was doubtless *de rigueur*. The archbishop is said by Murimuth to have been present at another "secret council," which met towards the beginning of October to discuss letters sent by Dean Offord, who remained at the curia. Precisely what transpired was unknown to Murimuth,[78] but a reply to proposals made by the pope was entrusted to M. John Thoresby and Sir Ralph Spigurnel, who were also instructed to secure dispensations for the Brabant marriages. From the relatively lowly status of these envoys Murimuth deduced that the suggestions forwarded by Offord were unacceptable. In fact he appears to have been mistaken, for the envoys were charged to deal with infringements of the truce more or less on the lines proposed by the pope and to seek its extension until mid-Lent 1345. Another decision allegedly arrived at by the royal council was that Edward should winter in England, despite the heavy expenditure, much of it now wasted, which had been incurred in preparations for his early departure for the continent.[79]

Clement, with Senecan stoicism, remained outwardly sanguine about his capacity to avert the threatened catastrophe of a full-scale war between Christian monarchs. John de Rippis, a Carmelite friar and papal chaplain, of whom Murimuth speaks disparagingly,[80] arrived in England at the beginning of November. His first call was on Stratford, after which he sought out the king.[81] The archbishop was one of many who had been forewarned of the Carmelite's coming. Clement urged him to cooperate in the struggle for peace, emphasizing the merit which would accrue in the sight of God to all who aided the cause.[82] Some part of the Carmelite's message concerned the earl of Derby's proposal for an assembly point for the crusading forces, to which the pope himself would come.[83] Clement declined to make any move in that direction until he could be assured of the peaceful intentions of the French and English towards each other.[84] It

---

[78] Ibid., p. 159: "Sed quae vel quales fuerunt dictae viae pacis oblatae, vel quae responsiones datae fuerunt, sciri non potuit in communi."

[79] Ibid., pp. 159-160; Déprez, "La conférence d'Avignon," pp. 318-319.

[80] *Murimuth*, p. 160: "Vir utique profanae religionis."

[81] Ibid.: "Primo venit ad archiepiscopum et postea accessit ad regem."

[82] Vatican Archives, *RV* 138, fol. 100ᵛ: 8 October 1344. The pope mentions the receipt at the hands of Rippis of letters from Stratford, the king, and the earl of Derby, which he discussed with the Carmelite and with John Offord. He expressed himself pleased with the content of Stratford's letters.

[83] Ibid. and cf. *Murimuth*, p. 184.

[84] Vatican Archives, *RV* 138, fol. 100ᵛ: "Nequaquam expediens visum fuit nos appropinquare ad locum de quo comes predictus nobis scripsit quousque super via pacis reformande aliqua de intentione partium magis pacifice sentiremus."

must have been shortly before Christmas that a further messenger reached England with a clutch of papal letters addressed to influential persons, including Stratford.[85] Their purport was to give notice of Clement's intention to send his nuncios Nicolino Canali, archbishop of Ravenna, and Pedro Alfonso, bishop of Astorga. Stratford was told that the pope had urged the king not to delay granting safe-conducts. Failure to act rapidly would prove expensive and bring opprobrium on the apostolic see; the archbishop was to exert his influence to see that the necessary letters were issued in the form appropriate for papal envoys. Thus ended ineffectually the papal attempt to arbitrate at Avignon.[86]

The threatened arrival of the nuncios was an embarrassment. Bent on prosecuting the war, Edward was none the less anxious to maintain the impression that it was not of his making. There was a flurry of activity. Edward hastened to join Stratford at Orsett, where the archbishop was staying with his nephew Ralph, the bishop of London. It was a small gathering but included three earls. Debate continued day and night. A council could not be summoned until after the Christmas festival, which Edward was to spend in Bishop Bateman's palace at Norwich. It was at that point – on Christmas Eve according to Murimuth – that a papal courier arrived with Clement's request for his nuncios' safe-conducts. Shortly thereafter a returning envoy, Hugh Neville, brought the latest news and further letters from the curia. It was decided to refer the matters which had arisen to a council in London on 10 January 1345.[87]

Stratford and his brother Robert are said to have been the only prelates at this council, though six earls and a few barons attended. It was agreed that safe-conducts should be issued for the nuncios, who were thought to be waiting expectantly at Wissant.[88] The initial idea was to summon a further council to the capital at the beginning of Lent, so that the papal ambassadors could be given a hearing. Only after that would envoys be sent to the curia. The king altered the arrangements by travelling towards Canterbury and intercepting the nuncios en route at Stratford's manor of Teynham.[89] If Murimuth is accurate the principal topic under discussion

---

[85] Ibid., fols. 135ʳ-136ʳ; *CPL 1342-1362*, pp. 12-13. The letter to Stratford is dated 21 November 1344. There is an earlier one (ibid., fol. 115ʳ⁻ᵛ) dated 3 November.

[86] Vatican Archives, *RV* 138, fol. 136ʳ: 21 November 1344. A copy of the form required was included with the archbishop's letters. See also Déprez, "La conférence d'Avignon," p. 309-310, 319.

[87] *Murimuth*, p. 160; Déprez, "La conférence d'Avignon," p. 319.

[88] *Murimuth*, p. 161.

[89] Ibid.: "Postmodum mutato consilio, direxit se rex versus Cantuariam, ipsoque constituto in manerio archiepiscopi apud Tenham."

was not peace but the question of royal permission for the continuance of papal provision and reservation of bishoprics and other benefices.[90] After consultation among the few councillors present – including Stratford, one surmises – the reply was given that the king had no knowledge of any injury done to the apostolic see, but would make enquiry and if necessary rectify anything of the kind. Naturally the nuncios were ill satisfied with such a devious reply and endeavoured to secure a statement from the king's own mouth. When Edward did respond personally it was in exactly the same terms, though coupled with a promise to discuss the business with the peers of the realm and then to provide a fuller answer. The nuncios were anxious to prolong their stay until this should be done, but the king would not allow them to remain. Instead he granted licence for their return to the pope with the message that he could not permit anything which might be to his prejudice or that of the crown. Before leaving the country the nuncios lingered at Canterbury, where Stratford provided them with suitable procurations with the intention, as Murimuth churlishly commented, of recouping himself later from the clergy of the province.[91]

An insight into the king's reasons for not giving the papal ambassadors a formal hearing is provided by Clement's letter, dated 30 January 1345, in which he denied a rumour that they were being sent to fulminate sentences against the king. No such authority had been granted, only that of using friendly and charitable persuasion.[92] The pope was clearly disappointed with the lack of response to his representations and after discussion with Bishop Bateman sent a much more conciliatory statement of his intentions. He would not accept any abridgment of his powers, but it was not his intention to be as liberal with provision to English benefices as he had been at the time of his promotion.[93] Conciliatory measures had

---

[90] Ibid.: "Rogabant et hortabantur quod dominus rex permitteret, sicut sui anteces-sores permiserunt, summam pontificem episcopatus, dignitates, prebendas, et ecclesias collationi sedis apostolicae reservare, conferre." Cf. Lunt, *Financial Relations* 2, pp. 335, 639.

[91] *Murimuth*, pp. 161-162. Their departure is said to have been followed by a "secret council."

[92] Vatican Archives, *RV* 138, fols. 191ᵛ-192ʳ; *CPL 1342-1362*, p. 15: 30 January 1345. Similar letters were sent to others in addition to the king, including Stratford.

[93] Vatican Archives, *RV* 138, fol. 245ᵛ; *CPL 1342-1362*, p. 17: 5 April 1345. "Pro parte nostra inter cetera verbotenus explicari quod licet non intenderemus sicut non intendere debebamus super collacionibus et provisionibus beneficiorum ecclesiasticorum vel aliis ad auctoritatem apostolicam spectantibus artare potestatem nostram vel etiam limitare quominus illa si quando et quociens nobis videretur honestum et expediens uteremur tamen super provisionibus huiusmodi de ipsis beneficiis in regno et terris tuis consistentibus indigenis vel extraneis faciendis non intendebamus extunc nos sic liberales sicut in nostre promocionis auspiciis...."

already been outstripped by events; the question of papal rights became overshadowed by the threat of war.

All the same, 1345 was to be the year in which the respective claims of pope and king were put to the test. It so happened that three major bishoprics were to fall vacant in quick succession. Murimuth, now an old man, was carpingly critical of papal procedures, particularly with regard to their impact on the English church. He watched the situation carefully and his chronicle gives a detailed if somewhat prejudiced summary in each instance. The see of Durham was the first to fall vacant with Richard de Bury's death on 14 April (not May as Murimuth says). The Benedictine chapter, though allegedly aware of papal reservation, without enthusiasm (magis concorditer quam hilariter) agreed to elect Thomas Hatfield, keeper of the privy seal. Although, states Murimuth, the pope declared the reservation, to please the king he conferred the see on Hatfield with licence to be consecrated where he wished. In fact Stratford conducted his consecration in the chapel of his Otford manor.[94] Then, on 20 June, Bishop Simon de Montacute died. This was unexpected, for he was comparatively young and vigorous (juvenis et fortis). Ely was also a monastic chapter, and the monks were brave enough to elect their prior. But fearing reservation, the elect did not pursue the matter energetically. Papal letters arrived on 29 July naming as bishop a papal penitentiary, the English Dominican Thomas de Lisle. When Thomas arrived in England Stratford as metropolitan surrendered to him the spiritualities and the king, allegedly at the prompting of his ministers, granted livery of the temporalities.[95] Seemingly there was no friction. Finally, on 18 July, the great bishopric of Winchester fell vacant with Adam Orleton's death. This time the situation was a little more complicated. William Edington had been acting as coadjutor for Orleton, who had also been assisted by his nephew, the new bishop of Hereford. Once again the chapter was a monastic one and the monks, by virtue of a congé d'élire issued in the name of Lionel, acting as custos in the king's absence, proceeded to elect one of their number, John Devenesch. The king, who had revoked his son's licence, was extremely angry and imposed a penalty of two thousand marks on the monastery. Undeterred, the elect left for Avignon. Not until Christmas Eve did papal letters of provision arrive.[96] These

[94] *Murimuth*, pp. 172-172; *Biog. Oxon.*, s.v.
[95] *Murimuth*, p. 172; *Biog. Cantab.*, s.v. A D.Th., he was provided 15 July, consecrated at Avignon 24 July, and received his temporalities 10 September 1345. Vatican Archives, *RV* 139, fols. 42ᵛ-43ʳ; *CPL 1342-1362*, p. 19.
[96] *Murimuth*, pp. 172-173.

nominated William of Edington, who in 1344 had become royal treasurer and whom Edward had recommended to the pope. The new bishop in his turn was consecrated by Stratford in the chapel at Otford.[97] As for the disappointed Devenesch, Clement conferred on him the abbacy of St. Augustine's Canterbury, where the inmates had just elected William de Kennington. The king, who claimed the rights of a patron, in a letter to the pope condemned Devenesch as an ambitious schemer and asked that Kennington's election be upheld. The monks were prohibited from allowing the papal provisor to administer the abbey's temporalities. In consequence the luckless Devenesch was confined to Nackington, a manor just outside Canterbury, from which he appointed Kennington as prior. As the king rightly pointed out to the pope, the situation was highly irregular. Devenesch was from another monastery and unknown to St. Augustine's.[98] The net result of all this was that at Durham the king had successfully secured the unopposed election of his nominee by a compliant chapter; at Winchester the pope, claiming reservation, had provided the royal candidate and endeavoured to accommodate the chapter's choice elsewhere; only at Ely had Clement enjoyed unrestricted exercise of his authority. It is evident that both pope and king were prepared to compromise. As usual the chapters were effectively deprived of their rights.

These events were central to Stratford's interests, but most people's concerns were concentrated elsewhere. John de Montfort escaped from his prison in France and on 20 May 1345 appeared before Stratford and other prominent members of the king's council at Lambeth, where he performed homage for the duchy of Brittany.[99] On 14 June Edward made formal declaration of Philip's rupture of the truce and embodied his arguments to that effect in latters patent directed to the cardinals.[100] At about the same time Stratford was required to offer the customary supplications for the royal success.[101] Lionel, the king's son, who was not

[97] On 14 May. Ibid., p. 192. The chronicler (p. 173) suggests that the pope delayed provision "exspectans preces magnorum et licitationes volentium plus offerre."

[98] Thorne, cols. 2081-2084. He comments: "Et predictus dominus Willelmus [Edington] sic episcopatum sortitus est quia sic honorabitur quem rex honorare voluerit." Clement vi in a bull dated 18 June 1348 asked Stratford to use his influence with the king on behalf of the "abbot of Canterbury" (presumably, St. Augustine's) whom allegedly Edward "himself had proposed for the bishopric of Winchester" [?]. See Sources ... Instrumenta Miscellanea, p. 54 no. 148 (I.M. 6316).

[99] Foedera 2, iv, p. 177.

[100] Murimuth, pp. 165-168.

[101] Foedera 2, iv, p. 180: 15 June 1345. The writ Cum sit militia vita hominis super terram and the action taken by virtue of it are recorded in various episcopal registers, e.g. Worcester Reg. Bransford, p. 315.

yet seven years old, became *custos* of the realm and two days later, 3 July, Edward sailed from Sandwich for an undisclosed destination, which turned out to be the Low Countries.[102] There Edward had an interview with his old ally van Artevelde, who shortly afterwards was murdered at Ghent. Angry at this blow to his plans, the king sailed back to Sandwich.[103] On the continent the English offensive was two-pronged. Henry, earl of Derby, accompanied by the earl of Pembroke, took a force to Gascony where he gained many successes and remained until January 1347.[104] The earl of Northampton, with the earls of Hereford and Devon, sailed from Porchester to Brittany, taking with them the Montfort claimant to the duchy.[105]

At home on 16 October 1345 a royal council met at Westminster. Stratford was in attendance with two other bishops, Hatfield of Durham and Bateman of Norwich. Also there were the earls of Warwick, Arundel and Huntingdon and M. John Offord, the dean of Lincoln, who was made chancellor at this time. On the agenda was a lengthy letter from Pope Clement. This constituted a review of events and of the negotiations for peace since the truce of Malestroit, in the context of the wider affairs of Christendom – the struggle in the East and the death of Henry, patriarch of Jerusalem. By implication Edward was blamed for the relapse into war, because following the return from the curia of John Thoresby and Ralph Spigurnel he had failed to send a more impressive embassy with Derby and Bartholomew Burghersh as members.[106] Murimuth regarded the papal interpretation as partial to the king of France.[107] The council was still in session when news arrived of the slaying by the Frisians of the count of Hainault, the queen's brother, and of the disaster to his army.

[102] *Murimuth*, pp. 164-165, 170. The chronicler gives 4 July as the date of sailing. *Foedera* 2, iv, p. 184, gives the date of the king's departure in the *Swallow* as Sunday 3 July at the ninth hour.

[103] *Murimuth*, pp. 164, 243-244 (from BL Cotton MS Nero D.x, fol. 135ʳ⁻ᵛ); ibid., pp. 164-165, 169-170. The king claimed to have rectified the situation in Flanders, but to have been blown onto the English shore while hastening "ad partes inimicorum." *Foedera* 2, iv, pp. 185-186: 3 August 1345; Lucas, *Low Countries*, pp. 524-525.

[104] *Avesbury*, pp. 355-357, 372-376, incorporating a letter from the earl which recounts his exploits.

[105] *Murimuth*, p. 164.

[106] Ibid., pp. 176-189. The "lowly courier of the pope" (quidam simplex cursor) brought not only the king's extensive letter (dated 25 July 1345) but also three others, addressed to Stratford, the bishop of Durham, and the earl of Arundel respectively. The date of the council is given as "Monday the feast of St. Michael in Monte Tumba," though this fell on Sunday (16 October) in 1345.

[107] Ibid., p. 188: "Ex praefatis literis colligeres evidenter quod papa regem Franciae ab omni culpa nititur excusare et regi Angliae impingere omnem culpam."

From Flanders came a request for the appointment of a leader to protect the inhabitants from their count and from the power of France. More cheerful was the news from Brittany – though the duke had died – and from Gascony.[108]

The king left for the Scottish border where his presence was urgently needed. King David's return in 1341 had been followed by Scottish raids on the northern counties of England. By the spring of 1342 the English, who possessed no system of fortified towns with integral castles readily supplied from the sea, such as existed in North Wales, were reduced to holding little more than the town of Berwick. Malestroit brought some respite, but raiding was resumed in strength during 1345.[109] In Edward's absence Stratford, the bishops of London and Norwich, the earls of Arundel and Huntingdon, Chancellor Offord and William of Edington, the treasurer, were deputed to receive the archbishop of Ravenna, the papal nuncio.[110] He arrived about Martinmas (11 November) but, according to Murimuth, was unwilling to divulge his business to the council in the king's absence and so remained in London.[111] Not until mid-December did Edward return from the north. Stratford, his nephew Ralph, the earls of Arundel and Suffolk were present with other members of the council when the nuncio outlined the papal plan for negotiating a truce in Brittany with the aid of the two cardinals, who were holding themselves in readiness to travel to any place that might be appointed.[112] Bartholomew Burghersh then spoke, arguing that Edward's adversary, who unjustly detained the realm of France, was responsible for breaking the truce by his capture and execution of men who were allies of the English king in Brittany and by other nefarious deeds on land and sea.[113] He added that because the king's allies were widespread no individual place could be assigned for peace talks; without their cooperation nothing could be decided. Finally, Burghersh is said to have declared that in

---

[108] Ibid., p. 189. With respect to Hainault the count, as we have seen above (n. 51), had ceased to be Edward's ally. In Flanders the internal strife which brought van Artevelde's death did not alter Edward's relationship with the Flemings. The king's financial policy of subsidizing the princes of the Low Countries and Germany had been abandoned. See Lucas, *Low Countries*, p. 525. In Brittany, Murimuth says, the inhabitants did homage to the earl of Northampton in the name of the English king and on behalf of the heir who was in England.

[109] For a summary of the Scottish situation see Campbell, "England, Scotland and Hundred Years War," pp. 189-193ff.

[110] *Foedera* 2, iv, p. 188: 8 November 1345.

[111] *Murimuth*, pp. 189-190.

[112] Ibid., pp. 190-191.

[113] For the execution of Breton nobles at Paris see *Jean le Bel* 2, p. 22 and n. 2.

pursuit of his right Edward would have to join his allies as soon as possible. If the pope were then to consider it appropriate he could send the cardinals, to whom the king might well give a hearing. The nuncio then asked when this was likely to be. Burghersh was enigmatic. When the king did come, the whole of Christendom would be aware of it, so no doubt would be left in the pope's mind! After which flamboyant utterance the envoy sought leave to depart.[114] Stratford was left to raise from the much taxed clergy of his province the procurations expected for his extended stay.[115]

Even then the pope did not abandon hope, but kept the cardinals hovering in the Low Countries ready to take advantage of the least opportunity to intervene. Meanwhile in England, on the pretext that the country had been constantly racked by war and that in consequence the treasury was empty, Edward declared it to be right and just that the goods of those in the realm should be utilized to defray the cost of defence. Following learned counsel's advice, he intended to apply the income of all benefices held by aliens, apart from the amount necessary to support essential outgoings, to the country's urgent needs.[116] As was to be anticipated, such outright confiscation of ecclesiastical goods brought a stern remonstrance from Pope Clement to Stratford. Would that those who advised the king to adopt such a course had been mindful of their own salvation! Occupiers of ecclesiastical goods were guilty of sacrilege and thereby incurred the church's penalties. God, in whose power lay the rights of all kingdoms, would not let such an evil go unpunished. These goods were taken without consent and those who kept them were in great danger for the offence to God's majesty. On his obedience Stratford was urged to do everything in his power to deflect the king from so misguided

---

[114] *Murimuth*, pp. 191-192.

[115] Ibid., p. 192: "Remansit tamen propter festa et procurationem quindecim florenum, quos recepit omni die." Stratford's mandate for the levying of procurations at this rate for fifty-five days is in Salisbury Reg. Wyville, fol. 164ʳ (al. 184ʳ), dated from Leicester, 15 January 1346. Cf. Ely Reg. Lisle, fols. 55ʳ-56ᵛ; Lunt, *Financial Relations* 2, pp. 639-640.

[116] *Foedera* 2, iv, p. 191: royal letter of explanation to the pope, 12 February 1346. All aliens, or the proctors of those abroad whose benefices were not yet in the king's hand, were to appear before the king and his council on 6 March. See, for instance, *Worcester Reg. Bransford*, where the bishop returned that the mandate had been received so late that the officials of the archdeacons could not execute it in time. A further writ of 15 September required the names of all aliens, the valuation of their benefices, and details of residence. Ibid., pp. 318, 322; also *Hereford Reg. Trillek*, p. 284, and for a very full return to the September writ, pp. 287-289.

a course.[117] The archbishop had already taken action by summoning a provincial assembly to meet on 4 May 1346. Some little time after the formal summons he wrote privately to his suffragans deprecating "certain novelties" introduced against God, His church and its ministers, and urging attendance at the council so that these could be resisted.[118] Stratford's uneasiness on the score of the church's liberties, even his spirited counteractions, were apparently insufficient to lose him the king's confidence or his position as principal councillor. In conjunction with Treasurer Edington and Chancellor Offord he was commissioned to raise loans from English and foreign merchants. In the same month, July 1346, with Edington and Ralph Stratford he was deputed to treat with the envoys of the kings of Spain and Hungary whose arrival was expected during the king's absence.[119]

At last Edward himself was ready to mount an expedition. He landed at La Hougue in the Cotentin on 12 July. By a strange irony one of those knighted on his landing was Roger Mortimer, grandson of the earl of March executed in 1330. The fact that it was to Stratford that Bartholomew Burghersh addressed newsletters with details of Edward's successes could indicate not merely the archbishop's prominence in the council, but also his sympathy with the policy that lay behind that baron's forceful intervention at the audience for the archbishop of Ravenna.[120] When the earl of Huntingdon returned to England from the scene of operations he brought with him a document fortuitously discovered at Caen. It was an agreement, dated 23 March 1339 from Bois-de-Vincennes, between the king of France and the duke of Normandy. Its purpose was an invasion of England, which if successful would have meant the country's subordination to the duke with the aid of France. Stratford, realizing its propaganda value, published it in St. Paul's

---

[117] Vatican Archives, *RV* 139, fols. 273ᵛ-274ʳ; *CPL 1342-1362*, p. 25: 24 April 1346. "Fraternitatem tuam requirimus monemus et in domino attencius exhortamur in virtute obediencie tibi nichilominus iniungentes quatinus super hiis te murum defensionis sicut teneris exhibens et exponens eundem regem qui utinam modicitatem utilitatis ordinacionis huiusmodi respectu tanti scandali meditacione pia et provida ponderaret ut nostris huiusmodi monitis effectualiter acquiescat inducere viis et modis quibus poteris non postponas."

[118] E.g. *Hereford Reg. Trillek*, pp. 272-273, dated 10 March.

[119] *Foedera* 2, iv, pp. 201-202.

[120] *Murimuth*, pp. 199ff. Two of Burghersh's letters to Stratford, one dated 12 [recte 17?] July from la Houghe, the other 29 July from Caen, are interpolated by Murimuth (ibid., pp. 200-201, 202-204). Burghersh was left a silver cup by Stratford in his will. At the beginning of August details of the landing were sent to the archbishop for publication, with the request that prayers, masses and processions (with litanies) be performed for the king's continued success. *Foedera* 2, iv, p. 203.

churchyard during the ceremonies marking the feast of the Assumption.[121] Its effect in arousing the crowd to vociferous support for their warrior-king can be imagined.[122]

Communications with the front were well maintained. Edward's continued successes on the continent were relayed to royal councillors and to the London house of the Dominicans by the king's confessor, Br. Richard de Wynkeleye (Winkley), and by M. Michael Northburgh, nephew of the bishop of Coventry and Lichfield. Winkley recounted the good fortune of the English from the capture of Caen until the victory of Crécy (26 August 1346), where two kings allegedly lay dead on the field of battle.[123] After this Calais was besieged, but not taken until the first week of August in the following year, 1347.[124] The successes of the earl of Lancaster, the title to which Derby succeeded on the death of his father, were only less striking. La Réole, lost to the French king as long before as 1325, was retaken and on 4 October 1346 Poitiers was captured.[125] A less predictable victory was achieved on 17 October 1346 when the local levies under the leadership of the archbishop of York and the lords Percy and Neville triumphed over the Scots at Neville's Cross, just outside Durham. King David was captured and brought to London.[126] The cup of Edward's success was not full even yet. Sir Thomas Dagworth, one of the king's ablest commanders, took the town of La Roche-Derien and captured Charles of Blois (20 June 1347).[127] Edward himself was investing Calais when towards the end of June Philip approached with a considerable army. The cardinals were quickly on the scene clamouring for a truce. Philip offered to do battle with four knights on either side.

---

[121] *Murimuth*, pp. 205-212; *Avesbury*, pp. 363-367. According to the former it was published 12 August; Avesbury gives the eve of the Assumption, i.e. the 14th. See above, "In the Seat of Power," n. 261.

[122] *Murimuth*, pp. 211-212, who says it was published "ut per hoc excitaret populum regni, ut eo ferventius diligerent regem et devotius pro prosperitate et expeditione ipsius orarent, qui ipse populum suum a dictis Gallicorum machinationibus conservavit indempnes."

[123] Ibid., pp. 211-217; *Avesbury*, pp. 358-363. The kings were those of Bohemia and Majorca, but the latter was not killed at that time (see *Knighton* 2, p. 38 n. 6; Viard, "Le siège de Calais," pp. 129, 144). BL Cotton MS Faustina B.v, fol. 92ʳ, rightly names the king of Bohemia only.

[124] According to *Avesbury*, p. 395, on 3 August; so too BL Cotton MS Vitellius A.xv, fol. 3ᵛ. A French source gives the 4th. Viard, "Le siège de Calais," unequivocally states that the siege lasted from 4 September 1346 until 4 August 1347.

[125] See the earl of Derby's account of the campaign: *Avesbury*, pp. 372-376; *Murimuth*, pp. 248-251 (from BL Cotton MS Nero D.x, fol. 137ʳ⁻ᵛ).

[126] *Murimuth*, pp. 218-219; ibid., pp. 252-253 (from BL Cotton MS Otho C.ii, fol. 102ʳ); *Avesbury*, pp. 376-377; and for a local account, *Rites of Durham*, pp. 23-29.

[127] *Avesbury*, pp. 388-390.

English sources report that Edward accepted the challenge only to find that the French army had slipped away quietly before morning.[128] The French chroniclers held that the English king prudently declined the contest.[129] News of these events was relayed by Edward to Stratford and to the chancellor and treasurer.[130] Even at that stage there were some last-minute alarms, revealed by Edward in an instruction to Stratford and his chief ministers. Intelligence suggested that Philip, under the impression that the English were deserting en masse, was intending to launch a vigorous offensive. The council of war determined that were battle to be offered it should be accepted. Edward demanded that promised reinforcements be sent to Calais in all haste.[131] But with no real hope of relief Calais could only surrender. Before August was out Edward sent an urgent request to Stratford and the ministers at home to send some English merchants, including the archbishop's close friend John Pulteney, so that they could stay for a month or six weeks in Calais and give advice on the settlement of the town from which the inhabitants had been ousted.[132] At last the cardinals' moment had arrived. Annibale Ceccano and Étienne Aubert were able to begin negotiations for a truce encompassing all the theatres of war. This was sealed on 28 September 1347. Edward was now free to return in triumph to England.[133]

While Edward was successfully engaged in war, Clement did not altogether despair of peace, or indeed of maintaining what he considered to be his lawful rights in England. In a letter to Stratford of April 1347 he made the suggestion that were the archbishop to join the king abroad and learn of a disposition towards peace, he might then travel to meet the pope. In any case, wrote Clement, he was sending Br. John de Rippis to the scene of hostilities with an oral message for Stratford.[134] The archbishop did not in practice leave England, nor is it likely that his physical condition would have permitted him to do so in safety. It need hardly be stressed that the meeting would have been an awkward one. Admittedly the pope did not openly suggest that Stratford was furthering the war, but he did take pains to impress on him the necessity to follow the ways of

---

[128] Ibid., p. 391 (also stated in the king's letter to Stratford, p. 393).

[129] See *Jean le Bel* 2, p. 158 n. 1. Froissart, following *Jean le Bel*, the *Chronique Normande* and *Chronographie*, says that he refused the offer of combat.

[130] *Avesbury*, pp. 391-395.

[131] *Jean le Bel* 2, pp. 350-351, App. 25; transcript of PRO C.81/324/18833 (Calais, 6 September 1347).

[132] *Jean le Bel* 2, p. 349, App. 24; transcript of PRO C.81/323/18790 (Calais, 27 August 1347).

[133] The text of the truce is in *Avesbury*, pp. 396-406. See also *Foedera* 3, i, pp. 20-22.

[134] Vatican Archives, *RV* 140, fol. 262^r; *CPL 1342-1362*, p. 32.

peace, emphasizing not for the first time the merits which would accrue to one who worked conscientiously in that cause.[135]

While the king was waging war Stratford was busy on the home front providing its sinews. So far as the clerical order was concerned, the biennial tenth of 1342 had been followed by the triennial tenth of 1344 and that in its turn by the biennial tenth of 1346 – granted at the October convocation.[136] The attempt to anticipate the dates of payment arranged for the tenth of 1342 ran into considerable opposition from the body of the clergy, despite the efforts of some of the bishops.[137] A similar anticipation of the 1346 grant was supported by Stratford, who sent letters urging those bishops who had been unable to persuade their clergy to respond to hold further meetings for the purpose.[138] Episcopal registers bear witness to the difficulty in collecting arrears of tenths, but the evidence has yet to be collated.[139] The chronicler Dene, though accepting the necessity, was uninhibited in his criticism of the weight of taxation.[140] The regular grants in parliament and convocation were supplemented by loans, such as those of 1342 and 1346, which were more forced than voluntary. For instance, in 1342 William de Neuwynham was pressing Bishop Bransford for a hundred marks on behalf of the king, but the diocesan was unable to meet the request in full.[141] Elsewhere Edward's

---

[135] "Quot et quanta bona tue saluti anime non parum utilia et eidem Christianitati multipliciter oportuna pacem procurando huiusmodi facere poteris si diligenter et fideliter laborare ut speramus curaveris in hac parte." Ibid.

[136] For the general question of royal taxation at this time see Harriss, *King, Parliament and Public Finance*, chaps. 13-14; also Stubbs, *Constitutional History* 2, pp. 394-395. Writs for the appointment of collectors of the tenth of 1342 were issued 30 November, for the triennial tenth of 1344, 18 December 1344; and for the biennial tenth of 1346, 14 May 1347. E.g. *Worcester Reg. Bransford*, subject index s.v. Taxation: tenths. See above, "Archbishop of Canterbury" for details of the convocations.

[137] The original terms were the Annunciation (25 March 1343) and the Baptist's Nativity (24 June 1344). The revised terms provisionally agreed to by the bishops in the council of October 1342 were 25 December 1342 and Pentecost (1 June) following. The writ for collection (30 November) named the original terms or "alios breviores." Bishop Hethe agreed to anticipate the dates, but his clergy complained that only with difficulty could the original ones be met. *Rochester Reg. Hethe*, pp. 691-695. The Worcester diocesan gave a similar response, though the abbots of Evesham and Pershore agreed to join him in discharging the tenth earlier. *Worcester Reg. Bransford*, pp. 206-207.

[138] E.g. Ely Reg. Lisle, fol. 72^r; Hereford Reg. Trillek, p. 277.

[139] Bishop Wyville in October 1345 excommunicated a number of persons for non-payment. Salisbury Reg. Wyville 1, fol. 116^v. Bishop Montacute did the same in Ely diocese early in 1342. Ely Reg. Montacute, fol. 74^r.

[140] BL Cotton MS Faustina B.v, fols. 94^v, 96^v.

[141] *Worcester Reg. Bransford*, p. 207. Cf. *Rochester Reg. Hethe*, pp. 688-691. The demand for £100 for the Brittany expedition involved Hethe (who pleaded inability to pay)

emissaries may have met with equally little success. The demands made in 1347 on Bishop Wyville of Salisbury – among others – were more peremptory. He was berated for not responding to an earlier writ requesting a loan of two hundred marks. It was pointed out to him that compared with the laity's response to royal needs that of the clergy had been niggardly. At the great council of 3 March 1347 laymen had loaned 20,000 sacks of wool, whereas the clergy had given nothing beyond the biennial tenth of the previous year. The bishop was to ensure that he had twenty sacks of wool at the collecting centre in London by Michaelmas.[142] Here surely we have a recurrence of the "unlawful exactions" to which Stratford objected in 1340-1341. Once again exigencies of war provided the excuse.

The parliament which began to assemble on 11 September 1346 was predictably to concern itself with the replenishing of the king's war treasury. From Calais Edward despatched a deputation led by Bartholomew Burghersh and John Darcy, the royal chamberlain.[143] Stratford and eight other bishops[144] were present when their authority was read out in parliament a couple of days later. The messengers then gave details of the events at Caen and of the ordinance for the annihilation of the English nation by nobles of France and Normandy – already published in August by Stratford at St. Paul's.[145] This document, coupled with the elation fostered by the successes of English arms, probably helped towards the commons' concession of two fifteenths; even so, this was accompanied by lengthy petitions which occupied Stratford and other councillors between 17 and 19 September. By the 20th the responses were ready. Naturally

in much correspondence with the *custos* of the realm, the queen, and a contact at court. Bishop Shrewsbury was asked for £300, but having nothing available asked to be excused. *Bath and Wells Reg. Shrewsbury*, p. 456. For lists of clergy asked for loans, the amounts demanded, and the names of those sent with the demands, see *Foedera* 2, iv, pp. 137 (for 1342), 191-192 (for 1346).

[142] Salisbury Reg. Wyville 1, original writ bound between fols. 164 and 165: 20 August 1347. Cf. *Hereford Reg. Trillek*, pp. 308-309. "Et quod non solum honori detraheretur regio set nos eciam, quod absit, confusione perpetua, anglicana[m]que ecclesia[m] ac ipsum regnum nostrum inevitabilibus involveremur perdicionis periculis si ab incepta guerra redire deficientibus guerrinis sumptibus cogeremur." Robert Stratford as bishop of Chichester loaned fifteen sacks. See *Foedera* 3, i, p. 23: 8 October 1347. See previous note for the 1346 loan.

[143] *Rot. Parl.* 2, pp. 157 no. 5, 158 no. 7. The other members were M. John Thoresby, keeper of the privy seal, and M. John de Carleton.

[144] Winchester (Edington), London (Ralph Stratford), Salisbury (Wyville), Norwich (Bateman), Chichester (Robert Stratford), Ely (Lisle), Hereford (John Trillek), St. Asaph (John Trevor) – who received his temporalities at this time.

[145] See above, n. 121; "In the Seat of Power," n. 261.

many petitions involved abuses of array, purveyance, or other war measures, but for Stratford the disturbing aspect was the well-orchestrated antipathy towards alien secular clergy, friars and monks – described as "no more than laymen." There were petitions against "our enemy" the abbot of Cluny on account of dues levied from English houses of the congregation,[146] against cardinals occupying English benefices, and in particular the two who had been granted two thousand marks from the provinces of Canterbury and York,[147] as well as against the Gascon M. Raymond Pelegrini,[148] alien occupiers of benefices, and payment of procuration to cardinals for their activities outside England. Many of the council's replies were evasive – it would be necessary to consult the king – but further collection of the deeply resented cardinals' procurations was disallowed.[149] Parliament closed with agreement to provide an aid for the knighting of the Prince of Wales, which had taken place on the king's landing at La Hougue.[150] It was also determined that alien benefices should be taken into the king's hand and that the bishops were to provide details of all such before the meeting of convocation.[151]

Stratford would certainly encounter difficulty in maintaining equilibrium between the king's needs, reinforced by popular xenophobia, and the papal insistence that he persuade Edward and the other councillors to safeguard the traditional liberties of the church. A possible source of dispute came with the death of Thomas Bek, bishop of Lincoln, in February 1347. Clement notified both Edward and the local cathedral chapter, one of secular canons this time, of his reservation of the see, to which he provided John Gynwell, who had served as chaplain and steward of the earl of Derby.[152] This last fact probably explains why there was no royal reaction, despite the method of promotion. The temporalities

---

[146] *Rot. Parl.* 2, pp. 160-163; for Cluny, ibid., p. 163 no. 41. The pope had been urging Stratford to act on Cluny's behalf. "Tu frater super amovendis impedimentis appositis in grangiis, maneriis, pensionibus, subsidiis et aliis bonis et iuribus suis in Anglia existentibus prout te rogaveramus per nostras litteras fideliter laborasti. Sane prout idem abbas asserit, nondum gentes sue super expedicione huiusmodi obtinere potuerunt a cancellaria regia litteras oportunas, fraternitatem tuam iterato rogamus quatinus super obtinendis eisdem litteris velis efficaciter interponere partes tuas." Vatican Archives, *RV* 139, fol. 20ʳ (cf. 19ʳ⁻ᵛ); *CPL 1342-1362*, p. 19: 14 June 1345.

[147] *Rot. Parl.* 2, p. 162 no. 35, and see above.

[148] *Rot. Parl.* 2, p. 163 no. 40.

[149] Ibid., p. 162 nos. 31-32; for the cardinals' procurations, n. 156 below.

[150] *Rot. Parl.* 2, p. 163 nos. 44-45.

[151] Ibid., p. 163 no. 46; also above, n. 116.

[152] Vatican Archives, *RV* 140, fol. 222ᵛ; *CPL 1342-1362*, p. 30: 1 February 1347; *Le Neve* 1, p. 1; *Biog. Oxon.*, s.v. Gynewell. He was provided 23 March 1347.

were restored without undue delay.[153] Stratford consecrated Gynwell at Otford on 23 September.[154] But two incidents do reveal the archbishop in conflict with secular authority. The first occurred in April 1347, when it was alleged that in contravention of the ordinance of the previous parliament at Westminster[155] proctors of the cardinals had clandestinely brought bulls to the archbishop, who had attempted to implement them. No such procurations were to be levied.[156] The second incident is more elusive. It concerns the provincial council – Stratford's last – which was summoned to St. Paul's for the first week of October.[157] Misgivings about the archbishop's intentions had been fostered in Edward's mind, but we know neither the precise grounds for these nor the persons responsible. From Calais the king instructed Chancellor Offord to gather together Chief Justice Thorp and other justices and councillors so that they could ensure that no ordinance prejudicial to the crown would be made by the provincial council. M. Thomas Bradwardine, theologian and future archbishop,[158] was sent to make the king's wishes known by word of mouth.[159] The incident might seem remarkable in view of Stratford's position as principal councillor. On the other hand, perhaps we should not read too much into the affair. Such precautions were not novel and the king was fully aware that some degree of ambivalence in Stratford's attitude was inevitable. Edward had shown similar perturbation when Stratford was about to hold the provincial council of October 1341.[160] What probably lay at the root of royal unease was the notion that Strat-

---

[153] 2 June 1347. *CPR 1345-1348*, p. 298; *Le Neve* 1, p. 1.

[154] *Biog. Oxon.*, s.v. Gynewell; Haines, *DHGE*, s.v.

[155] That of September 1346. *Rot. Parl.* 2, p. 162 no. 33.

[156] E.g. *Foedera* 3, i, pp. 9-10: 12 April 1347; *Hereford Reg. Trillek*, pp. 299-300; *Worcester Reg. Bransford*, p. 325 (cf. p. 317 for writ of September 1348 permitting collection of the procurations). For further details: Lunt, *Financial Relations* 2, pp. 641-642. For a time in 1347 the cardinals' proctors were imprisoned.

[157] Summons issued by Stratford; from Lambeth on 30 July 1347 for 1 October. E.g. *Bath and Wells Reg. Shrewsbury*, pp. 545-546; *Hereford Reg. Trillek*, pp. 306-308. See above, "Archbishop of Canterbury."

[158] Bradwardine was to be elected (for the second time) 4 June 1348 and provided on 19 June. He died 25-26 August in the same year. *Le Neve* 4, p. 30; and cf. *HBC*, p. 211; *Biog. Oxon.*, s.v. Bradwardine alias Beer de Hertefeld.

[159] The document printed by Wilkinson, *Chancery*, p. 118 n. 1 (from PRO S.C.1/39/198) is dated from Calais, 18 September 1347. It is said to have been delivered to Chancellor Offord only on 10 October – nine days *after* the provincial council was scheduled to begin. Wilkinson's observation (from a royal or curialist standpoint?) is: "Stratford and his supporters in the clergy may have again threatened to give trouble; but that only served to show the wisdom of Edward's return to clerical chancellors." See above, "Archbishop of Canterbury," n. 121.

[160] *CCR 1341-1343*, p. 335. See above, "The Crisis of 1341."

ford was intent on legislation which would exacerbate the conflict already in evidence between the commons, with their insular view, and ecclesiastics, who more readily worked within the context of western Christendom. The king wished for no contention at home, but he was determined to use secular criticism of papal "interference" as a political lever against Clement. Before long Edward was able to assess the primate's intentions for himself. On 12 October 1347 he landed at Sandwich; two days later he arrived in London.[161]

There remained one last shadow from the reign of the unfortunate Edward II. While at Sluys in 1345 the king and his barons had been approached by John Maltravers, condemned in 1330 for his part in deluding the earl of Kent and thereby causing his death.[162] The conviction "by notoriety" took place in parliament and Maltravers (wisely) had never stood trial. In their own interest the magnates appear to have exerted pressure in support of Maltravers' claim for a re-examination of the process by which he stood disinherited. Pending a reversal of judgment in parliament, he was permitted to stay in England. This interim arrangement is said to have been approved on the king's return by Stratford, his brother Robert, and other major councillors.[163] Maltravers' petition was presented in the parliament of January 1348, which Stratford attended,[164] but no pardon was issued until June of 1351.[165]

There is little further to record of Stratford's activities, either in the political or the ecclesiastical sphere. In July he was at his manor of Mayfield in Sussex, where he acquitted the executors of his old "enemy" Bishop Orleton.[166] He died there on 23 August 1348, within the confines of his brother's diocese of Chichester. And so, comments Dene, the man who in life was "dux regis" and Edward's principal councillor, in death suffered the confiscation of all his goods as a recompense.[167] This statement should not be taken too literally, for it lacks confirmation. What we

---

[161] *Foedera* 3, i, p. 23.

[162] See above, "Lancastrian Spokesman"; "In the Seat of Power."

[163] *Foedera* 3, i, p. 25: 28 December 1347.

[164] *Rot. Parl.* 2, p. 173 no. 65. Stratford was among those deputed to afforce the triers of petitions. Ibid., p. 164.

[165] The whole matter is reviewed by Bellamy, *The Law of Treason*, pp. 82-83. See also *CCR 1349-1354*, p. 312.

[166] *Hereford Reg. Trillek*, p. 135, and cf. pp. 123-124.

[167] BL Cotton MS Faustina B.v, fol. 96^{r-v}: "Obiit illo tempore Johannes de Stratford archiepiscopus Cantuar. apud Maghefeld dux regis et eius consiliarius principalis in vita sua, et ideo post mortem ipsius pro mercede sua omnia eius bona confiscantur, possessiones et predia destruuntur." Cf. *Vitae Arch. Cant.*, p. 41 (Lambeth MS 99, fol. 146^v).

do have is a copy of Stratford's will, made either in late 1347 or the early part of 1348,[168] and the inventory of his goods drawn up by his executors, or more correctly, by his residual executor Robert Stratford. In his will the archbishop conventionally left his soul to God, the Virgin Mary and to all the saints, in the hope that Christ who had suffered death for sinners would permit his unworthy soul to rest in the bosom of Abraham; his body he assigned for burial with the minimum of expense in Canterbury Cathedral.[169] His directions as to the exact place of burial have been obscured by damage to the manuscript, but it can be deduced that he wished his body to rest immediately to the west of the door which led through Prior Eastry's screen from the south ambulatory into the choir. There he was buried on 9 September – the Tuesday after the Nativity of Our Lady. Today the tomb is flanked on the east by that of Archbishop Sudbury, done to death by a mob in 1381, and on the west by that of Archbishop Kempe, who died in 1454, while the reset entry to the choir is between Kempe's tomb (to the east) and the archiepiscopal throne.[170] Prior Hathbrand wrote a letter of condolence to Robert Stratford, lamenting the death of the archbishop whom he described as a member of the Canterbury community, its leader and guardian,[171] and asking the bishop to let him know the date of burial so that the appointed site could be prepared and other arrangements made. Subsequently Hathbrand explained that an eminent position had been allotted to Stratford's tomb, but he was hesitant about beginning the task of construction in a manner which might later be criticized, since he lacked properly instructed workmen. He wished Bishop Robert to send him some without delay.[172]

[168] CCL W. 219:"Hac die Veneris ... anno domini 1347." The will is printed with many inaccuracies, some of them significant, in *Sede Vacante Wills*, pp. 72-76.

[169] There were to be few lights around the tomb, but the poor who came were to be given a penny each. "Quod ipsum corpus meum cum ... [gap here and below] sepeliant seu sepelire faciant quodque sumptus magnos circa cereos apponendos iuxta feretrum non apponeant, set ... [unum apud caput?] aliud ad pedes et unum ex utroque latere et non ultra in exequiis meis apponeant de convivio faciendo minime curantes ... sepulture mee pauperibus singulis venientibus singulis [sic] singulos denarios distribuant." There are various tears in the MS, CCL W. 219.

[170] "Item, lego corpus meum ad sepeliendum in ecclesia Cant. in parte occide... in d... parte hostii occidentalis iuxta ipsum hostium supradictum." Ibid. See Woodruff's introduction to *Sede Vacante Wills*, p. viii. He would appear to be right in placing the original entry through the screen east of Stratford's tomb, probably on the site now occupied by Sudbury's. For Canterbury's *pulpitum* and screens see Vallance, *Greater English Church Screens*, pp. 27ff.

[171] CCL Reg. L, fol. 81ᵛ:"Qui fuit nobis domesticus, dux et custos cui sumus parati pro viribus benivolenciam exhibere."

[172] "Quia timeremus incipere quod aliqui reprehenderent forsitan in eventum cum non reputemus apud nos constitutos artifices sic instructos quod superponeretis libenter eorum principio tantum opus."

From a copy of Prior Hathbrand's letter of thanks it would seem that Bishop Ralph Stratford was also solicitous about his uncle's burial arrangements.[173] The alabaster tomb, surmounted by an effigy of the archbishop in pontificals, is now much damaged – particularly the canopy.[174] According to a metal plate let into the floor it was restored in the time of Archbishop Randall Davidson (1903-1928) after six hundred years of disrepair, which can only be interpreted to mean that it was never finished.[175] Among other engravings of the tomb is one by Nicholas Battely in Somner's *Antiquities of Canterbury*, where we are told that the steps of St. Dunstan's altar were just beside it.[176] Indeed an honourable last resting place. In the priory's *obituarium* Stratford was commemorated as donor of a most precious cope, an excellent mitre, and copies of the *Decretum* and *Decretales*, and also as the procurer of an annual pension of a hundred shillings from the churches of Preston and Boughton. Every priest in the monastery was to say a mass for him and the others fifty psalms each.[177] Thus he was remembered kindly in the church of Canterbury, the rights and privileges of which he had stoutly defended. But Stratford's anonymous biographer goes much farther, adducing ample evidence that the archbishop died in the odour of sanctity. His concern for the church's future caused him to nominate Simon Islep as the man best suited to succeed him. Islep was to do so, thanks to unprecedented mortality among archbishops-elect. Stratford's death, of which he had frequently forewarned his *familia*, came at the first hour of

---

[173] CCL Liber L, fol. 86ᵛ. The rubric must be inaccurate as it suggests a letter *from* the bishop. "De multiplicibus benevolenciis vestris et gratitudinibus versus nos ostensis et de benigna solicitudine vestra circa opus sepulcri domini nostri prekarissimi defuncti, cordiales quantas possumus graciarum referrimus acciones."

[174] The effigy itself has lost a hand, the nose is damaged, and the crozier or cross is largely missing. Some of the alabaster decorative frieze is seemingly modern.

[175]   Sexcentis annis confracta est tumba Johannis
      Tandem Randallus sic reparavit opus,
      Venta prius sedes, nunc Christi copulat aedes
      In caelo praesul regnet uterque simul.

Archbishop Davidson died in 1930.

[176] *Antiquities*, pt. 2 facing p. 33. The engraving, described on the facing page, gives a pristine impression. Dart, *History and Antiquities of Canterbury* (1726), which includes an account of Stratford (pp. 144-148), has facing p. 144 an engraving of the tomb in which the figure and crozier or cross (the top is not seen) are likewise undamaged. Stothard, *Monumental Effigies of Great Britain* (1876), pl. 82, shows damage to the hands of the effigy and to the crozier or cross, but the nose is undamaged. Cf. n. 174 above.

[177] Lambeth MS 20, fol. 213ʳ; BL Arundel MS 68, fol. 39ʳ; *Anglia Sacra* 1, p. 59. The churches were appropriated to Faversham Abbey, which was to pay five marks to the infirmarian (in instalments at Michaelmas and Easter) and half that sum to the sacrist for the repair of the fabric (at the same terms). CCL P.32; Reg. D, fols. 464ᵛ-465ʳ.

the day after he had heard a mass of Our Lady, for whom apparently he nurtured a special devotion. While at Mayfield he is said to have made liberal distributions to the needy with his own hand. Every day in the morning thirteen poor received a penny and a loaf of bread each; at noon thirteen more in addition to a loaf of white bread were given a pottle of beer, soup, and a good helping of meat or fish; then after Vespers a further thirteen loaves and pennies were distributed. All this was over and above the customary disposal of "fragments" from his household to a throng of poor persons, not to mention the many charitable gifts to women in childbirth and private assistance to other indigent people. Towards his subjects he was gracious and merciful, taking nothing from them, but rather dispensing to all whatever he could.[178] However we interpret Stratford's life, which was always busy, often secular, and occasionally turbulent, if we believe his biographer he died in a manner in which in his better moments he would have wished to live. The alternative is to dismiss this deathbed panegyric. Indeed, one has to remember that elements of Stratford's biography owe not a little to the hagiographical tradition, while here and there one feels that the author is writing with an eye on a specific exemplar — the life of St. Thomas Becket.

[178] *Vitae Arch. Cant.*, p. 41 (Lambeth MS 99, fol. 146ᵛ).

5

Founder, Benefactor and Legislator

Roughly speaking it is possible to divide the beneficiaries of the archbishop's will into six categories, as follows: places and churches with
which he had been associated in the course of his career; religious houses,
particularly hospitals; relatives, friends and patrons; *familia* and servants;
the poor and needy; secular priests and friars deputed to pray for his soul.
Of course, some of these categories overlap somewhat, but the division is
a helpful one none the less.[1]

Stratford's birthplace figures largely in the list of benefactions. A
substantial sum was left to the poor of the town, but double the amount,
£40 that is, for the repair of the bridge over the Avon. The greatest single
beneficiary was understandably his chapel in the parish church, the
foundation of which will be dealt with below. Oxford, which had
provided Stratford's university education is marked by a gift of ten marks
(£6 13s 4d) to the scholars of Balliol Hall, and by the requirement that the
friars of the city should pray for his soul. That Balliol is singled out raises
the possibility that Stratford may have spent some of his time there as a
student, though there is no confirmation of this.[2] Stratford's Worcester
connection is inevitably overshadowed by the town of Stratford, which
lay within the medieval diocese, but it is remarkable that there was no
tangible remembrance of the cathedral priory which had assisted his early
career. Lincoln, where Stratford had been archdeacon, was left a cope of
red velvet embroidered with figures and many margarites. His former

---

[1] For discussions of beneficiaries see Sheehan, *Medieval Will*, chap. 6 sect. 2, and for
the devise of property, sect. 3. Stratford's will is summarized below, Appendix 7, where
some errors in *Sede Vacante Wills*, App. pp. 72-76, are corrected. The original will is not
extant. CCL. W.219 is a copy.

[2] See above, "The Making of a Career."

bishopric, Winchester, was marked by the gift of a set of white vestments to the cathedral church, and he did not forget two of the poorer religious houses of the diocese. Canterbury is particularly well represented among the beneficiaries. The prior and convent of Christ Church received a legacy of Stratford's new mitre, a new cope of velvet with gold figures and many margarites, together with his best copy of the *Decretum* and of the *Decretals*.[3] In addition small legacies were provided for many religious houses, both in the town and diocese, and two of the archiepiscopal churches, Mayfield and Cranbrook, were to receive five pounds each for the purchase of vestments.

Foundations for religious find a large place in the will. Thus in Winchester diocese Stratford left two pounds to the hospital of St. Mary Magdalene in the city and five marks to the nuns of Wintney. But for the most part the houses which benefited lay in Canterbury itself or its diocese. St. Nicholas, Harbledown, a hospital lying just to the west of the cathedral city received the largest sum – five pounds. Forty shillings were left to the Canterbury hospital of St. Thomas (Eastbridge); the same amount to the sisters of St. James, Thanington,[4] the Carmelites of Sandwich, and what is called the hospital of St. Edmund at "Maidenstood" or "Maidenstone."[5] The hospital of St. John the Baptist at Canterbury's north gate was left five marks (£3 6s 8d), the same amount as the nuns of the Holy Sepulchre in the town. The Carmelites of Aylesford, whose house Stratford regularly passed while travelling between his manors of Otford and Maidstone, received (surprisingly) a mere £1 6s 8d. The amount left to each of the mendicant houses in Canterbury has been lost owing to a tear in the manuscript.[6] But although the precise total left to all these religious houses cannot now be known, almost certainly it did not exceed the £40 contributed to Stratford bridge.

Three known relatives are mentioned in the will as legatees: Stratford's sister Alice, his brother Robert, and his nephew Ralph. Alice was allotted silver plates, silver salts, a silver cup, ten pounds of money, and the archbishop's best robe. Robert was to have the best Bible, a copy of *Sext*, a cup

---

[3] For the record of these gifts in the priory's *obituarium* see above, "Closing Years."

[4] For this nunnery or sisterhood see *Canterbury Chantries*, pp. 29-38; *Kent Chantries*, pp. 36-38. *Sede Vacante Wills*, p. 74, has "c marcas xl s.," which should be "xl s."

[5] It is not clear what hospital was intended. The dedication to St. Edmund is rare among hospitals, particularly in the south of England, being non-existent in Kent – though a parish church in Canterbury was so dedicated. This could well be an error for the hospital of St. Peter and St. Paul (also St. Thomas) at Maidstone, of which the archbishops were patrons.

[6] "Item lego fratribus mendicantibus in civitate Cant. cuilibet do[mo] ...."

enamelled outside and with various shields within, as well as an ornamental egg with cover and gilt base.[7] For Stratford's nephew there was Guido de Baysio's *Rosarium* and a special copy of the *Speculum Judiciale* produced in Bologna, where it had been purchased. The latter book may well have been brought back to England by Ralph himself, for he is known to have studied at Bologna University and could have taken his doctorate in canon and civil law there.[8] A cup, with a cover and enamelled all over, which Ralph had at some time given to his uncle, was likewise returned to him. To the king Stratford left gilt and enamelled bowls formerly in the possession of his "good lord" Simon de Montacute, the bishop of Ely, and also a silver-gilt troper.[9] For the Prince of Wales there was a fine missal, a "Resurrection" in silver gilt, which had also belonged to the bishop of Ely, and an ivory plaque with figures of mother of pearl. Bartholomew Burghersh, whom Stratford had entertained at Canterbury, was left a silver cup with gilt stand, at the base of which were two lions standing by a tree.[10] Stratford's friendship with the Pulteneys is reflected in their legacies. To John, the former mayor of London, he gave a godet or cup with other godets inside; to John's wife, Margaret, a silver vessel with a cover on which was a shield with a sword and key – objects depicted in saltire on the archbishop's seal; and to their son, William, his second-best palfrey. The archbishop's relationship with the Eccleshales is nowhere made clear, but it must have been a close one. Money was left to the poor relatives of Peter, former rector of Eccleshall, five marks to the person of the same name who had been the archbishop's chamberlain, while John de Eccleshale, a prominent member of his *familia*, was left a silver cup with cover and a peacock in the base. John was named one of the executors, as was Richard de Twyverton or Tiverton, who likewise received a cup. Three members of the archiepiscopal household were individually rewarded; William atte Fenne, the current chamberlain, John Latyn, the valet of the chamber, and Hugh Pode, the cameral page. Fenne was to have the archbishop's best bed and another red bed, the silver basin and washing bowl from the chamber, together with ten pounds; Latyn, the best robe and five marks; Pode, another robe and two pounds. M. John de Lecch, one of Stratford's principal clerks and at the time acting as official of the Court of Canterbury, was to receive a hundred and three

---

[7] Such "eggs" or cups featured in wills from time to time as can be seen from *Canterbury Reg. Chichele* 2, index p. 831 v-vi, where they are termed ostrich eggs.

[8] See *Biog. Oxon.*, s.v.

[9] A troper was a service book with musical notation, hence the description "silver-gilt" refers to decorative plates attached to the covers.

[10] "... pede duos leones stantes ad arborem."

(shillings?) and a copy of the *Novella* in two volumes.[11] So far nothing has come to light about the connection between John Pound or M. William de Derby and Stratford. The former was assigned the considerable sum of ten pounds, the latter the same number of marks (£6 13s 4d).[12] Distribution of £100 was to be made among those members of Stratford's *familia* for whom he had not made provision during his lifetime.

A substantial sum was to be given to the poor under a number of categories. Members of the archbishop's kin were to receive £100, distributed according to need rather than favour; the rector of Eccleshall's kin was to have twenty marks (£13 6s 8d); the indigent of Stratford twenty pounds; while £100 was to be distributed as dowry among needy girls who wished to marry. In addition the executors were instructed to apportion the residue of the archbishop's goods among the religious poor of Canterbury diocese, his kin living in that of Worcester, and girls needing dowries.

Apart from the five marks paid to each of fifty mass priests,[13] the friars of London, Oxford, and possibly Canterbury as well, were paid to pray for his soul. At London and Oxford the Dominicans and Franciscans were each paid five pounds, the Carmelites and Augustinians five marks (£3 6s 8d). The total, the Canterbury friars excepted, comes to the very large sum of £300 – a figure exceeding that allotted to the poor. From the executors' account we know that the total amount of the legacies and gifts determined in Stratford's life-time came to £1380 6s, and in addition to this were £30 paid in alms to the priors of the hospitals at the north gate in Canterbury and at Harbledown, and also £100 12s distributed as rewards to the archbishop's servants.[14]

Without doubt Stratford was generous to his *familia* and others in his service, but to what extent, if at all, his benefactions departed from the regular pattern of a man in his position and of similar background, can only be determined by an analysis of contemporary wills.[15]

---

[11] The MS reads "ciii ..." rather than the "civ" of *Sede Vacante Wills*, p. 76.

[12] M. William was a notary who on occasion acted for the Canterbury chapter. E.g. *Lit. Cant.* 2, p. 189 (unindexed); cf. ibid., p. 221.

[13] *Sede Vacante Wills* (p. 75) confuses this item, which should read: "Item, in virtute omnipotentis Dei onero ... executores meos quod statim post mortem meam ordinent .1. sacerdotes ad celebrandum continue pro anima mea eodem anno." In other words this was not a payment for fifty masses but for fifty stipendiaries to say masses for his soul throughout the year following his death. Cf. CCL A.37 (executors' account) where this item is costed at £166 13s 4d (five marks p.a. for each priest).

[14] The £30 mentioned here is additional to the £3 6s 8d and £5 payable in the will to the Northgate hospital and Harbledown respectively.

[15] Michael Sheehan is at present engaged on such a project. But it will be observed that grants made *inter vivos*, in Stratford's case considerable, inevitably obscure the real situation.

The College of St. Thomas the Martyr
at Stratford

It will be appreciated that Stratford's will concerned, indeed could only concern, movable property. His more lasting gift to posterity was the college of chantry priests in his native town. The first half of the fourteenth century saw a remarkable growth in chantry foundations, a growth which at one time was erroneously regarded as an aftermath of the Black Death.[1] Stratford's contemporaries and near-contemporaries were in the forefront of this development. For instance, Bishop Grandisson was buried in a chantry chapel which nestles obscurely between the west wall of his cathedral and the impressive stone screen newly built slightly beyond it. At nearby Ottery St. Mary he reconstructed the church on a grand scale and converted it into a college of canons with chantry and parochial functions.[2] Adam Orleton's successor at Winchester, Bishop Edington, was buried in an impressively simple chantry on the south side of the nave of his cathedral church, which he had helped to remodel in the perpendicular style. At his birthplace, Edington in Wiltshire, he established a college of chantry priests, though at the urging of the Black Prince this was soon changed into a house of Bonshommes.[3] Hamo de Hethe, the bishop of Rochester, had at one time been prior of his cathedral church and made a different type of arrangement. He left money to Lesnes Abbey from which an annual sum was to be made available to the monks of Rochester for a chantry priest to celebrate masses for his soul.[4] Laymen were equally to the fore in devoting their resources and energies to such

[1] E.g. Cook, *Chantry Chapels*, p. 17. Cf. Haines, *Worc. Admin.*, p. 231, where the table suggests that 1330-1339 was the peak decade for foundations. The fullest and most recent discussion of chantries is that of Wood-Legh, *Perpetual Chantries.*

[2] See Dalton, *The Collegiate Church of Ottery St. Mary*. There were eight canons in the college. Hamilton Thompson regarded the foundation as transitional between the "older cathedral model" and "a new type of collegiate establishment, the college composed of resident chantry priests" (as at Stratford). At Ottery, wrote Hamilton Thompson, "if its canonries and prebends were individual freehold benefices, the majority of their holders were intended to be resident" and there were distinct parochial obligations. *English Clergy*, p. 100.

[3] The chantry college seems to have lasted for barely a year. See Knowles and Hadcock, *Medieval Religious Houses*, pp. 179, 329. The chantry foundation (dated Southwark, 20 October 1351) is in Salisbury Reg. Wyville 1, fols. 175r-179v; see also ibid., fols. 180r-182v, 197r-203r. Prayers were to be offered for both Bishop Orleton and M. Gilbert de Middleton, an important secular clerk.

[4] Cook, *Chantry Chapels*, pp. 88-89; *CPR 1343-1345*, p. 307: 20 June 1344 (mortmain licence). For the chantry which Bishop Salmon founded at Norwich in the chapel of St. John the Evangelist, see *CPL 1305-1342*, p. 140; NNRO Episcopal charters, Box 2, nos. 1139, 4379.

projects. Among friends or colleagues of Stratford we can count Sir Thomas de Astley, Sir William de Clinton (later earl of Huntingdon), both from Warwickshire, Sir William de Montacute (later earl of Salisbury) and his brother the bishop of Worcester, as well as Sir John Pulteney, whose wife's family had Warwickshire connections. Astley founded a large chantry in his name-place, later converting it into a collegiate church. Among those for whom his chaplains were to pray are numbered both Stratford and the earl of Huntingdon.[5] At nearby Maxstoke Clinton himself founded a college of chantry priests, which a few years later he changed into an Augustinian priory. The principal endowment was provided by the appropriation of a number of churches and we know that in support of this process Stratford and his brother lent their influence.[6] William de Montacute's foundation was even more ambitious. The newly created earl founded a substantial Augustinian priory at his manor of Bisham in Berkshire. Among those who witnessed the foundation deed were Stratford and his brother Robert.[7] Stratford was as keen as his secular neighbours at Astley and Maxstoke to increase divine worship in his native town. His foundation, like some of the others mentioned, was carried out in two stages. The first is comprised in the chantry ordination of 1331, when he was bishop of Winchester.[8] This provided for five chaplains in priest's orders, one of whom was to be warden, another subwarden. It was presumably in the late 1320s that Stratford had constructed a chapel in honour of St. Thomas the Martyr in the south aisle

---

[5] *VCH Warwicks.* 2, p. 118. For Pulteney's foundations at St. Paul's (where Stratford was to be commemorated) and St. Laurence, Candlewick Street, see Dugdale, *St. Paul's*, pp. 33-34; Stow, *Survey* 1, p. 106; Haines, *Church and Politics*, p. 76. For his will (1348): Guildhall Lib. MS 66 A 35.

[6] The Worcester prior and chapter received a barrage of letters from the king, Archbishop Stratford, the bishop of Chichester, William de Clinton, and their own diocesan, Wolstan de Bransford, urging the appropriation of Tanworth church to Maxstoke. Prior John of Evesham wrote to Stratford and the bishops of Chichester (Robert Stratford) and London (Ralph Stratford) expressing his unwillingness to accede to the appropriation without compensation. Robert Stratford wrote that after much discussion a pension of 20s had been agreed upon and urged the prior to accept this as adequate in the circumstances. WoCL Liber Albus, fols. 172ᵛ-175ʳ; *Worcester Reg. Bransford* and *Worc. Admin.*, index s.v. Maxstoke; Holliday, "Maxstoke Priory." The year of Clinton's initial foundation coincides with that of Stratford's chantry.

[7] Dugdale, *Monasticon* 6, pp. 527-528.

[8] Southwark, 8 October 1331. Worcester Reg. Montacute 1, fols. 56ᵛii (al. p. 124) - 57ᵛii; WoCL Liber Albus, fols. 141ʳ-142ᵛ. The first chantry chaplain, John de Ofechurch, priest, was instituted at Stratford's presentation 22 October 1331 (*WRO*, p. 213), though the Worcester diocesan confirmed the foundation only in 1332 (not entered in his register but to be found in the priory's *Liber Albus*).

of the parish church of Holy Trinity.[9] With the consent of the bishop of
Worcester, Adam Orleton, that of the Worcester chapter, and of the rector
of Stratford, his college of chantry priests became a separate entity within
the parish church, but with ample provision for cooperation with the
parochial clergy. The chaplains were to pray for the welfare of the
founder and his brother, and for the souls of their parents Robert and
Isabel, as well as for the good estate of the king. The regulations for the
chantry's observance were precise; consistent with the experience of
someone who knew how often laxity led to irreversible decline.
Presentation of the warden was to be in the founder's hands during his
life-time and thereafter in those of the Worcester bishops, or during
vacancies of the see in those of the prior and chapter. Should they fail to
carry out the obligation within two months, presentation was to pass to
the archbishop of Canterbury and failing him to the prior and chapter of
Christ Church. At the time of his appointment the warden was to take an
oath to observe the ordinances and to be continually resident, unless
forced to be absent temporarily on business of the chapel. He was to
nominate a subwarden for presentation to the bishop.[10] Should he neglect
to do so within a month of a vacancy, the bishop of Worcester was to act.
Failing the bishop, the right of appointment was to follow the same
pattern as in the warden's case. It was the warden's responsibility to
provide the other chaplains with food and drink and to pay the subwarden
forty shillings a year and each of the chaplains two marks (£1 6s 8d) half
yearly at the Purification and the Nativity of St. John the Baptist.[11] After
deduction of his own expenses and those of a moderate *familia* the
warden was to use the remainder of the income for the benefit of the
chantry. To provide a check on administration there was to be an annual
inventory in the form of an indenture, one part of which was to remain in
the warden's charge, the other in that of the subwarden. All the chaplains,
including warden and subwarden, were to live in a house appointed for
the purpose, eating and sleeping communally. A clerk was to minister to
the chaplains both in their masses and in the residence. It was the
warden's duty to provide surplices and almuces lined with black fur for
use in the chapel and in the choir of the parish church. The books and

[9] Bishop Cobham issued an indulgence for the repair of the tower early in 1326. BRT
1/3/160; Fisher, *Antient Paintings*, pl. IX no. 6. Cf. *VCH Warwicks.* 6, p. 269.
[10] This was what happened in 1336 when John de Southwaltham was instituted on 12
July at Stratford's presentation, the subwarden on 15 July at Southwaltham's. The latter
was the second warden, the first of the augmented chantry. Worcester Reg. Montacute 1,
fol. 23ʳ.
[11] I.e. 2 February and 24 June.

ornaments of the chapel were to be in the subwarden's custody. He was in effect to act as sacrist, with authority to regulate the time and order of the masses and under obligation to make available the necessary bread, wine and water, though at the warden's expense. On the warden's death the subwarden was to act in his place, but to render an account to the next warden within a month of the latter's appointment. If both offices fell vacant at the same time the Worcester prior and convent were to step in.

The lengthiest part of the ordinances is concerned with details of liturgical observance. Daily between dinner and Vespers the chaplains were to say the office of the dead, together with the *Placebo* and *Dirige*, nine psalms and nine lessons, except on double feasts and at Easter time. After saying Vespers and Compline in the chancel of the parish church with the parochial clergy, the chaplains were to recite the commendation of the dead in their own chapel. Before dinner they were to say Matins and all the other canonical hours in the chancel with the parish clergy and then, in their own chapel, the seven penitential and fifteen gradual psalms with the litany and usual prayers. The chaplains' daily masses were to be celebrated in the chapel in accordance with a rota devised by the subwarden. The principal masses, all of them sung, were to be as follows: Monday, of requiem; Tuesday, of St. Thomas the Martyr; Wednesday, of St. Catherine, virgin and martyr; Thursday, of the Holy Spirit; Friday, of the Holy Cross; Saturday, of the glorious Virgin Mary; and Sunday, of St. John the Evangelist. There follow full instructions as to the six prayers which were to come after the principal collect – for the founder's welfare, the king, brothers and "parents" living,[12] peace, the faithful departed, and for the living and departed. All the chaplains were to have in mind the founder and his brother, the king, and the bishops of Worcester and Winchester, and were to pray especially in the *Memento* for the peace of the church and realm and for all the benefactors of the chapel.[13] After the founder's death they were to have him in mind first and then his father, mother and brother, the others mentioned above, benefactors of the chapel, and the souls of all the faithful departed.

---

[12] "Pro fratribus et parentibus vivis." This could be misleading. Both of the founder's parents were dead prior to the ordination, and there is no other mention of a brother apart from Robert. The six collects are as follows: Pro nostro statu, *Rege quesumus Domine famulum tuum*; pro rege, *Deus in cuius manu corda sunt regum*; pro fratribus et parentibus vivis, *Deus qui caritatis dona*; pro pace, *Deus a quo sancta desideria*; pro animabus omnium fidelium defunctorum, *Fidelium Deus omnium conditor et redemptor*; pro vivis et defunctis, *Omnipotens sempiterne Deus qui vivorum dominaris.*

[13] "Quodque in eodem memento rogent specialiter pro pace ecclesie et regni et pro benefactoribus dicte capelle quicumque fuerint."

Stratford was careful to avoid conflict with the observances of the parish church. Thus, on the greater or "double" feasts no mass was to be celebrated in the chapel, unless with the rector's consent, until the Gospel had been read at the parochial altars.[14] Such caveats were soon to be rendered unnecessary. The founder had reserved the right to modify his ordinances and by the augmentation deed of 1336 he effectively made the church collegiate with the appropriation of the rectory to the existing college of chantry priests.[15] From the time of the rector's resignation his place was to be taken by the warden of the chantry, who would become responsible for all parochial functions. The importance of this change is reflected in the heading of a separate quaternion of Bishop Simon de Montacute's register devoted to Stratford's chapel.[16]

The advowson of Stratford church belonged to the Worcester bishops and could not be alienated without appropriate compensation. Stratford himself granted a messuage, a carucate of land and ten shillings' worth of rent – together valued at ten marks a year – to the bishop and his successors,[17] and together with Robert Stratford, at the time archdeacon of Canterbury, restored lands and rents in the town of Stratford and in "Le Homme" which had been alienated by a former diocesan, Walter Maidstone.[18] Montacute's charter granting the advowson is dated 19 July

[14] This was basically a financial provision, to avoid the diversion of offerings from the parish to the chapel.

[15] Leicester, 1 October 1336, confirmed by Bishop Montacute at Hartlebury, 31 December 1336. Worcester Reg. Montacute 1, fols. 53^{r}ii (p. 119) - 56^{v}ii. Despite the new situation, institutions continued to be made to the "custodia" of the chapel within the church of Stratford (e.g. Worcester Reg. Brian 1, fol. 12^v). In 1413, under the wardenship of M. Simon Sloley, a royal *inspeximus* and confirmation of the chantry was secured (*CPR 1413-1416*, p. 154: 12 December 1413). According to *VCH Warwicks.* 2, p. 123 (apparently a misunderstanding of Dugdale, *Warwickshire* 2, p. 692) Sloley's successor, M. Richard Praty, was collated as "warden or dean." In fact he is termed "warden" (custos sive gardianus) but "of the collegiate church of Stratford." Worcester Reg. Morgan 1, fol. 22^v. Cf. Cook, *Chantry Chapels*, p. 53. It is to be noted that the term "gardianus" is used (idiosyncratically?) in 1349 (*Worcester Reg. Bransford*, p. 404). Dugdale, *Warwickshire* 2, p. 694, lists the incumbents from Praty's time as "custodes sive guardiani" of the collegiate church.

[16] Worcester Reg. Montacute 1, fol. 50^{r}ii. "Rubricella: Registrum domini Simonis Wygorniensis episcopi concernens capellam sancti Thome Martiris de Stretford et appropriacionem ecclesie de Stretford dicte capelle appropriate."

[17] Ibid. and fols. 58^{v}ii ff.

[18] Ibid. "Dedit eciam dictus pater ac magister Robertus de Stretford archidiaconus Cantuariensis dicto Simoni Wygorniensi episcopo terras et redditus in Stretford et in le Homme qui fuerunt aliquo tempore de mensa episcopi Wygorniensis." And see ibid., fols. 59^{v}ii ff. The alienations were made in 1317 to Walter de Frendesbury of Ingon and lay between Stratford bridge and Tiddington mill. Ibid., fol. 61^{v}ii.

1336.[19] Once legally in possession of the advowson Stratford proceeded to convey it to M. John de Southwaltham, warden of the chapel.[20] The next task in a lengthy and involved process was to secure the diocesan's formal assent to the appropriation of the rectory to the chantry. In order to do this canonically a case had to be made out and a well-established procedure followed. A petition was drawn up and despatched to the diocesan, although he must already have been fully aware of Stratford's intentions and the arguments to be advanced in justification. The main burden of the petition was that the chantry was insufficiently endowed for the services laid upon it. The full complement of servitors had not been recruited for lack of funds, and the buildings available were inadequate for the founder's purposes; the construction and maintenance of new ones being beyond the resources available. Bishop Montacute responded by deputing Walter de Morton, rector of Hampton, and Henry de Cokham, rector of Severn Stoke,[21] to hold the customary enquiry into the validity of the reasons for appropriation as contained in the petition. Of those who gave evidence,[22] Gilbert rector of Wilmcote was the most expansive. Describing the new chapel as "beautiful to look upon," he argued that it had served to increase the devotion of the people. But, he added, the houses in the warden's custody were small and inadequate, not to say largely ruinous. Furthermore, there was insufficient space for the servitors required by the chapel. The income of the chapel did not exceed ten marks and came from Ingon manor, consisting of arable land and a small rent from impoverished tenants.[23] This slenderness of resources had necessitated a subsidy from the founder, which he was still providing. But for this the chaplains might have been reduced to begging, to the disgrace of the clerical order.[24] The testimony of the other witnesses is mainly

[19] Ibid., fol. 50ʳii.

[20] Ibid., fol. 50ᵛii. Stratford, 21 July 1336.

[21] Ibid., fol. 51ʳii. Hartlebury, 23 July 1336. Cokham was to have a distinguished career as a clerk. When Robert Stratford was archdeacon of Canterbury he made Cokham his agent for Bishop Hemenhale's installation at Worcester (*Worcester Reg. Hemenhale*, fol. 10ʳ). As bishop of Chichester Robert made Cokham his chancellor.

[22] Twelve in all, including the rector of Wilmcote, the vicars of Bishopton and Luddington (all churches dependent on Stratford), two chaplains of Stratford church, a "literatus" (Adam de Styventon) who was a parishioner of Stratford, and six other parishioners.

[23] Worcester Reg. Montacute 1, fol. 51ᵛii. The Ingon manor, like Hatton which gave its name to a branch of the Stratford family, was a sub-manor of the episcopal manor of Hampton. Simon de Croome sold it to Robert Stratford in 1329. Robert later conveyed it to John Stratford, who in 1331 granted it to the chantry. Other small parcels of land were later transferred to the foundation. See *VCH Warwicks.* 3, p. 103.

[24] "Quod ipsi dim[i]tterent dictam cantariam inofficiatam et mendicarent in vituperium ordinis clericalis." This sentiment was not uncommon at the time.

confirmatory and repetitive, but Adam de Styventon claimed that there were insufficient priests in the church for the proper ministration of the sacrament. John Lacy made the telling point that in the normal course the staff of the parish church comprised a rector, who was frequently absent, and two chaplains, but if the church were to be appropriated there would be more chaplains than there had ever been before, and they bound to reside.[25] The arguments were judged acceptable; the bishop applauded the foundation's intention[26] and proceeded to appropriate the church. In his ratification of the process he declared that on the death or cession of the then rector, John Geraud, the rectory was to be united to the chapel and from the income the number of the chaplains was to be increased by eight, to form a college of thirteen priests. Again the warden was to be bound by an oath of residence, an obligation to be specified in his letters of appointment, and also by an oath of canonical obedience to the bishop. Church and chapel were to be subject to episcopal visitation and to that of the prior and convent of Worcester during the see's vacancy.[27]

Under the revised scheme Stratford's ordinances were to remain in force, but he took early opportunity to make lengthy modifications and additions. Basically these involved the arrangements of services and liturgical minutiae. The warden, or in his absence the subwarden, was to appoint a hebdomadary, or weekly officer, to have charge of church and chapel. Such hebdomadary was to celebrate daily the parochial high mass in the choir, which was to be sung with prayers and collects in accordance with the Sarum use. The mass on Sundays and double feasts was to be celebrated devoutly with a suitably vested deacon and subdeacon and in the presence of the other priests, or the greater part of them. Others of the priests were daily, except on double feasts, to say a mass *Salus populi* on behalf of the benefactors of the chapel, church and college, for the living

[25] The argument stresses, as do some other points in the chantry ordination itself, the importance of parochial duties in a college of this kind. It is to be noted that both John and Robert Stratford had been among the "largely absentee" rectors.

[26] Worcester Reg. Montacute 1, fol. 52ᵛii, where (in the words of Stratford's petition) the purposes are expressed as: "Ad divini cultus augmentum et ut Deo et matri sue beate Marie virgini gloriose beato Thome martiri et omnibus sanctis Dei in dicta capella laudabilius et dignius serviatur et ydoneorum ministrorum numerus augeatur in ea, nec non pro vivis et defunctis Deo placidum sacrificium offeratur, et ad exaltacionem fide[i] Christiani et devocionem Christi fidelium ampliandam, dictorum sustentacionem idoneam ministrorum hospitalitatem uberius procurandam, alia pietatis opera excercenda, et ad predicta onera vobis ut premittitur incumbencia facilius supportanda."

[27] The seals of Archbishop Stratford, the diocesan bishop, and the prior and chapter of Worcester were attached to the original document, dated in the chapter house at Worcester, 30 July 1336. Worcester Reg. Montacute 1, fol. 53ʳii.

and the departed, but especially for the king, the founder, M. Robert Stratford, John Geraud – described as lately rector of Stratford[28] – and after death for their souls and for those of the founder's predecessors as archbishops of Canterbury, the prior and chapter of Worcester, and all the faithful departed. The principal collect was to be *Omnipotens sempiterne Deus*, followed by the other collects prescribed in the primary ordination. Two priests were to be deputed by the warden or subwarden to celebrate masses in the chapel of St. Thomas; one of the Holy Trinity to be said, the other of St. John the Evangelist to be sung. On the other days the primary ordination was to be followed, with the prayer *Deus a quo sancta desideria* for the peace of the church and realm, and other prayers for Bishop Simon de Montacute, his brother William (later earl of Salisbury) and their mother, as well as a special prayer for their deceased father, William. After their decease the anniversary of Bishop Montacute and of other members of his family was to be kept with the office of the dead by all the priests, save for four[29] who were to say a daily mass at some altar in either church or chapel – as designated by the warden – for the founder, his successors as archbishops of Canterbury, and for all the faithful departed.

An outside notable could have arrangements made for a mass to be celebrated in place of one of the masses for the departed.[30] There was to be a daily sung mass of the Virgin at her altar in the church, at which at least four chaplains were to be present. But at times when the Mary Mass was celebrated in the choir a mass *Salus populi* was to take place at the altar of St. Thomas in the chapel. After Vespers on the eve of the anniversaries of the founder, his brother, their parents, and of M. John Geraud, the chaplains were to sing the *Placebo* and *Dirige* in the chancel, to be followed by a sung mass the next day. Each priest who took part in the celebration of the anniversary was to receive six pence. Daily after high mass in the chancel the chaplains, divided equally between the two sides of the choir, were to say the *De profundis*, the *Pater noster*, and other customary versicles. For the founder, his relatives, for benefactors and all the faithful departed, the celebrant was to say the collect *Fidelium Deus omnium conditor et redemptor*, and after the founder's death, *Deus qui inter apostolicos sacerdotes* instead, together with the collect *Fidelium*

---

[28] Ibid., fol. 53[v]ii and cf. fol. 53[r]ii.

[29] Ibid., fol. 53[v]ii: "Ac omnes dicti sacerdotes annuatim cum nota solempniter facient post eorum transitum ab hac vita anniversarium eorundem ... quatuor autem reliqui sacerdotes pro nobis ac predecessoribus nostris...."

[30] Ibid., fol. 54[r]ii: "Si aliqua extranea persona notalis [notabilis?] transitum faciens forte petat tempore competenti sibi missam celebrari."

Deus. On completion of these prayers the same priest was to say: "May
the soul of our founder John, the soul of his brother Robert, and the souls
of his parents and of their benefactors and ours, and those of all the
faithful departed, rest in peace." These words were to be repeated daily
after grace in the chaplains' house. Proper provision was to be made for
the eight priests, similar to that laid down for those of the original
foundation. But while the warden and subwarden were to be
"permanent," that is, having a benefice to which they were instituted, the
remainder of the chaplains were to be removable at will.

Daily throughout the year the community was to sing Matins in the
choir, the time varying with the season. In addition to the priests there
were to be a deacon, a subdeacon and an apparitor living and working on
the premises, as had been the case in the church prior to appropriation.[31]
Priests of both earlier and later foundations on double feasts of three
lessons, and on lesser festivals (profestivis diebus), were to say the seven
penitential psalms with the litany in the chapel. In Lent they were to do
this in the choir of the church but despite the injunction in the primary
ordination were not obliged to maintain the observance on other days.[32]

Most of the remainder of Stratford's ordination document is taken up
with regulations touching the behaviour, apparel, and community life of
the college. In church and chapel the priests were to wear capes, that is
"choir copes," with black almuces and white surplices underneath the
capes, in the same manner as the vicars in the church of Salisbury. On
Easter eve they were to discard the capes at the *Gloria in excelsis* and to
use only surplices and almuces until the Monday after the octaves of the
feast. They were to follow the same procedure on the vigil of
Pentecost – until the Monday after Trinity – and on all the double feasts
from Easter to Michaelmas and through the octaves of the Assumption
and Nativity of Our Lady.[33] These capes, almuces and surplices were to be
provided by the warden from the chantry's resources and to be returned
by the chaplains or their executors in the case of cession or death. Both the
original chaplains and the additional eight were to live in common, and

[31] Ibid. "Quod diaconus et subdiaconus et apparitor iuxta disposicionem dicti custodis
qui est et qui erit pro tempore sint in dictis capella et ecclesia ac vivant et deserviant in
eisdem sicut hactenus facere consueverant in ecclesia memorata."

[32] The primary ordination required them to say daily in chapel the seven penitential
and fifteen gradual psalms with the litany.

[33] Pentecost is the seventh Sunday after Easter; the Assumption falls on 15 August, the
Nativity on 8 September. For this practice see Frere, *The Use of Sarum* 1, p. 151; *Register
of St. Osmund* 1, pp. 34-37, which I follow in translating "cappe" (the *cappae nigrae* of
Salisbury) as "capes" rather than "copes."

since the house first assigned to them had proved inadequate, they were to occupy the rectory, eating there and sleeping in a single room or dormitory without partitions.[34] The infirm were to be allowed a separate chamber, as was the warden. If for reasonable cause a chaplain could not eat or sleep with the others he was to be excused. No corrody or pension was to be granted from the foundation's resources, and were anything of the kind to be attempted it would be void. Only the warden and subwarden were entitled to invite guests, but if a chaplain did introduce one, then he was to be charged three pence for the dinner and two pence for any other meal. In compliance with Bishop Montacute's appropriation settlement the warden was to take an oath of residence, and to him and to the subwarden the other chaplains were to swear obedience. It was not thought appropriate, on account of the smallness of their stipends, for chaplains to make frequent visits to friends. However, the revised ordination increased the meagre sums originally prescribed. The subwarden was to have an extra two marks (five marks in all) and each of the priests forty shillings (instead of two marks). Possibly the augmentation was intended as a stimulus to recruitment. If in the future the foundation's resources were to permit of a larger complement of chaplains, the additional ones were to be paid at the augmented rate.

It was the subwarden's duty to carry on the administration in the event of the warden's absence or following his resignation or death. The 1331 ordination had required the Worcester prior and convent to exercise this duty if there was neither a warden nor a subwarden. However, Stratford now considered that it would be inappropriate to bind the prior and convent by oath, so he decreed that the senior chaplain should act temporarily. To prevent drunkenness and insobriety – especially reprehensible among God's ministers – taverns were to be shunned by the chaplains. To avoid the occasion for such visits, no one was permitted to go to anyone's house without licence of the warden or subwarden. A bell was to be installed for summoning the community to meals (prandium, cena, collacio). It was also to be rung at a suitable time each day to ensure the return well before dusk of any chaplains who might be outside the house. Thereafter no one was to go out, unless with the specific permission of either warden or subwarden. The warden was entitled to will his goods and those derived from the chapel and church up to a value of ten marks, but was strictly forbidden, on the oath taken at his appointment, to call the goods of the chantry his own and to bequeath

[34] Worcester Reg. Montacute 1, fol. 54^{v}ii: "Et in una camera seu in uno dormitorio infra mansum eiusdem rectorie absque pariete intermedio simul dormiant."

them. No other administrator was to will any of the chantry's goods. Any residue of goods was to be utilized for the wardenship and for poor parishioners, particularly any of the archbishop's kin, and for hospitality. The warden was to provide four candles to burn before the altar of St. Thomas the Martyr and a further two at the burial place (sepulcrum) of the founder's father and mother,[35] one at the head, the other at the foot. These candles were to be lit during mass and the saying of the office of the dead in the chapel. Lastly Stratford sought to ensure that his wishes were both known and obeyed. The statutes and additions to them were to be read out four times a year while the chaplains were at table. Thereafter there was to be a daily reading from the Bible, the lives of the saints, or other holy writing, during which the other chaplains were to keep silence rather than arguing among themselves. The warden was enjoined to exercise correction, also four times a year, on the Friday following the reading of the statutes. During episcopal visitation enquiry was to be made as to the observance of the regulations.

As will have been gathered from the above summary, a chantry ordination was extensive and detailed, designed to meet every eventuality. Although Stratford's regulations are in many respects particular, in some others they reflect a pattern common among legislators.[36] There has been some confusion about the precise number of chantry chaplains and dependent clergy. So far as the founder's intentions are concerned, the 1331 foundation allowed for a warden, subwarden and three priests, with a clerk to minister to them. The 1336 augmentation added eight priests to the original number, making thirteen in all.[37] In addition, now that the church was appropriated, provision was made for a deacon, subdeacon and apparitor, taken over from the usual complement of parish clergy. Properly speaking the college consisted of the thirteen chantry chaplains, or as many as existed in practice, for evidence is hard to come by. The numbers which the founder envisaged may never have been achieved, though the rector of Wilmcote did state that the initial complement of five priests – which he deemed inadequate – had been reached by 1336.[38]

[35] This suggests that Stratford's parents may have been buried in the chapel.
[36] See, for instance, *Worcester Reg. Bransford*, subject index s.v. chantries; Hamilton Thompson, *English Clergy*, App. 5.
[37] Among annotations in the margin of Worcester Reg. Montacute at this point (1, fol. 53ᵛii) is one which reads: "Nota de octo capellanis novis additis quinque antiquis et eorum ministris ita quod sunt xiii capellani et eorum ministri." It was therefore a substantial foundation. *VCH Warwicks.* 2, pp. 123-124; Knowles and Hadcock, *Medieval Religious Houses*, pp. 310, 342 (following *VCH*); *Worc. Admin.*, pp. 233, 243-244; *CPP 1342-1419*, p. 94; Dugdale, *Monasticon* 6, p. 1471.
[38] Worcester Reg. Montacute 1, fol. 51ᵛii.

Another confusion has arisen with respect to the community life of the college, it having been suggested that this was not possible until the building of satisfactory premises by Bishop Ralph Stratford,[39] who surprisingly enough was not specifically included by his uncle among those whom the chantry was to commemorate. In fact there is no reason to doubt that the priests of the initial foundation lived together in the house provided. Its ruinous condition was doubtless exaggerated for the purposes of the appropriation, and when that was effected the rectoral buildings became available for communal living quarters. This availability depended upon the rector's resignation and the revised ordination shows that this had occurred by 1336. But even the rectory would have been far too small for the thirteen chaplains contemplated by Stratford, which explains why in May 1352 Ralph Stratford received royal protection for ten carpenters, ten masons, and the same number of carters, who were to be employed in bringing stone, timber and other necessaries for the buildings to be erected at Stratford for St. Thomas's chaplains.[40] It was these buildings which Leland described over a century and a half later.[41]

Before this provision of adequate living quarters Stratford himself had died, leaving a substantial legacy of valuable articles to his chapel. Some or all of them may already have been in use at Stratford. The archbishop bequeathed his best cope with figures worked in gold and silk and two "pairs" or sets of vestments with their accessories, one being of silk with lions and small peacocks in gold, the other of gold with birds and beasts. In addition he devised to his foundation all the missals, graduals, breviaries, legendaries, processionals and other books which would be needed for the services in church and chapel; also a cross of silver gilt with evangelists enamelled at its four extremities. The legacy included two chalices, one with a beryl, the other plain. But perhaps most esteemed of all the archbishop's gifts were the relics; their value was immeasurable, but they could be calculated to draw a steady stream of devout pilgrims. There was a head from (one of the martyrs of?) Cologne, enclosed within a silver-gilt reliquary, itself in the shape of a head; a portion of the Lord's cross in a cruciform receptacle of gold; relics of various saints in a crystal container; and finally the girdles of St. Edmund of Canterbury and of St. Richard of Chichester. To round off his gifts Stratford bequeathed a

[39] *VCH Warwicks.* 2, pp. 123-124.
[40] *CPR 1350-1354*, p. 262: 12 May 1352.
[41] *Itinerary* 2, pp. 48-49: "their [the chaplains'] mansyon place, an ancient pece of worke of square stone hard by the cemitory."

hundred pounds for the completion of the chapel, which suggests there was still some building work to be done as late as 1348.[42]

Once successfully established it was to be expected that further benefactions would accrue to the chantry. Such proved to be the case. In 1337, for instance, Stratford procured a royal charter permitting the chantry to receive the chattels of felons, fines for trespass, and other privileges normally reserved to the king, and leaving it quit of livery, pensions and corrodies, the imposition of which could be extremely burdensome, a fact to which many religious institutions bore witness.[43] In 1340 Stratford was probably instrumental in obtaining the mortmain licence which enabled the chantry warden to acquire twenty pounds' worth (in annual value) of land and rents. This produced a steady trickle of minor gifts of property and rent.[44] The archbishop's friends in Stratford were active in the matter, as is shown by the efforts of Adam de Styventon and John Nore.[45] The foundation had received the sanction of the Worcester bishops Orleton and Montacute, as well as the consent of the cathedral priory, and in 1345 a papal bull of confirmation was issued in response to a petition.[46] Legally the foundation's position was secure. But there was one endeavour which misfired. Stratford made an arrangement with John Pulteney for an exchange of the advowson of Napton in Warwickshire, a church about to be appropriated to that city merchant's chantry in St. Laurence, Candlewick Street, with that of Eastling in Kent. This would have enabled Stratford to appropriate Napton to his chantry. Had the exchange been effected both foundations would have benefited from greater ease of access to the respective properties.[47] But the archbishop's death intervened before the transaction could be completed and his brother Robert, for reasons which can only be surmised, granted the

[42] *CCL* W.219.

[43] *CChR 1327-1341*, pp. 422-423. Five years later the "Hall of the King's Scholars" at Cambridge was granted the same privileges conceded to the college of chaplains at Stratford. *CPR 1340-1343*, p. 466.

[44] *CPR 1338-1340*, p. 415: 8 February 1340. For the additions see, for instance, ibid. *1343-1345*, p. 439; ibid. *1345-1348*, pp. 430 (by Stratford himself of seven messuages in Stratford of 3s 4d annual value), 444 (by Adam de Styventon); ibid. *1348-1350*, pp. 46, 276, 281.

[45] *CPR 1345-1348*, p. 444; ibid. *1348-1350*, p. 281. John Nore alias "de Stratford" was the son of Adam of Shottery. See Worcester Reg. Hemenhale, fol. 23[r], where he is among those ordained to the diaconate.

[46] Vatican Archives, *RV* 172, fols. 207[r]-214[r]; *CPL 1342-1362*, p. 216: 23 June 1345; *CPP 1342-1419*, p. 94.

[47] *VCH Warwicks.* 6, p. 186. Members of Pulteney's mother's family, the Naptons, also merchants, were tenants in chief in Warwickshire. Thrupp, *The Merchant Class of Medieval London*, App. p. 361.

advowson to William Shareshull or Shareshill, the prominent justice. Shareshull, who came from his name-place near Wolverhampton, possessed property in Worcester diocese, including a house at Bromsgrove, and is believed by his biographer to have been a kinsman of Bishop Montacute.[48] Thus considerations of kinship or of political compatibility could have dictated Robert's concession, and in any case Shareshull was a powerful man who, on recovery from his temporary eclipse in 1340-1341, resumed a distinguished career.[49]

Another matter manipulated by the archbishop and his well-wishers was the wardenship of the chantry. John "called Geraud" was a Stratford man who had taken part in the complex interchange of benefices during 1319 and 1320 in which both John and Robert Stratford had been involved – and also the rectory of their native town.[50] Geraud ended up with the church of Overbury, but in 1334 he was instituted to Stratford at the king's presentation, and very possibly at the archbishop's prompting.[51] John's kinsman, possibly his brother, Henry Geraud, was instituted to the vacated Overbury.[52] Now this Henry can be identified with the chancery clerk Henry de Stratford, described by one authority as the archbishop's "cousin."[53] In other words, as might have been suspected, the Gerauds alias "de Stratfords" were kinsman of the founder of the Stratford chantry. Just before the augmentation document was drawn up John de Southwaltham and Robert de Lye were instituted as warden and subwarden respectively,[54] but the church could not be united with the chantry until Geraud either died or resigned. We are told in fact that Geraud had ceased to be rector before the revised deed was sealed on 1 October 1336.[55] Quite what happened to him then is not clear. He cannot be the man described as "M. John, son of Nicholas Geraud of Stratford," who was instituted to Ipsley in 1344 as rector and to Cherrington four years later, since he is recorded to have died by 21 April 1349.[56] Our John Geraud, given the prefix "magister" like his namesake, would appear to be the man

---

[48] Putnam, *Shareshull*, pp. 1, 5-6.

[49] Ibid., pp. 23, 137-140. Putnam suggests that his sympathies were Lancastrian. He was notably involved in the actions against Bishop Lisle of Ely for trespass. Ibid., pp. 30, 36, 140-142.

[50] See above, "The Making of a Career."

[51] Worcester Reg. Monacute 1, fol. 10^r: 16 June 1334.

[52] Ibid., fol. 10^v: 24 June 1334.

[53] See above, "Stratford's *Familia* and Administration," n. 3.

[54] Worcester Reg. Monacute 1, fol. 23^r.

[55] Ibid., fol. 53^vii. He was "nunc rector" 30 July 1336, ibid., fol. 52^vii.

[56] *Worcester Reg. Bransford*, pp. 380, 396, 402.

instituted warden of the Stratford chantry on 16 June 1349 at the height of the Black Death.[57] One can only assume that Bishop Bransford, who as the Worcester diocesan had the right of collation, acted as the Stratfords would have wished. Geraud was perhaps not entirely suitable for the wardenship. On 11 January 1355, when entitled "warden of the Stratford chantry of thirteen priests," he resigned for the purpose of visiting the shrines of the apostles Peter and Paul in Rome. Bishop Brian thereupon appointed Hugh de Ferrariis, rector of Hanbury-by-Droitwich, in his stead. But shortly afterwards, 5 February, he reinstated Geraud who was claiming that he had been denied right of passage abroad by the king.[58] The long-lived Geraud was returned in 1366 as a pluralist, since he was holding a canonry of Salisbury in conjunction with the chantry.[59]

The later history of the college need not detain us here, particularly as Dugdale in his *Antiquities of Warwickshire* has given a fairly full account.[60] Not so very long before the dissolution four choristers were added to the foundation by Dr. Ralph Collingwood, in accordance with the intention of his predecessor as master or warden, M. Thomas Balshall, who had been responsible for the rebuilding of the choir of Stratford church. The college was suppressed in 1546 and the site granted to the earl of Warwick four years later.[61] This, at any rate, was an eventuality which even the most prescient founder could not have foreseen.

Eastbridge Hospital and Other Benefactions

As early as 1326 Stratford, then bishop of Winchester, was engaged in the transfer of land to provide additional resources for the hospital of St.

---

[57] He was instituted in accordance with Stratford's 1336 ordinance. "Iuratusque de tenendo et observando quatenus in eo est ordinacionem dicte capelle iuxta disposicionem fundatoris, et de obediendo episcopo suisque successoribus et eorum ministris in licitis et canonicis mandatis." Ibid., p. 411. The date of institution is given as 16 June 1340 in *VCH Warwicks*. 2, p. 123, and in Dugdale, *Monasticon* 6, p. 1471, as 14 January 1339.

[58] Worcester Reg. Brian 1, fol. 12ᵛ (where his name is written as "Gerald") and cf. ibid., fol. 5ᵛ.

[59] *Worc. Admin.*, p. 234 n. 2; *Canterbury Reg. Langham*, p. 36. The wardenship was taxed at thirty-five marks (£23 6s 8d), the Salisbury prebend at £40.

[60] *Warwickshire* 2, pp. 692-694; cf. *VCH Warwicks*. 2, pp. 123-124. The *Registrum Album* cited by Dugdale and said in *VCH* (p. 123 n.36) to be "of the college," is in fact WoCL *Liber Albus*.

[61] Dugdale, *Monasticon* 6, p. 1471; idem, *Warwickshire* 2, p. 693; *CPR 1549-1551*, p. 374. Dr. Bell was warden at the time of the *Valor Ecclesiasticus* (1535), which also names a subwarden and four other chaplains. The taxed value of the foundation was £123 11s 9d. *Valor Eccles*. 3, p. 94; cf. *VCH Warwicks*. 2, pp. 123-124.

Thomas the Martyr at Southwark. This was a pious act performed, as was the custom of the day, not only for the bodily solace of the hospital's inmates, but also for Stratford's own spiritual welfare and that of others.[1] Five years later, in 1331, he secured royal licence for the grant of the advowson of Bishopstoke to the chantry of St. Stephen and St. Laurence in Marwell.[2] It was also as Winchester diocesan that he conceded a charter to the Augustinian friars of the city permitting the enlargement of their site by the acquisition of a lane contiguous to their house outside the south gate.[3] Subsequently, as we have seen, the archbishop's will included pious benefactions for his soul's salvation to hospitals, friaries and other religious houses. Among the hospitals which benefited was that of St. Thomas at Canterbury, commonly called Eastbridge Hospital. This still lies on the main east-west thoroughfare at the point where it inconspicuously crosses the River Stour not far from the Westgate, the only medieval city gate to survive.[4] A modern visitor to the hospital will see much of the fabric, basically transitional Norman in style, which we may assume was familiar to Stratford, though surprisingly he will find that the house does not openly record the archbishop among its benefactors. This, as we shall see, is less than just. Apart from the small legacy previously mentioned, Stratford's main contribution to Eastbridge was to appropriate to it the church of St. Nicholas, Harbledown, and at the same time, 1342, to draw up a set of ordinances for the conduct of its affairs.[5]

---

[1] *CPR 1327-1330*, p. 366: *inspeximus* and confirmation 17 February 1329 of a grant in free alms of 1 December 1326 for the salvation of Stratford's soul, those of his parents, and of Adam de Chaundeler and his wife Joan. Stratford and John of Windsor conveyed lands in Wimbledon which they had acquired by Joan's gift.

[2] Ibid. *1330-1334*, p. 165: 8 September 1331. For Stratford's attempt to appropriate Wonston to the prior and convent of Winchester in order to secure the annual payment of £25 19s 4d to the hospital of St. Mary Magdalene there see above, "Winchester 1323-1333."

[3] WinRS, fol. 36ᵛ; *CPR 1327-1330*, p. 307: *inspeximus* and confirmation 20 July 1328 of Stratford's charter of 9 May 1328.

[4] Leland, *Itinerary* 4, p. 59, wrote of the hospital of the Kingsbridge for poor pilgrims and wayfaring men. He enumerated six city gates.

[5] CCL Reg. H, fol. 88ᵛ; *Lit. Cant.* 2, pp. 251-257; Somner, *Antiquities*, App. to Supplement, pp. 13-15 no. 17. For the general history of the hospital see in particular Somner, *Antiquities*, pp. 62-70 nos. 36-38b; Duncombe and Battely, *The Three Archiepiscopal Hospitals*, pp. 297ff.; *Canterbury Chantries*, pp. 1-9; *Kent Chantries*, pp. 62-64. It is extremely likely that Stratford gave active support to the hospital's quaestors who sought aid in Lincoln diocese while he was official and subsequently in the later 1330s. E.g. Lincoln Reg. Dalderby 2 (Reg. 3), fol. 411ᵛ; Reg. Burghersh 2 (Reg. 5), fols. 541ᵛ, 549ʳ⁻ᵛ, 568ᵛ.

Stratford's special interest in this hospital is no doubt to be explained by the fact that it was dedicated to St. Thomas and had a particular function to perform with respect to the martyr's cult. As he tells us himself in the preamble to the ordinances, Stratford believed St. Thomas to have been the founder. In view of the hospital's avowed purpose – to provide a hostel for poor and sick pilgrims – it would seem more likely to have been established after the martyrdom of St. Thomas to accommodate the flood of visitors to his shrine. Indeed, it has now been shown that Eastbridge was built about 1175-1180 by one Edward Odbold, who held land in the parish of St. Peter's, Canterbury.[6]

While visiting Eastbridge, possibly in 1342, Stratford found many shortcomings with respect to divine service and the performance of works of charity. A petition claimed that the hospital was suffering from a lack of endowment and from the improvidence of former masters in cutting down woods and alienating other property; so much so, that it was allegedly reduced to a state of abject poverty. It was on these grounds that the archbishop consented to the appropriation of Harbledown rectory. He went further by taking the comparatively unusual step, because of the church's modest income,[7] of not ordaining a perpetual vicarage, merely requiring the hospital to provide a suitable priest to exercise the cure of souls.[8]

Stratford's ordinances are of interest on at least two counts; they provide insight into a rather special type of hospital and at some points they echo the regulations of the Stratford chantry. The master, who was to be appointed by Stratford and by his successors in the metropolitan see, had to be in priest's orders. Another chaplain, who could be removed at will, was to reside continually at Eastbridge with the master. Within a month of his appointment the master was to produce an inventory of the hospital's goods and to hand a copy to the prior of Canterbury on the archbishop's behalf. Annually between Michaelmas (29 September) and All Saints (1 November) he was to render a full account. Master and chaplain were to say or intone Matins and the other canonical hours in turn according to the Sarum use, as well as to celebrate a daily mass and a mass of St. Nicholas on Sundays.[9] On Tuesdays the mass was to be of St.

---

[6] *Canterbury Chantries*, pp. 7-9; W. G. Urry, *Archaeological Journal* 127 (1969), p. 237; Knowles and Hadcock, *Medieval Religious Houses* 2nd ed., p. 350.

[7] According to *Taxatio*, p. 1a, it was taxed at six pounds.

[8] "Salvo idoneo sacerdoti [?] servituro ecclesiae in divinis." Somner, *Antiquities*, no. 17. For Harbledown see *Canterbury Chantries*, pp. 38-44.

[9] "Unus eorum missa de die, alius vero diebus dominicis." Somner, *Antiquities*, no. 17.

Thomas, on Thursdays of St. Catherine, and for the remaining days of the week it was to be on behalf of the departed and the hospital's benefactors. The collect *Rege quesumus Domine famulum tuum pontificem nostrum* was to be said for the archbishop during his lifetime, and after his death *Deus qui inter apostolicos sacerdotes*.[10] In the canon of the mass the archbishop was to be prayed for and in all masses the chaplains were to keep him in mind. The master was to have the disposition of the goods of the house, but with the caveat that on ordinary days both he and the chaplain were to be content with one double course (de uno ferculo duplicato), with the addition of a pittance of similar quality on Sundays and feast days. There was to be no common seal in the house – presumably to avoid the alienation of hospital property. Poor pilgrims stricken by illness on the way, but not lepers, might be taken into the hospital, and should they die there were to be buried in the cemetery of the church in the place assigned of old for that purpose. Those pilgrims who were in good health were to stay only one night. Four pence a day was to be given to both categories of pilgrim, but the sick were to be given precedence over those in good health. Should there be only a few pilgrims at any one time, then the sum allotted could be increased on other occasions, provided that an overall average of four pence was maintained. There were to be twelve beds and a woman of upright life, over forty years of age, was to look after the pilgrims.[11] The master was to take an oath not to sell or make grants of the hospital's goods either in perpetuity or temporarily without first consulting the archbishop. Any committal of the hospital to someone who was not in priest's orders was to be void.

Despite its association with St. Thomas the Eastbridge hospital, like St. John's at the Northgate, also the subject of Stratford's interest, was to survive the sixteenth-century changes. In 1546, in answer to Henry VIII's commissioners, a book was produced which contained a copy of Stratford's ordinances, and he was claimed as founder.[12] At that time in addition to the master there was a chantry priest, while 34s 4d was paid annually to a Dominus George of Harbledown under the rubric "Rent due to Harbledown chantry." [13] When, in 1569, Archbishop Parker drew up fresh ordinances for Eastbridge, he duly acknowledged the regulations of his fourteenth-century predecessor, John Stratford.[14]

---

[10] As in the 1331 Stratford ordination. Worcester Reg. Montacute 1, fol. 57ᵛii.
[11] "Tam in lectis quam vitae necessariis." Somner, *Antiquities*, no. 17.
[12] *Canterbury Chantries*, p. 1. For St. John's hospital see ibid., pp. 12-19.
[13] Ibid., pp. 1, 5.
[14] Somner, *Antiquities*, App. to Supplement, pp. 63-65 no. 37a: 20 May 1569.

ORDINANCES FOR THE COURT OF CANTERBURY

In Stratford's time there were three archiepiscopal courts: the consistory court, the audience court, and the Court of Canterbury. About the first of these little is known, owing to the loss of the earlier act books, the visitation books, and the registers of wills.[1] From the extant commissions[2] – none of them from Stratford's archiepiscopate – it is clear that the commissary general acted in the consistory, being empowered to deal both with *ex officio* cases, that is those of correction brought on the archbishop's behalf, and cases introduced at the instance of parties. M. Thomas [Mason] of Canterbury was Stratford's commissary general round about 1340, as we know from some instructions issued to him in connection with audience court business, and he may well have acted throughout the archiepiscopate.[3] About the audience court there is rather more information, for some fragments of the proceedings have survived, possibly as a consequence of the prior's responsibility for audience cases *sede vacante*. Already they have provided information about the state of the diocese under Stratford's regimen.[4] The term "audience" refers to the archbishop's hearing of cases as he and his clerks made the circuit of the manorial residences. In practice, so far as we can judge, Stratford took part in only a limited number of cases, which were in the main conducted by his auditors.[5] The usual title given to the presiding judge was "auditor and special commissary." During the short time covered by the extant records[6] we find that M. Richard Vaughan acted in this capacity, but the bulk of the business was handled by M. John de Lecch and M. Laurence

---

[1] So far, that is, as the first half of the fourteenth century is concerned. *Cant. Admin.* 1, p. 60 n. 5. For the courts in general see ibid. 1, chaps. 9-11; Woodcock, *Medieval Courts*. The latter lists (pp. 139-142) the consistory court act books (1364-1536) and other records, and has much to say about the later history and practice of the court (ibid., index s.v. consistory).

[2] The earliest is dated 1282, but that of 1366 is the first to be explicit on the subject of the powers conferred. *Cant. Admin.* 2, pp. 13-16.

[3] Woodcock, *Medieval Courts*, pp. 113-123, lists commissaries general and other officers of the court including "M. Thomas of Canterbury" (p. 114). See also CCL A.36 IV, fols. 4ᵛ, 17ᵛ, and above, "Stratford's *Familia* and Administration."

[4] See above, "Archbishop of Canterbury."

[5] Ibid., n. 202.

[6] CCL A.36 III comprises three leaves; the first has writing on the recto with only a partial title on the verso, while the third is fragmentary and blank on the verso. The material dates from 1340-1341, but there is also mention of Stratford's mandate of 4 March 1339 from Antwerp. A.36 IV contains an entry from 1334 and considerable details of court proceedings particularly for the years 1340-1341 and 1347-1348. See above, "Archbishop of Canterbury," n. 202.

Fastolf.[7] In the audience, as in the consistory, both *ex officio* and instance cases were dealt with, but we are unlikely to discover why a particular case came into one court rather than the other. What we know of cases in the audience court does not substantiate the suggestion that they tended to be of the "weightier" kind.[8]

It is the third court, that of Canterbury or the Court of Arches, as it came to be called, which is of immediate concern as the object of Stratford's legislative activity. The earliest known archiepiscopal regulations for the court are those of Robert Kildwarby (1273-1278),[9] but the only extensive series of statutes were compiled under the aegis of Robert Winchelsey (1294-1313) and John Stratford respectively.[10] It goes almost without saying that Stratford's early experience as a practitioner in the court must have been invaluable when it came to legislation, and it is evident that he intended his ordinances to dovetail with those of his predecessor. From the preamble to the ordinances we learn that they arose from a personal visitation of the court which revealed, so Stratford tells us, a number of matters requiring correction and reformation.[11] It may well be that the busy archbishop left the detailed drafting to his clerks, but the assumption being made − for which there can be no definite proof − is that basically he was responsible for the substance of the ordinances.[12]

The Court of Canterbury was essentially an appeal court for the province. Cases came to it by appeal from a definitive sentence, more questionably by devolution from a lower court where a party suffered or thought he might suffer a defect of justice,[13] and by what was termed

---

[7] Vaughan is termed "auditor of the archbishop's court and commissary *in hac parte*" on 25 April 1340 and he acted in a case on the last day of July 1348. CCL A.36 IV, fols. 4ʳ, 105ᵛ. On 23 April 1340 Fastolf was appointed a proctor in the curia, but he was acting in the audience court at least by October of that year. Ibid., fols. 2ʳ, 5ʳ.

[8] Cf. Woodcock, *Medieval Courts*, p. 64.

[9] In the preamble to the ordinances the Court of Canterbury is described as: "In ecclesia beatae Mariae de Arcubus London. ab omni inferiorum ordinariorum jurisdictione exempta, et nostrae immediatae jurisdictioni subjecta." *Concilia* 2, p. 681. For Kilwardby's instruction about the admission of proctors and advocates see *Cant. Admin.* 1, pp. 426, 436; 2, p. 207; Lambeth, Black Book of the Arches, fol. 33ʳ.

[10] *Cant. Admin.* 1, pp. 435-436. Winchelsey's somewhat briefer statutes are printed in *Concilia* 2, pp. 204-213. Dr. Churchill used the versions to be found in the Black Book of the Arches (described by her in *Cant. Admin.* 2, pp. 206-210), fols. 42ʳ-62ʳ, 66ʳ-85ᵛ.

[11] "Ut ipsa nostrae visitationis ministerio, circa corrigenda in ea cultu justitiae illustretur, eandem curiam personaliter visitavimus, et nonnulla invenimus in personis et modis procedendi in causis et negotiis inibi ventilatis, reformatione, declaratione, et correctione condigna." *Concilia* 2, p. 681.

[12] The same problem of "authorship" arises with respect to Stratford's provincial constitutions.

[13] See *Cant. Admin.* 1, pp. 425, 427-428. There was much resistance to "short-

tuitorial appeal. This last was a means whereby appeal was made to the apostolic see and meanwhile for the protection of the Canterbury court. Such protection lasted for a year and a day after which, if the appellant had failed to prosecute his case in the curia, it would be remitted to the court from which it had been appealed. The manner in which this appellate jurisdiction was exercised provoked many complaints from suffragans. In Archbishop Pecham's time these were expressed in a schedule of articles.[14] Stratford himself was left in no doubt about Bishop Grandisson's opinion of the court's operation and of the manner in which appeals to Canterbury enabled clear-cut cases to be dragged on for the benefit of patent miscreants.[15] In 1333 Grandisson, irritated by the "odious" Mepham's attempt to visit Exeter diocese and to impose sentences in defiance of a papal bull of privilege, inhibited his archdeacons from obeying the Canterbury official. Stratford tried to mollify his suffragan. Reminding him of their long-standing friendship, he urged that as Archbishop Mepham had now died it was time to remove an inhibition which was at variance with any known law (dissonam omni iuri). Adam Murimuth and Wybert de Littleton were sent to support the archbishop's point of view.[16] Another quite different example comes from Worcester diocese where at times of vacancy the cathedral prior and chapter were impeded by tuitory appeals in their endeavour to exercise their lawful jurisdiction. These had the effect of depriving them of authority over certain religious houses for the whole of a vacancy, the disruptive process being set in motion again on the next occasion.[17]

A detailed examination of the complex ordinances devised by Stratford in 1342,[18] which in Wilkins' text are rendered manageable by no less than sixty rubrics,[19] is beyond the scope of the present enquiry, but something

circuiting" the hierarchy of courts and the phrase "omisso tamen medio" is often to be found in this connection.

[14] Ibid., pp. 427-430; *Councils and Synods*, pp. 921-932. The suffragans' articles presented at the provincial council of 1282 were met by unyielding replies. Subsequently arbitrators issued decisions with respect to "innovations" in the archbishops' courts. What is thought to have been a temporary ordinance for the Court of Canterbury was subsequently drawn up by Pecham (*Councils and Synods*, pp. 932-934).

[15] *Exeter Reg. Grandisson*, pp. 278-279. See above, "Archbishop of Canterbury."

[16] *Exeter Reg. Grandisson*, pp. 275-276.

[17] *Worc. Admin.*, pp. 304-309.

[18] Dated from Lambeth, 11 May 1342. See *Concilia* 2, p. 695. A rare slip in Cheney, *Notaries Public*, pp. 43-44, gives the date as 1345. Dr. Edwin Welch has edited the statutes in an unpublished University of Southampton thesis.

[19] I have numbered these 1-60, and in the notes which follow reference is made to those numbers together with the page of *Concilia* 2 on which the rubric in question appears. Spelman, *Concilia, Decreta, Leges*, pp. 550-571, has fifty-nine rubrics, omitting no. 32 in Wilkins (De advocatis et procuratoribus beneficiatis).

more than a cursory mention is called for. Stratford's aim was to ensure smoothness in the court's operation, the eradication of abuses, the minimizing of irritation to suffragans, the cutting down of delay in the conduct of cases, and the avoidance of unnecessary expenses for suitors. He sought to determine the competence of the court and the nature of its procedure, as well as to define the duties and qualifications of its officers. Throughout one senses a mixture of common sense, legal expertise, and a practical knowledge of the manner in which the court actually worked.

The official of Canterbury was set a high standard of duty. He was not to rescribe, that is to respond by drawing a case into his court, except when this was appropriate. In such matters he was to follow a path somewhere between excessive rigidity and too much pliancy. But there was to be no sacrifice of what Stratford felt to be the rights of his court. According to him the official was entitled as ordinary and immediate judge[20] to deal with cases brought against a suffragan by way of simple complaint (per viam querele simplicis), without mention of devolution.[21] Other cases involving a diocesan bishop might come to the official's cognizance by way of direct or tuitory appeal.[22] Appeals could also be made to him from episcopal officers, such as commissaries general, correctors or sequestrators, and he was entitled to respond should the bishop or his officers neglect to act. There were exceptions to the official's right of action; for instance, he was not to meddle in matters entrusted to papal delegates or executors of papal bulls, or in matrimonial suits still in process. With respect to the last the legislator claimed that whereas there could be no rescribing on account of *gravamina* (grievances) or the business of correction, an appeal could be made from definitive sentence.[23] By ancient custom, it was declared, the official had no right to proceed in matters of spoliation or molestation affecting possession of a benefice, tithes, or other spiritual rights, unless the instigator adduced canonical title and also specified the precise place where the alleged injuries had been sustained.[24] This was calculated to prevent vague or generalized complaints designed to serve the plaintiff's purpose and absorb the court's time. In all instances of tuition or devolution it was enough to

---

[20] "Judex ordinarius et immediatus." *Concilia* 2, p. 682 (no. 3 De querelis).
[21] Ibid. This was held to be in accordance with the *ius commune*. Bishops complained about the practice being a means to evade their lawful correction. Cf. art. 7 of the complaints of Pecham's suffragans, *Councils and Synods*, p. 923.
[22] *Concilia* 2, p. 682; Woodcock, *Medieval Courts*, pp. 64-65ff.
[23] *Concilia* 2, p. 683 (nos. 5 De consuetudinibus, 6 In quibus casibus).
[24] Ibid. (no. 7 De impetrantibus).

prove a single *gravamen*, thus relieving the parties of needless expense.[25] Although at least two witnesses were required for proof of grievance in a tuitory case, for lawful proof of the appeal the oath of a single witness coupled with that of the appellant was to suffice.[26]

Stratford devotes considerable space to the technicalities of tuitorial appeal. In doing so he claimed to be reiterating the customs observed by the court from time immemorial, though with amendments here and there. Appellants for tuition had developed means of slowing proceedings to prevent the remission of their cases to the court of origin. In future they were to produce all their supporting instruments on the first day of the hearing. Thereafter further proofs were to be inadmissible. The examination of witnesses had to be expeditious; no delay in proceedings was to be permitted for the production of instruments or letters, unless in circumstances ruled exceptional by the president.[27] A rescript was to be granted by the court on proof of *gravamina*, but those against whom nothing was proved were to be dismissed from its consideration. After concession by the court of protection or tuition all *gravamina* specified in the appeal, even those not proved, were to be revoked for the time being.[28] If, following the year allowed for tuition, the appellant had failed to prosecute his case in the Roman curia it was to be remitted.[29] To defeat the pretence that appeals had been renounced, Stratford ruled that tuition was to be withdrawn only on the appellant's appearance in court before the president.[30] A parallel abuse was the allegation, often with the support of forged letters, that a benefice had been resigned. In future the only acceptable evidence was to be the appellant's own admission before the court or letters of the ordinary within whose jurisdiction the benefice lay.[31]

A claim that the appellant was under excommunication did not debar prosecution of tuitory appeal, unless such sentence were promulgated on the authority of the apostolic see or of the Court of Canterbury itself and

---

[25] Ibid. (no. 8 Quod ad effectum).

[26] Ibid. p. 686 (no. 16 Quot testes).

[27] Ibid., p. 685 (nos. 12 De dilationibus, 13 Quod testes) and with respect to the "praiseworthy customs of the court from time immemorial," p. 683 (no. 5 De consuetudinibus).

[28] Ibid. (no. 15 De eodem, viz. De testibus). This was when the appellant alleged *gravamina* against more than one person (quodsi contra plures rescriptum fuerit impetratum).

[29] Ibid., p. 686 (no. 19 De effectu): "Tam pars, quam judex, a quibus extitit appellatum, libere possunt exequi et facere quod est suum."

[30] Ibid., p. 687 (no. 22 De renunciatione).

[31] Ibid. (no. 23 De resignatione).

properly substantiated. In the latter case the appellant was allowed three days in which to prove his absolution or the revocation of sentence.[32] Obviously a massive array of witnesses, some of whom might grow tired of waiting and slip away, retarded the judicial process – often by design. The parties were henceforth to be restricted to forty witnesses apiece for each article and, unless licensed by the president, the latter were not to withdraw from the court prior to examination.[33] Stratford took considerable pains over the issues raised by witnesses, for instance the problem of those who because of age or illness could not be examined in court. It was to rest with the president whether the examiner should go in person to such witnesses or whether, to obviate undue expense, the business could be entrusted to some other person agreeable to the parties in the suit. Should the examiner of the court have to make the journey, expenses for himself, his clerks, and his *familia* were to be limited to seven shillings a day. Moreover, the party involved was to be given the option of deciding whether he wanted to spend that much.[34]

Much of the remainder of the ordinances is concerned with the court's personnel. The official of Canterbury was, of course, the principal officer and mention of him, his authority and duties, occurs throughout the ordinances. His deputy – should he be absent – was the dean of the Arches, whom he was to constitute commissary general by means of a (written?) commission.[35] Appeal from *gravamina* could be made to the official against the dean of Arches or any other commissary of the court.[36]

Archbishop Winchelsey had legislated that there were to be sixteen advocates and ten proctors, the latter being forbidden to act without the former. The standard of expertise was set at a high level. Stratford decreed that no one was to be admitted as advocate unless he were a doctor or bachelor of either canon or civil law and had been in the court for a year learning its customs and practice. Preference was to be given to those entitled to the status of doctor or who for at least two years had lectured ordinarily (hora ordinaria) on the decretals. If, however, several doctors applied for a single vacancy, the choice was to be determined by the

---

[32] Ibid. (no. 21 Quae exceptio).

[33] Ibid., p. 688 (no. 27 De compulsione).

[34] Ibid., p. 690 (no. 36 De missione).

[35] Ibid., p. 694 (no. 58 De decano): "Officialis ... teneatur decanum ecclesiae beatae Mariae de Arcubus London. suum constituere in ipsius absentia commissarium generalem, qui habita commissione hujusmodi dicti officialis in ipsius absentia generalis commissarius nuncupetur." But Dr. Churchill suggests (*Cant. Admin.* 1, p. 443) that it was "either not enforced or it required the Archbishop's commission" – one such being issued in 1357.

[36] *Concilia* 2, p. 691 (no. 44 De causis).

reputation of the candidate for industry and satisfactory conduct. The clamorous and argumentative (clamosi, garrulosi) were to be passed over. Advocates were not to be absent without the president's licence or to frequent other courts while that of Canterbury was in session.[37] An advocate (as also a proctor) who held an uncontested benefice with cure of souls for a year was to surrender his office, whether he proceeded to the priesthood or not.[38] A blustering or verbose advocate was to be punished by suspension, as was one who knowingly falsified facts.[39]

Stratford defined the office of proctor in the court as being one of legal practice rather than speculation. To Winchelsey's regulation he added that no proctor general should be admitted unless he had stood in the court for at least a year for the purpose of mastering its business, regulations and statutes. Here again, a bachelor of canon or civil law was to be preferred to other candidates. Proctors were forbidden to introduce any case until their mandate to do so had been lodged with the judge, the opposing party, and the clerk of the court's registry. If such proctor acted under a special mandate – for the particular case – the original document was to be lodged with the registry and copies made for those who sought them, but at their own expense. But if the proctor's authority derived from a general mandate to act on his client's behalf, then a copy of such mandate was to be deposited prior to the return of the original. This would permit duplication for interested parties. Copies of all other instruments exhibited for judicial purposes were to receive like treatment, thus enabling the clerk of the registry to make duplicates available.[40] Whenever the court was in session proctors were to have access to the register of causes. Discrepancies between registration and the president's decrees were to be brought to the court's attention for correction.[41]

The examiner, Stratford asserts, was no routine officer, but a man who could act as judge and president of the court in the absence of both official and dean.[42] His office, which involved the personal and diligent

[37] Ibid., p. 688 (nos. 29 De postulando, 30 Quod advocati). Cf. *Cant. Admin.* 1, p. 452. For ordinary lectures see Rashdall, *Universities* 3, index s.v. Lectures.

[38] *Concilia* 2, p. 689 (no. 32 De advocatis).

[39] Ibid. (no. 33 De informationibus).

[40] Ibid., p. 690 (no. 39 De procuratoribus): "quorum officium magis in practica, quam in iuris speculatione constitit."

[41] Ibid. (no. 40 Quod procuratores).

[42] Ibid. (no. 35 De obtenta examinatorum): "... nomen examinatorum non ex nudo ministerio, sed ex officio sunt sortiti; ipsi (quoque) de antiquo more nostrae curiae in absentia officialis nostri, et decani ecclesiae beatae Mariae de Arcubus London. ejusdem officialis commissarii sunt dictae curiae praesidentes et judices." In *Cant. Admin.* 1, p. 448, it is noted that Archbishop Islep appointed examiners (1350) in accordance with Stratford's statutes. For the text: ibid., 2, pp. 192-193 (from Canterbury Reg. Islep, fol. 9ᵛ).

examination of witnesses, merited lengthy consideration and here again we have the feeling of an eye-witness's assessment of what occurred in the course of proceedings. For example, the examiner was not to allow his clerks to write down depositions in the absence of witnesses and then at a subsequent stage to read out what they had written, which often included matters which had never occurred to the deponents. They were to confine what they wrote to articles for the proof of which witnesses had been produced, and of which they had knowledge. As for interrogatories, these were to be written word for word, with the witnesses' responses to each individual article.[43] An examiner was not legally entitled to proceed to the concordance of such responses, but in the interest of economy, after the first witness had been fully recorded such examiner could note the agreement or disagreement of subsequent witnesses. To do this a special commission had to be procured from the official, which was to be deposited in the registry.[44]

The examiners' clerks, whose task was to record the responses of the parties to the various positions and interrogations, were to be nominated to the official by the principal clerk of the registry. The official was then to present them to the archbishop, who would constitute them notaries public and scribes under oath to record faithfully whatever pertained to them by virtue of their office.[45]

Like other ministers of the court, the registry clerks were to give their services free to the poor. They were to record the *acta* in full with the appearances, manner of pleading, the names of parties and proctors, and also the judgment. The parties involved were entitled to inspect the record and on payment to secure transcripts.[46]

Having dealt with the court's officers, much of what remains illustrates the technical details of pleading and the misdemeanours of litigants. In the event of the suborning of witnesses the promoter of the suit was to be summoned before the court and if unable to purge himself was to be severely punished. The testimony of any such witness was disallowed thereafter.[47] Should a notary public fabricate an instrument his name was

[43] *Concilia* 2, p. 689 (no. 34 De officio). See *Cant. Admin.* 1, p. 447. Churchill does not record (ibid. 2, p. 240) the names of any examiners from Stratford's archiepiscopate. In CCL A.36 IV, fol. 103ᵛ, is a copy of a commission to examine witnesses (17 May 1348) but the name of the recipient has been cut off.

[44] *Concilia* 2, p. 689 (no. 35 De obtenta): "Quod ad sic concordandum dicta testium ab officiali nostrae curiae dicti examinatores commissionem habeant specialem."

[45] Ibid., p. 690 (no. 38 De clericis).

[46] Ibid., p. 691 (no. 41 De registrariis). Cf. pp. 682 (no. 4 De expensis), 691 (no. 42 De actis); *Cant. Admin.* 1, pp. 453-455.

[47] *Concilia* 2, p. 692 (no. 48 De testibus).

to be entered in the register of the court with the reason for his conviction and his repudiated sign (signum damnatum) posted in a prominent place within the court. The names of witnesses or promoters implicated in deceit were likewise to be registered.[48] It was impossible, Stratford had to admit, to circumvent every evil related to the compulsion of witnesses, but to lessen the opportunity for fraud, subject to the president's determination there should be three citations only, the last being promulgated under penalty of deprivation of the right to give testimony. If apprehended, reluctant witnesses were to be compelled by ecclesiastical censures – aggravatory if need be – to put in an appearance.[49] In matters where the law required written documents, laymen alone would not suffice as witnesses. And, even if literate, they were not ordinarily to be given credence as to the lawfulness and sufficiency of exceptions and other propositions in the form of law.[50] Under Stratford's condemnation came the practice whereby appellants in cases of direct appeal deliberately delayed prosecution for three days until the final summons was issued under penalty of remitting the case. To circumvent this stratagem so far as was possible, the appellant in future would not be authorized to introduce his appeal until he had defrayed the expenses incurred on this account by the other party, that is unless he could provide good reason for his incapacity to introduce his suit on the first day.[51] For his part, the defendant was not to be permitted to admit some peccadillo for the purpose of excluding the appellant from the revocation of more serious *gravamina*.[52]

There is an interesting reference to the legate Otto's statute about the authenticity of seals, among which he numbered that of the rural dean. This, said Stratford, was not to be interpreted as referring to judicial acts within the Court of Canterbury. The rural dean's seal was of course to be accepted as adequate for citations and executions of mandates.[53]

The ordinances, as should now be evident, cover virtually every facet of court procedure, much of it in considerable detail. In default of other than fragmentary records they provide a valuable insight into the workings of the court, or perhaps more accurately, into what Stratford thought they ought to be. But it is clear that they are informed less by the wishful thinking of an armchair legislator than by an intimate knowledge

---

[48] Ibid. (no. 49 De notariis).
[49] Ibid. (no. 50 De compulsione).
[50] Ibid. (no. 51 In quibus).
[51] Ibid. (no. 43 De appellationibus).
[52] Ibid. (no. 45 De revocatione).
[53] Ibid., p. 694 (no. 59 De sigillis).

gained by a practitioner, supplemented by experience of complaints brought to him by such aggrieved litigants as Bishop Grandisson. As befits a legal man, Stratford shows himself respectful of his predecessor Winchelsey's ordinances, which for the most part he affirms, occasionally amends, frequently adds to, and in one instance seeks to elaborate in order to resolve an apparent conflict.[54] Stratford appreciated that if he was to uphold the dignity of his court he had to improve its functioning and to remove abuses which could only bring criticism and further litigation. How far he succeeded in such an aim can only be conjectured, but his ordinances none the less stand as an impressive monument to his care as a legislator.

PROVINCIAL CONSTITUTIONS

If, as has been implied above, Stratford's ordinances for the Court of Canterbury occupy a prominent place, arguably *the* most prominent place, in the legislative history of that institution, his relative superiority as a late-medieval legislator in the sphere of the Canterbury province is even more marked.

The monumental work undertaken by Professors Powicke and Cheney, among much other material, provides texts of the canons of councils and synods of the English church for the thirteenth century, and beyond to the year 1313.[1] This more than covers the great period of legatine, archiepiscopal and episcopal legislation.[2] What we have between 1313 and the Reformation is by comparison slight, whether at the provincial or the diocesan level. This is made abundantly clear by the number of canons glossed by the late-fourteenth/fifteenth-century lawyer and official of the Court of Canterbury, William Lyndwood, in his *Provinciale*.[3] In one of the preliminary tables in the 1679 edition the editor lists the more useful

---

[54] Ibid. (no. 57 De concordantia), which refers to Winchelsey's statutes *Diligenti* and *Praeterea*.

[1] *Councils and Synods* in two volumes paginated consecutively.

[2] See Gibbs and Lang, *Bishops and Reform*, for an examination of the impact on provincial and diocesan legislation of the canons of the Fourth Lateran Council (1215).

[3] The *Provinciale* (*seu Constitutiones Angliae*) of the fourteen archbishops from Langton to Chichele with Lyndwood's "summaries and erudite annotations" is published in the 1679 Oxford edition together with the legatine constitutions of Otto and Ottobon, glossed by John de Athon or Acton, and an unglossed edition of the archiepiscopal constitutions. Lyndwood, for whom see *Biog. Oxon.*, s.v., completed the *Provinciale* in 1430.

constitutions (constitutiones utiliores) with appropriate references to the body of the text. These include six constitutions attributed to Robert Winchelsey, ten (recte nine) to Walter Reynolds, eight to Simon Mepham, two to Simon Islep, one to Simon Langham, four to Simon Sudbury, eight to Thomas Arundel, and three to Henry Chichele – a total of forty-two. But the number of Lyndwood's chapters based on Stratford's constitutions is no fewer than thirty (one of them being repeated). The relative importance of Stratford's contribution is even greater than this calculation would suggest, since almost all of the "Winchelsey statutes" have been wrongly ascribed to that archbishop by Lyndwood. Moreover, those of Simon Langham as bishop of Ely, which are synodal rather than provincial, are now assigned to Robert Grosseteste, bishop of Lincoln, hence to the thirteenth century. Other problems arise with respect to certain statutes attributed to Archbishop Reynolds and/or his successor Simon Mepham, as well as to three of the four chapters ascribed to Sudbury.[4] In fact no less than forty-eight of Lyndwood's two hundred and forty chapters were not provincial legislation.[5]

Now in all legislation of this kind, as indeed in the case of ordinances for the Court of Canterbury, or even visitation injunctions, the question of authorship arises. In the context of thirteenth-century legislation Professor Cheney has warned that "we are incapable of answering it."[6] After all, archbishop and bishop had around them expert clerks, capable of framing such legislation themselves. But we also need to examine the meaning we attribute to "authorship." Are we thinking of the letter of the final draft, the basic ideas incorporated in it, or some mixture of the two? An archbishop had of necessity to delegate time-absorbing work to others, but that does not preclude authorship in a very real sense or the personal imprint provided by correction and modification at various stages of drafting. I suspect that we would be wide of the mark were we not to see the mind and hand of Stratford behind the legislation with which we are about to deal. There are many indications that the statutes reflect problems of which he was acutely aware during his period of office and to which he

---

[4] These matters have all been examined at length by C. R. Cheney, e.g. in "Legislation of the Medieval English Church," "The So-called Statutes of John Pecham and Robert Winchelsey," "Some Aspects of Diocesan Legislation during the Thirteenth Century," "William Lyndwood's *Provinciale*," *English Synodalia*, and at appropriate points in *Councils and Synods*.

[5] Cheney, "William Lyndwood's *Provinciale*," p. 173.

[6] *English Synodalia*, pp. 49-50, where he concludes: "If, to avoid intolerable circumlocution, we refer to a bishop as author of the statutes he promulgated, this must be taken as a mere form of words."

had on other occasions given attention. We also know that defects came to the archbishop's notice by means of a process whereby his suffragans deliberated with their clergy about matters which might require reformation. Unfortunately we seldom find returns of this kind, but some few have survived in episcopal registers.[7] Stratford's mandate of 23 July 1341 summoning a provincial council to St. Paul's for 19 October of that year includes a clause requiring such preliminary discussions at diocesan level. Matters calling for rectification were to be written down so that the information could be of use at the ensuing council.[8] In response to this instruction Bishop Orleton summoned his clergy to meet in Winchester Cathedral on 1st October and deputed his official to conduct the proceedings. As we shall see, the resulting return is concerned not so much with the reform of ecclesiastical abuses as with the redress of *gravamina* inflicted by secular authority.[9]

The Winchester return embodies three points, which are scarcely novel. The first required that liberties conceded to the church and to ecclesiastical persons should be preserved unharmed. Under the second item complaint is made that the king had alienated so many of the goods of his fisc that he was no longer able to support the duties incumbent upon him without imposing intolerable tallages and other burdens on the clergy and people of the realm. It was suggested that the royal council should order the restoration of such alienated goods, which were not to be re-granted in the future. Any who received such goods should be excommunicated unless the grant was by common consent of the whole parliament. Lastly, the king was to be petitioned not to burden abbots, priors and religious men who held their temporalities in free alms, or other ecclesiastics holding spiritual benefices. They should not be forced by such commissions to become involved in secular affairs contrary to the church's teaching.[10] How typical this return was it is impossible to say. The points submitted appear eminently suited to the parliamentary forum. Already the king was showing signs of alarm at the prospect of Stratford's

---

[7] E.g. *Hereford Reg. Trillek*, pp. 307-308, 309-310. From evidence of this kind Professor Cheney argued that "legatine and provincial canons were alike founded on the particular demands and deficiencies of the people concerned" and suggested the similarity of "injunctions issued by prelates after a visitation." "Legislation of the Medieval English Church," pp. 206-207.

[8] Ely Reg. Montacute, fol. 64ʳ (cf. *Concilia* 2, p. 680); WinRO 1, fol. 106ᵛ: "Super reformandis in concilio supradicto deliberetis et deliberent circumspecte ac in scriptis redigatis et redigant reformanda ut super illis dictis diebus et loco plenior et maturior informacio valeat optineri et quod expedit conveniencius ordinari."

[9] WinRO 1, fol. 107ʳ: Waltham 28 September 1341. See Appendix 1 below.

[10] WinRO 1, fol. 107ʳ.

council, allegedly convoked to arouse the people against the king by pressing the "pretended statutes" of 1341.[11] In the event the business seems to have taken a far less provocative turn.

Three sets of statutes are attributed to Stratford. The first of these comprises eight canons or chapters all save one of which, *De bigamia*, are to be found in modified form in the second series. It is a reasonable hypothesis that this initial series constituted a draft, in revising which some of the phraseology was toned down, or at any rate altered. Thus, as Professor Cheney has observed, "Apparitorum turba pestifera" becomes "Cum apparitorum onerosa multitudine";[12] though "Insatiabilis cupiditas" is no milder an expression than "Insatiabilis ambitio." [13] Murimuth's account lends credence to this view. He tells us that eight bishops attended the council and that they discussed many matters which involved the preservation of ecclesiastical liberty and the reformation of manners. Because the business could not be completed it was postponed to another council.[14]

According to the prefatory rubric in the edition by Wilkins the second series was issued (edite) in a provincial council at London on 10 October 1342. We know that two provincial assemblies were summoned for October 1342; the first for the 9th in response to a royal writ, the second for the 14th.[15] Wilkins also records that the third series of canons was issued in the London council on Wednesday after the feast of St. Edward king and martyr 1342, that is 19 March 1343, in the presence of ten

[11] *CCR 1341-1343*, p. 335: 1 October 1341. There "morrow of St. Lucy" should read "morrow of St. Luke" (cf. BL Cotton MS Nero D.x, fol. 125ʳ). See above, "The Crisis of 1341," for events leading up to the royal prohibition and for the council in general Bolton, "The Council of London, 1342." But "royal threats" did not necessarily deter episcopal attendance (the quorum was rarely more than ten for provincial or parliamentary assemblies). It is also doubtful whether the council was "virtually sabotaged" by the earlier political crisis (Bolton, "The Council of London, 1342," p. 151). Grandisson sent proctors (*Exeter Reg. Grandisson*, pp. 970-971), but the note (ibid., p. 971 n. 1) is erroneous in suggesting that he in fact attended the council.

[12] "Legislation of the Medieval English Church," pp. 415-417; *Concilia* 2, pp. 675-678.

[13] Caps. 4, 5, 10, 11, and 12 of the 1342 series are absent from the 1341 constitutions. In cap. 1 (1342) the final part of the equivalent cap. 6 (1341) is omitted. The closing paragraphs (as printed in *Concilia* 2) of caps. 7 and 8 (1342) are absent from the corresponding caps. 2 and 7 (1341). Cap. 12 (1342) is also printed separately in *Concilia* 2, pp. 679-680, from BL Cotton MS Vitellius A.ii, fol. 91ᵛ (al. 82ᵛ).

[14] *Murimuth*, pp. 122, 223 (additions from BL Cotton MS Nero D.x, fol. 125ʳ). "In quo consilio multa tractata fuerant pro libertatis ecclesiastice conservacione et morum reformacione, que tunc non poterant terminari usque ad aliud consilium fuerant prorogata." Cotton MS Nero D.x, fol. 125ʳ.

[15] Weske, *Convocation of the Clergy*, p. 251; below, Appendix 3; *Concilia* 2, p. 696.

bishops of English sees and the bishop of Bangor, called "David." [16] As Professor Cheney has pointed out, there is no independent record of a council at this time, and he suggests that perhaps we ought to read "Wednesday after the translation of Edward the king," that is to say 16 October 1342.[17] It so happens that we do not have to rely on conjecture. A rubric in the Salisbury register of Bishop Wyville states unequivocally that the constitutions of Archbishop Stratford (that is the third series) were issued in the council which began its deliberations on the Monday after the translation of St. Edward the king – in other words 14 October 1342.[18] However, it was not until 19 May of the following year that the archbishop sent copies of the constitutions to his suffragans, including Wyville. By means of his four archdeacons and the official of the dean of Salisbury Wyville assembled the clergy of his diocese in the cathedral on 14 July 1343. There the constitutions were read out word for word and a copy issued to each of the archdeacons for publication in their chapters. They were instructed in their turn to make available a copy to any ecclesiastical person within their jurisdiction who requested one. On 22 September Wyville was able to certify Stratford that he had implemented his instructions in full. The canons themselves are entered in the Salisbury register at this point, and although their rubrication differs from that of Wilkins the texts seem to coincide in all essentials.[19] This helps to clear up a number of points raised by Professor Cheney, and Wilkins' amended date for the issue of the constitutions, 16 October, now carries conviction.

The authority invoked for the implementation of the second and third series of constitutions merits examination. In the initial canon *Quam sit inhonestum* of the second series Stratford legislates "with the assent and counsel of his brother bishops and of the whole council." [20] Subsequently, when ordaining the remedy for an abuse, he uses the word "statuimus,"

---

[16] *Concilia* 2, p. 702 (Spelman, *Concilia, Decreta, Leges*, p. 581). Both Wilkins and Spelman used the fifteenth-century Cotton MS Otho A.xv, assumed to have been destroyed in the fire of 1731. Wilkins collated this MS with what he called Lambeth MS 17 (not the MS 17 noted by Todd, *Catalogue of the Archiepiscopal Manuscripts*, 1812, as missing), now Lambeth MS 538; Ely MS 235, now CUL MS Gg. vi 21; and Bodl. Lib. MS Digby 81. I am indebted to Johnstone, "Pecham and the Council of Lambeth," p. 179 nn. 3, 5, for the identification of the Lambeth and Ely MSS. "David Bangoren" (in both Spelman and Wilkins) is an error. Matthew de Englefield was bishop of Bangor at the time; Dafydd ap Bleddyn was the St. Asaph diocesan. But see above, p. 75 n. 105.

[17] "Legislation of the Medieval English Church," p. 416.

[18] Salisbury Reg. Wyville 1, fol. 128^r.

[19] Ibid., fols. 128^r-131^v. The Salisbury copy has ten rubrics instead of the seventeen of Wilkins. See below, Appendix 4b.

[20] *Concilia* 2, p. 696.

occasionally the phrase "statuimus approbante concilio." [21] There is no final chapter enjoining publication by the suffragans. The preamble to the third series declares Stratford to be acting "with the authority of the council and by the advice and assent of his suffragans";[22] throughout there is mention of the council's sanction in such expressions as "declaramus provisione concilii," "praesentis deliberatione concilii" and "praesentis auctoritate concilii." [23] The concluding chapter, 17, is a mandate to the comprovincial bishops to publish the statutes within their dioceses.[24] It has been held that a formal issue of the statutes, such as is recorded for both the second and third series, made them binding, not only perhaps on the auditors but also on those bishops who were merely represented by proctors. But this should not be taken to preclude subsequent modification or clarification by the archbishop.[25] The record of Wyville's process makes it clear that only the third series was published by virtue of Stratford's mandate of May 1343.[26] Evidence is lacking for the official dissemination of the second series at diocesan level.[27] Both series were glossed by Lynwood.

Now something has to be said about the contents of the constitutions. Broadly speaking the second series is concerned with matters of ecclesiastical administration and discipline, while the third is involved more with the maintenance of church liberties in general and with specific areas of friction between laymen and ecclesiastics. The second series comprises twelve canons, the third a proem and seventeen canons – the last being concerned solely with publication. In large measure the regulations of the second series constitute a condemnation of the cost of administration and the abuses to which it gave rise. Stratford names insatiable greed as the root cause of excessive fees. In future charges for enquiry into vacant benefices, for letters of institution, and for certificates of these processes, were not to exceed twelve pence. For letters of orders the maximum was to be half that sum. As for the ordinaries, they were to obviate the need for *douceurs* by paying their ministers suitable stipends.[28]

---

[21] Ibid., p. 697 passim.

[22] Ibid., p. 702.

[23] Ibid., p. 703 passim.

[24] Ibid., p. 709.

[25] Cheney, "Legislation of the Medieval English Church," p. 209. He is concerned specifically with thirteenth-century practice. I am also indebted to him for the qualification.

[26] Salisbury Reg. Wyville 1, fol. 128[r]: Lambeth 19 May 1343. There is no list of witnessing bishops.

[27] Cheney, "Legislation of the Medieval English Church," pp. 416-417.

[28] *Concilia* 2, pp. 696-697: *Nova et insatiabilis*. Lyndwood, p. 222, has *Saeva et insatiabilis* where, ad ver. *Ultra xii denarios*, he declares that sometimes less ought to be

For inductions an archdeacon was entitled to forty pence as seal fee and expenses, but if his official performed the task he was to have only two shillings. In the same way, unreasonable sums were being exacted for the probate of wills, and a scale of charges linked to the valuation in the inventory was laid down.[29] Here Stratford was reinforcing Archbishop Mepham's legislation. Visitation procurations provided another subject of criticism. There was to be a restriction to one procuration a day, and for a moderate number of familiars and carriages. Even then procuration was permissible only following diligent visitation conducted in person. In cases where there were defects in churches the monetary penalties imposed were to be used to defray the cost of reparations.[30] For notorious crimes it had been the practice to inflict a pecuniary penalty; Stratford forbade this for a second offence.[31] The initial canon of the series sought to remedy the abuse of saying masses in private oratories without the ordinary's licence. This was harmful to the rights and income of parish churches, and in any case the privilege was properly to be enjoyed only by magnates or nobles living at a distance from their parish churches.[32] Widespread support can be found for Stratford's contention that such chapels were becoming numerous and that they were being attended by other than lords and their immediate households.[33]

Another matter which attracted condemnation was the loss of alms to the poor occasioned by appropriation. This obligation incumbent on every benefice was to be maintained by appropriators on pain of sequestration.[34]

---

charged since letters of institution and collation or mandates of induction involved far less labour than certificates. Notices of stipends paid to episcopal officers are rare, but a later hand in *Worcester Reg. Wakefeld* (p. 8, fol. 10ʳ) lists £10 p.a. for the chancellor, £6 13s 4d for the commissary and £5 for the registrar, together with their fees. The official is not mentioned. When he became archbishop Stratford tried to secure support for the Canterbury official and the dean of Arches by means of appropriation. See PRO 31/9/17A, fols. 80ʳ-84ᵛ.

[29] *Concilia* 2, pp. 697-698. The canon *Adeo quorundam* refers back to and considerably modifies Mepham's canon with the same incipit. See also *Lyndwood*, p. 140, ad ver. *Quantitate pecuniae*.

[30] *Concilia* 2, p. 699: *Quamvis lex*. This constitution reflects papal legislation. Boniface's VIII's regulations are in *Sext* 3, 20, 3. In 1336 Benedict XII in his constitution *Vas electionis* (*Extrav. Commun.* 3, 10, 1) set upper limits for procuration.

[31] *Concilia* 2, p. 700: *Quoniam reus*.

[32] Ibid., p. 696: *Quam sit inhonestum*.

[33] In some cases chantry chapels were designed to provide services in remote areas and it is clear that a real need was felt for something more immediate than the parish church. On the other hand, chapels or oratories were regarded by rectors as a threat to their livelihood. See Lyndwood, p. 233 ad ver. *Oratoriis* and *Capellis*; Houghton, "Parochial Chapels."

[34] *Concilia* 2, p. 697: *In decimis*.

Another canon directed against the religious as the chief beneficiaries of appropriation claimed that insufficient income was being left for the maintenance of those parts of the church, such as the nave, roof, and tower, which by the custom of the province the parishioners were bound to repair.[35]

Other canons were intended to correct abuses of diocesan courts. The burden of maintaining consistory courts and archidiaconal chapters fell unevenly on individual areas, thus causing needless hardship. Those to whom the courts belonged were to provide what was required at the time of the sessions. Apparitors, so often given a bad reputation, were to be confined in number; one riding apparitor being permitted to each diocesan, while archdeacons were restricted to one foot apparitor in each deanery. Such officers were forbidden to stay more than a night and a day at the expense of rectors or vicars unless specifically requested to do so.[36] Purgation, it was suggested, had given rise to irregularities, including the demand for an excessive number of compurgators and the consequent expense of bringing them from long distances. So much so, that some preferred to confess to a fault they had not committed rather than to face the labour and expense involved. In future the limit in cases of fornication was to be six compurgators, for adultery twelve.[37] The final canon in the second series, *Esurientis avaritiae*, is of a different kind. Its preamble condemns the disgraceful scramble for benefices. Clerks were seeking to gain possession by means of royal presentation on the false grounds of vacancy long past or the custody of land. Or again, they sought writs of *Quare non admisit* or *Quare impedit*, thereby drawing bishops and others into the secular courts. Those who sued out such writs without first following the proper procedure of enquiry by the ordinary and removal of the occupier by process of the ecclesiastical courts were to be excommunicate. Anyone instituting or admitting a person to a benefice already occupied was to be suspended for two months if a bishop, or in the case of an inferior officer until all damage to the former possessor had been made good. The man admitted or instituted to a benefice already filled was to be deemed an intruder subject to the penalty prescribed by the legate Cardinal Ottobon.[38] But there was a caveat to the effect that

---

[35] Ibid.: *Licet parochiani*.

[36] Ibid., pp. 699-700: *Excussis subditorum*. In 1334 Bishop Montacute of Worcester ordered his sequestrator to defray the necessary expenses of the official or his commissary for the consistory out of the perquisites of his office. *Worc. Admin.*, p. 108.

[37] *Concilia* 2, pp. 700-701: *Item licet*.

[38] Ibid., pp. 701-702. For Ottobon's canon *Amoris proprii* see *Councils and Synods*, pp. 759-761. *Pace* Bolton, "Council of London," pp. 155-156, there seems to have been

there was no intention of derogating from the royal dignity. If a patron had recovered his right in the king's court and the ordinary was asked to admit, this was to be done provided no canonical obstacle existed. If, however, the benefice was not vacant, then the ordinary should excuse himself to the king or his justices on those grounds. A presentee who then proceeded further against the ordinary in the secular court, spurning the church's forum, was *ipso facto* under sentence of excommunication, coupled with other penalties of the law and constitutions.[39]

But it is the third series of statutes which from the point of view of the interaction of clerk and layman, of ecclesiastical and secular authority, is by far the most significant. The initial canon, *Superno Dei munere*, emphasizes the common interest in the maintenance of law and order. The king had asked for the cooperation of the bishops against malefactors, violators of the peace and false jurors. On the council's authority Stratford declared that all such incurred sentence of excommunication *ipso facto*. This was to be promulgated on the first Sunday in Lent and on other festivals in cathedral and capitular churches.[40]

But what constituted a clerk? This was a question raised in a canon with the incipit *Exterior habitus*. External appearance frequently revealed the inner reality; a disturbing observation which prefaces a rare exposition of clerical mores current among the trend-setters. Clergy with their long hair and extravagant bejewelled raiment were often indistinguishable from laymen. Fads of the kind had even spread to masters and scholars at the universities. Beneficed clerks, particularly those in holy orders, were to have a proper tonsure and to wear suitable clerical dress. Those who failed to mend their ways within six months were to suffer suspension and, after a further three months, deprivation. Those without benefices would disqualify themselves from holding them unless they too modified their behaviour within six months. Similar regulations were to apply in the universities. The only relaxation with respect to the length and cut of garments was for purposes of work and travel.[41]

Various chapters condemn the withdrawal of ecclesiastical rights, notably tithes, including the much disputed *silva cedua* or tithable underwood, and the offerings in porches, cemeteries and churches, which

---

no attempt to prohibit the use of such writs by clerics, providing that ecclesiastical processes had first been observed.

[39] *Concilia* 2, p. 702. The expansion of royal administration, hence the increase in clerks requiring support, may well have brought about this pressure on benefices. See Howell, *Regalian Right*, pp. 184-186.

[40] *Concilia* 2, pp. 702-703.

[41] Ibid., p. 703.

allegedly were being taken by laymen and used for their own purposes.[42]
An early invocation of this last canon, *Immoderatae temeritatis*, was by
Bishop Bransford of Worcester in 1344, when he declared *ipso facto*
excommunicate unknown persons who had carried off forty-nine wax
candles burning in Ipsley church on the feast of the Purification.[43]
Another infringement of clerical rights – which fell within the more
general condemnation made long before at the Council of Oxford and
subsequently by Cardinal Ottobon – was the practice whereby parishioners cut down grass or trees in churchyards.[44] Not so far removed from this
was the violation of sequestration of benefices, a canonical means of
coercion which often engendered reprisals.[45]

Wills provide the topic of three consecutive canons. The provisions are
both important and interesting. Stratford strove to reinforce the statute of
Archbishop Boniface, *Caeterum*, which asserted the right of those of
servile condition to make a will.[46] He also sought to maintain the rights
of intestates, both clerks and laymen, against lords who impeded the
ordinary's disposition of their goods for the benefit of wives, children or
parents. Moreover, men of servile status, women, whether married or
single, were to be allowed to make wills.[47] Such wills were to be proved
before the appropriate ordinary; interference with the process would
incur excommunication. In general, there was to be no administration of
goods prior to the making of an inventory, apart from the necessary
funeral expenses and the cost of valuing the deceased's effects. Religious
were not permitted to act as executors, and no executor was to appropriate
any of a testator's goods unless these were granted to him *inter vivos* or in
the will. The heaviest indictment was of ecclesiastical judges who

---

[42] Ibid., pp. 704-705: *Quanquam exsolventibus: Immoderatae temeritatis.* For a note
on *silva cedua* see Bolton, "Council of London," pp. 156-157 n. 3; also Lyndwood,
p. 190, ad ver. *Renascitur*.

[43] *Worcester Reg. Bransford*, p. 104.

[44] *Concilia* 2, p. 709: *Quia divinis.* Cf. *Councils and Synods*, pp. 106 (Council of
Oxford), 764 (legatine council at St. Paul's), to which reference is made in this canon.

[45] *Concilia* 2, p. 709: *Frequens perversorum.*

[46] *Councils and Synods*, p. 681; *Concilia* 2, p. 705. For this problem see Levett, "Wills
of Villeins and Copyholders," who cites (pp. 211-212) the passage beginning *Caeterum*
from the canon *Statutum*.

[47] Cf. the petition of 1344 (*Rot. Parl.* 2, p. 149 no. 9) which considered it "against
reason" that serfs and married women (neifs et femmes) should be allowed to make wills;
also the comments of Levett, "Wills of Villeins and Copyholders," pp. 210-212. Donahue,
"Lyndwood's Gloss *propriarum uxorum*" examines the canonist's meaning and motives.
He argues that Lyndwood is maintaining that the wife has goods of which she can dispose
by will, and suggests that he may have been attempting to "state the English practice of his
day in terms of the *ius commune*" (p. 32). On the enforcement of Stratford's constitution
see ibid., p. 32 n. 49.

hindered the carrying out of the wishes of a testator or the customary division of the goods of an intestate. Another malpractice was that of persons *in extremis* who distributed their goods *inter vivos* to the loss of their creditors and other rightful beneficiaries.[48] Even after death there were problems which merited the council's strictures. Vigils or wakes in private houses prior to burial, which gave opportunity for intercessory prayers, were indeed commendable, but too often the onslaught of the "enemy" had converted such wakes into illicit gatherings, the occasion for adultery, fornication and theft. Under pain of excommunication only friends and relatives of the deceased and those wishing to recite the psalter for the soul's benefit were to foregather round the corpse.[49]

Humana concupiscentia, the eleventh canon, sought to outlaw the practice of clandestine matrimony. Those who felt their marriages to be lawfully impeded by consanguinity or affinity, or some other debarment, were in the habit of leaving their parishes for remote places, particularly towns, where they were unknown. There they secured the solemnization of matrimony and even if they returned to their own parish the inhabitants did not wish or did not dare to make accusation. In this instance denunciation of the errant clergy was in reinforcement of Archbishop Mepham's canon of 1329, *Item quia ex contractibus*.[50]

The remaining canons, twelve, thirteen and sixteen, treat in detail of unsatisfactory aspects of the relationship between ecclesiastical and secular courts. The first of these, *Accidit novitate perversa*, is complex and lengthy. One of the principal infractions of ecclesiastical rights was said to be the manner in which landlords prevented their tenants and villeins from responding to courts outside their lordships, especially in testamentary matters. Not only did they hinder the exercise of jurisdiction within such areas, they even indicted judges for extortion by reason of their lawful imposition of monetary penalties. Others interrupted ecclesiastical proceedings, hindered the repression of transgressors, or brought cases in process before church courts to the secular justices, together with advocates, judges and other participants, whom they

[48] *Concilia* 2, pp. 705-706: *Statutum*. Lyndwood, p. 176, ad ver. *Prius* has some observations on the executors' right of action prior to commission of administration. See Sheehan, *Medieval Will*, pp. 213-214.

[49] *Concilia* 2, pp. 706-707: *Quia saepe*. The psalter elicits an approving gloss mentioning Richard Hampole: Lyndwood, p. 184, ad ver. *Psaltaria*.

[50] *Concilia* 2, p. 707. Lyndwood, p. 275 ad ver. *Solennizari facientes*, poses the question: "What if the parties only contracted marriage?" It seems that this would have been insufficient to attract the penalties imposed by Stratford. Cf. ibid., ad ver. *Impedimenta canonica*.

attached and imprisoned.[51] In towns and other places ecclesiastical jurisdiction was impeded, while lay lords or their bailiffs laid claim to the goods of intestates, in this way preventing their apportionment by the church for the benefit of the soul of the deceased.[52]

Saeculi principes, an almost equally lengthy canon, reviews the operation of the practice whereby the church invoked the aid of the secular arm to discipline excommunicate persons. It was being abused. Royal courts were falsely suggesting that those imprisoned were willing to obey the church's mandates and ordering their release. If excommunication had been pronounced in cases outside the church's forum, sheriffs were being instructed to free those sentenced without recourse to ecclesiastical judges.[53]

Another ruse practised by litigants was to secure royal writs for some transgression or other to be tried in counties remote from their adversaries, thus by default securing their outlawry or banishment. Clerks or laymen who practised such enormities or lent their aid or counsel to those who did so were to incur excommunication *ipso facto*.[54]

This impressive series of statutes with its resoundingly memorable incipits had an impact which cannot be assessed. From time to time episcopal registers illustrate the operation of individual canons, but their overall effect is another matter.[55] Even if diocesans were remiss in keeping them before the minds of their subjects – and we cannot know about this – time did not efface their memory. They came to be copied into numerous lawyers' collections and were eventually glossed by Lyndwood. In his will (1443) that eminent canonist expressed the wish that the *Provinciale* should be kept in St. Stephen's chapel, Westminster, as an exemplar. It is doubtful whether this was done, but in the 1480s a massive folio edition was printed at Oxford. A century after its first appearance the *Provinciale* must have enjoyed a wide circulation.[56] The effectiveness of Stratford's canons is another matter. However clearly abuses were defined, however severe the penalties prescribed, eradication of faults did not necessarily follow. For our purpose though, Stratford's constitutions provide a mirror of some of the less satisfactory aspects of the age and remain as a permanent memorial to an archbishop who recognized the situation and attempted to devise remedies for it.

---

[51] For Stratford's personal involvement in conflicts of this kind see above, "Archbishop of Canterbury."

[52] *Concilia* 2, pp. 707-708.

[53] Ibid., pp. 708-709.

[54] Ibid., p.709: *Dierum invalescens*.

[55] E.g. *Worcester Reg. Bransford*, p. 104 (above, n. 43); *Bath and Wells Reg. Shrewsbury*, p. 686.

[56] Cheney, "William Lyndwood's *Provinciale*," pp. 177-180.

6

Summing Up

Some reward is to be gleaned from a study of the manner in which Stratford was treated by contemporary or near-contemporary chroniclers, who at this time were for the most part secular clerks – men like Stratford himself. It will already be apparent that two such chroniclers are of special significance for Stratford's biographer. The first is the anonymous Canterbury monk usually referred to as "Birchington." [1] His work is conspicuously detailed, particularly with respect to the great political and personal struggle of 1340-1341. The other chronicler, author of the *Historia Roffensis*, is reliably taken to be William Dene, the archdeacon of Rochester, whose associations were with the diocese of that name, adjacent to Canterbury, within easy reach of London, and on the route to or from Dover and the continent.[2] Understandably he is well informed.

---

[1] I have abbreviated this chronicle as *Vitae* or *Vitae Arch. Cant.* and have referred to its author as the (anonymous) Canterbury chronicler or as Stratford's biographer. The question of authorship is discussed by Tait, *Chronica Johannis de Reading*, intro., pp. 63-75. He concludes (p. 68): "We have ventured therefore to disregard Wharton's attribution ... to Birchington and to restore to it the anonymity of the only manuscript." Another anonymous Canterbury chronicler (TCC MS R.5 41) shows no interest in Stratford's doings.

[2] The chronicle covers the years 1315 to 1350, commencing with Br. Hamo de Hethe's election as prior of Rochester in succession to John de Grenestrete and ending *in medias res* on a gloomy note: "Unde timetur quod Gog et Magog de inferno sint reversi ad consolandum tales et fovendum qui sint perversi." The author declares himself to be a notary (fol. 12ᵛ) on three occasions, but tantalizingly does not give his name. Dene originated in Winchester diocese. Hethe proved a valuable patron, securing for him the archdeaconry of Rochester by papal provision. Stratford as bishop of Winchester was one of the executors, the abbot of Langdon another. Vatican Archives, *RV* 76, fol. 22ʳ⁻ᵛ; *CPL 1305-1342*, p. 234; *Rochester Reg. Hethe*, p. 889 (cf. pp. 119-121 and index s.v.). Surprisingly Antonia Gransden, whose *Historical Writing* 2 reached me too late for appropriate citation, sums up Dene's chronicle thus: "The *Historia Roffensis* ... has some value for national events ... but concerns mainly local history" (Ibid., p. 3 n. 9).

Dene's chronicle, of which there is as yet no satisfactory edition,[3] has been much neglected. It constitutes a useful source of information about Stratford and a wide range of current affairs, though sometimes with a bizarre juxtaposition of purely local matters and those of national concern.

Most of the other major chroniclers such as Henry Knighton, Geoffrey le Baker and – so far as the 1320s and 1330s are concerned – Adam Murimuth, with respect to Stratford are to be consulted more on account of their omissions than any additional information they provide about one of the most important Englishmen of the century. For instance, if we take Knighton, the Leicester chronicler,[4] whose work prior to the fourth book and the year 1337 is in large measure derived from Hemingburgh and Higden,[5] we find that Stratford is rarely mentioned – only twice in fact. Under the year 1338, about the feast of Pentecost (31 May), there is record of his being sent to France with the bishop of Durham and in the company of the visiting cardinals.[6] Later in the same year – the chronicler's dating is again imprecise – he is said to have travelled with the same bishop to the parliament of Philip of France at Compiègne and again to that at Arras, with the avowed intention of procuring peace.[7] Stratford's expense account confirms his presence at both places.[8] After 1340 Knighton gives scant space to home affairs, none to Stratford's part in them. Events he considered worth mentioning were those taking place on the continent or in Scotland and along the northern march. While largely overlooking Stratford, Knighton lavishes praise on someone who has been taken to be the archbishop's enemy, Henry Burghersh, bishop of Lincoln.[9] This emphasis may in part explain his neglect of Stratford. On

---

[3] It was edited by Wharton, *Anglia Sacra* 1, pp. 356-383, but he omitted some passages. In the footnotes to this book reference is made only to the manuscript, BL Cotton MS Faustina B.v, which is foliated 2-101.

[4] Knighton or Cnitthon was a regular canon of the abbey of St. Mary-in-the-Meadows, Leicester, during the latter half of the fourteenth century. See Hamilton Thompson, *Leicester Abbey*, index s.v. Knighton; Gransden, *Historical Writing* 2, pp. 159-160 and index s.v. V. H. Galbraith maintained against J. R. Lumby (editor of the chronicle in the Rolls Series) that Knighton wrote the whole chronicle down to 1395, compiling the 1377-1395 portion first. See "The Chronicle of Henry Knighton," pp. 136-148, and also Tait's criticism of Lumby's edition in *EHR* 11 (1896), pp. 568-569. Lumby used BL Cotton MS Claudius E.iii (much damaged) and Tiberus C.vii (cf. Twysden's edition in *Historiae Anglicanae Scriptores Decem*).

[5] See the comparative table (Knighton, Hemingburgh) in *Knighton* 2, intro. p. xxxiii.

[6] *Knighton* 2, p. 4. Cf. *Murimuth*, p. 83.

[7] *Knighton* 2, p. 7. Apparently this statement is not to be found in other chronicles.

[8] PRO E.101/311/35.

[9] *Knighton* 2, p. 17: "Rex iter maris arripuit [1340] cum Henrico de Borugwas episcopo Lincolniensi, viro utique nobili, et sapienti consilio, eleganti audacia, praepotenti viribus, et retentione virorum fortium perspicuus."

account of his place of origin and because he espouses the cause both of Earl Thomas and of his younger brother Henry, Knighton is commonly taken for a "Lancastrian" chronicler. But Stratford, though regularly associated with the same "cause" both then and since, is of little interest to Knighton. Even in 1328, at the time of the insurrection against Mortimer and Isabella, he is no more than the bishop of Winchester, one of three members of the episcopate – the others being Archbishop Mepham and the bishop of London (Stephen Gravesend) – who are enumerated among Earl Henry's supporters.[10]

Geoffrey le Baker's treatment of Stratford is illuminating for different reasons. Baker was a minor clerk from Swinbrook in Oxfordshire and perhaps loosely connected with the Augustinian abbey of Osney.[11] No evidence has been found of his promotion to a benefice, but he could have been in the household of Sir Thomas Laurence de la More, whom he names as his patron. Sir Thomas was an Oxfordshire knight who was twice returned to parliament in 1338, twice in 1340, and again in 1343 and 1351.[12] Baker tells us that at the request of Sir Thomas he wrote a highly condensed *Chroniculum* found in conjunction with his substantial *Chronicon*. More was in Stratford's retinue in 1327, when the bishop travelled with the delegation from parliament to secure Edward II's abdication. It appears that he provided Baker with a copy in French of his recollection of that memorable occasion. Apart from his association with More Baker had an undefined connection with the much greater Bohun family, if we can judge from the reverential way in which he mentions members of it and from the provenance of the manuscript itself.[13] Since

[10] Ibid. 1, p. 450. Of course, at this point the chronicle is derivative.
[11] He finished his *Chroniculum* at Osney on 20 July 1347 (the year in which the latest recension of the Murimuth chronicle ends). *Chronicon*, p. 173; *Murimuth*, intro. p. xvii. For a not entirely satisfactory discussion of Baker see Gransden, *Historical Writing* 2, pp. 37-42. The author, with obvious justification, considers the chronicle attributed to Robert of Reading (*Flores Hist.* 3, pp. 137-235) to be an apologia for Mortimer and Isabella (*Historical Writing* 2, pp. 17-22). Baker's work, on the other hand, down to 1327 was anti-Isabella but not anti-Mortimer; anti-Orleton but not anti-Stratford.
[12] See above, "In the Seat of Power," n. 300. A writ to the sheriff of Oxford (19 February 1340) ordered payment to John Golafre and Thomas de la More, knights of the shire, of expenses for thirty-four days at 4s a day. *CCR 1339-1341*, p. 447. In the Lenten parliament of 1340 he was one of those deputed to reduce the petitions to statute form. *Chronicon*, intro. p. viii; *Rot. Parl.* 2, p. 113.
[13] See Maunde Thompson, *Chronicon*, intro. pp. viii-x, xii-xvi; *DNB*, s.v. More or Moore; n. 11 above. Bodley MS 761 alone contains the full text of the *Chronicon* together with the *Chroniculum*. BL Cotton MS App. LII has only the latter portion of the *Chronicon*. At Stratford's request Sir Thomas was granted exemption for life from being put on assizes, juries or recognizances, or being appointed sheriff. *CPR 1327-1330*, p. 184: 7 November 1327.

Maunde Thompson wrote his introduction to the *Chronicon* two further items of information have come to light, one concerning Baker, the other More. A "Geoffrey Pachon" of Swinbrook, chaplain, is one of a large group of malefactors pardoned by Edward II in 1326 on condition that they aided him against the insurgents – Queen Isabella and her forces. One can only guess that Baker's political affiliations had led him into some affray or other.[14] The other item is the appointment in 1329 by Stratford, as Winchester diocesan, of Thomas de la More as constable of his Somerset castle of Taunton.[15] The bishop addresses More as "nostre cher et bien aime neofeu." [16]

That Baker regarded Sir Thomas as his protector, as well as the provider of an eye-witness account of an important incident in his chronicle, and that the same Sir Thomas was Stratford's "nephew" and one of his household knights, helps to explain the somewhat selective attitude to Stratford's involvement in affairs. Down to 1341 Baker relies very much on Murimuth's chronicle, so much so that additions and omissions may be taken to indicate his own estimate of what was newsworthy, or alternatively what ought to be retailed to a wider audience. But first of all we must take note of some of Baker's prejudices with respect to certain of the *dramatis personae*. Thomas of Lancaster and his brother Henry are predictably held in high esteem,[17] so too are members of the Bohun family, as has already been mentioned, in particular Earl Humphrey who died at Boroughbridge.[18] Bishops Orleton and Burghersh, especially the former, are depicted as execrable villains on whom he foisted the main responsibility for Edward II's removal from the kingship and subsequent death.[19] Queen Isabella is the "iron woman," the vindictive virago, the female monster.[20] In short, the portion of the chronicle which is concerned with the years 1324-1327 departs substantially from the framework provided by Murimuth. It gives every appearance of being a piece of propaganda designed to fasten the blame for what happened on particular individuals and thus to deflect it from Stratford and the baronial supporters of Isabella and Mortimer.

[14] *CPR 1324-1327*, p. 331; Haines, *Church and Politics*, p. 105.
[15] WinRS, fol. 183ᵛ: Walton, 12 July 1329.
[16] Ibid. and see above, "Stratford's *Familia* and Administration," nn. 126, 128. "Nostre cher et bien amie" was the usual form of address.
[17] *Chronicon*, pp. 14, 42-43.
[18] Ibid., pp. 13-14.
[19] Ibid., pp. 18ff.; Haines, *Church and Politics*, chap. 4.
[20] *Chronicon*, pp. 20, 21, 24.

Stratford's name first occurs in 1327 in association with those of Bishops Orleton and Burghersh, allegedly principals in a deputation sent to Edward II at Kenilworth. It was on this occasion that Sir Thomas de la More, then a youngish man, travelled in Bishop Stratford's retinue. Although Stratford's part in the proceedings is revealed by other accounts to have been a major one, and Baker is clearly unhappy about the fate of the king, no hint of opprobrium is allowed to fall on him. On the contrary, it is Stratford and Henry earl of Leicester who exhibit an element of compassion for the swooning Edward.[21] Most of the other entries which concern Stratford are merely factual. They record his accompaniment of Edward III to do homage in 1331, his provision to Canterbury two years later, his embassy to France and supposedly Avignon in 1334,[22] his holding of a convocation in 1337, his crossing to France a year later and his subsequent discussions at Arras.[23] For Baker Stratford is a man of great wisdom and legal expertise.[24] Far more important from the point of view of the modern biographer is what one can only assume to be the deliberate omission from the *Chronicon* of Murimuth's recital of the king's spirited onslaught on Stratford's administration and the local officials. This does not prevent his noting the subsequent reconciliation when – according to Baker – Stratford swore that although the royal oath of homage for Gascony and Ponthieu was made by his counsel, this was not in order to accommodate the "tyrant"Philip, but solely in the interest of the English king.[25] Of Stratford Baker records nothing more. Clearly then, the *Chronicon* cannot be a yardstick of Stratford's influence on political events; certainly not for the crucial period 1340-1341. At the same time, Baker's personal associations provide obvious clues as to why he denigrated Orleton and Burghersh but looked with an indulgent eye on their fellow-revolutionary, Stratford.

Next something must be said about Baker's chief source, the chronicle of Adam Murimuth.[26] Murimuth was again a secular clerk, but a much

[21] Ibid., p. 27.

[22] In fact, Stratford seems to have gone no further than France. See above, "In the Seat of Power."

[23] *Chronicon*, pp. 59, 61-62.

[24] Ibid., p. 55: "Vir magne sapiencie et doctor egregius utriusque iuris."

[25] Compare *Chronicon*, p. 72, with *Murimuth*, pp. 117 (foot)-120 (foot). The declaration under oath by Stratford is recorded by Baker (*Chronicon*, p. 75) and would seem to refer to the archbishop's reconciliation with the king on 23 October 1341. See Harriss, *King, Parliament and Public Finance*, App. pp. 521-522.

[26] For him see *Biog. Oxon.*, s.v.; *Murimuth*, intro. pp. ix-xvi. Baker apparently used the recension of Murimuth's chronicle which terminates in 1341 as found, for instance, in BL Cotton MS Claudius E.viii (ca. 1400). See *Chronicon*, intro p. x. BL Harleian MS 3836 (ending 1347) provides the text for Maunde Thompson's edition in the Rolls Series.

more distinguished one that either Baker or even Dene. But his worldly rewards were by no means commensurate with his academic status and his obvious abilities, which is at least one reason why he was so scathing about papal provision. In looking at Murimuth's chronicle one is immediately struck by the vastly increased number of references to Stratford, references which Baker apparently chose to overlook. The initial mention of Stratford comes in 1323 at the time of his promotion to Winchester. Though inclined to be censorious in matters of this kind, Murimuth is content to allow that Edward II's letters in favour of another candidate, Robert Baldock, did arrive too late.[27] It was as a consequence of Stratford's recall, Murimuth remarks with affected modesty, that he himself was sent to conduct negotiations with the curia.[28] This chronicler has nothing to say about Stratford's participation in the political revolution of 1326-1327, nor does he include the bishop's name among those who adhered to the queen, even in the later stages.[29] Stratford's part in the Kenilworth mission is likewise omitted.[30] For the earlier part of Edward III's reign there are equally striking lacunas. Stratford is not connected with the abortive insurrections of 1328-1329, but two years later he is named as one of the king's companions on his secret journey to France.[31] Murimuth notes Stratford's election to Canterbury with a somewhat dry comment – the electors had no choice.[32] He is much more expansive on the topic of Orleton's consequent translation from Worcester to Winchester. No hint is dropped of Stratford's opposition to this move; instead Murimuth claims that the archbishop and other bishops intervened to secure the restitution of Orleton's temporalities.[33] There is record of Stratford's appointment in 1334 to treat with King Philip and of the usual enthronement festivities at Canterbury which preceded his embarkation at Dover.[34] Notes are made of the envoy's return, his subsequent visitation of his cathedral city and diocese, and of the king's anxiety to retain his services in government.[35] Mention of his journey from the north in 1337 for John of Eltham's burial at Westminster is

---

[27] Stratford's life-span was roughly coincident with that of Murimuth. See above, "The Making of a Career"; Smith, *Episcopal Appointments*, pp. 39-41.

[28] *Murimuth*, p. 41, where he describes himself as "unus simplex clericus" and goes on to relate his discomfiture of the Scottish envoys.

[29] Ibid., pp. 47-50; above, "From Conformist to Revolutionary."

[30] Cf. Baker, *Chronicon*, pp. 26-28, here avowedly relying on Thomas de la More.

[31] *Murimuth*, p. 63.

[32] Ibid., p. 69.

[33] Ibid., p. 70.

[34] Ibid., p. 73.

[35] Ibid., pp. 75-76.

followed by details of his accompanying the cardinals from Shooters Hill to London. Stratford's departure with the cardinals the following year, his stay at Arras, and his return to England about Michaelmas 1339 are all recorded.[36] There follows a break until a somewhat brief allusion to the conflict in 1341 between archbishop and king. But one version of the chronicle also contains (as does Avesbury[37]) a copy of Stratford's hortatory letter of 1 January 1341 in which he rebukes Edward for his unlawful acts.[38] Even so, the real nature of the dispute and its ramifications are not revealed. On the other hand, the committee of two bishops and four earls which adjourned *sine die* the hearing of Stratford's defence is given in full.[39] The provincial council of 1341 is reported with a degree of approval, but Stratford's subsequent accommodation with Edward was felt to have been to the church's detriment.[40] In 1342 Edward is stated to have taken his archbishop's advice about the proposed intervention of the cardinals; they were fobbed off with an excuse.[41] Stratford's attempted visitation of Norwich diocese in 1343 finds mention, so too its interruption by an urgent summons to the king's council.[42] Murimuth's remaining references to Stratford concern themselves with the papal negotiations of 1344 and 1345 and the archbishop's part in them as a royal councillor, together with two war despatches or "newsletters" addressed to him by Bartholomew Burghersh after the successful English landing on the coast of Normandy in 1346.[43] Here then are the lineaments of a biography, but disappointingly few indications of Stratford's character, his political objectives, or of his attitude to his ecclesiastical duties. Murimuth and Stratford had known each other since their early days as legal advocates, if not before. The chronicler must have been ideally suited to answer the sort of question we would wish to postulate.

William Dene's *Historia Roffensis* seemingly survives in a single manuscript. It is remarkably detailed and the author's prejudices overtly

---

[36] Ibid., pp. 78, 81, 83, 85, 90. Murimuth gives Stratford's return inaccurately as "before the feast of St. Michael." In fact he crossed from Wissant on 10 October. PRO E.101/311/35.

[37] *Avesbury*, pp. 324-329.

[38] *Murimuth*, p. 271 (from BL Cotton MS Claudius E.viii).

[39] Ibid., p. 120. At this point Murimuth gives the date of Geoffrey le Scrope's death as "about Christmas 1340" and that of Henry Burghersh as occurring "about the same time." Dene in the *Historia Roffensis* (BL Cotton MS Faustina B.v, fol. 88ʳ) is as vague, but *Vitae Arch. Cant.*, p. 21 (Lambeth MS 99, fol. 137ʳ) is precise to the day.

[40] *Murimuth*, p. 122 and cf. ibid., p. 223 (BL Cotton MS Nero D.x).

[41] Ibid., pp. 125-126.

[42] Ibid., pp. 147-148.

[43] Ibid., pp. 176-177, 190.

stated. Dene is sympathetic towards Edward II, sharply critical of Queen Isabella and Roger Mortimer, and keenly opposed to Archbishop Mepham and what he regarded as his jejune efforts to play the politician.[44] The bishop of Norwich, William Ayrminne, is the butt of some adverse remarks, mainly it would seem on account of his judicial conflict with Hamo de Hethe, the Rochester diocesan.[45] Hethe's activities, as one would expect, are reported in minute detail, as are the problems of the church of Rochester and the difficulties in the county of Kent created by the crippling burden of taxation.[46] Stratford's part in national affairs is not emphasized, rather the opposite. The conflict of 1341 is treated in a low key. Thus from the point of view of Stratford's biographer (though not of Hethe's) Dene is somewhat of a disappointment. Clearly he knew much more than he cared to tell. Such reticence is comparable to that of Murimuth.

By far the most revealing source for our purposes has been left until last; the *Lives of the Archbishops of Canterbury*, to use the English form. These *Lives* were printed by Henry Wharton in his *Anglia Sacra*[47] from Lambeth MS 99. Wharton was also well acquainted with John Joscelyn's *Lives* as contributed to Archbishop Matthew Parker's *De Antiquitate Britannicae Ecclesiae*.[48] Through his employer Joscelyn must have had access to a manuscript, cited as "Birchington," which has since disappeared.[49] This apparently contained passages lacking in the Lambeth manuscript and also continued to a later date.[50] Stephen Birchington, a monk of Christ Church, Canterbury, professed in the late-fourteenth century, may have appended his name to the extended account. This was

[44] E.g. BL Cotton MS Faustina B.v, fols. 46ᵛ-47ʳff., 51ᵛ-52ʳ.

[45] Ibid., fols. 55ᵛ, 59ʳ, 67ʳ-75ʳ, 78ʳ (where just before his death Ayrminne is said to have attended the Westminster parliament "licet graviter infirmus spe tamen officium in curia regis optinendi veniens, ut dicebatur").

[46] E.g. Ibid., fol. 81ᵛ.

[47] *Stephani Birchingtoni monachi Cantuariensis Historia de Archiepiscopis Cantuariensibus a prima sedis fundatione ad annum MCCCLXIX*, is at pp. 19-41 (Lambeth MS 99, fols. 136ʳ-146ᵛ). The shortened version of the *Lives* in BL Cotton MS Julius B.iii (item 2 at fol. 31ʳ) is attributed to Bishop Reed of Chichester.

[48] See Tait, *Chronica Johannis de Reading*, intro. pp. 63-75. Parker's *De Antiquitate* was published in 1572, three years before the archbishop's death, the four-hundredth anniversary of which was celebrated at Corpus Christi College by an exhibition "Matthew Parker's Legacy" (title of commemorative booklet, CCC Cambridge, 1975).

[49] Tait, *Chronica Johannis de Reading*, p. 64. However, it will be found that some passages ostensibly interpolated from Parker/Birchington (including a number in Stratford's *Vita*) are in fact in Lambeth MS 99.

[50] Wharton's edition of Stratford's *Vita* notes three passages as cited by Parker from "Birchington." See previous note.

what Wharton believed on the basis of Joscelyn's attribution.[51] But the Lambeth MS ends abruptly more than ten years prior to Birchington's profession. This and some other factors argue another author.[52] Whatever that author's name may have been, it is fairly clear that he was a monk of Canterbury. However, a number of rather obvious slips in the Lambeth manuscript suggest that it was merely a copy.[53]

The life of Stratford as printed by Wharton[54] falls fairly readily into distinct compartments. The introductory portion has no word of the origins of the archbishop, described as a "distinguished doctor of laws," and disposes of his career prior to his elevation to Canterbury by detailing his promotion to Winchester and giving a full account of his hair-raising flight from the Salisbury parliament of 1328. Only a thin factual narrative connects these major events. There follows a carefully dated description of the stages which led to his enthronement at Canterbury on 9 October 1334.[55] The death of Pope John XXII is then noted, as is Jacques Fournier's election in his stead on the 20th. After this comes a mention of the cardinals' abortive peace mission of 1337-1338 and of their procurations. The chronicler then summarizes the archbishop's preoccupations between 1334 and 1341 with chancery and other temporal business. Initially Stratford was concerned with such matters because of the king's youth, then in order to counteract what is termed the "dominatio effoeminatorum,"[56] and finally because of the diplomatic negotiations between England and France.[57] These concerns were secular; as archbishop, the author chides,

[51] Tait, *Chronica Johannis de Reading*, p. 64.

[52] Ibid., pp. 64-65 (and n. 2) gives the few known details of Birchington's life. He was professed in 1382, became treasurer and warden of the cathedral priory's manors, and at the time of his death, 21 August 1407, was cellarer and in priest's orders (as was usual at the time).

[53] E.g. the date of Stratford's flight from Wilton is given as 1329 rather than 1328, "Honiton" is written for "Downton," while the cardinals' arrival and departure are given as 1327 and 1328, rather than 1337 and 1338. Again September should be December in the account of the king's agents' seeking out Stratford at Lambeth in 1340. *Vitae Arch. Cant.*, pp. 19-20 (Lambeth MS 99, fol. 136^{r-v}).

[54] *Anglia Sacra* 1, pp. 19-41 (see above, n. 47).

[55] *Vitae Arch. Cant.*, p. 20 (Lambeth MS 99, fol. 136^v).

[56] Precisely what is meant by this is uncertain. It could refer to the laxity of manners and morals at court, or it may point more particularly to Edward's propensity for women, the topic of popular political songs at the time. *Murimuth*, pp. 155-156, has a remarkable description of the celebrations at Windsor in January 1344 to which a very large number of ladies was invited. See McKisack, *Fourteenth Century*, p. 167.

[57] "Tum idem archiepiscopus, a tempore translationis suae usque ad annum vii tam in partibus Angliae circa officium cancellarii ... quam aliqua alia negotia temporalia procuranda, tum propter juvenilem aetatem dicti regis, tum propter effoeminatorum in regno Angliae dominationem ... reprimendam, ac etiam in partibus Franciae negotia

he ought to have been engaged on ecclesiastical business. But the world which he had served turned on him with envy. Inciters of discord sowed their seeds in the hearts of the king and his *curiales* and an unprecedented dissension broke out. After this our anonymous author gives the best account of the troubles of 1340-1341, incorporating transcriptions of the *libellus famosus*, Stratford's *excusaciones*, and of the king's final thrust, the *Cicatrix cordium superbia*. With the archbishop's restoration to favour a brief postscript suffices for his few remaining years. The impression given is that Stratford resumed his position as chief councillor and worked with all his might for good government in the realm.[58] Much more than that, he became absorbed in pastoral care and daily works of charity.[59] All of this has a somewhat conventional ring, but it is strange that a chronicler so critical of Stratford's temporal involvement should give so little attention to his works as diocesan and metropolitan. There is no mention of the legislative activity of 1341 and 1342.

In conclusion it may be said that the chroniclers were more forbearing with respect to Stratford. He was not abused for securing the see of Winchester, as was his colleague Orleton, and on balance the report of his struggle with the king is more to his credit than to Edward's, which in view of the chroniclers' backgrounds is hardly surprising. Even the anonymous Canterbury biographer fails to do justice to his subject, but he does enshrine a salutary moral tale. Stratford like his exemplar Becket turned from the world and man's ingratitude to a life more appropriate to his calling as archbishop. Such a conclusion would have been welcomed by Stratford himself.

THE HISTORIANS' VERDICT

If we except Stratford's anonymous medieval biographer, the earliest historian worthy of consideration in this connection is John Joscelyn, the Latin secretary of Archbishop Matthew Parker. The title "historian" is probably defensible, though Henry Wharton, writing in the late-seventeenth century, adopted a description more appropriate to his day – the archbishop's household antiquarian (Antiquarius archiepiscopi domesticus). Joscelyn regarded Stratford as a conspicuous example of an upright and honourable man on whom suspicion and calumny had been

---

Angliae expedienda, multipliciter occupatus hujusmodi negotiis saecularibus, et non ecclesiasticis, ut debebat." *Vitae Arch. Cant.*, p. 20 (Lambeth MS 99, fol. 136ᵛ).

[58] Ibid., p. 41 (Lambeth MS 99, fol. 146ᵛ).

[59] Ibid. and see above, "Closing Years."

heaped. By and large though, Joscelyn's work, incorporated in Parker's *De Antiquitate Britannicae Ecclesiae* (1572),[1] is a paraphrase of the medieval biography. He even reiterates the texts of the *libellus famosus*, Stratford's *excusaciones*, and the concluding *Cicatrix cordium*. But he does provide a coherent biography, constituting an honest attempt at appraisal. The result is entirely favourable to Stratford.[2]

There the matter stood until almost three hundred years later, in 1865, Dean Hook included among his *Lives of the Archbishops* a lengthy account of John Stratford.[3] Hook made use of a number of chronicles, principally those of "de la More" (that is Baker's *Chronicon* in abbreviated form), "Birchington," Murimuth and Walsingham, but also that of the fifteenth-century Augustinian friar, John Caprave. Admittedly he used them uncritically, but he did not have the advantage of the work of such notable scholars as Stubbs, Tait, Maunde Thompson, Galbraith, Little, Richardson, and others, who have enabled modern historians to be far more conscious of the interrelationship of the various chronicles and of the manuscripts themselves. Hook's biography, a strictly chronological one, is carefully constructed, though here and there he embellishes his sources. There is a wonderfully evocative description of Stratford's proceedings at Canterbury when he published sentences of excommunication against all those who infringed Magna Carta and the laws and customs of the church.[4] Even more striking is his earlier conjuring-up of a Robin Hood-like figure in the Sussex woodlands taking refuge from Mortimer's assassins.[5]

> Under the greenwood-tree the bishop had the daily service performed; and as the chaplains chanted the psalms, they would compare their persecuted master to the outraged David when flying from the unjust wrath of Saul. Then would the dogs be called, and the bows were bent, and hunting became a business as well as a sport; for the venison, which the bishop, as a Stratford man, dearly loved, was to be supplied by the cross-bows pointed by his attendants – perhaps by his own right reverend hand.

[1] I have used the edition of Parker by Samuele Drake, London 1729. Cf. Wharton's introduction in *Anglia Sacra* 1, pp. xvii-xx; *Matthew Parker's Legacy*.
[2] *De Antiquitate*, ed. Drake, pp. 331-354.
[3] *Lives of the Archbishops of Canterbury* (1865) 4, pp. 1-79. I have omitted S. H. Cassan's short and somewhat inaccurate biography in *Lives of the Bishops of Winchester* (1827) 1, pp. 180-183. The statement that Stratford was appointed treasurer of the exchequer 12 Edward II arises from a confusion with John de Sandale, an earlier bishop of Winchester (ibid., p. 180). Another omission is the account of Stratford given by Campbell, *Lives of the Lord Chancellors* (1846) 1, pp. 215ff., which is even more erroneous.
[4] Hook, *Lives* 4, pp. 38-40.
[5] Ibid., p. 16.

But despite the occasional delightful flights of fancy this is a remarkably even account, firmly based not on the chroniclers alone but also to some extent on the public records. Stratford comes before us as a typical lawyer-statesman of his age, promoted to ecclesiastical office because of his career in royal service rather than on account of any vocation he might have had for the church. Once in a position of authority Stratford is seen to act with wisdom and in the church's interest. Even so, thought Hook, he was too much of a patriot to stomach the "abuse" of papal provision, however justified in theory. From King Edward's point of view English benefices were being diverted to foreigners, worse than that, to enemies. For Hook Stratford was a "friend of parliamentary government," as indeed in a sense he was, a man who ensured that the Court of Chancery should be stationary at Westminster, and who encouraged woollen manufacture in the English towns and countryside.[6] His "foreign policy" was to urge Edward to claim his right to the French throne as the means to an advantageous treaty. Once this was secured the claim was to be renounced, for its maintenance could benefit neither country.[7] This subtle policy cannot be substantiated from the records, though we know that Stratford was caught between the conflicting demands of peace and war.[8]

What is lacking from Hook's biography is an element so prevalent later – the constitutional interpretation. Nothing is to be learned about the "Lancastrian cause" or the prolonged "constitutional struggle" which was to culminate in the much admired political arrangements of nineteenth-century England. But Hook does claim Stratford as one of those who "sought, through the popular side of the constitution, to control the aristocracy."[9] Exactly a decade after the appearance of Hook's work all this was changed with the appearance of the second volume of Bishop Stubbs's classic *Constitutional History*.[10]

For Stubbs the fourteenth was one of three centuries of English history which lay uncomfortably "between the despotism of the Plantagenets and the despotism of the Tudors."[11] For him, as for Huizinga, "We pass from

---

[6] Ibid., pp. 20-21. Hook considered that Stratford was responsible for the regular proclamation against armed men coming to parliament. His other reference is to the statute of 11 Edward III (*Statutes* 1, pp. 280-281). But we cannot know to what extent Stratford was personally responsible for such regulations. The author of *VCH Hants.* 2, pp. 28-30, would appear to be following Hook fairly closely.

[7] Hook, *Lives* 4, p. 26.

[8] See above, "In the Seat of Power."

[9] Hook, *Lives* 4, p. 20.

[10] 3 vols., Oxford 1874-1878 (vol. 2, 1875). Here references are to this first edition.

[11] *Constitutional History* 2, p. 305.

the age of heroism to the age of chivalry, from a century ennobled by devotion and self-sacrifice to one in which the gloss of superficial refinement fails to hide the reality of heartless selfishness and moral degradation – an age of luxury and cruelty." [12] No longer are "great causes" the focal points of conflict, but instead "personal and family faction." The century does in practice produce "great constitutional results," but these emerge "from a confused mass of unconscious agencies rather than from the direct action of great lawgivers or from the victory of acknowledged principles." [13] The major "constitutional result" Stubbs sees as "the growth of the House of Commons into its full share of political power." [14]

It is against this unpromising backcloth that we must set Stubbs's estimate of Stratford. In the Victorian bishop's opinion men in general were of "meaner moral stature" in the fourteenth century. Even "patriots" had "lower objects" in view: "The baronial opposition is that of a faction rather than of an independent estate: the ecclesiastical champions aim at gaining class privilege and class isolation, not at securing their due share in the work of the nation." [15] These are resounding judgments, expressed with all the confidence of the era in which they were uttered. The truth may be somewhat less clear-cut.

The first notice of Stratford taken by Stubbs comes at the time of his provision to Winchester. "Instead of carrying out his master's wishes," the argument goes, "Stratford obtained Winchester for himself, and although after a year's resistance Edward admitted him to his temporalities, the new bishop let his resentment outweigh both gratitude and honesty." What is more, he set a bad example to others, notably the royal clerk, William Ayrminne. As a result Stubbs concluded that Stratford, Ayrminne and Henry de Beaumont were party to a "deliberate plan for the overthrow of the Despensers." [16] This allegation, so far as it concerns Ayrminne and Stratford, lacks confirmation. The evidence has already been analyzed.[17] Stratford did not move against Edward II even when the king's position had become untenable. Stubbs interprets this anomaly as the action of one "clinging to the old idea that in such cases it was the office of the clergy to arbitrate." [18] But this accords ill with the concept of a dedicated conspirator. Mention of Stratford's drawing up of

---

[12] Ibid., and cf. Huizinga, *Waning of the Middle Ages*, esp. chaps. 1-2.
[13] *Constitutional History* 2, p. 306.
[14] Ibid.
[15] Ibid., p. 309.
[16] Ibid., pp. 355-357.
[17] See above, "From Conformist to Revolutionary."
[18] *Constitutional History* 2, p. 359.

the six articles in justification of Edward II's removal from the kingship is accompanied by the guarded statement that though they contained "mere generalities on which no strictly legal proceedings could be based," none the less they "probably contain the germ of truth." [19] This is a remarkable understatement for a constitutional historian, though he later goes some way towards redressing the imbalance.[20] But the bishop cannot accept Stratford as a patriot, his Victorian background would not admit of such an estimate. While Orleton, Burghersh and Ayrminne "shared the triumph of their party," Stratford is regarded as having "reconciled himself ... to the patronage of the queen and her lover by the thought that the liberty of church and people had grown stronger by the change of masters." But, he concedes, the personal wrongs of Burghersh and the fears of Stratford provided some "slender justification" for their actions; whereas Orleton, dubbed "Mortimer's confidant," or Ayrminne "the queen's creature," had none. Stubbs saw in these men representatives of jealously warring factions, "the result of the party divisions and court intrigues" of Edward II's time. In Edward III's reign, Stratford "the champion of the constitutional administration" was matched against Burghersh "the spokesmen of the court" and Orleton "the agent of the queen." Through all this Stubbs sees the house of Lancaster emerging as "the mainstay of right government." [21]

The council of twelve, set up in 1327 to advise the youthful Edward III, included Stratford, whom Stubbs felt to be indispensable (together with Reynolds) on account of his "position and experience." [22] The more obvious reason for Stratford's inclusion is that he had taken a leading part in steering the political revolution to a successful conclusion. His experience of government since his assumption of the see of Winchester had been limited to diplomatic service abroad. Stubbs makes little of Stratford's part in the abortive rising of 1328-1329, though of the opinion that he was "still the most powerful adviser of the constitutional party." [23] With Mortimer's fall Stratford "as archbishop, chancellor, and president of the royal council" is seen as "supreme in the treasury as well as in the

---

[19] Ibid., pp. 361-363. Stubbs surmises that Stratford may have looked back to his predecessor Bishop Henry of Blois, who declared Stephen dethroned, or that he may have had in mind the deposition of the king of the Romans, Adolf of Nassau, in 1298 (ibid., pp. 364-365).

[20] Ibid., pp. 363-364.

[21] Ibid., pp. 367-368.

[22] Ibid., p. 369.

[23] Ibid., p. 371.

chancery." [24] He and his brother Robert are deemed to have been "honest if not brilliant administrators." It was as the "head of the Lancastrian or constitutional party" that Stratford came into conflict with Burghersh, said to have been his counterpart in the "court party," and with Orleton, Burghersh's ally.[25]

In his interpretation of the conflict of 1340-1341 Stubbs sees Stratford as courageously battling against the king, though on his own account. The barons watch from the sidelines, aware of a common interest. The outcome was a superficial victory for Stratford, mainly because the king wished to concentrate on other matters more central to his purposes. Stubbs regarded the combination of lords and commons in the petitions of 1340-1341 as leading to a situation in which the third estate acquired "its full share of parliamentary power." Yet the king emerged the ultimate victor. He had successfully defused the threatening onslaught and by a "piece of atrocious duplicity" nullified the concessions he had made. Stratford's constitutional stand was thus rendered nugatory, though he himself had come to terms with the king.[26]

Stubbs had a fervent belief in the onward-flowing stream of constitutional development. For him Stratford was a self-seeker, exhibiting some element of statesmanship; a man who for a brief moment rose to the surface before being submerged without trace. Against the weight of Stubbs's moral judgment he stands little chance of a fair hearing, but he is not denied all vestige of respectability.

The fourth edition of the second volume of the *Constitutional History* appeared in 1896, closely followed by C. L. Kingsford's summary biography of Stratford in the *Dictionary of National Biography*.[27] Nine years later T. F. Tout's contribution to the *Political History of England* was published.[28] Tout was strongly influenced, perhaps we might say taken in, by Baker, particularly with regard to the interpretation of Edward II's reign. Stratford scarcely figures in his narrative until the beginning of the following reign. From 1330, he declares, Stratford was "the guiding spirit of the administration." Like Stubbs Tout looks upon the Stratford brothers as "capable but not brilliant politicians." [29] He also follows Stubbs in regarding Stratford as the upholder of the Lancastrian party, while

[24] Ibid., p. 384.
[25] Ibid.
[26] Ibid., pp. 389-391.
[27] Vol. 55.
[28] *The History of England from the Accession of Henry III to the Death of Edward III*, London 1905. (*PHE*).
[29] *PHE* 3, p. 314.

Burghersh is seen to have connections – not only hereditary – with the old "middle party" of Pembroke and Badlesmere;[30] the very existence of which has in modern times been called into question.[31] Tout is a shade more expansive about the struggle of 1340-1341, when Stratford is said to have "brought the estates the greatest triumph over the prerogative won during Edward's reign." "It was," Tout concludes, "a strange irony of fate that this worldly and politic ecclesiastic should have perforce become the champion of the rights of the Church and the liberties of the nation." [32] A remark, incidentally, equally apposite in Becket's case. Thus Tout's estimate of Stratford is little more than a reiteraton of that of Stubbs.

Ten years later, in 1915, appeared a study by Dorothy Hughes of the "social and constitutional tendencies" of the early part of Edward III's reign. By the standard of Stubbs and Tout this is a pedestrian book; there are no magisterial generalizations or striking thumb-nail sketches, only measured discussion. As a result, Stratford passes largely unjudged. At one time, with Bishop Bury of Durham, he is a protector of privilege, at another (1341) he is credited with political principles.[33] But Miss Hughes was not concerned to give an overall assessment.

In 1928 was published the third volume of Tout's monumental *Chapters in the Administrative History of Mediaeval England*, which provided a detailed analysis of the early years of Edward III's reign and hence of the activities of Stratford in office.[34] As befits an administrative historian writing some ten years after the publication of Conway Davies' seminal study, *The Baronial Opposition to Edward II*, and some fourteen after his own *Place of Edward II in English History* (a debt to which was acknowledged by Davies in his preface), Tout envisages the early portion of Edward III's reign as a continuation of the struggles which convulsed that of his father. The official class, he argued, was barely disturbed at the lower levels, but among the great officials there was constant change, no fewer than five treasurers serving in the three years prior to the fall of Mortimer.[35] This is viewed as the consequence of a struggle between

[30] Ibid.
[31] Phillips, *Pembroke*, pp. 140-148. While dismissing the traditional "middle party," Phillips writes of three groups: 1. experienced councillors; 2. favourites dependent on the king's infatuation; 3. the prelates and papal envoys.
[32] *PHE* 3, p. 351.
[33] *A Study of Edward III*, pp. 80, 152. Her estimate of Stratford has to be carefully gleaned from widely-dispersed observations.
[34] See particularly Tout, *Chapters* 3, chap. 9, sections 1-3, and the beginning of chap. 4.
[35] Ibid., pp. 8ff.

political "parties." The outcome was that "a large share of the spoils of office was won by representatives of the baronial opposition." "The clearest proof of the influence of the Lancastrian magnates" Tout found in "the repudiation by the new rulers of the novel experiments of the Despensers, and the resumption of the good old ways which appealed to their conservative instincts." The "constitutional attitude" of the new government was in his opinion epitomized by the "frequency of representative parliaments and the great variety of business referred to them." [36] At the same time Tout emphasizes the "welter of self-seeking that mainly characterized the minority of Edward III," which makes it difficult to determine what lay behind individual appointments to office.[37] The fall of Mortimer in 1330 signalled the triumph of the Lancastrians and Stratford's promotion to the chancellorship gave them "the highest position in the state." [38] Because in the fourteenth century "earls were too dignified to be ministers" it was left to the "Lancastrian prelates" to make their influence felt. Stratford, according to Tout, was "the Lancastrian leader," who for the next ten years was to be "the dominating personality of the state." A lawyer and politician, who had "won his bishopric by despicable trickery," he is described as being "nearly as powerful in the ecclesiastical as in the political world." [39] In the third section of chapter nine, covering the years 1338 to 1343, Tout details Stratford's exercise of authority. By mid-Lent of 1340 his power was at its height: "If parliament was to control the king, the Stratfords were to control parliament." This power, thought Tout, was scarcely abated by Stratford's resignation of the great seal, his "diplomatic illness," and his attempt to restrain the king from re-crossing to Flanders.[40] Tout was able to expand his treatment of the conflict of 1340-1341 thanks mainly to the foundation laid by G. T. Lapsley's article of 1915 and the contemporaneous work of Miss Hughes.[41] By and large he is surprisingly fair to Stratford, finding praise for the restrained language of the *excusationes*, though describing his combination of "an assertion of extreme clerical doctrine" with "state-

[36] Ibid., pp. 11-12. "Under the active leadership of Henry of Lancaster and bishop Stratford, the baronial opposition which Thomas of Lancaster had once led, reformed its ranks and exerted overwhelming influence."

[37] Ibid., p. 15.

[38] Ibid., p. 35.

[39] Ibid., pp. 40-41.

[40] Ibid., pp. 106, 110-111.

[41] Ibid., pp. 118ff. At p. 126 n. 2 Tout acknowledges the work of Lapsley, "Archbishop Stratford"; Hughes, *A Study of Edward III*; Pike, *Constitutional History*; Harcourt, *His Grace the Steward*; and Barnes, *History of Edward III*.

ments of his political grievances" as an unnecessary complication, and dismissing his imitation of Becket as "ostentatious posing." At the same time he is prepared to concede "some nobility in the steadfastness with which he braved his former associates and maintained his position in the teeth of brutal threats." In Tout's analysis the outcome was the defeat of Edward III's attempt at despotism and "the acceptance of the archbishop's theory of the constitution." [42] Indeed, Stratford is considered to have achieved more than one of his most respected predecessors: "What Winchelsea and the ordainers had with difficulty enforced against a weakling, Stratford and his associates imposed on a vigorous and active king." [43] Tout's interest was that of a historian of his country's central administration; Stratford he looked upon as "formulating the baronial position, or more precisely, restating with greater precision that of Winchelsea and Thomas of Lancaster." [44]

In the fourteenth-century volume of the *Oxford History of England* May McKisack turned once more to a general assessment of Stratford in the style of Stubbs in the *Constitutional History* and Tout in the *Political History*. By that time (1959) Stratford was considered sufficiently important to merit a separate chapter.[45] Despite some aberrations in the account of her subject's activities during Edward II's reign, Professor McKisack is quite favourably disposed.[46] For her the "true causes" of the crisis of 1340 were fairly laid on the shoulders of Edward III.[47] The archbishop's manipulation of the events of the following year is favourably reviewed. He was not content with defensive action; rather, "with ingenuity and skill he sought to broaden the basis of his position so as to engage the sympathies of a wider public." [48] In the circumstances this was not particularly difficult; the commons were concerned about taxation and the king's arbitrary measures, the magnates about their own position in the light of the king's refusal to permit Stratford to enter parliament and to answer there for his conduct in office. McKisack is inclined to admit the genuineness of Stratford's concern for clerical interests. For the rest, his subsequent accommodation with the king and his failure to object to Edward's repeal of the statutes of 1341 are taken as

[42] Tout, *Chapters* 3, p. 126.
[43] Ibid., p. 127.
[44] Ibid.
[45] *Fourteenth Century*, chap. 6, "Edward III and Archbishop Stratford (1330-43)."
[46] Ibid., pp. 80-83. There is too much reliance on Geoffrey le Baker and the commonly held idea that Stratford remained an exile with the queen in Paris.
[47] Ibid., p. 166.
[48] Ibid., pp. 172-173.

an indication that he cared much for his own reputation and little for the maintenance of the concessions he had been instrumental in securing.[49] Stratford is felt to have continued in the royal service, albeit in a somewhat restricted role, almost to his death in 1348.[50] The conclusion is restrained. Stratford, "always the king's friend," was neither "a humbug" nor a "time-server." For his part the king was prepared to admit his minister's good intentions, however unfortunate their outcome. What had begun as an administrative crisis was turned by Stratford's ingenuity into a constitutional one.[51] Edward learned his lesson; "the king never repeated the mistakes of his early years and for a generation after the crisis, these issues lay dormant." It was none the less true, concludes McKisack, "that these opening years of the French war had afforded a striking demonstration of the dependence of the king on parliament," more particularly on the commons, "who took advantage of the opportunity to grant the king's financial necessities only in return for redress of grievances." [52] It will be observed that this treatment of Stratford's career entails a distinct shift of emphasis. There is far less concern for the so-called Lancastrian or baronial opposition, far more stress on the individual characters of Edward III and of Stratford.

A postscript is provided by two recent historians, Dr. G. L. Harriss and Mrs. Natalie Fryde. Dr. Harriss, whose concern is with national taxation and the effect upon it of the Hundred Years' War, devotes a chapter to Stratford's administration of 1340 and others to the events which both preceded and succeeded it.[53] As a preliminary he reviews the opinions of previous writers such as Stubbs, Tout, Hughes and Lapsley, but notably Bertie Wilkinson – to the effect that "for all his constitutional language Stratford appears as a lone and somewhat irresponsible demagogue; the Commons as independent and radical, if ultimately ineffective." [54] For Harriss the crises of 1311 and 1340 are markedly different; in the former the magnate opposition had forced a council on the king under the impetus of "popular clamour and grievance" but with the principal intention of removing Gaveston from Edward's side. Whereas in 1340, the home council "received plenary power on the petition of the Commons who saw it as the means of rescuing the community from royal

---

[49] Ibid., pp. 173-175.
[50] Ibid., pp. 177-179.
[51] Ibid., p. 179.
[52] Ibid., p. 180.
[53] *King, Parliament and Public Finance*, chap. 12; cf. chaps. 10-11, 13.
[54] Ibid., pp. 272-273.

exactions" and maintaining the country's internal security. Stratford, argues Harriss, made use of "the discontents of the home council" and of the commons "to re-establish his own position against the king's *familiares*." All the same, "the statutes and ordinances of 1340 embodied a reordering of royal government to reflect a constitutional ideal shared by the whole community." When the king returned in December 1340 he faced "an opposition with a coherent programme"; an opposition which comprised Stratford, the magnates, and the commons. In this view Stratford's position had been an impossible one; only by forceful exercise of authority could he have satisfied the king's financial needs and counteracted Edward's suspicions about his wholehearted support for the war; yet he was at the same time under obligation to mitigate the impact of war taxation on the community.[55]

Much of this is unexceptionable, but a number of highly debatable issues are raised, none of them entirely new. To what extent, for instance, did Stratford strive to play the demagogue? Was he in fact an exponent of the "Lancastrian tradition"; a man who forced Edward III to accept "the programme of Winchelsea and Thomas of Lancaster?"[56] Must we, in any case, regard him as leader of an "opposition," and if so, in what sense? Lastly, is it possible to account for the virulence of the king towards his archbishop? It may be that we need to move away from the conventional notion of the adoption by churchmen of "Lancastrian constitutionalism." Already, in Winchelsey's case, Dr. Denton has reacted against the assumption that he provided leadership for the ordaining movement. Winchelsey, he contends, was a sacerdotalist. As such he was not concerned to lead a lay movement against the crown.[57] In much that he did Stratford is patently Winchelsey's heir, but unfavourable and often quite unjust assessments of his character have led to undue suspicion of his motives, hence to conclusions that are ripe for re-examination or even rejection.

Mrs. Fryde's contribution to the evaluation of Stratford's life and work has been made principally in two articles and in the epilogue of a book devoted to the later years of Edward II's reign. The first of the articles deals with Stratford's career prior to his assumption of political authority in 1330.[58] The second concerns itself with the much discussed crisis of 1340-1341, of which the author takes a pragmatic view: "If we approach

[55] Ibid., p. 275.
[56] Ibid., p. 273.
[57] *Winchelsey*, pp. 256-257, 260-264.
[58] "John Stratford and the Crown," pp. 153-159.

the events ... without any constitutional hindsight, we find that we are dealing with a purely political crisis, a trial of strength between a king who meant to be complete master of his own kingdom and royal officials ... who had become unsatisfactory instruments." [59] In general Mrs. Fryde is markedly unsympathetic towards Stratford, whom she considered "very good at raising issues of principle to protect himself and his power." For her "the basic story of the crisis of 1341" was Edward's "victory in removing an old, wily but unreliable royal servant and a group of his associates and replacing them by men who served him better." [60] In fact, as we have seen, Stratford was by no means thrown on the political scrap-heap in 1341, but continued to exercise a not inconsiderable influence until his death.[61]

CONCLUSION

The arguments and, one hopes, most of the facts have been set before the reader. It may be presumptuous to influence him further. None the less, some onus lies on Stratford's latest biographer not to shirk the issue. The most difficult task is to cut a path through the undergrowth created by often wilfully misleading chroniclers or would-be helpful historians. When we have done this, what do we see? Possibly something along the following lines.

Stratford was an extremely able and intelligent man with a flair for administration and politics. Once equipped with the essential qualifications he launched himself on the world, in which he had every intention of making his way. In those days the road to advancement for someone of his birth and education could be only through the church. This does not mean to imply that for Stratford the church was merely a vehicle for personal advancement. That would be to jump to a conclusion for which there is no warrant; also it would be to misinterpret the attitude of the whole body of highly qualified clerks. They were quite certain that they *did* have something to offer the church, but they were not thinking in the narrowly spiritual terms, if one can so express it, which some critics have used to judge them. The "good" of the church could be achieved in a variety of ways: by increasing the opportunities for divine worship with the foundation of churches, chantries and religious institutions of all

---

[59] "Edward III's Removal of Ministers," p. 150.
[60] Ibid., p. 161. Cf. *Tyranny of Edward II*, pp. 226-227.
[61] See above, "Closing Years."

kinds; by preserving from secular encroachment its rights and privileges; and by ensuring the careful administration of ecclesiastical office and benefice so that, for instance, the canonical and customary functions of rector or vicar, archdeacon, bishop and metropolitan could be properly performed to the spiritual advantage of all concerned, laymen and clerk alike. It was a system which accommodated a great variety of talents; a system not calculated to foster saints, but one which did not preclude them.

Stratford's future was assured once he had secured the bishopric of Winchester. This wealthy see did not of itself guarantee Stratford's influence in matters of state, but combined with his own abilities and inclinations it provided in the long term a sound basis for political advancement. Not for him the life of a Murimuth who, gifted though he was, saw all the colleagues of his youth, including Stratford, leaving him behind, a somewhat carping and embittered man, whose chronicle ironically was to prove more enduring than some of the more immediately rewarding achievements of his contemporaries. And Murimuth was not the only man of ability whose career failed to match his talents. We need only mention the humble vicar of Winkfield in Berkshire, William de Pagula, whose erudition as a doctor of canon law must have been somewhat wasted on his humble parishioners (though their welfare was close to his heart) and whose pinnacle of preferment was a canonry of London.[1] In Stratford own entourage John le Brabazoun may well provide another instance. But we ought not to assume that all men of ability yearned for such national prominence as Stratford enjoyed, and for which on more than one occasion he suffered.

Those who criticize Stratford's actions at the time of his promotion to Winchester rather take for granted a royal right to the disposition of bishoprics. The acceptance of a bishopric contrary to the king's will provides an example not merely of a conflict of loyalties, but of a conflict of authority. A saint could either have withdrawn and risked the consequences of disobedience to papal command, or conscientiously assumed the "burden" – despite the king – on the basis that it was bestowed on him by an authority he ought not to resist. Stratford was no saint, but personal ambition and the acknowledgment of what he felt to be lawful authority combined at an early stage to provide him with opportunity and status. In this he proved more fortunate than the king's candidate, Robert Baldock, who not only failed to secure a bishopric

---

[1] See *Biog. Oxon.*, s.v. Paul; Pantin, *English Clergy*, pp. 195-202; Wright, *Church and Crown*, p. 199 n. 19; Boyle, "The *Oculus sacerdotis* and William of Pagula."

despite Edward II's sustained support, but ended his days miserably in a London gaol.[2]

Some historians have a tendency to assume that it is a sufficient explanation to label a man a careerist. Thus, by definition he is devoid of all moral scruple; his actions are open to the interpretation of being directed solely towards his own advancement. Both Bishop Stubbs and T. F. Tout with their too neatly-rounded judgments may be said to have been guilty of assumptions of this kind. In Stratford's career, as in Orleton's there came a time when a stand on a point of principle was necessary, whatever the consequences. Neither was found wanting but both, though more particularly Orleton, have been condemned for being primarily activated by self-interest. Reynolds was not prepared (with one possible exception) to make any stand against Edward II, whose rule after Boroughbridge has now been unequivocally stigmatized as tyrannous.[3] This is what marks him off from Stratford and Orleton, helping to explain why they attracted hostile criticism, Reynolds merely contempt.[4]

During Edward II's reign Stratford was content to endure the financial penalties imposed for his temerity in accepting the Winchester bishopric and to continue in the service of the crown. We lack evidence of his playing a double role; making no overt protest at home, but conspiring abroad with Isabella. Nor, I think, is there need to credit him with any ulterior motive in advocating the sending of the queen to negotiate in France. Hindsight serves to distort the intentions of those who favoured this diplomatic move, but had Isabella's estrangement from her husband been an open secret it is clear that she would not have been permitted to leave. Once the queen had landed safely in East Anglia Stratford must have been aware that the days of Edward II were numbered; the king lacked both baronial and popular support, the administrative class deserted him, the Londoners were hostile to his cause, and the leaders of the church were unable to decide on a common course of action. The panoply of kingship was speedily reduced to a forlorn group of dejected men drifting helplessly in the Bristol channel.[5] Meanwhile the bishops continued to vacillate; Stratford attracted no support for an approach to Queen Isabella and so he crossed his Rubicon and went alone. Orleton had no such compunction; he was with the queen in the early stages, though clearly he lacked prior intelligence of her landing.[6] And so it was

[2] *Biog. Oxon.*, s.v.; Haines, *Church and Politics*, pp. 111-112.
[3] See Fryde, *Tyranny of Edward II*.
[4] The best defence of Reynolds is that of Wright, *Church and Crown*, pp. 143-174.
[5] SA MS 122, fols. 43ᵛ-45ᵛ. See above, "From Conformist to Revolutionary," n. 44.
[6] Haines, *Church and Politics*, pp. 161, 164.

that two lawyer-bishops, Stratford and Orleton, came to provide the brains behind the displacement of Edward II. Now that the king's tyranny has been clearly delineated, the actions of these two men can be seen in a less unfavourable light. Do they not have some claim to a degree of patriotism, in the sense of having a care for their country's good government? Should they not be applauded for the skill with which the operation was conducted? Civil war was averted, though there was widespread violence of the kind inevitable when the reins of medieval government were seen to be relaxed. It is true that it was Edward's ineptitude rather than his tyranny that was chiefly stressed in the "articles of deposition," but this perhaps is only an indication of the caution exercised by those who devised them – principally Stratford, we are led to believe.

With the deposition Stratford's troubles were only just beginning. Like Orleton he withdrew from the political centre. His own view was that he was deliberately cold-shouldered. Not surprisingly the period of Mortimer and Isabella's dominance proved a difficult one. Despite the somewhat more favourable interpretation of this regime by some modern writers,[7] it is clear that Stratford was more impressed by what he felt to be the arbitrary conduct of affairs and the reappearance of the evils of the previous reign. At this point, some sources suggest, Stratford emerges as "Lancastrian spokesman"; hence he incurred the animosity of the new earl of March, Roger Mortimer, and was forced to flee from would-be assassins. Even so, the leadership of those few members of the episcopate who felt it necessary to act was assumed by Archbishop Mepham, a man singularly ill suited to the task, as a contemporary chronicler acidly observed.[8] Mepham's election as archbishop is thought to have been Henry of Lancaster's riposte to the prospective candidature of the bishop of Lincoln, Henry Burghersh, a close supporter of Queen Isabella.[9]

A word or two needs to be said at this point about Stratford and the "Lancastrian party." The concept of party has for too long bedevilled analysis of Edward II's difficult reign and the early years of that of his son. Thomas of Lancaster's biographer has credited him with a consciousness of history and of his being the heir to the ideals of Simon de Montfort.[10] The political programme of the Lancastrians, as they have been called, was manifested in the Ordinances and at the time of the conflict of 1340-

---

[7] E.g. Fryde, *Tyranny of Edward II*, chap. 15.
[8] See above, "Lancastrian Spokesman."
[9] See *Foedera* 2, iii, p. 11.
[10] Maddicott, *Lancaster*, pp. 321-322.

1341, as well as at other times. But one doubts very much whether Stratford was in any real sense a "Lancastrian," a firm follower of that baronial house.[11] In the early-fourteenth century ecclesiastical and other "liberties" were maintained by a balance of forces. When imbalance occurred, as in the reign of Edward II and during Mortimer and Isabella's regimen, elements of the baronage were certain to be alienated. In practice this meant the earl of Lancaster, the most powerful man in the land after the king. In practice too, it meant that certain bishops who considered that positive action ought to be taken in defence of the church's rights, and perhaps of those of others as well, were drawn into some form of coalition with disaffected secular lords. Some members of the episcopate shunned all such entanglements, preferring a policy of non-alignment. Among them we can probably number Archbishop Reynolds (with some qualification) and Bishop Hamo de Hethe of Rochester (with none). The latter apparently regarded his colleagues' involvement in politics as mere foolishness. Bishops such as Stratford and Cobham held that political decisions of magnitude should be taken in parliament. There were of course many other bishops, but closer examination of their actions has yet to be made; in many cases there will be insufficient evidence for judgment. What is being suggested is that Stratford and Cobham should not necessarily be dubbed "Lancastrian" because at critical moments they found themselves in association with Earl Thomas and his supporters.[12] The church's position could not be maintained in isolation; the lack of leadership evinced by Reynolds meant that certain stronger characters on the bench had to make an independent stand. Rarely indeed did the episcopate present anything approaching a united front.[13] It had become almost a commonplace of official phraseology that unwillingness to speak out on the one hand, and a degree of episcopal imprudence on the other, had been at the root of the disturbances of Edward II's reign.[14] Like Thomas of Lancaster, Stratford had a keen sense of historical continuity. He looked back for inspiration to that exemplar of resistance to secular, and notably royal coercion, Thomas Becket. But given the opportunity he was anxious to cooperate with a government which made this at all

[11] It is, of course, difficult to disentangle the constitutional attitude of the bishops from that of Thomas or Henry of Lancaster, but it would seem that they were not identical. Denton, *Winchelsey*, has made a distinction in that primate's case.
[12] It will be recalled that in the 1328-1329 affair Stratford retired to his diocese before the denouement.
[13] This was equally true under the leadership of Winchelsey, Reynolds, and Mepham, when there were deep divisions for differing reasons. See Haines, "Conflict in Government."
[14] E.g. *Foedera* 2, ii, p. 72; iii, pp. 4-5, 8-9.

possible. Some will argue, not without warrant, that in 1341 and subsequently he compromised too much. All the same, to the end of his life he was acutely aware of the need not to relax his vigilance for ecclesiastical liberty, and for his part Edward III kept a wary eye on his archbishop's activities in provincial council.

Stratford's involvement in the war with France, some say as instigator, certainly as spy, diplomatic envoy and fund-raiser, will be indefensible to the modern mind. Stratford rightly feared Edward III's impetuosity, but upheld the justice of his claim to the throne of France. It is scarcely conceivable that he could have adopted another course. There was, we know, a degree of ambivalence, for outwardly he expressed a strong desire for peace, in compliance with papal urging, while in the secrecy of the royal councils he was devising means to fend off the importunate visits of papal legates. The victory of Crécy, the high point of English success in this phase of the war, ostensibly gave opportunity for a favourable peace. This was not to be and before long, just about the time of Stratford's death, or shortly thereafter, the rapid onset of the Black Death was not only to hinder military operations but also to bring unprecedented mortality to the archbishop's flock. It was a timely release.[15]

Had it not been for William Shakespeare – a mighty exception it must be admitted – John Stratford would have been by far the best known of the sons of that Warwickshire town from which he took his name. He left his mark on its medieval buildings, notably the parish church, and has merited a not undistinguished place in English history. A determined man, not one to suffer fools gladly, at times he was irascible, even perhaps spiteful. Content on occasion to run before the wind, in an age when relatively few in high places would hazard their lives by confronting the king, he was not found unprepared for resistance to unlawful acts. Of course he had his faults; overmuch ambition some would say, others a too highly developed sense of his own importance. There is truth in such contentions. We have had occasion to observe an ambivalence in his attitude to important matters of national policy, as well as an approach to the church more administrative and legal than spiritual. But it can be said that Stratford did not shirk responsibility either in the ecclesiastical or the secular sphere. In both he was effective. If Stubbs was in a measure right in his estimate of the moral stature of men of the earlier fourteenth century, then it would have to be admitted that Stratford stands head and shoulders above most of his contemporaries.

[15] There is no reason to assume that Stratford died of the plague.

Appendix 1

Letters and Documents

9 Dec. 1317   Letters patent of John Stratford's appointment as official of
Newark   Lincoln diocese by Bishop Dalderby.

LAO Reg. Dalderby 2 (Reg. 3), fol. 376ʳ

Universis pateat per presentes quod nos Johannes permissione divina Lincolniensis episcopus dilectum in Christo filium magistrum Johannem de Stratford iuris civilis professorem officialem nostrum constituimus et eciam deputamus, omnibus et singulis subditis nostris in virtute obediencie firmiter iniungentes quatinus dicto magistro Johanni tanquam officiali nostro plenius obediant et intendant. In cuius rei testimonium sigillum nostrum presentibus est appensum. Dat' apud Newerk quinto Idus Decembris anno domini millesimo ccc^mo septimo decimo.

11 Dec. 1317   Bishop Dalderby authorizes Stratford, his official, to correct,
Newark   punish and reform his subjects; powers which he could not
                exercise merely by virtue of his commission as official.

LAO Reg. Dalderby 2 (Reg. 3), fol. 376ʳ

Johannes permissione divina Lincolniensis episcopus dilecto in Christo magistro Johanni de Stratford officiali nostro, salutem graciam et benediccionem. Licet per commissionem officii vestri vobis per nos factam excessus subditorum nostrorum corrigere nequeatis de iure, de zelo tamen quem vos ad salutem animarum gerere credimus confidentes, ad procedendum ex officio contra notatos quoscumque seculares subditos nostre diocesis ac eciam diffamatos super criminibus et excessibus super quibus fuerint diffamati, corrigendum puniendum et reformandum excessus huiusmodi subditorum de quibus credideritis expedire, ac cetera facienda et expedienda que in hac parte requiruntur agenda eciam si ad amocionem cuiusquam a beneficio de iure fuerit procedendum, vobis vices nostras committimus cum cohercionis canonice potestate. Valete. Dat' apud Newerk iii Idus Decembris anno domini millesimo ccc^mo septimo decimo et consecracionis nostre octavodecimo.

24 June 1318 Appointment of John Stratford, his fellow canon M. Thomas de
Stowe Park   Langetoft, and Ds. John de Clipston, canon of Penkridge, to grant
              absolution in cases reserved to the bishop during the period of
              visitation of Lincoln diocese which they have been empowered to
              undertake.

LAO Reg. Dalderby 2 (Reg. 3), fol. 391^r

Johannes permissione divina Lincolniensis episcopus dilectis in Christo filiis
magistris Johanni de Stretford officiali nostro et Thome de Langetoft canonicis
ecclesie nostre Linc' ac domino Johanni de Clipston canonico in ecclesia collegiata
de Penkrich Coventrensis et Lichfeldensis diocesis, salutem graciam et benediccionem. De vestra discrecione et serenitate zeli quem ad salutem animarum
procurandum vos habere credimus confidentes, ut parochianos nostros omnes et
singulos qui vobis voluerint confiteri a peccatorum suorum nexibus quorum
absolucio solis episcopis reservatur de consuetudine vel de iure, suspensionumque
et excommunicacionum sentenciis quibus fuerint involuti quatenus absolvendi
eosdem nobis est attributa potestas de iure, iniuncta sibi pro modo culparum
penitencia salutari prout rei convenit, absolvere valeatis vice nostra, plenam vobis
coniunctim et divisim et vestrum cuilibet in solidum durante visitacione cleri et
populi nostre diocesis quam nuper vobis sub certa forma commisimus
exequendum tenore presencium specialem concedimus facultatem. Dat' apud
Parcum Stowe viii Kalen' Julii anno domini millesimo ccc^{mo}xviii^o.

5 May 1324   Pope John XXII acknowledges the letters of the new bishop of
Avignon   Winchester, informing him of his own to Edward II, Bishop
             Ayrminne, Hugh d'Angoulême, and the younger Despenser. He
             declines to grant Stratford's request to be able to choose his
             installer, on the grounds that this might exacerbate the situation.

Vatican Archives, *RV* 112, fol. 192^v (al. xlviii).

Venerabili fratri Johanni episcopo Wintoniensi.

Fraternitatis tue litteris solita benignitate receptis et intellecta earum serie
diligenter super negotio tuo, tam carissimo in Christo filio nostro Edwardo regi
Anglie illustri quam venerabili fratri nostro Norwicensi episcopo, necnon et
dilecto filio magistro Hugoni de Engolisma sacriste Narbonensi apostolice sedis
nuncio, ac nobili viro Hugoni lo Despensier iuniori, nostras dirigimus litteras
oportunas. Sane si circa installacionem committendum alii quam ordinario tuo,
quem asseris tibi esse suspectum, precibus tuis annu[eri]mus proculdubio non
interis cum id nullatenus honestati congruet et ex ipsa commissione si fieret ipsum
contra te quod vitare nos condecet fortius provocares. Datum Avinion' ut supra.

18 July 1324 Faculty for Stratford's enthronement as bishop of Winchester by a
Avignon   suitable person of his choice.

Vatican Archives, *RV* 112, fol. 93^r (al. lxxxviii); duplicated (with slight verbal variations) at fol. 96ʳ (al. lxxxxi). See also *RV* 77, fol. 129ʳ⁻ᵛ and WinRS, fol. 8ᵛ, where the commission is copied and the words used by the installer, M. William Inge, are given.

Venerabili fratri ... episcopo Wintoniensi

Merita tue fraternitatis exposcunt ut personam tuam speciali benevolencia prosequentes ea que tuis oportunitatibus expedire videmus favorabiliter concedamus. Hinc est quod nos certis ex causis que ad hec nostrum animum induxerunt, ut a quocunque malueris antistite apostolice sedis graciam et communionem habente vel alia persona ecclesiastica in dignitate constituta intronisari hac vice in tua Wintoniensi ecclesia valeas, plenam tibi concedimus auctoritate presencium facultatem. Propter hoc tamen illius iuri cui alias intronizacio predicta facienda competit non intendimus imposterum derogare. Datum Avinion˙ xv Kal˙ Augusti anno octavo.

18 May [1325] Bishop Stratford requests Bishop Cobham of Worcester to grant
Brightwell   licence to M. John of Pershore, portionary in Leigh, so that he
               could study canon law. [Inserted in the register as an appropriate
               model.]

Worcester Reg. Cobham, fol. 102ʳ

Reverendo in Christo patri domino T[home] Dei gracia Wygorniensi episcopo J[ohannes] eiusdem permissione Wyntoniensis ecclesie minister humilis, salutem et fraternam in domino caritatem. Cum viris literatis per maxime fructum in ecclesia Dei affere cupientibus oportunum sit de pastoralis officii solicitudine omnis gracia et favor merito faciend*i*, vestram reverenciam ex corde requirimus et rogamus quatinus dilecto nostro magistro Johanni de Perschor˙ porcionario in ecclesia de Legh˙ vestre diocesis licenciam iuris canonici studio insistendi ubicumque studium viget generale, ut in eodem iure proficere valeat ac legere, de vestra solita bonitate ob nostri contemplacionem concedere dignetur vestra paternitas reverenda, quam ad ecclesie sue sancte regimen conservet in prosperis Jhesus Christus. Scriptum apud Brightewell xviii die Maii.

Undated   Mandate to the dean of Winchester. Stratford announces his
               intention to preach in his cathedral on Ash Wednesday [5
               February 1326] and directs the dean to summon the people to
               attend.

WinRS, fol. 15ʳ

Monicio ad audiendum predicacionem in festo Cinerum

Johannes *et cetera* decano Wynton˙ salutem. Angit nos cura potissima inter ceteras sollicitudines quibus assidue premimur ut nostris subditis exhibeamus nostram presenciam corporalem ipsos iuxta datam a Deo nobis prudenciam prout convenit instruendo verbis pariter et exemplis. Volentes igitur in hoc instanti festo

Cinerum in ecclesia nostra cathedrali Wynton' officium dicto diei conveniens peragere ut tenemur, tibi mandamus quatinus omnes parochianos nostros statim post recepcionem [MS "recepcionis"] presencium omnes et singulos parochianos nostros efficaciter moneas et inducas quod huiusmodi officio ut premittitur per nos dante domino faciendo cum summa devocione intersint audituri quod ibidem per nos ad eorum salutem annuente domino exponetur et ulterius facturi et recepturi *et cetera*.

20 May 1329   Royal writ requiring the return of the seal in use while Edward II
Westminster   was "outside the realm" and delivered to Stratford on 15
               November 1326.

WinRS, fol. 211ᵛ

Edwardus Dei gracia rex Anglie dominus Hibernie et dux Aquitanie venerabili in Christo patri Johanni Dei gracia episcopo Wynton', salutem. Cum celebris memorie dominus E[dwardus] nuper rex Anglie pater noster septimo die Novembris anno regni sui vicesimo mandasset tunc thesaurario et camerariis suis de scaccario quod illud sigillum quod alias ipso patre nostro extra regnum agente pro lege in eodem regno manutenenda et conservanda servire consuevit ad nos tunc custodem regni Anglie ipso patre nostro extra idem regnum tunc agente salvo et secure mitti facerent ac prefati camerarii sigillum predictum quintodecimo die Novembris eodem anno vicesimo vobis tunc tenenti locum thesaurarii scaccarii ipsius patris nostri liberaverint nobis tunc custodi regni predicti mittendum, prout per memoranda recepte scaccarii predicti est compertum, cumque nos ad partes transmarinas pro quibuscumque negociis arduis nos specialiter tangentibus in proximo Deo dante simus ituri et sigillo predicto pro lege in regno nostro conservanda indigeamus, vobis mandamus quod sigillum predictum si penes vos adhuc remaneat sub salva et secura custodia cum omni celeritate qua poteritis venire facias ad dictum scaccarium nostrum apud Westmonasterium thesaurario et camerariis de eodem scaccario ibidem liberandum, vel si forte dictum sigillum penes vos non remaneat, tunc prefatos thesaurarium et camerarios per vestras litteras distincte et aperte certificetis cui sigillum predictum liberastis et ubi et quo devenit. Et remittatis ibi tunc hoc breve. Teste venerabili patre T[homa] episcopo Herefordensi thesaurario nostro apud Westmonasterium vicesimo die Maii anno regni nostri tercio.

4 June 1329   Stratford's return of the above writ.
Farnham

Retornum eiusdem.

Venerabilibus et discretis viris dominis thesaurario et camerariis de scaccario domini nostri regis Anglie illustris Johannes permissione divina Wynton' episcopus, salutem in auctore salutis. Breve regium presentibus involutum tercio die instantis mensis Junii ad nos venit, super quo scire velit vestra discrecio reverenda quod sigillum de quo in dicto brevi fit mencio statim post recepcionem eiusdem sub nostro sigillo clausum misimus domine nostre domine Isabelle Dei gracia regine Anglie illustri apud Hereford' et illud sibi ibidem pro constanti liberari fecimus presencium per latores qui vobis plenam veritatem in hac parte noverint intimare. Et ubi dictum sigillum ulterius devenit totaliter ignoramus, quod vobis tenore presencium significamus. Dat' apud Farnham quarto die dicti mensis Junii anno domini millesimo CCC[mo] vicesimo nono.

Easter term   Stratford's response to the charge that he had left the Salisbury
1329   parliament of 1328 without the king's licence and hence was guilty
                 of contempt.

PRO K.B. 27/276/Rex m. 9[v] [Extract from proceedings].

Et predictus episcopus in propria persona sua venit et defendit contemptum et transgressionem et quicquid *et cetera*; et dicit quod ipse est unus de paribus regni et prelatus sacre ecclesie et eis inest venire ad parliamentum domini regis per summonitionem et pro voluntate ipsius domini regis cum sibi placuerit; et dicit quod si quis eorum deliquerit erga dominum regem in parliamento aliquo, in parliamento debet corrigi emendari et non alibi in minori curia quam in parliamento, per quod non intendit quod dominus rex velit in curia hic de huiusmodi transgressione et contemptu factis in parliamento responderi *et cetera*.

Oct. 1341   Topics from Winchester diocese intended for discussion at the
                 provincial council of 19 October. [In response to Archbishop Strat-
                 ford's mandate of 23 April 1341 Bishop Orleton had directed the
                 religious and secular clergy of his diocese to meet on 1 October to
                 deliberate on matters requiring reformation.]

WinRO 1, fol. 107[v]

Deliberata cleri diocesis Wynt' [margin]

Infrascripta sunt reformanda in concilio provinciali ex deliberacione cleri diocesis Wynton':

In primis quod libertates concesse per cartas regias ecclesiis et ecclesiasticis personis illibate serventur.

Item, quia dominus rex tot et tantas bonorum suorum fiscalium fecit alienaciones quod non habet unde incumbencia sibi onera supportare absque eo quod clero et populo regni sui tallias et alia imponat onera importabilia, ordinetur per concilium ut bona patrimonialia et fiscalia alienata ad statum pristinum revocentur et quod amplius nulla dentur et quod omnes huiusmodi bona de cetero recipientes excommunicentur nisi sit de communi consensu tocius parliamenti.

Item supplicetur domino regi quod non onerentur per commissiones regias abbates priores et alii viri religiosi qui in puram et perpetuam elemosinam temporalia tenent vel alii viri ecclesiastici quorum beneficia in spiritualibus consistunt et quod per dictas commissiones non artentur contra doctrinam ecclesiasticam se negociis secularibus immiscere.

13 Jan. 1344   Pope Clement VI complains about the "novelties" introduced in
Avignon   England against God and the Roman church. Some say that Stratford is their promoter, but from personal knowledge of him the
pope finds this hard to credit. He therefore urges the primate to
resist all such practices and to pay heed to M. William [Bateman]
of Norwich, whom he is sending to the king.

Vatican Archives, *RV* 137, fol. 172^v

Venerabili fratri Johanni archiepiscopo Cantuariensi.

Novitates contra Deum et sanctam Romanam ecclesiam attemptatas in partibus
regni Anglie hiis temporibus displicenter nimis audivimus non indigne. Et licet
assereretur ab aliquibus te frater promotorem ac patratorem novitatum
huiusmodi existere ac eciam extitisse, nosque a multis stimulati fuerimus ut
propterea contra te procedere deberemus, quia tamen iandudum cum status
inferior nos haberet [?] tuam circumspeccionem et prudenciam novimus ab
experto cadere in mente nostra fixa credulitate nequivit quod tu sic in virum
mutatus alterum contra eandem ecclesiam que te ad tante dignitatis tantique
status culmen graciose provexit ad tam grandis ingratitudinis vicium prorupisses
quomodolibet contra eam, et attendentes quod si procederemus adversum te sicut
nobis suggestum extitit ut prefertur lederetur non modicum fama tua quousque de
veritate informaremur plenius super hiis providimus desistendum. Quocirca
fraternitatem tuam rogamus, requirimus et hortamur attente quatinus circa
tollendas et revocandas novitates easdem que in divine maiestatis offensam et
eiusdem ecclesie contumeliam et iniuriam manifestam cedere proculdubio
dinoscuntur sic operose fideliter et sedule interponere studeas solicitudinis partes
tue quod inde tua clareat innocentia circa hec et culpa si forsan quod credere
nequimus precesserit penitus abstergatur, dilecto filio magistro Guillelmo de
Norwico decano ecclesie Lincolniensis capellano nostro, causarum apostolici
palacii auditori, zelatori tui honoris et commodi, super hiis que tibi pro parte
nostra explicanda duxerit adhibendo credulam et assistendo nichilominus super
aliis pro quibus ipsum ad carissimum in Christo filium nostrum Edwardum
regem Anglie illustrem et partes illas specialiter destinamus. Dat' Avinion' Id'
Januarii anno secundo.

Appendix 2

Stratford's Administration
at Winchester and Canterbury

A. Administrative and judicial officers

WINCHESTER

Vicars general

Date and place of commission	Appointee	Reference (WinRS)
2 Dec. 1324 Southwark	M. Robert Stratford	fol. 9^r
14 Feb. 1325 Southwark	M. Robert Stratford M. Richard of Chaddesley, chancellor	fol. 93^v fol. 93^v
7 July 1325 Southwark	M. Richard of Gloucester M. Richard of Chaddesley	fol. 95^v
23 Oct. 1325 Southwark	M. Richard of Gloucester, official M. Richard of Chaddesley, chancellor	fol. 97^r
23 Oct. 1326 Bristol	M. Robert Stratford M. Wybert de Littleton, chancellor	fol. 19^v
10 Mar. 1327 Dartford	M. Robert Stratford M. Richard of Gloucester, official M. Wybert de Littleton	fols. 24^v-25^r, 101^v
30 Jan. 1328 Witney	M. Richard of Gloucester, official M. Wybert de Littleton	fols. 35^v, 103^v
24 May 1331 Southwark	M. Robert Stratford M. Wybert de Littleton	fol. 123^r
2 Dec. 1331 Southwark	M. Robert Stratford M. Wybert de Littleton	fol. 126^r
27 Apr. 1332 Southwark	prior of Winchester M. Robert Stratford M. Wybert de Littleton	fols. 128^v-129^r
7 Feb. 1333 York	prior of Winchester M. Richard of Chaddesley, chancellor	fols. 77^r, 133^r

Chancellors

Acting:	Appointee	Reference
1325-1326	M. Richard of Chaddesley	"Stratford's *Familia* and Administration," n. 31
Oct. 1326 - ca. 30 Aug. 1332	M. Wybert de Littleton	ibid., n. 33
post Aug. 1332-1333	M. Richard of Chaddesley	ibid., n. 31

Officials

Acting	Appointee	Reference
by July 1325 until at least Jan. 1328	M. Richard of Gloucester	"Stratford's *Familia* and Administration," n. 35
by October 1329 until 1333	M. John de Lecch alias Loveryng of Northleach	ibid., n. 36

Commissaries general of the official

Commission/Acting	Appointee	Reference
19 March 1324 Southwark (temporary arrangement?)	M. Richard of Chaddesley	WinRS, fol. 2^r
acting by 13 Sept. 1324	M. Hugh Prany	ibid., fol. 8^v
acting 1325 until at least Jan. 1329	M. John de Lecch alias Loveryng of Northleach	E.g. ibid., fols. 11^r, 25^r, 33^v, 37^r, 40^v, 43^r, 95^r, 162^{r-v}, 171^v PRO C.115/K1/6681, fols. 15^r-17^r Also "Stratford's *Familia* and Administration," n. 30

President of consistory court in absence of the official and commissary general

Date and place of commission	Appointee	Reference
30 Jan. 1328 Witney	M. John de Shoreham	WinRS, fol. 35^r
5 July 1328 Wolvesey	M. Peter de Wymbourne (assessor to Shoreham)	ibid., fol. 39^r

Special commissaries

Date and place of commission	Appointee	Reference

i. For enquiry, correction and punishment of the bishop's subjects

5 Nov. 1324 Stockwell	M. John de Lecch alias Loveryng of Northleach	WinRS, fol. 7ᵛ

ii. To enquire into vacancies of benefices and to admit, institute and induct to them during the bishop's absence

2 Dec. 1324	idem	ibid., fol. 93ʳ

Sequestrators

Date and place of commisssion	Appointee	Reference (WinRS)

For whole diocese: (sequestrator general)

25 Jan. 1328 Crawley	M. Peter de Wymbourne	fol. 34ᵛ

(apparently not acting after 1328)

For Winchester archdeaconry:

10 Oct. 1324 Farnham (did not act)	vicar of Micheldever	fol. 7ᵛ
7 Nov. 1324 Stockwell (did not act)	M. Richard de Stokele	fol. 7ᵛ
29 Nov. 1324 Farnham	Thomas (de Bekford), vicar of Alton	fol. 7ᵛ
12 June 1325 Southwark	idem (renewal of commission, exception of Isle of Wight deanery)	fol. 11ᵛ
	(acquittance 23 Jan. 1328 for all the time he was sequestrator)	fol. 33ʳ
22 Apr. 1330 Southwark	M. William of Worcester (Ledbury) (appointed sequestrator general throughout the archdeaconry)	fol. 53ᵛ

For Surrey archdeaconry:

10 Oct. 1324 Farnham	Richard de Rudeham, rector of Compton-by-Guildford	fol. 7ᵛ
19 July 1326 Southwark	M. Gilbert de Kyrkeby, rector of Ash	fol. 16ʳ

Date and place of commisssion	Appointee	Reference (WinRS)
17 Dec. 1329 Highclere	idem	fol. 51ʳ

For Isle of Wight deanery:

10 Oct. 1324 Farnham	Nicholas de la Flode, rector of Newchurch	fol. 7ᵛ
acting Sept. 1327	H., vicar of Godshill	fol. 28ᵛ

Registrar

	Appointee	Reference
No record of appointment	Nicholas de Churchill alias Ystele	See "Stratford's *Familia* and Administration," nn. 63-64, 100

CANTERBURY

Vicars general

Commisssion/Acting	Appointee	Reference
probably dated from S.'s 1334-1335 absences	S[tephen Gravesend], bishop of London	*Lydford*, p. 119 no. 219
acting 12 Mar., 21 May 1334	M. Nicholas de Tarenta (Tarrant)	*Rochester Reg. Hethe*, pp. 1081 n. 1, 1173
acting Nov. 1334	M. Adam Murimuth	See "Archbishop of Canterbury," nn. 22, 65
acting Sept. 1335	M. Henry de Iddesworth M. Adam Murimuth	*Rochester Reg. Hethe*, pp. 1119, 1140
acting Dec. 1335	M. Adam Murimuth	*London Reg. Gravesend*, fol. 95ᵛ (p. 260)
acting Jan.-Feb. 1336	idem	E.g. CCL Reg. L, fol. 195ʳ; Reg. G., fol. 24ʳ⁻ᵛ; Lambeth Reg. Album, fols. 32ᵛ-33ʳ
acting Dec. 1336	idem	*London Reg. Gravesend*, fol. 99ᵛ (pp. 264-266)
acting 1338-1339	idem	WoCL *RSV*, fols. 147ʳ, 151ʳ (pp. 259, 264-265); *Rochester Reg. Hethe*, p. 1140
acting 1338-1340	M. Robert Stratford	See "Archbishop of Canterbury," nn. 69-70

Commissary general

Acting	Appointee	Reference
1336, 1340 and later	M. Thomas (Mason) of Canterbury (de Cant', Cantuaria)	CCL Reg. L, fol. 71ᵛ (*Lit. Cant.* 2, p. 183); A.36 IV, fols. 4ᵛ, 17ᵛ; *CPR 1340-1343*, p. 502; ibid. *1345-1348*, p. 203

Chancellors

Acting	Appointee	Reference
ca. 1334 ob. Aug. 1335	M. Wybert de Littleton	*HMCR* 10, App. 3, 1, p. 442 (cited *Cant. Admin.* 2, p. 244)
Apr., July 1340 memo. of commission: 24 Sept. 1341	M. John de Lecch	CCL Reg. L, fol. 75ʳ (*Lit. Cant.* 2, pp. 220-221); A.36 III, mm. 1ʳ, 3ʳ; WinRO 1, fol. 93ᵛ

Officials of the Court of Canterbury

Acting	Appointee	Reference
1335	M. Adam Murimuth	See "Stratford's *Familia* and Administration," nn. 93-94
1340s	M. Simon Islep	Ibid., n. 96 Black Book of the Arches (cited *Cant. Admin.* 2, p. 238) Linc. Reg. Bek 2 (Reg. 7), fol. 131ᵛ *CPP 1342-1419*, p. 35
ca. 1348	M. John de Lecch	CCL W.219

Dean of the Arches

Acting	Appointee	Reference
1333-1336	M. John de Offord	*HMCR* 10, App. 3, 1, p. 237 (cited *Cant. Admin.* 2, p. 239); above, p. 116 n. 97

Registrars and scribes

Acting	Appointee	Reference
i) Of the Court of Canterbury		
temp. Stratford	Robert de Avesbury	Black Book of the Arches, fol. 5^v (cited *Cant. Admin.* 2, p. 241)
	described as: "curie Cantuariensis registri custodem"	BL Harleian MS 200, fol. 76^v (*Avesbury*, p. 279)
ii) Of the archbishop		
Nov. 1340	M. Nicholas de Ystele (of Churchill)	CCL A.36 IV, fol. 24^r
iii) Of the acts of the Court of Canterbury		
temp. Stratford	M. Henry Bagworth	Black Book of the Arches, fol. 5^v (cited *Cant. Admin.* 2, p. 242) *Cant. Admin.* 1, p. 455

Note: For Canterbury registrars and the distinctions to be made see *Cant. Admin.* 1, pp. 21-25, 452-456; 2, pp. 199, 241-242.

Auditors and special commissaries in the Court of Audience

Commission/Acting	Appointee	Reference
21 Feb. 1335 Dover	M. Thomas de Astley M. Wybert de Littleton M. Laurence Fastolf	CCL R.20; Ducarel, "Fragmenta," 78^r
Apr. 1340, 1348	M. Richard Vaughan	CCL A.36 IV, fols. 4^r, 100^r, 104^{r}ff.
1340-1347	M. Laurence Fastolf	ibid., fols. 5^r, 9^{r}ff.
1340-1347	M. John de Lecch	ibid., fols. 4^r, 5^{r}ff.

B. Winchester ordinations

Date	Season	Place	Officiant	Ref. (fol.)
1324 10 Mar.	Sat. in Embertide 1st week of Lent	Southwark priory, infirmary chap. (afterwards one person ordained to first tonsure)	diocesan	WinRS 140^{r-v}

Date	Season	Place	Officiant	Ref. (fol.)
14 Apr.	Holy Saturday	Walton par. ch.	diocesan	141ʳ
1325				
2 Mar.	Sat. in Embertide 1st week of Lent	Southwark priory	Peter of Bologna, bp. of Corbavia, diocesan *in remotis*	141ᵛ-142ʳ
23 Mar.	Sat. (*Sitientes*), eve of Passion Sunday	Lambeth par. ch.	idem	142ʳ
21 Dec.	Sat. in Embertide	Farnham par. ch.	diocesan	142ᵛ-143ʳ
1326				
15 Feb.	Sat. in Embertide 1st week of Lent	Winchester cath.	diocesan	143ᵛ
16 Feb.	2nd Sunday in Lent	ibid. (first tonsure only)	diocesan	143ᵛ-144ʳ
20 Sept.	Sat. in Embertide	Kingsclere par. ch.	diocesan	144ᵛ
21 Sept.	Trinity 18	Highclere (first tonsure only)	diocesan	144ʳ
20 Dec.	Sat. in Embertide	Southwark priory	diocesan	145ʳ
1327				
7 Mar.	Sat. in Embertide 1st week of Lent	Southwark priory	diocesan	145ʳ-146ᵛ
6 June	Sat. in Embertide eve of Trinity	Southwark, chap. of bp.'s manor	Peter of Bologna, bp. of Corbavia	147ʳ⁻ᵛ
19 Sept.	Sat. in Embertide	Downton, chap. of bp.'s manor (ordines pro uno subdiacono)	idem	147ᵛ
1328				
19 Mar.	Sat. (*Sitientes*) eve of Passion Sunday	Crawley par. ch.	diocesan	148ʳ
2 Apr.	Holy Saturday	Waltham par. ch. (two persons ordained)	diocesan	148ʳ

Date	Season	Place	Officiant	Ref. (fol.)
17 Dec.	Sat. in Embertide	[Farnham] (first tonsure only)	diocesan	148^r
17 Dec.	Sat. in Embertide	Farnham par. ch.	diocesan	148^r-149^r
1329				
18 Mar.	Sat. in Embertide 1st week of Lent	Chertsey abbey	diocesan	149^v-150^r
8 Apr.	Sat. (*Sitientes*) eve of Passion Sunday	Walton par. ch.	diocesan	150^r
17 June	Sat. in Embertide eve of Trinity	Farnham par. ch.	diocesan	150^{r-v}
23 Sept.	Sat. in Embertide	Romsey abbey	diocesan	151^{r-v}
1330				
3 Mar.	Sat. in Embertide 1st week of Lent	Kingston par. ch.	diocesan	151^v-152^v
24 Mar.	Sat. (*Sitientes*) eve of Passion Sunday	Winchester cath.	diocesan	152^v-153^r
7 Apr.	Holy Saturday	Esher par. ch. (two persons ordained)	diocesan	153^r
22 Sept.	Sat. in Embertide	Farnham par. ch.	diocesan	153^{r-v}
1331				
23 Feb.	Sat. in Embertide 1st week of Lent	Southwark priory	diocesan	154^r-155^r
16 Mar.	Sat. (*Sitientes*) eve of Passion Sunday	Southwark priory	diocesan	155^{r-v}
30 Mar.	Holy Saturday	Southwark priory	diocesan	155^v
1332				
18 Apr.	Holy Saturday	Farnham par. ch.	diocesan	156^r
1333				
29 May	Sat. in Embertide eve of Trinity	Southwark priory	Benedict bp. of Sardica	156^r-157^v
18 Dec.	Sat. in Embertide	Farnham par. ch.	diocesan	157^v-159^r

Note: There were thirty-one ordinations – thirty-two if one counts the promotion of one man to the first tonsure in 1324. Of these, three (or four) were not "general" ordinations, being concerned only with the first tonsure. Of the twenty-eight general ordinations, all but five (one of them of one subdeacon only) were undertaken by Stratford himself. The number of those ordained was sometimes very small – two or even one – and large ordinations were rare, although there were over two hundred and thirty ordinands in Stratford's final ordination. No less than nine ordinations took place in Southwark, seven were in Farnham and three in Winchester cathedral, the remainder at various places throughout the diocese.

Appendix 3

Convocations, Provincial Councils, and Other Ecclesiastical Assemblies, 1334-1348

Although the scribes rubricating episcopal registers do not invariably make a distinction between convocation and provincial council, it is clear that the terms were not interchangeable at this time (e.g. *Exeter Reg. Grandisson*, p. 968, and see Kemp, *Counsel and Consent*, pp. 104-106). Apparently Reynolds did not hold a provincial council; indeed he was chary of doing so without the royal assent. Mepham, however, held two provincial councils (*Counsel and Consent*, pp. 97-100). Stratford summoned three such councils and a fourth assembly of a somewhat similar character. The king's attitude is revealed by the issue on two occasions of warnings not to infringe royal rights. The following table should be compared with that in Weske, *Convocation of the Clergy*, pp. 247-253, where the composition of each assembly is noted. Further references are to be found there. See also the printed registers of Bishops Shrewsbury (Bath and Wells) and Grandisson (Exeter); *HBC*, pp. 555-556; *Concilia* 2; and *CFR*.

	Type of assembly	Date, place and purpose	Grants	Abp.'s mandates	Royal writs	References
1	Clergy for parliament Convocation	19 Sept. 1334 St. Paul's, London		12 Aug. Lambeth	24 July Reading	WinRO 1, fols. 7ʳ-8ʳ, 13ᵛ; Worc. Reg. Montacute 2, fols. 2ᵛ-3ᵛ; Linc. Reg. Burghersh 2 (Reg. 5), fols. 481ʳ-482ᵛ; Salisb. Reg. Wyville 1, fols. 19ᵛ-20ʳ
		Business of the realm	Tenth (conceded			
2	Convocation	26 Sept. 1334 St. Paul's, London	at one or other assembly)		24 July Northampton (p.s.)	
		Purpose as above			(both incorporated in abp.'s mandate)	

	Type of assembly	Date, place and purpose	Grants	Abp.'s mandates	Royal writs	References
3	Clergy for parliament Convocation	11 Mar. 1336 St. Paul's, London Affairs of church and realm Clergy to come before abp. re business of parliament	Tenth	29 Jan. Bamburgh	22 Jan. Berwick	WinRO 1, fol. 33^{r-v}; Worc. Reg. Montacute 2, fol. 17^v; Linc. Reg. Burghersh 2 (Reg. 5), fols. 523^v-524^r
4	Convocation	30 Sept. 1336 St. Mary's Abbey, Leicester (prelates also summoned to great council at Nottingham for 23 Sept.) Urgent business of church and realm	Tenth	26 Aug. North-ampton	24 Aug. Perth	WinRO 1, fols. 43^v-44^r; Worc. Reg. Montacute 2, fols. 20^{r-v}, 38^v; Linc. Reg. Burghersh 2 (Reg. 5), fols. 539^v-540^v
5	Convocation	30 Sept. 1337 St. Paul's, London (also St. Bride's) (prelates also summoned to great council at Westminster for 26 Sept.) Defence of the realm in the king's absence	Three-year tenth	31 Aug. Lambeth	18 Aug. West-minster	Ely Reg. Montacute 2, fol. 38^{r-v}; Linc. Reg. Burghersh 2 (Reg. 5), fols. 550^{r-v}; WinRO 1, fol. 100c^{r-v}; *CFR 1337-1347*, p. 57
6	Quasi-legatine council	31 Jan. 1338 House of Carmelites, London (Cardinals Gomez and Montfavèz attempt to win bishops' support for papal peace policy)		None (cardinals' mandate 3 Jan.)	None	WinRO 2, fol. 20^v (dated January 1338/1339, an error followed by Weske, *Convocation of the Clergy*, p. 250)

	Type of assembly	Date, place and purpose	Grants	Abp.'s mandates	Royal writs	References
7	Convocation	1 Oct. 1338 St. Bride's, London (refers back to great council at Northampton on 26 July, in which defence of realm in the king's absence was discussed) King's financial requirements and anticipation of terms for tenths	Additional tenth	21 Aug. London (mandate of Robert Stratford as vicar general)	5 Aug. Northampton	WinRO 1, fol. 65^{r-v}; Linc. Reg. Burghersh 2 (Reg. 5), fols. 563^v-564^v; *CFR 1337-1347*, pp. 98-99; *Roch. Reg. Hethe*, pp. xxxvii-xxxix (Deliberacio cleri)
8	Convocation	27 Jan. 1340 St. Paul's, London (also Blackfriars) (prelates also summoned to Westminster parliament for 20 Jan.) For defence of realm and of royal rights	Tenth	15 Dec. 1339 Otford (sent to Orleton as dean of province on Bintworth's death)	28 Nov. 1339 Langley	WinRO 1, fols. 83^v-84^r; Linc. Reg. Burghersh 2 (Reg. 5), fols. 575^v-576^r; *Worc. Reg. Bransford*, pp. 289-290 (1142); *CFR 1337-1347*, p. 174
9	Provincial council	19 Oct. 1341 St. Paul's, London Preservation of ecclesiastical liberty; measures to be taken against "excesses" Lower clergy to come if their interests dictated or "si eis expediens videatur"		23 July Mayfield	None (1 Oct. prohibition against derogation of royal rights)	WinRO 1, fols. 106^r-107^r, 176^r (al. 48); Ely Reg. Montacute, fol. 64^r; *CCR 1341-1343*, p. 335

	Type of assembly	Date, place and purpose	Grants	Abp.'s mandates	Royal writs	References
10	Convocation	9 Oct. 1342* St. Paul's, London Warlike preparations against French and Scots Constitutions (2nd ser.) issued 10th	Tenth (conceded at this or next assembly)	23 Aug. Otford	15 Aug. Tower of London	WinRO 1, fols. 113ʳ-114ʳ; Linc. Reg. Bek 2 (Reg. 7), fols. 2ᵛ-3ʳ; *Worc. Reg. Bransford,* p. 205 (1043); *CFR 1337-1347,* p. 312
11	Provincial council	14 Oct. 1342 St. Paul's, London Correction and reformation begun in 1341 Sodbury case Lower clergy summoned "si eis utile videatur" Constitutions (3rd ser.) issued 16th		23 Aug. Otford	None	WinRO 1, fols. 114ʳ-115ʳ; Linc. Reg. Bek 2 (Reg. 7), fols. 1ʳ-ᵛff.; *Worc. Reg. Bransford,* pp. 205-206 (1044): ("general council" in rubric)
12	Convocation	31 May 1344 St. Paul's, London Onerous business touching king and defence of the realm	Three-year tenth	26 Apr. Lambeth	22 Apr. West-minster	Ely Reg. Montacute, fols. 91ᵛ-92ʳ; Linc. Reg. Bek 2 (Reg. 7), fol. 55ᵛ; *Worc. Reg. Bransford,* pp. 307-308 (1218); *Hereford Reg. Trillek,* pp. 6-9, 254; *CFR 1337-1347,* p. 384
13	Convocation or Provincial assembly (Council of bishops)	4 May 1346 St. Paul's, London Remedies for encroachment by laity, "novitates," and other urgent busi-ness of the church		23 Feb. Croydon 10 Mar. Lambeth (under S.'s p.s.)	None	Win. Reg. Edyndon 1, fol. 9ʳ; Ely Reg. Lisle, fols. 59ᵛ-60ʳ; *Worc. Reg. Bransford,* p. 131 (779); *Hereford Reg. Trillek,* pp. 15-16, 271-273, 275-278

* According to Weske, *Convocation of the Clergy,* p. 251, and Stubbs, *Constitutional History* 2, p. 392 n. 1, the royal writ stipulated 5 October, but the writ cited in episcopal registers gives the 9th.

Type of assembly	Date, place and purpose	Grants	Abp.'s mandates	Royal writs	References
	Anticipation of terms for tenth (not in abp.'s mandate) Only bishops summoned				
4 Convocation	16 Oct. 1346 St. Paul's, London Imminent perils to church and realm	Two-year tenth	15 Sept. Lambeth	8 Sept. West-minster	Win. Reg. Edyndon 2, fols. 10^v-11^r; Linc. Reg. Bek 2 (Reg. 7), fols. 86^v-87^r; Ely Reg. Lisle, fols. 62^v-63^r; *Hereford Reg. Trillek,* pp. 284-286; *CFR 1347-1356,* p. 33
5 Provincial council	1 Oct. 1347 St. Paul's, London Correction and reformation (Preamble refers to provincial council recently held in London) Lower clergy could come		30 July Lambeth	None (18 Sept. prohibi-tion against deroga-tion of royal rights)	Win. Reg. Edyndon 2, fols. 11^v-12^r; Linc. Reg. Gynwell 2 (Reg. 9), fol. 24^{r-v}; Ely Reg. Lisle, fols. 63^v-64^r; *Hereford Reg. Trillek,* pp. 306-308; PRO S.C.1/39/198

Appendix 4

Table of Stratford's Constitutions
and Concordance of Rubrics

A. Table of Stratford's Constitutions Glossed by Lyndwood

	Incipits (Lyndwood)	Wilkins' edition (caps. of 1341 draft in brackets)	Lyndwood *Provinciale* (1679 ed.)
1	Exterior habitus	703 c. 2	16
2	Hujus autem concilii	709 c. 17	18
3	Excussis	699 c. 8 (7)	90
4	Dierum invalescens	709 c. 16	97
5	Frequens perversorum	709 c. 15	104
5	idem	idem	114
1	Exterior habitus (repeated)	703 c. 2	122
6	In decimis	697 c. 4	133
7	Item quia archidiaconi	697 c. 3 (3)	140
8	Esurientis avaritiae	701 c. 12	143
9	Licet bonae memoriae	703 c. 3	154
10	Cordis dolore	706 c. 9	161
11	Statutum bonae memoriae	705 c. 7	171
12	Ita quorundam	706 c. 8	179
13	Adeo quorundam	698 c. 6 (1)	181
14	Quia saepe	706 c. 10	183
15	Erroris damnabilis	704 c. 4	187-188
16	Quanquam exsolventibus	704 c. 5	189-190
17	Immoderatae temeritatis	705 c. 6	191
18	Saeva et miserabilis (Wilkins: Nova et insatiabilis, as in [4])	696 c. 2 (4)	222

B. Concordance of rubrics for Stratford's constitutions (third series) in Salisbury Register Wyville with those in Wilkins, *Concilia* and BL Cotton MS Vitellius A.ii.

Salisbury Reg. Wyville 1, fols. 128ʳ-131ᵛ	Concilia 2, pp. 702-709; Cotton MS, not collated by Wilkins, in brackets
Prohemium: Sponsam Christi sacrosanctam	Sponsam Christi, sacrosanctam (Prohemium)
1 De pace ecclesie et regni Anglie conservanda	1 De pace ecclesiae et regni Angliae conservanda (De pace ecclesie et regni Anglie conservanda)
2 Rubrica: De honestate clericorum	2 De habitu et honestate clericorum (De honestate clericorum rubrica)
3 Rubrica: De dimissionibus beneficiorum ecclesiasticorum ad firmam	3 De dimissionibus beneficiorum ecclesiasticorum ad firmam (As in Wilkins)
4 Rubrica: De decimis et oblacionibus	4 De decimis et oblationibus (De decimis et oblacionibus)
	5 De sylva caedua decimanda (De silva cedua)
	6 De oblationibus per laicos occupatis (De oblacionibus a laicis nullatenus occupandis)
5 Rubrica: De testamentis	7 De debitis intestatorum solvendis (De testamentis)
	8 De testamentis et bonis testatorum et intestatorum
	9 De languidis in extremis sua bona in fraudem alienantibus et procurantibus (Contra donantes bona sua tempore mortis in fraudem vel eciam alienantes)
6 De vigiliis et exequiis mortuorum	10 Ne in vigiliis mortuorum fiant inhonesta (De vigiliis et exequiis mortuorum)
7 De celebrantibus matrimonia clandestina seu prohibita in ecclesiis oratoriis vel capellis	11 De celebrantibus matrimonia clandestina in ecclesiis, oratoriis, vel capellis (De celebrantibus clandestina matrimonia seu prohibita in ecclesiis oratoriis vel capellis)
8 De impedientibus iurisdiccionem ecclesiasticam et ecclesie libertatem	12 De impedientibus jurisdictionem ecclesiasticam (De impedientibus iurisdiccionem ecclesiasticam et ecclesie libertatem rubrica)

Salisbury Reg. Wyville 1, fols. 128ʳ-131ᵛ	Concilia 2, pp. 702-709; Cotton MS, not collated by Wilkins, in brackets
	13 De excommunicatis incarceratis sine praelato ecclesiae nullo modo liberandis (Contra dominos temporales usurpantes ius ecclesiasticum)
	14 De herbis et arboribus in coemiteriis crescentibus (Violatores libertatis ecclesiastice cense[a?]ntur qui contra voluntatem rectorum arbores de cimiteriis evellunt)
9 De violacione sequestri	15 De violatione sequestri (De violacione sequestrorum)
10 De impetrantibus et dolose prosequentibus brevia regia ut suos adversarios incarcerari faciant	16 De impetrantibus, et dolose prosequentibus breve regium contra adversarios in alienis comitatibus (De impetrantibus et dolose prosequentibus brevia regia ut suos adversarios incarcerari faciant et procurent)
[11] ... Huius autem	17 De publicatione constitutionum facienda (Conclusio finalis)

Note: Wilkins took his text from the now destroyed Cotton MS Otho A.xv, which he collated with Lambeth MS 17 (now MS 538), Ely MS 235 (now CUL MS Gg. vi 21), and Bodl. Lib. MS Digby 81. In other words his edition is derived from fifteenth-century copies. He was aware of BL Cotton MS Vitellius A.ii, which he used elsewhere. The index to fols. 1-6 of quire xlii, lost from the Winchester cartulary, precedes the text of the first volume as now rebound. It has been printed (*Winch. Chart.*, pp. 247-248) and given the date 1341. This index presumably incorporates the rubrics (twenty-one of them) from the lost quire, which suggest that the entry "De constitucionibus domini Johannis Cantuariensis archiepiscopi in suo consilio generali [sic]" was a conflation of the two sets of constitutions from 1342. Significantly, the distinguishing canon of the 1341 series (cap. 5 *De bigamia*) does not appear. However, in BL Harleian MS 52 is an entry which "combines the draft canons, as revised in 1342 (but including the chapter *de bigamia* then omitted)" with those chapters published in May 1343 by Stratford. Interestingly this MS has a Salisbury provenance. See Cheney, "Textual Problems," p. 127.

Appendix 5

Archiepiscopal *Acta* 1334-1348: a tentative list

Note: In this appendix and the following one "pp." and "fol(s)." have been omitted for the sake of brevity, except where confusion might arise.

For *acta* reference should also be made to Appendix 2 under Canterbury appointments and to Appendix 3.

A. Dated *acta*

Date and stated place of issue	Details	Reference
1334		
Feb. 6 Woodstock	Archbishop-elect's friendly letter to the Canterbury prior, promising to make his excuses for absence from the York parliament	CCL Reg. Q, 183^v (al. 187)
Mar. 30 Otford	Commission as archbishop-elect to Bishop Gravesend for an exchange of benefices	*London Reg. Gravesend*, 88^{r-v} (p. 257)
May 18 Senlis (cf. "Itinerary" under this date)	Request for Bishop Grandisson to licence the absence from the Exeter precentorship of Adam Murimuth, designated official of the Court of Canterbury	*Exeter Reg. Grandisson*, 276-277
June 12 Wingham	Letter requesting Grandisson to relax sequestration of church attached to the Exeter chancellorship (on behalf of Walter de Meriet)	Ibid., 274
June 22 Lambeth	Request to the same to remove inhibition (by reason of his privilege) against mandates of the Court of Canterbury	Ibid., 275-276
July 24 Lambeth	Prior of Canterbury forbidden to admit monks without archiepiscopal permission	CCL Reg. L, 68^r; *Lit. Cant.* 2, 160-161 (630)
Aug. 12 Lambeth	Mandate incorporating summons of clergy to parliament and convocation	*Concilia* 2, 575-576; and see Appendix 3

Date and stated place of issue	Details	Reference
Aug. 20 Lambeth	Mandate for attendance at the archbishop's enthronement	Worc. Reg. Montacute 2, 4ᵛ
Oct. 16 Charing	Request for consent of prior and convent of Christ Church to appropriation of Herriard church to Wintney Priory	*Winch. Chart.*, 261
Oct. 17 Charing	Sentence in Reculver-Herne dispute re burial rights	CCL R.20; Ducarel, "Fragmenta," 82ʳ⁻ᵛ
Nov. 23 Paris	Commission to M. Wybert de Littleton, chancellor, for execution of bull for appropriation of Chew church to *mensa* of bishop of Bath and Wells	*HMCR* 10, App. 3, 1, 442-443; *CPL 1305-1342*, 411
1335		
Jan. 11 Saltwood	Commission to Bishop Gravesend for an exchange of benefices	London Reg. Gravesend, 91ʳ (p. 257)
[Feb. 3-8 Canterbury]	Visitation of Canterbury Cathedral Priory: process incorporated in Simon of Charing's notarial instrument	CCL A.197; Reg. Q, 197ᵛ (201) - 198ʳ al. xxviii-xxix
Feb. 21 Dover	Appointment of Masters Astley, Littleton and Fastolf as auditors in the audience court	CCL R.20; Ducarel, "Fragmenta," 78ʳ
Mar. 6 Faversham	Letter to prior and convent of Canterbury opposing jurisdictional claims of the archdeacon of Canterbury	CCL Reg. L, 39ᵛ; *Lit. Cant.* 2, 81 (564)
May 8 Huntingdon	Recension of crusading bulls including *Non absque grandi*: levying of sexennial tenth, preaching, prayers and collections. Mandate for implementation by suffragans	WinRO 2, 9ʳ-14ᵛ; Linc. Reg. Burghersh 2 (Reg. 5), 509ᵛ-513ʳ, also 513ᵛ; Salisbury Reg. Wyville 1, 27ʳ-30ʳ
May 22 Acomb-by-York	do.	Worc. Reg. Montacute 2, 11ʳ-14ᵛ; cf. *Bath and Wells Reg. Shrewsbury*, 246-247
June 6 Acomb	Letter to prior and convent of Canterbury: is remaining in north and will keep horses loaned by them	CCL Reg. L, 109ʳ; *Lit. Cant.* 2, 96 (575)
[June 8 York]	[Witnesses confirmation of liberties of church of Winchester]	WinRO 1, 134ᵛ-135ʳ
June 11 Acomb	Letter to prior and convent of Canterbury answering queries and assuring them of his good health	CCL Reg. L, 108ᵛ; *Lit. Cant.* 2, 98-99 (578)
July 18 York	Request for intervention of secular arm in defence of M. Roger de Aston, whose right to Tong church had been upheld by Court of Canterbury	PRO S.C.8/267/13350

Date and stated place of issue	Details	Reference
Aug. 14 York	Request to prior and convent of Winchester for consent to appropriation of Herriard church to Wintney Priory (see above, 16 Oct. 1334)	*Winch. Chart.*, 271
Aug. 28 York	Letter to the prior and convent of Canterbury rejoicing in the tranquillity of their house	CCL Reg. L, 108^v; *Lit. Cant.* 2, 100-101 (580)
Oct. 22 Warkworth	Commission to abbot of Faversham as collector of sexennial tenth	CCL Reg. L, 191^r-194^r
Oct. 30 Warkworth	Letter to Bishop Grandisson explaining his absolution of the bishop's officers	*Exeter Reg. Grandisson*, 292-293
1336 Jan. 29 Bamburgh	Transmission of summons to parliament and mandate to attend convocation	*Concilia* 2, 581 and see Appendix 3
Mar. 15 Lambeth	Mandate to commissary general in Reculver-Herne case	CCL R.20; Ducarel, "Fragmenta," 79^r
Mar. 18 Lambeth	Mandate for correction in case of adultery	WinRO 1, 38^{r-v}
Mar. 21 Lambeth	Revocation on papal authority of collection of sexennial crusading tenth. Mandate to collect tenth for king "in necessariam defensionem ecclesie Anglicane"	Worc. Reg. Montacute 1, 34^r; cf. *Bath and Wells Reg. Shrewsbury*, 301
Mar. 23 Lambeth	Commission to Bishop Orleton for an exchange of benefices	WinRO 2, 52^v-53^r
Apr. 2 Otford	Mandate for collection of procurations of papal nuncios: Hugh, bishop of St. Paul-Trois-Châteaux, and Roland of Asti, canon of Lodi	Worc. Reg. Montacute 2, 18^v-19^r; WinRO 1, 36^{r-v}. Cf. *Bath and Wells Reg. Shrewsbury*, 281-282
Apr. 4 London	In conjunction with bishops of London (Gravesend), Winchester (Orleton), Lincoln (Burghersh), Rochester (Hethe), requests pope for postponement of payment of first year of sexennial tenth	*Rochester Reg. Hethe*, 423-424
May 4 London, New Temple	Commission to Bishop Burghersh for an exchange of benefices by reason of vacancy of Norwich diocese	Lincoln Reg. Burghersh 1 (Reg. 4), 215^v
June 10 Eynsham	Commission to Bishop Montacute for an exchange of benefices	Worc. Reg. Montacute 1, 23^v
July 2 Northampton, Abbey of St. James nearby	Commission to Bishop Burghersh for an exchange of benefices by reason of vacancy of Norwich diocese	Lincoln Reg. Burghersh 1 (Reg. 4), 386^v

Date and stated place of issue	Details	Reference
July 13 Stratford	Grant of land to Bishop Montacute in connection with foundation of Stratford chantry	Worc. Reg. Montacute 1, 59ʳii ff. (p. 129)
July 19 Stratford	Appointment of Robert Stratford as proctor to receive seisin of advowson of Stratford church	Ibid., 50ᵛii (p. 114)
July 19 Stratford	Appointment of the same to grant seisin of the advowson to John de Southwaltham, warden of Stratford chantry	Ibid., 51ʳii (p. 115)
July 21 Stratford	Letters patent of grant of Stratford advowson to John de Southwaltham as warden	Ibid., 50ᵛii-51ʳii (p. 114-115)
[July 30 Stratford]	[Bishop Montacute's ratification of appropriation of Stratford to the chantry, witnessed by the archbishop]	Ibid., 52ᵛii-53ʳii (p. 118-119)
Aug. 2 Stratford	Letters patent of grant of advowson of chapel of St. Thomas the Martyr, Stratford, to Bishop Montacute	Ibid., 58ʳii (p. 127)
Aug. 10 Kenilworth	Mandate enjoining prayers to be offered for royal success against the Scots: *Superni providencia iudicis*	Ibid. 2, 21ʳ (*Concilia* 2, 582); WinRO 1, 43ʳ⁻ᵛ; *Bath and Wells Reg. Shrewsbury*, 272; *Winch. Chart.*, 105
Aug. 14 Leicester	Instruction re payment of sexennial tenth to Bardi	Worc. Reg. Montacute 2, 17ᵛ (*Concilia* 2, 582); *Bath and Wells Reg. Shrewsbury*, 275-276
Aug. 20 Northampton	Further instruction re payment of tenth to Bardi	*Exeter Reg. Grandisson*, 295-296
Aug. 26 Northampton	Mandate for assembly of convocation at Leicester	*Concilia* 2, 582-583; and see Appendix 3
Sept. 27 Lenton	Mandate to Bishop Burghersh for an exchange of benefices by reason of vacancy of Norwich diocese	Lincoln Reg. Burghersh 1 (Reg. 4), 387ʳ
Oct. 1 Leicester	Reordination of Stratford chantry	Worc. Reg. Montacute 1, 53ʳii-56ᵛii
Nov. 8 York	Claim against prior for horse, being chattel of a felon	ccl Reg. L, 67ʳ; *Lit. Cant.* 2, 140 (609)
Nov. 27 York	Commission to Bishop Orleton for an exchange of benefices	WinRO 2, 56ᵛ
1337		
Jan. 29	Letter to king requiring return of William Rouland taken from sanctuary at Otford church and imprisoned at Maidstone	pro S.C.8/235/11719

Date and stated place of issue	Details	Reference
Feb. 11 Saltwood	Commission to Bishop Hethe for an exchange of benefices	*Rochester Reg. Hethe*, 570-571
Feb. 26 Lambeth	Letter to prior of Christ Church about appointment of a pententiary	CCL Reg. L, 107^r; *Lit. Cant.* 2, 144 (615)
Mar. 21 Lambeth	Revocation of sexennial tenth on papal authority	WinRO 1, 52^v; *Bath and Wells Reg. Shrewsbury*, 305-306
June 2 Uffington-by-Stamford	Mandate for processions and prayers for the king's success against the Scots	*Bath and Wells Reg. Shrewsbury*, 305-306
June 24 Uffington-by-Stamford	Mandate to prior for reconciliation of Canterbury Cathedral churchyard	CCL Reg. L; 67^v; *Litt. Cant.* 2, 155-156 (622)
July 24 Lambeth	Letter forbidding prior of Christ Church to admit monks without archiepiscopal licence	CCL Reg. L, 68^r; *Lit. Cant.* 2, 160-161 (630)
Aug. 31 Lambeth	Mandate for convocation	*Concilia* 2, 623; and see Appendix 3
Sept. 27 Lambeth	Letter to prior and convent of Christ Church announcing intended visitation	CCL Reg. L, 69^r; *Lit. Cant.* 2, 166 (636a)
Oct. 9 Mortlake	Commission to Bishop Orleton for an exchange of benefices	WinRO 2, 61^{r-v}
Oct. 26 Otford	Mandate to prior and convent of Christ Church and commissary general of Canterbury for excommunication of those impending sanctuary at All Saints, Canterbury	CCL Reg. I, 442^v-443^r
Oct. 27 Otford	Mandate re forthcoming consecration of Robert Stratford as bishop of Chichester	WinRO 1, 100D^{r-v}; Ely Reg. Montacute, 38^v; *Bath and Wells Reg. Shrewsbury*, 312
Dec. 27 Otford	Advice to prior of Christ Church to examine registers for procurations paid to papal nuncii in the past	CCL Reg. L, 70^r; *Lit. Cant.* 2, 174 (644)
1338		
Jan. 19 Lambeth	Mandate for pronouncement of excommunication and interdict in Romsey	CCL Reg. L, 70^v-71^r; *Lit. Cant.* 2, 179-183 (652)
Feb. 15 Lambeth	Letter to abbot and convent of Bury about diversion of a watercourse to the detriment of Christ Church	CCL Reg. L, 71^r; *Lit. Cant.* 2, 179 (651)
Apr. 16 Lambeth	Probate of Bishop Gravesend's will	Guildhall Lib. MS 66 A. 27
May 13 Lambeth	Mandate for excommunication of pirates for killing a cardinal's commensal chaplain and some thirty others in defiance for royal safe-conduct	WinRO 1, 60^{r-v}

Date and stated place of issue	Details	Reference
May 25 Lambeth	Mandate empowering commissary general to absolve fishermen from excommunication	Lambeth MS 241, 39ᵛ
June 14 Hadleigh	Mandate re forthcoming consecration of Richard Bintworth as bishop of London	WinRO 1, 62ᵛ
July 10 Dover, St. Radegund's Abbey	Appointment of Robert Stratford, bishop of Chichester, to act in the event of the election of a prior at Christ Church	CCL Reg. L, 104ᵛ; *Lit. Cant.* 2, 192-194 (661)
Aug. 26 Valenciennes	Letter to Prior Hathbrand of Christ Church accepting his election despite doubts as to the procedure	CCL Reg. L, 86ʳ; *Lit. Cant.* 2, 215 (679)
1339		
March 24 Antwerp	Mandate deprecating direct approach to bishops for taxation	WinRO 2, 30ʳ-31ʳ; *Bath and Wells Reg. Shrewsbury*, 357-358
May 5 Antwerp	Mandate for excommunication of those removing goods from ecclesiastical places	Salisbury Reg. Wyville 1, 53ᵛ; *Bath and Wells Reg. Shrewsbury*, 358; *Exeter Reg. Grandisson*, 914-915
Nov. 10 Canterbury	Recension of process of Prior Hathbrand's election	CCL C.1300
Nov. 30 Otford	Commission to Bishop Orleton for an exchange of benefices	WinRO 2, 79ᵛ
Dec. 9 Lambeth	Letter under archbishop's privy seal to Bishop Orleton for summoning convocation following death of Bishop Bintworth, dean of the province	Ibid. 1, 83ʳ
Dec. 15 Otford	Mandate to Bishop Orleton as acting dean of the province for summoning convocation	See Appendix 3
Dec. 29 Maidstone	Appointment of Alexander de Stratford to office of janitor in Christ Church	CCL Reg. L, 74ᵛ; *Lit. Cant.* 2, 217 (681)
1340		
Feb. 9 Lambeth	Confirmation of sentence in Reculver-Herne case	CCL R.20; Ducarel, "Fragmenta," 82ʳ-ᵛ
Feb. 13 Lambeth	Mandate re forthcoming consecration of Raph Stratford as bishop of London	WinRO 1, 86ᵛ-87ʳ
Mar. 13 *Chercham*	Mandate for citation of executor of Alice de Columbers	*Bath and Wells Reg. Shrewsbury*, 367
Mar. 27 Lambeth	Mandate to rector of Charing in case concerning prioress and convent of Davington	CCL A.36 IV, 4ᵛ

Date and stated place of issue	Details	Reference
Apr. 3 Lambeth	Confirmation to abbot and convent of Faversham of churches of Boughton-under-Blean and Preston-by-Ospringe	CCL Reg. L, 75^r; *Lit. Cant.* 2, 219-220 (686); Bodl. Lib. Kent Rolls 8, *ff*
Apr. 18 Lambeth	Mandate to commissary general re sentence of excommunication in tithes case	CCL A.36 IV, 4^v
Apr. 23 Lambeth	Appointment of M. Laurence Fastolf and M. Robert de Tresk as proctors in the curia	Ibid., 2^r
May 6 Lambeth	Letter to Bishop Hethe re "excesses" of abbot of Lesnes, sent under private seal	*Rochester Reg. Hethe,* 646
May 10 Lambeth	Mandate to dean of Sittingbourne for imposition of a penance	CCL A.36 IV, 61^r
May 12 London	Mandate to Robert Wyville, bishop of Salisbury, re execution of papal bull and sequestration of prebend	Ibid., 61^v
May 29 Lambeth	Mandate to commissary general for citation	Ibid., 60^v
May 30 Lambeth	Private letter, accompanied by charter of liberties, advising bishops to retain a portion of the tenth to repay cardinals' procurations	WinRO 1, 91^v; *Worc. Reg. Bransford,* 511-512. For the charter (among other places): Salisbury Reg. Wyville 1, 51^{r-v}; WinRO 1, 91^v-92^v
June 1 Lambeth	Letters patent of obligation of rector of St. Mary Aldermarychurch to pay an annual pension to Canterbury Cathedral Priory	CCL L.88
July 20 Lambeth	Intimation to Bishop Orleton of the archbishop's appointment of a prior of Twynham (Christchurch)	WinRO 1, 93^r
July 26 Lambeth	Letter to Bishop Orleton about Twynham appointment (above) and the sending of his chancellor, M. John de Lecch	Ibid., 93^v
July 30 Lambeth	Letter to Bishop Orleton for settlement of the dispute about Twynham)	Ibid., 94^r
Aug. 7 Maidstone	Further letter to Orleton suggesting despatch of his commission for appointment of the Twynham prior	Ibid., 94^r
Aug. 8 [?] Maidstone	Mandate to official of archdeacon of Canterbury for carrying out testator's wishes re celebration for his soul	CCL A.36 IV, 62^v
Aug. 12 Saltwood	Letter to Bishop Orleton detailing the compromise with respect to the Twynham election	WinRO 1, 94^v

Date and stated place of issue	Details	Reference
Aug. 19 Charing	Certification of process of election of prior of Twynham	Ibid., 94ᵛ-95ʳ
Sept. 26 Otford	Commission of administration of goods of James de Cobham to executors	CCL A.36 IV, 24ʳ⁻ᵛ
Oct. 12 Otford	Mandate to dean of Elham for citation	Ibid., 6ʳ
	Similar mandate to dean of Shoreham	Ibid., 6ᵛ
Oct. 19 Maidstone	Commission to Bishop Hethe for an exchange of benefices	*Rochester Reg. Hethe*, 666
Oct. 23 Maidstone	Mandate to official of Bishop Hethe for citation of abbot of Lesnes	CCL A.36 IV, 62ʳ
Oct. 26 Charing	Mandate to dean of Lympne for enforcement of payment of tithes	Ibid., 63ʳ
Nov. 7 Charing	Mandate re dispensation and promotion to orders	Ibid., 14ʳ
Nov. 19 Charing	Mandate for publication of Benedict XII's bull for peace, with grant of forty days' indulgence	WinRO 2, 35ʳ⁻ᵛ; Salisbury Reg. Wyville 1, 59ʳ⁻ᵛ
Nov. 20 Charing	Confirmation of Bishop Orleton's appropriation of Tytherington (Glos.) to Llanthony Priory	PRO C.115/K1/6683, 306ʳ-307ʳ
Nov. 21 Charing	Confirmation of appropriation of Barton Stacey church to the same	Ibid. 6681, 19ʳ-20ʳ
Nov. 22 Charing	Confirmation of appropriation of Kington church and its chapels to the same	Ibid., 29ʳ-30ʳ
Nov. 27 Charing	Confirmation of tithes from manor of Bransbury and Ford and from land in Barton Stacey granted to the same	Ibid., 20ʳ-22ʳ (cf. *Winch. Chart.* 323; WinRS, 23ᵛ, 34ʳ)
Nov. 29 Charing	Mandate to dean of Canterbury for enquiry	CCL A.36 IV, 22ʳ
Nov. 29 Charing	Mandate to bishops for collection of the biennial tenth and the discharge of cardinals' procurations from it	Ely Reg. Montacute, 52ᵛ-53ʳ; *Exeter Reg. Grandisson*, 931-932
Dec. 1 Charing	Mandate to commissary general re prior and brethren of St. John of Jerusalem	CCL A.36 IV, 17ᵛ
Dec. 10 Canterbury	Mandate to dean of Dover for citation	Ibid., 60ᵛ
Dec. 11 Canterbury	Stratford's arbitration between the bishop and the dean and chapter of Chichester about rights of episcopal visitation	WSRO Liber E, 196ᵛ-197ʳ
Dec. 20 Canterbury	Mandate to Robert de Valognes, rector of Northfleet, for holding an enquiry re violence of a priest who	CCL A.36 IV, 21ᵛ

Date and stated place of issue	Details	Reference
	continued to exercise sacerdotal functions	
Dec. 22 Canterbury	Decree concerning rights of Llanthony Priory in Barton Stacey (see above, 21 Nov.)	PRO C.115/K1/6681, 22ʳ-24ᵛ
Dec. 31 Canterbury	Mandate *Sacrosancta ecclesia* in defence of church liberties, with recension of sentences of excommunication published on the 29th	Salisbury Reg. Wyville 1, 60ʳ-61ʳ; WinRO 1, 99ᵛ-100ʳ; *Walsingham* 1, 237-240, collated by Charles Johnson with Rochester copy in *Rochester Reg. Hethe*, 653-655
1341		
Jan. 1 Canterbury	Letter remonstrating with the king about breaches of the charters and choice of unsuitable ministers: *Dominacioni vestre scire placeat*	*Foedera* 2, ii, 1143 (French); *Hemingburgh* 2, 363ff.; *Walsingham* 1, 231-234; *Avesbury*, 324ff.; and cf. *Rochester Reg. Hethe*, 653
Jan. 28 Canterbury	Letter to Chancellor Bourchier setting out the terms on which the additional tenth and the ninth had been granted	*Hemingburgh* 2, 367-369; *Walsingham* 1, 234-235
Jan. 29 Canterbury	Letter to suffragans about exaction of the ninth and tenth contrary to conditions of the grants: *Cum animosa guerrarum*	Salisbury Reg. Wyville 1, 61ʳ⁻ᵛ; WinRO 1, 100ᵛ, 101ʳ; *Bath and Wells Reg. Shrewsbury*, 428. Cf. *Rochester Reg. Hethe*, 657, collated with *Hemingburgh* 2, 371-375; *Concilia* 2, 659-660 (*Exeter Reg. Grandisson*, 937-938)
Jan. 30 Canterbury	Letter to suffragans denouncing those who oppress the church by exacting money not granted and urging maintenance of ecclesiastical liberties: *Christi legacione fungentes episcopi*	Salisbury Reg. Wyville 1, 61ᵛ; WinRO 1, 100ᵛ; *Bath and Wells Reg. Shrewsbury*, 428; *Concilia* 2, 659 (*Exeter Reg. Grandisson*, 937-939)
Mar. 8 Canterbury	Mandate to suffragans warning against quaestors who allege fabric of churches to be destroyed to the foundations "eciam si dicti domini archiepiscopi effigiem obtineant litterarum."	Salisbury Reg. Wyville 1, 65ᵛ-66ʳ; WinRO 1, 104ʳ (s.a. 1342); *Bath and Wells Reg. Shrewsbury*, 453

Date and stated place of issue	Details	Reference
Mar. 10 Canterbury	Letter to suffragans against publication of *libellus famosus: Purioris nitore luminis*	Salisbury Reg. Wyville 1, 67^{r-v}; WinRO 1, 102^{r-v}; *Concilia* 2, 670-671 (*Bath and Wells Reg. Shrewsbury*, 432)
Mar. 13 Canterbury	Letter condemning the incarceration of clerks: *Adhec nos Deus pretulit*	Salisbury Reg. Wyville 1, 64^{r-v}; WinRO 1, 103^{r-v}
Mar. 23 Maidstone	Request to prior of Canterbury for copy of mandate for collection of cardinals' procurations	CCL Reg. L, 75^v; *Lit. Cant.* 2, 238 (704)
Apr. 17 Canterbury	Confirmation of sentence in Herne-Reculver dispute	CCL R.20; Ducarel, "Fragmenta," 82^{r-v}
May 21 Lambeth	Commission as papal delegate to subdelegates for appropriation of Chew church	*HMCR* 10, App. 3, 1, 442-443, 550
June 28 Canterbury	Confirmation of composition between the parishioners of Reculver and Herne	CCL R.20; Ducarel, "Fragmenta," 82^v-84^r
July 17 Mayfield	Mandate for appointment of coadjutors to Bishop Orleton	*Winch. Chart.*, 525
July 23 Mayfield	Summons to provincial council at St. Paul's	See Appendix 3
Sept. 2 Mayfield	Renewed commission (see 21 May above) for Chew appropriation	*HMCR* 10, App. 3, 1, 442-443, 550
Sept. 24 Mayfield	M. John de Lecch appointed chancellor	CCL A.36 III, mm. 1^r, 3^r
Nov. 9 Mayfield	Notification to Chew parishioners of appropriation of their church to the *mensa* of the bishops of Bath and Wells. Ratification of process	*HMCR* 10, App. 3, 1, 442-443, 550
1342		
Mar. 4 Mayfield	Mandate to commissary general in case concerning tithes of great fish	Lambeth MS 241, 38^v-39^r
May 11 Lambeth	Mandate to Court of Arches with instruction for publication of statutes for the court	Black Book of Arches, 66^r-85^v; *Concilia* 2, 681-695
July 30 Canterbury	Augmentation of vicarage of St. Dunstan's, Canterbury, appropriated to St. Gregory's Priory	Somner, *Antiquities*, App. 75 (70b)
Aug. 17 Mayfield	Mandate directed against Archbishop Zouche's openly carrying his cross in the southern province	Lincoln Reg. Bek 2 (Reg. 7), 4^v
Aug. 23 Otford	Summons to convocation and provincial council at St. Paul's	See Appendix 3

Date and stated place of issue	Details	Reference
Aug. 23 Otford	Mandate for prayers and pious exercises on the king's behalf in response to writ *Terribilis in iudiciis*	WinRO 1, 116ᵛ-117ʳ; Lincoln Reg. Bek 2 (Reg. 7), 3ᵛ-4ʳ; *Worc. Reg. Bransford*, 206 (1045)
Sept. 23 Canterbury	Regulations for Eastbridge hospital and appropriation to it of St. Nicholas, Harbledown	CCL Reg. H, 88ᵛ-90ʳ; *Lit. Cant.* 2, 251-257 (719); Somner, *Antiquities*, App. 13-15 (17)
1343		
Mar. 9 Otford	Decision in dispute between dean and chapter of Lincoln re sequestration of prebends and dignities	LAO Dij/60/2/14, 16
May 19 Lambeth	Letter accompanying provincial constitutions with instructions to publish them	Salisbury Reg. Wyville 1, 128ʳ; Lincoln Reg. Bek 2 (Reg. 7), 39ʳ; *Bath and Wells Reg. Shrewsbury*, 463
Oct. 20 Immingham	Letter to suffragans about payment of procurations of ¹/₄d in £ to the cardinals	Lincoln Reg. Bek 2 (Reg. 7), 49ʳ⁻ᵛ; WinRO 2, 42ʳ⁻ᵛ; Salisbury Reg. Wyville 1, 121ʳ; *Bath and Wells Reg. Shrewsbury*, 480-481
Dec. 27 Immingham	Process against Louis of Bavaria incorporated in public instrument	Salisbury Reg. Wyville 1, 96ʳ-99ʳ
1344		
Jan. 9 Immingham	Mandate to suffragans for publication of papal process against Louis of Bavaria	*Ibid.*, 96ʳ
Mar. 27 Mayfield	Confirmation of M. John de Trillek as bishop of Hereford	*Hereford Reg. Trillek*, 1
Apr. 26 Lambeth	Summons to convocation at St. Paul's	See Appendix 3
June 13 Lambeth	Mandate for levying arrears of cardinals' procurations and those of bishop-elect of Norwich	Salisbury Reg. Wyville 1, 122ʳ-123ʳ; Lunt, *Financial Relations* 2, 638-639
June 21 Lambeth	Request to Bishop Bek for customary payment of a choir cope following his consecration	Lincoln Reg. Bek 2 (Reg. 7), 77ʳ
July 1	Agreement with John Darcy re the archbishop's franchise at Menhill, county York	Lambeth Cart. Misc. VI 80
1345		
Mar. 8	Mandate for collection of ¹/₄d in £2 for cardinals' procurations [incorporat-	Salisbury Reg. Wyville 1, 91ʳ⁻ᵛ, 123ᵛ-124ᵛ;

Date and stated place of issue	Details	Reference
	ed in mandate of official of Court of Canterbury]	*Exeter Reg. Grandisson*, 992-995
May 6 Mayfield	Mandate for caption of Thomas de Haselsshawe, brother of the rector of Chew	*Bath and Wells Reg. Shrewsbury*, 515
July 28 Lambeth	Signification of excommunication of four men from Lincoln diocese	Logan, *Excommunication*, 163-164 (PRO C.85/9/71)
Oct. 21 Lambeth	Letter requesting Bishop Hethe's assent to Edward III's foundation of a house of Dominican sisters at Dartford according to his father's intention	*Rochester Register Hethe*, 758
Dec. 19 Mayfield	Ordination of Hougham vicarage	Lambeth MS 241, 192^{r-v}
1346		
Jan. 15 Leicester	Mandate for collection of $^1/_4$d in £ for archbishop of Ravenna's procurations: *Pridem venerabilis*	Salisbury Reg. Wyville 1, 164^r; Ely Reg. Lisle, 55^r-56^v; Lincoln Reg. Bek 2 (Reg. 7), 78^r-79^r
Feb. 3 Lambeth	Mandate for levying of $^1/_4$d in £ for the above legate	*Hereford Reg. Trillek*, 63-66
Feb. 8 Lambeth	Mandate for citation of executors of Bishop Thomas Charlton (Hereford)	Ibid., 66-67
Feb. 10 Lambeth	Commission to abbot of Leicester for probate of will of Henry of Lancaster, without prejudice to the composition between Bishop Dalderby and Archbishop Reynolds (1320)	Lincoln Reg. Bek 2 (Reg. 7), 215^v
Feb. 13 Lambeth	Ordination of Chislet vicarage	*Thorne*, 2081 [has 5 Feb.], 2115-2116; ed. Davis, pp. 504, 555
Feb. 15 Croydon	Notification to his vicar general in spirituals and to the official of Winchester (both deputed by S. by reason of the vacancy) of Edington's appointment to Winchester	Winchester Reg. Edyndon 1, 3^r
Feb. 16 Croydon	Mandate for payment of $^1/_4$d in £ for procurations (cf. Jan. 15, Feb. 3 above)	Ibid., 5^v-6^r
Feb. 23 Croydon	Summons for convocation or council at St. Paul's	Ibid., fol. 9^r; *Concilia* 2, 727; and see Appendix 3
Mar. 4 Lambeth	Request for prayers and pious exercises for safe return of king's army	*Hereford Reg. Trillek*, 273-274; Ely Reg. Lisle, 58^{r-v}

Date and stated place of issue	Details	Reference
Mar. 8 [Lambeth?]	Ordination of Littlebourne vicarage	*Thorne*, 2108; ed. Davis, pp. 543-544
Mar. 10 Lambeth	Private letter deprecating novelties practised against the church and urging attendance at councils	*Hereford Reg. Trillek*, 272-273
Mar. 16	Ordination of Milton vicarage	*Thorne*, 2093-2094; ed. Davis, p. 523 n. 1
Mar. 20 Croydon	Mandate to commissary general re rector of Blackmanstone	CCL A.36 IV, 103^r
Mar. 21 Croydon	Appropriation of Leatherhead church to the prior and convent of Leeds, Kent	Bodl. Lib. Kent Rolls 8, *g, hhh*
Mar. 21 Croydon	Allotment of pension to the Winchester bishops following papal appropriation of above church to Leeds Priory	Winchester Reg. Edyndon 2, 3^v-4^r
Mar. 29 Lambeth	Letter urging anticipation of terms of last year of triennial tenth	*Hereford Reg. Trillek*, 268-269
May 10 Lambeth	Signification of excommunication of Richard Freiselle alias Fresel, clerk	*YB 20 Edw. III*, 219-220 no. 3
May 14 Otford	Letters testimonial as to the consecration and oath of fealty to the pope taken by Edington, bishop of Winchester	Winchester Reg. Edyndon 2, 54^r
June 8 Otford	Mandate for surrender by those detaining them of goods of the late Bishop Montacute	Ely Reg. Lisle, 60^v-61^r
June 26 Maidstone	Commission to Bishop Hethe for an exchange of benefices	*Rochester Reg. Hethe*, 787
Aug. 15 Lambeth	Condemnation of prior of St. Martin's, Dover, to pay six marks to vicar of Coldred	Lambeth MS 241, 251^v-252^r
Sept. 15 Lambeth	Summons to convocation at St. Paul's	*Concilia* 2, 728 and see Appendix 3
Sept. 16 Lambeth	Authority for Bishop Trillek to absolve from sentences for non-payment of legates' procurations	*Hereford Reg. Trillek*, 87-88
Oct. 25 Lambeth	Mandate to commissary general for payment of pension to vicar of Coldred	Lambeth MS 241, 251^r
Oct. 29 [Lambeth]	Recommendation for Order of St. John of Jerusalem notwithstanding aid given by some members to the king of France	*Hereford Reg. Trillek*, 289-290
Oct. 30 Lambeth	Private letter on the Order's behalf despite adhesion of French prior to king of France at Crécy	Ibid., 290-291

Date and stated place of issue	Details	Reference
Nov. 4	Ordination of vicarage of St. Mary Northgate in Canterbury	Somner, *Antiquities*, App. 73-74 (68)
Dec. 8 Lambeth	Mandate to commissary general re vicar of Coldred (see 15 Aug., 25 Oct.)	Lambeth MS 241, 251^v
1347		
Jan. 20 Lambeth	Commission to Bishop Hethe for an exchange of benefices	*Rochester Reg. Hethe*, 798
Apr. 12 Lambeth	Mandate for the denunciation as excommunicate of raptors of lady Margaret de la Beche from Beaumes manor	Winchester Reg. Edyndon 2, 7^{r-v}
Apr. 23 Lambeth	Letters testimonial re clause in will of Thomas Romayn, citizen of London, re right of presentation to Clapham	Ibid. 1, 24^r
May 4 Lambeth	Commission to Bishop Ralph of Shrewsbury for an exchange of benefices	*Bath and Wells Reg. Shrewsbury*, 541
June 9 Saltwood	Ordination of vicarage of Holy Cross church in Westgate, Canterbury	Somner, *Antiquities*, App. 74 (69)
July 8 Croydon	Mandate to the bishop of Lincoln for custody of goods of the earl of Warenne (Stratford an executor)	Lincoln Reg. Gynwell 2 (Reg. 9), 24^v
July 10 Lambeth	Signification of restoration of Richard de Weston as abbot of Dore	PRO S.C.8/235/11740
July 28 Lambeth	Sentence in dispute between Thomas, vicar of Farningham, and the prior and convent of Christ Church	CCL F.18
July 30 Lambeth	Summons to provincial council at St. Paul's	See Appendix 3
July 31 Lambeth	Mandate for citation of executors of late bishop of Lincoln, Thomas Bek	Lincoln Reg. Gynwell 2 (Reg. 9), 24^v
Aug. 9 Lambeth	Probate of will of Hugh de Hastings, knight	York Reg. Zouche, 319^r
Aug. 21 Headstone (*Heggeston*)	Sentence of suspension against rector of Eastling in pension dispute with Leeds priory	Lambeth Cart. Misc. XII 17
Dec. Otford	Mandate to Bishop Gynwell for citation of legatees of late bishop [Original, the base excised with loss of day of month]	Lincoln Reg. Gynwell 2 (Reg. 9), 39^r
1348		
Jan. 19	Citation of Bishop Trillek and co-executors of Bishop Orleton of Winchester	*Hereford Reg. Trillek*, 123-124

Date and stated place of issue	Details	Reference
Apr. 9 Lambeth	Mandate for prevention of misappropriation of goods of Hugh Audley, late earl of Gloucester	Bodl. Lib. Kent Rolls 8, *e*
May 4 Maidstone	Commission to bishop of Winchester to receive vow of chastity of Eleanor Giffard	Winchester Reg. Edyndon 2, 15^r
May 17 Maidstone	Mandate for the examination of witnesses in audience court case	CCL A.36 IV, 103^v
May 20 Maidstone	Confirmation of sentence in dispute between vicar of Farningham and Canterbury Cathedral Priory [see above, 28 July 1347]	CCL F.18; *Exchequer Ancient Deeds* (PRO E.211/519), 263
May 24 Maidstone	Arbitration in dispute between Bishop Edington and M. Richard Vaughan, archdeacon of Surrey	*Lydford* 134-141; Winchester Reg. Edyndon 1, 12^r-13^v
June 12 Maidstone	Ordination of vicarage of Croydon church, appropriated to Bermondsey Priory	Canterbury Reg. Courtenay, 176^v; Ducarel, "Fragmenta," 62^v-66^v
July 6 Mayfield	Acquittance granted to executors of Bishop Orleton (see 19 Jan.)	*Hereford Reg. Trillek*, 135
[Aug. 23 Mayfield]	[Death of Archbishop Stratford]	

B. Some undated *acta*

Note: I have not included a number of the undated *acta* in CCL A.36 IV concerned with routine court procedure, citation, etc.

Date and stated place of issue	Details	Reference
[May 1335]	Letter asking the prior of Canterbury to provide a palfrey for the archbishop's journey to York	CCL Reg. L, 109^r; *Lit. Cant.* 2, 95 (573)
[*post* 11 July 1337]	Indulgence of 40 days granted to those assisting Tonbridge Priory following the fire there	Bodl. Lib. Kent Rolls 7, *l* and cf. 8, *zz*
[1341]	Letter to the king and council about the imprisonment of clerks: *Quod cum omnes clericos capientes*	*Hemingburgh* 2, 369-371
	Ordinations of vicarages of:	
	Kennington-by-Ashford	*Thorne*, 2104-2105
[1342]	Northbourne	Ibid., 2081, 2111-2113
[1346?]	Preston-by-Wingham	Ibid., 2109-2110
1347 Lambeth	Probate of will of Thomas Bek, bishop of Lincoln	York Reg. Zouche, 311^v

Appendix 6

Itinerary 1323-1348

Note: No finality is claimed for the following itinerary. Only the outside dates of Stratford's stay in a particular place during any one month have usually been given.
In the "reference" column "pp." and "fol(s)." have been omitted (as in Appendix 5)
for the sake of brevity. In the case of *Lit. Cant.* the MS citation (ascertainable from
the printed edition) has been omitted. Fuller references for the *acta* are in Appendix
5.
Some difficulty arises from the use of lists of witnesses to charters (PRO C.53). It is
quite clear that on many occasions when a charter was tested by Stratford he was
not in fact present. None the less I have made considerable use of the handwritten
PRO list 25/50, but the "*at* Woodstock" etc. does not mean that he was necessarily
there. For Archbishop Reynolds' itinerary Robert Wright found fewer discrepancies than I have done. He has a useful "Note on the Charter Rolls," *Church and
Crown*, pp. 365-367.

Date	Place	Details	Reference
1323			
June 20	Avignon	Bulls of provision to Win-chester	*Foedera* 2, ii, 77; *RA* 19, 108^v-109^r; *RV* 75, 26^v-27^v
26	Avignon	Consecration by Bertrand, car-dinal bishop of Tusculum	*RA* 19, 81^v-82^r; *RV* 75, 46^v-47^r; WinRS, 1^r
July 12	Avignon	S.'s account as royal envoy: "quo die electus fuit in episcopum Wynton."	PRO E.101/309/27 m.3
Nov. before 22	Nottingham	Justice Scrope and Ayleston interrogate S.	PRO K.B. 27/255/Rex mm. 38^r-39^r; *Foe-dera* 2, ii, 89
23	Nottingham	Carmelite cloister. S. cited be-fore Staunton *ubicumque*	*Foedera* 2, ii, 90
25		S. fails to respond	Ibid., 89-90
28		S. appears before justices; declared guilty of double contempt	Ibid., 90
		Brings instructions as envoy into court. Case adjourned to 20 Jan.	Ibid.

Date	Place	Details	Reference
Dec. 7		S. comes into court in response to writ of 26 Nov. Adjourned as above	Ibid., 91
1324			
Jan. 20	Hereford	S. appears before Justice Staunton	Ibid.
Feb. 9	[Hereford?]	Appears again. Adjournment on account of king's writ of 15 Jan.	Ibid.
23	Westminster	Case continued in parliament	Ibid.
23-29	Southwark	Appoints as penitentiary M. Nicholas de Heytesbury, monk of St. Swithun's	*Winch. Chart*, 249; WinRS, 1^{r-v}
Mar. 7-30	Southwark	Ordination (10th)	1^v-2^r, 101^r, 140^{r-v}
		Appointment of officers; Chaddesley to act in consistory (19th)	
Apr. 1-7	Southwark		3^r, 89^v, 101^r
10	Ewell		3^v
11-14	Walton	Ordination (14th)	3^v, 141^r
20	Cobham		4^r
25	Frensham		4^r
30	Hursley		4^v, 90^r
May 4	Alton		90^r
5	Stoke-by-Guildford		90^r
7-16	Southwark	Audience court session	4^v-5^r, 90^v
23	Southwark		90^v
27-31	Battersea	Prelates, magnates, etc. at Westminster assembly. S. supports Canterbury province's petition for peace to pope	5^r; 90^v; *Roch. Reg. Hethe*, 339-341
June 1-13	Battersea	Audience court session	WinRS, 4^v, 10^r, 90^v, 101^r, 160^v
16	Southwark		90^v
26		S. said to be outside diocese	161^v
27	Penshurst		90^v
28-29	Tonbridge	Writs for livery of temporalities. S. performs fealty. Submits to recognizance (see below, 30th)	*Foedera* 2, ii, 101 ; *CCR 1323-1327*, 117, 198; *Vitae Arch. Cant.*, 19 (s.a. 1323)
29	Stockwell		WinRS, 90^v
30	Westminster	S. renounces prejudicial clauses in his bull	PRO S.C.7/56/17 (notarial instrument attached)
July 1		Admitted to his temporalities	WinRS, 182^r
2-3	Stockwell	Commission for Robert Stratford to receive homage, appoint temporal officers, and hold courts	90^v-91^r, 182^r

Date		Place	Details	Reference
	6	Wavcrlcy		91ʳ
	6-7	Durford (Suss.)		6ʳ, 91ʳ
	8-10	Southwark	Appointment of Thomas de Fulquardeby as treasurer of Wolvesey (8th)	6ʳ, 163ᵛ, 182ʳ
	13	Selborne (Hants)		91ʳ⁻ᵛ; York Reg. Melton 1, 101ᵛ
	15	Esher		WinRS, 91ʳ
	15	Battersea		10ʳ
	17	Stockwell		91ʳ
	18-20	Lambeth	Election of Walter de Lisle as prior of Selborne	6ʳ
	19-23	Stockwell		91ʳ⁻ᵛ
	28	Esher		5ᵛ
	31	Shalford		91ᵛ
Aug.	1-4	Shalford	Appoints coadjutor of vicar of Twyford	6ᵛ, 92ʳ, 182ʳ
	4-8	Guildford		6ʳ
	8	Esher		6ᵛ
	9	Southwark		182ʳ
	17-19	Southwark		7ʳ
	26	Esher		7ʳ
Sept.	13	Farnham		7ʳ
	21	Waltham		92ʳ
	30	Farnham		92ʳ
Oct.	2	Farnham		92ʳ
	3	Waltham		182ᵛ
	9-10	Farnham		7ᵛ, 92ʳ
	10	Stockwell		8ʳ
	21-28	Southwark	Assembly of prelates, magnates, knights, in London	8ʳ, 10ʳ, 92ʳ
Nov.	4-7	Stockwell		7ᵛ-8ʳ, 92ᵛ
	11-20	Southwark and Westminster	Cardinals meet king. Asssembly (S. present) of Canterbury province at Westminster	8ʳ; CCL Reg. I, 401ᵛ-402ᵛ; BL Egerton MS 2814
	23	Marwell		WinRS, 8ʳ, 10ʳ
	25	Winchester	Enthronement by William Inge, archd. of Surrey	8ᵛ
	26-27	Wolvesey		8ᵛ, 92ᵛ
	27-28	Cheriton		8ʳ, 92ᵛ
	29	Farnham		8ʳ, 92ᵛ
Dec.	1	Mortlake	Profession of obedience to Abp. Reynolds	Cant. Prof. 96, no. 272
	1-3	Southwark	Appoints vicars general (2nd)	WinRS, 8ᵛ, 9ʳ, 93ʳ
	4	Dartford		8ᵛ
	4-5	Rochester		92ᵛ
	7-8	Canterbury	Recitation of profession before high altar of cathedral (7th)	PRO E.101/309/27 m.1ʳ; Cant. Prof., 96 no. 272

Date		Place	Details	Reference
	10-11	Dover-Wissant	Crosses the channel on 11th	PRO E.101/309/27 m.1ʳ; WinRS, 92ᵛ
	ca. 26	Paris		PRO E.101/309/27 m.1ʳ
1325				
Jan.	13	Wissant-Dover		ibid.
	20-27	Southwark and Westminster	Meeting at Westminster (S. present) to discuss French negotiations	WinRS, 93ʳ; *War St. Sardos*, 195
	29	Stockwell	Benediction of abbot of Quarr	WinRS, 11ᵛ
Feb.	2-9	Stockwell		9ᵛ, 92ᵛ, 93ʳ⁻ᵛ
	14	Southwark	Appointment of vicars general. "Illo die arripuit iter suum versus Franciam."	93ᵛ, 141ʳ
	16	Newington		93ᵛ
	18	Dover-Wissant		PRO E.101/309/27 m.1ᵛ
Mar.		Paris		Ibid.
	22-24	Poissy	With Qu. Isabella and Bp. Ayrminne, John of Brittany	*War St. Sardos*, 267 (mainly from PRO E.101/380/9,10)
	30	Poissy	With Qu. Isabella and Bp. Ayrminne	Ibid.
	31	Poissy	Agreements drawn up by papal envoys and envoys of king of France	*War St. Sardos*, 199-205
Apr.	1	St-Germain-en-Laye		WinRS, 94ᵛ; PRO E.101/309/27 m.1ᵛ
	10-13	Wissant-Dover		Ibid.
	13	Southwark	Returns "negociis regiis feliciter expeditis"	WinRS, 10ᵛ, 94ᵛ
	14	London		PRO E.101/309/27 m.1ᵛ
	14	Beaulieu	With king "et cum maioribus regni per dies aliquot"	WinRS, 10ᵛ
	28	Winchester	King at Winchester on 27th	10ᵛ; BL Egerton MS 2814
	28-29	Wolvesey		WinRS, 10ᵛ, 144ʳ
		Wolverton (?)	Mandate to dean of Winchester to receive criminous clerks	*SCKB* 4, 162
	30	Marwell		WinRS, 95ʳ
May	2-3	Winchester	Response of king in presence of papal and French envoys. S. appointed to continue negotiations	*War St. Sardos*, 205-207
	5-6	Marwell		WinRS, 10ᵛ, 95ʳ
	8	Wolvesey	S. attends royal council at Winchester	*War St. Sardos*, 199-200; WinRS, 144ʳ
	16	Highclere		11ʳ
	18	Brightwell		*Worc. Reg. Cobham,*

Date		Place	Details	Reference
				102r, 262; WinRS, 95r
	21	Farnham		11v
	26-29	Southwark	Appoints administrator of hospital of St. Thomas, Southwark	11v, 12v, 95r
June	6	Stockwell		95r
	9-12	Southwark		11v, 12r-v, 95r
	23-27	Stockwell	Parliament at Westminster	11r, 95r
July	3	Stockwell		95v
	7-8	Southwark	Appoints vicars general (7th). Begins his journey abroad on royal affairs. S.'s decision re prior of Llanthony	95r; Worc. Reg. Cobham, 118r-119r, 235-237
	13	Dover-Wissant		PRO E.101/309/27 m.2r
Aug.	–	Jargeau	Queen there 21st (and 18 July)	Ibid.; War St. Sardos, 268
	–	Marchenoir	Queen there 22nd	
	–	Beaugency by Orléans	Queen there 23rd	
	–	Saint-Riquier		
	–	Châteauneuf-sur-Loire	Queen there 24th (and 18 July)	
Sept.	2	Châteauneuf-sur-Loire	S. dines with queen	War St. Sardos, 268
	14		S. appointed with Bp. Stapeldon and Beaumont as guardian of king's son	CPR 1324-1327, 174
Oct.	12	Wissant-Dover		PRO E.101/309/27 m.2r
	15	Sheen	S. reports to king	Foedera 2, ii, 144
	17-24	Southwark	Returns to diocese "negociis regiis expeditis." Appoints vicars general (23rd). Sets out on further journey to France	PRO E.101/309/27 m.2v (and for following dates)
	28	Dover-Wissant		
		Montreuil-sur-Mer	Queen there 30th	
Nov.	–	Noyon	(Letters sent to or from S. at this and following places)	
	–	Amiens		
	–	Senlis		
	–	Paris		
	–	St. Cristophe		
	18	Wissant-Dover		
	22-26	Southwark	"Venit ... de partibus transmarinis negociis regiis pro quibus ivit prospere expeditis" (22nd)	WinRS, 12v, 13v, 97r

Date		Place	Details	Reference
Dec.	3-5	Southwark		97[r]
	9	New Place (Guildford)		97[v]
	13	Farnham		97[v]
	21-29	Farnham	Ordination (21st) in parish church	12[v], 13[r], 97[v], 142[v]-143[r]
1326				
Jan.	1-2	Farnham		13[r], 97[v]
	5-20	Waltham	Preparations for primary visitation. Mandate to cathedral priory (11th)	12[v]-14[v], 143[r]
	22	Wolvesey		15[r]
	25-28	Waltham		14[r], 97[v]
Feb.	1	Marwell		14[r]
	3	Winchester	Visitation of cathedral priory	13[v]
	5	Wihchester	Preaches Ash Wednesday sermon in cathedral	15[r]
	6-13	Wolvesey	Licenses friars to hear confessions (13th)	15[r], 97[v]
	16	Winchester	Ordination in cathedral	143[r-v]
	16-23	Wolvesey	Visitation of Hyde Abbey (21st)	13[v], 14[r]
Mar.	1-5	Wolvesey		13[v], 14[r], 97[v]
	19	Wolvesey		28[v]
	29	Highclere		13[v], 98[r]
Apr.	8-10	Thelsford-by-Warwick		15[v], 98[r]
	14	Stratford-on-Avon		15[v]
	17-22	Witney		16[r], 98[r]
	28	Oxford		98[r]
May	14-16	Wargrave		16[r], 98[r], 144[r]
	29-31	Esher	Appoints deputies to act in Hyde Abbey case	98[r-v], 162[v]
June	2	Esher	Papal envoys with bishops at Canterbury (9th)	TCC R.5 41, 120[v]
	15-21	Southwark	Commission for Lecch to act in audience court	WinRS, 16[r], 98[v], 162[v]
	30	Wargrave		16[r]
July	1	Wargrave	Injunctions issued for cathedral priory	174[r]
	10	Merton Priory	Audience court case in chapel B.V.M. re Kingston vicarage	164[r]
	13-16	Stockwell		16[v], 98[v]
	18-20	Southwark		16[r], 99[r]
	21	Merton Priory		164[r]
	21-22	Esher	S. agrees to purchase 50 sacks of wool from Abp. Melton (21st)	99[r] (York Reg. Melton, 33[r])
	24-25	Farnham		16[v]
	27	Sutton		99[r]
	31	Waltham		99[r-v]

Date		Place	Details	Reference
Aug.	4	Winchester	S. suspends penalties imposed on cathedral monks	174^r
	8-9	Hursley		17^r, 99^v
	12	Downton		17^r
	15-29	Waltham		17^{r-v}, 99^v, 100^r
Sept.	2	Waltham	S. issues injunctions for St. Mary's, Winchester	177^r
	7-12	Farnham		18^v, 144^r
	13	Porchester (?)	Acknowledges obligation of £2000 to younger Despenser (by proxy?)	CCR 1323-1327, 647
	14	Farnham	Citation of friars to audience court	WinRS, 162^r
	15-17	Waltham	Session of audience court in chapel of manor (15th)	19^r, 164^v
	20	Kingsclere	Ordination	144^v
	21	Highclere	Minor ordination	18^v, 144^r
	24	Southwark	Qu. Isabella at Orwell haven	22^v
	30	London	Publication of bull of excommunication at St. Paul's	Ann. Paul., 315
Oct.	1-4	Southwark	Deprivation of warden of St. Elizabeth's college (2nd) Edward II leaves London	WinRS, 18^v, 19^r, 99^v
	6-10	Farnham	Abbot of Hyde before S. in audience court within parish church (7th)	19^r, 22^r, 144^r, 162^v
	12	Esher		100^r
	13-15	Southwark	S. at St. Mary's Southwark and later at Lambeth for assembly of bishops of Canterbury province. Murder of Bp. Stapeldon (15th)	19^v, 100^r; BL Cotton MS Faustina B.v, 47^v-48^r
	23-26	Bristol	At insurgents' recognition of Edward II's son as custos (26th) Appoints vicars general (23rd)	WinRS, 19^{r-v}; Foedera 2, ii, 169
Nov.	6	Hereford	Writ of appointment as deputy treasurer	PRO E.403/220 (Davies, Baronial Opposition, 568, no. 49); CMRE, no. 832
	14	Westminster	S. presents writ	Ibid.
	15-17	London and Southwark	Receives livery of seal (15th)	WinRS, 163^r, 211^v; Ann. Paul., 318; Appendix 1
	23-30	Southwark		WinRS, 20^v, 28^v, 100^r, 144^v
Dec.	5	Westminster	S. as deputy-treasurer issues commission	Cal. Inqu. Misc., no. 922
	5-22	Southwark	S. delivers jewels of younger Despenser to Qu. Isabella's wardrobe (5th).	CPR 1324-1327, 339-340; WinRS, 19^v, 100^r, 144^r-145^r, 163^r

Date		Place	Details	Reference
			Ordination in priory (20th).	
			S. said to have been at Guildhall making contribution to rebuilding of chapel	*Cal. Letter Books E*, 215
	25	Wallingford	S. said by Orleton to have been with Qu. Isabella	*Responsiones*, 2766-2767
	28-29	Brightwell	John de Rasne appointed to collect debts due to bp. and king from episcopal franchise	WinRS, 20ᵛ, 183ʳ
	31	Wargrave		21ʳ
1327				
Jan.		London	S. attends parliament at Westminster (7 Jan. - 9 Mar.)	See footnotes to "From Conformist to Revolutionary"
	16	Southwark	Excuses himself from convocation summoned to St. Paul's (for 16th)	WinRS, 21ʳ
	ca. 20	Kenilworth	With delegation sent to Edward II	
		[London]	Canterbury date for Edward II's renunciation of realm (24th). S. relinquishes deputy-treasurership (28th)	BL Cotton MS Galba E.iv, fol. 183ᵛ
Feb.	2-26	Southwark	S. assists at Edward III's coronation (1 Feb.)	WinRS, 21ᵛ-23ᵛ, 101ʳ, 144ᵛ, 183ᵛ; *Foedera* 2, ii, 172
			Cancellation of S.'s recognizances	*CCR 1327-1330*, 24, 93, 100
			Appointed member of embassy to France (22nd)	*Foedera* 2, ii, 180
Mar.	2-9	Southwark	Ordination in priory (7th). "Arripuit iter" (9th)	WinRS, 24ʳ, 101ʳ⁻ᵛ, 145ʳ-146ᵛ, 183ʳ
	10	Dartford	Appoints vicars general	25ʳ, 101ᵛ
		Dover-Wissant		PRO E.101/309/40
	15	Wissant		(inferred from "vadia nunciorum")
	20	Beauvais		
	29-31	Paris	S. seals treaty with France (31st)	*Foedera* 2, ii, 185-186
Apr.	6-29	Paris		PRO E.101/309/40 (and for following dates)
May	1-11	Paris		
	16-19	Clermont		
	30	Wissant-Dover	"Negociis regiis et regni Anglie ac pace terre Vascon' finaliter reformata prospere expeditis" (the account – PRO E.101/309/40 – runs to 31st).	WinRS, 26ʳ

Date		Place	Details	Reference
June	1	Canterbury		PRO E.101/309/40
	2	Wargrave (?)		WinRS, 102ʳ
	3	Rochester		26ᵛ
	8-25	Wargrave	Execution (8th) of Reynolds' mandate for peace: *Quoniam Scoti arma summentes*	PRO E.101/309/40; WinRS, 27ᵛ-28ʳ, 102ʳ, 183ʳ
	26	Southcot		178ʳ; *Winch. Chart.*, 251
July	2-5	Wargrave		WinRS, 28ʳ, 102ʳ, 183ʳ
	11-14	Witney		102ᵛ, 147ʳ, 183ʳ
	15-26	Wargrave		26ᵛ, 102ʳ
	29	York	With royal council and Qu. Isabella	*CCR 1327-1330*, 214
Aug.		Lincoln (?)	S. summoned to council re Scottish affairs (for 17th)	Ibid., 207-208
	21	Farnham		WinRS, 27ᵛ
	22	Alton		103ʳ
	23-30	Waltham		27ᵛ, 28ᵛ
Sept.	2	Hursley		28ᵛ, 102ᵛ
	2-11	Waltham	S. appoints proctors (11th) for Lincoln parliament (15th)	28ᵛ, 29ᵛ, 102ᵛ, 103ᵛ, 104ʳ
	15	Farnham		
	17-19	Downton	Ordination in chapel of bp.'s manor (19th)	32ʳ, 102ᵛ-103ʳ, 147ᵛ
	20	Twynham	Death of Edward of Carnarvon (21st)	*Winch. Chart.*, 139
	22	Knoyle		WinRS, 104ᵛ
	30	Rimpton		29ʳ
Oct.	8-12	Downton		29ʳ, 32ᵛ, 35ʳ, 102ᵛ-103ʳ
	12	Mottisfont		103ʳ
	13	Timsbury		33ᵛ, 104ᵛ
	19-22	Twynham		32ᵛ, 105ʳ⁻ᵛ
	26-27	Waltham		32ᵛ, 183ᵛ
	27-30	Highclere		33ᵛ, 102ᵛ
Nov.	1	Adderbury (*Abberbury*)		32ᵛ
	3	Aylestone	Return of summons to convocation (for 4th) at Leicester. S. one of those asked to act for indisposed Reynolds	WinRS, 29ᵛ; Cant. Reg. Reynolds, 207ᵛ (29 Sept., Otford)
	20	Farnham	Death of Archbishop Reynolds (16th)	WinRS, 147ʳ
	26	Southwark		28ᵛ
Dec.	6	Farnham		33ᵛ
	7	St. Denys, Southampton		103ʳ
	10-13	Farnham	Injunctions for Breamore priory (11th)	33ᵛ, 178ᵛ
	15	Newbury		104ʳ

Date		Place	Details	Reference
	20-21	Gloucester	Writ ordering respite for S. for 500 marks on acc. of wages while in royal service (Worcester, 23rd)	*CCR 1327-1330*, 241
1328				
Jan.	1-6	Waltham		WinRS, 33^{r-v}, 35^r, 103^r
	8	Bitterne		34^r
	15-25	Waltham	S. declares himself ready to set out for York parl. (19th). Interrupts visitation. Injunctions for Twynham priory (25th)	*Winch. Chart.*, 323; WinRS, 33^r, 34^v-35^r, 103^v, 147^r, 179^r-180^r, 183^v; PRO C.115/K1/6681, 15^r-17^r
	25	Crawley		WinRS, 35^v
	29-30	Witney	Appoints vicars general	33^r, 35^r, 103^v, 183^v
Feb.		York	S. attends parliament at York (7 Feb. - 5 Mar.)	103^v
	26-28	York		PRO C.53 (list 25/50)
Mar.	1-6	York	Borrows £100 from Abp. Melton (6th)	Ibid.; York Reg. Melton, 40^r
	9-15	Wolvesey		WinRS, 103^v-104^r
	18-19	Crawley	Ordination in parish church (19th)	147^r, 148^r
Apr.	2-6	Waltham	Ordination in parish church (2nd)	35^v-36^r, 38^r, 103^v
	8	Alton		36^r, 38^r
	9	Wargrave		106^r
	20-22	Wargrave		36^v-37^r, 106^r
	23	Wycombe	Parliament at Northampton (24 Apr. - 14 May)	106^r
	30	East Haddon		38^r
May	3-13	East Haddon		36^v-37^v, 106^v
		Northampton		PRO C.53 (list 25/50)
	14	Northampton	Acknowledges debt of 500 marks to John Grantham, citizen of London (mayor in 1329)	*CCR 1327-1330*, 386
	26-27	Wargrave		WinRS, 37^{r-v}, 106^v
June	1	Wargrave	S. "gravi infirmitate corporis prepediti." Gives approval but unable to attend consecration of bps. of St. David's and Bangor (12th, Canterbury)	37^v
	15	Highclere		38^r
	15-16	Wolvesey		38^r, 106^v
	17-20	Winchester		109^r
	24-30	Wolvesey	Resignation of Richard de En-	38^{r-v}, 106^v-107^r

Date		Place	Details	Reference
			ford, prior of Winchester (25th)	
July	1-5	Wolvesey		38^r, 39^r
	5	Wargrave		40^r
	8-13	Marwell	Examination of election process of prior of Winchester (conf. 13th)	38^r, 40^r, 107^{r-v}
	15	Winchester	Enthronement of Alexander Heriard as prior	107^r, 108^r
	16-31	Waltham	Parliament/Council summoned to York (31 July - 6 Aug.). S. appoints proctors (19th); busy with affairs of his church (cf. above, June 1)	37^v-38^v, 39^v-40^r, 110^r
Aug.	5-27	Waltham		38^v, 40^{r-v}, 110^r
Sept.	2	Waltham		40^v
	11	Higham Ferrers	Discussions with Henry, earl of Lancaster?	110^r
	14	London	At the Guildhall	*Cal. PMR*, 68
	(16	Wisbech)		PRO C.53 (list 25/50)
	17	London	Addresses citizens with Thomas Wake	*Cal. PMR*, 66, 68-69
	17-20	Southwark		WinRS, 40^v, 110^{r-v}
	23	Kennington		40^v
Oct.	6-13	Southwark		40^v, 41^r, 110^v, 111^v
	13-14	Farnham		40^v, 111^r
	16-17	Wolvesey		40^v-41^r, 111^r
	21	Salisbury	Salisbury parliament (16-31 Oct.) attended after opening stages by S.	PRO C.53 (list 25/50)
	25	Southwark (?)	[These entries do not coincide with the chronicle evidence]	WinRS, 41^r
	27	Wolvesey (1327?)		40^v 183^v
		Wilton	S. there during Salisbury parl. from which he flees (31st?)	*Vitae Arch. Cant.*, 19 (Lambeth MS 99, 136^r)
		Downton		Ibid. (MS)
Nov.	by 3	Winchester		Ibid.; *Cal. Inqu. Misc.*, 1039
		Waltham	S. said to have hidden in Waltham Chase	*Vitae Arch. Cant.*, 19 (Lambeth MS 99, 136^r)
	6	Brockhampton		WinRS, 111^v
	8-13	Wolvesey	Writ to sheriff of Hampshire (11th) to bring S. *coram rege* 20 Jan. for leaving parl. without licence	41^r, 41^v, 111^{r-v}; *CCR 1327-1330*, 420
	18	Farnham		WinRS, 112^r

Date		Place	Details	Reference
	20	Wolvesey		112^r
	28	Farnham		111^v
Dec.	6-7	Farnham	Mortimer leaves London with Qu. Isabella (1st)	41^v, 112^r
	17	Farnham	Ordination (to first tonsure)	148^r-149^r
	19	London	"Lancastrians" assemble in London, S. present	Ann. Paul., 343
	23-24	Southwark		WinRS, 43^r, 112^v
1329				
Jan.	1-2	Southwark		112^v
	2	London	S. at St. Paul's with "Lancastrians"	Ann. Paul., 344
	8	Guildford		WinRS, 41^v
	12	Farnham	Submission of "Lancastrians" at Bedford (ca. 19th)	112^v
	29-31	Southwark	Abp. Mepham's provincial council at St. Paul's (27 Jan. - 10 Feb.)	42^r, 112^v
Feb.	5-27	Southwark	Parliament at Westminster (9th-22nd)	42^{r-v}, 43^v, 113^{r-v}, 168^r; WAM 6672
			S. grants indulgence to those making pilgrimage to the relics at Westminster Abbey (22nd)	
Mar.	1	Staines		WinRS, 168^r
	6	Wargrave		42^v
	17	Wargrave		116^r
	18	Chertsey		149^v-150^r
	18-21	Walton		42^v, 113^v, 114^v, 116^r
	27	Kingston		114^r
	27-31	Walton		42^v, 114^r; PRO S.C.8/ 236/11778
Apr.	7-9	Walton		WinRS, 114^{r-v}, 150^r
	20	Chertsey		114^r
May	1	Witney		47^r
	5-9	Walton		114^{r-v}
	ca. 10	Westminster	S. defends himself in Court of King's Bench for withdrawal from Salisbury parl.	PRO K.B.27/276/Rex m.9^v
	25	Farnham		WinRS, 45^v, 114^v-115^r
June	3	Wintney	Election of prioress	115^r
	4-6	Farnham		45^v, 115^r, 211^v
	17-21	Farnham	Ordination in parish ch. (17th)	45^v, 46^v, 115^r, 150^{r-v}
July	1-12	Walton	Appoints Thomas de la More constable of Taunton (12th)	46^r, 115^{r-v}, 183^v
	19	Farnham		46^v
	20-22	Walton		115^v

Date		Place	Details	Reference
Aug.	2	Walton		115ᵛ
	6-18	Farnham		46ᵛ, 47ᵛ, 115ᵛ-116ʳ
Sept.	3-8	Waltham		47ʳ, 116ʳ, 183ᵛ
	19	Michelmersh		116ʳ
	20-23	Romsey		116ʳ, 151ʳ⁻ᵛ
	26	Chilbolton		47ʳ
Oct.	15-29	Walton		47ʳ⁻ᵛ
Nov.	2	Walton		47ᵛ
	3	Southwark		116ʳ⁻ᵛ
	15-16	Highclere		116ᵛ-117ʳ
	21	Wolvesey		116ᵛ
Dec.	1	Hurstbourne (Priors)		50ʳ; PRO C.115/K1/ 6681, 17ʳ⁻ᵛ
	5-19	Highclere		WinRS, 47ʳ, 116ᵛ-117ʳ
1330				
Jan.	8	Wolvesey		*Winch. Chart*, 148
	15	Cheriton		WinRS, 117ᵛ
	16	Selborne		117ᵛ
	17	Highclere		117ᵛ
	21-26	Southwark		53ᵛ, 117ᵛ-118ʳ
Feb.	1	Southwark		53ᵛ
	22	Esher		118ʳ
Mar.	3	Kingston	Ordination in parish ch.	151ᵛ-152ʳ
	15	Winchester	Parliament at Winchester (11-21 Mar.)	118ʳ
	21	Marwell		118ᵛ
	24	Winchester	Ordination in cathedral	152ᵛ-153ʳ
	25	Esher		118ᵛ
	26-31	Marwell		118ʳ⁻ᵛ; *Exeter Reg. Grandisson*, 561-562
Apr.	6-7	Esher	Ordination in parish ch.	WinRS, 153ʳ; PRO S.C.8/235/11722
	16	Esher		WinRS, 53ᵛ
	22	Southwark		53ᵛ
	25	Brightwell		118ᵛ
	27	Woodstock		PRO C.53 (list 25/50)
May	1-4	Woodstock		Ibid.
	20-31			WinRS, 118ᵛ, 119ʳ
June	1-28	Esher	Composition between A. & C. Chertsey and rector of Esher (18th)	51ʳ, 53ʳ, 119ʳ; *Winch. Chart.*, 130; *Chertsey Cart.*, 46
July	10	Marwell		WinRS, 119ʳ
	19-22	Esher		51ʳ, 52ᵛ, 53ᵛ
	26	Wargrave		119ʳ⁻ᵛ
	29	Farnham		45ᵛ
Aug.	1-29	Farnham	S. publishes sentences of excommunication in Alton parish ch. (19th)	45ᵛ, 49ʳ, 51ᵛ, 119ᵛ

Date		Place	Details	Reference
Sept.	2-20	Farnham		50^r, 52^{r-v}, 119^v
	21	Michelmersh (error for 1329?)		49^v
	22	Marwell		120^v
	22-24	Farnham	Ordination in parish ch. (22nd)	49^r, 153^{r-v}
	25	Esher		49^r
	26	Farnham		119^v
Oct.	2-4	Farnham		50^r, 120^r
	13	Southwark		50^r
	16	Nottingham (?)		PRO C.53 (list 25/50)
	22	Marwell		WinRS, 53^v
Nov.	1	Esher		54^r
	3	Southwark		53^v
	4	Farnham		120^r
	22	Wolvesey		
	26	Westminster Southwark	Parliament at Westminster (26 Nov. - 9 Dec.)	PRO C.53 (list 25/50); WinRS, 59^r
	28	Westminster Southwark	S. assumes seal as chancellor in royal palace	Foedera 2, iii, 52
	(30-24 Jan. 1331)		(charters witnessed by S. as chancellor at Westminster)	PRO C.53 (list 25/50)
Dec.	1	Westminster	Witnesses charter granting lands to John of Eltham, earl of Cornwall	WAM 1946
			Pardon of Henry of Lancaster and others; S. to cancel recognizances	CCR 1327-1330, 530-531
	5	Southwark		WinRS, 120^v
	10-31	Southwark		49^v, 52^v, 53^v, 120^v
1331				
Jan.			Letter from Winchester prior congratulating S. on his improved circumstances (9th)	Winch. Chart., 151
	11	Southwark		WinRS, 52^r
	15	Cheriton (1330?)		50^v
	17-29	Southwark		51^r, 52^v, 53^v, 54^r
	30-31	Esher		50^v
Feb.	1-9	Southwark	Election of prior of Mottisfont (8th)	53^v, 121^{r-v}
	10-28	Southwark	Ordination in the priory (23rd)	51^r, 52^v, 53^v, 54^r, 122^r, 154^r-155^r
Mar.	1	Eltham		PRO C.53 (list 25/50)
	13	Otford (?)		Ibid.
	14	Marwell		WinRS, 50^v
	16	Southwark	Ordination in the priory	155^{r-v}
	17-21	Marwell		50^v, 53^v
	25-30	Southwark	Ordination in the priory (30th)	54^r, 122^r, 155^v
	27	Esher		64^r

Date		Place	Details	Reference
Apr.	1	Southwark	Great seal placed in custody of Robert Stratford (until 7 May)	*Foedera* 2, iii, 62; *CCR 1330-1333*, 299
	2	Marwell		WinRS, 51^r
	4	Dover-Wissant	Embarks with king's flotilla	*Foedera* 2, iii, 62; *CCR 1330-1333*, 299
	7	St. Just-en-Chaussée		Déprez, *Les prélimi-naires*, 75-76
	12-16	Pont-Sainte-Maxence		Ibid.
	20	Wissant-Dover		*Foedera* 2, iii, 62; *CCR 1330-1333*, 299
	21-24	Wingham (?)		Ibid. and PRO C.53 (list 25/50)
	30	Southwark		WinRS, 52^v
May	(4-24)		(charters witnessed by S. *at* Havering)	PRO C.53 (list 25/50)
	8	Esher		WinRS, 51^r
	16	Farnham		122^v
	20	Esher		53^v
	21-22	Southwark		53^v, 122^v
	24	Southwark	"Episcopus Wynton. tunc cancellarius Anglie arripuit iter suum versus Norf[olk] et generales vicarios deputavit [24th]"	56^r, 122^v
	30	Bury St. Edmunds	Agreement before S. and others of the king's council (in Edward III's presence) in dispute between abbey and townsmen	*CCR 1330-1333*, 320
June	3	Norwich	Ordinances re Great Yarmouth dispute with John of Brittany	*CPR 1330-1334*, 124
	4	Bury St. Edmunds		PRO C.53 (list 25/50)
	11	Norwich	Enquiry before S. re rights of Great and Little Yarmouth	*Cal. Inqu. Misc.*, 1199 (PRO C.145/116/6)
	28	Lynn		PRO C.53 (list 25/50)
July	4	Lincoln		WinRS, 57^v
	(14-31)		(charters witnessed by S. *at* Lincoln)	PRO C.53 (list 25/50)
Aug.	2-4	Highclere	S. returns from Norfolk to his diocese.	WinRS, 57^v, 123^v
			Confirmation of process re appropriation of Barton Stacey (4th)	PRO C.115/K1/6681, 19^{r-v}
	6-21	Farnham	Augmentation of Chobham vic. (21st)	WinRS, 50^v, 51^v, 56^v, 58^r, 124^r; *Chertsey Cart.*, 68
	23	Selborne		WinRS, 58^v
	24-25	Marwell		71^v, 124^r
	28-29	Marwell		58^v, 59^r

Date		Place	Details	Reference
Sept.	3	Marwell		63ᵛ
	6	Highclere		63ʳ⁻ᵛ, 124ʳ
	11	Wargrave		62ᵛ
	21-27	Esher		64ʳ, 124ʳ
	30	Westminster	S. as chancellor opens parliament (30 Sept. - 9 Oct.)	*Rot. Parl.* 2, 60ff.
Oct.	(2-18)		(charters witnessed by S. *at* Westminster)	PRO C.53 (list 25/50)
	5-8	Southwark	Appointed with others to treat with Ct. of Guelders	*Foedera* 2, iii, 70; WinRS, 63ʳ, 64ᵛ, 67ᵛ, 124ᵛ
			Primary ordination of Stratford chantry (8th)	66ᵛ-67ᵛ (Worc. Reg. Montacute 1, 56ᵛii-57ᵛ)
	15-29	Southwark	Appointment of prior (25th)	WinRS, 62ᵛ, 64ʳ, 124ᵛ, 125ʳ⁻ᵛ
			Agreement for marriage with Ct. of Guelders (20th)	*Foedera* 2, ii, 75-76
Nov.	1-17	Southwark		WinRS, 62ᵛ, 63ʳ⁻ᵛ, 64ʳ, 75ᵛ, 125ᵛ
	16	Windsor (?)		PRO C.53 (list 25/50)
	17	Guildford		Ibid.
	23-27	Farnham	Henry Cliff and Robert Stratford custodians of great seal (21st)	WinRS, 64ʳ, 65ʳ⁻ᵛ, 126ʳ; *Winch. Chart.*, 436; *CCR 1330-1333*, 421
	30	Esher		WinRS, 126ʳ, 127ʳ
		Clarendon		PRO C.53 (list 25/50)
Dec.	1	Southwark		WinRS, 65ᵛ
	2	Southwark	S. sets out for France and	126ʳ
		London	appoints vicars general	PRO E.372/176/67ᵛ; *CCR 1330-1333*, 428-429
		Dover-Wissant		
1332				
Jan.	15	Bramford	S. returns to his diocese (16th)	PRO E.372/176/67ᵛ
	16-29	Southwark	Council at Westminster (20th)	WinRS, 64ʳ⁻ᵛ, 67ᵛ, 126ᵛ, 127ʳ
	(26-6 Feb.)		(charters witnessed by S. *at* Westminster)	PRO C.53 (list 25/50)
Feb.	1-28	Southwark	Bp. Grandisson lands at Sandwich en route from curia (9th)	WinRS, 65ᵛ, 67ᵛ, 68ʳ⁻ᵛ, 127ʳ; *Exeter Reg. Grandisson*, 638, 646
Mar.	12-31	Southwark	S. opens parliament at Westminster (16-21 March). Arrives late	WinRS, 66ʳ, 68ʳ, 73ʳ, 127ʳ⁻ᵛ; *Rot. Parl.* 2, 64ff.
		London		
	(16-27)		(charters witnessed by S. *at* Westminster)	PRO C.53 (list 25/50)

Date	Place	Details	Reference
Apr. 1	London	S. delivers great seal to Henry Cliff in house of Carmelites	*CCR 1330-1333*, 452, 550-551
3-7	Farnham		WinRS, 68v
14-22	Farnham	Ordination in parish ch. (18th)	128v, 156r, 186v
22	New Place (Guildford)		71r
23-27	Southwark	S. appoints vicars general and departs for France (27th)	68v, 69v, 128v, 132v; PRO E.372/177/40
	Dover-Wissant		PRO E.372/177/40
May	Wissant-Dover		
26	Woodstock		PRO C.53 (list 25/50)
30	Southwark	S. returns to his diocese	WinRS, 129r
June 6	Woodstock	S. reports on his mission to the king	PRO E.372/177/40
9	Woodstock		PRO C.53 (list 25/50)
	Witney	Warning of impending visitation sent to cathedral priory	WinRS, 69v
23		Robert Stratford given custody of great seal (until 17 Dec.: see below). S. said to be engaged on royal business	*Foedera* 2, iii, 79; *CCR 1330-1333*, 573
23-30	Farnham		WinRS, 69v, 71r, 73r, 129r-v
July 2	Farnham		71r
8-9	Wolvesey	Visitation of cathedral priory	69v, 73r, 129v, 130r
	Winchester		*Winch. Chart.*, 200; *York Reg. Melton* 2, 150 no. 398
10-13	Wolvesey		WinRS, 71r, 73r, 130r
(20-24)		(S. witnesses charters *at* Woodstock)	PRO C.53 (list 25/50)
20	Oxford	Mepham's summons to provincial council	WinRS, 74r
23	Godstow	S. excommunicates those breaching the park of the bishop of Bath and Wells at Dogmersfield	*Bath and Wells Reg. Shrewsbury*, 100
28	Esher		WinRS, 131r
Aug. 6-8	Southwark	Earl of Norfolk acknowledges deed of surrender of lands granted by king (5th)	72r, 74v; *CCR 1330-1333*, 587
12	Farnham		WinRS, 131v
16	Bishops Waltham		PRO S.C.1/39/1
17	Hambledon		WinRS, 131v
21	Waltham		75r
26	Crawley		74v
27	Highclere		74v
28	Esher		74r

Date		Place	Details	Reference
	30	Witney	S. excuses himself from attendance at provincial council on account of king's business	72^v
		Adderbury		74^v
Sept.	2	Northampton	Provincial council at St. Paul's (4th)	74^r
	9	Southwark	Parliament at Westminster (9-12 Sept.)	131^v; *Rot. Parl.* 2, 66-67
	(8-25)		(S. witnesses charters *at* Woodstock)	PRO C.53 (list 25/50)
	12	Waltham		WinRS, 156^r
	14	Farnham		74^v
	15-26	Southwark		74^v, 75^{r-v}, 131^v, 132^r
Oct.	2	Esher		132^v
	16-29	Farnham		74^v-76^r, 132^v
Nov.	3-24	Farnham	On account of illness S. appoints proctors for York parliament summoned for 4 Dec. (18th)	73^r, 74^v-75^r, 132^v, 136^r; PRO S.C.10/ 17/813
Dec.			Parliament at York (4-11 Dec.). Robert Stratford surrenders great seal until 8 Jan. 1333 in order to travel to Stratford (York, 17th)	*CCR 1330-1333*, 619-620
	26	Farnham		WinRS, 74^v, 132^v
1333				
Jan.	1-4	Reading		132^v, 133^r
	14	Doncaster		75^v
	22-30	York	Parliament at York (reconvened 20-27 Jan.)	74^v, 135^r; WSRO Ep. VI/1/6, 116^{r-v}; *Rot. Parl.* 2, 67ff.; PRO C.53 (list 25/ 50)
Feb.	1-7	York	Appointment of vicars general (7th)	Ibid. (PRO); WinRS, 76^r, 77^r, 133^r
	19	York	S. and others acknowledge debt of £1000 to Abp. Melton	*CCR 1333-1337*, 89
Mar.	10	Pontefract		PRO C.53 (list 25/50)
	18	Pontefract		Ibid.
Apr.	6	Helperby		Ibid.
	8	York		WinRS, 133*
	16	Durham		PRO C.53 (list 25/50)
May	5	York	Exchequer moved to York	WinRS, 133*
July	18-28	Berwick		PRO C.53 (list 25/50)
Aug.	2-3	Newcastle		Ibid.
	6	Northallerton		Ibid.

Date		Place	Details	Reference
	10	York	S. licensed to return to his diocese; surrenders seal in St. Mary's Abbey to Abp. Melton	*CCR 1333-1337*, 129-130
	12	Pontefract		PRO S.C.1/36/110
	23-31	Farnham	Returns to diocese eve of St. Bartholomew (23rd)	WinRS, 82^v, 83^r, 135^v
Sept.	3	Farnham		135^v
	3-13	Waltham		83^v, 84^r, 136^r
	17-18	Marwell		84^r, 86^r
	22	Bishops Sutton		85^v
	26	Chertsey		85^v
	30	*Coppedehall* (Copped Hall?)		86^r
Oct.	7	Canterbury		86^r
	13-25	Farnham		85^v-86^r, 87^r; PRO S.C.1/39/109
	25	Maidstone		WinRS, 85^v
	26-31	Farnham		85^v-86^r
Nov.	2-4	Wolvesey	Appointment of Robert of Chertsey as bailiff for life of soke of Winchester (2nd)	86^v, 138^r; *CPR 1330-1334*, 567
			S. postulated as abp. (3rd)	
	5-14	Farnham	Canterbury monks inform S. of his postulation (10th)	WinRS, 85^v, 86^r-87^r, 136^v, 137^r, 138^v
	17	Wolvesey		138^r; *Winch. Chart.*, 184, 420
	18	Clarendon	Kings sends letters to pope recommending S. as abp.	WinRS, 136^v
	26	Timsbury	(date of S.'s bulls of provision)	86^v
	28	Hursley		137^v
		Winchetser		*Winch. Chart.*, 437
	30	Wolvesey		WinRS, 138^r
Dec.	2	Wolvesey		138^r
	4	Winchester		88^r
	5	Wolvesey		138^r
	13-30	Farnham	Ordination in parish ch. (18th)	88^v, 138^v, 139^r, 157^v-159^r
			S. consecrates Richard de Bury as bp. of Durham at Chertsey (19th)	*Murimuth*, 71; *Biog. Oxon.*, s.v. Bury
1334				
Jan.	(4-10)		(S. witnesses charters *at* Wallingford)	PRO C.53 (list 25/50)
	15	Farnham		WinRS, 139^v
	26	Farnham		Ibid.
Feb.	1	Chertsey	Arrival of provisory bulls	*Vitae Arch. Cant.*, 20
	2	Woodstock	Mandate for livery of Canterbury temporalities (5th)	PRO C.53 (list 25/50); *Vitae Arch. Cant.*, 20

Date	Place	Details	Reference
6	Woodstock		CCL Reg. Q, 187^v
17	York	Chancery clerks deliver great seal to S. in St. Mary's Abbey	CCR 1333-1337, 296
21-28	York	Parliament at York (21 Feb. - 2 Mar.)	Ibid., 297; PRO C.53 (list 25/50)
Mar. 2-4	York	S. instructs Bp. Hethe to deliver pallium to York. S. receives £100 for expenses of forthcoming mission abroad (9th)	Ibid. (PRO); BL Cotton MS Faustina B.v, 75^r; PRO E.372/179/34
18	Northampton	S. appointed to continue diplomatic processes (26th)	PRO C.53 (list 25/50)
Apr. 6	Otford	S. delivers great seal to Robert Stratford	CCR 1333-1337, 309
	Charing		PRO E.101/311/6 (and for dates below)
8	Dover		
10	Wissant-Le Crotoy		
15	Montreuil		
17-20	Garde		
23	Rue prope La Garde	S. receives pallium from Bp. Hethe	BL Cotton MS Faustina B.v, 75^r
25	St. Riquier		
May 1-4	Creil (Craele)		
8-23	Senlis or St. Louis	(Identified by Déprez as St. Louis, hamlet of Egreville, Seine-et-Marne. But see text.)	Déprez, Études, 146-147; idem, Les préliminaires, 97 n. 1; PRO S.C.1/39/56-57; Exeter Reg. Grandisson, 269-271, 276-277
June 7	Le Crotoy-Dover		PRO E.101/311/6
10-12	Wingham		Exeter Reg. Grandisson, 274
22	Lambeth		Ibid., 275-276
July 5	Doncaster		PRO E.101/311/6
12-17	Nottingham		PRO C.53 (list 25/50); cf. Chronicon, 53
Aug. 5	Windsor		PRO C.53 (list 25/50)
12	Lambeth	S.'s mandate for convocation	E.g. Worc. Reg. Montacute 2, 3^v. See Appendix 3
20	Lambeth	Summons to attend S.'s enthronement as abp.	Worc. Reg. Montacute 2, 4^v
Sept. 13-30	Westminster	Parliament (19-23 Sept.) Convocation (26th) S. delivers great seal to Bp. Bury in royal palace (28th)	Ibid., 2^v-4^r; PRO C.53 (list 25/50); CCR 1333-1337, 346; and see Appendix 3

Date		Place	Details	Reference
Oct.	9	Canterbury	S. enthroned as abp.	BL Cotton MS Faustina B.v, 75ᵛ; *Vitae Arch. Cant.*, 20
	12-24	Charing		WinRO 1, 17ʳ; *Winch. Chart.*, 261; CCL R.20 (Ducarel, "Fragmenta," 79ʳ); PRO E.101/311/6 (and for dates which follow)
	26	Dover-Le Crotoy		
	30	Rue in Ponthieu		
Nov.	4	Poix (dép. Somme)		
	10	Beaumont		
	20-23	Paris		*HMCR* 12, App. 3, 1, 442-443
Dec.	8	Paris		PRO E.101/311/6 (and for dates which follow)
	19	Beaumont		
	22	Poix		
	24	Garde		
	29	Garde		
1335				
Jan.	?	Wissant-Dover		
	15	Saltwood		
Feb.	3-8	Canterbury	Visitation of cathedral priory	*Lit. Cant.* 2, 558; CCL A.197
	21	Dover		CCL R.20 (Ducarel, "Fragmenta," 78ʳ)
Mar.	6	Faversham		*Lit. Cant.* 2, 564
	26	Nottingham (?)	Council held to which S. summoned	*CCR 1333-1337*, 468
Apr.	20	Nottingham		PRO C.53 (list 25/50)
May	8	Huntingdon		WinRO 2, 13ᵛ
	20	York		PRO C.53 (list 25/50)
	22	Acomb-by-York	S.'s recension of crusading bulls	E.g. Worc. Reg. Montacute 2, 11ʳ-14ᵛ
	24-26	York	Parliament at York (26 May - 3 June)	PRO C.53 (list 25/50); *CCR 1333-1337*, 481
June	4-8	York and Acomb	Great seal handed to S. (6th), reappointed chancellor, in house of Friars Minor Witnesses confirmation of liberties of church of Winchester	*CCR 1333-1337*, 493; *Lit. Cant.* 2, 575; WinRO 1, 134ᵛ-135ʳ
	11	Acomb-by-York		*Lit. Cant.* 2, 578
	25	York	By indenture S. acknowledges debt to William de North-	*CCR 1333-1337*, 498

Date		Place	Details	Reference
			well on acc. of late Robert de Tauton	
	30	Newcastle		PRO C.53 (list 25/50)
July	2	Newcastle		Ibid.
	18	York		PRO S.C.8/267/13350
	29	Airth (Stirling)		PRO C.53 (list 25/50)
Aug.	5	Carlisle		Ibid.
	14	York		*Winch. Chart.*, 271
	23	York	Great council London (25th). S. too busy to attend	*Bath and Wells Reg. Shrewsbury*, 246-247
	28	York	(*Cal. PMR*, 92-93) (Note: PRO C.53 (list 25/50) gives S. as witnessing *at* Perth 20 and 27 Aug.)	*Lit. Cant.* 2, 580
Sept.	6	Linlithgow		PRO C.53 (list 25/50)
	18-24	Cockburnspath		Ibid.
Oct.	1	Bamburgh		Ibid.
	3-15	Berwick		Ibid.; *Foedera* 2, iii, 136-137
	21	Roxburgh		PRO C.53 (list 25/50)
	22	Warkworth		CCL Reg. L, 191^r-194^r
	29-30	Warkworth		*Exeter Reg. Grandisson*, 292-293
Nov.	1	Doddington (Northumberland)		PRO C.53 (list 25/50)
	15-26	Newcastle		Ibid.
Dec.	18	Bishop Auckland		Ibid.
	28	Newcastle		Ibid.
1336				
Jan.	11	Newcastle		*Cal. Inqu. Misc.*, 1447
	11-12	Berwick		Ibid.
	27	Berwick		Ibid.
	29	Bamburgh	S. summons convocation	E.g. Worc. Reg. Montacute 2, 17^v. See Appendix 3
Feb.	6	Knaresborough		PRO C.53 (list 25/50)
Mar.	(5-24)		(Charters witnessed by S. *at* Westminster)	Ibid.
	11	London, St. Paul's	Convocation	*Concilia* 2, 581. See Appendix 3
	15	Lambeth	Parliament at Westminster (11-20 Mar.)	CCL R.20 (Ducarel, "Fragmenta," 79^r)
	18-23	Lambeth		WinRO 1, 38^{r-v}; Worc. Reg. Montacute 1, 34^r; WinRO 2, 52^v-53^r
Apr.	2	Otford		Worc. Reg. Montacute 2, 18^v-19^r; *Bath and Wells Reg. Shrewsbury*, 281-282

Date		Place	Details	Reference
	4	London		*Rochester Reg. Hethe*, 423-424
	8-12	Waltham		PRO C.53 (list 25/50)
	13	Westminster		Ibid.
	16	London	S. determines dispute about dower between Margaret late wife of John de Bohun, earl of Hereford, and Humphrey de Bohun	*CCR 1333-1337*, 568-569; PRO C.53 (list 25/50)
	18	Guildford		Ibid.
May	1	Westminster		Ibid.
	4	New Temple, London		Linc. Reg. Burghersh 1 (Reg. 4), 215ᵛ
	4-6	Westminster		PRO C.53 (list 25/50)
	24	Westminster		Ibid.
	25-29	Woodstock	Council at Oxford (27th)	Ibid.
June	1-3	Woodstock		Ibid.
	10	Woodstock Eynsham		Ibid.; Worc. Reg. Montacute 1, 23ᵛ
	25	Northampton	S. present at royal council	*Rot. Parl. Inediti*, 240
July	2-9	Northampton, St. James's abbey		Linc. Reg. Burghersh 1 (Reg. 4), 386ᵛ; PRO C.53 (list 25/50)
	13-21	Stratford	Engaged in foundation of Stratford chantry (Note: PRO C.53 (list 25/50) gives S. as witnessing *at* Perth 1st, Nottingham 9th July)	Worc. Reg. Montacute 1, 50ᵛ(ii) ff.
Aug.	2	Stratford		Ibid., 58ʳ⁻ᵛ (ii)
	10	Kenilworth		E.g. ibid. 2, 21ʳ
	14	Leicester		E.g. ibid. 2, 17ᵛ
	20	Northampton		*Exeter Reg. Grandisson*, 295-296
	26	Northampton	S. summons convocation	E.g. Worc. Reg. Montacute 2, 20ʳ⁻ᵛ. See Appendix 3
Sept.	22-27	Nottingham		PRO C.53 (list 25/50)
	27	Lenton (Nottingham)	Great council at Nottingham (23-27 Sept.)	Linc. Reg. Burghersh 1 (Reg. 4), 387ʳ
	28	Nottingham		PRO C.53 (list 25/50)
	30	Leicester	Convocation of Canterbury province	*Concilia* 2, 582. See Appendix 3
Oct.	1-2	Leicester	Reordination of Stratford chantry (1st)	Worc. Reg. Montacute 1, 53ʳ (ii) ff.; PRO C.53 (list 25/50)
	3	Nottingham		Ibid.; WAM 1946
Nov.	8	York		*Lit. Cant.* 2, 609
	16-20	Bothwell		PRO C.53 (list 25/50)
	27	York		WinRO 2, 56ᵛ

Date		Place	Details	Reference
Dec.	6	Bothwell		PRO C.53 (list 25/50)
1337				
Jan.	3	London	Council. S. deputed with others to preside	*Foedera* 2, iii, 155-156
	10-15	London, Tower Westminster	S. celebrates requiem mass for John of Eltham (*Ann. Paul.* has 13th, *Hist. Roff.* 27th)	PRO C.53 (list 25/50); *Ann. Paul.*, 365; BL Cotton MS Faustina B.v, 79^v
	29	Otford	Visit from envoy John de Thrandeston	PRO S.C.8/235/11719; *Froissart*, ed. Lettenhove 18, 155ff. no. 41; *deutsch-englische Bündnis* 1, 484
Feb.	11	Saltwood		*Rochester Reg. Hethe*, 570-571
	17	Maidstone	Further visit from John de Thrandeston	Froissart 18, 155ff. no. 41; *deutsch-englische Bündnis* 1, 484
	26	Lambeth		*Lit. Cant.* 2, 615
	27	London, Tower		PRO C.53 (list 25/50)
Mar.	3-24	Westminster	Parliament meets (3rd) S. surrenders great seal, then delivered to his brother Robert (24th)	Ibid. *CCR 1337-1339*, 117
	21	Lambeth	Mandate for revocation of sexennial tenth	WinRO 1, 52^v
Apr.	1	London, Tower		PRO C.53 (list 25/50)
	18-22	Westminster		Ibid.
	28	Mortlake	S. present for oath of *custos rotulorum*	*CCR 1337-1339*, 130
	30	Westminster		PRO C.53 (list 25/50)
May	10	Mayfield		PRO S.C.1/39/54
	12	South Malling		Ibid., 1/39/55
	15	Mayfield		Ibid., 1/39/58
	30	Stamford	Council to which S. summoned	*CCR 1337-1339*, 129
June	1	Grantham		PRO C.53 (list 25/50)
	2	Uffington-by-Stamford		*Bath and Wells Reg. Shrewsbury*, 305-306
	16	Stamford		*CCR 1337-1339*, 131
	20-26	Stamford Uffington-by-Stamford		PRO C.53 (list 25/50); *Lit. Cant.* 2, 622
	28	Kingscliffe		PRO C.53 (list 25/50); *Placita de Quo Warranto*, 820
July	3	Westminster		PRO C.53 (list 25/50)
	10	Westminster		*CCR 1337-1339*, 140

Date		Place	Details	Reference
	15	London, Tower		PRO C.53 (list 25/50)
	21	Westminster	Council to which S. summoned	*CCR 1337-1339*, 139
	24	Lambeth		*Lit. Cant.* 2, 630
	25	London, Tower	Witness with Robert Stratford of Bp. Hemenhale's oath renouncing prejudicial clauses in his bull	*Foedera* 2, iii, 182
Aug.	8-25	Westminster London, Tower		PRO C.53 (list 25/50)
	31	Lambeth	S. summons convocation	E.g. Worc. Reg. Montacute 2, 38^{r-v}. See Appendix 3
Sept.	1-4	Westminster		PRO C.53 (list 25/50)
	27	Lambeth	Great council at Westminster (26 Sept. - 4 Oct.)	*Lit. Cant.* 2, 636a
	30	London, St. Paul's	Convocation	E.g. Ely Reg. Montacute, 38^{r-v}. See Appendix 3
Oct.	1-6	Westminster London, Tower		PRO C.53 (list 25/50)
	9	Mortlake		WinRO 2, 61^{r-v}
	26-27	Otford	Mandate for attendance at Robert Stratford's consecration	CCL. Reg. I, 442^v-443^r; Ely Reg. Montacute, 38^v
	27	Dartford		Ely Reg. Montacute, 38^v
Nov.	22	Westminster	S. witnesses earl of Salisbury's grant to his foundation at Bisham	*CCR 1337-1339*, 277
	28	Wingham	Robert Stratford's consecration and profession at Canterbury (30th)	PRO S.C.1/39/199
Dec.	16	Westminster		PRO C.53 (list 25/50)
	27	Otford		*Lit. Cant.* 2, 644
1338				
Jan.	19	Lambeth		*Ibid.*, 652
	31	London	Quasi-legatine council	WinRO 2, 20^v. See Appendix 3
Feb.	7-14	Westminster	Parliament (3-14 Feb.)	PRO C.53 (list 25/50)
	15	Lambeth		*Lit. Cant.* 2, 651
	21-26	Westminster		PRO C.53 (list 25/50); *Chichester Cart.*, 795
Mar.	2	Westminster		PRO C.53 (list 25/50)
	10-12	London, Tower		*Ibid.*; *Chichester Cart.*, 1074
Apr.	5	Langley		PRO C.53 (list 25/50)
	16	Lambeth		Guildhall Lib. MS 66 A. 27

Date		Place	Details	Reference
	22-24	Westminster		PRO C.53 (list 25/50)
	27	London, St. Paul's,	S. buries Bp. Gravesend in presence of the king, two cardinals, many bishops, priors, earls and barons	*Ann. Paul.*, 367
May	1	Westminster		PRO C.53 (list 25/50)
	ca. 21	Oxford	S. confirms election of Bintworth as bp. of London	*Historia Eduardi*, 418
	25	Westminster Lambeth		PRO C.53 (list 25/50) Lambeth MS 241, 39ᵛ
	28	Lambeth		PRO S.C.1/39/64
June	8	Lopham		PRO C.53 (list 25/50)
	14	Hadleigh		WinRO 1, 62ᵛ
	17	Ipswich		PRO C.53 (list 25/50)
	19-29	Walton	S. witnesses earl of Salisbury's charter founding Bisham Priory (Bisham, 21st), also Edward III's confirmation of liberties of the see of London (Walton, 25th)	Ibid. *Monasticon* 6, 527-528 Guildhall Lib. MS 8762
July	(1-13)		(S. witnesses charters *at* Walton) Robert Stratford surrenders great seal at Walton (6th). Bintworth made chancellor	PRO C.53 (list 25/50)
	10	Dover, St. Radegund's Abbey		*Lit. Cant.* 2, 661; CCL C.1300
	11	Dover- Wissant	S. embarks for France with Bp. Bury and the cardinals	PRO E.372/184/42; E.101/311/35 (and for what follows)
		Amiens Paris	(Note: S. was abroad until Oct. 1339 engaged with the cardinals in peace negotiations and in spying. Dates to plot his itinerary are few, but he seems to have been mainly at Arras.)	
[Sept.]			[Edward III with Emperor at Coblence]	
			S. appointed to negotiate with Philip, Antwerp 15 Nov.	*Foedera* 2, iv, 39
1339				
Jan.-Feb.			(Note: S. was at Arras, Valenciennes, Compiègne, Antwerp, Brussels, Diest, and various other places, but we have no precise dates.)	PRO E.372/184/42; E.101/311/35

Date		Place	Details	Reference
Mar.	4	Antwerp		CCL A.36 III, 2ʳ
	24	Antwerp		*Bath and Wells Reg. Shrewsbury*, 357-358; WinRO 2, 30ʳ-31ᵛ
Apr.	9	Antwerp	Guarantor of royal debt	*CPR 1338-1340*, 371
May	5	Antwerp		Salisbury Reg. Wyville 1, 53ᵛ; *Bath and Wells Reg. Shrewsbury*, 358
	10-13	Antwerp Malines	S. acts as guarantor of royal debts and witnesses grant to de la Poles	*Foedera* 2, iv, 46; *CPR 1338-1340*, 383-385
June	22	Brussels	S. as guarantor of agreement with John, duke of Lorraine	*Foedera* 2, iv, 47-48
July	1	Antwerp	S. at instance of cardinals among those appointed to negotiate peace	Ibid., 49
	22	Antwerp	Revocation of S.'s authority to treat with pope	*CPR 1338-1340*, 190
Aug.	4	Brussels	S. among those guaranteeing the king's agreement with the Bardi	Ibid., 391; WinRO 1, 159ʳ
	26	Valenciennes		*Lit. Cant.* 2, 679
Sept.	26	Marcoing	S. named principal councillor of duke of Cornwall. Pardon at his request of minor debts to exchequer	*CPR 1338-1340*, 394; *Foedera* 2, iv, 51
Oct.	⁓10	(Wissant-Dover)		
Nov.	5	Maidstone	(Apparently refers to 1339)	PRO S.C.1/39/84
	10	Canterbury		CCL C.1300
Dec.	8-9	Lambeth	Great seal brought from Southwark where Chancellor Bintworth died to S. at Lambeth (8th)	*CCR 1339-1341*, 339; WinRO 1, 83ʳ
	15	Otford	S. summons convocation	E.g. WinRO 1, 84ʳ. See Appendix 3
	17	Maidstone		PRO S.C.1/39/104
	29	Maidstone		*Lit. Cant.* 2, 681
1340				
Jan.	20	Westminster	Parliament (to 19 Feb.)	*Rot. Parl.* 2, 107ff.
	27	London, St. Pauls, Blackfriars	Convocation	See Appendix 3
Feb.			Parliament and convocation in session	
	9	Lambeth		CCL R.20
	13	Lambeth		WinRO 1, 86ᵛ-87ʳ
	14	Kennington		PRO C.53 (list 25/50)

Date		Place	Details	Reference
Mar.	4-6	Westminster		Ibid.
	12	Canterbury	Ralph Stratford's profession of obedience as bishop-elect of London before S. and his brother Robert	WinRO 1, 86ᵛ-87ʳ; *Cant. Prof.*, 101-102 no. 286
	13	*Chercham*		*Bath and Wells Reg. Shrewsbury*, 367
	27	Lambeth	Parliament at Westminster (29 Mar. - 10 May)	CCL A.36 IV, 4ᵛ
	30	Westminster		PRO C.53 (list 25/50)
Apr.	3	Lambeth		Bodl. Lib. Kent Rolls 8 *ff*; *Lit. Cant.* 2, 686
	4	Westminster	S. witnesses confirmation of privileges of St. Martin's-le-Grand	WAM 13159
	(4-25)		(S. witnesses charters *at* Westminster)	PRO C.53 (list 25/50)
	10	Westminster	S. witnesses confirmation of charters of Llanthony Priory	PRO C.115/K1/6681, 237ʳ-238ʳ
	18-23	Lambeth		CCL A.36 IV, 2ʳ⁻ᵛ, 4ᵛ
	28	Westminster	S. resumes great seal (28th)	*CCR 1339-1341*, 467; *Foedera* 2, iv, 72-73
	29	Lambeth		Ibid.
May	6	Lambeth		*Rochester Reg. Hethe*, 646
	7	Westminster		PRO C.53 (list 25/50)
	12	London		CCL A.36 IV, 61ᵛ
	18	Canterbury		Bodl. Lib. Kent Rolls 8 *hh*
	23-24	Westminster		PRO C.53 (list 25/50)
	29-30	Lambeth		WinRO 1, 91ᵛ; Worc. Reg. Bransford, 511-512; CCL A.36 IV, 60ᵛ
June	1	Lambeth		CCL L.88
	20	Orwell haven	S. fails to dissuade Edward from sailing. Surrenders great seal	*Foedera* 2, iv, 78; *Avesbury*, 310-312
	21	Shotley	Battle of Sluys (24th)	PRO C.53 (list 25/50)
July	12-16	Westminster	Parliament at Westminster (12th-26th)	Ibid.
	20	Lambeth		WinRO 1, 93ʳ
	25	Kennington		*Exeter Reg. Grandisson*, 63
	26-30	Lambeth Westminster		WinRO 1, 93ᵛ-94ʳ *Rot. Parl.* 2, 122
Aug.	3	Trottiscliffe	S. at Bp. Hethe's manor	BL Cotton MS Faustina B.v, 88ʳ

Date	Place	Details	Reference
7-8 (?)	Maidstone		WinRO 1, 94ʳ; CCL. A.36 IV, 62ᵛ
12	Saltwood		WinRO 1, 94ᵛ
13	London (?)		Rot. Parl. 2, 122
19	Charing		WinRO 1, 95ʳ
20	Maidstone		Ibid., 94ᵛ
Sept.		Truce of Espléchin (25th)	
26	Otford		CCL. A.36 IV, 24ʳ
Oct. 1		Council scheduled for punishment of "faux ministres"	WAM 12195; cf. CCR 1339-1341, 624
(1-12)		(S. witnesses charters at Wallingford 1st, 12th; at Andover 2nd, 8th)	PRO C.53 (list 25/50)
9	Lambeth		CCL. A.36 IV, 28ᵛ
12	Otford		Ibid., 6ʳ
19	Maidstone		Rochester Reg. Hethe, 666
23	Maidstone		CCL. A.36 IV, 62ʳ
26	London, Tower (?)		PRO C.53 (list 25/50)
Nov. 3-29	Charing	Mandate for publication of bull enjoining peace (19th) King lands secretly at Tower Steps night of 29/30 Nov.	CCL. A.36 IV, 14ʳ, 24ʳ, 26ᵛ; CCR 1339-1341, 640; Bath and Wells Reg. Shrewsbury, 425; Ely Reg. Montacute, 52ᵛ-53ʳ; PRO C.115/K1/6681, 19ᵛ-22ʳ; WinRO 2, 35ʳ⁻ᵛ
Dec. 1	Charing		CCL. A.36 IV, 17ᵛ, 34ʳ; Vitae Arch. Cant., 20
2-31	Canterbury, Christ Church	Arrival of Nicholas de Cantilupe (2nd) S. preaches and publishes sentences (29th) Mandate Sacrosancta ecclesia (31st)	Ibid., 20-21; CCL. A.36 IV, 21ᵛ; PRO C.115/K1/6681, 22ʳ-24ʳ; Bath and Wells Reg. Shrewsbury, 426-427
1341			
Jan. 1-30	Canterbury	Arrival of Ralph Baron Stafford (4th)	Foedera 2, ii, 1143; Hemingburgh 2, 363ff.; Vitae Arch. Cant., 22; CCL. A.36 IV, 11ᵛ; WinRO 1, 100ᵛ
Feb.	Canterbury	Publication of libellus famosus (10th-12th)	Vitae Arch. Cant., 27
18-21	Canterbury	Arrival of William Kilsby (18th). S. preaches sermon Ash Wednesday (21st)	Ibid., 22-23

Date		Place	Details	Reference
Mar.	8-14	Canterbury	Parliament summoned (3rd)	*Bath and Wells Reg. Shrewsbury*, 433; WinRO 1, 102^r-103^v
	23 (?)	Maidstone	["1341" supplied by editor of *Lit. Cant.* and accepted Lunt, *Financial Relations* 2, 625]	*Lit. Cant.* 2, 704
			Publication by king of *Cicatrix cordium* (31st)	
Apr.			Rapprochement of Emperor Louis and Philip leading to revocation of vicariate	*Froissart* ed. Letten-hove 18, 186-188ff. nos. 48-51
	17	Canterbury	Said to have been S.'s last day here (*Vitae*)	CCL R.20 (Ducarel, "Fragmenta," 82^v); *Vitae Arch. Cant.*, 38
	23	Lambeth		Ibid.
	24	Westminster	S. arrives for parliament (23 Apr. - 27/28 May)	Ibid.
May	(1-26)		(S. witnesses charters *at* West-minster)	PRO C.53 (list 25/50)
	3	Westminster	S. reconciled with king	*Vitae Arch. Cant.*, 40
	21	Lambeth		*HMCR* 10, App. 3, 1, 442-443
June	8	Hadleigh		PRO C.53 (list 25/50)
	10	Langley		Ibid.
	14	Westminster		Ibid.
	18-24	Woodstock	Intimation to king of rev-ocation of vicariate (25th, Frankfurt)	Ibid.; *Foedera* 2, iv, 104
	28	Canterbury		CCL R.20 (Ducarel, "Fragmenta," 82^v-84^r)
July			Council at London (12th)	*Foedera* 2, iv, 105-106
			Edward's response to emperor re vicariate (14th)	
	17	Mayfield		*Winch. Chart.*, 525
	23-24	Mayfield	S. summons provincial coun-cil	Ibid., 524, 528; Ely Reg. Montacute, 64^r; PRO C.85/9/44. See Appendix 3
Sept.	2	Mayfield		*HMCR* 10, App. 3, 1, 442-443
	20	Eastry		PRO C.53 (list 25/50)
	24	Mayfield	M. John de Lecch diocesan chancellor	CCL A.36 III, mm. 1^r, 3^r
Oct.	19	London, St. Paul's	Provincial council	E.g. *Concilia* 2, 680; *Murimuth*, 122, 223. See Appendix 3

Date		Place	Details	Reference
	23	Kennington Westminster	S. justifies conduct before king and barons	PRO C.53 (list 25/50) *Winch. Chart.*, 518
	31	Canterbury	Reconciliation with Kilsby at royal request	Ibid.
Nov.	5-9	Mayfield		CCL A.36 III, m. 2ᵛ; *HMCR* 10, App. 3, 1, 442-443
1342				
Mar.	4	Mayfield		Lambeth MS 241, 38ᵛ- 39ʳ
Apr.			Royal council at Westminster (29th)	
May	11	Lambeth	Statutes for Court of Arches published	Black Book of Arches, 66ʳ-85ᵛ
	29	Lambeth		CCL A.36 IV, 60ᵛ
June	14	Saltwood	Session of audience court be- fore S.	Ibid., 55ʳ
July	30	Canterbury		Ducarel, "Fragmenta," 59 (Somner, *Anti- quities*, App., 75)
Aug.	15	London	Cardinals' envoys arrive. King consults S.	*Murimuth*, 125, 227
	17	Mayfield		Lincoln Reg. Bek 2, 4ᵛ
	23	Otford	S. summons provincial coun- cil and convocation	E.g. *Bath and Wells Reg. Shrewsbury*, 452-454. See Ap- pendix 3
Sept.	23	Canterbury		*Lit. Cant.* 2, 719
Oct.	9	London, St. Paul's	Constitutions issued (10th) at convocation	See Appendix 3
	14	London, St. Paul's	Provincial council Constitutions issued (16th) King lands in Brittany (30th)	Ibid.
	21	Ibid., chapel of B.V.M.	Great council at Westminster (16th) Sodbury case	*Exeter Reg. Gran- disson*, 968
Dec.	14	Westminster	S. summoned to council meet- ing morrow of St. Lucy. Supersession of demand on S. for biennial tenth, prelates having granted a ninth for two years (15th)	Ibid., 612-613
1343				
Jan.			Truce of Malestroit (19th) until Michaelmas	
Mar.	1-2	Otford		WAM 9222 (and for fol- lowing dates in March)
	3-6	Maidstone		
	7	Otford		

Date		Place	Details	Reference
	8-16	Lambeth		(LAO Dij/60/2/14, 16
	17-18	Croydon		dated 9 Mar. from
	19	Otford		Otford)
	20	Maidstone		
	22-25	Canterbury		
	26	Charing		
	27	Maidstone		
	28-31	Otford		
Apr.	8	Westminster		PRO C.53 (list 25/50)
	18	Havering		Ibid.
	28	Westminster	Parliament (28 Apr. - 20 May)	Ibid.
May	(1-21)		(S. witnesses charters *at* Westminster)	PRO C.53 (list 25/50)
	19	Lambeth	S. sends copies of constitutions	E.g. Salisbury Reg. Wyville 1, 128^r. See Appendix 3
	24	Westminster	Witnesses *inspeximus* of grants to nuns of Sheppey	WAM 5107
	30	Westminster		PRO C.53 (list 25/50)
June	4	Westminster		Ibid.
July	26	Clarendon		Ibid.
Aug.	1	Clarendon	Writ permitting S. to take such armed men as necessary on journey to Canterbury (26th)	Ibid.; *CPR 1343-1345*, 115
	(20-24)		(S. witnesses charters *at* Westminster)	PRO C.53 (list 25/50)
Sept.	(15-20)		(S. witnesses charters *at* Westminster)	Ibid.
	20	Westminster	Attests charter reaffirming rights of abbot of Cirencester against townsmen	*Cirencester Cart.*, 123
Oct.	ca. 1	Norwich	S. attempts to carry out visitation of the chapter and diocese of Norwich	*Murimuth*, 147
	20	Immingham		E.g. WinRO 2, 42^{r-v}
Nov.	21-28	Westminster	S. attends council concerning papal negotiations and missions of Andrew Offord and John de Schordich	*Murimuth*, 147-148ff.
	28		S. returns to Norwich	Ibid., 147
Dec.	10	Norwich	Witnesses charter	Blomefield, *Norfolk* 3, 86-88
	16	Westminster		PRO C.53 (list 25/50)
	22	Westminster		Ibid.
	27	Immingham	Publication of processes against Louis of Bavaria	Salisbury Reg. Wyville 1, 96^r-99^r

Date	Place	Details	Reference
1344			
Jan. 9	Immingham		Ibid.
30		Royal prohibition against provisions	*Murimuth*, 153-154
Feb. 1	Westminster		PRO C.53 (list 25/50)
post 2	Otford	William Bateman, newly provided to Norwich, sent with royal councillors to S.	*Murimuth*, 157
(16)	London	Royal council: action to be taken against provisors	Ibid., 233
25	Westminster		PRO C.53 (list 25/50)
Mar. 27	Mayfield		*Hereford Reg. Trillek*, 1
Apr. 14	Westminster		PRO C.53 (list 25/50)
18	Westminster	Council. S. summoned	*Rot. Parl.* 2, 146; *CCR 1343-1346*, 350
23	Westminster		PRO C.53 (list 25/50)
26	Lambeth	S. summons convocation	E.g. *Hereford Reg. Trillek*, 6-9. See Appendix 3
May 4	Westminster		PRO C.53 (list 25/50)
31	London, St. Paul's	Convocation	See Appendix 3
June (1-23)		(S. witnesses charters *at* Westminster)	PRO C.53 (list 25/50)
13	Lambeth	Parliament at Westminster (7th-28th)	Salisbury Reg. Wyville 1, 122ʳ-123ʳ
21	Lambeth		Lincoln Reg. Bek 2, 77ʳ
July (1-11)		(S. witnesses charters *at* Westminster)	PRO C.53 (list 25/50)
Aug. 11	London	Council on return of earl of Derby from curia	*Murimuth*, 158-159
19	Westminster		PRO C.53 (list 25/50)
23	Westminster		Ibid.
Oct. 15	Westminster		Ibid.
23	Westminster	Secret council, S. present. Decision to send Thoresby and Spigurnell to curia (19th) Papal arbitration between French and English (22 Oct. - 29 Nov.)	Ibid.; *Murimuth*, 159; Déprez, "La conférence d'Avignon," 326 n. 5 (PRO C.81/300/16428); ibid., 305 n. 8
Nov.		Arrival of papal envoy John de Rippis who calls on S. (ca. 3rd)	*Murimuth*, 160
Dec. before 25	Orsett	S. in manor of Ralph Stratford to discuss papal negotiations	Ibid.
26	Norwich		PRO C.53 (list 25/50)

Date		Place	Details	Reference
1345				
Jan.	3	Norwich		PRO C.53 (list 25/50)
	10	London	S. at royal council. Decision to allow safe-conduct to papal envoys	*Murimuth*, 160-161
	12-20	Westminster		PRO C.53 (list 25/50)
Feb.	ca. 9	Teynham	Papal nuncios with S. and the king	*Murimuth*, 161
	ca. 20	Canterbury (?)	Prior to their departure (24th) papal nuncios stay at S.'s expense	Ibid., 162; cf. Lunt, *Financial Relations* 2, 639
Mar.	ca. 6	London	Secret council	*Murimuth*, 162
	8		Arrangements for cardinals' procurations	Salisbury Reg. Wyville 1, 123ᵛ-124ᵛ; *Exeter Reg. Grandisson*, 992-993
	10	Westminster		PRO C.53 (list 25/50)
	20	Windsor		Ibid.
	29	Guildford		Ibid.
May	6	Mayfield	Request for caption of parson of Chew's brother	*Bath and Wells Reg. Shrewsbury*, 515; *CCR 1339-1341*, 484-485
	7	Reading (?)		PRO C.53 (list 25/50)
	10	Westminster		Ibid.
	16	Eltham		Ibid.
	20	Westminster		Ibid.
		Lambeth	Homage to king performed by John de Montfort, duke of Brittany	*Foedera* 2, iv, 177; *CCR 1343-1346*, 569
June	15	Westminster		PRO C.53 (list 25/50)
	16	London, Tower		Ibid.
	25	Sandwich		Ibid.
July	6	Reading	Death of Bp. Orleton (18th)	Ibid.
	28	Lambeth	Signification of excommunication	Logan, *Excommunication*, 163-164 (PRO C.85/9/71)
Aug.	7	Otford	Consecration of Thomas Hatfield, bp. of Durham	*Murimuth*, 172
	9	Hertford	Witnesses Norwich charter	Blomefield, *Norfolk* 3, 89-92; PRO C.53 (list 25/50)
	26	Westminster		Ibid.; *CCR 1343-1346*, 604
	31	Westminster	Debtors acknowledge sum due to S. in his presence	*CCR 1343-1346*, 649
Oct.	(4-26)		(S. witnesses charters *at* Westminster)	PRO C.53 (list 25/50)
	16	Westminster	S. attends (with other "secret councillors") meeting for discussion of papal letters	*Murimuth*, 177

Date		Place	Details	Reference
	21	Lambeth		*Rochester Reg. Hethe*, 758
	26	Westminster	John Offord made chancellor (26th)	*CCR 1343-1346*, 661
Nov.	5	Mortlake		PRO C.53 (list 25/50)
	8		S. with bps. of London and Norwich to receive papal nuncio, abp. of Ravenna	*Foedera* 2, iv, 188; cf. Lunt, *Financial Relations* 2, 639-640
Dec.	7	Clipstone		PRO C.53 (list 25/50)
	18	Westminster	Present with Robert Stratford at audience for papal nuncio	*Murimuth*, 190
	19	Mayfield		Lambeth MS 241, 192^{r-v}
1346				
Jan.	15	Leicester	Council. Mandate for cardinal's procurations	Ely Reg. Lisle, 55^r-56^v; Salisbury Reg. Wyville 1, 164^r
Feb.	1-6	Westminster	Council at Westminster (3rd)	PRO C.53 (list 25/50)
	8-13	Lambeth		*Hereford Reg. Trillek*, 66-67; *Thorne*, 2115-2116; *Bath and Wells Reg. Shrewsbury*, 524-525
	15-16	Croydon		Winchester Reg. Edyndon 1, 3^r, 5^v-6^r
	(16)		(S. witnesses charters *at* Westminster)	PRO C.53 (list 25/50)
	23	Croydon	S. summons convocation or council	*Bath and Wells Reg. Shrewsbury*, 526. See Appendix 3
Mar.	4	Lambeth	Prayers enjoined for king's safe return	*Hereford Reg. Trillek*, 273-274
	8	(Lambeth?)		*Thorne*, 2108
	10	Lambeth	S. deprecates novelties injuring rights of church	*Hereford Reg. Trillek*, 272-273
	20-21	Croydon		Winchester Reg. Edyndon 2, 4^r; CCL A.36 IV, 103^r; Bodl. Lib. Kent Rolls 8, *hhh*
	23-29	Westminster		PRO C.53 (list 25/50)
	29	Lambeth		*Hereford Reg. Trillek*, 268-269
Apr.	2	Lambeth		Ibid., 63-66
	11	London, Tower		PRO C.53 (list 25/50)
May	1	London, Tower		Ibid.
	4	London, St. Paul's	Convocation or council	E.g. Winchester Reg. Edyndon 1, 9^r. See Appendix 3

Date		Place	Details	Reference
	10	Lambeth	Signification of excommunication	*YB 20 Edward III*, 219-220
	14	Otford	S. consecrates (with Ralph S. of London and Robert S. of Chichester) Edington as bp. of Winchester	*Murimuth*, 192; Winchester Reg. Edyndon 2, 54ʳ; *Le Neve* 4, 46
June	(6-7)		(S. witnesses charters *at* Porchester)	PRO C.53 (list 25/50)
	8	Otford		Ely Reg. Lisle, 60ᵛ-61ʳ
	(20-28)		(S. witnesses charters *at* Porchester)	PRO C.53 (list 25/50)
	26	Maidstone		*Rochester Reg. Hethe*, 787
July	1	(from Porchester)	Appointed to treat with merchants for loans to king	*Foedera* 2, iv, 202
	11	(from St. Helen's, Isle of Wight)	S. with Bps. Edington and Ralph Stratford to negotiate with envoys of Hungary and Spain	Ibid.
	(12-16)		(S. witnesses charters *at* Windsor)	PRO C.53 (list 25/50)
Aug.	12	London	S. publishes invasion plan captured at Caen	*Murimuth*, 211
	15	Lambeth	Battle of Crécy (26th)	Lambeth MS 241, 251ᵛ-252ʳ
Sept.			Parliament at Westminster (11-20 Sept.)	*Rot. Parl.* 2, 157ff.
	15-16	Lambeth	S. summons convocation (15th)	E.g. *Hereford Reg. Trillek*, 284-286; ibid., 87-88. See Appendix 3
	20	Westminster	S. witnesses charter of liberties for bp. of Bath and Wells	*CChR 1341-1417*, 52; *SCKB* 6, 121-122
Oct.	16	London, St. Paul's	Convocation	E.g. Lincoln Reg. Bek 2, 86ᵛ-87ʳ. See Appendix 3
			Battle of Neville's Cross (17th)	*Murimuth*, 218
	25	Lambeth		Lambeth MS 241, 251ʳ
	27	Westminster		PRO S.C.1/56/6
	29-30	[Lambeth]	S. recommends Order of St. John	*Hereford Reg. Trillek*, 289-291
Nov.	4			Ducarel, "Fragmenta," 59ᵛ; Somner, *Antiquities*, App., 73-74
	18	London, Tower		PRO C.53 (list 25/50)
Dec.	8	Lambeth		Lambeth MS 241, 251ᵛ
	29	Eltham		PRO C.53 (list 25/50)
1347				
Jan.	1	Eltham		Ibid.

Date	Place	Details	Reference
20	Lambeth		*Rochester Reg. Hethe,* 798
Mar. 26	Westminster		PRO C.53 (list 25/50)
		Great council at Westminster (3rd): loan to king of 20,000 sacks of wool	*CFR 1347-1356,* 1-2; Lloyd, *English Wool Trade,* 200-201
27	Reading		PRO C.53 (list 25/50)
Apr. 12	Lambeth*		Winchester Reg. Edyndon 2, 7^{r-v}
19	Reading		PRO C.53 (list 25/50)
May 4	Lambeth		*Bath and Wells Reg. Shrewsbury,* 541
8-30	Reading		PRO C.53 (list 25/50)
June 9	Saltwood		Ducarel, "Fragmenta," 59^v (Somner, *Antiquities,* App., 74)
16	Reading		PRO C.53 (list 25/50)
July 8	Croydon		Lincoln Reg. Gynwell 2 (Reg. 9), 24^v
10	Lambeth		PRO S.C.8/235/11740
12	Reading		PRO C.53 (list 25/50)
23	Reading		Ibid.
28-31	Lambeth	S. summons provincial council (30th)	CCL F.18; e.g. Lincoln Reg. Gynwell 2 (Reg. 9), 24^{r-v}; *Bath and Wells Reg. Shrewsbury,* 545-546. See Appendix 3
Aug. 6	Reading		PRO C.53 (list 25/50)
9	Lambeth	Grant of probate	York Reg. Zouche, 319^r
13	Bristol		PRO C.53 (list 25/50)
21	Headstone (*Heggeston*)		Lambeth Cart. Misc. XII 17
Sept.		Hugh, abp. of Damascus, appears before Lecch and Fastolf at Croydon (4th)	*Exeter Reg. Grandisson,* 1030
20	Westminster		PRO C.53 (list 25/50)
23	Otford	Consecration of John Gynwell, bp. of Lincoln	*Biog. Oxon.,* s.v.
		Truce of Calais (28th)	
Oct. 1	London, St. Paul's	Provincial council	See Appendix 3

* At this time the archbishop was clearly in the neighbourhood of Reading and his mandate concerns the local manor of Beaumes.

Date		Place	Details	Reference
	3	Lambeth	Hugh, abp. of Damascus, appears before S. and other bishops	*Exeter Reg. Grandisson*, 1030-1031
	(16-28)		(S. witnesses charters *at* Westminster)	PRO C.53 (list 25/50)
			Edward III back in England (from 12th)	
Nov.	(10-18)		(S. witnesses charters *at* Westminster)	Ibid.
Dec.	(1 and 17)		do.	Ibid.
	1-10	Croydon		WAM 9223
	13-15	Otford		Ibid. (dorse)
	25	Maidstone	[inferred]	Ibid.
1348				
Jan.	19	Lambeth	Parliament at Westminster (14 Jan.-12 Feb.). S. one of those deputed to afforce the auditors and triers of petitions	*Hereford Reg. Trillek*, 123-124; *Rot. Parl.* 2, 164
	(20-30)		(S. witnesses charters *at* Westminster)	PRO C.53 (list 25/50)
Feb.	(7-17)		do.	Ibid.
Mar.	(8-15)		do.	Ibid.
Apr.	(6-8)		do.	Ibid.
	9	Lambeth		Bodl. Lib. Kent Rolls 8 *e*
	(10-19)		(S. witnesses charters *at* Westminster)	PRO C.53 (list 25/50)
	24	Windsor		Ibid.
May	4	Maidstone		Winchester Reg. Edyndon 2, 15ʳ
	8	Lichfield (?)		PRO C.53 (list 25/50)
	17	Maidstone		CCL A.36 IV, 103ᵛ
	18	Westminster (?)		PRO C.53 (list 25/50)
	20	Maidstone		CCL F.18
	24	Maidstone	Arbitration between Edington, bp. of Winchester, and M. Richard Vaughan, archdeacon of Surrey	*Lydford*, 134-141
June	12	Maidstone	Here S. fell ill according to the *Vitae*	Canterbury Reg. Courtenay, 176ᵛ; *Vitae Arch. Cant.*, 41
July	1	Westminster (?)		PRO C.53 (list 25/50)
	6	Mayfield		*Hereford Reg. Trillek*, 135
	12	Mayfield	Fenne granted abp.'s liberty of Southwark	*CPR 1348-1350*, 306
	17	Westminster (?)		PRO C.53 (list 25/50)

Date	Place	Details	Reference
Aug. 23	Mayfield	S. dies about the first hour of the day	BL. Cotton MS Faustina B.v, 96ʳ; *Vitae Arch. Cant.*, 41 (Lambeth MS 99, 146ᵛ)
Sept. 9*	Canterbury	Burial in choir of cathedral	Ibid.

* "Die Martis in crastino Nativitatis" (*Vitae*). This can only refer to the Nativity of Our Lady, which did fall on Monday in 1348. But there are difficulties here. The interval between death and burial is somewhat long (17 days) and Stratford's successor (Bradwardine) was elected 30 August (not 29th as in *HBC*). The corresponding intervals following the deaths of Winchelsey, Reynolds and Mepham were respectively 12, 11, and 14 days (counting the burial day itself). In each case election day came at a decent interval thereafter. But there seems to be no reason to doubt the *Vitae*, since in Stratford's case no *Instrumentum de sepultura* is to be found among the election documents. In short, there seems to have been a technical irregularity and some reason for advancing the election. The Black Death?

Appendix 7

Summary of Stratford's Will
and Inventory of his Goods

A. Summary of the provisions of Stratford's will

(CCL W.219; cf. *Sede Vacante Wills*, App. pp. 72-76)

Beneficiary	Legacy
Canterbury, prior and convent of	His new and best mitre. This they might lend to future archbishops, but it was to remain in possession of the priory for the benefit of the church of Canterbury His new cope of purple velvet with gold figures and many margarites His best and finest copy of the *Decretum* and *Decretales*
Winchester, church of	His set of white vestments with all its accessories (cum omnibus apparamentis eius)
Lincoln, church of	A cope of red velvet embroidered with figures and many margarites
Stratford, chapel of St. Thomas at	His best cope of gold and silk with figures (de auro et serico con...xta cum ymaginibus) Two sets of vestments; one of silk (panno serico) with lions and small peacocks in gold, another of cloth of gold with birds and other beasts, together with all the accessories Missals, graduals, breviaries, legendaries, processionals, and all the other books belonging to his chapel A cross of silver-gilt with evangelists at its four extremities Two chalices in the chapel; one with a beryl, the other plain All the relics: A head ... from Cologne enclosed within a silver-gilt head A portion of the Lord's cross within a gold cross Many relics of various saints in a crystal (reliquary) The girdles of St. Edmund of Canterbury and of St. Richard of Chichester £100 for the completion of work on the chapel
Mayfield church	£5 for the purchase of a set of vestments
Cranbrook church	The same
The king	Gilt and enamelled bowls formerly belonging to the archbishop's good lord Simon (de Montacute), bishop of Ely A silver-gilt troper with ... (MS torn)

Beneficiary	Legacy
Edward Prince of Wales	One good missal
	A "Resurrection" in silver-gilt which belonged to the bishop of Ely
	An ivory plaque (tabula) with figures of mother of pearl
Bartholomew Burghersh	A silver cup with gilt stand (cum tripode) ... at the base two lions standing by a tree
Religious houses in Canterbury and the diocese:	
Mendicant friars of the city	To each ... (amount lost through tear in MS)
Nuns (Ben.) of Holy Sepulchre	5 marks (£3 6s 8d)
Nuns of St. James (Thanington)	£2
Hospital of St. Thomas (Eastbridge)	£2
Hospital of (St. Nicholas) Harbledown	£5
Hospital of (St. John the Baptist) Northgate	5 marks (£3 6s 8d)
Carmelites of Sandwich	£2
Carmelites of Aylesford	£1 6s 8d
Hospital of St. Edmund sic) at "Maidenstood" or "Maidenston"	£2
Alice, his sister	6 silver plates, 6 silver salts of moderate size
	A silver bowl "weighing" £2 8s 4d
	A white silver cup "weighing" £1 19s 8d with an armed lion in the base
	£10 and his best robe
Indigent of his blood	£100 – to be distributed according to need
Indigent of kin of Peter, formerly rector of Eccleshall	20 marks (£13 6s 8d)
Robert (Stratford), bishop of Chichester, his brother	His good Bible and a *Liber Sext*
	One cup with cover, the base enamelled outside and with various shields within
	One egg with cover and gilt base having a tooth with four cusps (habens dentem cum quatuor foliis)
Ralph (Stratford), bishop of London, his nephew	The *Rosarium* of Guy (de Baysio) covered with untanned hide (pelle viridi)
	A *Speculum Judiciale* in a hand of Bologna and bought there
	A great cup with cover, enamelled all over, given to him by the same bishop
John de Pulteney	One cup (godet) with cover and with godets inside
Margaret Pulteney, wife of John	A silver vessel, its cover having a shield with a sword and key
	An egg with stand (cum pede) and gilt cover with an acorn and four leaves (glandem cum quatuor foliis)

Beneficiary	Legacy
William son of John Pulteney	His second best palfrey
John de Eccleshall	A cup and cover with a peacock in the base
Richard de Twyverton	A cup with a star in the base
Injured parties	Enquiry was to be made as to any of his tenants who had suffered injury so that recompense could be made
Dowries for girls to be married	£100 to be distributed at the discretion of his executors
Priests	Executors to provide 50 to say masses continually for his soul throughout the year (following his death)
Mendicants of London:	
Preachers (Dominicans)	£5
Minors (Franciscans)	£5
Carmelites	5 marks (£3 6s 8d)
Augustinians	5 marks
Mendicants of Oxford	Corresponding amount of money to be distributed among the same orders in the University of Oxford
Stratford bridge	£40
Stratford poor	£20
Winchester, hospital of St. Mary Magdalene	£2
Executors of Walter Stapeldon), bishop of Exeter	His executors are to come to an accommodation (composicio) with respect to the good cope (formerly Stapeldon's) which the archbishop received from the hands of Robert de Tauton
Familia	£100 for distribution among those for whom he had not made provision in his lifetime, at the executors' discretion
William atte Frenn [Fenne], the chamberlain	His best bed, another red bed (lectum meum rubeum), the silver basin and washing bowl (pelvim et lavatorium) from the chamber, and £10
John Latyn, valet of the chamber	His best robe and 5 marks (£3 6s 8d)
Hugh Pode, page of the chamber	A suitable robe and £2
Prioress and nuns of Wintney	5 marks (£3 6s 8d)
M. John de Lecch, official of the Court of Canterbury	£5 3s and his Novella in two volumes
"Scholars" of Balliol hall	10 marks (£6 13s 4d)
John Pound	£10
M. William de Derby	10 marks (£6 13s 4d)
Peter de Eccleshall, formerly his chamberlain	5 marks (£3 6s 8d)

Beneficiary	Legacy
Religious poor in Canterbury diocese, poor of his kin in Worcester diocese, poor girls needing dowries	Residue of his goods to be distributed among them at the executors' discretion

B. Inventory of Stratford's goods made by his executors in 1349 (CCL A.37)

RECEIPTS

Treasury:	£303	15s	0d
Debts due to deceased	£402	13s	4d
Chapel and its books (libri eiusdem):			
Books, vestments and various other things (alia diversa)	£1100	3s	8d
Books on various subjects (libri diverse facultat')	£200	6s	0d
Silver vessels (vasa argent')	£684	1s	9d
Precious objects/jewels (iocalia)	£406	10s	0d
Wardrobe and armoury (armatur'):			
Robes, beds, cloths (pann', counterpanes?) and armour	£200	14s	0d
Hall:			
Various hangings and benchcovers (dorsor', bancar')	£26	13s	4d
Pantry, buttery:			
Cloths, towels and other vessels (mappe, tuell' et alia vasa)	£20	16s	8d
Kitchen:			
Brass vessels and various others (vasa enea et alia diversa)	£20	1s	8d
Larder:			
Carcasses of oxen (boum) and bacon	£13	6s	8d
Stable:			
Palfreys and other horses with carts	£181	3s	4d
Granaries:			
Various kinds of grain	£112	10s	0d
Granges:			
Various kinds of grain	£1333	6s	8d
All manors:			
Livestock of various kinds	£1203	12s	3d
Wool:			
Sheep wool (lana grossa) and lambswool	£300	0s	0d
Total of receipts	£6509	14s	4d

EXPENDITURES

Expenses after death of the lord and for the funeral	£782	4s	2¼d
Debts paid to various creditors	£1100	13s	9d

Legacies and other things determined in the lord's lifetime	£1380	6s	0d
Alms paid to the priors of Northgate and Harbledown (hospitals)	£30	0s	0d
Paid to various stewards (diversis sen') and others for fees in arrears	£184	3s	4d
Rewards: various gifts to servants for their great labour	£100	12s	0d
Expenses for forfeitures: various after the lord's death	£837	14s	1d
Paid to 50 chaplains celebrating masses for the deceased's soul	£166	13s	4d
Paid to the lord king in grain sold to him for unpaid tenths	£1333	6s	8d
Total expenditures	£5925	13s	$4^1/_4$d
(Credit balance)	(£584	0s	$11^3/_4$d)

Bibliography

Note: Certain items included in the list of abbreviations are not repeated here. Full details of printed and manuscript episcopal registers are now to be found in D. M. Smith, *Guide to Bishops' Registers of England and Wales* (London 1981). In view of this the printed registers are omitted from "Collections of Documents and Calendars," below, pp. 525-529, being adequately identified in the footnotes.

Manuscript Sources

Great Britain:

Cambridge

University Library

Registers of Simon de Montacute (1337-1345) and Thomas de Lisle (1345-1361)

MS Gg. vi 21. Contains Stratford's constitutions (cited by Wilkins as Ely MS 235). Cf. copies in Dd. ix 38, Ii. ii 7, Ii. iii 14. Dd. ix 38 also contains much material from the 1340s (including *Cum animosa guerrarum* and *Christi legacione fungentes*)

Corpus Christi College

MS 174 (Brut chronicle)

Trinity College

R.5 41 (Canterbury-based chronicle)

Canterbury

Cathedral Library and Archives

Registers:

    D Cartulary

    G *Sede vacante* material (initial quaternion of archiepiscopal privileges)

    H Cartulary with later additions including Eastbridge Hospital material

    I Copies of documents of political interest from Edward II's reign

    L Paper letter-book of Priors Oxenden and Hathbrand

    Q *Sede vacante* and election material, much of it duplicated in "G"

Audience Court Books (Chartae Antiquae):

    A.36 III Fragments (3 membranes) 1339-1341

    A.36 IV Composite volume containing material chiefly from 1340-1343 and 1347-1348 (bound without indication as to original arrangement)

Domestic Economy:
    D.E.3   Draft account book of Priors Oxenden and Hathbrand
Miscellaneous MSS (Chartae Antiquae):
    A.37   Inventory and valuation of Archbishop Stratford's goods
    A.40a   Process of securing the pallium and delivering it to an archbishop
    A.196   Proxy for two monks to present Stratford's postulation at the curia
    A.197   Simon de Charing's notarial instrument of Stratford's visitation process at Christ Church
    C.1300   Stratford's confirmation of Hathbrand's election as prior of Christ Church (1339)
    F.18   Stratford's exemplification and confirmation of a decision in a suit between Christ Church and the vicar of Farningham (1348) (Fine pendent great seal of the archbishop, virtually undamaged)
    L.88   Stratford's letters patent of the acknowledgment by the rector of St. Mary Aldermary church of his obligation to pay a pension to Christ Church (1340) (Counterseal with Becket martyrdom)
    P.32   Notarial instrument and attached agreement (1340) between abbot of Faversham and Archbishop Stratford (seal as in F.18) with respect to payment of 100s. p.a. compensation to Christ Church for Boughton and Preston appropriation (also Reg. D, fols. 464^v-465^r)
    R.20   Exemplification (1389) of Reculver-Herne process re relationship of vicar and parishioners of Herne to mother church of Reculver (also Ducarel, "Fragmenta," fols. 78^r-86^r)
    W.219   Copy of Archbishop Stratford's will and probate by Prior Hathbrand
    W.222   Prior Hathbrand's letters patent of M. Richard Vaughan's renunciation of his position as one of Stratford's's executors (1348)

Chichester

West Sussex Record Office
    Ep. VI/2/2 Liber B
    Ep. VI/1/4 Liber E
    Ep. VI/1/6 Liber Y
    Cap. 1/12/2 (Register K) "Swayne's Book"
    See F. W. Steer, *Diocese of Chichester: a Catalogue of the Records of the Bishop, Archdeacons and Former Exempt Jurisdictions*; Peckham, *Chartulary of Chichester*

Exeter

Devon Record Office
    Chanter MSS 723   "Precedent book" of John Lydford (see Owen, *Lydford*)
              1030   Grant of Bosham chapel in free alms

Cathedral Library
   MS 2227 *Libellus famosus* (10 February 1341)

Hereford

Cathedral Library
   MS P.5 XII   Contains sermons attributed to Stratford

Lichfield

Lichfield Joint Record Office
   B/A/1/1   Register of Walter Langton (1296-1321)
   B/A/1/1-3   Register of Roger Northburgh (1322-1358)

Lincoln

Lincolnshire Archives Office
   Register of John Dalderby (1300-1320) 1-2 (Regs. 2-3)
   Register of Henry Burghersh (1320-1340) 1-3 (Regs. 4-5, 5b)
   Register of Thomas Bek (1342-1347) 2 (Reg. 7)
   Register of John Gynwell (1347-1362) 2-4 (Regs. 9, 9b, 9c)
   A/2/3   John de Schalby's book
   A/2/122   Portion of Norwich register (1340-1343 temp. Anthony Bek)
   A/2/182   Fragment of notarial documents (temp. Stratford's tenure of
      Lincoln archdeaconry)
   Bj/2/5   Volume of common fund accounts (re fruits of Archdeacon Strat-
      ford's prebend on elevation to Winchester
   Dj/20/2/B1-3   Documents about Bishop Dalderby's projected canoniza-
      tion
   Dij/60/2/14, 16   Archbishop Stratford's decision (1343) in dispute be-
      tween Dean William (Bateman) of Norwich and his chapter with regard
      to vacant prebends and the exercise of jurisdiction (cf. Wright, *Church
      and Crown*, p. 331 no. 69)
   Dij/62/1/12, 13   *Inspeximus* (1320) by Archbishop Reynolds of the
      sentences of his commissary, Stratford, with respect to churches,
      pensions, etc., belonging to the dean and chapter

London

British Library
Add. MSS:
   4162   Ely diocesan material of the 14th century
   5844   William Cole of Milton's transcripts (1771)
   6066   Andrew Coltée Ducarel, "Fragmenta sequentia registrorum
           Simonis de Mepeham et Johannis de Stratford Cantuar. archiepis-
           coporum" (1756)
   24510   *Collectanea Hunteriana* (Joseph Hunter's transcripts)
   35114   Wardrobe receipt book, 17 Edward II (1323-1324)
   35296   Spalding cartulary (pt. 1). Cf. Harleian MS 742

Add. charters:

23340   Grant in farm to Archbishop Stratford of lands in Burstow and Horne

33675   Stratford witnesses charter (1338)

44694   Stratford witnesses charter (1345)

Seals:

Detached XXXV 42 modern impression of common seal of college of Stratford-on-Avon

LXXVIII 6 do. of Robert Stratford, bishop of Chichester as his brother's vicar general

See also Birch, *Catalogue* 1, pp. 164-165, 353, nos.:

1221 (Stratford's archiepiscopal seal; cf. Canterbury MS F.18)

1222 Fragmentary seal

2249 Cast of Stratford's seal as bishop of Winchester (1323)

And see *PSA* 11 (2nd ser.), pp. 285, 289

Arundel MS:

68   Christ Church martyrology with obituaries of the archbishops and others (cf. Lambeth MS 20)

Cotton MSS:

Appendix LII   Damaged fragment of Baker's Chronicon for the reign of Edward III

Claudius A.v   Peterborough chronicle

Claudius D.vi   St. Albans chronicles, Trokelowe and Blaneforde

Claudius D.vii   Lanercost chronicle (fols. 172ᵛ-245ᵛ printed by Joseph Stevenson)

Claudius E.iii   Knighton's chronicle (cf. the damaged Tiberius C.vii)

Cleopatra A.xvi   Anonymous Westminster chronicle

Cleopatra D.iii   Hales chronicle

Faustina B.v   *Historia Roffensis*

Galba E.iv   Prior Henry of Eastry's (Canterbury) register

Julius A.i   French chronicle (Pipewell)

Julius B.iii   Abbreviated version of *Vitae Arch. Cant.* (cf. Lambeth MS 99), attributed to Bishop William Reed of Chichester

Nero D.x   Continuator of Nicholas Trivet or Trevet

Vespasian C.xii   Details of Castilian negotiations at fol. 60 (1325)

Vitellius A.ii   Copy of Stratford's constitutions

Vitellius A.xv   Chronicle

Vitellius E.iv 9   Mutilated letter of Bishop Orleton to Pope John XXII

Egerton MSS:

2032   W. T. Alchin's index to Winchester registers Sandale, Stratford, and Orleton

2814   Roll of controller of wardrobe (daybook) 1324-1325

Harleian charters:

43 I 40   Stratford's purchase of horses for Queen Isabella (1326)
43 H 1   Letters patent of Robert Stratford's confirmation of Caldecote
           manor (Cambridge) to Robert de Thorp, formerly held for life by
           Alice wife of Philip de Barton
83 C 29   Archbishop Stratford's grant to John Darcy and his wife Elizabeth
           of lands at Seamer in "Canterburyfee" (1346)

Harleian MSS:

200   Chronicle of Robert of Avesbury
742   Spalding cartulary (pt. 2). Cf. Add. MS 35296
1729   Chronicle (Hearne's *Hemingford*, first continuation of Higden)
3836   Version of Murimuth's chronicle

Harleian roll:

V 13   Stratford's award in a suit concerning tithes of Little Wolston,
           Bucks. (copy)

Royal MSS:

App. 88   Leaves from a Winchester register (temp. Orleton) containing
           transcripts of papal bulls
11 D.vi   Stratford's *repetitio* written on flyleaf of *Digestum Vetus*
12 D.xi   "Bishop Bintworth's formulary"

Stowe MS:

533   Wardrobe book, 15-17 Edward II (1321-1324)

Guildhall Library

MSS 8762   Charter of Edward III confirming liberties of the see of London,
           Walton 25 June 1338. Stratford witnesses.
9531/1   Register of Bishop Stephen Gravesend (1319-1338). Contained in
           composite volume

St. Paul's Cathedral MSS:

66 A 27   Will of Bishop Stephen Gravesend, 19 February 1337, with
           bequest to Archbishop Stratford: "Unum anulum magnum cum
           saphiro qui fuit bone memorie domini Thome Herefordensis
           episcopi." Probate by Stratford, 16 April 1338 (dorse).
66 A 35   Will of John de Pulteney (Poultney), knight, 14 November 1348.
           Mentions his chantry, which included commemoration of Strat-
           ford, recently deceased.

Lambeth Palace Library

Register of Walter Reynolds (1313-1327)
Register of Simon Islep (1349-1366)
Register of William Courtenay (1381-1396)
Black Book of the Arches (S.R. 137)
Registrum Album

MSS 20   Martyrology of Christ Church (cf. Arundel MS 68)
61   M. Henry de Harclay's sermon in Oxford University (fols. 143ʳ al.
           144-147ᵛ). Cf. Hereford MS P.5 XII

99	*Vitae Arch. Cant.* ("Birchington") and other material
241	Cartulary of Dover Priory
538	Contains Stratford's constitutions (cited by Wilkins as MS 17)
1213	*Diversi tractatus* (from St. Augustine's Abbey, Canterbury)

Misc. charters (page references are to Owen, *Catalogue*):

VI 80 (p. 84)	Agreement between Archbishop Stratford and John Darcy about the Canterbury franchise at Menhill, co. York (1344). Cf. Harleian charter 83 C 29
VI 116 (p. 88)	*Inspeximus* re archbishop's claim to wardship in Menhill lands (1342)
XI 55 (p. 131)	Licence for Faversham Abbey to exchange Tring manor for the advowson of Boughton-under-Blean and Preston-next-Ospringe (1340)
XI 58 (p. 131)	St. Augustine's Abbey nominates a proctor to exhibit its privileges before the archbishop (1340)
XI 78 (p. 133)	Royal grant of market and fair at Archbishop Stratford's manor of St. Nicholas-in-Thanet (1336)
XII 17 (p. 137)	Suspension by Stratford of rector of Eastling (1347)
XVII 2 1433 2 mm. (p. 160)	Alienation of *Caldecote* (Calcott) manor to Christ Church (1359 *not* 1339)

Public Record Office

Chancery:

C.47	Miscellanea. Bundles 27-32 diplomatic documents
C.49	Parliamentary and Council proceedings (rolls and files)
C.53	Charter rolls. (*CChR* omits witnesses: see PRO typescript list shelved under no. 25/50)
C.70	Roman rolls
C.76	Treaty rolls
C.81	Warrants for the great seal
C.85	Significations of excommunication
C.115	Master's exhibits (Duchess of Norfolk deeds)
C.145	Miscellaneous inquisitions
C.202	Chancery files, Petty Bag series

Exchequer:

E.30	Diplomatic documents
E.36	Wardrobe accounts
E.101	Various accounts (includes those of *nuncii*)
E.159	Memoranda rolls, King's Remembrancer
E.163	Exchequer miscellanea
E.315	Miscellaneous books (E.315/63 Liber Ecclesie Wygorniensis)
E.352	Chancellor's rolls, Lord Treasurer's Remembrancer
E.372	Pipe rolls (includes enrolled accounts of *nuncii*)

E.403   Issue rolls
E.404   Wardrobe debentures
Justices Itinerant:
Just. 1/1338   Inquisitions by Hervy de Staunton and his associates, 1324
King's Bench:
K.B. 27   *Coram Rege* rolls
Special Collections:
S.C.1   Ancient correspondence
S.C.7   Papal bulls
S.C.8   Ancient petitions
S.C.10   Parliamentary proxies
Transcripts:
PRO 31/8/142   Archives de la ville de Gand
PRO 31/9/17A   Copy of Andrea Sapiti's register of petitions (extracts)

St. Paul's Cathedral Library (see *Guildhall Library*)

Society of Antiquaries
MS 122   Chamber account book, 18-20 Edward II, 1324-1326
MS 845   H. R. Hubbard, Farnham Castle (typescript)

Westminster Abbey Muniment Room
MSS 146   John Cok assigned by royal writ to sell goods of late Robert de Sauton and to pay proceeds to Archbishop Stratford (1335)
596   Document concerning John Geraud and Stratford chantry
605   do.
1851   Ordination of Morden vicarage (1331)
1894   Acquittance by Bermondsey Priory as commissaries of Bishop Stratford for collection of papal tenths in Surrey archdeaconry (1330)
1946A   Stratford witnesses grants of land to John of Eltham (1330)
1946B   do. with respect to Geoffrey le Scrope (1336)
4193   Stratford witnesses settlement re lands at Mimms, Herts.
4940   Abbot of Chertsey writes to Stratford as bishop of Winchester re ordination of monks (1333)
5107   Stratford witnesses *inspeximus* of grants to nuns of Sheppey (1343)
6672   Grant of indulgence by Bishop Stratford to Westminster Abbey pilgrims (1329)
9222   Archbishop Stratford's household/wardrobe account [March 1343]
9223   do. for part of December [1347]
12194   *La vis de conseil*. Copy of parliamentary petitions and responses, 1341 (*Rot. Parl.* 2, pp. 131-134)
12195   Undated letter from a prominent member of the council in England to someone abroad close to the king [1340]
13159   Stratford witnesses confirmation of privileges of St. Martin's le Grand (1340)

20344   Br. Robert de Beby's account for going to Nottingham in an attempt to secure Edward II's body

32741   Re M. John Geraud, warden of Stratford chantry. Cf. 596, 605

Norwich

Norfolk and Norwich Record Office

Register of John Salmon (1299-1325)
Register of Robert Baldock, bishop-elect and -confirmed (1325)
Register of William Ayrminne (1325-1336)
Register of Anthony Bek (1337-1343)
Register of William Bateman (1344-1355)

DCN Confirmations and Settlements box:

MS 3856   Notarial instrument of judgment in curia nullifying Stratford's sentences against the late bishop of Norwich, Anthony Bek

MS 3864   Dodnash visitation document

DCN Episcopal charters:

Box 2, MSS 1139, 4379   Bishop Salmon's chantry at Norwich

Oxford

Bodleian Library

Ashmole MS 1146   Liber Cicestrensis (Liber D, see above, Chichester) attributed to Bishop Reed, containing Stratford's constitutions and his ordinances for the Arches (inchoate)

Bodley MSS:

761   Baker's *Chronicon* and *Chroniculum*
956   Lichfield chronicle

Digby MS 81   Cited by Wilkins for text of Stratford's constitutions
Laud MS Misc. 529   Evesham version of Higden's *Polychronicon*
Kent Rolls 6-8   Enrolment of documents concerning Tonbridge Priory, Kent

Salisbury

Diocesan Registry

The episcopal registers, which I consulted at Wren Hall, are now at Trowbridge, q.v.

Stratford-on-Avon

Shakespeare's Birthplace Trust Records Department

These MSS are too many to enumerate. They are cited with the prefix BRT
See Wellstood, "Stratford: Calendar of Medieval Records"; Hardy, "Calendar"; Fisher, *Antient Paintings*

Trowbridge

Wiltshire County Record Office

Register of Roger Wyville (1330-1375)

Winchester

Hampshire Record Office

    Register of John Stratford (1323-1333)
    Register of Adam Orleton (1333-1345)
    Register of William de Edington (Edyndon) (1345-1366)
    Winchester Pipe Rolls (1324-1333), nos. 159336-159345
See A. J. Willis, Handlist of the Episcopal Records of the Diocese of Winchester,
    1964 (typescript); Beveridge, "Winchester Rolls and their Dating."

Cathedral Library

    Winchester cartulary

Worcester

Hereford and Worcester Record Office, St. Helen's

    Register of Godfrey Giffard (1268-1302)
    Register of Walter Reynolds (1308-1313)
    Register of Walter Maidstone (1314-1317)
    Register of Thomas de Cobham (1317-1327)
    Register of Adam Orleton (1327-1333)
    Register of Simon de Montacute (1333-1337)
    Register of Thomas de Hemenhale (1337-1338)
    Register of Wolstan de Bransford (1339-1349)
    Register of Reginald Brian (1353-1361)
    Register of Philip Morgan (1419-1426)
    Register of Thomas Polton (1426-1433)

Cathedral Library

    Liber Albus
    Registrum Sede Vacante (*RSV*)
    C482   Compotus roll of cellarer and bursar

York

Borthwick Institute of Historical Research, St. Anthony's Hall

    Register of William Melton (1317-1340)
    This contains a number of entries relating to Melton's sale of 50 sacks of
    wool at £9 a sack to Stratford (21 July 1326) and also to the various loans he
    made to him (1328-1338). There is an acquittance for £100, part payment of
    a recognizance of 1,000 marks (4 Feb. 1327) entered into by Stratford. See
    fols. 33 (inserted indenture), 40^r, 57^r, 71^r, 79^v, 716^v.
    Register of William Zouche (1342-1352)

Italy:

Vatican Archives (Archivio Segreto Vaticano)

 RA Registra Avenionensia
 RV Registra Vaticana

See Boyle, *Vatican Archives*; *Sources ... Instrumenta Miscellanea* (ed. Burns)

Printed Sources

Note: To save space printed episcopal registers are not included (see note preceding "Manuscript Sources," p. 514). Likewise the papal registers are not listed; full references are readily available in L. E. Boyle, *A Survey of the Vatican Archives and of its Medieval Holdings* (Toronto 1972), pp. 125-127 and general bibliography.

Chronicles

Annales London.: *Annales Londonienses*, see *Chronicles of the Reigns of Edward I and Edward II*, 1.

Annales Paulini: see *Chronicles of the Reigns of Edward I and Edward II*, 1.

Anonimalle Chronicle: *The Anonimalle Chronicle 1333 to 1381*. Ed. V. H. Galbraith. Manchester 1927.

Avesbury: *Robertus de Avesbury, De Gestis Mirabilibus Regis Edwardi Tertii*. Ed. E. Maunde Thompson. RS 93. London 1889.

Baker, *Chronicon*: *Chronicon Galfridi le Baker de Swynebroke*; Baker, *Chroniculum*: *Chroniculum Galfridi le Baker de Swynebroke*. Ed. E. Maunde Thompson. Oxford 1889.

Birchington: see *Vitae Arch. Cant.*

Blaneforde: see *Trokelowe*

Bridlington: *Gesta Edwardi de Carnarvon auctore Canonico Bridlingtoniensi*, see *Chronicles of the Reigns of Edward I and Edward II*, 2.

Bruce, The: *The Bruce ... compiled by Master John Barbour*. Ed. W. W. Skeat. 3 vols. (cont. pagination). EETS O.S. xi, xxi, xxix. London 1870-1877.

Brut: *The Brut or Chronicles of England*. Ed. F. W. D. Brie. 2 vols. (cont. pagination). EETS O.S. 131, 136. London 1906, 1908. (See Cambridge, CCC MS 174.)

Canonici Lichfeldensis Indiculus de Successione Archiepiscoporum Cantuariensium. Ed. H. Wharton. *Anglia Sacra*, 1. London 1691.

Cartulaire des comtes de Hainaut de 1337 à 1436, 1. Ed. L. Devillers. Brussels 1881 (Collection de chroniques Belges inédites).

Chronica Johannis de Reading et anonymi Cantuariensis 1346-1367. Ed. J. Tait. Manchester 1914.

Chronicle of London: *A Chronicle of London from 1089 to 1483*. [Ed. E. Tyrell, H. Nicolas]. London 1827.

Chronicles of the Mayors and Sheriffs of London 1188-1274; *The French Chronicle of London 1259-1343*. Trans. H. T. Riley. London 1863. (See *French Chronicle*.)

Chronicles of the Reigns of Edward I and Edward II. Ed. W. Stubbs. 2 vols. RS 76. London 1882, 1883.

Chronicon, Chroniculum: see Baker.

Chronique anonyme de la guerre entre Philippe le Bel et Gui de Dampierre. Ed. J.-J. de Smet. *Recueil des chroniques de Flandre*, 4. Brussels 1865 (Collection de chroniques Belges inédites).

Chronique des Pays-Bas, de France, d'Angleterre et de Tournai d'après un ms. de la bibliothèque de Bourgogne. Ed. J.-J. de Smet, *Recueil des chroniques de Flandre*, 3. Brussels 1856 (Collection de chroniques Belges inédites).

Continuatio Historiae Bartholomaei Cotton de Episcopis Norwicensibus. Ed. H. Wharton. *Anglia Sacra*, 1. London 1691.

Flores Historiarum, 3 (1265-1326). Ed. H. R. Luard. RS 95. London 1890.

French Chronicle: Chroniques de London. Ed. G. J. Aungier. Camden Soc. o.s. 28. London 1844.

Froissart (ed. Lettenhove): *Œuvres de Froissart: Chroniques....* Ed. J. B. M. C. Kervyn de Lettenhove. 25 vols. in 26 (5 to 1356, vol. 18 pièces justificatives 1319-1399). Brussels 1867-1877.

Froissart (ed. Luce): *Chroniques....* Ed. S. Luce, G. Raynaud. 11 vols. (4 to 1356). Paris 1869-1899 (Société de l'histoire de France).

Graystanes: Roberti de Graystanes Dunelmensis Episcopi Historia de Statu Ecclesiae Dunelmensis. Ed. H. Wharton. *Anglia Sacra*, 1. London 1691 (cf. *Historiae Dunelmensis Scriptores Tres.* Ed. J. Raine. Surtees Soc. 9, London/Edinburgh 1839, pp. 35-123).

Great Chronicle: The Great Chronicle of London. Ed. A. H. Thomas, I. D. Thornley. London 1938.

Hemingburgh: Chronicon domini Walteri de Hemingburgh, vulgo Hemingford nuncupati. Ed. H. C. Hamilton. Eng. Hist. Soc., London 1849 (cf. *The Chronicle of Walter of Guisborough, previously edited as the Chronicle of Walter of Hemingford or Hemingburgh.* Ed. H. Rothwell. Camden 3rd ser. 89, 1957).

Historia de Episcopis Bathoniensisbus et Wellensibus. Ed. H. Wharton. *Anglia Sacra*, 1. London 1691.

Historia Decanorum et Priorum Ecclesiae Christi Cantuariensis. Ed. H. Wharton. *Anglia Sacra*, 1. London 1691.

Historia Eduardi: Anonymi Historia Eduardi Tertii, in *Walteri Hemingford ... Historia* [etc.]. Ed. T. Hearne. 2 vols. Oxford 1731.

Historia Roffensis: Willielmi de Dene Historia Roffensis. Ed. H. Wharton. *Anglia Sacra*, 1 (with omissions). London 1691. See London, BL Cotton MS Faustina B.v.

Historiae Anglicanae Scriptores Decem. Ed. R. Twysden. London 1652 (contains Orleton's *responsiones*).

Jean le Bel: Chronique de Jean le Bel. Ed. J. Viard, E. Déprez. 2 vols. Paris 1904-1905 (Société de l'histoire de France).

Knighton: Chronicon Henrici Knighton. Ed. J. R. Lumby. 2 vols. RS 92. London 1889, 1895.

Lanercost: *Chronicon de Lanercost*. Ed. J. Stevenson. Bannatyne Club. Edinburgh 1839.

Lichfield Chronicle: Extracts ed. M. V. Clarke, "Committees of Estates" (see below). See Oxford, Bodleian Library, Bodley MS 956.

Melsa: *Chronicon Monasterii de Melsa auctore Thoma de Burton abbate* [continuation to 1406], 2. Ed. E. A. Bond. RS 43. London 1867.

Murimuth: *Adae Murimuth, Continuatio Chronicarum*. Ed. E. Maunde Thompson. RS 93. London 1889.

Peterborough Chronicle: *Chronicon Angliae Petriburgense*. Ed. J. A. Giles. Caxton Soc. London 1845. See London, BL Cotton MS Claudius A.v.

Pipewell Chronicle: Extracts ed. M. V. Clarke, "Committees of Estates" (see below) and J. Taylor, "Judgment on Hugh Despenser" (see below). See London, BL Cotton MS Julius A.i.

Rites of Durham. Ed. J. T. Fowler. Surtees Soc. 107. Durham 1903; repr. Durham and London 1964.

Scalacronica: *Scalacronica by Sir Thomas Gray of Heton, Knight*. Ed. J. Stevenson. Maitland Club. Edinburgh 1836.

Scotichronicon: *Johannis de Fordun Scotichronici* 4. Ed. T. Hearne. Oxford 1722. See also idem (*cum supplementis ac continuatione Walteri Boweri*). Ed. W. Goodall. 2 vols. Edinburgh 1759.

Thorne: *Chronica Guillelmi Thorne Monachi Sancti Augustini Canturiae*. Ed. R. Twysden. In *Historiae Anglicanae*... (q.v.). Also trans. A. H. Davis. *William Thorne's Chronicle of St. Augustine's Abbey, Canterbury*. Oxford 1934.

Trivet: *Nicolai Triveti Annalium Continuatio*. Ed. A. Hall. Oxford 1722.

Trokelowe: *Johannis de Trokelowe et Henrici de Blaneforde ... Chronica et Annales*. Ed. H. T. Riley. RS 28, 3. London 1866.

Vita: *Vita Edwardi Secundi*. Ed. N. Denholm Young. London 1957.

Vita et Mors: *Vita et Mors Edwardi II conscripta a Thoma de la Moore*. See *Chronicles of the Reigns of Edward I and Edward II*, 2.

Vitae Arch. Cant.: *Stephani Birchingtoni Monachi Cantuariensis Historia de Archiepiscopis* .... Ed. H. Wharton. *Anglia Sacra*, 1. London 1691. See Lambeth Palace Library MS 99.

Walsingham: *Thomae Walsingham Historia Anglicana*. Ed. H. T. Riley. 2 vols. RS 28, 1. London 1863. See also *Gesta Abbatum Monasterii S. Albani a Thoma Walsingham ... compilata*. Ed. H. T. Riley. 3 vols. RS 28, 4. London 1867-1869.

Collections of Documents and Calendars

Acta Aragonensia. Ed. H. Finke. 3 vols. Berlin-Leipzig 1908-1922.

Anglia Sacra. Ed. H. Wharton. 2 vols. London 1691.

Antient Paintings: *A Series of Ancient Allegorical, Historical, and Legendary Paintings ... discovered ... 1804, on the walls of the Chapel of the Trinity, belonging to the Gilde of the Holy Cross at Stratford-upon-Avon ....* Etched and ed. T. Fisher. London 1836 (with letterpress by J. Gough Nichols. London 1838).

Calendar of Ancient Petitions relating to Wales. Ed. W. Rees. Cardiff 1975.

Calendar of Chancery Warrants, 1, 1244-1326. London 1927.

Calendar of Charter Rolls, 4, 1327-1341; 5, 1341-1417. London 1912, 1916.

Calendar of Fine Rolls, 2-6, 1307-1356. London 1912-1922.

Calendar of Inquisitions (Miscellaneous), 2, 1307-1349. London 1916.

Calendar of Letter Books of the City of London, E (1314-1337), F (1337-1352). Ed. R. R. Sharpe. London 1902-1904.

Calendar of Memoranda Rolls (Exchequer), 1326-1327. London 1968.

Canterbury Chantries and Hospitals ... in 1546. Transcribed E. L. Holland, ed. C. Cotton. Kent. Arch. Soc. add. vol. Ashford 1934.

Canterbury Professions. Ed. M. Richter. CYS 1973.

Catalogue of Lambeth Manuscripts 889 to 901, A. Ed. D. M. Owen. London 1968.

Chertsey Cartularies 1. [Ed. M. S. Giuseppi]. Surrey Rec. Soc. 12. Frome 1933.

Chichester Cart[ulary]: The Chartulary of the High Church of Chichester. Ed. W. D. Peckham. Sussex Rec. Soc. 46. Lewes 1946.

Cirencester Cartulary: The Cartulary of Cirencester Abbey. Ed. C. D. Ross. 2 vols. London 1964.

Collectanea. 2nd ser. Ed. M. Burrows. OHS 16. Oxford 1890.

Compotus Rolls of the Priory of Worcester, Early 13th Century. Ed. J. M. Wilson, C. Gordon. WHS. Oxford 1908.

Compotus Rolls of the Priory of Worcester, 14th-15th Centuries. Ed. S. G. Hamilton. WHS. Oxford 1910.

Concilia, Decreta, Leges. Ed. H. Spelman. London 1664.

Concilia Magnae Britanniae et Hiberniae. Ed. D. Wilkins. 4 vols. London 1737.

Constitutiones Legatinae; Constitutiones Provinciales. See *Provinciale*.

Councils and Synods. Ed. F. M. Powicke, C. R. Cheney. 2 vols. Oxford 1964.

Das deutsch-englische Bündnis von 1335-1342. Ed. F. Bock. Quellen und Erörterungen zur bayerischen Geschichte, neue Folge, Band 12. Munich 1956.

Documents Illustrating the Activities of the General and Provincial Chapters of the English Black Monks, 1215-1540. Ed. W. A. Pantin. Camden 3rd ser. 45, 47, 59. London 1931-1937.

Documents Illustrating the History of St. Paul's Cathedral. Ed. W. S. Simpson. Camden Soc. n.s. 26. London 1880.

Documents Illustrative of English History in the 13th and 14th Centuries. Ed. H. Cole. London 1844.

"Documents Relating to Edward II." Ed. S. A. Moore. *Archaeologia* 50 (1887), 215-226.

Dugdale Soc. 6: see *Lay Subsidy Roll for Warwickshire*.

Early Rolls of Merton College, Oxford, The. Ed. J. R. L. Highfield. OHS n.s. 18. Oxford 1964.

English Medieval Diplomatic Practice, pt. 1 (2 vols); pt. 2 (plates). Ed. P. Chaplais. London 1975, 1982.

Études de diplomatique anglaise Edward ɪ-Henry vɪɪ (1272-1485). Ed. E. Déprez. Paris 1908.

Exact Abridgement of the Records in the Tower of London.... Ed. W. Prynne. London 1657.

Exchequer Ancient Deeds, DD Series 1101-1645 (pro E.211), List and Index Soc. 200. London 1983.

Extenta Manerii de Stratford 1252. Middle Hill Press. ca. 1846 [See below, *Red Book of Worcester*.]

Formularies: see *Oxford Formularies*.

"Fragmenta," ed. Ducarel. See ms bibliography s.v. London, British Library.

Gascon Calendar of 1322. Ed. G. P. Cuttino. Camden 3rd ser. 70. London 1949.

Hemingby's Register. Ed. H. M. Chew. Wiltshire Arch. and Nat. Hist. Soc. Records Branch 18. Devizes 1963.

Hereford Cathedral Charters: Charters and Records of Hereford Cathedral. Ed. W. W. Capes. Hereford 1908.

Historical Papers and Letters from Northern Registers. Ed. J. Raine. rs 61. London 1873.

Historical Poems of the 14th and 15th Centuries. Ed. R. H. Robbins. New York 1959.

Index of British Treaties 1101-1968. Ed. C. Parry, C. Hopkins. 3 vols. London 1970.

Kent Chantries. Ed. A. Hussey. Kent Arch. Soc. 12. Ashford 1936.

Lay Subsidy Roll for Warwickshire of 6 Edward ɪɪɪ 1332. Trans. and ed. W. F. Carter. *... Appendix Containing Three Early Subsidy Rolls for Stratford on Avon*. Ed. F. C. Wellstood. Dugdale Soc. 6. London 1926.

Lay Subsidy Roll, a.d. 1332-3, and 'Nonarum Inquisitiones,' 1340, for the County of Worcester. Ed. J. Amphlett. whs. Oxford 1899.

Letters from Northern Registers. See *Historical Papers and Letters*.

Lettres de rois, reines et autres personnages des cours de France et d'Angleterre ... tirés des archives de Londres par [O. F. de] Bréquigny, 2 (1301-1515). Ed. M. Champollion-Figeac. Paris 1847.

Liber Albus of Worcester Priory [calendar]. Ed. J. M. Wilson. whs. Oxford 1919. (See also *Worcester Liber Albus*.)

Liber Ecclesiae Wigorniensis, a Letter Book of the Priors of Worcester. Ed. J. H. Bloom, collated E. Stokes. whs. Oxford 1912. (See ms bibliography s.v. London, pro E.315/63.)

Liber Pensionum Prioratus Wigorn. Ed. C. Price. whs. Oxford 1925.

Memorials of Merton College. Ed. G. C. Brodrick. ohs. Oxford 1885.

Monasticon Anglicanum. Ed. W. Dugdale, rev. J. Caley et al. 6 vols. in 8. London 1817-1830.

Nonarum Inquisitiones in curia Scaccarii tempore regis Edwardi ɪɪɪ. Rec. Comm. London 1807.

Obituaries at Canterbury: *Dies Obituales Archiepiscoporum Cantuariensium ex Martyrologio et Obituario Ecclesiae Christi Cantuariensis*. Ed. H. Wharton, *Anglia Sacra*, 1. London 1691 (see MS bibliography s.v. London, British Library, Arundel MS 68; Lambeth Palace, Lambeth MS 20).

Original Papal Documents in the Lambeth Palace Library. Ed. J. E. Sayers, *BIHR* spec. supp. 1967.

Oxford Formularies: Formularies Which Bear on the History of Oxford c. 1204-1420, 1. Ed. H. E. Salter et al. OHS. Oxford 1942.

Parliamentary Texts of the Later Middle Ages. Ed. N. Pronay, J. Taylor. Oxford 1980.

Parliamentary Writs. Ed. F. Palgrave. 2 vols. in 4. Rec. Comm. London 1827-1844.

Placita de Quo Warranto temporibus Edward I, II, and III. Ed. W. Illingworth, J. Caley. Rec. Comm. London 1818.

Political Poems and Songs Relating to English History. Ed. T. Wright. 2 vols. RS 14. London 1859-1861. [Vol. 1 contains the "Vows of the Heron," pp. 1-25, and John of Bridlington's satire on the acts of Edward III, pp. 123-215.]

Political Songs of England. Ed. T. Wright. Camden Soc. 6. London 1839.

Provinciale. W. Lyndwood. Oxford 1679. [Contains: *Provinciale seu Constitutiones Angliae*; *Constitutiones Legatinae Othonis et Othoboni*, with John of Athon's gloss; text of *Constitutiones Provinciales*.]

Records of Merton Priory, The. Ed. A. Heales. London 1898.

Recueil de lettres Anglo-Françaises (1265-1399). Ed. F. J. Tanquerey. Paris 1916.

Red Book of Worcester, The. Ed. M. Hollings. WHS. Oxford 1934-1950. [Pt. 3 contains extents of Old Stratford 1252 and 1299.]

Register of the Gild of the Holy Cross, the Blessed Mary and St. John the Baptist, of Stratford on Avon, The. Ed. J. H. Bloom. London 1907. [See also *English Gilds*. Ed. L. Toulmin Smith. EETS O.S. 40. London 1870; repr. 1963: pp. 211-225, Stratford on Avon, Gild of the Holy Cross.]

Register of St. Osmund. Ed. W. H. Rich Jones. 2 vols. RS 78. London 1883-1884.

Registrum Sede Vacante: The Register of the Diocese of Worcester during the Vacancy of the See. Ed. J. W. Willis-Bund. WHS. Oxford 1893-1897.

Reports ... Touching the Dignity of a Peer. 5 vols. London 1920-1929.

Return of Members of Parliament, 1 (1213-1702). 1878.

Rotuli Parliamentorum. Ed. J. Strachey et al. 6 vols. London 1767.

Rotuli Parliamentorum Anglie Hactenus Inediti. Ed. H. G. Richardson, G. O. Sayles. Camden 3rd ser. 51. London 1935.

Sede Vacante Wills: A Calendar of Wills Proved before the Commissary of the Prior and Convent of Christ Church. Ed. C. E. Woodruff. Kent Arch. Soc. Records Branch 3. Canterbury 1914.

Sources of British and Irish History in the Instrumenta Miscellanea of the Vatican Archives. C. Burns. Archivium Historiae Pontificiae 9. Rome 1971.

Statutes of the Realm. Rec. Comm. London 1810-1828.

Survey of the Vatican Archives and of its Medieval Holdings, A. L. E. Boyle. Toronto 1972.

"Table of Canterbury Archbishopric Charters." I. J. Churchill. Camden Misc. 15, 3rd ser. 41. London 1929, pp. i-x, 1-27.

Taxatio Ecclesiastica Angliae et Walliae ... circa 1291. Rec. Comm. London 1802.

Testamenta Eboracensia 1. [Ed. J. Raine]. Surtees Soc. 4. 1836.

Treaty Rolls, 1, *1234-1325*. Ed. P. Chaplais. London 1955.

Treaty Rolls, 2, *1337-1339*. Ed. J. Ferguson. London 1972.

Valor Ecclesiasticus, temp. Henrici VIII. Rec. Comm. London 1810-1834.

Vatican Archives: see *Survey of the Vatican Archives*.

Vatikanische Akten zur deutschen Geschichte in der Zeit Kaiser Ludwigs des Bayern. Ed. S. von Riezler. Innsbruck 1891; repr. 1973.

War of Saint Sardos. Ed. P. Chaplais. Camden 3rd ser. 87. London 1954.

Wardrobe Book of William de Norwell (1338-1340). Ed. M. Lyon, B. Lyon, H. S. Lucas. Brussels 1983.

Worcester Liber Albus. Ed. J. M. Wilson. London 1920 (see also *Liber Albus of Worcester Priory*).

Secondary Sources

Akerman, J. Y. [Note on a document relating to the election of Archbishop Stratford], *PSA* 2nd ser. 4 (1867-1870), 413-415.

Ames, E. "The Sterling Crisis of 1337-1339." *Journal of Economic History* 25 (1965), 496-522.

Atiya, A. S. *The Crusade in the Later Middle Ages*. London 1938.

Baker, R. L. *The English Customs Service, 1307-1343: A Study of Medieval Administration*. American Phil. Soc. n.s. 51 pt. 6. Philadelphia 1961.

Baldwin, J. F. "The King's Council." In Willard and Morris eds., *English Government at Work, 1327-1336*. 1, pp. 129-161. Cambridge, Mass. 1940.

———. *The King's Council in England during the Middle Ages*. Oxford 1913.

Balfour-Melville, E. W. M. *Edward III and David II*. Historical Assoc. London 1954.

Barnes, F. R. "The Taxation of Wool, 1327-1348." In Unwin, ed., *Finance and Trade under Edward III*, pp. 137-177. Manchester 1918; repr. London 1962.

Barrow, G. W. S. *Robert Bruce and the Community of the Realm of Scotland*. London 1965.

Baumgarten, P. M. *Von der apostolischen Kanzlei*. Cologne 1908.

Beardwood, A. *The Trial of Walter Langton, Bishop of Lichfield, 1307-1312*. American Phil. Soc. n.s. 54 pt. 3. Philadelphia 1964.

Bellamy, J. G. *The Law of Treason in England in the Later Middle Ages*. Cambridge 1970.

Beveridge, W. H. "Memoranda. The Winchester Rolls and their Dating." *EcHR* 11 (1929), 93-113 (cf. H. Hall, "The Winchester Rent Rolls," *Economica* 10 [1924], 52-61).

Blackley, F. D. "Isabella and the Bishop of Exeter." In Sandquist and Powicke, eds., *Essays ... Presented to Bertie Wilkinson*, pp. 220-235. Toronto 1969.

Blomefield, F. *An Essay towards a Topographical History of the County of Norfolk*, 3. London 1806.

Bolton B. "The Council of London of 1342." In *Councils and Assemblies. SCH* 7 (1971), 147-160.

Boyle, L. E. "Aspects of Clerical Education in Fourteenth-Century England." In *The Fourteenth Century Acta IV*, pp. 19-32. Centre for Medieval and Early Renaissance Studies. Binghampton, New York 1977.

——. "The Constitution *Cum ex eo* of Boniface VIII: Education of Parochial Clergy." *Mediaeval Studies* 24 (1962), 262-302.

——. "The *Oculus sacerdotis* and some other Works of William of Pagula." *TRHS* 5th ser. 5 (1955), 81-110.

——. *Pastoral Care, Clerical Education and Canon Law.* Variorum. London 1981 [contains all three studies above with original pagination].

——. "William of Pagula and the *Speculum Regis Edwardi III.*" *Mediaeval Studies* 32 (1970), 329-336.

Broome, D. M. "Exchequer Migrations to York in the Thirteenth and Fourteenth Centuries." In Little and Powicke, eds., *Essays in Medieval History Presented to T. F. Tout*, pp. 291-300. Manchester 1925; repr. New York 1967.

Brown, E. A. R. "Gascon Subsidies and the Finances of the English Dominions, 1315-1324." In Adelson, ed., *Studies in Medieval and Renaissance History*, 8. Lincoln, Nebraska 1971.

Brownbill, J. "An Old English Canonist." *The Antiquary* 24 (1891), 164-167.

Bryant, W. N. "Some Earlier Examples of Intercommuning in Parliament." *EHR* 85 (1970), 54-58.

——. "The Financial Dealings of Edward III with the County Communities, 1330-60." *EHR* 83 (1968), 760-771.

Buck, M. *Politics, Finance and the Church in the Reign of Edward II: Walter de Stapeldon, Treasurer of England.* Cambridge 1983.

Bullough, D. A. and R. L. Storey, eds. *The Study of Medieval Records: Essays in Honour of Kathleen Major.* Oxford 1971.

Cam, H. "The General Eyres of 1329-30." *EHR* 39 (1924), 241-251.

Campbell, J. "England, Scotland and the Hundred Years War in the 14th Century." In Hale, Highfield, Smalley, eds., *Europe in the Later Middle Ages*, pp. 184-216. Evanston 1963.

Campbell, J. Lord. *Lives of the Lord Chancellors and Keepers of the Great Seal of England*, 1. London 1846.

Carte, T. *A General History of England.* 4 vols. London 1747-1755.

Cassan, S. H. *The Lives of the Bishops of Winchester.* 2 vols. London 1827.

Chaplais, P. "Le Duché-Pairie de Guyenne: l'hommage et les services féodaux de 1303 à 1337" (pt. 2). *Annales du Midi* 70 (1958), 135-160 [both parts now included in Chaplais, *Essays in Medieval Diplomacy and Administration*, London 1981].

——. "English Arguments concerning the Feudal Status of Aquitaine in the 14th Century." *BIHR* 21 (1948), 203-213.

——. "English Diplomatic Documents to the End of Edward III's Reign." In Bullough, Storey, eds., *The Study of Medieval Records: Essays in Honour of Kathleen Major*, pp. 22-56. Oxford 1971.

Cheney, C. R. *English Bishops' Chanceries 1100-1250*. Manchester 1950.

——. *The English Church and its Laws, 12th-14th Centuries*, Variorum. London 1982 [contains "Legislation of the Medieval English Church," "Norwich Cathedral Priory" and "The So-called Statutes of Pecham and Winchelsey."].

——. *English Synodalia of the Thirteenth Century*. Oxford 1941.

——. "Legislation of the Medieval English Church." *EHR* 50 (1935), 193-224, 385-417.

——. *Medieval Texts and Studies*. Oxford 1973 [includes "Textual Problems of the English Provincial Canons," pp. 111-137; "William Lyndwood's *Provinciale*," pp. 158-184 (*The Jurist* 21 [1961], 405-434), "Some Aspects of Diocesan Legislation during the Thirteenth Century," pp. 185-202].

——. "Norwich Cathedral Priory in the 14th Century." *BJRL* 20 (1936), 93-120.

——. *Notaries Public in England in the 13th and 14th Centuries*. Oxford 1972.

——. "The So-called Statutes of John Pecham and Robert Winchelsey for the Province of Canterbury." *JEH* 12 (1961), 14-34.

Cheyette, F. "Kings, Courts, Cures and Sinecures: the Statute of Provisors and the Common Law." *Traditio* 19 (1963), 295-349.

Clarke, M. V. "Committees of Estates and the Deposition of Edward II." In Edwards et al., eds., *Historical Essays in Honour of James Tait*, pp. 27-45. Manchester 1933.

——. "The Deposition of Richard II" (with V. H. Galbraith). *BJRL* 14 (1930), 125-181.

——. *Fourteenth Century Studies*. Ed. L. S. Sutherland and M. McKisack. Oxford 1937; repr. 1968 [reprints "The Deposition of Richard II" and "The Origin of Impeachment" at pp. 53-98, 242-271 respectively].

——. *Medieval Representation and Consent*. London/New York 1936; repr. 1964 [reprints the "Committees of Estates" at pp. 173-195].

——. "The Origin of Impeachment." In *Oxford Essays in Medieval History presented to H. E. Salter*, pp. 164-189. Oxford 1934.

Clay, R. M. *The Medieval Hospitals of England*. 2nd impr. 1966.

Cohn, N. *The Pursuit of the Millennium*. Oxford 1970.

Colvin, H. M. *The History of the King's Works* 2. London 1963.

Cook, G. H. *Mediaeval Chantries and Chantry Chapels*. London 1947.

Coulton, G. G. *Five Centuries of Religion*. 4 vols. Cambridge 1923/1929-1930.

Cristofori, E. *Storia dei Cardinali di Santa Romana Chiesa*. Rome 1888.

Crump, C. G. "The Arrest of Roger Mortimer and Queen Isabel." *EHR* 26 (1911), 331-332.

Curtis, E. *History of Mediaeval Ireland (1110-1513)*. Dublin 1923.

Cuttino, G. P. *English Diplomatic Administration 1259-1339*. 2nd ed., Oxford 1971.

——. "Henry of Canterbury." *EHR* 57 (1942), 298-311.

——. "Historical Revision: The Causes of the Hundred Years War." *Speculum* 31 (1956), 463-477.

Cuttino, G. P. and T. W. Lyman. "Where is Edward ɪɪ ?" *Speculum* 53 (1978), 522-544.

Dalton, J. N. *The Collegiate Church of Ottery St. Mary*. Cambridge 1917.

Dart, J. *History and Antiquities of the Cathedral Church of Canterbury*. London 1726.

Davies, J. C. *The Baronial Opposition to Edward ɪɪ*. Cambridge 1918.

Davies, R. R. *Lordship and Society in the March of Wales*. Oxford 1978.

Davis, H. W. C. ed., *Essays in History Presented to R. L. Poole*. Oxford 1927; repr. New York 1969.

Davis, R. H. C. and J. M. Wallace-Hadrill, eds. *The Writing of History in the Middle Ages*. Oxford 1981.

Dean, R. J. "Nicholas Trevet, Historian." In Alexander and Gibson, eds., *Medieval Learning and Literature. Essays Presented to Richard William Hunt*. Oxford 1976.

Deeley, A. "Papal Provision and Royal Rights of Patronage in the Early Fourteenth Century." *EHR* 43 (1928), 497-527.

Denholm-Young, N. "The Authorship of the *Vita Edwardi Secundi*." *EHR* 71 (1956), 189-211.

——. *Collected Papers on Medieval Subjects*. New ed. Cardiff 1969 [reprints the above at pp. 267-289 and "Richard de Bury" at pp. 1-25].

——. "Richard de Bury (1287-1345)." *TRHS* 4th ser. 20 (1937), 135-168.

Denton, J. H. *English Royal Free Chapels 1100-1300*. Manchester 1970.

——. *Robert Winchelsey and the Crown 1294-1313*. Cambridge 1980.

——. "Walter Reynolds and Ecclesiastical Politics 1313-1316: A Postscript to *Councils and Synods*, II." In Brooke et al., eds., *Church and Government in the Middle Ages. Essays Presented to C. R. Cheney*, pp. 247-274. Cambridge 1976.

Déprez, E. "La conférence d'Avignon (1344); l'arbitrage pontifical entre la France et l'Angleterre." In Little and Powicke, eds., *Essays in Medieval History Presented to T. F. Tout*, pp. 301-302. Manchester 1925; repr. New York 1967.

——. *Les préliminaires de la Guerre de Cent Ans*. Bibliothèque des Écoles Françaises d'Athènes et de Rome 96. Paris 1902.

Diller, G. T. "Robert d'Artois et l'historicité des Chroniques de Froissart." *Le Moyen Âge* 86 (1980), 217-231.

Doherty, P. C. "The Date of the Birth of Isabella, Queen of England (1308-58)." *BIHR* 48 (1975), 246-248.

Donahue, C. "Lyndwood's Gloss *propriarum uxorum*: Marital Property and the Ius Commune in Fifteenth-Century England." In Horn, ed., *Europäisches*

Rechtsdenken in Geschichte und Gegenwart, Festschrift für Helmut Coing, pp. 19-37. Munich 1982.

Donahue, C. and J. P. Gordus. "A Case from Archbishop Stratford's Audience Book and some Comments on the Book and its Value." *Bulletin of Medieval Canon Law* n.s. 2 (1972), 45-59.

Du Boulay, F. R. H. *The Lordship of Canterbury*. London 1966.

Dugdale, W. *The Antiquities of Warwickshire*. 2nd ed. rev. W. Thomas. London 1730.

——. *The Baronage of England*. 2 vols. London 1675-1676.

——. *History of St. Paul's Cathedral*. London 1716.

Duncombe, J. and N. Battely. *The History and Antiquities of the Three Archiepiscopal Hospitals at or near Canterbury*. London 1785.

Dyer, C. *Lords and Peasants in a Changing Society: The Estates of the Bishopric of Worcester 680-1540*. Cambridge 1980.

Edwards, J. G. "The Negotiating of the Treaty of Leake, 1318." In Davis, ed., *Essays in History Presented to R. L. Poole*, pp. 360-378. Oxford 1927; repr. New York 1969.

——. "Sir Gruffyd Llwyd." *EHR* 30 (1915), 589-601.

Edwards, J. G., V. H. Galbraith and E. F. Jacob, eds. *Historical Essays in Honour of James Tait*. Manchester 1933.

Edwards, K. *English Secular Cathedrals*. 2nd ed. New York 1967.

——. "The Political Importance of the English Bishops during the Reign of Edward ii." *EHR* 59 (1944), 311-347.

Emden, *Biog. Cantab., Biog; Oxon*. See Abbreviations.

Fairbank, F. R. "The Last Earl of Warenne and Surrey and the Distribution of his Possessions." *Yorkshire Archaeological Journal* 19 (1907), 193-264.

Flahiff, G. B. "The Use of Prohibition by Clerics against Ecclesiastical Courts in England." *Mediaeval Studies* 3 (1941), 101-116.

——. "The Writ of Prohibition to Court Christian in the Thirteenth Century." *Mediaeval Studies* 6 (1944), 261-313; 7 (1945), 229-290.

Fowler, K. *The King's Lieutenant: Henry of Grosmont, First Duke of Lancaster, 1310-1361*. London/New York 1969.

Frame, R. *English Lordship in Ireland 1318-1361*. Oxford 1982.

Frere, W. H. *The Use of Sarum*. 2 vols. Cambridge 1898, 1901.

Fryde, E. B. "The Dismissal of Robert de Wodehouse from the Office of Treasurer, December 1338." *EHR* 67 (1952), 74-78.

——. "Edward iii's Wool Monopoly of 1337." *History* 37 (1952), 8-24.

——. "The English Farmers of the Customs 1343-51." *TRHS* 5th ser. 9 (1959), 1-17.

——. "Financial Resources of Edward i in the Netherlands 1294-98: Main Problems and some Comparisons with Edward iii in 1337-40." *Revue Belge de philologie et d'histoire* 40 (1962), 1168-1187; 45 (1967), 1142-1193, followed by tables pp. 1194-1216.

——. "The Last Trials of Sir William de la Pole." *EcHR* 15 (1962), 17-30.

——. "Materials for the Study of Edward III's Credit Operations, 1327-48." *BIHR* 22 (1949), 105-138; 23 (1950), 1-30.

——. "Parliament and the French War, 1336-40." In Sandquist and Powicke, eds., *Essays in Medieval History Presented to Bertie Wilkinson*, pp. 250-269. Toronto 1969.

——. *The Wool Accounts of William de la Pole*. St. Anthony's Hall Pubns. York 1964.

Fryde, E. B. and E. Miller, eds. *Historical Studies of the English Parliament 1: Origins to 1399*. Cambridge 1970.

Fryde, N. M. "Antonio Pessagno of Genoa, King's Merchant of Edward II in England." In *Studi in Memoria di Federigo Melis* 2, pp. 159-178. Naples 1978.

——. "Edward III's Removal of his Ministers and Judges, 1340-1341." *BIHR* 48 (1975), 149-161.

——. "John Stratford, Bishop of Winchester, and the Crown, 1323-30." *BIHR* 44 (1971), 153-159.

——. "A Medieval Robber Baron: Sir John Molyns of Stoke Poges, Buckinghamshire." In *Medieval Legal Records Edited in Memory of C. A. F. Meekings* by R. F. Hunnisett and J. B. Post, pp. 198-207, 211-221 (text). London 1978.

——. *The Tyranny and Fall of Edward II, 1321-1326*. Cambridge/New York 1979.

Fuller, T. *The History of the Worthies of England*, 2. [London] 1811.

Galbraith, V. H. "The Chronicle of Henry Knighton." In Gordon, ed., *Fritz Saxl, a Volume of Memorial Essays*, pp. 136-148. London 1957.

——. "Extracts from the *Historia Aurea* and a French *Brut*." *EHR* 43 (1928), 203-217.

——. "The *Historia Aurea* of John, Vicar of Tynemouth, and the Sources of the St. Albans Chronicle (1327-1377). In Davis, ed., *Essays in History Presented to R. L. Poole*, pp. 379-398. Oxford 1927; repr. New York 1968.

——. "Statutes of Edward I: Huntingdon Library MS H.M. 25872." In Sandquist and Powicke, eds., *Essays in Medieval History Presented to Bertie Wilkinson*, pp. 176-191. Toronto 1969.

Gibbs, M. and J. Lang. *Bishops and Reform 1215-1272*. London 1934.

Giesey, R. E. *The Juristic Basis of Dynastic Right to the French Throne*. American Phil. Soc. n.s. 51 pt. 6. Philadelphia 1961.

Godfrey, W. H. "Some Medieval Hospitals of East Kent." *Arch. Jnl.* 2nd ser. 86 (1929), 99-100.

Gough, R. *Sepulchral Monuments in Great Britain*. 2 vols. London 1786-1796.

Gransden, A. "The Continuation of the *Flores Historiarum* from 1265 to 1327." *Mediaeval Studies* 36 (1974), 472-492.

——. *Historical Writing in England*, 2: *c. 1307 to the Early Sixteenth Century*. London 1982.

——. "Propaganda in English Medieval Historiography." *Journal of Medieval History* 1 (1975), 363-381.

Grassi, J. L. "William Airmyn and the Bishopric of Norwich." *EHR* 70 (1955), 550-561.

Graves, E. B. *A Bibliography of English History to 1485*. Oxford 1975.

——. "Circumspecte Agatis." *EHR* 43 (1928), 1-20.

Haines, C. R. *Dover Priory*. Cambridge 1930.

Haines, R. M. "Adam Orleton and the Diocese of Winchester." *JEH* 23 (1972), 1-30.

——. "The Administration of the Diocese of Worcester 'Sede Vacante' 1266-1350." *JEH* 13 (1962), 156-171.

——. "An Appeal of 1334 against the Bishop of Winchester." Forthcoming.

——. "The Appropriation of Longdon Church to Westminster Abbey." *Trans. Worcs. Arch. Soc.* 38 (1961), 39-52 [a revised version is incorporated in my forthcoming *Ecclesia Anglicana: Studies in the English Church of the Later Middle Ages*].

——. *The Church and Politics in Fourteenth-Century England: The Career of Adam Orleton c. 1275-1345*. Cambridge 1978.

——. "Conflict in Government: Archbishops versus Kings 1279-1348." Forthcoming.

——. "A Defence Brief for Bishop Adam de Orleton." *BIHR* 50 (1977), 232-242.

——. "The Education of the English Clergy during the Later Middle Ages: Some Observations on the Operation of Boniface VIII's Constitution *Cum ex eo* (1298)." *Canadian Journal of History* 4 (1969), 1-22 [revised version in *Ecclesia Anglicana*].

——. "An English Archbishop and the Cerberus of War." In *The Church and War, SCH* 20 (1983), 153-170.

——. "Some Sermons at Hereford Attributed to Archbishop John Stratford." *JEH* 34 (1983), 425-437.

——. "Wolstan de Bransford, Prior and Bishop of Worcester, c. 1280-1349." *University of Birmingham Historical Journal* (1962), 97-113.

Hale, J. R., J. R.L. Highfield and B. Smalley, eds. *Europe in the Late Middle Ages*. Evanston 1963.

Harcourt, L. W. V. *His Grace the Steward and the Trial of Peers*. London 1907.

Harding, A. "Political Liberty in the Middle Ages." *Speculum* 55 (1980), 423-443.

Harriss, G. L. "The Commons' Petitions of 1340." *EHR* 88 (1963), 625-654.

——. *King, Parliament and Public Finance in Medieval England to 1369*. Oxford 1975.

Haskins, G. L. "A Chronicle of the Civil Wars of Edward II." *Speculum* 14 (1939), 73-81.

Hasted, E. *History and Topographical Survey of the County of Kent*, 12. Canterbury 1801.

Hewitt, H. J. *The Organisation of War under Edward III*. Manchester 1966.

Highfield, J. R. L. "The English Hierarchy in the Reign of Edward III." *TRHS* 5th ser. 6 (1956), 115-138.

Hill, M. C. "Jack Faukes, King's Messenger and his Journey to Avignon in 1343." *EHR* 57 (1942), 19-30.

Hilton, R. H., ed. *Peasants, Knights and Heretics: Studies in Medieval English Social History.* Cambridge 1976.

Holliday, J. R. "Maxstoke Priory." *Birmingham and Midland Institute Arch. Section Trans.* 5 (1874), 56-105.

Holmes, G. A. "Judgment on the Younger Despenser." *EHR* 70 (1955), 261-267.

——. "The Rebellion of the Earl of Lancaster, 1328-9." *BIHR* 28 (1955), 84-89.

Hook, W. F. *Lives of the Archbishops of Canterbury*, 4. London 1865.

Houghton, F. T. S. "The Parochial and Other Chapels of the County of Worcester." *Birmingham and Midland Institute Arch. Section Trans.* 45 (1919), 22-114.

Howell, M. E. *Regalian Right in Medieval England.* London 1962.

Hoyt, R. S. "Royal Taxation and the Growth of the Realm in Medieval England." *Speculum* 25 (1950), 36-48.

Hughes, D. *A Study of Social and Constitutional Tendencies in the Early Years of Edward III.* London 1915.

Huizinga, J. *The Waning of the Middle Ages.* Harmondsworth 1955.

Hunt, R. W., W. A. Pantin and R. W. Southern, eds. *Studies in Medieval History Presented to F. M. Powicke.* Oxford 1948; repr. 1969.

Hunter, J. "Journal of the Mission of Queen Isabella to the Court of France and of her Long Residence in that Country." *Archaeologia* 36 (1855), 242-257.

——. "On the Measures taken for the Apprehension of Sir Thomas de Gournay, One of the Murderers of King Edward the Second...." *Archaeologia* 27 (1838), 274-297.

Johnstone, H. "Archbishop Pecham and the Council of Lambeth of 1281." In Little and Powicke, eds., *Essays in Medieval History Presented to T. F. Tout*, pp. 171-188. Manchester 1925; repr. New York 1967.

Jones, M. "Some Documents relating to the Disputed Succession to the Duchy of Brittany." In *Camden Miscellany*, 24, pp. 1-78. Camden 4th ser. 9. London 1972.

Jones, W. R. "Bishops, Politics and the Two Laws; the *Gravamina* of the English Clergy 1237-1399." *Speculum* 41 (1966), 209-245.

——. "The English Church and Royal Propaganda during the Hundred Years War." *Journal of British Studies* 19 (1979), 18-30.

——. "Relations of the Two Jurisdictions: Conflict and Co-operation in England during the Thirteenth and Fourteenth Centuries." *Studies in Medieval and Renaissance History* 7 (1970), 77-210.

——. "*Rex et Ministri*: English Local Government and the Crisis of 1341." *Journal of British Studies* 13 (1973), 1-20.

Kaeuper, R. W. "Law and Order in Fourteenth-Century England: the Evidence of Special Commissions of Oyer and Terminer." *Speculum* 54 (1979), 734-784.

Keen, M. M. *The Outlaws of Medieval England*. Toronto 1961.

Keeney, B. C. "Military Service and the Development of Nationalism in England, 1272-1327." *Speculum* 22 (1947), 534-549.

Kemp, E. W. *Counsel and Consent*. London 1961.

——. "History and Action in the Sermons of a Medieval Archbishop." In Davis and Wallace-Hadrill, eds., *Writing of History in the Middle Ages*, pp. 349-365. Oxford 1981.

Kershaw, I. "The Great Famine and Agrarian Crisis in England 1315-1322." In Hilton, ed., *Peasants, Knights and Heretics*, pp. 85-132. Cambridge 1976.

King, A. A. *Liturgies of the Primatial Sees*. London 1957.

Kirsch, J. B. "Andreas Sapiti, englischer Prokurator an der Kurie im 14. Jahrhundert." *Historisches Jahrbuch* 14 (1893), 582-595.

Knowles, D. and R. N. Hadcock. *Medieval Religious Houses*. Cambridge 1953; 2nd ed. London 1971.

Lapsley, G. T. "Archbishop Stratford and the Parliamentary Crisis of 1341." *EHR* 30 (1915), 6-18, 193-215 (reprinted in *Crown, Community and Parliament*, ed. H. M. Cam, G. Barraclough, pp. 231-272. Oxford 1951).

Larson, A. "English Embassies during the Hundred Years War." *EHR* 55 (1940), 423-431.

——. "Payment of Fourteenth-Century English Envoys." *EHR* 54 (1939), 403-414.

Leland, J. *Itinerary*, 2. Ed. L. T. Smith. London 1907-1910.

Levett, A. E. "Wills of Villeins and Copyholders." In *Studies in Manorial History*, pp. 208-234. Oxford 1938; repr. London 1963.

Lewis, N. B. "The Recruitment and Organisation of a Contract Army, May to November 1337." *BIHR* 37 (1964), 1-19.

Little, A. G. "The Authorship of the Lanercost Chronicle." *EHR* 31 (1916), 269-279; 32 (1917), 48-49 (reprinted *Franciscan Papers*, pp. 42-54. Manchester 1943).

——, and F. M. Powicke, eds. *Essays in Medieval History Presented to T. F. Tout*. Manchester, 1925; repr. New York, 1967.

Lloyd, T. H. *The English Wool Trade in the Middle Ages*. Cambridge 1977.

Lobel, M. D. "A Detailed Account of the 1327 Rising at Bury St. Edmund's and the Subsequent Trial." *Proc. Suffolk Inst. of Arch. and Nat. Hist.* 21 (1933), 215-231.

Logan, F. D. *Excommunication and the Secular Arm in Medieval England*. Toronto 1968.

Lowry, E. C. "Clerical Proctors in Parliament and the Knights of the Shire, 1280-1374." *EHR* 48 (1933), 443-455.

Lucas, H. S. "Diplomatic Relations between England and Flanders from 1329 to 1336." *Speculum* 11 (1936), 59-87.

———. "The European Famine of 1315, 1316, and 1317." *Speculum* 5 (1930), 343-377.

———. *The Low Countries and the Hundred Years War, 1326-1347.* Michigan 1929.

———. "The Machinery of Diplomatic Intercourse." In Willard and Morris, eds., *English Government at Work 1327-1336*, 1, pp. 300-331. Cambridge, Mass. 1940.

Lunt, W. E. *Accounts Rendered by Papal Collectors in England 1317-78.* Ed. E. B. Graves. Philadelphia 1968.

———. *Financial Relations of the Papacy with England to 1327, 1327-1534.* 2 vols. Cambridge Mass. 1939, 1962.

———. *Papal Revenues in the Middle Ages.* 2 vols. New York 1934.

Luttrell, A. "The Crusade in the Fourteenth Century." In Hale et al., eds., *Europe in the Late Middle Ages*, pp. 122-154. Evanston 1963.

Lyubimenko, I. I. *Jean de Bretagne, Comte de Richmond.* Lille 1908.

Macray, W. D. "Sermons for the Festivals of St. Thomas Becket." Notes and Documents *EHR* 8 (1893), 85-91.

Maddicott, J. R. *Thomas of Lancaster 1307-1322: A Study in the Reign of Edward II.* London 1970.

Marsden, R. G. "The Mythical Town of Orwell." *EHR* 21 (1906), 93-98.

McKisack, M. *The Fourteenth Century 1307-1399.* Oxford 1959.

Mirot, L. and E. Déprez. "Les ambassades anglaises pendant la Guerre de Cent Ans: catalogue chronologique (1327-1450)." *Bibliothèque de l'École des Chartes* 59 (1898), 550-577.

Moille, L. C. "The Liturgies of Lyons." *The Month* 151 (1928), 402-408.

Mollat, G. *The Popes at Avignon 1305-1378.* New York 1965 (French 9th ed. Paris 1949, with bibliography).

Moore, S. A. "Documents relating to the Death and Burial of King Edward II." *Archaeologia* 50 (1887), 215-226.

Morgan, R. "The Barony of Powys, 1275-1360." *Welsh History Review/ Cylchgrawn Hanes Cymru* 10 (1980), 1-32.

Morris, W. A. "Magnates and Community of the Realm in Parliament, 1264-1327." *Mediaevalia et Humanistica* 1 (1943), 58-94.

Nash, T. *Collections for the History of Worcestershire.* 2 vols. 1781-1782 (supplement 1799).

Nicholson, R. *Edward III and the Scots.* Oxford 1965.

Offler, H. O. "England and Germany at the Beginning of the Hundred Years War." *EHR* 54 (1939), 608-631.

Oliver, G. *Lives of the Bishops of Exeter.* Exeter 1861-1887.

Orpen, G. H. *Ireland under the Normans (1169-1333).* 4 vols. Oxford 1911-1920.

Owen, D. M. *Church and Society in Medieval Lincolnshire.* Lincoln 1971.

Pantin, W. A. "English Monastic Letter-Books." In Edwards et al., eds., *Historical Essays in Honour of James Tait*, pp. 201-222. Manchester 1933.

———. "The Letters of John Mason: a Fourteenth-Century Formulary from St. Augustine's Canterbury." In Sandquist and Powicke, eds., *Essays in Medieval History Presented to Bertie Wilkinson*, pp. 192-219. Toronto 1969.

Parker, M. *De Antiquitate Britannicae Ecclesiae* [1572]. Ed. S. Drake. London 1729.

Parry, C. H. *The Parliaments and Councils of England*. London 1839.

Patourel, J. le. "Edward III and the Kingdom of France." *History* 43 (1958), 173-189.

Pearce, E. H. *Thomas de Cobham*. London 1923.

Perroy, E. *The Hundred Years War*. London 1951.

Phillips, J. R. S. *Aymer de Valence, Earl of Pembroke 1307-1324*. Oxford 1972.

Pike, L. O. *Constitutional History of the House of Lords*. London 1894.

Plucknett, T. F. T. "The Origins of Impeachment." *TRHS* 4th ser. 24 (1942), 47-71.

———. "Parliament." In Willard and Morris, eds., *English Government at Work 1327-1336*, 1, pp. 82-128. Cambridge Mass. 1940 (also in Fryde and Miller, eds., *Historical Studies of the English Parliament*, 1, pp. 195-241. Cambridge 1970).

———. *Statutes and their Interpretation in the First Half of the Fourteenth Century*. Cambridge 1922.

Powell, J. E. and K. Wallis. *The House of Lords in the Middle Ages*. London 1968.

Prestwich, M. "English Armies in the Early Stages of the Hundred Years War: a Scheme in 1341." *BIHR* 56 (1983), 102-113.

Prince, A. E. "The Payment of Army Wages in Edward III's Reign." *Speculum* 19 (1944), 137-160.

Putnam, B. H. *The Place in Legal History of Sir William Shareshull....* Cambridge 1950.

———. *Proceedings before the Justices of the Peace in the Fourteenth and Fifteenth Centuries*. London 1938.

———. "The Transformation of the Keepers of the Peace." *TRHS* 4th ser. (1929), 19-48.

Queller, D. *The Office of Ambassador in the Middle Ages*. Princeton 1967.

Rashdall, H. *The Universities of Europe in the Middle Ages*. Ed. F. M. Powicke and E. B. Emden. 3 vols. London 1936.

Rayner, D. "The Forms and Machinery of the *Commune Petition* in the Fourteenth Century." *EHR* 56 (1941), 198-233, 549-570.

Re, N. del. *La Curia Romana: Lineamenti Storico-Giuridici*. Ser. Sussidi Eruditi 23. 3rd ed. Rome 1970.

Redstone, V. B. "Some Mercenaries of Henry of Lancaster." *TRHS* 3rd ser. 7 (1913), 151-166.

Richardson, H. G. "The *Annales Paulini*." *Speculum* 23 (1948), 630-640.

Richardson, H. G. and G. O. Sayles. "The Early Statutes." *Law Quarterly Review* 50 (1934), 201-223, 540-571.

———. "The King's Ministers in Parliament, 1272-1377." *EHR* 46 (1931), 529-550; 47 (1932), 194-203, 377-397.

———. "Parliaments and Great Councils." *Law Quarterly Review* 77 (1961), 213-236, 401-426. (The above are now incorporated with other material in Richardson and Sayles, *The English Parliament in the Middle Ages* [London 1981]).

———. "The Parliaments of Edward III." *BIHR* 8 (1930), 65-82; 9 (1931), 1-18.

Riesenberg, P. N. *Inalienability of Sovereignty in Medieval Political Thought.* New York 1956.

Robo, E. *Mediaeval Farnham: Everyday Life on an Episcopal Manor.* Farnham 1935; repr. 1949.

Round, J. H. "Landing of Queen Isabella in 1326." *EHR* 14 (1899), 104-105.

Russell, F. H. *The Just War in the Middle Ages.* Cambridge 1975.

Sandquist, T. A. and M. R. Powicke. *Essays in Medieval History Presented to Bertie Wilkinson.* Toronto 1969.

Sayles, G. O. "The 'English Company' of 1341 and a Merchant's Oath." *Speculum* 6 (1931), 177-205.

———. "The Formal Judgement on the Traitors of 1322." *Speculum* 16 (1941), 57-63.

See also: Richardson, Sayles.

Sheehan, M. M. *The Will in Medieval England.* Toronto 1963.

Smallwood, T. M. "The Lament of Edward II." *Modern Languages Review* 68 (1973), 521-529.

Smith, J. B. "Edward II and the Allegiance of Wales." *Welsh History Review/ Cylchgrawn Hanes Cymru* 8 (1976), 139-171.

Smith, W. E. L. *Episcopal Appointments and Patronage in the Reign of Edward II.* Chicago 1938.

Smyth, J. *The Lives of the Berkeleys.* Ed. Sir J. Maclean. Gloucester 1883-1885.

Somner, W. *The Antiquities of Canterbury* [1 *The Antiquities of Canterbury* with Appendix; 2 Supplement, *Cantuaria Sacra*; 3 Appendix to Supplement]. Rev. and enlarged by N. Battely. London 1703. (See also reproduction of 1703 ed. without *Cantuaria Sacra* but with Battely's plates; intro. W. Urry, 1977.)

Southern, R. W. *Western Society and the Church in the Middle Ages.* Harmondsworth 1970.

Stanley, A. P. *Historical Memorials of Westminster Abbey.* 6th ed. London 1886.

Stones, E. L. G. *Anglo-Scottish Relations 1174-1328.* [London] 1965; repr. 1971.

———. "The English Mission to Edinburgh in 1328." *Scottish Historical Review* 28 (1949), 121-132.

———. "The Folvilles of Ashby-Folville, Leicestershire, and their Associates in Crime, 1326-47." *TRHS* 5th ser. 7 (1957), 117-136.

———. "Sir Geoffrey le Scrope, *c.* 1285-1346." *EHR* 69 (1954), 1-17.

——. "The Treaty of Northampton, 1328." *History* n.s. 38 (1953), 54-61.

Stothard, C. A. *The Monumental Effigies of Great Britain*. New ed. by John Hewitt. London 1876.

Stow, J. *Survey of London*. 2 vols. Oxford 1971.

Stuart, E. Pole. "The Interview between Philip v and Edward ii at Amiens in 1320." *EHR* 41 (1926), 412-415.

Stubbs, W. *The Constitutional History of England*. 3 vols. Oxford 1874-1878 (other editions as cited).

Swainson, C. A. *History and Constitution of a Cathedral of the Old Foundation ... the Cathedral of Chichester*, pt. 1 (to 1503). London 1880.

Tanquerey, F. J. "The Conspiracy of Thomas Dunheved, 1327." *EHR* 31 (1916), 119-124.

Taylor, J. "The French *Brut* and the Reign of Edward ii." *EHR* 72 (1957), 423-437.

——. "The Judgment of Hugh Despenser, the Younger." *Medievalia et Humanistica* 12 (1958), 70-77.

——. *The Use of Medieval Chronicles*. London 1965.

Templeman, G. "Edward iii and the Beginnings of the Hundred Years War." *TRHS* 5th ser. 2 (1952), 69-88.

Thompson, A. Hamilton. *The Abbey of St. Mary of the Meadows, Leicester*. Leicester 1949.

——. *The English Clergy and their Organisation in the Later Middle Ages*. Oxford 1947.

——. "Pluralism in the Mediaeval Church." *Associated Architectural Societies' Reports and Papers* 33 (1915-1916), 35-73; 34 (1917-1918), 1-26; 35 (1919-1920), 87-108; 36 (1921-1922), 1-41.

Titow, J. Z. *Winchester Yields: A Study in Medieval Agricultural Productivity*. Cambridge 1972.

Tout, T. F. "The Captivity and Death of Edward of Carnarvon." *BJRL* 6 (1920), 69-113.

——. *Chapters in Medieval Administrative History*. 6 vols. Manchester 1920-1933.

——. *Collected Papers*. 3 vols. Manchester 1932-1934; incorporates: "The Captivity and Death of Edward Carnavon," 3, pp. 145-190, and "The Westminster Chronicle Attributed to Robert of Reading," 2, pp. 289-304.

——. *The Place of the Reign of Edward ii in English History*. Manchester 1914. 2nd ed. revised H. Johnstone. Manchester 1936.

——. "The Westminster Chronicle Attributed to Robert of Reading." *EHR* 31 (1916), 450-464.

Thrupp, S. L. *The Merchant Class of Medieval London*. Ann Arbor 1962.

Ullmann, W. *The Growth of Papal Government in the Middle Ages*. 2nd ed. London 1965.

Unwin, G., ed. *Finance and Trade under Edward iii*. Manchester 1918; repr. London 1962.

Vallance, W. H. A. *Greater English Church Screens*. London 1947.

Viard, J. "Le siège de Calais 4 Septembre – 4 Août 1347." *Le Moyen Âge* 39 (1929), 129-189.

Wake, W. *The State of the Church and Clergy of England*. London 1703.

Waugh, S. L. "The Profits of Violence: the Minor Gentry in the Rebellion of 1321-1322 in Gloucestershire and Herefordshire." *Speculum* 52 (1977), 843-869.

Weinbaum, M. *London under Eduard I und II*. Stuttgart 1933.

Weske, D. B. *Convocation of the Clergy*. London 1937.

Whiting, B. J. "The Vows of the Heron." *Speculum* 20 (1945), 261-278.

Wilkinson, B. "The Authorisation of Chancery Writs under Edward III." *BJRL* 8 (1924), 107-139.

——. "The Chancery." In Willard and Morris, eds., *English Government at Work 1327-1336*, 1, pp. 162-205. Cambridge Mass. 1940.

——. *The Chancery under Edward III*. Manchester 1929.

——. "The Deposition of Richard II and the Accession of Henry IV." *EHR* 54 (1939), 215-239 (also in Fryde and Miller, eds., *Historical Studies of the English Parliament*, 1, pp. 330-353. Cambridge 1970).

——. "The Negotiations preceding the 'Treaty' of Leake, August 1318." In Hunt et al., eds., *Studies in Medieval History Presented to F. M. Powicke*, pp. 333-353. Oxford 1948; repr. 1969.

——. "The Protest of the Earls of Arundel and Surrey in the Crisis of 1341." *EHR* 46 (1931), 181-193.

——. *Studies in the Constitutional History of the Thirteenth and Fourteenth Centuries*. Manchester 1937.

Wilks, M. J. *The Problem of Sovereignty in the Later Middle Ages*. Cambridge 1963.

Willard, J. F. "Edward III's Negotiations for a Grant in 1337." *EHR* 21 (1906), 727-731.

Willard, J. F. and W. A. Morris, *The English Government at Work 1327-1336*, 1. Cambridge, Mass. 1940.

Williams, G. A. *Medieval London: From Commune to Capital*; London 1963.

Williams, W. R. *The Parliamentary History of the County of Oxford 1213-1899*. Brecknock 1899.

Willis, Browne. *An History of the Mitred Parliamentary Abbies and Conventual Cathedral Churches*. 2 vols. London 1718-1719.

Woodcock, B. L. *Medieval Ecclesiastical Courts in the Diocese of Canterbury*. London 1952.

Wood-Legh, K. L. *Perpetual Chantries in Britain*. Cambridge 1965.

Woodruff, C. E. "Notes from a Fourteenth Century Act-Book of the Consistory Court of Canterbury." *Archaeologia Cantiana* 40 (1928), 53-64.

Wright, J. R. *The Church and the English Crown, 1305-1334: A Study based on the Register of Archbishop Walter Reynolds*. Toronto 1980.

Index

Abingdon (Berks.), Benedictine abbey, sacking of, 207

Abingdon, John de, deputises for Bradeweye (q.v.), 123n

Acomb-by-York, 456, 490

Adderbury (Oxon.), 478, 487

Addington (Surrey), vicarage of, 39

Adisham (Kent), rector of, 117n

Adolf of Nassau, king of the Romans 1292-1298, 419n

Agde (dép. Herault), provost of, *see* Canale

Agen (dep. Lot-et-Garonne), process of, 233

Agenais, the (Gascony), 155, 160

Aimery, Hugh, bp. of St. Paul-Trois-Châteaux, 241, 457

Airth (Stirling), 491

Aka (Rock), M. Nicholas de, Stratford's clerk, rector of Avington, Bentworth, Brighstone, Hadleigh, 13n, 38, 109n, 111 and n, 223

Aldingbourne (Sussex), 92

Aledon, Thomas de, 204

Alexander III (Rolando Bandinelli), pope 1159-1181, 79

Alfonso, infante of Aragon (King Alfonso IV 1327-1336), his son's proposed marriage to Joan of the Tower, 154, 164n

Alfonso XI, king of Castile 1312-1350, 154, 164n, 339, 352, 505; Eleanor, sister of, 154

Alfonso, Pedro, bp. of Astorga, 345

Alresford (Hants), 121. *See also* New Alresford

Alresford, M. William de, 76

Alton (Hants), 25n, 45, 478, 489; Stratford publishes excommunication in church of, 482; vicar of, *see* Bekford

Alvechurch (Worcs.), Worcester bps.' manor, 10n

Amiens (Picardy, dép. Somme), 162, 163n, 223, 255, 256, 474, 493; oath of homage at (1329), 207, 219, 220

Andover (Hants), 498; rectory of, 40n

Angelic Salutation, the, 44

Angoulême (dép. Charente), dean of, 46n. *See also* Genest

Angoulême, M. Hugh d', 149, 150n, 433

Angus, earl of, *see* Umfraville

Anonimalle chronicle, the, 182n

Antwerp (Belgium), 213n, 255-258, 460, 495, 496

Antwerp, Lionel of, third son of Edward III, *see* Lionel

Aquitaine, duchy of, 150, 152, 158, 159, 226, 251, 340. *See also* Gascony

Aquitaine, duke of, *see* Edward III

Aragon, king of, *see* Peter IV

Aragon, projected English marriages with, 154n, 161n, 164n

Arches, court of (the), dean of, *see* Canterbury, courts of the diocese and province

Armenia, king of, *see* Leo IV

Arras (dép. Pas de Calais), 256, 257 and n, 407, 496; talks at (1339), 259

Artevelde, Jacob van, 267, 348, 350n

Artois, Robert d', 248 and n, 257, 271

Arundel, earl of, *see* FitzAlan

Ash (Surrey), rector of, 109n. *See also* Kyrkeby

Ashford (Kent), 283

Askeby, M. Robert de, 279

Assamari, Peter, 256

Assier (de Asserio) Rigaud d', bp. of Winchester 1319-1323, 29, 128, 130, 131, 136, 140, 142; death of at Avignon, 136, 143

Asti, Roland d', canon of Lodi, 241, 457

Astley (War.), 113n, 368

Astley, M. Thomas de, canon of Lichfield and London, 30n, 46, 56, 107n, 111-113, 114n, 115n, 122, 153n, 154n, 155; auditor and special commissary in Canterbury audience court, 116, 443, 456

Astley, Sir Thomas, 113n; his foundation at Astley, 368

Aston, M. Roger de, 456

Astorga (Léon), bp. of, *see* Alfonso

Atholl, earl of, *see* Strathbogie

Athon or Acton, M. John de, canonist, 7

Aubert, cardinal Étienne, 354

Aubrey, Andrew, mayor of London, 282

supposed champion of commons, 276; surety at Antwerp (1339), 258; surrenders great seal (1340), 270; sympathies of in 1330, 217; warns against publication of *libellus famosus*, 464

— final years 1342-1348, 328-362: acquits Orleton's executors, 359; appearance before of John de Montfort, 348; attempts to raise money for Edward III's campaigns (1342-1346), 355; death of at Mayfield, 359, 362, 469, 508; deprecates novelties injurious to the church, 504; entitled "dux regis," 359; falls ill at Maidstone, 507; irenic policy towards the king, 328-329ff.; ordinances for the Court of Canterbury, *see under* abp. of Canterbury; present at 1344 council at Westminster, 342; present at 1345 council in London, 345; principal councillor (1342), 328; provincial councils (1341-1347), *see under* abp. of Canterbury; publishes invasion plan of 1339, 352-353, 356; receives clandestine bulls (1347), 358; tomb in Canterbury cathedral, 360-361 and n; urged by Pope Clement to resist novelties, 335-336; will and benefactions, 360, 363-366, 509-513

Stratford, M. Ralph, bp. of London, *see* Hatton

Stratford, M. Robert, Sch. Th., rector of Stratford, archdeacon of Canterbury, bp. of Chichester 1337-1362, chancellor of Oxford 1335-1338, keeper of the great seal 1331-1332, 1335, chancellor 1337-1338, 1340, 1, 3, 29n, 46, 63-64 and n, 74n, 75n, 78n, 85-86, 92, 105n, 113n, 114n, 263, 272, 329, 332 and n, 342, 372n, 373n, 485, 486, 494; accompanies his brother abroad (1320), 101-102; acknowledges debt to Italian merchants, 103n; acts as his brother's attorney, 112; acts as his brother's steward, 29, 119 and n; appointed to receive homage of Winchester tenants, 28, 471; arranges details of his brother's tomb, 360; attends Westminster council (1344), 342; attends London council (1345), 345; baggage of pillaged, 336-337; chancellor, 249, 270, 272; claims deanery of Wells, 114n; commemorated at Astley, 113n; consecrated bp. of Chichester, 252, 459, 494; convenes convocation, 72; cooperation of in foundation of Stratford chantry, 86, 371; death of, 97; declines grant to his

brother of Leeds castle, 257; deputed by his brother to act in Christ Church election, 460; escorts cardinals (1337), 253; exchanges benefices (1319), 15 and n, 131n; executor of bull for citation of Kilsbys, 280n; keeper of great seal, 234; loan by of wool to king (1340), 271; present at parliament of 1339, 261n; — of 1341, 312ff., 315, 318n, 319, 321 and nn, 322; — of 1343, 332n; — of 1346, 356; proctor of his brother for opening York parliament (1332), 225; refuses to appear before council, 283; residual executor of his brother, 360; surrenders great seal (1332), 254, 274; — (1338), 487; temporary keeper of great seal, 224; urges Maxstoke foundation, 368n; vicar general of Canterbury, 61 and n, 66, 116, 257, 275, 441; vicar general at Winchester, 25n, 438

Stratford, M. Robert de, master of Stratford hospital, 2 and n, 7

Stratford, Nicholas de, 102. *See also* Geraud, Nicholas; Shottery, Nicholas de

Stratford, Old, manor, 1n; Thurstan messuage in, 4n

Stratford, Robert, father of John and Robert S., 1ff., 369; Isabel, wife of, 1, 369

Stratford-on-Avon, Stratford (War.), 1ff., 371, 458, 475, 492; bailiffs of, *see* Hatton, Henry de; Peyto, John de; bridge over River Avon at, 1, 364, 371n, 511; Clopton bridge, 1n; confraternity of Holy Cross in, 1-2 and nn.; Guild chapel in, 1n, 2n; Holy Trinity church, 6, 15, 363, 369; — appropriated to Stratford chantry (q.v.), 15, 458; — rectors of, 369; *see also* Greenfield, Stratford John and Robert; — schoolmaster possibly attached to, 6; manor, 4n; Stratford's benefactions to, 363, 511

Stratford-on-Avon, chantry and college of St. Thomas the Martyr, 83, 86, 90, 103, 367-381, 458, 492; assignment of rents to in Stratford and "Le Homme," 371; primary ordination of (1331), 368ff., 485; — augmentation of, 371ff., 458, 492; seal of, 517; Stratford's legacy to, 363, 509

Strathbogie, David, earl of Atholl (ob. 1326), 137

Strathbogie, David de, earl of Atholl (ob. 1335), 225; death of, 241, 251

Stratton, John de, 103n